principles of macroeconomics

seventh edition

JOHN B. TAYLOR

Stanford University

AKILA WEERAPANA

Wellesley College

SOUTH-WESTERN
CENGAGE Learning™

Australia • Brazil • Japan • Korea • Mexico • Singapore • Spain • United Kingdom • United States

SOUTH-WESTERN
CENGAGE Learning™

Principles of Macroeconomics, Seventh Edition

John B. Taylor, Akila Weerapana

VP/Editorial Director: Jack W. Calhoun

Publisher: Joe Sabatino

Executive Editor: Mike Worls

Developmental Editor: Julie Warwick

Editorial Assistant: Allyn Bissmeyer

Sr. Marketing Manager: John Carey

Sr. Content Project Manager: Cliff Kallemeyn

Media Editor: Sharon Morgan

Sr. Frontlist Buyer: Kevin Kluck

Sr. Marketing Communications Manager: Sarah Greber

Sr. Rights Specialist: Deanna Ettinger

Production Service: Cenveo Publisher Services

Sr. Art Director: Michelle Kunkler

For product information and technology assistance, contact us at **Cengage Learning Customer & Sales Support, 1-800-354-9706**

For permission to use material from this text or product, submit all requests online at **www.cengage.com/permissions**
Further permissions questions can be emailed to
permissionrequest@cengage.com

Library of Congress Control Number: 2011935465

ISBN-13: 978-0-538-45355-4

ISBN-10: 0-538-45355-9

South-Western Cengage Learning
5191 Natorp Boulevard
Mason, OH 45040
USA

Cengage Learning products are represented in Canada by Nelson Education, Ltd.

For your course and learning solutions, visit **www.cengage.com**
Purchase any of our products at your local college store or at our preferred online store **www.cengagebrain.com**

Printed in the United States of America
1 2 3 4 5 6 7 15 14 13 12 11

ABOUT THE AUTHORS

John B. Taylor

is one of the field's most inspiring teachers. As the Raymond Professor of Economics at Stanford University, his distinctive instructional methods have made him a legend among introductory economics students and have won him both the Hoagland and Rhodes prizes for teaching excellence.

Professor Taylor is also widely recognized for his research on the foundations of modern monetary theory and policy. One of his well-known research contributions is a rule—now widely called the Taylor Rule—used at central banks around the world.

Taylor has had an active career in public service, recently completing a four-year stint as the head of the International Affairs division at the United States Treasury, where he had responsibility for currency policy, international debt, and oversight of the International Monetary Fund and the World Bank and worked closely with leaders and policymakers from countries throughout the world. He has also served as economic adviser to the governor of California, to the U.S. Congressional Budget Office, and to the President of the United States and has served on several boards and as a consultant to private industry.

Professor Taylor began his career at Princeton, where he graduated with highest honors in economics. He then received his Ph.D. from Stanford and taught at Columbia, Yale, and Princeton before returning to Stanford.

Akila Weerapana

is an Associate Professor of Economics at Wellesley College. He was born and raised in Sri Lanka and came to the United States to do his undergraduate work at Oberlin College, where he earned a B.A. with highest honors in Economics and Computer Science in 1994. He received his Ph.D. in Economics from Stanford in 1999, writing his dissertation on monetary economics under the mentorship of John Taylor.

Since then, Professor Weerapana has taught in the Economics Department at Wellesley College. His teaching interests span all levels of the department's curriculum, including introductory and intermediate macroeconomics, international finance, monetary economics, and mathematical economics. He was awarded Wellesley's Pinanski Prize for Excellence in Teaching in 2002. He also enjoys working with thesis students, advising projects ranging from a study of the economic benefits of eradication of river blindness in Ghana to an analysis of the determinants of enterprise performance in Russia.

In addition to teaching, Professor Weerapana has research interests in macroeconomics, specifically in the areas of monetary economics, international finance, and political economy.

PREFACE

Our goal in this book is to present modern economics in a form that is intuitive, relevant, and memorable to students who have had no prior exposure to the subject. We both teach introductory economics—Taylor at Stanford, Weerapana at Wellesley—and we enjoy teaching greatly. We especially enjoy interacting with students in the classroom as we endeavor to make the basic economic ideas as clear and understandable as possible. In this book we aim for that same clarity and teacher-student interaction, often imagining that we are talking with students or responding to their questions as we write.

The New Economics from Generation to Generation

We remember what it was like when we first took introductory economics—Taylor in the 1960s, Weerapana in the 1990s. People called 1960s-vintage economics the "new economics," because many new ideas, including those put forth by John Maynard Keynes, were being applied to public policy for the first time. By the 1990s there was a "new" new economics, stressing incentives, expectations, long-run fundamentals, institutions, and the importance of stable, predictable economic policies. Now, as we begin the second decade of the twenty-first century, the global financial crisis, the great recessions in the United States and Europe, and explosive growth in emerging markets have additional implications for economics.

In the 1980s and 1990s, the United States experienced far fewer recessions than in the 1960s and 1970s and the recessions were relatively short and mild. But instability returned with the crisis and recession of 2007–2009—one of the longest and deepest in American history—and the slow recovery from the recession, causing a great deal of harm to millions of people. This poor economic performance has again raised many questions about the effectiveness of economic policy. Economists are engaged in a vigorous debate about what caused the crisis and how best to prevent future crises, accelerate economic growth, and keep unemployment low. Europe has also been grappling with economic policy especially the appropriate responses to the mounting debt accumulated by Greece and Ireland during the crisis.

In this Seventh Edition, we give these and other recent developments a prominent, clearly explained place within the basic tradition of economics. We emphasize the central idea of economics: that people make purposeful choices with scarce resources and interact with other people when they make these choices. We explain this idea using examples of choices that students actually face. We give real-world examples of how markets work, and we explain why markets are efficient when the incentives are right and inefficient when the incentives are wrong. We stress long-run fundamentals, but we also discuss current public policy issues relating to the crisis where the short run matters. The big policy questions about the role of government being debated by economists and others today receive special attention. We know from our teaching experience that examples of how economic ideas are used in practice make economics more interesting to students, thereby making learning economics easier.

Summary of Changes from the Sixth to the Seventh Edition

Here we provide a summary of the revisions in Seventh Edition.

Chapter 1 of our text has traditionally begun with a story of real people making real choices. Here we tell the story of several entrepreneurs who made different choices about college which had profound effects on their lives. Then throughout the chapter we add text and new box material to show how recent real world events affect opportunity costs, cause inefficiencies, and influence the economic debate about market economies and government intervention.

In Chapter 2 we provide a new empirical case study on the effect of gasoline prices on the number of miles people drive. We also add a new box on the President's Council of Economic Advisers, and we update the appendix to include the most recent government debt projections for the graphing tutorial.

In Chapters 3 and 4, the changes mainly consist of updated examples and data corresponding to recent developments.

Chapter 5 is substantially updated with descriptions of the 2007–2009 recession, contrasting it with the Great Moderation that preceded it. GDP data have been updated to incorporate a discussion of the slow recovery. We have added a new section on how recessions are defined and updated references in several sections to incorporate the 2007–2009 recession and compare and contrast it with past recessions. We have updated data on unemployment, inflation and interest rates and give an overview of fiscal and monetary policy.

Chapter 6 on macroeconomic measurement has been updated with the latest GDP and inflation data to incorporate the recent events. Changes in the basic long-run macro Chapters 7 through 9 are relatively small, with updates of data on spending shares, employment and unemployment.

Chapter 10, "Money and Inflation," has been updated to show the rapid increase in bank reserves in 2009 and 2010 as the Fed expanded its loans to private firms and increased its purchases of assets—the so-called quantitative easing programs. It explains the reason for the increase in excess reserves at banks and the increase in the money supply at that time.

Chapter 11, which we have renamed "Recessions, Recoveries, and Expansions," has a new chapter opening focusing on the recent recession A new discussion of temporary tax cuts and rebates based on the Stimulus Act of 2008 is added to the section on the permanent income model in the Appendix.

Chapter 12 has a new introduction focusing on the stimulus bill passed in February 2009 as a motivation for why we study the economic fluctuations model. The box is updated to include more recent monetary policy decisions; the discussion of the target inflation rate incorporates recent actions by the Fed.

Chapter 13 also has a new chapter opening, focusing on current macro-economic developments. There is a new section on using the economic fluctuations model to analyze the recent economic downturn, covering both causes and remedies. A new box describes how monetary policy may have contributed to the boom/bust in the housing market.

A new chapter opening in Chapter 14 uses examples from the 2008 and 2009 stimulus acts in the United States. The data on the budget deficit and debt situation are updated to show these large increases. The analysis of counter-cyclical policy with the economic fluctuations model focuses on the 2009 stimulus plan. There are new boxes describing stimulus plans and arguments for and against them.

Chapter 15, "Monetary Policy and the Financial Crisis," is perhaps the most substantially updated chapter. There is a new chapter opener explaining the unprecedented ways in which the Fed responded to the financial crisis. There is a new section on the Federal Reserve's balance sheet which enables the student to understand and to compare the Fed's traditional tools such as open market operations with the Fed's new tools. A simple version of the Fed's balance sheet appears as a new Table 1 along with a graph showing the "size" of the Fed's balance sheet. There is a new section on the liquidity trap and the zero lower bound on the interest rate and a new section on "quantitative easing." Finally, there is new material on central bank independence, including a new box on implications of new Fed actions for its independence. The chapter was reorganized to put more emphasis on the new operations at the front.

Chapter 16, "Capital and Financial Markets," is substantially updated. There is a new chapter opening with charts showing the volatility of the stock market and the housing market in 2008 and early 2009. There is a new section called "The Housing Market," which explains why the demand for housing is negatively related to the interest rate, enabling a discussion of the housing boom of 2003–2006 which led up to the housing bust and the financial crisis. There is a new section on "The Role of Government in Financial Markets" which discusses how risky mortgage loans were made and sold off to other investors and also how government intervened to prevent spillover from the crisis but perhaps caused moral hazard. We also add a new box on the causes of the stock market panic of September–October 2008.

Chapter 17 also has a new opening stressing the interconnectedness of the global economic downturn. The discussion of catch-up has been re-organized to show that, while there has not been broad-based catch-up across the globe, the East Asian economies have made remarkable strides in a single generation to catch-up with more advanced nations. The section on economic development has also been updated to reflect the rapid rise of India and China as well as a discussion of the recent signs of encouraging economic growth in more than a dozen sub-Saharan African nations.

Chapter 18 has changed substantially in terms of structure. The 6th edition had two separate chapters on international trade and trade policy and these have been combined into a single chapter.

Last but not least, we have added a completely new Chapter 19 on International Finance. The 6th edition covered exchange rates in all the relevant places but we wanted instructors to have a stand-alone chapter exploring exchange rate issues in more depth. This chapter presents the basics of exchange rates and how interest differentials and relative price differentials can influence the determination of exchange rate patterns over time. It also provides students with a detailed discussion of fixed exchange rates, undervaluation and overvaluation of a currency and the resulting consequences. Finally, the chapter provides a discussion of a single currency area like the European Economic and Monetary Union (EMU), which has been in the forefront of news in 2011 as the crisis in Greece developed.

A Brief Tour

The basic workings of markets and the reasons they improve people's lives are the subjects of Part One. Chapter 1 outlines the unifying themes of economics: scarcity, choice, and economic interaction. The role of prices, the inherent international aspect of economics, the importance of property rights and incentives, and the difference between central planning and markets are some of the key ideas in this chapter. Chapter 2 introduces the field of economics through a case study showing how economists observe and explain economic puzzles. Chapters 3 and 4 cover the basic supply and demand model and elasticity. Here, the goal is to show how to use the supply and demand model to make sense of the world—and to learn how to "think like an economist." The concept of elasticity is now wholly contained in Chapter 4.

The study of macroeconomics begins with Chapter 5. This chapter gives an overview of the facts, emphasizing that macroeconomics is concerned with the growth and fluctuations in the economy as a whole. Chapter 6 shows how GDP and other variables are measured.

Chapter 7 starts with the first macro model to determine the long-run shares of GDP. Chapter 8 gives an analysis of how the level of unemployment in the economy as a whole is determined. Labor, capital, and technology are then presented in Chapter 9 as the fundamental determinants of the economy's growth path. One clear advantage of this approach is that it allows students to focus first on issues about which there is general agreement among economists. Moreover, this ordering helps students better understand short-term economic fluctuations. Similarly, the long-run treatment of money, presented in Chapter 10, sets the stage for the discussion of economic fluctuations.

As shown in Part Three (Chapters 11 through 16), the economy does fluctuate as it grows over time. Declines in production and increases in unemployment (characteristics of recessions) have not vanished from the landscape as long-term growth issues have come to the fore. Part Three delves into the causes of these fluctuations and proposes an analysis of why they end. It begins by explaining why shifts in aggregate demand may cause the economy to fluctuate and ends by showing that price adjustment plays a significant role in the end of recessions.

Ever-increasing global economic linkages will be one of the hallmarks of the world that today's students of economics will grow up to live in. Part Four (Chapters 17 through 19) aims to equip students with a better understanding of the economic relationships among countries. With issues about which there are many differing opinions, the text tries to explain these opinions as clearly and as objectively as possible; it also stresses the areas of agreement.

Pedagogical Features

The following pedagogical features are designed to help students learn economics.

Examples within the text. Illustrations of real-world situations help explain economic ideas and models. We have attempted to include a wide variety of brief examples and case studies throughout the text. Examples include a look at the gasoline market in Chapter 2 and a case study on unemployment among young people around the world in Chapter 8. Many other examples are simply woven into the text.

Boxed examples to give real-life perspectives. Economics in Action boxes examine current issues and debates, and also give examples of recent news stories relating to economic concepts.

Stimulating vignettes at the beginning of each chapter. Examples of opening vignettes include explanation of economic events such as the price of Super Bowl tickets in Chapter 2 and discussions on how unemployment affects different individuals during a recession in Chapter 8.

Complete captions and small conversation boxes in graphs. The captions and small green-shaded conversation boxes make many of the figures completely self-contained. In some graphs, sequential numbering of these conversation boxes stresses the dynamic nature of the curves. Figure 4-7 in Chapter 4 provides a good example.

Use of photos and cartoons to illustrate abstract ideas. Special care has gone into the search for and selection of photos and cartoons to illustrate difficult economic ideas, such as inelastic supply curves or opportunity costs. Many text photos or photo spreads have short titles and captions to explain their relevance to the text discussion.

Key term definitions. Definitions of key terms appear in the margins next to where the key term is presented in the text as well as in the end of each Chapter, complete with page references. All key terms and definitions are also found in the alphabetized glossary in the back of the book.

Brief reviews at the end of each major section. These reviews summarize the key points in abbreviated form as the chapter evolves; they are useful for preliminary skim reading as well as for review.

Questions for review at the end of every chapter. These are tests of recall and require only short answers; they can be used for oral review or as a quick self-check.

Problems. An essential tool in learning economics, the problems have been carefully selected, revised, and tested for this edition. An ample supply of these problems appears at the end of every chapter and appendix. Some of the problems ask the reader to work out examples that are slightly different from the ones given in the text; others require a more critical thinking approach.

Enhanced Teaching and Learning Package

Cengage Learning's CourseMate

Multiple resources for learning and reinforcing principle concepts are now available in one place! CourseMate equips students with a wealth of resources that help them study and apply economic concepts. As they read the chapters, students can go online and access ABC News videos, Economic News articles, Economic debates, interactive quizzes and flashcards. Students also have access to graphing tutorials to aid the in understanding how graphs are used. Test your student's research skills with Internet activities. Chapter questions and solutions are available for individual assignments or group projects. The following resources also come with your CourseMate purchase:

Engagement Tracker How do you know your students have read the material or viewed the resources you've assigned? Engagement Tracker assesses student preparation and engagement. Use the tracking tools to see progress for the class as a whole or for individual students. Identify students at risk early in the course. Uncover which concepts are most difficult for your class. Monitor time on task. Keep your students engaged in economics!

Global Economic Watch This groundbreaking resource stimulates discussion and understanding of the global downturn with easy-to-integrate teaching solutions. It includes a content-rich blog, real-time database with hundreds of relevant and vetted articles, videos and podcasts, a timeline, and overview of events leading to today's global economic crisis.

Interactive e-Book Students can take notes, highlight, search and interact with embedded media specific to this book.

Study Guide Through CourseMate, students also have access to the Study Guide (Micro and Macro) which provides another learning opportunity for additional practice and also to aid in the preparation of exams.

Aplia

Founded in 2000 by economist and Stanford Professor Paul Romer, Aplia™ is dedicated to improving learning by increasing student effort and engagement. The most successful online product in Economics by far Aplia has been used by more than 1,000,000 students at over 1800 institutions. Visit **www.aplia.com/cengage** for more details.

For help, questions, or a live demonstration, please contact Aplia at **support@aplia.com**

Cengage Compose

Cengage Compose a custom format of Cengage Learning's online digital content. Compose provides the fastest, easiest way for you to create your own learning materials. Choose content from hundreds of best-selling titles, material from numerous databases — even add your own material — to create an accompaniment textbook that is perfectly customized to your course. Learn more at http://compose.cengage.com.

Student Resources

Study Guide

Revised and updated by Tori Knight of Carson-Newman College. The Study Guide provides a wonderful learning opportunity that many students will value. Each chapter contains an overview, an informal chapter review, and a section called 'Zeroing In' that harnesses students' intuition to explain the chapter's most important concepts. The Study Guide also provides ample means for practice in using the economic ideas and graphs introduced in each text chapter and address a variety of learning needs through graph-based questions and problems as well as multiple-choice practice tests. A section called 'Working It Out' provides worked problems that take the student step-by-step through the analytical process needed for real-world application of the core concepts covered in the chapter. These are followed by practice problems that require students to use the same analytical tools on their own. Detailed answers are provided for all review and practice questions. End-of-part quizzes offer students yet another chance to test their retention of material before taking in-class exams. The Study Guide is available for both the Macro and Micro textbooks as well as the Principles of Economics book. Students may purchase the Study Guide online at CengageBrain.com. IAC: 9781133311850. The Study Guide comes along with your CourseMate purchase.

Tomlinson Economics Videos "Like Office Hours 24/7"

Award winning teacher, actor and professional communicator, Steven Tomlinson (Ph.D. Economics, Stanford) walks students through all of the topics covered in principles of economics in an online video format. Segments are organized to follow the organization of the Taylor text and most videos include class notes that students can download and quizzes for students to test their understanding which can be sent to the professor if required. Tomlinson Videos can be purchased through CengageBrain .com. PAC: 9781428275379, IAC: 9781428275249. Find out more at www.cengage.com/economics/tomlinson.

The Global Economic Watch

Learn lessons as real life happens—from the declining housing market, to the recession—today's financial turmoil transforms academic theory into intense real life challenges. The Global Economic Watch includes a content-rich blog, real-time database with hundreds of relevant and vetted articles, videos and podcasts, a timeline, and an overview of events leading to today's global economic crisis.

You can purchase The Watch through Cengagebrain.com and it is also available within a CourseMate purchase. IAC: 1439040745, PAC: 1439040753.

Taylor Companion Web Site

The student section of the Taylor Companion Website which can be accessed through CengageBrain.com, provides additional study tools, including interactive quizzes, flashcards and crossword puzzles.

Instructor Resources

Test Bank

A reliable test bank is the most important resource for efficient and effective teaching and learning. The Test Bank has been revised by Jim Lee at Texas A&M, Corpus Christi for the 7th edition. It contains more than 5,000 test questions—including multiple-choice, true/false, and short answer problems—many of which are based on graphs. All Test Bank questions are tagged by topic, difficulty (easy, moderate, and challenging), AACSB learning standards, Bloom's Taxonomy and Course Outcomes.

The test banks also include a set of parallel problems that match the end-of-chapter problems from the text. The Test Bank is available on the Instructor's Resource CD-ROM and also available on the password protected portion of the text website.

ExamView

ExamView Computerized Testing Software contains all of the questions from the Test Bank. ExamView is an easy-to-use test creation software compatible with both Microsoft Windows and Apple Macintosh.

Create and administer quizzes online. Easily test your students understanding of today's economic skills and developments with this electronic testing system. Easy-to-use test creation software allows you to add or edit questions, instructions and answers. You can select questions (randomly or numerically) by previewing them on the screen. ExamView is only available on the Instructor's Resource CD-ROM.

Instructor's Resource and Solutions Manual

Revised for the 7th edition by Chuck Parker at Wayne State College, the Instructor's Resource Solutions Manual provides solutions to end-of-chapter exercises and problems are located in this manual, complete with figures and diagrams. Each chapter also provides valuable resources including a brief overview, teaching objectives, key terms from the text, and suggested topics to discuss in class. The Instructor's Resource Solutions Manual is available on the Instructor's Resource CD-ROM and also available on the password protected portion of the text website.

PowerPoint Lecture Slides

Complete with a new design and revised by Amy Chataginer of Mississippi Gulf Coast Community College, these vivid slides contain key highlights of important concepts. Slides are organized by chapter for your convenience and may be modified or expanded to meet your individual classroom needs. The slides are complete with figures and tables from the book to help make your lectures come to life! The PowerPoint slides are available on the Instructor's Resource CD-ROM and also available on the password protected portion of the text website.

Instructor's Resource CD-ROM

Get quick access to all instructor ancillaries from your desktop. This easy-to-use CD lets you review, edit, and copy exactly what you need in the format you want. This supplement contains the Instructor's Resource Solutions Manual, Test Bank, Examview Testing software, and the PowerPoint lecture slides. IRCD ISBN: 09781111969745.

Taylor Companion Web Site

The instructor section of the Taylor Companion Website which can be accessed at http://login.cengage.com, allows for easy online access to the following supplemental materials: PowerPoint Lecture Slides, Test Bank and the Instructor's Resource Solutions Manual.

Acknowledgments

Completing a project like this is a team effort, and we both have been blessed with good students and colleagues who have given us advice and encouragement.

John B. Taylor I am grateful to many colleagues and students, whom I have consulted over the years, including Don Brown, Tim Breshanan, Marcelo Clerici-Arias, Anne Kreuger, Tom McCurdy, Paul Milgrom, Roger Noll, John Pencavel, Paul Romer, Nate Rosenberg, Mark Tendell and Frank Wolak. I must acknowledge with very special gratitude Akila's partnership in this project. Akila first demonstrated his extraordinary teaching and writing skills even before completing his PhD at Stanford. After receiving his PhD, Akila joined the faculty at Wellesley College, where he has taught the Principles course for many semesters and further established his reputation for teaching excellence, and in 2002, received the Anna and Samuel Pinanski Teaching Award. His ability to get complex topics across to his students and his enthusiasm for bringing policy implications alive is clearly reflected in our new coauthored book.

Akila Weerapana I am exceedingly grateful to John for giving me the opportunity to communicate my enthusiasm for teaching economics to a broader audience than the students in my classes at Wellesley. My passion for economics stems from the inspiration I received from my economics professors: Barbara Craig and Peter Montiel at the undergraduate level, and John Taylor, Frank Wolak, and Chad Jones at the graduate level. I too have benefited immensely from working with my colleagues. The faculty members in the Economics Department at Wellesley live up to the liberal arts ideal that I aspire to, combining excellent teaching with active research. Special thanks are owed to Courtney Coile and David Lindauer for the time they spent helping me understand how best to pitch topics in microeconomics that I am less familiar with teaching than they are. The real inspirations for this book, however, are the students that I have taught over the past decade—two years at Stanford, but especially, the last eight years at Wellesley. Without their enthusiasm for economics, their willingness to be continually challenged, and their need to better understand an ever-changing world, none of this would be possible. My contributions to this book are shaped by countless hours spent talking economics with my students. Through this book, I hope that this conversation extends to many others. Along these lines, special thanks go to Helena Steinberg, Class of 2008 at Wellesley. She served as an invaluable and patient resource for how students would react to and understand economic concepts, examples, newspaper articles, photographs, cartoons, and study questions.

We would also like to thank William B. Stronge of Florida Atlantic University, who provided wonderful end-of-chapter problems that are conceptually challenging and require students to think more deeply about the concepts. Bill's efforts helped us meet an incredibly demanding schedule, and we are grateful for his contributions. Numerous reviewers provided insights, suggestions, and feedback along the way—often at critical points in product and supplement development. These individuals include

Mohsen Bahmani-Oskooee, University of Wisconsin, Milwaukee
Erik Craft, University of Richmond
David H. Eaton, Murray State University
Lewis Freiberg, Northeastern Illinois University
Wang Fuzhong, Beijing University of Aeronautics & Astronautics
Janet Gerson, University of Michigan
Lisa Grobar, California State University, Long Beach
Ritika Gugnani, Jaipuria Institute of Management (Noida)
Gautam Hazarika, University of Texas, Brownsville
Aaron Johnson, Missouri State University
Jacob Kurien, Rockhurst University
Babu Nahata, University of Louisville
Soloman Namala, Cerritos College
Sebastien Oleas, University of Minnesota, Duluth
Greg Pratt, Mesa Community College
Virginia Reilly, Ocean County College
Brian Rosario, University of California, Davis
William B. Stronge, Florida Atlantic University
Della Lee Sue, Marist College
J. S. Uppal, State University of New York, Albany
Michele T. Villinski, DePauw University
Laura Wolff, Southern Illinois University, Edwardsville

We are grateful to Sarah L. Stafford of the College of William and Mary and Robert J. Rossana of Wayne State University for their detailed and timely accuracy checks of the main texts and several key supplements. We are especially appreciative of the contributions of the Sixth Edition supplements authors for their creativity, dedication, and careful coordination of content; this group includes

Sarah E. Culver, University of Alabama, Birmingham
David H. Eaton, Murray State University
John Kane, State University of New York, Oswego
Jim Lee, Texas A&M University, Corpus Christi
John S. Min, Northern Virginia Community College
Wm. Stewart Mounts, Jr., Mercer University
David H. Papell, University of Houston

Virginia Reilly, Ocean County College Center for Economic
    Education
Brian Rosario, University of California, Davis
John Solow, University of Iowa
William B. Stronge, Florida Atlantic University
Eugenio D. Suarez, Trinity University
Laura Wolff, Southern Illinois University, Edwardsville

We would also like to thank Edward Gullason of Dowling College for reviewing many of these supplements and Matthew Berg and Julia Ong for copyediting them.

REVIEWERS

Matthew Alford *Southeastern Louisiana University*

Charles Anderson *Kean University*

Len Anyanwu *Union County College*

Kenneth Ardon *Salem State College*

Sukhwinder Bagi *Bloomsburg University*

Gaurango Banerjee *University of Texas at Brownsville*

Kevin Beckwith *Salem State College*

Charles A. Bennett *Gannon University*

Derek Berry *Calhoun Community College*

Charles Bondi *Morgan State University*

Joyce Bremer *Oakton Community College*

Amy Chataginer *MS Gulf Coast Community College*

Paul Clement *Fashion Institute of Technology-SUNY*

Marcelo Clerici-Arias *Stanford University*

Barbara Collister-Priestley *Concordia University Ann Arbor*

Mitchell Dudley *The College of William & Mary*

Dr. J. Pat Fuller *Brevard CC*

Cynthia Gamez *The University of Texas at El Paso*

Lara Gardner *Southeastern Louisiana University*

Dale Garrett *Evangel University*

Satyajit Ghosh *University of Scranton*

Sarah Ghosh *University of Scranton*

Alan Gin *University of San Diego*

Judith Grenkowicz *Kirtland Community College*

Curry Hilton *Guilford Technical Community College*

James Holcomb *University of Texas at El Paso*

Gokhan Karahan *Delta State University*

Ghebre Keleta *Grambling State University*

Deborah Kelly *University of San Diego*

Tori Knight *Carson-Newman College*

Viju Kulkarni *Mesa College*

Sonja Langley *Prairie View A&M University*

Sang Lee *Southeastern Louisiana University*

Charles Link *University of Delaware*

Linda Loubert *Morgan State University*

Farzin Madjidi *Pepperdine University/GSEP*

Tim McCabe *Tompkins Cortland Community College*

Todd McFall *Wake Forest University*

Daniel Morvey *Piedmont Technical College*

Shahriar Mostashari *Campbell University*

Francis Mummery *Fullerton College*

Pattabiraman Neelakantan *East Stroudsburg University*

Ogbonnaya Nwoha *Grambling State University*

Olugbenga Onafowora *Susquehanna University*

Chuck Parker *Wayne State College*

Van Pham *Salem State College*

Roxana Postolache *Capital University*

Rahim Quazi *Prairie View A&M University*

MG Quibria *Morgan State University*

David Rodgers *Northwestern Connecticut Community College*

S. Scanlon Romer *Delta College*

Daniel Saros *Valparaiso University*

Mark Scanlan *Stephen F. Austin State University*

Ted Scheinman *Mt. Hood Community College*

Virginia Shingleton *Valparaiso University*

Noel Smith *Palm Beach State College*

Donald Sparks *The Citadel*

Mark Steckbeck *Campbell University*

TaMika Steward *Tarrant County College*

Chin-Chyuan Tai *Averett University*

Robert Tansky *St. Clair Community College*

Jill Trask *Tarrant County College*

Margie Vance *North Arkansas College*

Lisa Verdon *College of Wooster*

Ann Wimmer *Iowa Lakes Community College*

Benaiah YongoBure *Kettering University*

BRIEF CONTENTS

CONTENTS

part one
INTRODUCTION TO ECONOMICS 1

part two
PRINCIPLES OF MACROECONOMICS   105

CHAPTER 7
The Spending Allocation Model 156

CHAPTER 19

International Finance 464

CHAPTER 18
International Trade   424

part four
TRADE AND GLOBAL MARKETS   403

CHAPTER 17
Economic Growth and Globalization   404

CHAPTER 14

Fiscal Policy   324

APPENDIX TO CHAPTER 11

Deriving the Formula for the Keynesian Multiplier and the Forward-Looking Consumption Model   275

principles of macroeconomics

part one

INTRODUCTION TO ECONOMICS

The Central Idea

At the center of **economics** is the idea that people make *purposeful choices* with *scarce resources* and *interact with others* when they make these choices. Consider the people in the photo below—including the President of the United States, entrepreneurs, and chief executives from top technology firms such as Apple, Cisco, Facebook, Genentech, Google, Netflix, Oracle, Twitter, and Yahoo!—who are meeting over dinner to talk about the economy.

Everyone at the table had experiences in making choices with scarce resources. Mark Zuckerberg, sitting to President Obama's right, faced a big *choice* when he was in college in 2004: that is, whether to finish his degree or to drop out and devote all his time to trans-

form a novel idea into a start-up firm. Completing college while pursuing the start-up was not an option because time is *scarce,* only 24 hours in a day, and he did not have enough time to do both activities and sleep a bit. So he had to make a choice. In choosing one activity, he would have to incur the cost of giving up the other activity. Dropping out of college would mean passing up a degree that would help him get a good job. Staying in college would mean he could not start up a new firm. Zuckerberg chose to drop out of college, and it looks like he made the right choice: His firm, Facebook, is now worth billions of dollars.

Steve Jobs, sitting to the left of the president in the photo, also dropped out of college, but for a different reason. He felt the cost of tuition was too high compared to what he was getting out of the formal courses. Better, he thought, to let his parents keep the money. A couple of years later, Jobs founded Apple computer, but he credits its success to the freedom he gained to explore new activities without the structure of a college degree. Larry Ellison of Oracle, sitting right across from the president, also chose not to complete a college degree.

Of course, not every executive in the photo chose to drop out of college. Carol Bartz, at the far end of the

Pete Souza/White House via Bloomberg/Getty Images

table, earned a degree in computer science, earning tuition money as a cocktail waitress. Years later, it seems clear that she also made the right choice: The college degree prepared her to become the CEO of Yahoo! Dick Costolo of Twitter also finished college. Others chose not only to finish college, but also to earn more advanced degrees. Reed Hastings of Netflix pursued a master's degree in business. President Obama chose to go to law school. Eric Schmidt of Google and Art Levinson of Genentech both chose to get doctorates.

Whatever their choice, these people were able to reap economic gains from their ideas or degrees because of the opportunities they had to *interact with people*. Hundreds of millions of people around the world interact through Facebook, Google, Yahoo! or Twitter. Even politicians like President Obama benefit from the social networking made possible by these firms. Zuckerberg, Schmidt, Bartz, and Costolo benefit from this interaction, too, in part because people pay them to advertise products on their sites. Indeed, these social networking firms depend on interactions with other firms represented at the table, including Apple's display devices and Cisco's networking equipment that powers the Internet. So behind the people in the photo are many stories of scarcity, choice, and economic interaction.

Scarcity is a situation in which people's resources are limited. People always face a scarcity of some sort. Scarcity implies that people must make a **choice** to forgo, or give up, one thing in favor of another. As you read this text, you may find yourself reflecting on decisions that you have to make—whether to major in economics or biology, whether to take all your classes after 10:00 A.M. or to schedule them all before noon, whether to search the Internet or to study.

Economic interactions between people occur every time they trade or exchange goods with each other. A college student buys education services from a university in exchange for tuition. A teenager sells labor services to Taco Bell in exchange for cash. Within a household, one member may agree to cook dinner in exchange for the other person agreeing to wash the dishes. Economic interactions typically take place in a **market**. A market is simply an arrangement by which buyers and sellers can interact and exchange goods and services with each other. There are many types of markets, ranging from the New York stock market to a local flea market. Interactions do not have to take place with the buyer and seller in physical proximity to each other; the Internet, for example, greatly enhances the opportunities for economic interaction.

The purpose of this book is to introduce you to the field of economics, to provide you with the knowledge that will help you understand how so much of what happens in the world is shaped by the actions of people who had to make choices when confronted by scarcity. A better understanding of economics will equip you to handle the opportunities and challenges you face—should you continue with schooling if the economy is weak and it is hard to find a job? It also will leave you better informed about the challenges that the nation faces—should the government intervene in the economy to regulate businesses, or should it provide economic stimulus packages to help the economy? Soon you will find yourself viewing the world through the lens of economics. Your friends may tell you that you are "thinking like an economist." You should take that as a compliment. The first step on this path is to understand the enormous power of the central ideas of scarcity, choice, and economic interactions. That's the purpose of this chapter.

economics
the study of how people deal with scarcity.

scarcity
the situation in which the quantity of resources is insufficient to meet all wants.

choice
a selection among alternative goods, services, or actions.

economic interactions
exchanges of goods and services between people.

market
an arrangement by which economic exchanges between people take place.

opportunity cost
the value of the next-best forgone alternative that was not chosen because something else was chosen.

Scarcity and Choice for Individuals

It is easy to find everyday examples of how people make purposeful choices when they are confronted with a scarcity of time or resources. A choice that may be on your mind when you study economics is how much time to spend on these studies versus other activities. If you spend all your time on economics, you may get a 100 percent on the final exam, but a 0 percent in biology. If you spend all your time on biology, then you may get a 100 percent in biology and a 0 percent in economics. Most people resolve the choice by *balancing* out their time to get a decent grade in both subjects. If you are premed, then you probably will devote more time to biology. If you are interested in business, then devoting more time to economics might be appropriate.

Now let us apply this basic principle to two fundamental economic problems: individual choices about what to *consume* and what to *produce*. For each type of economic problem, we first show how scarcity forces one to make a choice, and then we show how people gain from interacting with other people.

Consumer Decisions

Consider Maria, who is going for a walk in a park on a sunny day. Maria would love to wear a hat (baseball style with her school logo) and sunglasses on the hike, but she forgot them at home. Maria has brought $20 with her, however, and there is a store in the park that is having a "two-for-one" sale. She can buy two hats for $20 or two pairs of sunglasses for $20. She would prefer to buy one hat and one pair of sunglasses, but that is not possible. Her scarcity of funds causes her to make a choice. The $20 limit on her spending is an example of a *budget constraint*, a scarcity of funds that limits her to spending no more than this amount. Her choice will depend on her tastes. Let us assume that when she is forced by scarcity to make a choice, she will choose the sunglasses.

Opportunity Cost Maria's decision is an example of an economic problem that all people face: A budget constraint forces them to make a choice between different items that they want. Choosing one item means that you have to give up other items. The **opportunity cost** of a choice is the value of the next-best forgone alternative that was not chosen. The opportunity cost of the hats is the loss from not being able to wear the sunglasses. An opportunity cost occurs every time there is a choice. For example, the opportunity cost of waking up to attend an 8:00 A.M. class rather than sleeping in is the hours of sleep you lose when you get up early. The opportunity cost of Mark Zuckerberg's staying in college versus pursuing his start-up would have been the money he earned from Facebook. In many cases involving choice and scarcity, you have to choose from among many more than two options. If you choose vanilla ice cream out of a list of many possible flavors, then the opportunity cost is the loss from not being able to consume the *next-best* flavor, perhaps strawberry.

Now, suppose Maria is not the only hiker. Also in the park is Adam, who also has $20 to spend. Adam also loves both hats and sunglasses, but he likes hats more than sunglasses. When forced to make a choice, he buys the hats. His decision is shaped by scarcity just as Maria's is: Scarcity comes from the budget constraint. He must make a choice, and each choice has an opportunity cost.

Gains from Trade: A Better Allocation Now suppose that Adam and Maria meet each other in the park. Let's consider the possibility of economic interaction between them. Maria has two pairs of sunglasses and Adam has two hats, so Maria and Adam can trade with each other. Maria can trade one of her pairs of sunglasses for one of Adam's hats, as shown in Figure 1-1. Through such a trade, both Maria and Adam

Figure 1-1

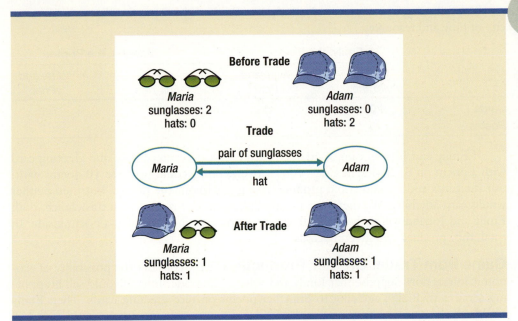

Gains from Trade through a Better Allocation of Goods
Without trade, Maria has more pairs of sunglasses than she would like, and Adam has more hats than he would like. By trading a hat for a pair of sunglasses, they both gain.

can improve their situation. There are **gains from trade** because the trade reallocates goods between the two individuals in a way that they both prefer. Trade occurs because Maria is willing to exchange one pair of sunglasses for one hat, and Adam is willing to exchange one hat for one pair of sunglasses. Because trade is mutually advantageous for both Maria and Adam, they will voluntarily engage in it if they are able to. In fact, if they do not gain from the trade, then neither will bother to make the trade.

This trade is an example of an economic interaction in which a reallocation of goods through trade makes both people better off. The total quantity of goods produced does not change. The number of hats and sunglasses has remained the same. Trade simply reallocates existing goods.

The trade between Maria and Adam is typical of many economic interactions that we will study in this book. Thinking like an economist in this example means recognizing that a voluntary exchange of goods between people must make them better off. Many economic exchanges are like this, even though they are more complicated than the exchange of hats and sunglasses.

gains from trade
improvements in income, production, or satisfaction owing to the exchange of goods or services.

Producer Decisions

Now consider two producers—Emily, a poet, and Johann, a printer. Both face scarcity and must make choices. Because of differences in training, abilities, or inclination, Emily is much better at writing poetry than Johann is, but Johann is much better at printing greeting cards than Emily is.

If Emily writes poetry full time, she can produce 10 poems in a day; but if she wants to make and sell greeting cards with her poems in them, she must spend some time printing cards and thereby spend less time writing poems. However, Emily is not very good at printing cards; it takes her so much time to do so that if she prints one card, she has time to write only one poem rather than 10 poems during the day.

If Johann prints full time, he can produce 10 different greeting cards in a day. However, if he wants to sell greeting cards, he must write poems to put inside them. Johann is so poor at writing poems that if he writes only one poem a day, his production of greeting cards drops from 10 to one per day.

The following is a summary of the choices Emily and Johann face because of a scarcity of time and resources.

	Emily, the Poet		Johann, the Printer	
	Write Full Time	Write and Print	Print Full Time	Write and Print
Cards	0	1	10	1
Poems	10	1	0	1

If Emily and Johann cannot interact, then each can produce only one greeting card with a poem on the inside in a day. Alternatively, Emily could produce 10 poems without the cards and Johann could produce 10 cards without the poems, but then neither would earn anything. We therefore assume that when confronted with this choice, both Emily and Johann will each choose to produce one greeting card with a poem inside. In total, they produce two greeting cards.

Gains from Trade: Greater Production Now consider the possibility of economic interaction. Suppose that Emily and Johann can trade. Johann could sell his printing services to Emily, agreeing to print her poems on nice greeting cards. Then Emily could sell the greeting cards to people. Under this arrangement, Emily could spend all day writing poetry, and Johann could spend all day printing. In total, they could produce 10 different greeting cards together, expending the same time and effort it took to produce two greeting cards when they could not trade.

Note that in this example the interaction took place in a market: Johann sold his print jobs to Emily. Another approach would be for Emily and Johann to go into business together, forming a firm, Dickinson and Gutenberg Greetings, Inc. Then their economic interaction would occur within the firm, without buying or selling in the market. Whether in a market or within a firm, the gains from trade in this example are huge. By trading, Emily and Johann can increase their production of greeting cards fivefold, from two cards to 10 cards.

Specialization, Division of Labor, and Comparative Advantage This example illustrates another way in which economic interaction improves people's lives. Economic interaction allows for **specialization**: people concentrating their production efforts on what they are good at. Emily specializes in poetry, and Johann specializes in printing. The specialization creates a division of labor. A **division of labor** occurs when some workers specialize in one task while others specialize in another task. They divide the overall production into parts, with some workers concentrating on one part (printing cards) and other workers concentrating on another part (writing poetry).

The writing-printing example of Emily and Johann also illustrates another economic concept, **comparative advantage**. In general, a person or group of people has a comparative advantage in producing one good relative to another good if that person or group can produce that good with comparatively less time, effort, or resources than another person or group can produce that good. For example, compared with Johann, Emily has a comparative advantage in writing relative to printing. And compared with Emily, Johann has a comparative advantage in printing relative to writing. As this example shows, production can be increased if people specialize in the skill in which they have a comparative advantage[1]—that is, if Emily specializes in writing and Johann in printing.

specialization
a concentration of production effort on a single specific task.

division of labor
the division of production into various parts in which different groups of workers specialize.

comparative advantage
a situation in which a person or group can produce one good at a lower opportunity cost than another person or group.

---

[1] Chapter 18 explores other examples illustrating that comparative advantage also can occur when one person is absolutely better at both activities.

ECONOMICS *IN ACTION*

Gains from Trade on the Internet

The Internet has created many new opportunities for gains from trade. Internet auction sites like eBay allow sellers a way to offer their goods for sale and buyers a way to make bids on sale items. The gains are similar to those of Maria and Adam as they trade sunglasses for hats. Hundreds of different types of sunglasses and baseball hats (and millions of other things) can be bought and sold on eBay—nearly 39,000 types of sunglasses and 5,900 types of baseball hats were for sale at last count.

eBay founder Pierre Omidyar.

If you—like Maria—want to sell a pair of sunglasses and buy a baseball hat, you can simply go to www.ebay.com, offer a pair of sunglasses to sell, and search for the hat you would like to buy. The computer screen will show photos of some of the sunglasses and baseball hats that are offered. You also may find yourself looking through other categories, like baseball cards or beachwear, and decide to enter into another economic transaction, simply because eBay is an extremely large marketplace that lets you interact with more individuals than you had intended to when you first decided to look for a baseball hat.

Another successful online trading site is StubHub, a market for tickets to concerts and sporting events from Phish to football to figure skating. As in other markets, the prices on StubHub convey useful information. Ticket prices on StubHub for the 2009 Super Bowl averaged $2,500, down from $3,500 in 2008. Tickets for the 2011 Super Bowl rebounded to an average of $4,700. Economists surmised that the financial crisis and weak economy in 2009 cut into the price people were willing to pay to go to the Super Bowl.

Another site that has been phenomenally successful at bringing individuals together to gain from trade is Craigslist. Craig Newmark, the founder of Craigslist, saw the power of the Internet for bringing together buyers and sellers who previously had interacted through classified advertisements in newspapers. Craigslist has become one of the first places that people go when they are looking for an apartment to rent or a used car to buy (or, for

Craigslist founder, Craig Newmark.

that matter, looking to rent out their apartment or to sell their used car). Furthermore, Craigslist was quick to exploit the fact that for certain goods and services (apartment sublets, secondhand furniture, used cars), it was more important to reach a group of buyers and sellers who lived in geographic proximity to the person initiating the transaction than it was to reach millions of people all over the world, as eBay did. Newspapers lost millions of dollars in classified advertising revenue as a result of economic transactions switching over to Craigslist.

Perhaps the main reason for the success of these online marketplaces is their underlying simplicity. They provide information and a means for buyers and sellers to interact with each other, just as markets have done throughout history, but the scale of these virtual flea markets dwarfs what was possible before the Internet. The Internet will only continue to grow as a technology that enhances economic interactions. Social networking sites like Facebook, Twitter, and MySpace are extremely popular. The vast sums of money that companies are prepared to pay to own these sites indicates that they, too, will become important online locations for economic interactions to take place in the future. eBay paid $310 million for StubHub in 2007.

Questions to Ponder

1. Can you think of potential gains from trade for you (or for a friend or a family member) that can be realized by using eBay or Craigslist or StubHub?
2. Why do the prices of Super Bowl tickets fall during an economic crisis?

International Trade

international trade
the exchange of goods and
services between people or firms
in different nations.

Thus far, we have said nothing about where Emily and Johann live or work. They could reside in the same country, but they also could reside in different countries. Emily could live in the United States; Johann, in Germany. If this is so, when Emily purchases Johann's printing service, **international trade** will take place because the trade is between people in two different countries.

The gains from international trade are thus of the same kind as the gains from trade within a country. By trading, people can better satisfy their preferences for goods (as in the case of Maria and Adam), or they can better utilize their comparative advantage (as in the case of Emily and Johann). In either situation, both participants can gain from trade.

REVIEW

- All individuals face scarcity in one form or another. Scarcity forces people to make choices. For every choice that is made, there is also an opportunity cost of not doing one thing because another thing has been chosen.
- People benefit from economic interactions—trading goods and services—with other people.

- Gains from trade occur because goods and services can be allocated in ways that are more satisfactory to people.
- Gains from trade also occur because trade permits specialization through the division of labor. People should specialize in the production of goods in which they have a comparative advantage.

Scarcity and Choice for the Economy as a Whole

Just as individuals face scarcity and choice, so too does the economy as a whole. The total amount of resources in an economy—workers, land, machinery, and factories—is limited. Thus, the economy cannot produce all the health care, crime prevention, education, or entertainment that people want. A choice must be made. Let us first consider how to represent scarcity and choice in the whole economy and then consider alternative ways to make those choices.

Production Possibilities

To simplify things, let us suppose that production in the economy can be divided into two broad categories. Suppose the economy can produce either computers (laptops, desktops, servers) or movies (thrillers, love stories, mysteries, musicals). The choice between computers and movies is symbolic of one of the most fundamental choices individuals in any society must face: how much to invest to produce more or better goods in the future versus how much to consume in the present. Computers help people produce more or better goods. Movies are a form of consumption. Other pairs of goods also could be used in our example. Another popular example is guns versus butter, representing defense goods versus nondefense goods.

production possibilities
alternative combinations of
production of various goods that
are possible, given the economy's
resources.

With a scarcity of resources, such as labor and capital, a choice exists between producing some goods, such as computers, versus other goods, such as movies. If the economy produces more of one, then it must produce less of the other. Table 1-1 gives an example of the alternative choices, or the **production possibilities**, for computers and movies. Observe that six different choices could be made, some with more computers and fewer movies, others with fewer computers and more movies.

Table 1-1 tells us what happens as available resources in the economy are moved from movie production to computer production or vice versa. If resources move from producing movies to producing computers, then fewer movies are produced. For example, if all of the resources are used to produce computers, then 25,000 computers and zero movies can be produced, according to the table. If all resources are used to produce movies, then no computers can be produced. These are two extremes, of course. If 100 movies are produced, then we can produce 24,000 computers rather than 25,000 computers. If 200 movies are produced, then computer production must fall to 22,000.

Increasing Opportunity Costs

The production possibilities in Table 1-1 illustrate the concept of opportunity cost for the economy as a whole. The opportunity cost of producing more movies is the value of the forgone computers. For example, the opportunity cost of producing 200 movies rather than 100 movies is 2,000 computers.

An important economic idea about opportunity costs is demonstrated in Table 1-1. Observe that movie production increases as we move down the table. As we move from row to row, movie production increases by the same number: 100 movies. The decline in computer production between the first and second rows—from 25,000 to 24,000 computers—is 1,000 computers. The decline between the second and third rows—from 24,000 to 22,000 computers—is 2,000 computers. Thus, the decline in computer production gets greater as we produce more movies. As we move from 400 movies to 500 movies, we lose 13,000 computers. In other words, the opportunity cost, in terms of computers, of producing more movies increases as we produce more movies. Each extra movie requires a loss of more and more computers. What we have just described is called **increasing opportunity costs**, with an emphasis on the word *increasing*.

Why do opportunity costs increase? You can think about it in the following way. Some of the available resources are better suited for movie production than for computer production, and vice versa. Workers who are good at building computers might not be so good at acting, for example, or moviemaking may require an area with a dry, sunny climate. As more and more resources go into making movies, we are forced to take resources that are much better at computer making and use them for moviemaking. Thus, more and more computer production must be lost to increase movie production by a given amount. Adding specialized computer designers to a movie cast would be quite costly in terms of lost computers, and it might add little to movie production.

increasing opportunity cost a situation in which producing more of one good requires giving up an increasing amount of production of another good.

Table 1-1

Production Possibilities

	Movies	Computers
A	0	25,000
B	100	24,000
C	200	22,000
D	300	18,000
E	400	13,000
F	500	0

ECONOMICS *IN ACTION*

Community College Enrollments and the Economic Downturn

The fall term of the 2008–2009 academic year saw record enrollment increases at community colleges throughout the United States. Enrollment at Delaware Community College in Media, Pennsylvania, was up 8.5 percent compared with typical increases of 3 percent. Enrollment was up an estimated 16 percent at Palm Beach Community College, in Lake Worth, Florida. According to an August 2008 report from *Inside Higher Education,* "Though most colleges only have estimates for their enrollments this fall, many colleges are projecting increases of around 10 percent over last fall."

What explains this enrollment boom? Changing opportunity costs is the most likely explanation. Grace Truman, the spokesperson for Palm Beach Community College, put it this way, "Our enrollment growth strongly correlates to downturns in the economy. Locally, we have had significant slumps and layoffs, particularly in the housing and construction related industries. Our housing, food and gasoline costs have risen sharply in the same time period."

In other words, the downturn in the economy reduced the opportunity cost of going to community college because it made jobs harder to find and less attractive. The unemployment rate in Florida jumped from 4.5 percent to 8.1 percent during the 12 months ending in December 2008. In Pennsylvania, it rose from 4.4 to 6.7 percent and in the nation as a whole from 4.9 to 7.2 percent. The unemployment rate for teenagers (ages 16 to 19) is always higher than the average and it equaled 21 percent at the end of 2008. In these circumstances, finding a job may take a long time and, when you do find one, it may not pay as much as in good economic times.

Question to Ponder

1. Enrollment at community colleges also grew more rapidly than at four-year colleges. Can you use opportunity costs to explain that growth?

iStockphoto.com/Moodboard_Images

The Production Possibilities Curve

Figure 1-2 is a graphical representation of the production possibilities in Table 1-1 that nicely illustrates increasing opportunity costs. We put movies on the horizontal axis and computers on the vertical axis of the figure. Each pair of numbers in a row of the table becomes a point on the graph. For example, point *A* on the graph is from row A of the table. Point *B* is from row B, and so on.

When we connect the points in Figure 1-2, we obtain the **production possibilities curve**. This curve shows the maximum number of computers that can be produced for each quantity of movies produced. Note that the curve in Figure 1-2 slopes downward and is bowed out from the origin. That the curve is bowed out indicates that the opportunity cost of producing movies increases as more movies are produced. As resources move from computer making to moviemaking, each additional movie means a greater loss of computer production.

production possibilities curve

a curve showing the maximum combinations of production of two goods that are possible, given the economy's resources.

Figure 1-2

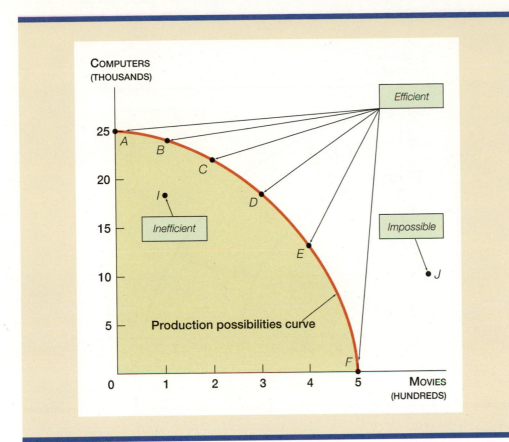

COMPUTERS
(THOUSANDS)

Efficient

Inefficient

Impossible

Production possibilities curve

MOVIES
(HUNDREDS)

The Production Possibilities Curve

Each point on the curve shows the maximum number of computers that can be produced when a given amount of movies is produced. The points with letters are the same as those in Table 1-1 and are connected by smooth lines. Points in the shaded area inside the curve are inefficient. Points outside the curve are impossible. For the efficient points on the curve, the more movies that are produced, the fewer computers that are produced. The curve is bowed out because of increasing opportunity costs.

Inefficient, Efficient, or Impossible? The production possibilities curve shows the effects of scarcity and choice in the economy as a whole. Three situations can be distinguished in Figure 1-2, depending on whether production is in the shaded area, on the curve, or outside the curve.

First, imagine production at point *I*. This point, with 100 movies and 18,000 computers, is inside the curve. But the production possibilities curve tells us that it is possible to produce more computers, more movies, or both with the same amount of resources. For some reason, the economy is not working well at point *I*. For example, a talented movie director may be working on a computer assembly line because her short film has not yet been seen by studio executives, or perhaps a financial crisis has prevented computer companies from getting loans and thus disrupted all production of computer chips. Points inside the curve, like point *I*, are *inefficient* because the economy could produce a larger number of movies, as at point *D*, or a larger number of computers, as at point *B*. Points inside the production possibilities curve are possible, but they are inefficient.

Second, consider points on the production possibilities curve. These points are *efficient*. They represent the maximum amount that can be produced with available resources. The only way to raise production of one good is to lower production of the other good. Thus, points on the curve show a *trade-off* between one good and another.

Third, consider points to the right and above the production possibilities curve, like point *J* in Figure 1-2. These points are *impossible*. The economy does not have the resources to produce those quantities.

Shifts in the Production Possibilities Curve The production possibilities curve is not immovable. It can *shift* out or in. For example, the curve is shown to shift out

Figure 1-3

Shifts in the Production Possibilities Curve
The production possibilities curve shifts out as the economy grows. The maximum numbers of movies and computers that can be produced increase. Improvements in technology, more machines, or more labor permits the economy to produce more.

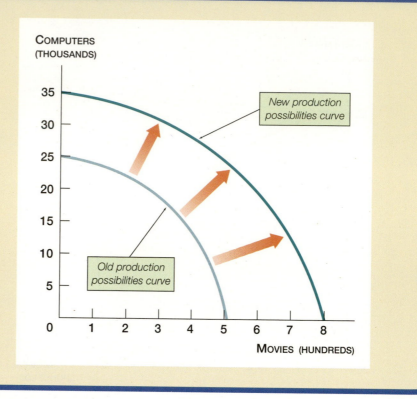

in Figure 1-3. More resources—more workers, for example, or more cameras, lights, and studios—would shift the production possibilities curve out. A technological innovation that allowed one to edit movies faster also would shift the curve outward. When the production possibilities curve shifts out, the economy grows because more goods and services can be produced. The production possibilities curve need not shift outward by the same amount in all directions. The curve could move up more than it moves to the right, for example.

As the production possibilities curve shifts out, impossibilities are converted into possibilities. Some of what was impossible for the U.S. economy in 1975 is possible now. Some of what is impossible now will be possible in 2035. Hence, the economists' notion of possibilities is a temporary one. When we say that a certain combination of computers and movies is impossible, we do not mean "forever impossible," we mean only "currently impossible."

Scarcity, Choice, and Economic Progress

However, the conversion of impossibilities into possibilities is also an economic problem of choice and scarcity: If we invest less now—in machines, in education, in children, in technology—and consume more now, then we will have less available in the future. If we take computers and movies as symbolic of investment and consumption, then choosing more investment will result in a larger outward shift of the production possibilities curve, as illustrated in Figure 1-4. More investment enables the economy to produce more in the future.

The production possibilities curve represents a *trade-off*, but it does not mean that some people win only if others lose. First, it is not necessary for someone to lose in order for the production possibilities curve to shift out. When the curve shifts out, the production of both items increases. Although some people may fare better than others as the production possibilities curve is pushed out, no one necessarily loses. In principle, everyone can gain. Second, if the economy is at an inefficient point (like point *I* in Figure 1-2), then production of both goods can be increased with no trade-off. In general, therefore, the economy is more like a win-win situation, where everyone can achieve a gain.

Figure 1-4

Shifts in the Production Possibilities Curve Depend on Choices

On the left, few resources are devoted to investment for the future; hence, the production possibilities curve shifts only a little over time. On the right, more resources are devoted to investment and less to consumption; hence, the production possibilities curve shifts out by a larger amount over time.

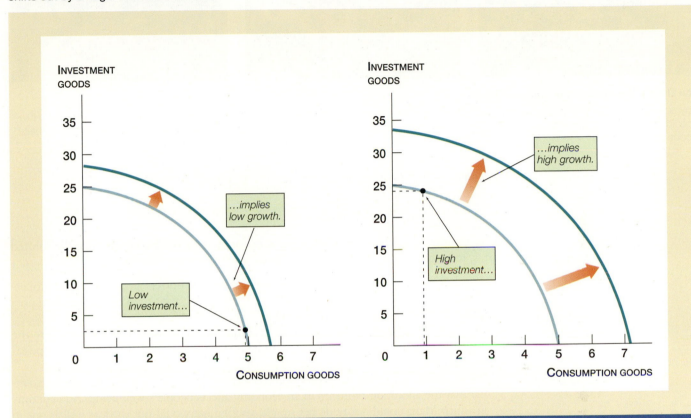

REVIEW

- The production possibilities curve represents the choices open to a whole economy when it is confronted with a scarcity of resources. As more of one item is produced, less of another item must be produced. The opportunity cost of producing more of one item is the reduced production of another item.

- The production possibilities curve is bowed out because of increasing opportunity costs.

- Points inside the curve are inefficient. Points on the curve are efficient. Points outside the curve are impossible.

- The production possibilities curve shifts out as resources increase.

- Outward shifts of the production possibilities curve or moves from inefficient to efficient points are the reasons why the economy is not a zero-sum game, despite the existence of scarcity and choice.

What?

How?

For Whom?

The Three Fundamental Economic Questions

Any economic system has to answer three questions: What goods and services should be produced—cars, movies, or something else? How should these goods or services be produced—in what type of factory, and with how much equipment and labor? And for whom should these goods be produced?

Market Economies and the Price System

Every economy, whether it is a small island economy or a large economy like the United States, must find a way to solve three essential questions or problems.

- *What* is to be produced: movies, computers, guns, butter, greeting cards, Rollerblades, health care, or something else? In other words, where on the production possibilities curve should an economy be?
- *How* are these goods to be produced? In other words, how can an economy use the available resources so that it is not at an inefficient point inside the production possibilities curve?
- *For whom* are the goods to be produced? We know from the hat versus sunglasses example that the allocation of goods in an economy affects people's well-being. An economy in which Maria could not trade her sunglasses for a hat would not work as well as one in which such trades and reallocations are possible. Moreover, an economy in which some people get everything and others get virtually nothing also is not working well.

market economy
an economy characterized by freely determined prices and the free exchange of goods and services in markets.

command economy
an economy in which the government determines prices and production; also called a centrally planned economy.

Broadly speaking, the **market economy** and the **command economy** are two alternative approaches to answering these questions. In a market economy, most decisions about what, how, and for whom to produce are made by individual consumers, firms, governments, and other organizations interacting in markets. In a command, or centrally planned, economy, most decisions about what, how, and for whom to produce are made by those who control the government, which, through a central plan, commands and controls what people do.

Command economies are much less common in the twenty-first century than they were in the mid-twentieth century, when nearly half the world's population, including the residents of Eastern Europe, the Soviet Union, and China, lived in centrally planned economies. After many decades of struggling to make this system work, leaders of the command economies gradually grew disillusioned with the high degree of inefficiency resulting from the planned approach, which required that the state, or central planners, make critical detailed production decisions; this often resulted in shortages or surplus of products and, as a by-product, in political unrest. Since 1990, most command economies have, with varying degrees of success, tried to convert from a command to a market system. The difficulties with converting these systems are partly due to the fact that these economies have none or few of the social, legal, or political fixtures critical to the market system. China has been by far the most successful of these economies at making the

cannot know the exact reasons why prices for certain goods rise or fall. Hence, it is rather amazing that prices can signal this information.

Incentives Now let's use this example to consider how prices provide incentives. A higher price for bicycles will increase the incentives for firms to produce bicycles. Because they receive more for each bicycle, they produce more. If there is a large price increase that is not merely temporary, new firms may enter the bicycle business. In contrast, the reduced prices for cars signal to car producers that production should decrease.

Distribution How do prices affect the distribution of income? On the one hand, workers who find the production of the good they make increasing because of the higher demand for bicycles will earn more. On the other hand, income will be reduced for those who make cars or who have to pay more for bicycles. Local delivery services that use bicycles will see their costs increase.

Financial Crises and Recessions

Economies are sometimes hit by **financial crises**. When the World Trade Center was destroyed by terrorists in September 2001, the financial markets in New York had to close down because trading rooms and electronic networks for making trades were destroyed. However, backup facilities were soon made operational and the markets reopened after only a few days. Fortunately, the financial crisis was over soon after it began.

In August 2007 another financial crisis began, but this one lasted much longer and its causes are more difficult to determine. Most likely a fall in home prices in 2006 and 2007 following a prior rapid rise caused people to stop making payments on their home loans; banks and other financial institutions then became reluctant to lend. As a result people throughout the economy had trouble getting loans, and they reduced their purchases of goods and services. This meant that firms had to cut production of these goods and services and they laid off people who were employed producing them. A **recession**—a period of declining production and employment—thus began in December 2007 and ended in June 2009.

Economies have been subject to financial crises and recessions for hundreds of years. By far the worst in the United States was the Great Depression of the 1930s, but comparably serious financial crises have occurred in other regions and countries, most recently in Latin America, Asia, and Russia in the 1990s. The 1980s and 1990s in the United States was a period of unusual financial calm with few recessions. There is a great debate about whether financial crises are inevitable—a kind of market failure where the market economy does not work well—and government has a role to play in trying to prevent them and mitigate them, or whether the crises are due to government actions which make things worse—a kind of government failure.

financial crises
disruptions to financial markets which make it difficult for people and business firms to borrow and obtain loans.

recession
a decline in production and employment that lasts for six months or more.

REVIEW

- The market economy and the command economy are two alternative systems for addressing the questions any economy must face: what to produce, how to produce, and for whom to produce.

- A market economy is characterized by several key elements, such as freely determined prices, property rights, and freedom to trade at home and abroad.

- For a market economy to work well, markets should be competitive and the government should play a role when there is a market failure.

- Prices are signals, they provide incentives, and they affect the distribution of income.

- Market economies are sometimes hit by financial crises and recessions, creating another role for government in preventing or alleviating them.

CONCLUSION

One basic idea lies at the center of economics: People make purposeful choices with scarce resources, and interact with other people when they make these choices.

This introductory chapter illustrates this idea, starting with decisions by Steve Jobs and Mark Zuckerberg about whether to leave school and continuing with simple examples of people making choices about what to consume or produce.

From this central idea, many other powerful ideas follow, as summarized visually in Figure 1-5. An *opportunity cost* exists every time a choice is made. People *gain from trade*, both through a *better allocation* of goods and through *comparative advantage*. Every society faces trade-offs described by *production possibilities curves*. Every society faces three fundamental questions: *what*, *how*, and *for whom* to produce. Market economies—characterized by *freely determined prices, property rights, freedom to trade*, and *a role for both government and private organizations*—provide answers to these three questions. The price system helps a market economy work by providing *incentives*, sending *signals*, and affecting the *distribution* of income.

You will see this central idea again and again as you continue to study economics.

Figure 1-5

From One Central Idea, Many Powerful Ideas Follow

As you study economics, you will see the same central idea again and again. This figure illustrates how many powerful economic ideas are connected to the one in the center.

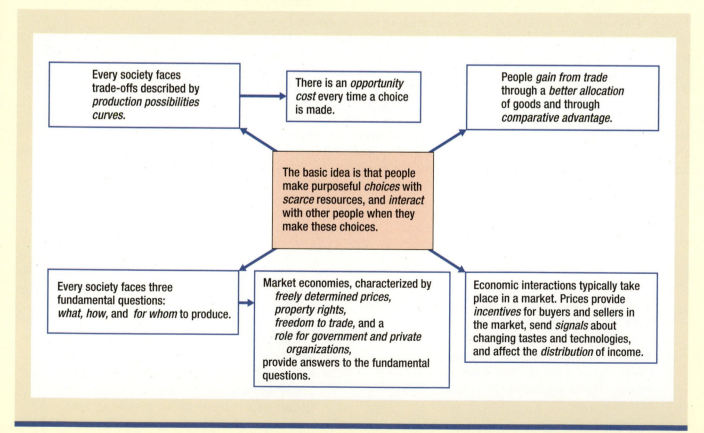

KEY POINTS

1. Everyone faces a scarcity of something, usually time or resources.
2. Scarcity leads to choice, and choice leads to opportunity costs.
3. Trade leads to gains because it allows goods and services to be reallocated in a way that improves people's well-being.
4. Trade also leads to gains because it permits people to specialize in what they are relatively good at.
5. The production possibilities curve summarizes the trade-offs in the whole economy because of scarcity.
6. Economic production is efficient if the economy is on the production possibilities curve. Production is inefficient if the economy is inside the production possibilities curve.
7. Points outside the production possibilities curve currently are impossible. More investment, more workers, or better technology can shift the production possibilities curve out and make the impossible possible.
8. The three basic questions that any economy must face are what, how, and for whom production should take place.
9. A well-functioning market system, involving freely determined prices, property rights, freedom to trade, and a role for government and private organizations, can answer these basic questions.
10. Prices transmit signals, provide incentives, and affect the distribution of income in a market economy. If prices are set at incorrect levels by government, waste and inefficiency—such as feeding bread to livestock—will result.

KEY TERMS

choice, 3
command economy, 14
comparative advantage, 6
division of labor, 6
economic interactions, 3
economics, 2
financial crises, 17
freely determined prices, 15
gains from trade, 5
government failure, 16
incentive, 15
increasing opportunity costs, 9

international trade, 8
market, 3
market economy, 14
market failure, 16
opportunity cost, 4
production possibilities, 8
production possibilities curve, 10
property rights, 15
recession, 17
scarcity, 3
specialization, 6

QUESTIONS FOR REVIEW

1. What is the basic idea at the center of economics?
2. Why does scarcity imply a choice among alternatives?
3. What is the opportunity cost of making a choice?
4. How can gains be achieved from trade even when total production of goods and services does not change?
5. How can specialization lead to gains from trade?
6. What is the principle of increasing opportunity costs?
7. Why is the production of a combination of goods that is located inside the production possibilities curve considered to be inefficient?
8. How can financial crises cause inefficiencies?
9. What are the key ingredients of a market economy?
10. What are the three basic questions that any economic system must address?
11. What roles do prices play in a market economy?

PROBLEMS

1. Suppose that you are president of the student government, and you have to decide how to allocate a $20,000 fund for guest speakers for the year. Conan O'Brien and Will Ferrell each cost $10,000 per appearance, Stephen Colbert costs $20,000 per appearance, and former economic advisers to the government charge $1,000 per lecture. Explain the economic problem of choice and scarcity in this case. What issues would you consider in arriving at a decision?

2. Michelle Wie, a teenage golf prodigy who earned $16 million in endorsements and $4 million in prize money and appearance fees in 2006, announced that she would enroll as a student at Stanford University in the fall of 2007. What was her opportunity cost of a year of college? How does it compare to your opportunity cost of a year of college?

3. Allison will graduate from high school next June. She has ranked her three possible postgraduation plans in the following order: (1) work for two years at a consulting job in her hometown paying $20,000 per year, (2) attend a local community college for two years, spending $5,000 per year on tuition and expenses, and (3) travel around the world tutoring a rock star's child for pay of $5,000 per year. What is the opportunity cost of her choice?

4. Suppose you have two boxes of chocolate chip cookies and a friend of yours has 2 gallons of milk. Explain how you can both gain from trade. Is this a gain from trade through *better allocation* or *greater production?*

5. Suppose Tina and Julia can produce brownies and romantic poems (which can be combined to make a lovely gift) in the following combinations in a given week:

Tina		Julia	
Brownies	*Poems*	*Brownies*	*Poems*
50	0	25	0
40	1	20	1
30	2	15	2
20	3	10	3
10	4	5	4
0	5	0	5

a. If Tina and Julia are each currently producing two poems per week, how many brownies are they producing? What is the total production of brownies and poems between them?

b. Is there a possibility for increasing production? Why or why not?

c. Suppose Julia completely specializes in producing poems and Tina completely specializes in producing brownies. What will be their total production of brownies and poems?

6. Suppose you must divide your time between studying for your math final and writing a final paper for your English class. The fraction of time that you spend studying math and its relation to your grade in the two classes are given in the table below.

Fraction of Time Spent on Math	Math Grade	English Grade
0	0	97
20	45	92
40	65	85
60	75	70
80	82	50
100	88	0

a. Draw a trade-off curve for the math grade versus the English grade.

b. What is the opportunity cost of increasing the time spent on math from 80 to 100 percent? What is the opportunity cost of increasing the time spent on math from 60 to 80 percent?

c. Are there increasing opportunity costs from spending more time on math? Explain.

d. Suppose your parents want you to get a 92 percent in both subjects. What would you tell them?

7. A small country produces only two goods, cars and cakes. Given its limited resources, this country has the following production possibilities:

Cars	Cakes
0	200
25	180
50	130
75	70
100	0

a. Draw the production possibilities curve.

b. Suppose car production uses mainly machines and cake production uses mainly labor. Show what happens to the curve when the number of machines increases, but the amount of labor remains unchanged.

8. Tracy tells Huey that he can improve his economics grade without sacrificing fun activities or his grades in other courses. Can you imagine ways in which this might be possible? What does that imply about the initial situation? If Huey is taking just two courses and he can improve his economics grade without hurting his math grade, how could you represent this situation graphically?

9. Suppose decreased production of oil in the Middle East causes the price of oil to rise around the world. Explain how this change in the price signals information to U.S. producers of various goods, provides incentives to U.S. producers of various goods, and affects the distribution of income.

10. When you look at the economies of the United States, Europe, or Japan, you see most of the ingredients of a market economy. For example, consider bicycles. Prices in the bicycle market are free to vary; people have property rights to the bicycles they buy; many people sell bicycles; many bicycles sold in the United States, Europe, and Japan come from other countries; the government regulates bicycle use (no bicycles on the freeways, for example); and bicycle production takes place within firms with many workers. Replace bicycles with another good or service of your choosing and comment on whether the statement is still true.

2 Observing and Explaining the Economy

Just as physicists try to explain the existence of black holes in outer space and biologists try to explain why dinosaurs became extinct, economists try to explain interesting observations and facts about the economy. One reason is pure intellectual excitement: It can be fun to solve economic puzzles. But understanding economic events or trends is also essential for making sound policy recommendations, whether in business or government. An incorrect explanation for the financial crisis in 2008, for example, could bring about harmful policy responses in the future with unintended consequences despite the best of intentions.

To explain economic events, economists use the ideas introduced in the previous chapter—from opportunity cost to incentives to the price system of a market economy. Why does community college enrollment increase in recessions? Because the lack of jobs lowers the opportunity cost of staying in school. Why did the price of Super Bowl tickets fall sharply in 2009 and then rise again? Probably because many people who usually go to the Super Bowl lost money in the financial crisis in fall 2008 and decided not to go. Why has health care spending increased faster than the rest of the U.S. economy? In part, because people have less incentive to watch what they spend on health care compared with other goods and services. Why did economic growth increase dramatically in China in the past 30 years? Because China moved from a command economy toward a market economy.

Learning to apply economic ideas to such real-world questions is an important part of learning economics, but it also is one of the most challenging parts because the real world is never quite as tidy as we would like and usually the explanation has several factors. In this chapter, we explain some of the ways that economists explain the facts in practice, and we point out some of the key pitfalls.

We start by using a practical example to show how economists document and quantify their observations. As we will see, even documenting the facts can be tricky.

Why Has Driving Shifted into Reverse?

According to data from the Federal Highway Administration, Americans have been driving less in recent years. Graphs are a helpful way to document and pinpoint such trends. Figure 2-1 plots the total miles traveled by all the vehicles—cars, trucks, and motorcycles—on all the streets, roads, and highways in the United States from 1993 to 2010. The vertical axis is measured in billions of miles; the horizontal axis is measured in years. Observe that after rising for many years, "vehicle miles traveled" reached a peak in 2007 and then started to decline. At the peak, about 3,000 billion, or 3 trillion, miles were driven. Why did the driving trend reverse after moving up for many years?

The first thing to investigate is whether changes in the number of people in the United States may have been a factor in the changes in the miles traveled. You would expect that more people would lead to more total driving and fewer people to less total driving. To test this possibility, one can simply divide vehicle miles traveled by the population of the United States. In 2007, when total miles traveled were 3,000 billion, around 300 million people lived in the United States; this implies that the average miles traveled per person were about 10,000, which probably is a more understandable number than 3 trillion. Vehicle miles traveled per person for the other years from 1993 to 2010 are plotted in Figure 2-2. Now note something important about Figure 2-2 compared with Figure 2-1: Vehicle miles traveled *per person* reaches a peak in 2005 rather than 2007. Thus, miles traveled started growing more slowly than the population in that year. So we should think of 2005 rather than 2007 as the turning point to try to explain the change in miles traveled. Another difference between Figure 2-1 and Figure 2-2 is that the line graph in Figure 2-2 shows a continued fall in 2010, illustrating that, relative to the population, driving continued to decline in 2010.

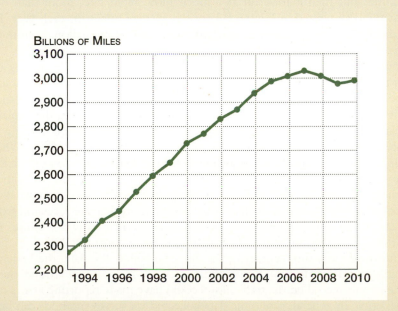

Figure 2-1

"Vehicle Miles Traveled" in the United States, 1993–2010

For each year from 1993 through 2010, the total amount of miles traveled in vehicles on U.S. roads and streets is plotted; a line then connects the points to better visualize the trends and turning points.

Source: Federal Highway Administration.

Figure 2-2

Vehicle Miles Traveled Per Person

For each year, vehicle miles traveled from Figure 2-1 is divided by the population of the United States and plotted in the graph.

Source: Figure 1 and Bureau of the Census.

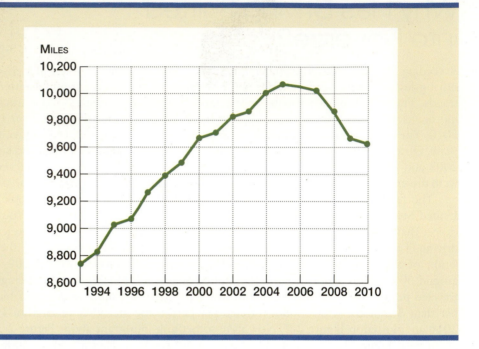

We can look in many places for an explanation of the reversal in this trend, but the first obvious place is the price of gasoline. If the price of gasoline increases, then people will have a greater incentive to walk or ride a bike or take a train or plane rather than drive their car, truck or motorcycle. So let's look at the price of gasoline. Figure 2-3 plots the average price of gasoline for the same years as Figures 2-1 and 2-2 in the United States; dollars per gallon are now on the vertical axis. Look carefully at the pattern of the price of gasoline. Note that the price did not rise much at all for nearly 10 years from 1993 to 2002, but then it took off at a much more rapid rate, more than doubling. Recall that the data plotted in Figure 2-3 are the average prices for each year. In 2008, the price during the summer months reached more than $4 per gallon, even though the average for the year was $3.30.

By comparing Figures 2-2 and 2-3, one can see that the peak in driving occurred soon after the price of gasoline started to rise rapidly. Based on the data in these figures, one can begin to make a plausible case that higher gasoline prices are the explanation for the decline in driving. But, as with many real-world economic events, the explanation is not as clear and obvious as one might hope. One problem is that the turning point in driving occurred in 2005, several years after prices started rising rapidly. What could cause such a lag? Perhaps people took awhile to adjust; commuters may have had to wait until they could find a place to live closer to the train station. Perhaps some people thought the high price of gasoline was temporary. In fact, the price did partially reverse in 2009 before rising again in 2010. Another possibility is that the recession from 2007 to 2009, and the resulting high unemployment rates, led to fewer commutes to work, although the peak in driving occurred before the recession began.

Yet another issue is the accuracy of the data. To collect the data, the Federal Highway Administration set up monitoring stations at 4,000 locations around the United States. The people recording the traffic flows could have made reporting errors or missed key intersections. In general, economic data collected via survey methods can be inaccurate; people sometimes do not understand the questions, or they do not have the correct

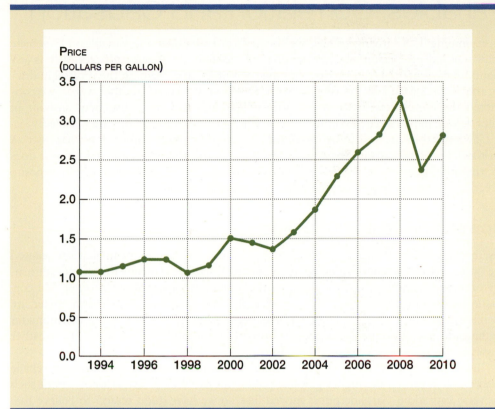

Figure 2-3

Average Retail Price of Gasoline in the United States, 1993–2010
For each year, the price of a gallon of gasoline is averaged across the year and across all grades and plotted in the graph.

Source: Department of Energy.

information. Sometimes, data may be more aggregated than you would like them to be; for example, the average price of a gallon of gasoline during a given year conceals the substantial variation in gasoline prices that occur within a year (as was true in 2008). By using the annual average, one might miss potentially important patterns in the data.

It is also important to check the difference between the price of gasoline and the *relative* price of gasoline compared with other goods. If you find that the price of other forms of transportation—trains, planes, or bicycles—rose just as fast as gasoline, then the rising price of gasoline would not be a good explanation for the decline in driving. In sum, although it seems quite reasonable that an explanation for the reversal in driving trends was the rise in the price of gasoline, as always in economics, there are other possible competing views to discuss and assess.

REVIEW

- Explaining real-world economic trends and events is both interesting in its own right and essential for sound policy making. The first step is to find good data to describe the trend or event, then to identify what factors may have caused the trend, and finally to assess how changes elsewhere in the economy could affect the explanation.

- When applying economic ideas to explain real-world trends and events, it is best to recognize the limitations of the analysis and think critically about all possible causal factors. For example, when studying changes over time, it is important to take account of changes in the population which have large effects.

Variables, Correlation and Causation

economic variable
any economic measure that can vary over a range of values.

In examining U.S. driving trends, we focused on two economic variables: (1) vehicle miles traveled per person and (2) the price of gasoline. An **economic variable** is any economic measure that can vary over a range of values. In explaining the reversal in driving trends, we noted a relationship between these two variables. In other words, we considered the correlation between the price of gasoline and the subsequent amount of miles driven; in particular, we noted that, when prices rose rapidly, driving declined.

Two variables are said to be *correlated* if they tend to move up or down together. A *positive correlation* exists if the two variables move in the same direction—when one goes up, the other goes up. A *negative correlation* exists if the two variables move in opposite directions—when one goes up, the other goes down.

Correlation versus Causation

Just because two variables are correlated it does not necessarily mean that one caused the other. *Causation* and *correlation* are different. *Correlation* means that one event usually occurs with another. *Causation* means that one event brings about another. But correlation does not imply causation. For example, high readings on a thermometer are correlated with hot weather: High readings occur when it is hot. But the thermometer readings do not cause the hot weather. Causation is the other way around: Hot weather causes the reading on the thermometer to be high.

In the example of miles driven, one might be concerned that the decline in vehicle miles traveled caused the higher gasoline prices, but the timing raises doubts about such a reverse causation: Gasoline prices moved first, so we have good reason to believe that gasoline prices caused the change in driving trends. In many instances, determining causation is difficult.

The Lack of Controlled Experiments in Economics

controlled experiments
empirical tests of theories in a controlled setting in which particular effects can be isolated.

In many sciences—psychology, physics, and biology—investigators perform **controlled experiments** to determine whether one event causes another event. An example of a controlled experiment is the clinical trial of a new drug. New drugs are tested by trying them out on two groups of individuals. One group gets the new drug; the other group, the control group, gets a placebo (a pill without the drug). If the experiment results in a significantly greater number of people being cured among the group taking the drug than among the group taking the placebo, investigators conclude that the drug causes the cure.

Controlled experiments are rare in economics. When faced with a situation with limited data (say, data for one country over a particular time period), causation is hard to determine. In these circumstances, we can try to look at other countries' experiences, or we can look at the experiences of different states within the United States. But, unfortunately, no two countries or states are alike in all respects. Thus, attempting to control for other factors is not as easy as in the case of clinical trials.

experimental economics
a branch of economics that uses laboratory experiments to analyze economic behavior.

In recent years, economists have adapted some of the methods of experimental science and have begun to conduct economic experiments in laboratory settings that are similar to the real world. These experiments can be repeated, and various effects can be controlled for. **Experimental economics** is a growing area of economics. The findings of experimental economics have affected economists' understanding of how the economy works. Experiments in economics also provide an excellent way to *learn* how the economy works, much as experiments in science courses can help one learn about gravity

or the structure of plant cells. But because it is difficult to replicate real-world settings as precisely as in such experiments, they have yet to be applied as widely as the clinical or laboratory experiments in other sciences.

Economic Models

To explain economic facts and observations, one needs an economic theory, or *model*. An **economic model** is an explanation of how the economy or a part of the economy works. In practice, most economists use the terms *theory* and *model* interchangeably, although sometimes the term *theory* suggests a general explanation and the term *model* suggests a more specific explanation. The term *law* also is used interchangeably with the terms *model* and *theory* in economics.

Economic models are always abstractions, or simplifications, of the real world. They take complicated phenomena, such as the behavior of people, firms, and governments, and simplify them. Economists like to draw an analogy between a model and a road map—both are abstractions of a much more complex reality. Some maps (like some models) can be detailed; others are just broad abstractions. No single model is "correct," just like no single map is "correct." If you wanted to drive from New York to California, you would need an interstate map, one that ignores the details of individual streets within a city to show the main highways. In contrast, if you were headed from one neighborhood of Chicago to another, an interstate map would be of no use; instead, you would need a map that showed city streets in greater detail.

Microeconomic versus Macroeconomic Models
There are two types of models corresponding to the two main branches of economics: microeconomics and macroeconomics. They each have their purpose.

Microeconomics studies the behavior of individual firms and households or specific markets like the health care market or the college graduate market. It looks at variables such as the price of a college education or the reason for increased wages of college graduates. Microeconomic models explain why the price of gasoline varies from station to station and why airfares are discounted. The analogy in the map world is to the city street map.

Macroeconomics focuses on the whole economy—the whole national economy or even the whole world economy. The most comprehensive measure of the size of an economy is the **gross domestic product (GDP)**. GDP is the total value of all goods and services made in the country during a specific period of time, such as a year. GDP includes all newly made goods, such as cars, shoes, gasoline, airplanes, and houses; it also includes services like health care, education, and auto repair. Macroeconomics tries to explain the changes in GDP over time rather than the changes in a part of the GDP, like health care spending. It looks at questions such as, what causes the GDP to grow and why many more workers are unemployed in Europe than in the United States? The analogy in the map world is to the interstate map.

economic model
an explanation of how the economy or part of the economy works.

microeconomics
the branch of economics that examines individual decision making at firms and households and the way they interact in specific industries and markets.

macroeconomics
the branch of economics that examines the workings and problems of the economy as a whole–GDP growth and unemployment.

gross domestic product (GDP)
a measure of the value of all the goods and services newly produced in an economy during a specified period of time.

ECONOMICS *IN ACTION*

An Economic Experiment to Study Discrimination

As you know by now, economists are hampered by their inability to run controlled experiments. Without controlled experiments, it is always a challenge to definitively establish whether one variable has a causal impact on another. However, even though good experiments are rare in economics, they are by no means nonexistent. In 2004, economists Marianne Bertrand and Sendhil Mullainathan published a paper[1] that described a labor market experiment they ran to study discrimination patterns in labor markets.

The title of Bertrand and Mullainathan's research paper, "Are Emily and Greg More Employable Than Lakisha and Jamal?" gives an idea of what their experiment was about. They wanted to test whether résumés that were attached to African American–sounding names (like Lakisha Washington and Jamal Jones) got fewer callbacks for interviews than did identical-quality résumés attached to names that were associated more typically as white-sounding (like Emily Walsh and Greg Baker). This was a controlled experiment in that the only difference between the two résumés was the name of the candidate. If the résumés with African American–sounding names got fewer callbacks than the résumés with white-sounding names, then that would provide evidence of differential treatment simply on the basis of race.

A controlled labor market experiment like this is a much better way to test for differential treatment than looking at the observed labor market outcomes of whites and African Americans. After all, in many cases, a researcher would not be able to get data on applicants for a position. Even if the researcher got the data, the applicants would have very different profiles and qualifications. Furthermore, it would be difficult for the researcher to know how to judge whether one candidate was more qualified than another across a variety of job types.

An overview of Bertrand and Mullainathan's project is given here; you can search the internet to find the complete version of the paper.

- Bertrand and Mullainathan sent out nearly 5,000 résumés in response to 1,300 help wanted advertisements in Boston and Chicago.

- The résumés were of two types: one containing education and work experience for a highly qualified worker, and the other containing information for a less-qualified worker.

- Each position received four résumés, two high-quality ones and two low-quality ones. One résumé of each type was randomly assigned one of a set of names commonly associated with whites, and the other was assigned a name from a set of names commonly associated with African Americans.

- The results of the experiment showed that applicants with white-sounding names had to send out about 10 résumés before getting a callback, whereas applicants with African American–sounding names had to send out around 15 résumés.

- The researchers found that white-sounding names with a higher-quality résumé had a much higher probability of being called back (almost 30 percent) for an interview than whites with a lower-quality résumé. The gap between African Americans with high-quality résumés and African Americans with low-quality résumés was smaller, implying that the gap between the races is even wider at the top end of the quality distribution.

- The results held true across different industries and different occupations.

- The researchers also looked at the issue of class by choosing white and African American–sounding names that are associated with relatively low levels of parental education and names associated with high levels of education. The differences in perceived class were nowhere near as important as the differences in perceived race.

This research provides an example of how creative, interesting, and influential good economics research can be. The results provided compelling evidence of labor market access differentials across race. Because this was an experiment, we can be much more certain that the causal factor behind the differential treatment was the perceived race. Furthermore, the pernicious effect of this lack of equal access is quite substantial: Mullainathan and Bertrand estimate that it takes eight years of extra experience on a résumé to make up for having an African American–sounding name. They also point out that standard policy recommendations for minority unemployment, which include better training and education programs, will not necessarily be the solution, because the rewards for having more experience and skills seem to be smaller for African American workers than for white workers. Although the results of the research may be dismaying, its insights represent an important step in making people aware of the extent of unequal access to labor markets and encourage people to work toward bettering the situation.

[1] Marianne Bertrand and Sendhil Mullainathan, "Are Emily and Greg More Employable Than Lakisha and Jamal? A Field Experiment on Labor Market Discrimination," *American Economic Review*, 94, no. 4 (September 2004).

Figure 2-4

A Model with Two Positively Related Variables

The upward-sloping line shows how the variables are related. When one variable increases from *A* to *B*, the other variable increases from *C* to *D*. If one variable declines from *B* to *A*, the other variable declines from *D* to *C*. We say that Variable 1 is positively related to Variable 2, or that Variable 1 varies directly with Variable 2.

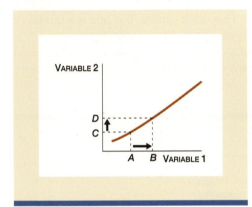

Figure 2-5

A Model with Two Negatively Related Variables

When one variable increases from *A* to *B*, the other variable decreases from *D* to *C*. Likewise, when one variable decreases from *B* to *A*, the other variable increases from *C* to *D*. We say that Variable 1 is negatively related to Variable 2, or that Variable 1 varies inversely with Variable 2.

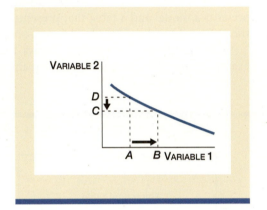

Do not be critical of economic models just because they are simplifications. In every science, models are simplifications of reality. Models are successful if they explain reality reasonably well. In fact, if they were not simplifications, models would be hard to use effectively. Economic models differ from those in the physical sciences because they endeavor to explain human behavior, which is complex and often unpredictable. It is for this reason that the brilliant physicist Max Planck said that economics was harder than physics.

Economic models can be described with words, numerical tables, graphs, or algebra. To use economics, it is important to be able to work with these different descriptions. Figures 2-4 and 2-5 show how models can be illustrated with graphs. By looking at a graph, we can see quickly whether the model has an inverse or a direct relationship. If a model says that one variable varies inversely with the other, this means that if the first variable rises, then the second falls. If a model says that one variable varies directly with another, this means that if one variable rises, the other also rises. In economics, the expression "is positively related to" is frequently used in place of the phrase "varies directly with," which is more common in other sciences. Similarly, the expression "is negatively related to" is frequently used in place of "varies inversely with."

In Figure 2-4, two variables are shown to be **positively related**. In other words, when Variable 1 increases from *A* to *B*, Variable 2 increases from *C* to *D* by the specific amount given by the curve. Likewise, when Variable 1 decreases from *B* to *A*, Variable 2 decreases from *D* to *C*. In Figure 2-5, a model with two variables that are **negatively related** is shown. Here, when Variable 1 increases from *A* to *B*, Variable 2 decreases from *D* to *C*. Likewise, when Variable 1 decreases from *B* to *A*, Variable 2 increases from *C* to *D*. Models have *constants* as well as variables. The constants in the models in Figures 2-4 and 2-5 are the positions and shapes of the curves.

positively related
a situation in which an increase in one variable is associated with an increase in another variable; also called *directly related*.

negatively related
a situation in which an increase in one variable is associated with a decrease in another variable; also called *inversely related*.

An Example: A Model with Two Variables Figure 2-6 shows a model describing how doctors employed in a health maintenance organization (HMO) provide physical examinations. The model illustrates that the more doctors who are employed at the HMO, the more physical exams can be given. The model is represented in four different ways: (1) words, (2) a numerical table, (3) a graph, and (4) algebra.

A verbal description appears on the lower right of Figure 2-6: More doctors mean more physical exams, but additional doctors increase the number of exams by smaller amounts, presumably because the diagnostic facilities at the HMO are limited; for example, only so many rooms are available for physical exams.

On the upper left, a table with numbers shows how the number of examinations depends on the number of doctors. Exactly how many examinations can be given by each number of doctors is shown in the table. Clearly, this table is much more specific than the verbal description. Be sure to distinguish between the meaning of a table that presents a model and a table that presents data. They look similar, but one is a model of the real world and the other represents observations about the real world.

On the upper right, a curve shows the relationship between doctors and physical examinations. The curve shows how many exams each number of doctors can perform.

Figure 2-6

Economic Models in Four Ways

Each model has advantages and disadvantages; this book focuses mostly on verbal descriptions, graphs, and numerical tables, but occasionally some algebra will be used to help explain things.

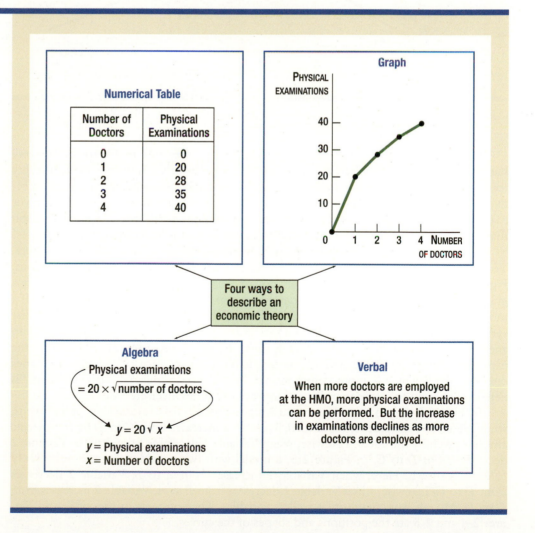

Numerical Table

Number of Doctors	Physical Examinations
0	0
1	20
2	28
3	35
4	40

Graph

PHYSICAL EXAMINATIONS / NUMBER OF DOCTORS

Four ways to describe an economic theory

Algebra

Physical examinations
$= 20 \times \sqrt{\text{number of doctors}}$

$$y = 20\sqrt{x}$$

y = Physical examinations
x = Number of doctors

Verbal

When more doctors are employed at the HMO, more physical examinations can be performed. But the increase in examinations declines as more doctors are employed.

The points on the curve are plotted from the information in the table. The vertical axis has the number of examinations; the horizontal axis has the number of doctors. The points are connected with a line to help visualize the curve.

Finally, the lower left shows the doctor-examination relationship in algebraic form. In this case, the number of exams is equal to the square root of the number of doctors times 20. If we use the symbol **y** for the number of exams and **x** for the number of doctors, the model looks a lot like the equations in an algebra course.

All four ways of representing models have advantages and disadvantages. The advantage of the verbal representation is that we usually communicate with people in words, and if we want our economic models to have any use, we need to communicate with people who have not studied economics. The verbal representation, however, is not as precise as the other three models. In addition to verbal analysis, in this book we focus on tabular and graphical representations and, when appropriate, algebraic descriptions as well.

The *Ceteris Paribus* Assumption

To use models for prediction, economists use the assumption of **ceteris paribus**, which means "all other things being equal." For example, the prediction that Variable 2 will fall from *D* to *C* assumes that the curve in Figure 2-5 does not shift: The position of the curve when Variable 1 is at *A* is *equal* to the position of the curve when Variable 1 is at *B*. If other things were not equal—if the curve shifted—then we could not predict that Variable 2 would fall from *D* to *C* when Variable 1 rose from *A* to *B*. Similarly, predicting that more doctors can produce more physical exams assumes that there is no power outage that would cause the diagnostic equipment to stop operating.

ceteris paribus
"all other things being equal"; refers to holding all other variables constant or keeping all other things the same when one variable is changed.

The Use of Existing Models

Because economics has been around for a long time, many existing models can be applied to explain observations or make predictions that are useful to decision makers. In practice, whether in government or business or universities, economists use models that are already in existence.

The models are used in many different types of applications, from determining the effects of discrimination in the workplace to evaluating the gains from lower health care prices. Frequently, the models are applied in new and clever ways.

The Development of New Models

Like models in other sciences, economic models change and new models are developed. Many of the models in this book are different from the models in books published 40 years ago. New economic models evolve because some new observations cannot be explained by existing models.

The process of the development of new models or theories in economics proceeds much like that in any other science. First one develops a *hypothesis*, or a hunch, to explain a puzzling observation. Then one tests the hypothesis by seeing if its predictions of other observations are good. If the hypothesis passes this test, then it becomes accepted. In practice, however, this is at best a rough description of the process of scientific discovery in economics. Existing models are constantly re-examined and tested. Some economists specialize in testing models; others specialize in developing them. The process of creating and testing of models in economics is ongoing. In the next chapter, you will be introduced to the supply and demand model, and how it can be applied to understanding the gasoline market.

Recommending Appropriate Policies

Ever since the birth of economics as a field—around 1776, when Adam Smith published the *Wealth of Nations*—economists have been concerned about and motivated by a desire to improve the economic policy of governments. In fact, economics originally was called *political economy*. Much of the *Wealth of Nations* is about what the government should or should not do to affect the domestic and international economy.

capitalism

an economic system based on a market economy in which capital is individually owned, and production and employment decisions are decentralized.

socialism

an economic system in which the government owns and controls all the capital and makes decisions about prices and quantities as part of a central plan.

mixed economy

a market economy in which the government plays a very large role.

positive economics

economic analysis that explains what happens in the economy and why, without making recommendations about economic policy.

normative economics

economic analysis that makes recommendations about economic policy.

Adam Smith argued for a system of *laissez faire*—little government control—in which the role of the government is mainly to promote competition, provide for national defense, and reduce restrictions on the exchange of goods and services. More than one hundred years later, Karl Marx brought an alternative perspective to Smith's (and other classical economists') view of political economy, arguing against the laissez-faire approach. His analysis of market economies, or **capitalism**, centered on the contradictions that he saw arising out of such a system, particularly the conflict between the owners of production and the laborers. He argued that these contradictions would result in the inevitable collapse of capitalism and the emergence of a new economic system, called **socialism**, in which government essentially would own and control all production. Although Marx actually wrote little about what a Socialist or Communist economy would look like, the centrally planned economies that arose in the Soviet Union, Eastern Europe, and China in the twentieth century can be traced to Marx's ideas.

In the twenty-first century, most countries have rejected the command economy and have moved toward market economies, but the debate about the role of government continues. In many modern market economies, the government plays a large role, and for this reason, such economies are sometimes called **mixed economies**. How great should the role of government be in a market economy? Should the government provide health care services? Should it try to break up large firms? The answers to these questions are difficult to comprehend and have been debated for years.

Positive versus Normative Economics

In debating the role of government in the economy, economists distinguish between positive and normative economics. **Positive economics** is about what *is*; **normative economics** is about what *should be*. For example, positive economics endeavors to explain why driving declined in 2005. Normative economics aims to develop and recommend policies that might prevent driving from increasing in the future, perhaps with the aim of improving the environment. In general, normative economics is concerned with making recommendations about what the government should do—whether it should control the price of gasoline or health care, for example. Economists who advise governments spend much of their time doing normative economics. In the United States, the president's **Council of Economic Advisers** has legal responsibility for advising the president about which economic policies are beneficial and which policies are detrimental to the economy.

Positive economics also can be used to explain *why* governments do what they do. Why were tax rates cut in the 1980s, increased in the 1990s, and then cut again in the 2000s? Positive analysis of government policy requires a mixture of both political science and economic science, with a focus on what motivates voters and the politicians they elect.

Economics as a Science versus a Partisan Policy Tool

Although economics, like any other science, is based on facts and theories, it is not always used in a purely scientific way.

In political campaigns, economists put forth arguments in favor of one candidate, emphasizing the good side of their candidate's ideas and de-emphasizing the bad side. In a court of law, one economist may help a defendant—making the best case possible—and another economist may help the plaintiff—again, making the best case possible. In other words, economics is not always used objectively. A good reason to learn economics for yourself is to see through fallacious arguments.

But economics is not the only science that is used in these two entirely different modes. For example, there is currently a great controversy about the use of biology and chemistry to make estimates of the costs and benefits of different environmental policies. This is a politically controversial subject, and some on both sides of the controversy have been accused of using science in nonobjective ways.

Economics Is Not the Only Factor in Policy Issues

Although economics can be useful in policy decisions, it frequently is not the only factor. For example, national security sometimes calls for a recommendation on a policy issue different from one based on a purely economic point of view. Although most economists recommend free exchange of goods between countries, the U.S. government restricted exports of high-technology goods such as computers during the Cold War because defense specialists worried that the technology could help the military in the Soviet Union, and this was viewed as more important than the economic argument. The government still places heavy restrictions on trade in nuclear fuels for fear of the proliferation of nuclear weapons.

Disagreement between Economists

Watching economists debate issues on television or reading their opinions in a newspaper or magazine certainly gives the impression that they rarely agree. There are major controversies in economics, and we will examine them in this book. But when people survey economists' beliefs, they find a surprising amount of agreement.

Why, then, is there the popular impression of disagreement? Because there are many economists, and one can always find an economist with a different viewpoint. When people sue other people in court and economics is an issue, it is always possible to find economists who will testify for each side, even if 99 percent of economists would agree with one side. Similarly, television interviews or news shows want to give both sides of public policy issues. Thus, even if 99 percent of economists agree with one side, the producers are able to find at least one who holds the opposing view.

Economists are human beings with varying moral beliefs and different backgrounds and political views that frequently are unrelated to economic models. For example, an

Council of Economic Advisers
a three-member group of economists appointed by the president of the United States to analyze the economy and make recommendations about economic policy.

economist who is concerned about the importation of drugs into the United States might appear to be more willing to condone a restriction on coffee exports from Brazil and other coffee-exporting countries to give Colombia a higher price for its coffee to offset a loss in revenue from cocaine. Another economist, who felt less strongly about drug imports, might argue strongly against such a restriction on coffee. But if they were asked about restrictions on trade in the abstract, both economists probably would argue for government policies that prevent such restrictions.

ECONOMICS *IN ACTION*

The President's Council of Economic Advisers in Action

The President's Council of Economic Advisers (CEA), founded more than 60 years ago by the Employment Act of 1946, is a unique organization. Over the years, through many ups and downs in the economy, it has rarely wavered from its primary mission, which is to give the best economic advice to the president of the United States. It has not grown in size, as many other government agencies have; it has a small staff and three members, one of whom is the chair. And it does not represent any particular group, as the Department of Commerce does with businesses and the Department of Labor does with labor.

Some have likened the CEA to the Central Intelligence Agency (CIA), the mission of which is to provide information, but not policy advice, to the president. Although separation between facts and policy might work for security agencies, it does not work for economics, as should be clear from this chapter. So the CEA has never shied away from policy positions.

For many years the CEA occupied the Old Executive Office Building right next to the White House, but after the terrorist attacks of September 11, 2001, it moved to quarters outside the White House complex to make room for more staff of the National Security Council. Some pundits argued that the CEA lost influence with that move, but there is no real evidence of that. There are other economists close to the president. For example, economist Lawrence Summers, former president of Harvard and secretary of the treasury under President Clinton, was chosen by President Barack Obama to work in the White House during the first two years of his administration.

At the start of his administration, President Obama chose three distinguished economists for his CEA. His choice for chair was Christina Romer, a professor at the University of California at Berkeley and a specialist in economic history. One of her research papers showed that recessions were no milder in the 1950s and 1960s than they were before the Great Depression, as many had argued. Another showed how the recovery from the

Austan Goolsbee, chair of the Council of Economic Advisers, speaks during an onstage interview at the 2010 meeting of the Wall Street Journal CEO Council in Washington, November 16, 2010.

Great Depression was mainly due to financial factors rather than to government spending. Romer received her doctorate in economics at MIT.

President Obama's two other choices for the CEA were Austan Goolsbee and Cecelia Rouse. Goolsbee, a professor at University of Chicago, was an economic adviser to Barack Obama's 2004 Senate campaign and a senior economic adviser to his 2008 presidential campaign. His research expertise is taxes, technology, and government policy. He also received a doctorate in economics from MIT. Rouse, a professor at Princeton University, is a specialist in labor economics and the economics of education. In addition, she also works on discrimination issues similar to those discussed in the box on page 28. She received a doctorate in economics from Harvard.

CEA members usually return to academia after serving a few years. In 2010, Christina Romer returned to Berkeley and President Obama appointed Austan Goolsbee to replace her.

CONCLUSION: A READER'S GUIDE

In Chapter 1, we explored the central idea of economics: scarcity, choice, and economic interaction. In this chapter, we discussed how economists observe economic events and use economic models to explain these phenomena. It is now time to move on and learn more about the models and application of the central idea. As you study economic models in the following chapters, it will be useful to keep three points in mind, which are implied by the ideas raised in this chapter.

First, *economics—more than other subjects—requires a mixture of verbal and quantitative skills.* Frequently, those who come to economics with a good background in physical science and algebra find the mix of formal models with more informal verbal descriptions of markets and institutions unusual and perhaps a little difficult. If you are one of these people, you might wish for a more cut-and-dry, or algebraic, approach.

In contrast, those who are good at history or philosophy may find the emphasis on formal models and graphs difficult and might even prefer a more historical approach that looked more at watershed events and famous individuals and less at formal models of how many individuals behave. If you are one of these people, you might wish that economic models were less abstract.

In reality, however, economics is a mixture of formal modeling, historical analysis, and philosophy. If you are good at algebra and you think the symbols and graphs of elementary economics are too simple, think of Max Planck's comment about economics and focus on the complexity of the economic phenomena that these simple models and graphs are explaining. Then when you are asked an open-ended question about government policy that does not have a simple yes or no answer, you will not be caught off guard. Or if your advantage is in history or philosophy, you should spend more time honing your skills at using models and graphs. Then when you are asked to solve a cut-and-dry economic problem with an exact answer requiring graphic analysis, you will not be caught off guard.

Second, *economics is a wide-ranging discipline.* When your friends or relatives hear that you are taking economics, they may ask you for advice about what stock to buy. Economists' friends and relatives are always asking for such advice. Some topics that you study in economics will help you answer questions about whether to invest in the stock market or put your money in a bank or how many stocks to buy. But even these areas of economics will not offer any predictions about the success of particular companies. Rather, what economics gives you is a set of tools that you can use to obtain information about companies, industries, or countries and to analyze them yourself. Furthermore, the scope of economics is vast. Even among the faculty in a small college, you will find economists who study childhood obesity, trade barriers, real estate markets, abortion policy, the formation of American corporations, economic growth, international lending agencies, social security, agricultural pollution, and school choice.

Third, and perhaps most important, *the study of economics is an intellectually fascinating adventure in its own right.* Yes, economics is highly relevant, and it affects people's lives. But once you learn how economic models work, you will find that they actually are fun to use. Every now and then, just after you have learned about a new economic model, put the book down and think of the economic model independent of its message or relevance to society—try to enjoy it the way you would a good movie. In this way, too, you will be learning to think like an economist.

KEY POINTS

1. Economics is a way of thinking that requires observation (describing economic events), explanation (identifying variables that are potential explanatory variables of the event), prediction (building and using economic models to predict future events), and policy recommendations (courses of action for government—and business—to follow, based on these observations and models).

2. Finding the appropriate data series to explain economic events is a challenge because data often can be hard to find or incomplete, or can be misleading if they are not appropriately transformed.

3. Finding explanations for why an economic event occurred is challenging because even if you can find variables that are correlated with the variable in which you are interested, correlation does not imply causation. The inability to run controlled experiments also makes it difficult for economists to definitively establish a causal explanation for an economic event.

4. Economists have to explain the complex behavior of humans in economic situations. They often use models that are abstractions, or simplifications, of reality in their work. Economic models, like models in other sciences, can be described with words, tables, graphs, or algebra. All four ways are important and complement each other.

5. Economists use the tools of economic analysis to come up with policy insights concerning what the government is doing, or what the government should be doing, with regard to the economist's area

of interest. Improving economic policy has been a goal of economists since the time of Adam Smith.

6. Economics is a discipline that requires a combination of analytical, algebraic, and verbal skills. You can apply the tools of economics to almost any problem that involves decision making by individuals. Many students are interested in studying economics because they find it relevant to events that occur in the world, but the study of economics can be an intellectually stimulating exercise in its own right.

KEY TERMS

capitalism, 32
ceteris paribus, 31
controlled experiments, 26
council of economic advisers, 33
economic model, 27
economic variable, 26
experimental economics, 26
gross domestic product (GDP), 27

macroeconomics, 27
microeconomics, 27
mixed economies, 32
negatively related, 29
normative economics, 32
positive economics, 32
positively related, 29
socialism, 32

QUESTIONS FOR REVIEW

1. How do economists typically approach an economics-related problem?
2. What are the challenges that economists face in trying to describe an economic event?
3. What is meant by a relative price, and why is it important in certain situations to look at the relative price of a good instead of the actual price of that good?
4. What does it mean for two variables to be correlated? What is the difference between positive and negative correlation?
5. Why doesn't correlation imply causation? Can you come up with your own example of why correlation does not imply causation?
6. Why do economists use economic models? Can you come up with some reasons why economists should be careful in using models?

7. What is the *ceteris paribus* assumption? Why is it so important in economics?
8. What is the difference between macroeconomics and microeconomics? Between positive and normative economics?
9. What academic disciplines do you think of as being more scientific than economics? Why do you think so? Which disciplines do you consider to be less scientific, and why?
10. Look through the research and teaching interests of the economics faculty members in your department. Collectively, how wide-ranging are those interests? Were you surprised to find that the tools of economics could be applied to a particular area?

PROBLEMS

1. Which of the following variables are studied as part of microeconomics, and which are studied as part of macroeconomics?
   a. The U.S. unemployment rate.
   b. The amount of tips earned by a waiter.
   c. The national rate of inflation.
   d. The number of hours worked by a student.
   e. The price paid to obtain this economics textbook.

2. Consider the following table, which provides the price of chicken and the price of all foods from 1996 to 2006.

   a. Calculate the relative price of chicken for each year.
   b. Plot the relative price of chicken as in Figure 2-2.
   c. What can you say about how the price of chicken has varied in comparison to the price of all foods in the decade from 1996 to 2006?

Year	Price of All Foods	Price of Chicken	Relative Price
1996	92	95	
1997	93	98	
1998	96	98	
1999	97	99	
2000	100	100	
2001	103	103	
2002	104	105	
2003	108	106	
2004	111	114	
2005	113	116	
2006	116	114	

3. A change in the relative price of a good matters more than the change in the price of a good in analyzing the change in spending on that good. Show that the relative price of a good can fall on occasions when the price of that good is rising, falling, or remaining unchanged, using numerical examples from the table in Problem 2.

4. Indicate whether you expect positive or negative correlation for the following pairs of variables, labeled X and Y. For each pair, state whether X causes Y, Y causes X, or both.

   a. Sunrise (X) and crowing roosters (Y).
   b. The use of umbrellas (X) and a thunderstorm (Y).
   c. The price of theater tickets (X) and the number of theatergoers (Y).
   d. Weekly earnings of a worker (X) and the number of hours a week she works at her job (Y).
   e. The number of children who were vaccinated against a disease (X) and the number of children who currently suffer from that disease (Y).

5. Consider an economic model of donut production. Show how to represent this model graphically, algebraically, and verbally, as in Figure 2-6.

Number of Workers	Number of Donuts Produced
0	0
1	100
4	200
9	300
16	400

6. Suppose you decide to build a model to explain why the average worker in a particular occupation works more hours during some weeks than during others.

   a. What data would you collect to describe this phenomenon?
   b. What variable do you believe would supply the major part of the explanation of the variation in hours worked?
   c. If you graph the data with hours worked on the vertical axis and your explanatory variable on the horizontal axis, will the relationship be upward-sloping or downward-sloping?
   d. What does your answer to part c imply for whether the data on hours worked and the data on your explanatory variable are positively or negatively correlated?

7. Why is it typical for economists to make the *ceteris paribus* assumption when making predictions? Now consider the statement: "If the local McDonald's reduces the price of a Big Mac hamburger, it will sell a lot more hamburgers." What other variables are most likely being held fixed under the *ceteris paribus* assumption when this statement is being made?

8. Suppose you wanted to modify the Bertrand and Mullainathan study to focus on gender discrimination. Describe the "experiment" that you would run. Also be sure to explain how the *ceteris paribus* assumption is involved in terms of the names you would choose for the men and for the women.

9. Identify whether the following policy statements are positive or normative. Explain.

   a. The price of gasoline is too high.
   b. The average price of gasoline rose to a record high of $4.02 in June 2008.
   c. Forty-four million Americans lack access to health insurance.
   d. The government needs to provide basic health care to the uninsured.

e.   The collapse in the real estate market will affect many Americans.

10.   Suppose an economic study shows that increasing the tax rate on cigarettes will reduce the amount of smoking. Which of the following statements can be validly made on the basis of the study because they are positive statements, and which cannot be validly made because they are normative statements?

a.   Increasing the cigarette tax rate is a method of reducing smoking.

b.   If the government wishes to reduce smoking, it should raise the cigarette tax.

c.   If the government wishes to reduce smoking, it can raise the cigarette tax.

d.   The government should reduce smoking by raising the cigarette tax.

e.   The government should not raise the cigarette tax on low-income smokers.

Appendix to Chapter 2

Reading, Understanding, and Creating Graphs

Whether you follow the stock market, the health care market, or the whole economy, graphs are needed to understand what is going on. That is why the financial pages of newspapers contain so many graphs. Knowing how to read, understand, and even create your own graphs is part of learning to "think like an economist." Graphs help us see correlations, or patterns, in economic observations. Graphs also are useful for understanding economic models. They help us see how variables in the model behave. They help us describe assumptions about what firms and consumers do.

Computer software to create graphs is now widely available. To understand how helpful graphs can be, you might want to create a few of your own graphs. Here we provide a short review of elementary graphing techniques.

Visualizing Observations with Graphs

Most economic graphs are drawn in two dimensions, like the surface of this page, and are constructed using a **Cartesian coordinate system**. The idea of Cartesian coordinates is that pairs of observations on variables can be represented in a plane by designating one axis for one variable and the other axis for the other variable. Each point, or coordinate, on the plane corresponds to a pair of observations.

Time-Series Graphs

In many instances, we want to see how a variable changes over time. Consider the federal debt held by the public—all the outstanding borrowing of the federal government that has not yet been paid back. Table A.2-1 shows observations of the U.S. federal debt. The observations are for every ten years. The observations in Table A.2-1 are graphed in Figure A.2-1. The graph in Figure A.2-1 is called a **time-series graph** because it plots a series—that is, several values of the variable—over time.

Table A.2-1

U.S. Federal Government Debt

Year	Debt (billions of dollars)
1960	237
1970	283
1980	712
1990	2,412
2000	3,410
2010	9,018
2020 (Projected)	17,392

Source: Congressional Budget Office.

Figure A.2-1

U.S. Federal Debt
Each point corresponds to a pair of observations—the year and the debt—from Table A.2-1.

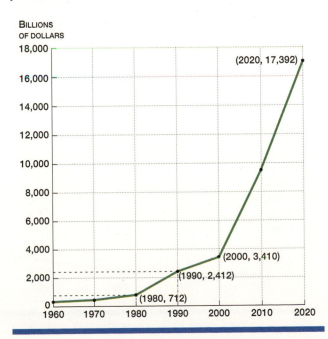

Observe the scales on the horizontal and vertical axes in Figure A.2-1. The seven years are put on the horizontal axis, spread evenly from the year 1960 to the year 2020. The last year is a forecast. For the vertical axis, one needs to decide on a scale. The range of variation for the debt in Table A.2-1 is wide—from a minimum of $237 billion to a maximum of $17,392 billion. Thus, the range on the vertical axis—from $0 to $18,000 billion in Figure A.2-1—must be wide enough to contain all these points.

Now observe how each pair of points from Table A.2-1 is plotted in Figure A.2-1. The point for the pair of observations for the year 1960 and the debt of $237 billion is found by going over to 1960 on the horizontal axis, then going up to $237 billion and putting a dot there. The point for 1970 and $283 billion and all the other points are found in the same way. To better visualize the points, they can be connected with lines. These lines are not part of the observations; they are only a convenience to help in eyeballing the observations. The points for 1980, 1990, and 2000 are labeled with the pairs of observations corresponding to Table A.2-1, but in general, such labels are not needed.

One could choose scales different from those in Figure A.2-1, and if you plotted your own graph from the data in Table A.2-1 without looking at Figure A.2-1,

your scales probably would be different. The scales determine the amount of movement in a time-series graph. For example, Figure A.2-2 shows two ways to stretch the scales to make the increase in the debt look more or less dramatic. So as not to be fooled by graphs, it is important to look at the scales and think about what they mean.

As an alternative to time-series graphs with dots connected by a line, the observations can be shown on a bar graph, as in Figure A.2-3. Some people prefer the visual look of a bar graph, but, as is clear from a comparison of Figure A.2-1 and A.2-3, they provide the same information as time-series graphs.

The debt as a percentage of GDP is given in Table A.2-2 and graphed in Figure A.2-4. Note that this figure makes the debt look different from the way it looks in the first one. As a percentage of GDP, the debt fell from the end of World War II (when it was large because of the war debt) until around 1980. It increased during the 1980s and declined in the 1990s, but started to increase again in the 2000s.

Some data to be graphed have no observations close to 0, in which case including 0 on the vertical axis would leave some wasted space at the bottom of the graph. To eliminate this space and have more room to see the graph, we can start the range near the minimum value and end it

Figure A.2-2

Stretching the Debt Story in Two Ways

The points in both graphs are identical to those in Figure A.2-1, but by stretching or shrinking the scales, the problem can be made to look either less dramatic or more dramatic.

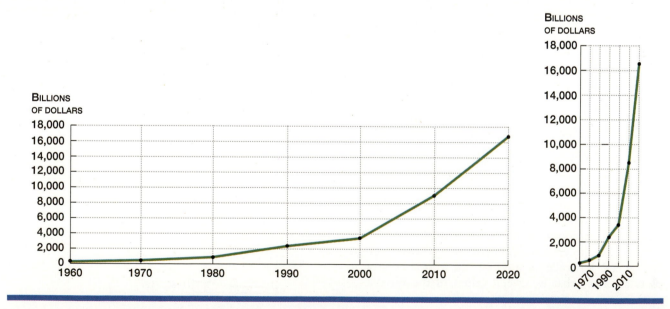

near the maximum value. This is done in Figure A.2-5, where the debt as a percentage of GDP is shown up to 1990. Note, however, that cutting off the bottom of the scale could be misleading to people who do not look at the axis. In particular, 0 percent is no longer at the point where the horizontal and vertical axes intersect. To warn people about the missing part of the scale, a little cut is sometimes put on the axis, as is done in Figure A.2-5, but you have to look carefully at the scale.

Figure A.2-4

U.S. Federal Debt as a Percentage of GDP
Each point corresponds to a pair of observations from Table A.2-2.

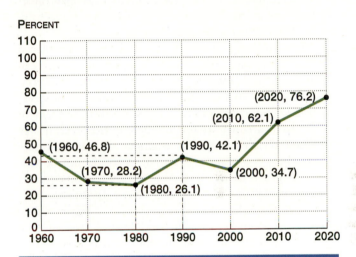

Figure A.2-3

U.S. Federal Debt in Bars
The observations are identical to those in Figure A.2-1.

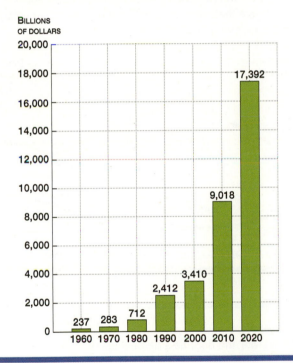

Figure A.2-5

A Look at Debt as a Percentage of GDP from 1960 to 1990

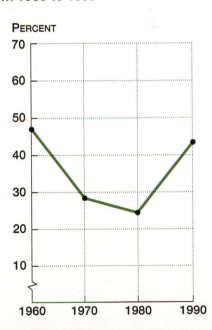

(*Note:* To alert the reader that the bottom part of the axis is not shown, a break point is sometimes used, as shown here.)

Table A.2-2

U.S. Federal Debt as a Percentage of GDP

Year	Debt (percent of GDP)
1960	46.8
1970	28.2
1980	26.1
1990	42.1
2000	34.7
2010	62.1
2020 (Projected)	76.2

Source: Congressional Budget Office.

Time-Series Graphs Showing Two or More Variables

So far, we have shown how a graph can be used to show observations on one variable over time. What if we want to see how two or more variables change over time together? Suppose, for example, we want to look at how observations on debt as a percentage of GDP compare with the interest rate the government must pay on its debt. (The interest rate for 2020 is, of course, a forecast.) The two variables are shown in Table A.2-3.

The two sets of observations can easily be placed on the same time-series graph. In other words, we can plot the observations on the debt percentage and connect the dots and then plot the interest rate observations and connect the dots. If the scales of measurement of the two variables are much different, however, it may be hard to see both. For example, the interest rate ranges between 1 and 12 percent; it would not be visible on a graph going all the way from 0 to 100 percent, a range that is fine for the debt percentage. In this situation, a **dual scale** can be used, as shown in Figure A.2-6. One scale is put on the left-hand vertical axis, and the other scale is put on the right-hand vertical axis. With a dual-scale diagram, it is essential to be aware of the two scales. In Figure A.2-6, we emphasize the different axes by the color line segment at the top of each vertical axis. The color line segment corresponds to the color of the curve plotted using that scale.

Scatter Plots

Finally, two variables can be usefully compared with a **scatter plot**. The Cartesian coordinate method is used,

as in the time-series graph; however, we do not put the year on one of the axes. Instead, the horizontal axis is used for one of the variables and the vertical axis for the other variable. We do this for the debt percentage and the interest rate in Figure A.2-7. The interest rate is on the vertical axis, and the debt percentage is on the horizontal axis. For example, the point at the upper left is

Figure A.2-6

Comparing Two Time Series with a Dual Scale
When two variables have different scales, a dual scale is useful. Here the interest rate and the debt as a percentage of GDP are plotted from Table A.2-3.

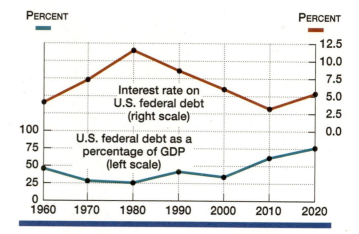

Figure A.2-7

Scatter Plot
Interest rate and debt as a percentage of GDP are shown.

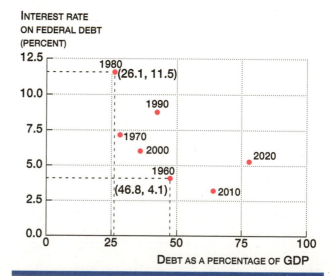

Table A.2-3

Interest Rate and Federal Debt as a Percentage of GDP

Year	Debt (percent of GDP)	Interest Rate (percent)
1960	46.8	4.1
1970	28.2	7.3
1980	26.1	11.5
1990	42.1	8.6
2000	34.7	6.0
2010	62.1	3.2
2020 (Projected)	76.2	5.4

Source: Federal Reserve Board and Table A.2-2.
Note: Interest rate is on 10-year bonds.

26.1 percent for the debt as a percentage of GDP and 11.5 percent for the interest rate.

Visualizing Models with Graphs

Graphs also can represent models. Like graphs showing observations, graphs showing models usually are restricted to curves in two dimensions.

Slopes of Curves

Does a curve slope up or down? How steep is it? These questions are important in economics, as in other sciences. The **slope** of a curve tells us how much the variable on the vertical axis changes when we change the variable on the horizontal axis by one unit.

The slope is computed as follows:

$$\text{Slope} = \frac{\text{change in variable on vertical axis}}{\text{change in variable on horizontal axis}}$$

In most algebra courses, the vertical axis is usually called the y-axis and the horizontal axis is called the x-axis. Thus, the slope is sometime described as

$$\text{Slope} = \frac{\text{change in y}}{\text{change in x}} = \frac{\Delta y}{\Delta x}$$

where the Greek letter Δ (delta) means "change in." In other words, the slope is the ratio of the "rise" (vertical change) to the "run" (horizontal change).

Figure A.2-8 shows how to compute the slope. In this case, the slope declines as the variable on the x-axis increases.

Observe that *the steeper the curve, the larger the slope.* When the curve gets very flat, the slope gets close to zero. Curves can either be upward-sloping or downward-sloping. If the curve slopes up from left to right, as in Figure A.2-8, it has a **positive slope**, and we say that the two variables are positively related. If the curve slopes down from left to right, it has a **negative slope**, and we say that the two variables are negatively related. Figure A.2-9 shows a case where the slope is negative. When x increases by 1 unit ($\Delta x = 1$), y declines by 2 units ($\Delta y = -2$). Thus, the slope equals –2; it is negative. Observe how the curve slopes down from left to right.

If the curve is a straight line, then the slope is a constant. Curves that are straight lines—like that in Figure A.2-9—are called **linear**. But economic relationships do not need to be linear, as the example in Figure A.2-8 makes clear. Figure A.2-10 shows six different examples of curves and indicates how they are described.

Figure A.2-8

Measuring the Slope
The slope between two points is given by the change along the vertical axis divided by the change along the horizontal axis. In this example, the slope declines as x increases. Because the curve slopes up from left to right, it has a positive slope.

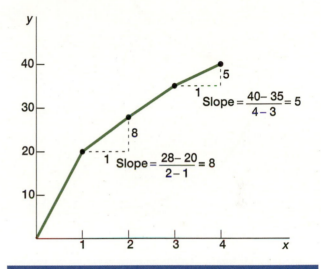

Figure A.2-9

A Relationship with a Negative Slope
Here the slope is negative: $(\Delta y)/(\Delta x) = -2$. As x increases, y falls. The line slopes down from left to right. In this case, y and x are inversely, or negatively, related.

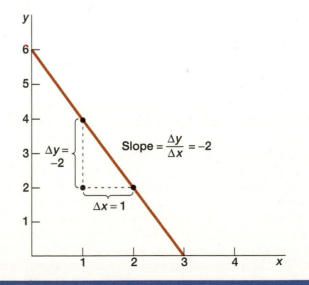

Six Types of Relationships
In the top row, the variables are positively related. In the bottom row, they are negatively related.

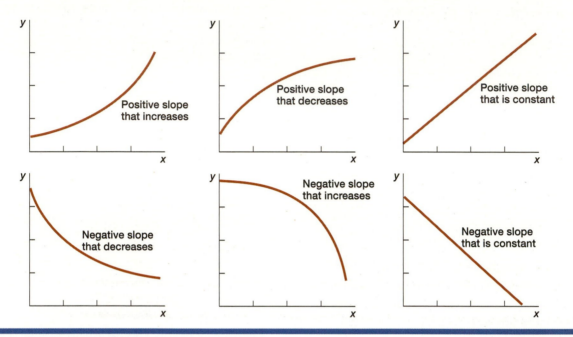

Graphs of Models with More Than Two Variables

In most cases, economic models involve more than two variables. For example, the number of physical examinations could depend on the number of nurses as well as the number of doctors. Or the amount of lemonade demanded might depend on the weather as well as on the price.

Economists have devised several methods for representing models with more than two variables with two-dimensional graphs. Suppose, for example, that the relationship between y and x in Figure A.2-9 depends on a third variable z. For a given value of x, larger values of z lead to larger values of y. This example is graphed in Figure A.2-11. As in Figure A.2-9, when x increases, y falls. This is a **movement along the curve**. But what if z changes? We represent this as a **shift of the curve**. An increase in z shifts the curve up; a decrease in z shifts the curve down.

Thus, by distinguishing between shifts of and movements along a curve, economists represent models with more than two variables in only two dimensions. Only two variables (x and y) are shown explicitly on the graph, and when the third (z) is fixed, changes in x and y are movements along the curve. When z changes, the curve shifts. The distinction between "movements along" and "shifts of" curves comes up many times in economics.

A Third Variable Shifts the Curve
To represent models with three variables (x, y, and z) on a two-dimensional graph, economists distinguish between movements along the curve (when x and y change, holding z unchanged) and shifts of the curve (when z changes).

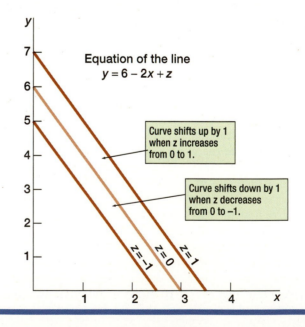

KEY TERMS AND DEFINITIONS

Cartesian coordinate system: a graphing system in which ordered pairs of numbers are represented on a plane by the distances from a point to two perpendicular lines, called axes.

time-series graph: a graph that plots a variable over time, usually with time on the horizontal axis.

dual scale: a graph that uses time on the horizontal axis and different scales on the left and right vertical axes to compare the movements of two variables over time.

scatter plot: a graph in which points in a Cartesian coordinate system represent the values of two variables.

slope: a characteristic of a curve that is defined as the change in the variable on the vertical axis divided by the change in the variable on the horizontal axis.

positive slope: a slope of a curve that is greater than zero, representing a positive or direct relationship between two variables.

negative slope: a slope of a curve that is less than zero, representing a negative or inverse relationship between two variables.

linear: a situation in which a curve is straight, with a constant slope.

movement along the curve: a situation in which a change in the variable on one axis causes a change in the variable on the other axis, but the position of the curve is maintained.

shift of the curve: a change in the position of a curve, usually caused by a change in a variable not represented on either axis.

QUESTIONS FOR REVIEW

1. What is the difference between a scatter plot and a time-series graph?
2. Why are dual scales sometimes necessary?
3. What is the advantage of graphs over verbal representations of models?
4. What does a curve with a negative slope look like?
5. What is the difference between a shift in a curve and a movement along a curve?

PROBLEMS

1. The following table presents data on the debt (in billions of dollars), the debt to GDP ratio, and the interest rate predicted by the Congressional Budget Office for the United States for each year through 2021.

Year	Debt	Debt to GDP Ratio (percent)	Interest Rate
2010	9,018	62.1%	3.2
2011	10,439	69.4%	3.4
2012	11,598	73.9%	3.8
2013	12,386	75.5%	4.2
2014	12,996	75.3%	4.6
2015	13,625	74.9%	5.0
2016	14,358	75.0%	5.3
2017	15,064	75.2%	5.4
2018	15,767	75.3%	5.4
2019	16,557	75.8%	5.4
2020	17,392	76.2%	5.4
2021	18,253	76.7%	5.4

Source: Congressional Budget Office.

a. Construct a time-series plot of the ratio of government debt to GDP.
b. Construct a time-series plot of the debt.
c. Construct a scatter plot of the debt ratio and the interest rate.

2. The following table shows the number of physical examinations given by doctors at health maintenance organization with three different-size clinics: small, medium, and large. The larger the clinic, the more patients the doctors can handle.

Exams per Small Clinic	Exams per Medium Clinic	Exams per Large Clinic	Number of Doctors
0	0	0	0
20	30	35	1
28	42	49	2
35	53	62	3
40	60	70	4

a. Show the relationship between doctors and physical exams given with *three* curves, where the number of doctors is on the horizontal axis and the number of examinations is on the vertical axis.
b. Describe how the three relationships compare with one another.
c. Is a change in the number of doctors a shift of or a movement along the curve?
d. Is a change in the size of the clinic a shift of or a movement along the curve?

3 The Supply and Demand Model

The "Super Bowl" is an appropriate name for what is the biggest annual sporting event in the United States. Every winter, in late January or early February, the last two teams left standing in the National Football League (NFL) meet in a neutral site to play in a football game that is watched by more than 100 million people on television. The 2010 Super Bowl between the New Orleans Saints and the Indianapolis Colts was the most widely viewed network telecast, and three other Super Bowls are featured in the top 10 list of most widely viewed telecasts in the United States. The Super Bowl is also the biggest advertising target of the year. The price for a 30-second commercial shown during the Super Bowl telecast averages around $3 million, or about $100,000 per second of television time. Even though 100 million people are able to watch the Super Bowl on television, only about 100,000 people were able to watch the 2011 Super Bowl in person at Cowboys Stadium, the opulent new home arena of the Dallas Cowboys. How does one become a fortunate one in a thousand to attend the Super Bowl in person? It turns out that the NFL does not sell Super Bowl tickets directly to the general public. You could be one of the lucky fans to win a lottery for 10,000 tickets held directly by the NFL. Or you could be a lucky season ticket holder for one of

Kevin C. Cox/Getty Images

the two participating teams, which typically get about a third of the tickets between them. If you were a season ticket holder who won the lottery you then would have to decide between going to the Super Bowl or reselling the ticket for a staggeringly high price and join the tens of millions watching the game at home. The *New Orleans Times-Picayune* reported that a New Orleans Saints fan who won the ticket lottery for the 2010 Super Bowl was able to purchase tickets for $800 apiece.[1] That fan would soon find out that plenty of people would pay $5,000 to $10,000 for those tickets, quite a temptation for even the most devoted fan. On the other hand, if you were a devoted football fan who did not win the lottery, you would find yourself having to pay several

---

[1] "New Orleans Saints fans win Super Bowl lottery," *The Times-Picayune*, January 27, 2010.

thousand dollars for a Super Bowl ticket, either to an online ticket broker or to a seller on an online auction site.

Why does a Super Bowl ticket cost so much? Why does it cost so much to buy a 30-second television commercial to be shown during the Super Bowl? Who decides what price to charge for a Super Bowl ticket? Why do the NFL and the participating teams use a lottery system to select fans who are then permitted to buy tickets at a much lower price than that charged by a street seller or by an online ticket broker? Who ends up going to the Super Bowl, and who ends up selling their ticket and watching the game and the commercials on television? The purpose of this chapter is to show how to find the answers to such questions using the *supply and demand model*.

Recall from Chapter 2 that a model is a simplified description of a more complex reality. The supply and demand model is what economists use to explain how prices are determined in a market. We can use this model to understand the market for Super Bowl tickets or Final Four tickets, as well as in a variety of other settings. What causes the price of gasoline to fluctuate? What causes the price of computers to fall over time, even though the prices of most other goods seem to rise over time? Why do roses cost more on Valentine's Day? Once you understand how the model works, you will find yourself using it over and over again to understand the markets that you come across in your everyday life.

The supply and demand model consists of three elements: *demand*, describing the behavior of consumers in the market; *supply*, describing the behavior of firms in the market; and *market equilibrium*, connecting supply and demand and describing how consumers and firms interact in the market. Economists like to compare the supply and demand model to a pair of scissors. Demand is one blade of the scissors, and supply is the other. Either blade alone is incomplete and virtually useless; however, when the two blades of a pair of scissors are connected to form the scissors, they become an amazingly useful, yet simple, tool. So it is with the supply and demand model.

Demand

To an economist, the term *demand*—whether the demand for tickets or the demand for roses—has a very specific meaning. **Demand** is a relationship between two economic variables: (1) *the price of a particular good* and (2) *the quantity of that good that consumers are willing to buy at that price during a specific time period*, all other things being equal. For short, we call the first variable the **price** and the second variable the **quantity demanded**. The phrase *all other things being equal*, or *ceteris paribus*, is appended to the definition of demand because the quantity that consumers are willing to buy depends on many other things besides the price of the good; we want to hold these other things constant, or equal, while we examine the relationship between price and quantity demanded.

Demand can be represented by a numerical table or by a graph. In either case, demand describes how much of a good consumers will purchase at each price. Consider the demand for bicycles in a particular country, as presented in Table 3-1. Of course, because of the many kinds of bicycles—mountain bikes, racing bikes, children's bikes, and inexpensive one-speed bikes with cruiser brakes—you need to simplify and think about this table as describing demand for an average, or typical, bike.

demand
a relationship between **price** and **quantity demanded.**

price
the amount of money or other goods that one must pay to obtain a particular good.

quantity demanded
the quantity of a good that people want to buy at a given price during a specific time period.

Observe that, as the price rises, the quantity demanded by consumers goes down. If the price goes up from $180 to $200 per bicycle, for example, the quantity demanded goes down from 11 million to 9 million bicycles. On the other hand, if the price goes down, the quantity demanded goes up. If the price falls from $180 to $160, for example, the quantity demanded rises from 11 million to 14 million bicycles.

demand schedule
a tabular presentation of demand showing the price and quantity demanded for a particular good, all else being equal.

The relationship between price and quantity demanded in Table 3-1 is called a **demand schedule**. The relationship shows price and quantity demanded moving in opposite directions, and this is an example of the law of demand. The **law of demand** says that the higher the price, the lower the quantity demanded in the market; and the lower the price, the higher the quantity demanded in the market. In other words, the law of demand says that the price and the quantity demanded are negatively related, all other things being equal.

law of demand
the tendency for the quantity demanded of a good in a market to decline as its price rises.

The Demand Curve

Figure 3-1 represents demand graphically. The price of the good appears on the vertical axis and the quantity demanded of the good appears on the horizontal axis. It shows the demand for bicycles given in Table 3-1. Each of the nine rows in Table 3-1 corresponds to one of the nine points in Figure 3-1. For example, the point at the lower right part of the graph corresponds to the first row of the table, where the price is $140 and the quantity demanded is 18 million bicycles. The resulting curve showing all the combinations of price and quantity demanded is the **demand curve**. It slopes downward from left to right because the quantity demanded is negatively related to the price.

demand curve
a graph of demand showing the downward-sloping relationship between price and quantity demanded.

Why does the demand curve slope downward? When economists draw a demand curve, they hold constant the price of other goods: running shoes, in-line skates, motor scooters, and so on. Consumers have scarce resources and need to choose between bicycles and other goods. If the price of bicycles falls, then bicycles become more attractive to people in comparison with these other goods—some consumers who previously found the price of bicycles too high may decide to buy a bicycle rather than buy other goods. Conversely, when the price of bicycles increases, then bicycles become less attractive to people in comparison with other goods—some consumers may decide to buy in-line skates or motor scooters instead of bicycles. As a result, quantity demanded declines when the price rises and vice versa.

Plenty of real-world evidence indicates that demand curves are downward sloping. In the summer of 2008, vehicle sales at General Motors were slowing. In August, General Motors announced that they were extending their "employee pricing" deal on most trucks and cars to all prospective buyers. Calculations by *Consumer Reports* estimated this to be a 13 percent decrease in the price of a vehicle. You might (correctly) speculate that this reduction in the price of vehicles was intended to increase vehicle sales.

Table 3-1

Demand Schedule for Bicycles (millions of bicycles per year)

Price	Quantity Demanded	Price	Quantity Demanded
$140	18	$240	5
$160	14	$260	3
$180	11	$280	2
$200	9	$300	1
$220	7		

Figure 3-1

The Demand Curve

The demand curve shows that the price of a good and the quantity demanded by consumers are negatively related—the curve slopes down. For each price, the demand curve gives the quantity demanded, or the quantity that consumers are willing to buy at that price. The points along the demand curve for bicycles shown here are the same as the pairs of numbers in Table 3-1.

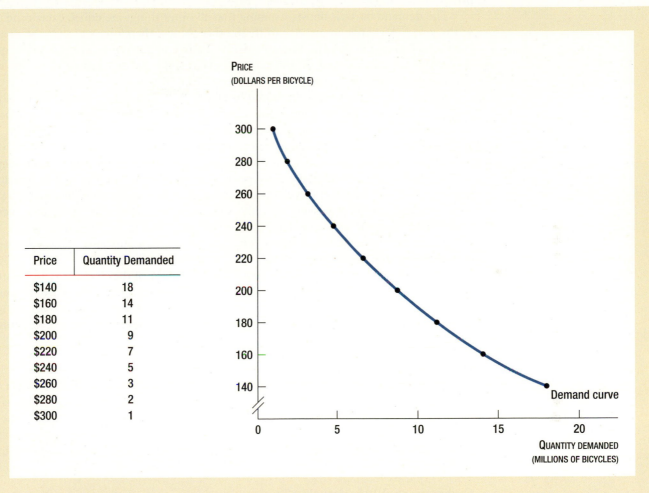

Price	Quantity Demanded
$140	18
$160	14
$180	11
$200	9
$220	7
$240	5
$260	3
$280	2
$300	1

Similarly, policies designed to reduce smoking by teenagers or to cut down on drinking on college campuses often aim to do this by raising the price of cigarettes and alcohol. The idea, of course, is that teens would buy fewer cigarettes and students would buy less alcohol if these goods were more expensive.

Shifts in Demand

Price is not the only thing that affects the quantity of a good that people buy. Weather conditions, concerns about the environment, or the availability of bike lanes on roads can influence people's decisions to purchase bicycles, for example. If climate change brought on an extended period of warm weather, people would have more opportunities to ride their bicycles. As a result, more bicycles would be purchased at any given price. Or perhaps increased awareness of the health benefits of exercise might lead people to ride their bicycles to work rather than drive their cars. This also would lead to more purchases of bicycles at any given price. Alternatively, if bike lanes are taken away to allow for an extra lane of cars on the road, fewer bicycles would be purchased at any given price.

The demand curve is drawn assuming that all other things are equal, except the price of the good. A change in any one of these other things, therefore, will shift the demand curve. An increase in demand shifts the demand curve to the right—at every price, quantity demanded will increase. A decrease in demand shifts the demand curve to the left—at every price, quantity demanded will decrease.

An increase in demand is illustrated in Figure 3-2. The lightly shaded curve labeled "old demand curve" is the same as the demand curve in Figure 3-1. An extended period of warm weather will increase demand and shift the demand curve to the right. The arrow shows how this curve has shifted to the right to the more darkly shaded curve labeled "new demand curve." When the demand curve shifts to the right, more bicycles are purchased than before at any given price. For example, before the shift in demand, a $200 price led to 9 million bicycles being purchased. But when the demand curve shifts to the right because of warmer weather, that same price leads to 13 million bicycles being purchased. On the other hand, if bicycle lanes were taken away from roads, then the demand curve would shift to the left because people's purchases of bicycles would now be less at any given price.

The demand curve may shift for many reasons. Most of these reasons can be attributed to one of several sources: *consumers' preferences, consumers' information, consumers' incomes, the number of consumers in the market, consumers' expectations of future prices*, and *the price of related goods*. Let us briefly consider each source of shifts in demand.

Consumers' Preferences

In general, a change in people's tastes or preferences for a product compared with other products will change the amount of the product they purchase at any given price. On many college campuses, demand for clothing that is certified as not having been produced in "sweatshops" has increased. Also, over the last couple of decades, consumers have shown a great deal of interest in buying "organically grown" fruits and vegetables, which are produced without using artificial pesticides or fertilizers.

Consumers' Information

A change in information relating to a product also can cause the demand curve to shift. For example, when people learned about the dangers of smoking, the demand for cigarettes declined. Shortly after an outbreak of *E. coli* in parts of the United States was linked to contaminated spinach, demand for spinach at grocery stores decreased. A number of fatal car accidents in 2009 and 2010 were linked to a possible problem with the accelerator pedals of some models of cars made by Toyota. The demand for Toyota automobiles fell sharply.

Consumers' Incomes

If people's incomes change, then their purchases of goods usually change. An increase in income increases the demand for most goods, while a decline in income reduces the demand for these goods. Goods for which demand increases when income rises and decreases when income falls are called **normal goods** by economists. Many of the goods that people typically purchase—shoes, clothing, jewelry—fall into the category of normal goods.

However, the demand for some goods may decline when income increases. Such goods are called **inferior goods** by economists. The demand for inferior goods declines

normal good
a good for which demand increases when income rises and decreases when income falls.

inferior good
a good for which demand decreases when income rises and increases when income falls.

Figure 3-2

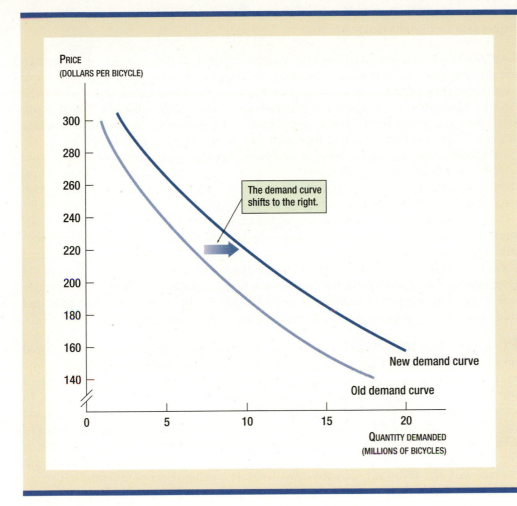

PRICE
(DOLLARS PER BICYCLE)

The demand curve shifts to the right.

New demand curve

Old demand curve

QUANTITY DEMANDED
(MILLIONS OF BICYCLES)

A Shift in the Demand Curve

The demand curve shows how the quantity demanded of a good is related to the price of the good, all other things being equal. A change in one of these other things—the weather or people's tastes, for example—will shift the demand curve, as shown in the graph. In this case, the demand for bicycles increases; the demand curve for bicycles shifts to the right.

when people's income increases because they can afford more attractive goods. For example, instant noodles form the basis of many college students' diets. After these students leave college and start working and earning a salary, however, many will switch over to eating microwavable meals or to eating out in restaurants. Thus, the demand for instant noodles will fall as income rises. Another example of an inferior good that is familiar to many college students in Boston and New York is the cheap bus service that runs between the Chinatowns in the two cities; a bus ticket may cost as little as $10, whereas a plane ticket between the two cities may cost $150. As students graduate and start earning money, however, they often buy more of the $150 plane tickets and fewer of the $10 bus tickets. In this case, the plane ticket is categorized as a normal good, and the bus ticket is categorized as an inferior good.

Number of Consumers in the Market Demand is a relationship between price and the quantity demanded by *all* consumers in the market. If the number of consumers increases, then demand will increase. If the number of consumers falls, then demand will decrease. For example, the number of teenagers in the U.S. population expanded sharply in the late 1990s. This increased the demand for *Seventeen* magazine, Rollerblades, Clearasil, and other goods that teenagers tend to buy. As the baby boom generation in the United States ages, the demand for health care, hair coloring kits, and luxury skin care products is increasing.

Consumers' Expectations of Future Prices

If people expect the price of a good to increase, they will want to buy it before the price increases. Conversely, if people expect the price of goods to decline, they will purchase fewer items and wait for the decline. One often sees this effect of expectations of future price changes. "We'd better buy before the price goes up" is a common reason for purchasing items during a clearance sale. Or, "Let's put off buying that flat-screen television until the post-holiday sales."

In general, it is difficult to forecast the future, but consumers sometimes know quite a bit about whether the price of a good will rise or fall, and they react accordingly. Thus, demand increases if people expect the *future* price of the good to rise. And demand decreases if people expect the *future* price of the good to fall.

In 2009, Congress created a program that aimed to provide incentives for U.S. consumers to buy new, more fuel-efficient cars by trading in their older, less fuel-efficient vehicles. This program, popularly known as "Cash for Clunkers," offered customers about a $4,000 discount for buying a new car. Many people moved up their planned car purchases to take advantage of the "Cash for Clunkers" program. The program, which was planned to run for five months, exhausted all the available funds allocated to it, and $2 billion more in additional allocations, in less than two months.

Prices of Closely Related Goods

substitute
a good that has many of the same characteristics as, and can be used in place of, another good.

A change in the price of a closely related good can increase or decrease demand for another good, depending on whether the good is a substitute or a complement. A **substitute** is a good that provides some of the same uses or enjoyment as another good. Butter and margarine are substitutes. In general, the demand for a good will increase if the price of a substitute for the good rises, and the demand for a good will decrease if the price of a substitute falls. Sales of CDs and downloaded music are substitutes. You therefore would expect a decrease in the price of downloaded music to decrease the demand for CDs. This may help explain why the recording industry filed lawsuits against users of online file-sharing software in 2003.

Substitutes and Complements

Music CDs and downloaded music are examples of substitutes; they share similar characteristics. You would expect, therefore, that a rise in the price of CDs would result in an increase in the sale of downloaded music—and vice versa. SUVs and gasoline are examples of complements; they tend to be consumed together. With an increase in gasoline prices in 2004 and 2005, consumers were less eager to purchase SUVs, and their sales declined.

A **complement** is a good that tends to be consumed together with another good. Gasoline and sport utility vehicles (SUVs) are complements. The rapid increase in gasoline prices in 2007 and the early part of 2008 led to a decrease in demand for SUVs.

complement
a good that usually is consumed or used together with another good.

Movements Along versus Shifts of the Demand Curve

We have shown that the demand curve can shift, and we have given many possible reasons for such shifts. As you begin to use demand curves, it is important that you be able to distinguish *shifts* of the demand curve from *movements along* the demand curve. This distinction is illustrated in Figure 3-3.

A *movement along* the demand curve occurs when the quantity demanded changes as a result of a *change in the price of the good*. For example, if the price of bicycles rises, causing the quantity demanded by consumers to fall, then there is a movement along the demand curve. You can see in Figure 3-3 that at point *A*, the price is $200 and the quantity demanded is 9 million. Now suppose the price rises to $220. The quantity demanded then falls from 9 million to 7 million. This can be shown as a movement along the demand curve for bicycles from point *A* to point *B*. Conversely, if the price of a bicycle falls to $180, then the quantity demanded will increase to 11 million bicycles.

Figure 3-3

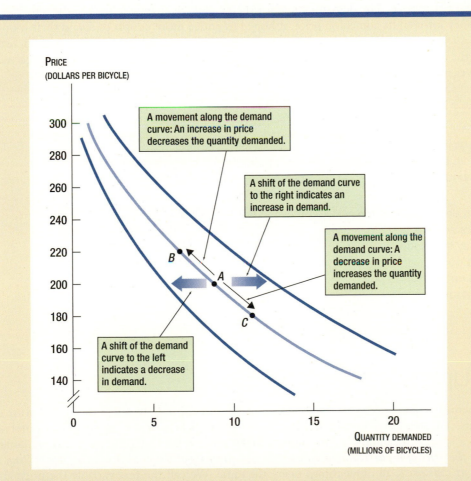

Shifts of versus Movements Along the Demand Curve
A *shift* of the demand curve occurs when a change in something (other than the good's own price) affects the quantity of a good that consumers are willing to buy. An increase in demand is a shift to the right of the demand curve. A decrease in demand is a shift to the left of the demand curve. A *movement along* the demand curve occurs when the price of the good changes, causing the quantity demanded to change, as, for example, from point *A* to point *B* or *C*.

This can be shown as an increase from point *A* to point *C* in Figure 3-3. Economists refer to a movement along the demand curve as a *change in the quantity demanded*.

A *shift* of the demand curve, on the other hand, occurs when a change is caused by *any source except the price*. Remember, the term *demand* refers to the entire curve or schedule relating price and quantity demanded, whereas the term *quantity demanded* refers to a single point on the demand curve. As we discussed, if warm weather increases, people would be more likely to buy bicycles at any given price. This means that the entire demand curve would shift to the right. On the other hand, if bicycle lanes are eliminated, people would be less likely to buy bicycles at any given price. The entire demand curve would shift to the left. Economists refer to a shift in the demand curve as a *change in demand*.

You should be able to tell whether an economic event causes (1) a change in demand or (2) a change in the quantity demanded; or, equivalently, whether an event causes (1) a shift in the demand curve or (2) a movement along the demand curve. Use the following example to test your understanding of demand shifts and movement along the demand curve. In 2001, Disney's theme park attendance was lower than in previous years as a result of the weak economy. Because of the fall in attendance, Disney lowered the adult admission price at its California Adventure park, which helped increase attendance. Which of these was a *change in demand* and which was a *change in the quantity demanded* in the market for theme parks?

The decrease in attendance caused by the weak economy in 2001 was a decrease in demand—fewer people were going to theme parks in 2001 than in prior years for any given ticket price. The demand curve for theme park visits thus shifted to the left. When Disney lowered its admission price, it hoped to entice more people to spend their money on a trip to its California Adventure park instead of on other goods. This is an increase in the quantity demanded—the park management anticipated more attendance at a lower price. This was a movement along the demand curve for theme park visits.

REVIEW

- Demand is a negative relationship between the price of a good and the quantity demanded, all other things being equal.

- The demand curve slopes down because when the price of a good rises, consumers are less likely to use their scarce resources to buy that good. Conversely, when the price of a good falls, some consumers who previously had not chosen to buy the good because the price was too high may decide to buy the good.

- It is important to distinguish shifts of the demand curve from movements along the demand curve. When the quantity demanded changes as a result of a price change, we have a movement along the demand curve. When a change in demand is brought about by something other than a price change, we have a shift of the demand curve.

Supply

supply
a relationship between price and quantity supplied.

quantity supplied
the quantity of a good that firms are willing to sell at a given price.

Whereas demand refers to the behavior of consumers, supply refers to the behavior of firms. The term *supply*—whether it is the supply of tickets or the supply of computers—has a specific meaning for economists. **Supply** is a relationship between two variables: (1) *the price of a particular good* and (2) *the quantity of the good that firms are willing to sell at that price*, all other things being the same. We call the first variable the price and the second variable the **quantity supplied**.

Supply can be represented by a numerical table or by a graph. An example of the quantity supplied (in millions of bicycles) in the entire market by bicycle-producing firms at each price is shown in Table 3-2. For example, at a price of $180, the quantity supplied is 7 million bicycles. Observe that as the price increases, the quantity supplied increases, and that as the price decreases, the quantity supplied decreases. For example, if the price rises from $180 to $200, the quantity supplied increases from 7 to 9 million bicycles. The relationship between price and quantity supplied in Table 3-2 is called a **supply schedule**. The relationship shows price and quantity supplied moving in the same direction, and this is an example of the law of supply. The **law of supply** says that the higher the price, the higher the quantity supplied; and the lower the price, the lower the quantity supplied. In other words, the law of supply says that the price and the quantity supplied are positively related, all other things being equal.

The Supply Curve

We can represent the supply schedule in Table 3-2 graphically by plotting the price and quantity supplied on a graph, as shown in Figure 3-4. The scales of each axis in Figure 3-4 are exactly the same as those in Figure 3-1, except that Figure 3-4 shows the quantity supplied, whereas Figure 3-1 shows the quantity demanded. Each pair of numbers in Table 3-2 is plotted as a point in Figure 3-4. The resulting curve showing all the combinations of prices and quantities supplied is the **supply curve**. Note that the curve slopes upward: At a price of $280, the quantity supplied is high—16 million bicycles. If the price were $160 a bicycle, then firms would be willing to sell only 4 million bicycles.

Why does the supply curve slope upward? Imagine yourself running a firm that produces and sells bicycles. If the price of the bicycles goes up from $180 to $280, then you can earn $100 more for each bicycle you produce and sell. Given your production costs, if you earn more from each bicycle, you will have a greater incentive to produce and sell more bicycles. If producing more bicycles increases the costs of producing each bicycle, perhaps because you must pay the bike assembly workers a higher wage for working overtime, the higher price will give you the incentive to incur these costs. Other bicycle firms will be thinking the same way. Thus, firms are willing to sell more bicycles as the price rises. Conversely, the incentive for firms to sell bicycles will decline as the price falls. Basically, that is why a positive relationship exists between price and quantity supplied.

When formulating economic policy, it is important to remember this supply relationship. When the price of a good increases, it leads to an increase in the quantity supplied. If U.S. agricultural policy results in the U.S. government offering to pay farmers a higher price for their corn, then the farmers will respond by increasing their production of corn. If coffee prices on the world market collapse, some coffee farmers in developing countries will switch to producing other crops instead of coffee.

Shifts in Supply

The supply curve is a relationship between price and the quantity supplied drawn on the assumption that all other things are held constant. If any one of these other things changes, then the supply curve shifts. For example, suppose a new machine is invented that makes it possible to produce bicycle frames at less cost; then firms would have more incentive at any given price to produce and sell more bicycles. Supply would increase, and the supply curve would shift to the right.

---

supply schedule
a tabular presentation of supply showing the price and quantity supplied of a particular good, all else being equal.

law of supply
the tendency for the quantity supplied of a good in a market to increase as its price rises.

Table 3-2

Supply Schedule for Bicycles (millions of bicycles per year)

Price	Quantity Supplied
$140	1
$160	4
$180	7
$200	9
$220	11
$240	13
$260	15
$280	16
$300	17

supply curve
a graph of supply showing the upward-sloping relationship between price and quantity supplied.

Figure 3-4

The Supply Curve

The supply curve shows that the price and the quantity supplied by firms in the market are positively related. The curve slopes up. For each price on the vertical axis, the supply curve shows the quantity that firms are willing to sell along the horizontal axis. The points along the supply curve for bicycles match the pairs of numbers in Table 3-2.

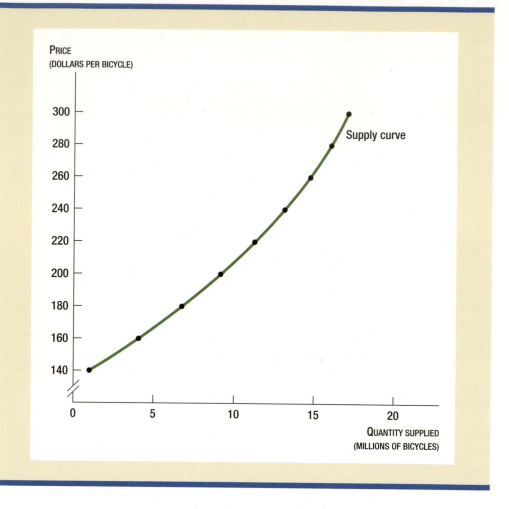

Figure 3-5 shows that the supply curve for bicycles would shift to the right because of a new cost-reducing machine. The supply curve would shift to the left if supply decreased. Supply would decrease, for example, if bicycle-producing firms suddenly found that their existing machines would break down unless they were oiled with an expensive lubricant each time a bicycle was produced. This would raise costs, lower supply, and shift the supply curve to the left.

Many things can cause the supply curve to shift. Most of these can be categorized by the source of the change in supply: *technology, weather conditions, the price of inputs used in production, the number of firms in the market, expectations of future prices*, and *government taxes, subsidies, and regulations*. Let us briefly consider the sources of shifts in supply.

Technology Anything that changes the amount a firm can produce with a given amount of inputs to production can be considered a change in technology. The Harbour Report, a study that examines the number of labor hours needed to produce an automobile, calculated that in 2005, General Motors needed 34 hours per vehicle, while Toyota needed only 28 hours per vehicle. Suppose an improvement in technology enabled General Motors to reduce the time it took to produce a car by six hours per vehicle. This improvement in technology would correspond to an increase

Figure 3-5

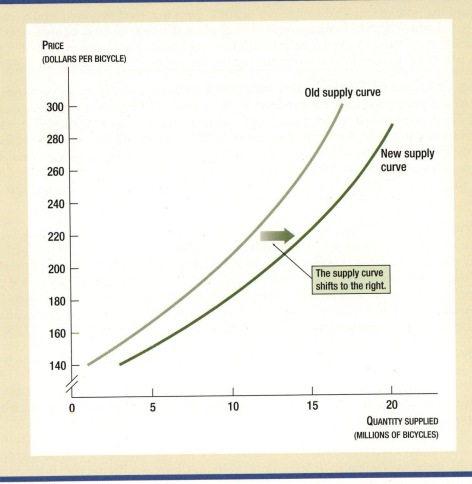

A Shift in the Supply Curve
The supply curve is a relationship between the quantity supplied of a good and the price of the good, all other things being equal. A change in one of these other things (other than the good's price) will shift the supply curve, as shown in the graph. In this case, the supply of bicycles increases; the supply curve for bicycles shifts to the right.

supply, a shift in the supply curve to the right. Another way of viewing an increase in supply is that producers are willing to sell any given quantity at a lower price than before. This makes sense, because production costs are lower with the improvement in technology.

Weather Conditions Droughts, earthquakes, and hurricanes also affect how much of certain types of goods can be produced with given inputs. A drought can reduce the amount of wheat that can be produced on a farm in the Midwest. The floods that devastated some regions in Australia in early 2011 resulted in a fall in cotton supplies on the world market, for which Australia is a leading producer and exporter. Hurricanes Katrina and Rita disrupted oil drilling and refining activities in Texas and Louisiana. Because such events change the amount that can be produced with a given amount of inputs, they are similar to changes in technology. In the examples just given, the supply curve shifted to the left, although you could have favorable weather conditions that would shift the supply curve for a particular good to the right.

The Price of Inputs Used in Production If the prices of the inputs to production—raw materials, labor, and capital—increase, then it becomes more costly to produce goods, and firms will produce less at any given price. In this case, the supply curve will shift to the left. When the U.S. government imposed trade restrictions that caused the price of imported steel to rise in 2002, firms that used imported steel to produce household appliances were unwilling to produce the same quantity of appliances at existing price levels. So an increase in production costs causes the supply curve to shift to the left, and a decrease in production costs causes the supply curve to shift to the right.

The Number of Firms in the Market Remember that the supply curve refers to *all* the firms producing the product. If the number of firms increases, then more goods will be produced at each price: supply increases, and the supply curve shifts to the right. A decline in the number of firms, on the other hand, would shift the supply curve to the left. For example, if a country removes barriers that prevent foreign car manufacturers from selling cars to the domestic market, then the number of firms producing cars for that country's domestic market will increase, and the supply curve for cars in that economy will shift to the right.

Expectations of Future Prices If firms expect the price of the good they produce to rise in the future, then they will hold off selling at least part of their production until the price rises. For example, farmers in the United States who anticipate an increase in wheat prices because of political turbulence in the Russian Federation may decide to store more wheat in silos and sell it later, after the price rises. Thus, expectations of *future* price increases tend to reduce supply. Conversely, expectations of *future* price decreases tend to increase supply.

Government Taxes, Subsidies, and Regulations The government has the ability to affect the supply of particular goods produced by firms. For example, the government imposes taxes on firms to pay for such government services as education, police, and national defense. These taxes increase firms' costs and reduce supply. The supply curve shifts to the left when a tax on what firms sell in the market increases.

The government also makes payments—subsidies—to firms to encourage those firms to produce certain goods. Such subsidies have the opposite effect of taxes on supply. An increase in subsidies reduces firms' costs and increases the supply. If the U.S. government provided subsidies for corn production to encourage the use of ethanol, an alternative fuel for cars that is produced from corn, this would increase the production of corn. On the other hand, when the U.S. government imposes a tax on cigarettes, the supply of cigarettes will decrease.

Governments also regulate firms. In some cases, such regulations can change the firms' costs of production or their ability to produce goods and thereby affect supply. For example, if a city government decides that only vendors who successfully pass a health and sanitation inspection are allowed to sell food from street carts, the supply curve for street-vendor food will shift to the left.

Movements Along versus Shifts of the Supply Curve

As with the demand curve, it is important that you understand how to distinguish between *shifts* of the supply curve and *movements along* the supply curve. This distinction is illustrated in Figure 3-6.

A *movement along* the supply curve occurs when the quantity supplied changes as a result of a *change in the price of the good*. For example, if a copper mine in Zambia increases its production because the price of copper has increased on the world market, then that indicates a movement along the supply curve. In our bicycle example, an increase in the price of bicycles from $200 to $220 would increase the quantity supplied

Figure 3-6

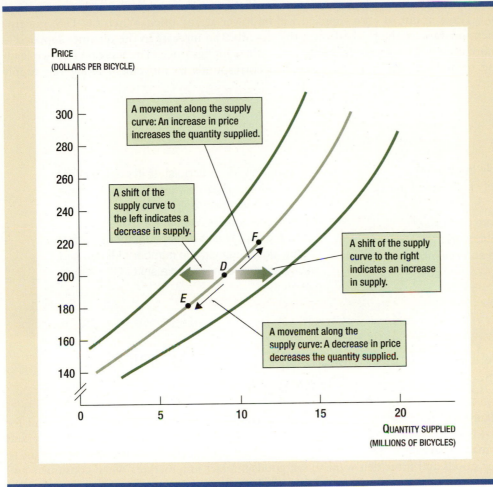

PRICE
(DOLLARS PER BICYCLE)

A movement along the supply curve: An increase in price increases the quantity supplied.

A shift of the supply curve to the left indicates a decrease in supply.

A shift of the supply curve to the right indicates an increase in supply.

A movement along the supply curve: A decrease in price decreases the quantity supplied.

QUANTITY SUPPLIED
(MILLIONS OF BICYCLES)

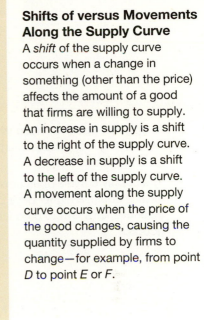

Shifts of versus Movements Along the Supply Curve
A *shift* of the supply curve occurs when a change in something (other than the price) affects the amount of a good that firms are willing to supply. An increase in supply is a shift to the right of the supply curve. A decrease in supply is a shift to the left of the supply curve. A movement along the supply curve occurs when the price of the good changes, causing the quantity supplied by firms to change—for example, from point *D* to point *E* or *F*.

from 9 million bicycles to 11 million bicycles. This can be shown as a movement along the supply curve for bicycles from point *D* to point *F*. Conversely, if the price of a bicycle were to fall from $200 to $180, then the quantity supplied would decrease to 7 million bicycles. This can be shown as movement from point *D* to point *E* in Figure 3-6. Economists refer to a movement along the supply curve as a *change in the quantity supplied*.

A *shift* of the supply curve, on the other hand, occurs if a change is caused by *any source except the price*. An unexpected winter freeze in California will mean that farmers will be able to produce fewer oranges at any given price. This means that the supply curve of oranges will shift to the left. When the supply curve shifts, economists call that a *change in supply*.

You should be able to tell whether a change in something causes (1) a change in supply or (2) a change in the quantity supplied; or, equivalently, if a change causes (1) a shift in the supply curve or (2) a movement along the supply curve. The following example will test your ability to distinguish between movement along a supply curve and a shift in the supply curve. Suppose that U.S. agricultural policy guarantees farmers a specific price on certain crops. An economist suggested that the government instead should pay farmers to not plant some of their fields. Which policy is describing a *change in supply* and which is describing a *change in the quantity supplied* in the market for corn?

A policy that pays farmers to leave cornfields unplanted describes a decrease in supply. The amount of corn supplied will be lower at any price. When the U.S. government guarantees the price of corn, this describes an increase in the quantity supplied—more corn will be grown in anticipation of the higher price. The increase in price leading to an increase in quantity supplied corresponds to movement along the supply curve.

REVIEW

- Supply is a positive relationship between the price of a good and the quantity supplied of the good by firms.

- The supply curve slopes upward because, all else equal, a higher price offers greater incentive for a firm to produce and sell more goods.

- It is important to distinguish shifts of the supply curve from movements along the supply curve. When the quantity supplied changes because of a change in price, we have a movement along the supply curve. Other factors—such as technology, weather, the number of firms, and expectations—can lead to a shift in the supply curve.

Market Equilibrium: Combining Supply and Demand

Figure 3-7 summarizes what you have learned thus far about consumers' demand for goods in a market and firms' supply of goods in a market. Now, we put supply and demand together to complete the supply and demand model. Consumers who want to buy goods and firms that want to sell goods interact in a market. When consumers and firms interact, a price is determined at which the transaction occurs. Recall that a market does not need to be located at one place; the U.S. bicycle market consists of all the bicycle firms that sell bicycles and all the consumers who buy bicycles.

Fascinatingly, no single person or firm determines the price in the market. Instead, the market determines the price. As buyers and sellers interact, prices may go up for a while and then go down. Alfred Marshall, the economist who did the most to develop the supply and demand model in the late nineteenth century, called this process the "higgling and bargaining" of the market. The assumption underlying the supply and demand model is that, in the give and take of the marketplace, prices adjust until they settle down at a level at which the quantity supplied by firms equals the quantity demanded by consumers. Let's see how.

Determination of the Market Price

To determine the market price, we combine the demand relationship with the supply relationship. We can do this using either a table or a diagram. First consider Table 3-3, which combines the demand schedule from Table 3-1 with the supply schedule from Table 3-2. The price is in the first column, the quantity demanded by consumers is in the second column, and the quantity supplied by firms is in the third column. Observe that the quantity that consumers are willing to buy is shown to decline with the price, whereas the quantity that firms are willing to sell is shown to increase with the price.

Finding the Market Price Pick a price in Table 3-3, any price. Suppose the price you choose is $160. Then the quantity demanded by consumers (14 million bicycles) is greater than the quantity supplied by firms (4 million bicycles). In other words, there is a shortage of 14 − 4 = 10 million bicycles. A **shortage**, or **excess demand**, is a situation

shortage (excess demand)
a situation in which quantity demanded is greater than quantity supplied.

Figure 3-7

Overview of Supply and Demand

<u>SUPPLY</u>

Supply describes firms.

The supply curve looks like this:

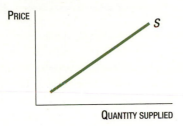

<u>DEMAND</u>

Demand describes consumers.

The demand curve looks like this:

Law of Supply

Price and quantity supplied are positively related.

Movements along supply curve occur

when price rises and quantity supplied rises or when price falls and quantity supplied falls.

Shifts in supply are due to:

Technology (new inventions)

Weather (especially for agricultural products)

Number of firms in market

Price of goods used in production (inputs such as fertilizer, labor)

Expectations of future prices (firms will sell less now if prices are expected to rise; for example, farmers may store goods to sell next year)

Government taxes, subsidies, regulations (commodity taxes, agricultural subsidies, safety regulations)

Law of Demand

Price and quantity demanded are negatively related.

Movements along demand curve occur

when price rises and quantity demanded falls or when price falls and quantity demanded rises.

Shifts in demand are due to:

Preferences (changes in consumers' tastes)

Number of consumers in market

Consumers' information (about smoking, or faulty products, for example)

Consumers' income (normal goods versus inferior goods)

Expectations of future prices (consumers will buy more now if prices are expected to rise in the future)

Price of related goods (both substitutes, like butter and margarine, and complements, like gasoline and SUVs)

Table 3-3

Finding the Market Equilibrium

Price	Quantity Demanded	Quantity Supplied	Shortage, Surplus, or Equilibrium	Price Rises or Falls
$140	18	1	Shortage = 17	Price rises
$160	14	4	Shortage = 10	Price rises
$180	11	7	Shortage = 4	Price rises
$200*	9*	9*	Equilibrium*	No change*
$220	7	11	Surplus = 4	Price falls
$240	5	13	Surplus = 8	Price falls
$260	3	15	Surplus = 12	Price falls
$280	2	16	Surplus = 14	Price falls
$300	1	17	Surplus = 16	Price falls

*Note: Quantity supplied equals quantity demanded.

in which the quantity demanded is greater than the quantity supplied. With a shortage of bicycles, buyers who really need a bicycle will start to offer to pay more to acquire a bicycle, while firms that are faced with an abundance of potential customers wanting to buy their bicycles will begin to charge higher prices. Thus, $160 cannot last as the market price. Observe that as the price rises above $160, the quantity demanded falls and the quantity supplied rises. Thus, as the price rises, the shortage begins to decrease. Suppose the price increases to $180. At that price, the quantity demanded falls to 11 million bicycles and the quantity supplied rises to 7 million bicycles. A shortage still exists and the price still will rise, but the shortage is now much less, at 11 − 7 = 4 million bicycles. The shortage will disappear only when the price rises to $200, as shown in Table 3-3.

Suppose instead that you had picked a price above $200, let's say $260. Then the quantity demanded by consumers (3 million bicycles) is less than the quantity supplied by firms (15 million bicycles). In other words, there is a surplus of 12 million bicycles. A **surplus,** or **excess supply**, is a situation in which the quantity supplied is greater than the quantity demanded. With a surplus of bicycles, buyers who really need a bicycle have an abundance of sellers who are eager to sell them a bicycle, while firms have to compete with one another to entice buyers for their products. Therefore, the price of bicycles will fall: Firms that are willing to sell bicycles for less than $260 will offer to sell to consumers at lower prices. Thus, $260 cannot be the market price either. Observe that as the price falls below $260, the quantity demanded rises and the quantity supplied falls. Thus, the surplus decreases. If you choose any price above $200, the same thing will happen: A surplus will exist, and the price will fall. The surplus disappears only when the price falls to $200.

Thus, we have shown that for any price below $200, a shortage exists, and the price rises, while for any price above $200, a surplus exists, and the price falls. What if the market price is $200? Then the quantity supplied equals the quantity demanded; there is not a shortage or a surplus, and there is no reason for the price to rise or fall. This price of $200 is called the **equilibrium price** because, at this price, the quantity supplied equals the quantity demanded, and the price has no tendency to change. There is no other price for which quantity supplied equals quantity demanded. If you look at all the other prices, you will see either a shortage or a surplus, and thus the price has a tendency to either rise or fall.

The quantity bought and sold at the equilibrium price is 9 million bicycles. This is the **equilibrium quantity**. When the price equals the equilibrium price and the quantity bought and sold equals the equilibrium quantity, economists call this a **market equilibrium**.

Our discussion of the determination of the equilibrium price shows how the market price coordinates the buying and selling decisions of many firms and consumers. We see

surplus (excess supply)
a situation in which quantity supplied is greater than quantity demanded.

equilibrium price
the price at which quantity supplied equals quantity demanded.

equilibrium quantity
the quantity traded at the equilibrium price.

market equilibrium
the situation in which the price is equal to the equilibrium price and the quantity traded equals the equilibrium quantity.

that the price serves a *rationing function*. When a shortage exists, a higher price reduces the quantity demanded and increases the quantity supplied to eliminate the shortage. Similarly, when a surplus exists, a lower price increases the quantity demanded and decreases the quantity supplied to eliminate the surplus. Thus, both shortages and surpluses are eliminated by the forces of supply and demand.

Two Predictions By combining supply and demand, we have completed the supply and demand model. The model can be applied to many markets, not just the example of the bicycle market. One prediction of the supply and demand model is that *the equilibrium price in the market will be the price for which the quantity supplied equals the quantity demanded.* Thus, the model provides an answer to the question of what determines the price in the market. Another prediction of the model is that *the equilibrium quantity bought and sold in the market is the quantity for which the quantity supplied equals the quantity demanded.*

Finding the Equilibrium with a Supply and Demand Diagram

The equilibrium price and quantity in a market also can be found with the help of a graph. Figure 3-8 combines the demand curve from Figure 3-1 and the supply curve from Figure 3-4 in the same diagram. Observe that the downward-sloping demand curve

Figure 3-8

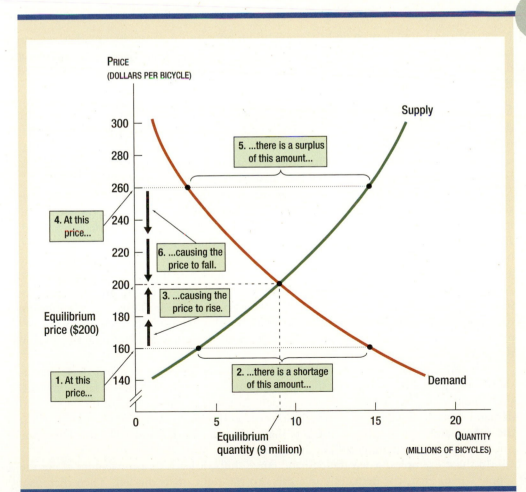

Equilibrium Price and Equilibrium Quantity
When buyers and sellers interact in the market, the equilibrium price is at the point of intersection of the supply curve and the demand curve. At this point, the quantity supplied equals the quantity demanded. The equilibrium quantity also is determined at that point. At a higher price, the quantity demanded will be less than the quantity supplied; a surplus will exist. At a lower price, the quantity demanded will be greater than the quantity supplied; a shortage will exist.

intersects the upward-sloping supply curve at a single point. At that point of intersection, the quantity supplied equals the quantity demanded. Hence, the *equilibrium price is at the intersection of the supply curve and the demand curve*. The equilibrium price of $200 is shown in Figure 3-8. At that price, the quantity demanded is 9 million bicycles, and the quantity supplied is 9 million bicycles. This is the equilibrium quantity.

If the price were lower than this equilibrium price, say, $160, then the quantity demanded would be greater than the quantity supplied. A shortage would exist, and demand would pressure the price to increase, as shown in the graph. The increase in gasoline prices in 2007 and the early part of 2008 led to an increase in demand for hybrid automobiles. With a shortage of hybrid vehicles and long waiting lists, some automobile sellers increased the price of the hybrids.

On the other hand, if the price were above the equilibrium price, say, $260, then the quantity supplied would be greater than the quantity demanded. A surplus would exist, and excess quantity would pressure the price to fall. After September 11, 2001, a large number of vacationers canceled vacation plans that involved air travel. Caribbean hotels, with a surplus of vacant hotel rooms following this decrease in demand, began to offer big discounts.

Thus, the market price will tend to move toward the equilibrium price at the intersection of the supply curve and the demand curve. We can calculate exactly what the equilibrium price is in Figure 3-8 by drawing a line over to the vertical axis. And we can calculate the equilibrium quantity by drawing a line down to the horizontal axis.

Market Outcomes When Supply or Demand Changes

Now that you know how to find the equilibrium price and quantity in a market, we can use the supply and demand model to analyze the impact of factors that change supply or demand on equilibrium price and quantity. We first consider a change in demand and then a change in supply.

Effects of a Change in Demand
Figure 3-9 shows the effects of a shift in the demand curve for bicycles. Suppose that a shift occurs because of a fitness craze that increases the demand for bicycles. The demand curve shifts to the right, as shown in Figure 3-9(a). The demand curve before the shift and the demand curve after the shift are labeled the "old demand curve" and the "new demand curve," respectively.

If you look at the graph, you can see that something must happen to the equilibrium price when the demand curve shifts. The equilibrium price is determined at the intersection of the supply curve and the demand curve. With the new demand curve, there is a new intersection and, therefore, a new equilibrium price. The equilibrium price is no longer $200 in Figure 3-9(a); it is up to $220 per bicycle. Thus, the supply and demand model predicts that the price in the market will rise if demand increases. Note also that the equilibrium quantity of bicycles changes. The quantity of bicycles sold and bought has increased from 9 million to 11 million. Thus, the equilibrium quantity has increased along with the equilibrium price. The supply and demand model predicts that an increase in demand will raise both the price and the quantity sold in the market.

We can use the same method to find out what happens if demand decreases, as shown in Figure 3-9(b). Suppose that the elimination of dedicated bicycle lanes on roads shifts the demand curve for bicycles to the left. At the new intersection of the supply and demand curves, the equilibrium price is lower, and the quantity sold also is lower. Thus, the supply and demand model predicts that a decrease in demand will both lower the price and lower the quantity sold in the market.

In these examples, when the demand curve shifts, it leads to a movement along the supply curve. First, the demand curve shifts to the right or to the left. Then there is a

Figure 3-9

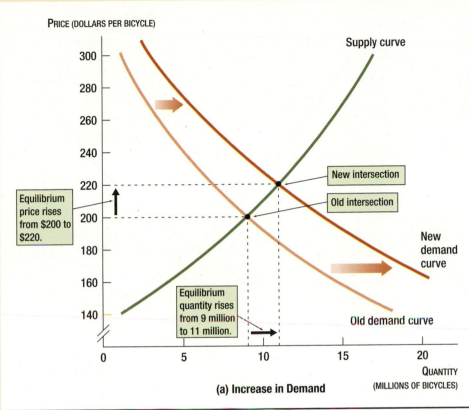

(a) **Increase in Demand**

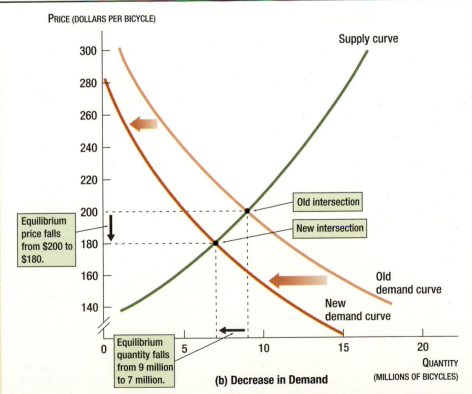

(b) **Decrease in Demand**

Effects of a Shift in Demand

When demand increases, as in graph (a), the demand curve shifts to the right. The equilibrium price rises, and the equilibrium quantity also rises. When demand decreases, as in graph (b), the demand curve shifts to the left. The equilibrium price falls, and the equilibrium quantity also falls.

Figure 3-10

Effects of a Shift in Supply

When supply increases, as in graph (a), the supply curve shifts to the right, the equilibrium price falls, and the equilibrium quantity rises. When supply decreases, as in graph (b), the supply curve shifts to the left, the equilibrium price rises, and the equilibrium quantity falls.

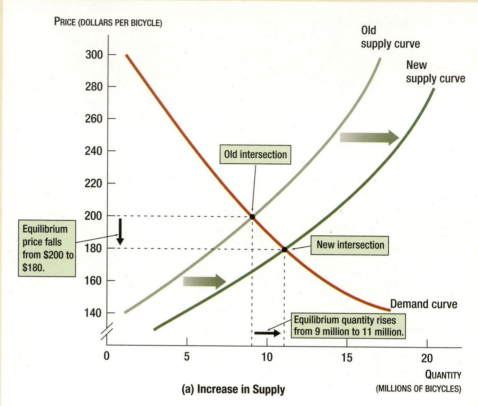

PRICE (DOLLARS PER BICYCLE)

Old supply curve

New supply curve

Old intersection

New intersection

Equilibrium price falls from $200 to $180.

Demand curve

Equilibrium quantity rises from 9 million to 11 million.

QUANTITY (MILLIONS OF BICYCLES)

(a) Increase in Supply

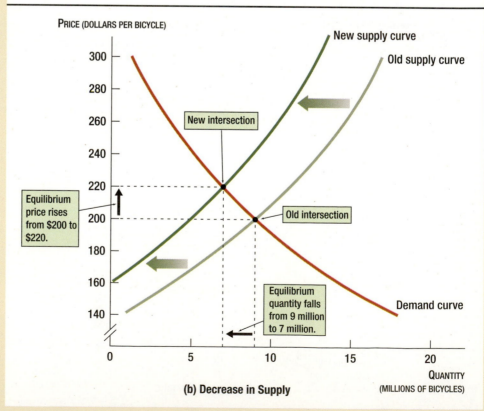

PRICE (DOLLARS PER BICYCLE)

New supply curve

Old supply curve

New intersection

Old intersection

Equilibrium price rises from $200 to $220.

Equilibrium quantity falls from 9 million to 7 million.

Demand curve

QUANTITY (MILLIONS OF BICYCLES)

(b) Decrease in Supply

Table 3-4

Effects of Shifts in Demand and Supply Curves

Shift	Effect on Equilibrium Price	Effect on Equilibrium Quantity
Increase in demand	Up	Up
Decrease in demand	Down	Down
Increase in supply	Down	Up
Decrease in supply	Up	Down

movement along the supply curve because the change in the price affects the quantity of bicycles that firms will sell.

Effects of a Change in Supply

Figure 3-10 shows what happens when a change in the market shifts the supply curve. Suppose a new technology reduces the cost of producing bicycles, resulting in the supply curve for bicycles shifting to the right. Figure 10(a) shows that that a new equilibrium price is lower than the old equilibrium price. In addition, the equilibrium quantity rises. Thus, the supply and demand model predicts that an increase in the supply of bicycles will lower the price and raise the quantity of bicycles sold.

Suppose instead that an increase in the cost of bicycle tires increases the cost of producing bicycles, resulting in the supply curve for bicycles shifting to the left. Figure 10(b) shows that the equilibrium price rises, and the equilibrium quantity falls. Thus, the model predicts that a decrease in the supply of bicycles will raise the price of bicycles and lower the quantity of bicycles sold.

Table 3-4 summarizes the results of this analysis of shifts in the supply and demand curves.

When Both Curves Shift

The supply and demand model is easiest to use when you are analyzing a factor that shifts either demand or supply, but not both. In reality, however, it is possible for something or several different things to simultaneously shift both supply and demand. To predict whether the price or the quantity rises or falls in such cases, we need to know whether demand or supply shifts by a larger amount. Dealing with the possibility of simultaneous shifts in demand and supply curves is important in practice, as we show in the following example.

REVIEW

- The supply and demand model is used to predict the price and the quantity that result from interactions of consumers and producers in a market.

- In a market, the price will adjust upward or downward until the quantity supplied equals the quantity demanded. This price is called the equilibrium price, and the corresponding quantity is called the equilibrium quantity.

- Changes in the economy that cause the demand curve to shift to the right will raise both the equilibrium price and the equilibrium quantity. Changes that cause the demand curve to shift to the left will lower both the equilibrium price and the equilibrium quantity.

- Changes in the economy that cause the supply curve to shift to the right will lower the equilibrium price and raise the equilibrium quantity. Changes that cause the supply curve to shift to the left will raise the equilibrium price and lower the equilibrium quantity.

ECONOMICS *IN ACTION*

Using the Supply and Demand Model to Analyze Real-World Issues

Between January and October of 2005, a period of eight months, the average price of a gallon of gasoline in the United States rose from $1.75 to $2.92 a gallon, an increase of almost 60 percent, according to data gathered by the Department of Energy. Rising gasoline prices are of critical importance to the American people. If you own a car, rising gasoline prices have a direct impact on you—you may have to cut back on driving, or ask your parents for more money to buy gasoline, or spend less on other things because you are spending more on gasoline. Even if you do not own a car, rising gasoline prices can affect you. The prices of goods and services will rise because the cost of transportation increases. Bus fares, taxi fares, and airplane tickets all may rise in price because of the high price of gasoline.

Why did the price of gasoline go up so rapidly in 2005? How long did the high price of gasoline last? What could policy makers do to lower the price of gasoline? The model of supply and demand gives us a tool to model the market for gasoline, to examine the causes of the high price, to understand the impact on U.S. people and businesses, and to focus on what policy makers can do to lower the price of gasoline.

As President Bush pointed out in an April 2005 press conference, "Over the past decade, America's energy consumption has been growing about 40 times faster than our energy production." Demand for gasoline had been increasing, as more Americans were driving gas-guzzling SUVs and people were driving more miles. These factors shifted the demand curve for gasoline to the right.

On the supply side, the destruction caused by Hurricane Katrina disrupted drilling on oil rigs and shut down refineries along the Gulf Coast. This reduction in supply added to a long-term trend whereby the supply of gasoline was being lowered as a result of a reduction in U.S. refining capacity. In addition, both stricter environmental regulations for refining gasoline and the increasing price of oil led to an increase in production costs for gasoline. All of these factors combined to cause the supply of gasoline to shift to the left.

Figure 3-11

Combined Effect of a Simultaneous Increase in Demand and Decrease in Supply of Gasoline

When demand for gasoline increases and, at the same time, the supply of gasoline *decreases* because of decreased refining capacity, the supply curve will shift to the left. The equilibrium price increases, and the equilibrium quantity also increases. In this situation, the increase in demand is larger than the decrease in supply.

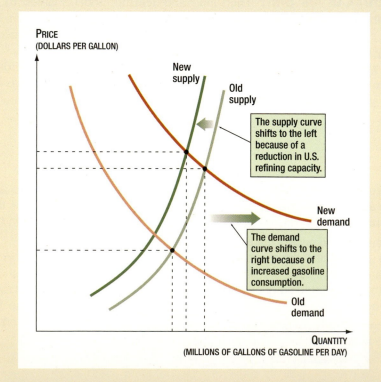

Figure 3-11 illustrates the events that led to the rapid increase in gasoline prices, using a supply and demand model. The equilibrium price will unambiguously be higher: The increase in demand and the decrease in supply both will tend to push the price higher. The impact on equilibrium quantity will be ambiguous: The increase in demand would push the equilibrium quantity higher, but the decrease in supply would push the equilibrium quantity lower. Figure 3-11 illustrates a possible outcome in which the increase in demand is larger than the decrease in supply, leading to a rise in the equilibrium quantity.

What could policy makers have done to lower the price of gasoline? President Bush stressed in his press conference that Congress needed to pass an energy bill to address the high price of energy. President Bush stated, ''You can't wave a magic wand. I wish I could.'' A magic wand won't work, but the model of supply and demand can predict what will. Policies that encourage the development of new technologies for conservation of energy and the development of new sources of energy that would reduce the demand for gasoline eventually can help decrease the equilibrium price of oil. President Bush pointed out that the best way to get the price of gasoline to fall quickly would be to encourage oil-producing nations to increase their supply of oil. An increase in the supply of oil would lead to an increase in the supply of gasoline and a reduction in its price.

Figure 3-12 illustrates the gasoline market with a simultaneous decrease in demand and increase in supply. Both the decrease in the demand for gasoline and the increase in the supply of gasoline would lead to a decrease in the equilibrium price of gasoline. This is a prediction that policy makers easily could make. What if they wanted also to predict the change in the consumption of gasoline resulting from this energy bill? A decrease in demand would decrease equilibrium consumption, while an increase in supply would increase equilibrium consumption. Policy makers therefore could not predict whether gasoline consumption would rise or fall without knowing whether demand or supply would shift by a larger amount. Figure 3-12 shows a resulting increase in the consumption of gasoline because the supply increase is greater in magnitude than the demand decrease.

Now draw your own graph, but make the demand decrease larger than the supply increase. You will see a resulting decrease in the consumption of gasoline. If policy makers want an energy bill that both reduces the price of gasoline and reduces the quantity of gasoline consumed, they need to ensure that conservation efforts are the primary focus of the plan.

Figure 3-12

Predicted Effects of Energy Policy

The supply and demand model also can be used to predict what would happen with a successful energy policy that promoted the development of new sources of energy and energy conservation. Here, demand decreases slightly because of the effects of energy conservation, and supply increases because of the development of new technology for energy development. When demand decreases and supply increases, the equilibrium price goes down and the equilibrium quantity increases.

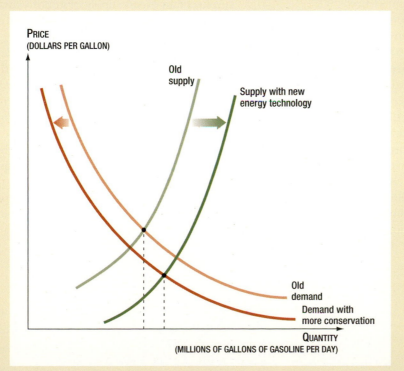

PRICE
(DOLLARS PER GALLON)

Old supply

Supply with new energy technology

Old demand

Demand with more conservation

QUANTITY
(MILLIONS OF GALLONS OF GASOLINE PER DAY)

CONCLUSION

This chapter has shown how to use the supply and demand model to find out how equilibrium price and quantity are determined in markets in which buyers and sellers interact freely. The supply and demand model is probably the most frequently used model in economics, and it has been in existence for more than 100 years in pretty much the same form as economists use it now. You will come to appreciate it more and more as you study economics.

A key feature of the model is that the equilibrium price and quantity are found at the intersection of the supply and demand curves. We can use the model to analyze how a change in factors that shift either the supply curve or the demand curve (or both) will affect equilibrium price and quantity in the market.

In later chapters, we will take a closer look at the supply and demand model to understand issues like how much equilibrium price or quantity changes when the demand curve or the supply curve shifts. We also can look at whether a market in which buyers and sellers interact freely can deliver the best outcomes for society, or whether their outcomes can be improved.

We also will look at what happens when buyers and sellers are not able to interact freely because of restrictions that limit how much a seller can charge for a good or how much a buyer has to pay for a good. This examination will enable you to better understand policy debates about minimum wages and rent controls.

KEY POINTS

1. Demand is a negative relationship between the price of a good and the quantity demanded by consumers. It can be shown graphically by a downward-sloping demand curve.

2. A movement along the demand curve occurs when a higher price reduces the quantity demanded or a lower price increases the quantity demanded.

3. A shift of the demand curve occurs when something besides a change in price changes the quantity of a good that people are willing to buy.

4. Supply is a positive relationship between the price of a good and the quantity supplied by firms. It can be shown graphically by an upward-sloping supply curve.

5. A movement along the supply curve occurs when a higher price increases the quantity supplied or a lower price decreases the quantity supplied.

6. A shift of the supply curve occurs when something besides a change in price changes the quantity of a good that firms are willing to sell.

7. The equilibrium price and equilibrium quantity are determined by the intersection of the supply curve and the demand curve. At this intersection point, the quantity supplied equals the quantity demanded—no shortages or surpluses exist.

8. The adjustment of prices moves the market into equilibrium. In situations in which a shortage or an excess demand exists for goods, price will rise, increasing the quantity supplied and reducing the quantity demanded. In situations in which a surplus or an excess supply of goods exists, price will fall, decreasing the quantity supplied and increasing the quantity demanded.

9. We can use the supply and demand model to analyze the impact of changes in factors that move the supply curve or the demand curve or both. By shifting either the supply curve or the demand curve, observations of prices can be explained and predictions about prices can be made.

10. When the demand curve shifts to the right (left), both equilibrium price and equilibrium quantity will increase (decrease). When the supply curve shifts to the right (left), the equilibrium price will fall (rise), and the equilibrium quantity will rise (fall).

KEY TERMS

complement, 53
demand, 47
demand curve, 48

demand schedule, 48
equilibrium price, 62
equilibrium quantity, 62

inferior goods, 50

law of demand, 48

law of supply, 55

market equilibrium, 62

normal goods, 50

price, 47

quantity demanded, 47

quantity supplied, 54

shortage, or excess demand, 61

substitute, 52

supply, 54

supply curve, 55

supply schedule, 55

surplus, or excess supply, 62

QUESTIONS FOR REVIEW

1. Why does the demand curve slope downward?
2. Why does the supply curve slope upward?
3. What is the difference between a shift in the demand curve and a movement along the demand curve?
4. What are four things that cause a demand curve to shift?
5. What is the difference between a shift in the supply curve and a movement along the supply curve?

6. What are four things that cause a supply curve to shift?
7. How can one find the equilibrium price and equilibrium quantity?
8. What happens to the equilibrium price if the supply curve shifts to the right?
9. What happens to the equilibrium price if the demand curve shifts to the right?
10. If both the supply curve and the demand curve shift to the right, what happens to the equilibrium quantity? What about the equilibrium price?

PROBLEMS

1. For each of the following markets, indicate whether the stated change causes a shift in the supply curve, a shift in the demand curve, a movement along the supply curve, or a movement along the demand curve.

   a. The housing market: Consumers' incomes fall.
   b. The tea market: The price of sugar goes down.
   c. The coffee market: A freeze in Brazil severely damages the coffee crop.
   d. The fast-food market: The number of fast-food restaurants in an area decreases.
   e. The peanut market in the U.S. Southeast: A drought lowers supply.

2. Determine which of the following four sentences use the terminology of the supply and demand model correctly.

   a. The price of bicycles rose, and therefore the demand for bicycles went down.
   b. The demand for bicycles increased, and therefore the price went up.
   c. The price of bicycles fell, decreasing the supply of bicycles.
   d. The supply of bicycles increased, and therefore the price of bicycles fell.

3. Use the supply and demand model to explain what happens to the equilibrium price and the equilibrium quantity for frozen yogurt in the following cases:

   a. The number of firms producing frozen yogurt expands significantly.
   b. It is widely publicized in the press that frozen yogurt is not more healthy for you than ice cream.
   c. It is widely publicized in the press that people who eat a cup of frozen yogurt a day live to be much happier in their retirement years.
   d. The price of milk used to produce frozen yogurt suddenly increases.
   e. Frozen yogurt suddenly becomes popular because a movie idol promotes it in television commercials.

4. Suppose a decrease in consumers' incomes causes a decrease in the demand for chicken and an increase in the demand for potatoes. Which good is inferior and which is normal? How will the equilibrium price and quantity change for each good?

5. Consider the following supply and demand model of the world tea market (in billions of pounds):

Price per Pound	Quantity Supplied	Quantity Demanded
$0.38	1,500	525
$0.37	1,000	600
$0.36	700	700
$0.35	600	900
$0.34	550	1,200

a. Is there a shortage or a surplus when the price is $0.38? What about $0.34?
b. What are the equilibrium price and the equilibrium quantity?
c. Graph the supply curve and the demand curve.
d. Show how the equilibrium price and quantity can be found on the graph.
e. If there is a shortage or surplus at a price of $0.38, calculate its size in billions of pounds and show it on the graph.

6. Consider Problem 5. Suppose that there is a drought in Sri Lanka that reduces the supply of tea by 400 billion pounds at every price. Suppose demand does not change.

a. Write down in a table the new supply schedule for tea.
b. Find the new equilibrium price and the new equilibrium quantity. Explain how the market adjusts to the new equilibrium.
c. Graph the new supply curve along with the old supply curve and the demand curve.
d. Show the change in the equilibrium price and the equilibrium quantity on the graph.
e. Did the equilibrium quantity change by more or less than the change in supply? Show how you arrived at your answer using both the table and the supply and demand diagram that you drew.

7. Suppose you notice that the prices of fresh fish have been rising while the amounts sold have been falling in recent years. Which of the following is the best explanation for this?

a. Consumer preferences have shifted in favor of fish because it is healthier than red meat.
b. Fishermen are prevented from using the most advanced equipment because of concerns about overfishing.
c. Consumers' incomes have risen faster than inflation.
d. Consumers have become worried about mercury levels in fish.

8. Suppose the prices of illegal drugs fall in your community at the same time that police drug seizures increase. Which is the best explanation for this?

a. Fewer drugs are being supplied locally.
b. Police arrests are removing more drug dealers.
c. Police arrests are reducing drug consumption sharply.
d. More drugs are being supplied locally.

9. In the United States, corn often is used as an ingredient in animal feed for livestock. Why does an increase in the use of corn to make ethanol, an additive that is used in gasoline, raise the price of meat? Use supply and demand curves for the corn market and the meat market to explain your answer.

10. Using the demand and supply diagrams (one for each market), show what short-run changes in price and quantity would be expected in the following markets if terrorism-related worries about air safety cause travelers to shy away from air travel. Each graph should contain the original and new demand and supply curves, and the original and new equilibrium prices and quantities. For each market, write one sentence explaining why each curve shifts or does not shift.

a. The market for air travel.
b. The market for rail travel.
c. The market for hotel rooms in Hawaii.
d. The market for gasoline.

4 Subtleties of the Supply and Demand Model: Price Floors, Price Ceilings, and Elasticity

In June of 2009, the federal minimum wage increased to $7.25 per hour. This was the culmination of a legislative process that began in May 2007 when the bill was signed into law by President George W. Bush. When congressional Democrats initially introduced the bill in the early days of the 110th Congress, the minimum wage was $5.15 per hour. The bill required that the minimum wage rise to $5.85 in 2007, $6.55 in 2008 and, finally, to $7.25 in 2009. Supporters of the legislation argued that an increase in the legally mandated minimum wage was needed to help low-income workers. Without this intervention, some workers would earn a wage that was "too low"; the higher wage would boost the incomes of these workers and help improve their lives. Opponents of the plan, and skeptics, argued that intervening in the labor market would not help these workers and might even end up hurting them. They pointed out that raising the minimum wage would result in some low-income workers losing their jobs. They also argued that a minimum-wage increase was a poorly targeted policy—most of the benefits, in fact, would not accrue to those who were truly in need. To add to the debate, when the last stage of the three-step increase came up in June 2009, unemployment in the United States had surged to 9.5 percent. To supporters of the bill, this was all the more reason to support the bill—more money in the pockets of working consumers would enable them to support their families in tough economic times and also provide a welcome boost to sales in the economy as a whole. Others argued that raising the cost of employing workers was too much of a burden for firms struggling to survive in the recession, and thus would end up raising unemployment more and hurting low-income workers by costing them their jobs.

Were the supporters of the plan correct in their claim that many poor people's lives could be improved by instituting a higher minimum wage? Or were the opponents correct to claim that a higher minimum wage could end up hurting more people than it helped? In this chapter, we look at more sophisticated aspects of the supply and demand model that are helpful in understanding policy debates, like the minimum-wage increase. We first look at how to use the supply and demand model in situations in which government policies do not allow price to be freely determined in a market. These interventions can take the form of a *price ceiling*, a maximum price imposed by the government when it feels that the equilibrium price is "too high," or a *price floor,* a minimum price imposed by the government when it feels that the equilibrium price is "too low," as in the case of the minimum wage. This extension of the supply and demand model also will be helpful in solidifying your understanding of the important role played by prices in the allocation of resources.

We then move on to discussing an elegant, and remarkably useful, economic concept called *elasticity* that economists use when they work with the supply and demand model. In economics, elasticity is a measure of how sensitive one variable is to another. In the case of the supply and demand model, elasticity measures how sensitive the quantity of a good that people demand, or that firms supply, is to the price of the good. In this chapter, we show how the concept of elasticity can be used to answer the question raised earlier about how much unemployment is caused when the minimum wage is raised. You will learn a formula that shows how elasticity is calculated and then learn how to work with and talk about elasticity.

Interference with Market Prices

Thus far, we have used the supply and demand model in situations in which the price is freely determined without government control. But at many times throughout history, and around the world in the twenty-first century, governments have attempted to control market prices. The usual reasons are that government leaders were not happy with the outcome of the market or were pressured by groups who would benefit from price controls.

Price Ceilings and Price Floors

In general, the government imposes two broad types of **price controls**. Controls can stipulate either a **price ceiling**, a maximum price at which a good can be bought and sold, or a **price floor**, a minimum price at which a good can be bought and sold. Why would a government choose to intervene in the market and put in a price floor or a price ceiling? What happens when such an intervention is made?

Ostensibly, the primary purpose of a price ceiling is to help consumers in situations in which the government thinks that the equilibrium price is "too high" or is inundated with consumer complaints that the equilibrium price is too high. For example, the U.S. government controlled oil prices in the early 1970s, stipulating that firms could not charge more than a stated maximum price of $5.25 per barrel of crude oil at a time when the equilibrium price was well over $10 per barrel. As another example, some cities in the United States place price controls on rental apartments; landlords are not permitted to charge a rent higher than the maximum stipulated by the **rent control** law in these

price control
a government law or regulation that sets or limits the price to be charged for a particular good.

price ceiling
a government price control that sets the maximum allowable price for a good.

price floor
a government price control that sets the minimum allowable price for a good.

rent control
a government price control that sets the maximum allowable rent on a house or apartment.

cities. Tenants living in rent-controlled units pay less than the market equilibrium rent that would prevail in the absence of the price ceiling.

Conversely, governments impose price floors to help the suppliers of goods and services in situations in which the government feels that the equilibrium price is "too low" or is influenced by complaints from producers that the equilibrium price is too low. For example, the U.S. government requires that the price of sugar in the United States not fall below a certain amount. Another example can be found in the labor market, in which the U.S. government requires that firms pay workers a wage of at least a given level, called the **minimum wage**.

Side Effects of Price Ceilings

Even though price ceilings typically are implemented with the idea of helping consumers, they often end up having harmful side effects that hurt the consumers that the ceiling was put in place to help. If the price ceiling that the government puts in place to prevent firms from charging more than a certain amount for their products is lower than the equilibrium price, then a shortage is likely to result, as illustrated in Figure 4-1. The situation of a persistent shortage, in which sellers are unwilling to supply as much as buyers want to buy, is illustrated for the general case of any good in the top graph in Figure 4-1 and for the specific case of rent control in the bottom graph.

Dealing with Persistent Shortages
Because higher prices are not allowed, the shortage must be dealt with in other ways. Sometimes the government issues a limited amount of ration coupons, which do not exceed the quantity supplied at the restricted maximum price, to people to alleviate the shortage. This was done in World War II when people had to present these ration coupons at stores to buy certain goods, and only those individuals who had ration coupons could buy those goods. If the price ceiling had not been in place, the shortage would have driven prices higher, and those who were willing and able to pay the higher price would have been able to buy the goods without the need for a ration coupon.

Alternatively, if ration coupons are not issued, then the shortage might result in long waiting lines. In the past, in centrally planned economies, long lines for bread frequently were observed because of price controls on bread. Sometimes black markets develop, in which people buy and sell goods outside the watch of the government and charge whatever price they want. In the past, this was typical in command economies. In the twenty-first century, black markets are common in less-developed countries when the governments in these countries impose price controls.

Another effect of price ceilings is a reduction in the quality of the good sold. By lowering the quality of the good, the producer can reduce the costs of producing it. A frequent criticism of rent control is that it can lower the quality of housing—landlords are more reluctant to paint the walls or to repair the elevator because they are prevented from charging a higher rent.

Making Things Worse
Although the stated purpose of price ceilings is to help people who have to pay high prices, the preceding examples indicate how price ceilings can make things worse. Issuing ration coupons raises difficult problems about who gets the coupons. In the case of a price ceiling on gasoline, for example, should the government give more coupons to those who use a lot of gasoline because they drive vehicles with poor gas mileage than to those who use less gasoline because they drive more fuel-efficient cars or use public transportation for their daily commute? Rationing by waiting in line also is an undesirable outcome. People who are waiting in line could be doing more enjoyable or more useful things. Similarly, black markets, being illegal, encourage

minimum wage
a wage per hour below which it is illegal to pay workers.

Figure 4-1

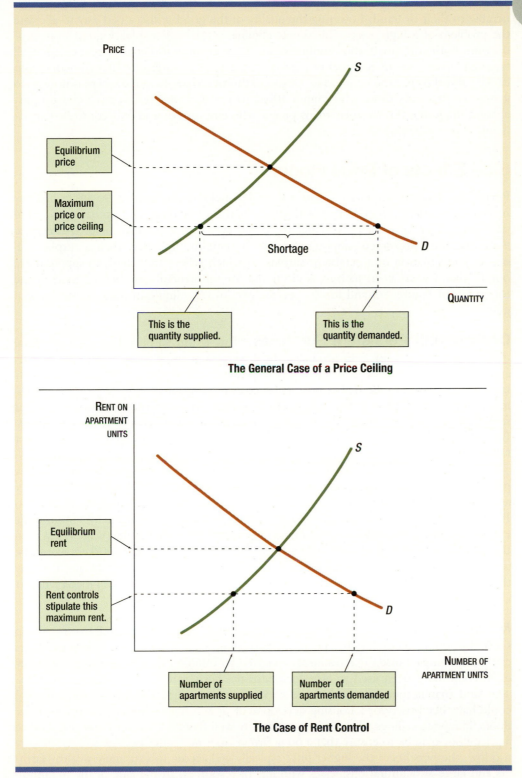

The General Case of a Price Ceiling

The Case of Rent Control

Effects of a Maximum-Price Law

The top diagram shows the general case when the government prevents the market price from rising above a particular maximum price, or sets a price ceiling below the equilibrium price. The lower diagram shows a particular example of a price ceiling, rent controls on apartment units. The supply and demand model predicts a shortage. The shortage occurs because the quantity supplied is less than consumers are willing to buy at that price. The shortage leads to rationing, black markets, or lower product quality.

people to go outside the law. People transacting in black markets also may be more vulnerable to theft or fraud. Lowering the quality of the good is also a bad way to alleviate the problem of a high price. This simply eliminates the higher-quality good from production; both consumers and producers lose. Price ceilings also are not particularly well targeted. Even though the goal of a price ceiling may be to ensure that someone who cannot afford to pay the equilibrium price still can purchase the good, there is no way to guarantee that only those who cannot afford to pay the equilibrium price end up purchasing the good. For instance, many people who end up living in rent-controlled apartments may not be poor at all.

Side Effects of Price Floors

Price floors typically are enacted with the goal of helping producers who are facing low market equilibrium prices, but, as with price ceilings, they often end up having harmful side effects that hurt the people that the policy was put in place to help. If the price floor that the government imposes exceeds the equilibrium price, then a surplus will occur. The situation of a persistent surplus, in which sellers are willing to supply more output than buyers want to buy, is illustrated for the general case of any good in the top graph of Figure 4-2 and for the specific case of the minimum wage in the bottom graph.

Dealing with Persistent Surpluses
How is this surplus dealt with in actual markets? In markets for farm products, the government usually has to buy the surplus and, perhaps, put it in storage. Buying farm products above the equilibrium price costs taxpayers money, and the higher price raises costs to consumers. For this reason, economists argue against price floors on agricultural goods. As an alternative, the government sometimes reduces the supply by telling farms to plant fewer acres or to destroy crops. But government requirements that land be kept idle or crops destroyed in exchange for taxpayer's money are particularly repugnant to most people.

When the supply and demand model is applied to labor markets, the price is the price of labor (or the wage) and a minimum wage is a price floor. What does the supply and demand model predict about the effects of a minimum wage? The lower diagram in Figure 4-2 shows that a minimum wage can cause unemployment. If the minimum wage exceeds the equilibrium wage, the number of workers demanded at that wage is less than the number of workers who are willing to work. Even though some workers would be willing to work for less than the minimum wage, employers are not permitted to pay them less than the minimum wage. Therefore, there is a surplus of unemployed workers at the minimum wage.

Making Things Worse
Even though the stated purpose of price floors is to help sellers by paying them a higher price, the preceding examples indicate how price floors can make things worse. The resources allocated to building grain silos to store surplus grain could have been used to hire doctors or teachers or to build low-income houses. The land that farmers are encouraged to keep in an undeveloped yet unfarmed state could have been used for a housing development or as a high school athletic field. Price floors, like price ceilings, also are not particularly well targeted. Even though the goal of a price floor may be to ensure that a poor farmer does not suffer because crop prices are too low, the benefits of the higher price typically will accrue to extremely wealthy farmers and large agricultural businesses with lots of resources. In the case of the minimum wage, teenagers from relatively well-off families may end up earning a higher salary as a result of the minimum wage, but a poor parent may end up losing his or her job and joining the ranks of the unemployed.

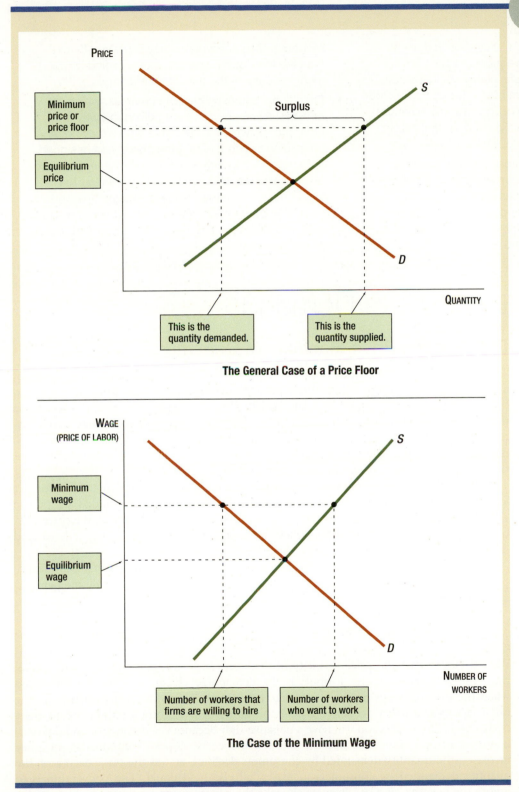

The General Case of a Price Floor

The Case of the Minimum Wage

Figure 4-2

Effects of a Minimum-Price Law

The top diagram shows the general case when the government prevents the market price from falling below a particular minimum price, or sets a price floor above the equilibrium price. The lower diagram shows a particular example when the price of labor—the wage—cannot fall below the minimum wage. The supply and demand model predicts that sellers are willing to sell a greater quantity than buyers are willing to buy at that price. Thus, there is a surplus of the good or, in the case of labor, unemployment for some of those who would be hired only at a lower wage.

REVIEW

- Governments occasionally will intervene in markets because they think that the equilibrium price is too high or too low. In some instances in which the government thinks the price that buyers have to pay is too high, it may impose a price ceiling. In some instances in which the government thinks the price that sellers are receiving is too low, it may impose a price floor.

- Price ceilings cause persistent shortages, which, in turn, cause rationing, black markets, and a reduced quality of goods and services. Price ceilings also may not end up helping the people that the policy was designed to benefit. In the case of rent control, for example, the people who end up in

rent-controlled apartments may be more affluent than the individuals who are unable to find an apartment because of the persistent shortages.

- Price floors cause persistent surpluses, which, in turn, result in resources being diverted away from other productive activities. Price floors may not end up helping the people that the policy was designed to benefit. In the case of a minimum wage, for example, the workers who end up in jobs earning the higher minimum wage may be teenagers from relatively well-off families, while a poor worker may be unable to find a job because of the surplus of unemployed workers.

Elasticity of Demand

Defining the Price Elasticity of Demand

The price elasticity of demand is a measure of the sensitivity of the *quantity demanded* of a good to the *price* of the good. "Price elasticity of demand" is sometimes shortened to "elasticity of demand," the "demand elasticity," or even simply "elasticity" when the meaning is clear from the context. The price elasticity of demand always refers to a particular demand curve or demand schedule, such as the world demand for oil or the U.S. demand for bicycles. The price elasticity of demand is a measure of *how much* the quantity demanded changes when the price changes.

For example, when economists report that the price elasticity of demand for contact lenses is high, they mean that the quantity of contact lenses demanded by people changes by a large amount when the price changes. Or if they report that the price elasticity of demand for bread is low, they mean that the quantity of bread demanded changes by only a small amount when the price of bread changes.

price elasticity of demand the percentage change in the quantity demanded of a good divided by the percentage change in the price of that good.

We can define the price elasticity of demand clearly with a formula: **Price elasticity of demand** is the percentage change in the quantity demanded divided by the percentage change in the price. That is,

$$\text{Price elasticity of demand} = \frac{\text{percentage change in quantity demanded}}{\text{percentage change in price}}$$

We emphasize that the price elasticity of demand refers to a particular demand curve; thus, the numerator of this formula is the percentage change in quantity demanded when the price changes by the percentage amount shown in the denominator. All the other factors that affect demand are held constant when we compute the price elasticity of demand. This expression will have a negative sign because the numerator and denominator are of opposite signs. Because the demand curve slopes downward, as the price increases, the quantity demanded by consumers declines, and as the price decreases, the quantity demanded by consumers increases, all else held equal. The convention is to ignore the negative sign or, alternatively, take the negative sign for granted when we discuss the elasticity of demand.

For example, if the price elasticity of demand for gasoline is said to be about 0.2, that means that if the price of gasoline increases by 10 percent, the quantity of gasoline demanded will fall by 2 percent (0.2 × 10). If the price elasticity of demand for alcoholic beverages is said to be about 1.5, that means that when the price of alcoholic beverages rises by 10 percent, the quantity demanded will fall by 15 percent (1.5 × 10). As you can see from these examples, knowing the elasticity of demand enables us to determine how much the *quantity demanded* changes when the price changes.

The Size of the Elasticity: High versus Low

The two graphs in Figure 4-3 each show a different possible demand curve for oil in the world. We want to show why it is important to know which of these two demand curves gives a better description of economic behavior in the oil market. Each graph has the price of oil on the vertical axis (in dollars per barrel) and the quantity of oil demanded on the horizontal axis (in millions of barrels of oil a day).

Figure 4-3

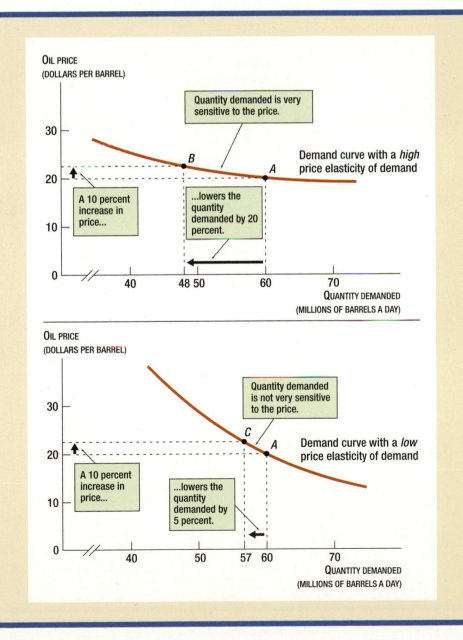

Comparing Different Sizes of the Price Elasticity of Demand
Both sets of axes have exactly the same scale. In the top graph, the quantity demanded is sensitive to the price; the elasticity is high. In the bottom graph, the quantity demanded is not sensitive to the price; the elasticity is low. Thus, the same increase in price ($2, or 10 percent) reduces the quantity demanded much more when the elasticity is high (top graph) than when it is low (bottom graph).

Both of the demand curves pass through the same point *A*, where the price of oil is $20 per barrel and the quantity demanded is 60 million barrels per day. But observe that the two curves show different degrees of sensitivity of the quantity demanded to the price. In the top graph, where the demand curve is relatively flat, the quantity demanded of oil is sensitive to the price; in other words, the demand curve has a high elasticity. For example, consider a change from point *A* to point *B*: When the price rises by $2, from $20 to $22, the quantity demanded falls by 12 million, from 60 million to 48 million barrels a day. In percentage terms, when the price rises by 10 percent ($2/20 = 0.10$, or 10 percent), the quantity demanded falls by 20 percent ($12/60 = 0.20$, or 20 percent).

On the other hand, in the bottom graph, the quantity demanded is not quite as sensitive to the price; in other words, the demand curve has a low elasticity. It is relatively steep. When the price rises by $2 from point *A* to point *C*, the quantity demanded falls by

Figure 4-4

The Importance of the Size of the Price Elasticity of Demand

The impact on the oil price of a reduction in oil supply is shown for two different demand curves. The reduction in supply is the same for both graphs. When the price elasticity of demand is high (top graph), there is only a small increase in the price. When the price elasticity of demand is low (bottom graph), the price rises by much more.

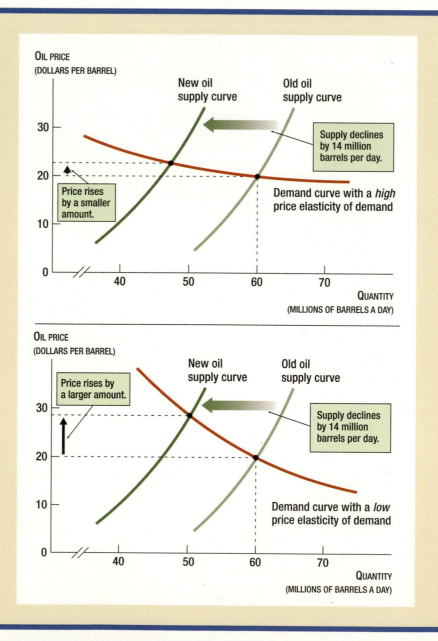

3 million barrels. In percentage terms, the same 10 percent increase in price reduces the quantity demanded by only 5 percent ($3/60 = 0.05$, or 5 percent). Thus, the sensitivity of the quantity to the price, or the size of the elasticity, is what distinguishes these two graphs.

The Impact of a Change in Supply on the Price of Oil

Now consider what happens when there is a decline in supply in the world oil market. In Figure 4-4, we combine the supply curve for oil with the two demand curves for oil from Figure 4-3. Initially the oil market is in equilibrium in Figure 4-4; in both graphs, the quantity demanded equals the quantity supplied. The equilibrium price is $20 per barrel, and the equilibrium quantity is 60 million barrels a day, just like at point A in Figure 4-3. A reduction in the supply of oil—perhaps because of the reduction in Iraqi oil production or the shutdown of refineries following Hurricane Katrina—is also shown. The exact same leftward shift in supply is shown in the top and bottom graphs of Figure 4-4.

Now, observe how the equilibrium price changes in the two graphs. Recall that this change is our prediction—using the supply and demand model—of what would happen to the price of oil if the supply declined. We know that a decrease in supply will lead to an increase in the equilibrium price and a decrease in the equilibrium quantity. As the two graphs show, however, there is a huge difference in the size of the predicted price increase. In the top graph, the oil price increases only a little. If the elasticity is very high, then even a small increase in the price is enough to get people to reduce their use of oil and thereby bring the quantity demanded down to the lower quantity supplied. On the other hand, in the bottom diagram, the price rises by much more. Here the elasticity is very low, and thus a large increase in price is needed to get people to reduce their use of oil and bring the quantity demanded down to the quantity supplied.

Thus, to determine how much the price will rise in response to a shift in oil supply, we need to know how sensitive the quantity demanded is to the price, or the size of the elasticity of demand.

REVIEW

- We know that an increase in price will lower the quantity demanded, whereas a decrease in price will increase the quantity demanded. The price elasticity of demand is a number that tells us by how much the quantity demanded changes when the price changes.

- The price elasticity of demand, which we also refer to as "elasticity of demand" or just as "elasticity," is defined as the percentage change in the quantity demanded divided by the percentage change in the price.

- A given change in price has a larger impact on quantity demanded when the elasticity of demand is higher.

- A given shift of the supply curve will have a larger impact on equilibrium quantity (and a smaller impact on equilibrium price) when the elasticity of demand is higher.

Working with Demand Elasticities

Having demonstrated the practical importance of elasticity, let us examine the concept in more detail and show how to use it. Some symbols will be helpful.

If we let the symbol e_d represent the price elasticity of demand, then we can write the definition as

$$e_d = \frac{\Delta Q_d}{Q_d} \div \frac{\Delta P}{P} = \frac{\Delta Q_d/Q_d}{\Delta P/P}$$

ECONOMICS *IN ACTION*

Predicting the Size of a Price Increase

Economists used a numerical value of elasticity to predict the size of the oil price rise caused by the Iraqi invasion of Kuwait in 1990. Here are the steps they took:

- First, they determined—after looking at historical studies of oil prices and quantities—that the price elasticity of the demand for oil was 0.1. In other words, $e_d = 0.1$.

- Second, they calculated—after consulting with oil producers—that the invasion of Kuwait would reduce the world oil supply by 7 percent. They assumed that this 7 percent would also be the percentage decline in the quantity of oil demanded because other sources of oil could not increase in a short period of time. In other words, $\Delta Q_d / Q_d = 0.07$, or 7 percent.

- Third, they plugged these numbers into the formula for elasticity to calculate that the oil price would rise by 70 percent. Here is the exact calculation behind this step: Rearrange the definition of elasticity, $e_d = (\Delta Q_d/Q_d)/(\Delta P/P)$, to put the percentage change in the price on the left. That is, $\Delta P/P = (\Delta Q_d/Q_d)/e_d$. Now plug in $\Delta Q_d/Q_d = 0.07$ and $e_d = 0.1$ to get $0.07/(0.1) = 0.70$, or 70 percent.

The 70 percent price rise predicted might seem large. In fact, the actual rise in the price of oil in 1990 was large, even larger than 70 percent: The price of oil rose from \$17 per barrel in July 1990 to \$36 in October 1990, or about 112 percent. (The larger-than-predicted price increase may have been due to worries that Iraq also would invade Saudi Arabia and reduce the oil supply even further.)

This type of calculation—showing that a huge oil price increase could be caused by the 7 percent reduction in oil supply—was a factor in the decision by the United States and its allies to send troops to the Middle East to halt the Iraqi invasion of Saudi Arabia and eventually to force Iraq out of Kuwait.

where Q_d is the quantity demanded, P is the price, and Δ means "change in." In other words, the elasticity of demand equals the "percentage change in the quantity demanded" divided by the "percentage change in the price." Observe that to compute the percentage change in the numerator and the denominator, we need to divide the change in the variable (ΔP or ΔQ_d) by the variable (P or Q_d).

Keep in mind again that because the quantity demanded is negatively related to the price, the elasticity of demand is a negative number: When $\Delta P/P$ is positive, $\Delta Q_d/Q_d$ is negative. But when economists write or talk about elasticity, they usually ignore the negative sign and report the absolute value of the number. Because the demand curve always slopes downward, this nearly universal convention need not cause any confusion, as long as you remember it.

It is easy to do back-of-the-envelope computations of price elasticity of demand. Suppose a study shows that when the price of Australian wine fell by 8 percent, the quantity of Australian wine demanded increased by 12 percent. The price elasticity of demand for Australian wine is

$$e_d = \frac{\Delta Q_d/Q_d}{\Delta P/P} = \frac{12}{8} = 1.5$$

Suppose your university raises student season ticket prices from \$50 to \$60, which results in the quantity of season tickets sold falling from 2,000 to 1,800. The price elasticity of demand for season ticket prices would be

$$e_d = \frac{\Delta Q_d/Q_d}{\Delta P/P} = \frac{200/2,000}{10/50} = \frac{.1}{.2} = .5$$

Notice that measured in percentage changes, the demand for Australian wine is responsive to changes in the price, and the demand for season tickets is not responsive to changes in the price.

The Advantage of a Unit-Free Measure

An attractive feature of the price elasticity of demand is that it does not depend on the units of measurement of the quantity demanded—whether barrels of oil or pounds of peanuts. It is a **unit-free measure** because it uses percentage changes in price and quantity demanded. Thus, it provides a way to compare the price sensitivity of the demand for many different goods. It even allows us to compare the price sensitivity of less expensive goods—like rice—with that of more expensive goods—like steak.

> **unit-free measure**
> a measure that does not depend on a unit of measurement.

For example, suppose that when the price of rice rises from $0.50 to $0.60 per pound, the quantity demanded falls from 20 tons to 19 tons—that is, a decline of 1 ton for a *$0.10* price increase. In contrast, suppose that when the price of steak rises by $1, from $5 to $6 per pound, the quantity demanded falls by 1 ton, from 20 tons to 19 tons of steak—that is, a decline of 1 ton for a *$1* price increase.

Using these numbers, the price sensitivity of the demand for steak and the demand for rice might appear to be different: $0.10 to get a ton of reduced purchases versus $1 to get a ton of reduced purchases. Yet the elasticities are the same. The percentage change in price is 20 percent in each case ($1/$5 = $0.10/$0.50 = 0.20, or 20 percent), and the percentage change in quantity is 5 percent in each case: 1 ton of rice/20 tons of rice = 1 ton of steak/20 tons of steak = 0.05, or 5 percent. Hence, the elasticity is 5/20 = 1/4 in both cases.

Elasticity allows us to compare the price sensitivity of different goods by looking at ratios of percentage changes regardless of the units for measuring either price or quantity. With millions of different goods and hundreds of different units of measurement, this is indeed a major advantage.

Elasticity versus Slope

After looking at Figure 4-3, you might be tempted to say that demand curves that are steep have a low elasticity, and demand curves that are flat have a high elasticity. That turns out not to be the case, so you have to be careful not to simply look at a flat demand curve and say that it has a high elasticity. You need to understand why the *elasticity of the demand curve* is not the same as the *slope of the demand curve*. Remember that the slope of a curve is the change in the y variable over the change in the x variable; in the case of the demand curve, the slope is defined as the change in price divided by the change in quantity demanded. The slope is not a unit-free measure—it depends on how the price and quantity are measured. Elasticity, on the other hand, is a unit-free measure.

To illustrate the difference between slope and elasticity, we show in Figure 4-5 a demand curve for rice and a demand curve for steak. The two demand curves have different slopes because the prices are so different. When the price of rice increases by $0.10, the quantity demanded of rice falls by 1 ton, whereas when the price of steak increases by $1 (or 100 cents), the quantity demanded of steak falls by 1 ton. The slope of the steak demand curve is (–$1 a ton), which is 10 times greater than the slope of the rice demand curve (–$0.10 cents a ton). Yet the elasticity is the same for the change from A to B for both demand curves—the price of rice and the price of steak both increased by 20 percent, while the quantity demanded of rice and the quantity demanded of steak both decreased by 5 percent.

Calculating the Elasticity with a Midpoint Formula

To calculate the elasticity, we need to find the percentage change in the quantity demanded and divide it by the percentage change in the price. As we have illustrated with examples, to get the percentage change in the price or quantity, we need to divide the change in price (ΔP) by the price (P) or the change in quantity demanded (ΔQ_d) by

Figure 4-5

Different Slopes and Same Elasticities

The slope of the steak demand curve in the bottom graph is greater than the slope of the rice demand curve in the top graph. The price elasticity of demand for rice and steak from point *A* to point *B* is the same, however. From point *A* to point *B*, the price rises by 20 percent and the quantity demanded decreases by 5 percent. Thus, the elasticity is one fourth for both rice and steak at these points.

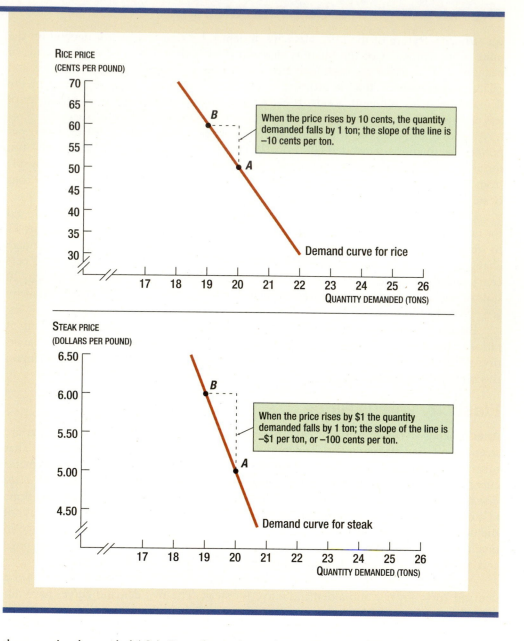

When the price rises by 10 cents, the quantity demanded falls by 1 ton; the slope of the line is −10 cents per ton.

When the price rises by $1 the quantity demanded falls by 1 ton; the slope of the line is −$1 per ton, or −100 cents per ton.

the quantity demanded (*Q_d*). But when price and quantity demanded change, a question arises about what to use for *P* and *Q_d*. Should we use the old price and the old quantity demanded before the change, or should we use the new price and the new quantity demanded after the change?

The most common convention that economists use is a compromise between these two alternatives. They take the *average,* or the *midpoint,* of the old and new quantities demanded and the old and new prices. That is, they compute the elasticity using the following formula, called the *midpoint formula:*

$$\text{Price elasticity of demand} = \frac{\dfrac{\text{change in quantity}}{\text{average of old and new quantities}}}{\div \dfrac{\text{change in price}}{\text{average of old and new prices}}}$$

For example, if we use the midpoint formula to calculate the price elasticity of demand for oil when the price changes from \$20 to \$22 and the quantity demanded changes from 60 million to 48 million barrels a day, we get

$$\left[\frac{12}{(60+48)/2}\right] \div \left[\frac{2}{(20+22)/2}\right] = 0.2222 \div 0.0952 = 2.33$$

That is, the price elasticity of demand is 2.33 using the midpoint formula. When we originally calculated the elasticity using the old price and the old quantity demanded, we came up with an elasticity of

$$\left[\frac{12}{60}\right] \div \left[\frac{2}{20}\right] = 0.2 \div 0.1 = 2$$

If we had used the new price and the new quantity, we would have calculated the elasticity to be

$$\left[\frac{12}{48}\right] \div \left[\frac{2}{22}\right] = 0.25 \div 0.0909 = 2.75$$

So the elasticity calculated using the midpoint formula turns out to be in between these two values, as you would expect.

Talking about Elasticities

Economists classify demand curves by the size of the price elasticities of demand, and they have developed a very precise terminology for doing so.

Elastic versus Inelastic Demand
Goods for which the price elasticity is greater than one have an **elastic demand**. For example, the quantity of foreign travel demanded decreases by more than 1 percent when the price rises by 1 percent because many people tend to travel at home rather than abroad when the price of foreign travel rises.

Goods for which the price elasticity of demand is less than one have an **inelastic demand**. For example, the quantity of eggs demanded decreases by less than 1 percent when the price of eggs rises by 1 percent because many people do not want to substitute other things for eggs at breakfast.

Perfectly Elastic versus Perfectly Inelastic Demand
A demand curve that is vertical is called **perfectly inelastic**. Figure 4-6 shows a perfectly inelastic demand curve. The elasticity is zero because when the price changes, the quantity demanded does not change at all. No matter what the price, the same quantity is demanded. People who need insulin have a perfectly inelastic demand for insulin. As long as there are no substitutes for insulin, they will pay whatever they have to for the insulin.

A demand curve that is horizontal is called **perfectly elastic**. Figure 4-6 also shows a perfectly elastic demand curve. The elasticity is infinite. The perfectly flat demand curve is sometimes hard to imagine because it entails infinitely large movements of quantity for tiny changes in price. To better visualize this case, you can imagine that the curve is tilted ever so slightly. Goods that have a lot of comparable substitutes are likely to have high elasticities of demand.

Table 4-1 summarizes the terminology about elasticities.

Revenue and the Price Elasticity of Demand

When people purchase 60 million barrels of oil at \$20 a barrel, they must pay a total of \$1,200 million (\$20 × 60 million). This is a payment to the oil producers and is the

elastic demand
demand for which the price elasticity is greater than one.

inelastic demand
demand for which the price elasticity is less than one.

perfectly inelastic demand
demand for which the price elasticity is zero, indicating no response to a change in price and therefore a vertical demand curve.

perfectly elastic demand
demand for which the price elasticity is infinite, indicating an infinite response to a change in price and therefore a horizontal demand curve.

Figure 4-6

Perfectly Elastic and Perfectly Inelastic Demand

A perfectly inelastic demand curve is a vertical line at a certain quantity. The quantity demanded is completely insensitive to the price: Whatever happens to the price, the quantity demanded does not change. A perfectly elastic demand curve is a flat line at a certain price. An increase in price reduces the quantity demanded to zero; a small decrease in price raises the quantity demanded by a huge (literally infinite) amount.

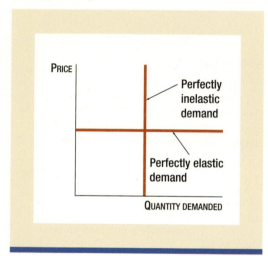

Table 4-1

Terminology for Price Elasticity of Demand

Term	Value of Price Elasticity of Demand (e_d)
Perfectly inelastic	0 (vertical demand curve)
Inelastic	Less than 1
Elastic	Greater than 1
Perfectly elastic	Infinity (horizontal demand curve)

producers' revenue. In general, revenue is the price (P) times the quantity (Q), or $P \times Q$. A change in price therefore will affect revenue. Although this seems obvious, it is important that you understand exactly how price affects revenue. In fact, a change in price has two opposite effects on revenue. For instance, when the price increases, people pay more for each item, which increases revenue; but they buy fewer items, which in turn reduces revenue. The price elasticity of demand determines which of these two opposite effects dominates, because elasticity is a measure of how much the quantity demanded changes when price changes.

Figure 4-7, which is a replica of Figure 4-3 with the scales changed, illustrates the effects on revenue. In the top graph, revenue went from $1.2 billion (60 million × $20 = $1,200 million) to $1.056 billion (48 million × $22 = $1,056 million). In other words, revenue declined by $144 million even though price increased. Now compare this to the revenue changes in the bottom graph. There revenue went from $1.2 billion to $1.254 billion (57 million × $22 = $1,254 million), an increase of $54 million. Using the old price and the old quantity demanded, you can show that the elasticity of demand in the top graph is 2 while the elasticity of demand in the bottom graph is 0.5. We can see from this example that, following a price increase, revenue fell in the case where the elasticity was greater than one, and revenue rose when elasticity was less than one.

Is this always the case? We can illustrate the relationship between elasticity and revenue better by using a simple straight-line demand curve, as shown in Figure 4-8. Because this is a straight line, the slope is identical at all points on the demand curve—a $1 change in price will change quantity demanded by two units.

If you calculate the elasticity of demand at each point along the line, what you will find is that the elasticity of demand is equal to one at a price of $5 and a quantity demanded of 10. At this point, a $1 change in price (which is equivalent to a 20 percent change in the price) results in a two-unit change in quantity demanded (which is also equivalent to a 20 percent change in the quantity demanded). To the left of this point, the elasticity of demand is greater than one. You can see this by considering what happens at a price of $6 and a quantity demanded of eight. A $1 change in price will continue to bring about a two-unit change in quantity demanded, but the percentage change in price is smaller ($1/$6 = 16.66 percent instead of 20 percent), and the percentage change in quantity is larger (2/8 = 25 percent instead of 20 percent). Thus, the elasticity will now be greater than one. To the right of this point, the elasticity of demand is less than one. You can see this by considering what happens at a price of $4 and a quantity demanded of twelve. A $1 change in price will continue to bring about a two-unit change in quantity demanded, but the percentage change in price is larger ($1/$4 = 25 percent instead of 20 percent), and the percentage change in quantity is

Figure 4-7

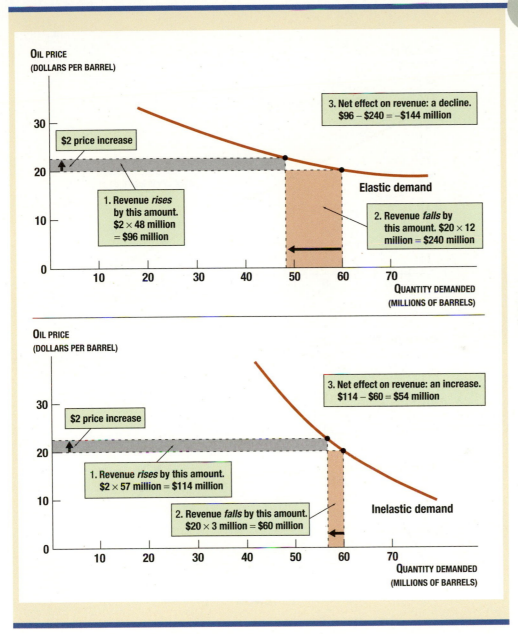

OIL PRICE
(DOLLARS PER BARREL)

3. Net effect on revenue: a decline.
$96 − $240 = −$144 million

$2 price increase

Elastic demand

1. Revenue *rises*
by this amount.
$2 × 48 million
= $96 million

2. Revenue *falls* by
this amount. $20 × 12
million = $240 million

QUANTITY DEMANDED
(MILLIONS OF BARRELS)

OIL PRICE
(DOLLARS PER BARREL)

3. Net effect on revenue: an increase.
$114 − $60 = $54 million

$2 price increase

1. Revenue *rises* by this amount.
$2 × 57 million = $114 million

2. Revenue *falls* by this amount.
$20 × 3 million = $60 million

Inelastic demand

QUANTITY DEMANDED
(MILLIONS OF BARRELS)

Effects of an Increase in the Price of Oil on Revenue

These graphs are replicas of the demand curves for oil shown in Figure 4-3, with the scale changed to show the change in revenue when the price of oil is increased. An increase in the price has two effects on revenue, as shown by the gray- and peach-shaded rectangles. The increase in revenue (gray rectangle) is due to the higher price. The decrease in revenue (peach rectangle) is due to the decline in the quantity demanded as the price is increased. In the top graph, where elasticity is greater than one, the net effect is a decline in revenue; in the bottom graph, where elasticity is less than one, the net effect is an increase in revenue.

smaller (2/12 = 16.67 percent instead of 20 percent). Thus, the elasticity will now be less than one.

For each point along the demand curve, you can calculate revenue by simply multiplying price and quantity. The bottom panel of Figure 4-8 shows how revenue changes as the quantity demanded changes. Revenue begins at $0 (at a price of $10, quantity demanded is zero), increases for a while as quantity demanded increases, starts decreasing again, and ends up at $0 (because quantity demanded of 20 corresponds to a price of zero). Interestingly, you can see that the range over which revenue is rising with quantity demanded corresponds exactly with the range at which the elasticity is greater than one. Similarly, the range over which revenue is falling corresponds with the region of the demand curve at which the elasticity is less than one. Table 4-2 summarizes the

Figure 4-8

Revenue and Elasticity of a Straight-Line Demand Curve

Along the straight-line demand curve in the top panel, the price elasticity ranges from above 1 (to the left) to below 1 (to the right). When the price elasticity is greater than 1 an increase in the price will reduce revenue, as shown in the lower panel.

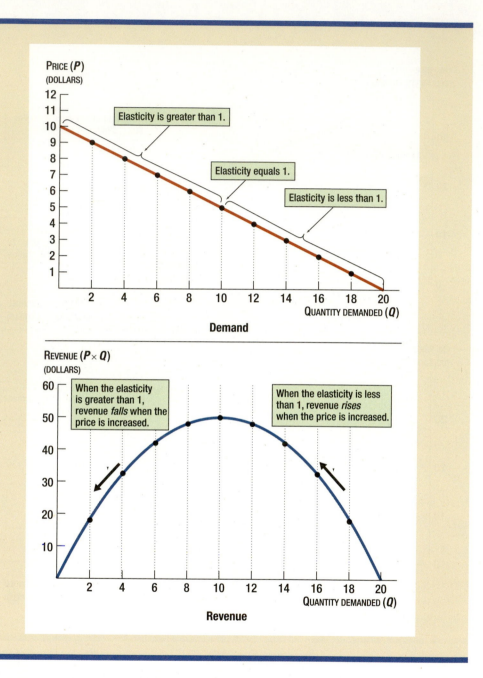

Table 4-2

Revenue and the Price Elasticity of Demand

Elasticity Is	Effect of a Price Increase on Revenue	Effect of a Price Decrease on Revenue
Less than 1 (< 1)	Revenue increases	Revenue decreases
Equal to 1 ($= 1$)	No change in revenue	No change in revenue
Greater than 1 (> 1)	Revenue decreases	Revenue increases

relationship between revenue and the price elasticity of demand. An increase in price will raise revenue if the elasticity is less than one and will lower revenue if the elasticity is greater than one.

This relationship between the elasticity of demand and the revenue impact of a price change is important. Businesses need to know the price elasticity of demand for their products to understand the implications of raising or lowering prices. For instance, in June 2010, Amazon.com announced that it would sharply cut the price of its new e-book reader, the Kindle, from $259 to $189, a drop of about 30 percent. Would the lower price entice more people to buy a Kindle? If so, would the increase in customers lead to an increase or a decrease in Amazon.com's revenue? The answer depends on the price elasticity of demand for Amazon's e-book readers. Similarly, in 2009, Apple, Inc. announced that it was raising the price for downloading a popular song from $0.99 to $1.29, an increase of around 26 percent using the midprice formula. Could this increase drive away many iTunes customers to rival music-downloading sites? If so, would the decrease in customers be so large as to lower Apple's revenue? The answer depends on the price elasticity of demand for music downloads on iTunes.

If demand for Amazon's e-book readers is price elastic and the demand for music downloads on iTunes is price inelastic, then both Amazon and Apple changed prices to increase revenue—Amazon cut the price of e-book readers to increase revenue, taking advantage of price-elastic demand, and Apple increased the price of music downloads to increase revenue, taking advantage of price-inelastic demand. How would Amazon or Apple know whether demand would be elastic or inelastic? The next section discusses the determinants of price elasticity of demand. You should judge as you read this chapter whether demand for business air travel and demand for pay phone calls are likely to be price elastic or price inelastic.

What Determines the Size of the Price Elasticity of Demand?

Table 4-3 shows price elasticities of demand for several different goods and services. The price elasticity for jewelry, for example, is 2.6. This means that for each percentage increase in the price of jewelry, the quantity demanded will fall by 2.6 percent. Compared with other elasticities, this is large. On the other hand, the price elasticity of eggs is very small. For each percentage increase in the price of eggs, the quantity of eggs demanded falls by only 0.1 percent.

Why do these elasticities differ in size? Several factors determine a good's elasticity.

The Degree of Substitutability   A key factor is whether the item in question has good substitutes. Can people easily find a substitute when the price goes up? If the answer is yes, then the price elasticity will be high. Foreign travel has a high elasticity because it has a reasonably good substitute: domestic travel.

On the other hand, the low price elasticity for eggs can be explained by the lack of good substitutes. As many fans of eggs know, these items are unique; synthetic eggs are not good substitutes. Hence, the price elasticity of eggs is small. People will continue to buy them even if the price rises a lot.

The degree of substitutability depends in part on whether a good is a necessity or a luxury. If you want to easily preserve food for more than a few hours, a refrigerator has no good substitute. A fancy refrigerator with an exterior that blends in with the rest of your kitchen, however, is more of a luxury and likely will have a higher price elasticity.

Table 4-3

Estimated Price Elasticities of Demand

Type of Good or Service	Price Elasticity
Jewelry	2.6
Eggs	0.1
Telephone (first line)	0.1
Telephone (second line)	0.4
Foreign travel	1.2
Cigarettes (ages 18–24)	0.6
Cigarettes (ages 25–39)	0.4
Cigarettes (ages 40–older)	0.1
Gasoline (short run)	0.2
Gasoline (long run)	0.7

Price Elasticity of Cell Phone Service in the Desert

There's probably not much of a substitute available for long-distance communication in the desert, which would make the price elasticity of the cell phone used here quite low. Do you think the caller in this picture would be equally insensitive to an increase of $0.10 per minute in the price of her calls if she were seated in her apartment in Chicago?

Big-Ticket versus Little-Ticket Items

If a good represents a large fraction of people's income, then the price elasticity will be high. If the price of foreign travel doubles, many people will not be able to afford to travel abroad. On the other hand, if the good represents a small fraction of income, the elasticity will be low. For example, if the price of eggs doubles, most people still will be able to afford to buy as many eggs as before the price increase.

Temporary versus Permanent Price Changes

If a change in price is known to be temporary, the price elasticity of demand will tend to be high, because many people can easily shift their purchases either later or earlier. For example, suppose a sewing machine store announces a discount price that will last only one day. Then people will shift their sewing machine purchase to the day of the sale. On the other hand, if the price cut is permanent, the price elasticity will be smaller. People who expect the price decrease to be permanent will not find it advantageous to buy sooner rather than later.

Differences in Preferences

Different groups of consumers may have different levels of elasticity. For example, young cigarette smokers, whose habit of smoking may not be entrenched, are more sensitive to changes in prices than older smokers. Table 4-3 shows that the price elasticity of demand for cigarettes for young adults between 18 and 24 years old is much higher than the very low price elasticity for people more than 40 years old.

Long-Run versus Short-Run Elasticity

Frequently the price elasticity of demand is low immediately after a price change, but then it increases after a period of time has passed. To analyze these changes, economists distinguish between the *short run* and the *long run*. The short run is simply a period of time before people have made all their adjustments or changed their habits; the long run is a period of time long enough for people to make such adjustments or change their habits.

Many personal adjustments to a change in prices take a long time. For example, when the price of gas increases, people can reduce the quantity demanded in the short run only by driving less and using other forms of transportation more, or by reducing the heating in their homes. This may be inconvenient or impossible. In the long run, however, when it comes time to buy a new car or a new heating system, they can buy a more fuel-efficient item or one that uses an alternative energy source. Thus, the quantity of gas demanded falls by larger amounts in the long run than in the short run (see Table 4-3).

Habits that are difficult to break also cause differences between short-run and long-run elasticity. Even a large increase in the price of tobacco may have a small effect on the quantity purchased because people cannot break the smoking habit quickly. But after a period of time, the high price of cigarettes may encourage them to break the habit, while discouraging potential new users. Thus, the long-run elasticity for tobacco is higher than the short-run elasticity.

The following examples will test your understanding of the determinants of the price elasticity of demand. The movie industry reported that its summer revenue was 3 percent higher than the previous year. A closer analysis reveals that ticket sales were down 1 percent. How could ticket revenue increase at the same time that the number of tickets sold decreased? The ticket price must have increased. Demand for movies also must be price inelastic, so that the reduction in ticket sales was more than offset by the increase in the price of the movie tickets. Does this make sense for the movie industry? It is plausible that some people feel that they *must see* the newest release and that the cost of the movie is a little-ticket item for many people who go to the movies. This would make the price elasticity of demand low and plausibly make demand price inelastic.

What Is the Price Elasticity of Demand for the *Harry Potter* Book Series?

For these loyal fans, attending a book-release party for the 2007 book release *Harry Potter and the Deathly Hallows*, demand is price inelastic. For readers in general, the answer to that question may say a lot about the future of the book industry. If the price of books goes up, and at the same time, revenue from book sales increases, then demand for the purchase of books is price inelastic.

General Motors Corporation reported that revenues rose by more than 10 percent in the first half of 2010 compared with the second half of 2009. This occurred even though General Motors cut prices on many models of cars. At the same time, General Motors offered large discounts to customers purchasing cars. How could revenue increase while the price of cars was going down? It must be that more cars were sold at the lower price and that demand for these cars is price elastic. The reduction in price therefore was offset by the increase in cars sold, and revenue increased. Does this make sense for General Motors' cars? It is plausible that customers feel that cars have close substitutes and that this is a big-ticket purchase for many customers. This would make the price elasticity of demand high and demand plausibly price elastic.

Income Elasticity and Cross-Price Elasticity of Demand

Recall that the price elasticity of demand refers to movements along the demand curve. We emphasized in Chapter 3 the difference between a shift in the demand curve and a movement along the demand curve. A *shift* in the demand curve occurs when the quantity that people are willing to buy changes because of a change in anything except the price—for example, a change in income.

The concept of elasticity also can be applied to measure how changes in the quantity that consumers are willing to buy respond to changes in income. This elasticity must be distinguished from the price elasticity of demand. The **income elasticity of demand** is the percentage change in the quantity of a good demanded at any given price divided by a percentage change in income. That is,

$$\text{Income elasticity of demand} = \frac{\text{percentage change in quantity demanded}}{\text{percentage change in income}}$$

income elasticity of demand

the percentage change in quantity demanded of a good divided by the percentage change in income.

ECONOMICS *IN ACTION*

Elasticity of Demand and Teen Smoking

Policy makers use information about the price elasticity of demand in many ways. Take the government's continuing efforts to reduce smoking. Although many tools have been employed in the campaign to reduce cigarette smoking—health warnings, restrictions on vending machines, age limits for tobacco purchases, public health–related advertising campaigns—the method that researchers think is particularly effective at reducing teenage smoking is to raise cigarette taxes. Diagram A shows the impact of a new cigarette tax (modeled as a decrease in supply) raising the price for which cigarettes sell.

How effective cigarette taxes are in reducing smoking by teens depends on their price elasticity of demand. If the price elasticity of demand for cigarettes is higher for teenagers than for the rest of the smoking population, then the impact of the cigarette taxes will result in a greater reduction in cigarette purchases by teens. See the diagram below.

Why might the price elasticity of demand be higher for teenage smokers than for adult smokers? One reason may be that since teenagers have not been smoking for very long, the habit may not be as entrenched as for adults; hence, it may be easier for them to give up the habit. Another reason may be that for a teenager on a limited income or an allowance, the price of cigarettes is likely to be a bigger-ticket item than for an adult. Economist Frank Chaloupka has estimated that a 10 percent increase in cigarette prices increases the likelihood that a teen would give up smoking by between 6 and 9 percent, about twice as large an effect as for adults.

These significant effects of higher prices on cigarette smoking have led many states to impose cigarette taxes. As the recession worsened and governments faced budgetary concerns, taxes on cigarettes became an even more attractive prospect, as well as their teen smoking reduction potential. In June 2010, new taxes imposed by the State of New York raised cigarette prices to almost $9.50 a pack, and additional taxes in New York City raised the price to almost $11 a pack. Whenever a tax is imposed in a particular locale, buyers will try to avoid the tax by purchasing cigarettes elsewhere. Policy makers recognized this loophole and moved to close it with the Prevent All Cigarette Trafficking (PACT) act of 2010, which banned the U.S. Postal Service from shipping cigarettes and required anyone selling cigarettes over the Internet to pay all applicable federal and state taxes.

Some states and cities have also passed price floors on cigarettes—preventing sellers from selling at prices low enough to attract young smokers. This is yet another example of how the lessons learned about supply, demand, price floors, and elasticity of demand are invaluable in understanding public policy actions and their consequences.

A

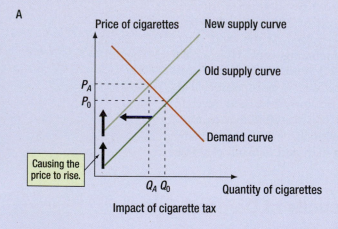

Impact of cigarette tax

B

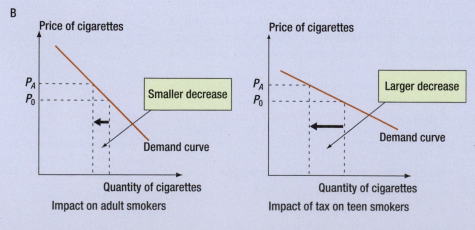

Impact on adult smokers   Impact of tax on teen smokers

For example, if incomes rise by 10 percent and, as a result, people purchase 15 percent more health care at a given price, the income elasticity of health care is 1.5. Table 4-4 lists income elasticities of demand for several different goods and services.

As discussed in Chapter 3, the demand for most goods increases when people's incomes increase. If you have more income, your demand for movies probably will increase at each price. Recall that a normal good is a good or service whose demand increases as income increases. But not every good is a normal good; if the demand for a good declines when income increases, the good is called an inferior good. The income elasticity of demand for an inferior good is negative and is reported as a negative number by economists.

Another type of elasticity relating to shifts in the demand curve is the **cross-price elasticity of demand**, which is defined as the percentage change in the quantity demanded divided by the percentage change in the price of another good. For example, an increase in the price of Rollerblades would *increase* the quantity demanded of bicycles at every price as people shift away from Rollerblading to bicycle riding. Rollerblades are a substitute for bicycles. A cross-price elasticity also can go in the other direction. An increase in the price of bicycle helmets may *reduce* the demand for bicycles. Bicycle helmets and bicycles are complements. For a complement, the cross-price elasticity of demand is negative.

Table 4-4

Estimated Income Elasticities of Demand

Type of Good or Service	Income Elasticity
Food	0.58
Clothing/ footwear	0.88
Transport	1.18
Medical care	1.35
Recreation	1.42

cross-price elasticity of demand
the percentage change in the quantity demanded of one good divided by the percentage change in the price of another good.

REVIEW

- The price elasticity of demand, or elasticity, is used to measure how much the quantity demanded changes when the price changes. Elasticity also helps determine how large a price increase will occur as a result of a shift in supply, and by how much revenue will change when the price rises.

- Elasticity is a unit-free measure—it is the ratio of the percentage change in quantity demanded to the percentage change in price. In other words, it measures by what percentage quantity demanded changes when the price changes by 1 percent.

- Horizontal demand curves have infinite price elasticity. Vertical demand curves have zero price elasticity. Most products have a price elasticity between these two extremes. We use the term *elastic demand* to refer to an elasticity of demand that is greater than one and *inelastic demand* to refer to an elasticity of demand that is less than one.

- Other than the horizontal and vertical cases, elasticity is different from the slope of the demand curve, however. A demand curve that is a straight line has a different elasticity of demand at each point.

- The size of the price elasticity of demand depends on the availability of substitutes for the item, whether the item represents a large fraction of income, and whether the price change is temporary or permanent.

- Whereas the price elasticity of demand refers to movements along the demand curve, the income elasticity of demand refers to shifts in the demand curve caused by changes in income. Most goods are normal and have a positive income elasticity of demand. Inferior goods have a negative income elasticity of demand.

- The cross-price elasticity of demand also relates to shifts in the demand curve, in this case, a change in the price of a complement or substitute good.

Elasticity of Supply

Knowing how sensitive the quantity supplied is to a change in price is just as important as knowing how sensitive the quantity demanded is. The price elasticity of supply measures this sensitivity. "Price elasticity of supply" is sometimes shortened to "supply elasticity" or "elasticity of supply." Supply describes the behavior of firms that produce

ECONOMICS *IN ACTION*

Will an Increase in the Minimum Wage Benefit Poor Workers?

When the 110th Congress took office in January 2007, the first bill brought to the floor by the newly elected Democratic majority was an increase in the federal minimum wage from $5.15 to $7.25. The federal minimum wage is a floor on wages that applies to most workers. Supporters of the minimum wage increase, like the Washington, D.C. based think tank EPI, argue that the increase in the minimum wage would raise the hourly wage rate of almost 11 percent of the work force, either directly because they earn the minimum wage or indirectly because they earn a wage that is just above the current minimum wage or that is tied to the minimum wage. The EPI also argued that the gains would also accrue more to women, minorities, and working households at the bottom of the income distribution.

Not everyone agreed with the arguments made by the proponents of the plan. The economist David Neumark pointed out that workers making the current minimum wage may lose their jobs and end up earning zero dollars instead of the higher minimum wage. The higher minimum wage may also make it hard for young workers to find jobs, thus denying them the experience and training needed to eventually obtain a higher-paying position.

The arguments for and against the minimum-wage increase rest on an economic concept that is familiar to you: the elasticity of demand. If the elasticity of demand for labor is large, then the imposition of a higher minimum wage that increases the price of hiring workers will lead to a substantial decrease in the demand for workers. On the other hand, if the demand for labor is relatively inelastic, then an increase in the price of labor will not lead to much of a decrease in the demand for labor.

How do economists settle disputes like this? Once the theory behind the opposing sides of an argument is understood, the best way to settle the debate is to use data to settle it empirically. In other words, use past experiences with minimum-wage increases, along with the tools of statistical and economic analysis, to estimate the magnitude of the elasticity of demand for minimum-wage labor.

There have been a plethora of empirical studies estimating the impact of a minimum-wage increase on the labor market. Perhaps the work that has had the most impact in recent years is a study by David Card and Alan Krueger, who showed that an increase in the state minimum wage in New Jersey had no impact on the employment of minimum-wage workers in the fast-food industry. Their study surveyed fast-food establishments located along the New Jersey/Pennsylvania border, comparing the response by employers in New Jersey (where wages went up) to the response by employers in Pennsylvania (who did not have to pay higher wages).

A more recent paper by the same authors concluded that recent increases in the minimum wage had indicated an elasticity of demand for teenage labor of between –0.1 and –0.3 and of around –0.1 for workers who made close to the existing minimum wage. They also find generally larger effects on hours (firms are more likely to cut back on the number of hours in response to a higher minimum wage) and more long-term effects (over time, firms are more likely to substitute away from minimum-wage workers to more productive, higher-paid workers or to invest in machines and equipment that do the job that minimum-wage workers do).

goods. A high price elasticity of supply means that firms raise their production by a large amount if the price increases. A low price elasticity of supply means that firms raise their production only a little if the price increases.

price elasticity of supply
the percentage change in quantity supplied divided by the percentage change in price.

The **price elasticity of supply** is defined as the percentage change in the quantity supplied divided by the percentage change in the price. That is,

$$\text{Price elasticity of supply} = \frac{\text{percentage change in quantity supplied}}{\text{percentage change in the price}}$$

The price elasticity of supply refers to a particular supply curve, such as the supply curve for gasoline or video games. All other things that affect supply are held constant when we compute the price elasticity of supply. For example, suppose the price elasticity of supply for video games is 0.5. Then, if the price of video games rises by 10 percent, the quantity of video games supplied will increase by 5 percent (0.5×10).

Working with Supply Elasticities

All the attractive features of the price elasticity of demand also apply to the price elasticity of supply. To see this, let us first take a look at the definition of the price elasticity of supply using symbols. If we let the symbol e_s be the price elasticity of supply, then it can be written as

$$e_s = \frac{\Delta Q_s}{Q_s} \div \frac{\Delta P}{P} = \frac{\Delta Q_s / Q_s}{\Delta P / P}$$

where Q_s is the quantity supplied and P is the price. In other words, the price elasticity of supply is the percentage change in the quantity supplied divided by the percentage change in price. Observe the similarity of this expression to the analogous expression for the price elasticity of demand on page 80: The only difference is the use of quantity supplied (Q_s) rather than quantity demanded (Q_d). This means that the concepts and terminology for supply elasticity are very similar to those for demand elasticity. For example, in Table 4-1, if you replace "Demand" with "Supply," you have the terminology for the price elasticity of supply. Moreover, like the price elasticity of demand, the price elasticity of supply is a unit-free measure, and the elasticity of supply and the slope of the supply curve are not the same thing.

Because of this similarity, our discussion of supply elasticity can be brief. It is useful to consider the extreme cases of perfectly elastic supply and perfectly inelastic supply, and then to go through an example illustrating the importance of knowing the size of the price elasticity of supply.

Perfectly Elastic and Perfectly Inelastic Supply As in the case of demand, there can be **perfectly elastic supply** or **perfectly inelastic supply**, as shown in Figure 4-9. The vertical supply curve is perfectly inelastic; it has zero elasticity. Such supply curves are not unusual. For example, only one *Mona Lisa* exists. A higher price cannot bring about a higher quantity supplied, not even one more *Mona Lisa*. But the supply curve for most goods is not vertical. Higher prices will encourage coffee producers to use more fertilizer, hire more workers, and eventually plant more coffee trees. Thus, the quantity supplied increases when the price rises.

The horizontal supply curve is perfectly elastic. In this case, the price does not change at all. It is the same regardless of the quantity supplied. It is easier to understand the horizontal supply curve if you view it as an approximation to a supply curve that is *nearly* horizontal, one with a very high elasticity. Then, only a small increase in price brings forth a huge increase in the quantity supplied by firms.

Why the Size of the Price Elasticity of Supply Is Important Now let us look at the importance of knowing the size of the supply elasticity even if it is not at one of these two extremes. Figure 4-10 shows two different supply curves for coffee. The horizontal axis shows the quantity of coffee supplied around the world in billions of pounds; the vertical axis shows the price in dollars per pound of coffee. For the supply curve in the top graph, the quantity supplied is very sensitive to the price; the price

perfectly elastic supply
supply for which the price elasticity is infinite, indicating an infinite response of quantity supplied to a change in price and therefore a horizontal supply curve.

perfectly inelastic supply
supply for which the price elasticity is zero, indicating no response of quantity supplied to a change in price and therefore a vertical supply curve.

Rostislav Glinsky/Shutterstock.com

Perfectly Inelastic Supply

The paintings of Leonardo da Vinci provide an example of a good with a perfectly inelastic supply. The supply curve is vertical because no matter how high the price, no more *Mona Lisas* can be produced. However, what about the demand to see the *Mona Lisa* at the Louvre? Is it perfectly inelastic? Will raising the price of admission charged by the Louvre Museum in Paris reduce the number of people coming to see the painting?

elasticity of supply is high. For the supply curve in the bottom graph, the price elasticity of supply is much lower.

The price elasticity of supply is important for finding the response of price to shifts in demand. This is shown in Figure 4-11, in which the demand for coffee declines, perhaps because of concerns about the effect of the caffeine in coffee or because of a

Figure 4-9

Perfectly Elastic and Perfectly Inelastic Supply

When the quantity supplied is completely unresponsive to the price, the supply curve is vertical and the price elasticity of supply is zero; this case is called perfectly inelastic supply. When the quantity supplied responds by large amounts to a price change, the supply curve is horizontal; economists say that supply is perfectly elastic.

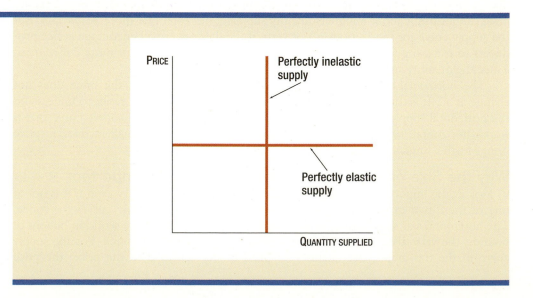

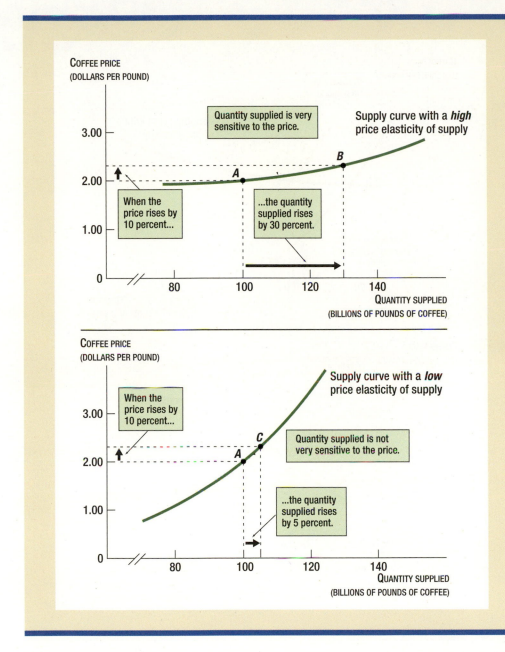

Figure 4-10

Comparing Different Sizes of the Price Elasticities of Supply

In the top graph, the quantity supplied is much more sensitive to price than in the bottom graph. The price elasticity of supply is greater between points *A* and *B* at the top than between points *A* and *C* at the bottom.

decrease in the price of caffeine-free substitutes for coffee. In either case, if the price elasticity of supply is high, as in the top graph, the price does not change as much as when the price elasticity of supply is low, as in the bottom graph. With a high price elasticity, a small change in price is enough to get firms to bring the quantity supplied down to the lower quantity demanded.

Figure 4-11

Importance of Knowing the Size of the Price Elasticity of Supply

When demand changes, the price also will change. If the price elasticity of supply is high, a small change in price will result. If the price elasticity of supply is low, a large change in price will result.

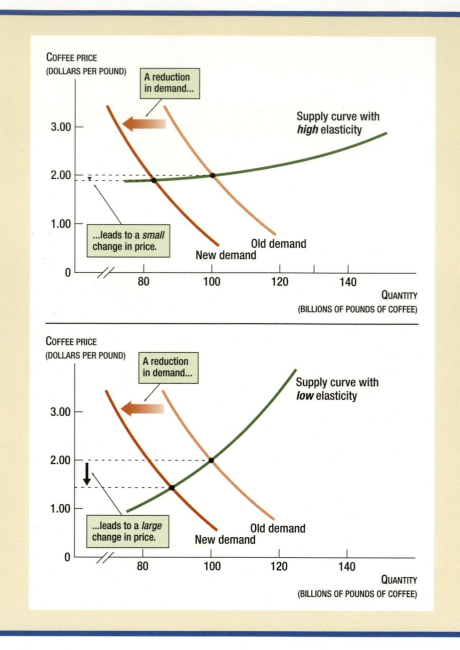

REVIEW

- The price elasticity of supply is a number that tells us how sensitive the quantity supplied is to the price. It is defined as the percentage change in the quantity supplied divided by the percentage change in the price.

- The attractive features of the price elasticity of demand are also true for the price elasticity

of supply. Its size does not depend on the units of measurement of either price or quantity.

- The price elasticity of supply is useful for determining how much prices will change when demand changes.

CONCLUSION

In this chapter, we have extended our analysis of the supply and demand model in two directions. We first learned about what happens when the government intervenes to put a price ceiling or a price floor into the economy. Understanding how to use the supply and demand model with price floors and ceilings enables us to better understand policy debates such as the one surrounding the increase in the minimum wage.

The second extension was to develop an understanding of *how much* the equilibrium price and quantity change in response to changes in supply or demand. The concept of price elasticity of demand helps us understand what happens to the quantity demanded when price changes or when the supply of a good changes. We also can predict whether revenue will increase or decrease when prices are cut or raised. The related concept of the elasticity of supply is also useful in understanding what happens to the quantity supplied when price changes or when the demand for a good changes. We also discussed the concept of an income elasticity of demand, which can clarify how the quantity demanded for various goods will change as incomes rise, and the cross-price elasticity of demand, which tells us how much the quantity demanded of a good changes as prices for substitute or complementary goods change.

KEY POINTS

1. Governments occasionally will intervene in markets because they think that the equilibrium price is too high or too low. When they act to impose a maximum price on a market, because they think the price that buyers have to pay is too high, they are said to be imposing a price ceiling. When they act to impose a minimum price on a market, because they think the price that sellers are receiving is too low, they are said to be imposing a price floor.

2. Price ceilings cause shortages, with the quantity supplied being less than the quantity demanded. Shortages lead to rationing or black markets. Price floors cause surpluses, with the quantity supplied being greater than the quantity demanded. Surpluses lead to resources being diverted away from other productive activities to deal with the extra output that needs to be stored or disposed of.

3. Rent controls are a classic application of a price ceiling, and minimum wages are a classic application of a price floor. The supply model helps us understand some basic issues related to these policies, which frequently appear in the news. We will develop the supply and demand model further, which will allow us to do a more sophisticated analysis of minimum-wage laws, for example, than we have done in this chapter.

4. Elasticity is a measure of the sensitivity of one economic variable to another. For example, the price elasticity of demand measures how much the quantity demanded changes when the price changes.

5. Elasticity is a unit-free measure. The price elasticity of demand is the percentage change in the quantity demanded divided by the percentage change in price. It refers to changes in price and quantity demanded along the demand curve, all other things being equal.

6. Demand is said to be elastic if the price elasticity of demand is greater than one and inelastic if the price elasticity of demand is less than one.

7. When the elasticity is greater than one, an increase in the price reduces the quantity demanded by a percentage greater than the percentage increase in the price, thereby reducing revenue. When the elasticity is less than one, an increase in the price reduces the quantity demanded by a percentage less than the percentage increase in the price, thereby increasing revenue.

8. The elasticity of demand for a good depends on whether the good has close substitutes, whether its value is a large or a small fraction of total income, and the time period of the change.

9. Whereas the price elasticity of demand refers to movements along the demand curve, the income elasticity of demand refers to shifts in the demand curve caused by changes in income, and the cross-price elasticity of demand refers to shifts in the demand curve caused by changes in the price of other goods. Most goods are normal and have a positive income elasticity of demand. Inferior

goods have a negative income elasticity of demand.

10. The price elasticity of supply is defined as the percentage change in the quantity supplied divided by the percentage change in the price. If a good has a high price elasticity of supply, then a change in price will cause a big change in the quantity supplied. Conversely, if a good has a low price elasticity of supply, then a change in price will have only a small impact on the quantity supplied.

KEY TERMS

cross-price elasticity of demand, 95

elastic demand, 87

income elasticity of demand, 93

inelastic demand, 87

minimum wage, 76

perfectly elastic demand, 87

perfectly elastic supply, 97

perfectly inelastic demand, 87

perfectly inelastic supply, 97

price ceiling, 75

price controls, 75

price elasticity of demand, 80

price elasticity of supply, 96

price floor, 75

rent control, 75

unit-free measure, 85

QUESTIONS FOR REVIEW

1. Why is the price elasticity of demand a unit-free measure of the sensitivity of the quantity demanded to a price change?
2. What factors determine whether the price elasticity of demand is high or low?
3. What is the difference between elastic and inelastic demand?
4. Why is the price elasticity of demand useful for finding the size of the price change that occurs when supply shifts?
5. If the price elasticity of demand for textbooks is two and the price of textbooks increases by 10 percent, by how much does the quantity demanded fall?
6. Why is the price elasticity of demand lower in the short run than in the long run?
7. For what values of the price elasticity of demand do increases in the price increase revenue?
8. What is the income elasticity of demand?
9. What is the difference between the price elasticity of demand and the income elasticity of demand?
10. What is the slope of a perfectly elastic supply curve?

PROBLEMS

1. Consider the market for automatic teller machine (ATM) services in a city. The price is the fee for a cash withdrawal.

    a. Sketch the demand curve and the supply curve for ATM transactions.
    b. How is the equilibrium price determined?
    c. If the town council imposes a ban on ATM fees— equivalent to a price ceiling in this market—what happens to quantity supplied and quantity demanded?
    d. Economists frequently argue against price controls because of the shortages and associated problems that they create. What are some of the potentially negative side effects of interference in the ATM market?

2. In 1991, the price of milk fell 30 percent. Senator Leahy of Vermont, a big milk-producing state, supported a law in the U.S. Congress to put a floor on the price. The floor was $13.09 per hundred pounds of milk. The market price was $11.47.

    a. Draw a supply and demand diagram for milk and show how the equilibrium price and quantity would be determined in the absence of the price floor.
    b. Using the diagram you just drew, explain the effects of the legislation.

c. The dairy farmers supported the legislation, while consumer groups opposed it. Why?

d. Economists frequently argue against price floors because of the surpluses and associated problems that they create. What are some of the potentially negative side effects of interference in the milk market?

3. More than 20 states have laws outlawing price gouging during a state of emergency, which might be declared after a hurricane or an earthquake. These laws prohibit price increases on basic necessities, such as gasoline. Which of the arguments against price ceilings might not be significant during a state of emergency?

4. Donors of organs for transplantation or medical research are prohibited from charging a price for these organs (there is a price ceiling of zero). Will this result in a shortage? How will the market cope with the shortage?

5. Consider the following data for a demand curve:

Price	Quantity
11	10
10	20
9	30
8	40
7	50
6	60
5	70
4	80
3	90

a. Use the midpoint formula to calculate the elasticity between a price of $10 and $11.

b. Use the midpoint formula to calculate the elasticity between a price of $3 and $4.

c. Because this is a linear demand curve, why does the elasticity change?

d. At what point is price times quantity maximized? What is the elasticity at that point?

6. Consider the following data for a supply curve:

Price	Quantity Supplied
2	10
3	20
4	30
5	40
6	50
7	60
8	70
9	80

a. Use the midpoint formula to calculate the price elasticity of supply between a price of $7 and $8.

b. Use the midpoint formula to calculate the price elasticity of supply between a price of $3 and $4.

c. How does supply elasticity change as you move up the supply curve?

d. Why does the supply elasticity change even though the slope of the supply curve is unchanged as you move up the supply curve?

7. Given the following income elasticities of demand, would you classify the following goods as normal or inferior goods?

a. Potatoes: elasticity = 0.5

b. Pinto beans: elasticity = −0.1

c. Bottled water: elasticity = 1.1

d. Video cameras: elasticity = 1.4

8. Calculate the cross-price elasticity for the following goods. Are they substitutes or complements?

a. The price of movie theater tickets goes up by 10 percent, causing the quantity demanded for video rentals to go up by 4 percent.

b. The price of computers falls by 20 percent, causing the quantity demanded of software to increase by 15 percent.

c. The price of apples falls by 5 percent, causing the quantity demanded of pears to fall by 5 percent.

d. The price of ice cream falls by 6 percent, causing the quantity demanded of frozen yogurt to fall by 1 percent.

9. Food items often have low elasticities of demand. Suppose excellent weather leads to bumper yields of agricultural crops. Why might farmers complain about market conditions?

10. The board of directors of an airline wishes to increase revenue. One group favors cutting airfares, and the other group favors raising airfares. What are the assumptions each group is making about the price elasticity of demand?

11. Compare a market in which supply and demand are very (but not perfectly) inelastic to one in which supply and demand are very (but not perfectly) elastic. Suppose the government decides to impose a price floor $1 above the equilibrium price in each of these markets. Compare, diagrammatically, the surpluses that result. In which market is the surplus larger?

12. In 1992, the federal government placed a tax of 10 percent on goods like luxury automobiles and yachts. The yacht-manufacturing industry had huge declines in orders for yachts and laid off many workers, whereas the reaction in the auto industry was much milder. (The tax on yachts was subsequently removed.) Explain this situation using two supply and demand diagrams. Compare the elasticity of demand for luxury autos with that for yachts based on the experience with the luxury tax.

part two

PRINCIPLES OF MACROECONOMICS

5 Macroeconomics: The Big Picture

How times change! At the end of 2006, when the final touches were being added to the sixth edition of this textbook, this introductory macroeconomics chapter talked about how the U.S. economy had been basking in the glow of a period known as "the Great Moderation." During this period of a quarter century, following the serious economic downturn of 1981–1982, the economy only experienced two minor recessions (in 1990–1991 and in 2001), both of which were much milder than previous recessions. The Great Moderation saw almost continuous economic growth, accompanied by declining rates of inflation and unemployment, as well as greater stability—the economy was less likely to experience significant ups and downs—over this period. This growth was in sharp contrast to the turbulent decade of the 1970s, leading up to the 1981–1982 recession, when double-digit inflation, high unemployment, and economic volatility were the norm.

A little over four years later, in the early months of 2011 as the seventh edition of the textbook takes shape, the Great Moderation seems like a distant memory. Now the discussion is far more likely to be about the "Great Recession" rather than the "Great Moderation." The headlines over the last three years have told a dismal tale: "U.S. GDP fall at record rate," "U.S. stocks suffer worst year since Great Depression," "Rise in U.S. unemployment tipped to be biggest for 60 years," "New home sales set record low last year." In the first few weeks after taking office, President Obama, along with Congress, worked out the details of two important pieces of legislation—a stimulus package worth hundreds of billions of dollars and a plan, also in the hundreds of billions of dollars, to help the troubled banking system. Many were hopeful that these new policies would help the economy recover, but no one at that time knew for sure whether they would.

Eighteen months after the recession ended, doubts still remain about the health of the U.S. economy. In December 2010, the unemployment rate was still above 9 percent. More than 6 million Americans had been unemployed for more than 26 weeks, and the nation was not optimistic that unemployment would come down below 7 percent anytime soon. In addition to the short-term concerns about the labor market and the pace of recovery, there were long-term concerns about the impact of rising government debt, widening economic inequality, the impact of an aging population with rising health bills and dwindling savings, and U.S. children falling further behind in education outcomes.

Furthermore, the recent slowdown was a global phenomenon. It affected most industrial nations, including the United Kingdom, Japan, and the countries in the European Monetary Union; emerging market economies like the Republic of Korea, the Russian Federation, and Brazil; poor countries that rely on exports to rich countries; and even the highest flyers, China and India. Many of the emerging market economies and the export-oriented economies have recovered, but the industrial world still faces major economic challenges. Ireland, Greece, and the United Kingdom have embarked on large programs of fiscal austerity in which the government has cut spending drastically, raised some taxes, and tried to reduce the path of budget deficits and government debt. Japan, after showing the first signs of finally being able to overcome an economic slump that lasted almost two decades, was hit by a triple shock of an earthquake, a tsunami, and potential nuclear catastrophe.

It is important, however, not to let gloomy stories about the economy obscure the happier stories about economic progress over a longer term. The period since 1980 is filled with remarkable economic developments, none more remarkable than the rapid economic growth of developing economies, such as China. According to data collected by the International Monetary Fund, production per person in China in 2005 was 15 times as large as it had been in 1980. The economy of the second most populous nation in the world, India, also grew at a rapid pace. Production per person in India in 2005 was almost five times as large as it had been in 1980. Such rapid rates of economic growth in China, India, and several other countries mean a better quality of life for hundreds of millions of people. The World Bank calculated that the number of people living on an income of less than $1 a day fell by almost 200 million even as the world population increased by more than a billion people over this period. We should be delighted that the progress made by China and India has given so many of their people a brighter future. Sub-Saharan African countries like Sierra Leone, Togo, and Niger—economies that essentially are producing as much output per person in the twenty-first century as they produced in 1980—can benefit from a better understanding of why China and India grew so fast, so that they, too, can achieve even moderate rates of growth. An increase in economic growth over the next decade or two is vital for improving the living conditions of the world's poorest.

Macroeconomics is the study of the whole market economy. Like other parts of economics, macroeconomics uses the central idea that people make purposeful decisions with scarce resources. However, instead of focusing on the workings of one market—whether the market for peanuts or the market for bicycles—macroeconomics focuses on the economy as a whole. Macroeconomics looks at the big picture: Economic growth, recessions, unemployment, and inflation are among its subject matter. You should accordingly put on your "big picture glasses" when you study macroeconomics.

By studying macroeconomics, you can better understand the changes that are taking place in the economy, better understand the role of good economic policies in driving economic growth and reducing unemployment, and become a more informed and educated citizen. Hopefully, you will be inspired by the study of macroeconomics to do your part to bring about strong economic growth, which in turn can help alleviate poverty, free up resources to improve the environment, and lead to a brighter future for your generation.

This chapter summarizes the overall workings of the economy, highlighting key facts to remember. It also provides a brief preview of the macroeconomic theory designed to explain these facts. The theory will be developed in later chapters.

Measuring the "Size" of an Economy

To understand why some economies have done so much better than others, we first need to understand how macroeconomists measure the size of an economy. Gross domestic product (GDP) is the economic variable that is of most interest to macroeconomists. GDP is the total value of all new goods and services produced in the economy during a specified period of time, usually a year or a quarter. The total value of goods and services can change either because the quantities of goods and services are changing or because their prices are changing. As a result, economists often prefer to use **real gross domestic product (real GDP)** as the measure of production; the adjective *real* means that we adjust the measure of production to account for changes in prices over time. Real GDP, also called *output* or *production*, is the most comprehensive measure of how well the economy is doing.

Figure 5-1 shows the changes in real GDP in recent years in the United States. When you look at real GDP over time, as in Figure 5-1, you notice two simultaneous patterns emerging. Over the long term, increases in real GDP demonstrate an upward trend, which economists call long-term **economic growth**. In the short term, you notice more transient increases or decreases in real GDP, called **economic fluctuations**. These short-term fluctuations in real GDP also are called *business cycles*. The difference between the long-term economic growth trend and the economic fluctuations can be better seen by drawing a relatively smooth line between the observations on real GDP. Such a smooth trend line is shown in Figure 5-1. Sometimes real GDP fluctuates above the trend line, and sometimes it fluctuates below the trend line. In this section, we look more closely at these two patterns: economic growth and economic fluctuations.

Economic Growth: The Relentless Uphill Climb

The large increase in real GDP shown in Figure 5-1 means that people in the United States now produce a much greater amount of goods and services each year than they did 40 years ago. Improvements in the economic well-being of individuals in any society cannot occur without such an increase in real GDP. To get a better measure of how individuals benefit from increases in real GDP, we consider average production per person, or *real GDP per capita*. Real GDP per capita is real GDP divided by the number of people in the economy. It is the total production of all food, clothes, cars, houses, compact discs, concerts, education, computers, and so on per person. When real GDP per capita is increasing, then the well-being—or the standard of living—of individuals in the economy, at least on average, is improving.

real gross domestic product (real GDP)
a measure of the value of all the goods and services newly produced in a country during some period of time, adjusted for changes in prices over time.

economic growth
an upward trend in real GDP, reflecting expansion in the economy over time.

economic fluctuations
swings in real GDP that lead to deviations of the economy from its long-term growth trend.

Figure 5-1

Economic Growth and Fluctuations

Real GDP has grown by more than $10 trillion during the last 50 years. The trend in growth is shown by the blue line. At the same time, the economy has fluctuated up and down as it has grown, with eight recessions—marked by the vertical shaded bars—and eight subsequent expansions (the most recent expansion was ongoing at the end of 2010).

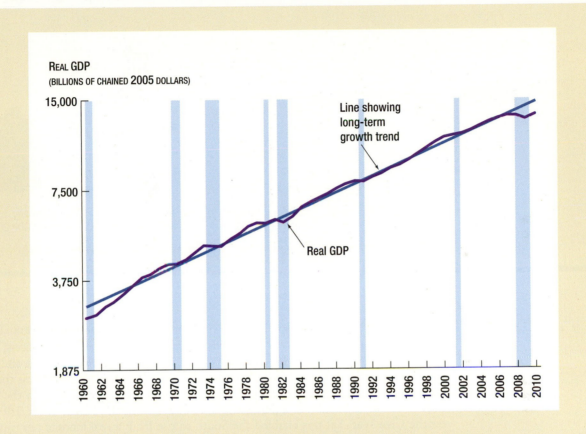

REAL GDP
(BILLIONS OF CHAINED 2005 DOLLARS)

Line showing long-term growth trend

Real GDP

Source: Bureau of Economic Analysis, "National Income and Product Accounts," Table 1.1.6.

How much economic growth has occurred during the last 40 years in the United States? The annual *economic growth rate*—the percentage increase in real GDP each year—provides a good measure. On average, for the last 40 years, the annual economic growth rate has been a little under 3 percent per year. This growth may not sound like much, but it means that real GDP has more than tripled. The increase in production in the United States over the past 40 years is larger than what Japan and Germany together now produce. It is as if all the production of Japan and Germany—what is made by all the workers, machines, and technology in these countries—were annexed to the U.S. economy, as illustrated in Figure 5-2.

How much did real GDP *per capita* increase during this period? Because the U.S. population grew by more than 100 million people during this period, the increase in real GDP per capita has been less dramatic than the increase in real GDP, but it is impressive nonetheless. The annual growth rate of real GDP per capita is the percentage increase in real GDP per capita each year. It has averaged just under 2 percent per year. Again, this might not sound like much, but it has meant that real GDP per capita more than doubled,

Figure 5-2

Visualizing Economic Growth

Over the last 40 years, production in the U.S. economy has increased by more than the total current production of the Japanese and German economies combined. It is as if the United States had annexed Germany and Japan.

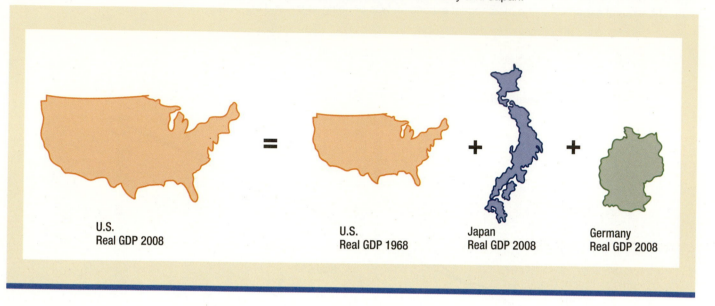

U.S.
Real GDP 2008

=

U.S.
Real GDP 1968

+

Japan
Real GDP 2008

+

Germany
Real GDP 2008

from about $21,000 per person in 1970 to about $43,000 per person in 2008. That extra $22,000 per person represents increased opportunities for travel, televisions, housing, washing machines, aerobics classes, health care, antipollution devices for cars, and so on.

Over long time spans, small differences in economic growth—even less than 1 percent per year—can transform societies. For example, economic growth in the southern states was only a fraction of a percent greater than that in the North in the 100 years after the Civil War. Yet this enabled the South to rise from a real income per capita about half that of the North after the Civil War to one about the same as that of the North in the twenty-first century. Economic growth is the reason that fast-growing countries like Korea can catch up with and even surpass slow-growing countries like Mexico. Data from the International Monetary Fund show that in 1980, Korea had a real GDP per capita that was about 60 percent of Mexico's real GDP per capita, but by 2005, Korea's real GDP per capita was almost twice as large as Mexico's real GDP. Economic growth is also key to improvements in the less-developed countries in Sub-Saharan Africa, South Asia, and Latin America. Because economic growth has been lagging in many of these countries, their real GDP per capita is considerably less than that of the United States.

Economic Fluctuations: Temporary Setbacks and Recoveries

Clearly, real GDP grows over time, but every now and then real GDP stops growing, falls, and then starts increasing rapidly again. These ups and downs in the economy— that is, economic fluctuations or business cycles—can be seen in Figure 5-1.

One of these business cycles, the one in 2008–2009, is blown up for closer examination in Figure 5-3. No two business cycles are alike. Certain phases are common to all business cycles, however. These common phases are shown in the diagram in the margin. In the

Figure 5-3

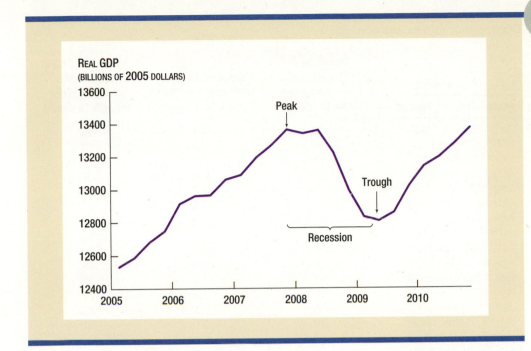

REAL GDP
(BILLIONS OF 2005 DOLLARS)

The Phases of Business Cycles
Although no two business cycles are alike, they have common features, including the *peak, recession,* and *trough,* shown here for the 2008–2009 recession.

United States, the "official designator" of business cycles is the National Bureau of Economic Research (NBER)'s Business Cycle Dating Committee. Economists on this committee try to identify key turning points in overall economic activity to identify, and designate as, recessions and expansions. In the definitions that follow, economic activity is usually, but not always, synonymous with real GDP.

When economic activity falls, economists call this a **recession**; a rule of thumb says that the fall must last for a half year or more before the decline is considered a recession. The highest point in economic activity before the start of a recession is called the **peak**. The lowest point in economic activity at the end of a recession is called the **trough**, a term that may cause you to imagine water accumulating at the bottom of one of the dips. The period between recessions—from the trough to the next peak—is called an **expansion**, as shown for a typical fluctuation in the margin. The early part of an expansion usually is called a **recovery** because the economy is just recovering from the recession.

The peaks and troughs of the seven recessions since the mid-1960s are shown by vertical bars in Figure 5-1. The shaded areas represent the recessions. The areas between the shaded bars show the expansions. The dates of all peaks and troughs back to 1920 are shown in Table 5-1. The average length of each business cycle from peak to peak is slightly more than five years, but it is clear from Table 5-1 that business cycles are not regularly occurring ups and downs, like sunup and sundown. Recessions occur irregularly. There were only 12 months between the back-to-back recessions of the early 1980s, while 58 months of uninterrupted growth occurred between the 1973–1975 recession and the 1980 recession. The recession phases of business cycles also vary in duration and depth. The 1990–1991 recession, for example, was not nearly as long or as deep as the 1973–1975 recession.

Table 5-1 illustrates how much less volatile the U.S. economy had been in recent times, at least until the most recent recession. The 1990–1991 recession and the 2001 recession were among the shortest recessions in U.S. history, each lasting about eight months. Both of these recessions were preceded by long economic expansions lasting between seven and ten years. The economic expansion that began after the 2001

recession
a decline in economic activity that lasts for at least six months.

peak
the highest point in economic activity before a recession.

trough
the lowest point of economic activity at the end of a recession.

expansion
the period between the trough of a recession and the next peak, consisting of a general rise in output and employment.

recovery
the early part of an economic expansion, immediately after the trough of the recession.

Table 5-1

Comparison of Recessions

Recession		Duration of Recession (months from peak to trough)	Decline in Real GDP (percent from peak to trough)	Duration of Next Expansion (months from trough to peak)
Peak	**Trough**			
Jan 1920–Jul 1921		18	8.7	22
May 1923–Jul 1924		14	4.1	27
Oct 1926–Nov 1927		13	2.0	21
Aug 1929–Mar 1933		43	32.6	50
May 1937–Jun 1938		13	18.2	80
Feb 1945–Oct 1945		8	11.0	37
Nov 1948–Oct 1949		11	1.5	45
Jul 1953–May 1954		10	3.2	39
Aug 1957–Apr 1958		8	3.3	24
Apr 1960–Feb 1961		10	1.2	106
Dec 1969–Nov 1970		11	1.0	36
Nov 1973–Mar 1975		16	4.9	58
Jan 1980–Jul 1980		6	2.5	12
Jul 1981–Nov 1982		16	3.0	92
Jul 1990–Mar 1991		8	1.4	120
Mar 2001–Nov 2001		8	0.0	72
Dec 2007–June 2009		18	4.1	21*

*As of March 2011.
Source: Columns 1, 2, and 4, National Bureau of Economic Research.

recession lasted almost six years before the economy went into recession at the end of 2007. That recession lasted 18 months (exceeding the 1990–1991 and 2001 recessions in duration), ending in the middle of 2009.

Amid the euphoria of the Great Moderation, economists debated whether economic policies were responsible for the length of the recent expansions and the brevity of the recent recessions. Was this "Great Moderation" the result of better policy making by the Federal Reserve and by our elected leaders? Or was it because we benefited from technological advances like more effective pharmaceuticals, the invention of the personal computer, or the creation of the Internet? Or was it simply the result of "good luck" in terms of the economy being hit by less disruptive shocks than in the 1970s?

When the economy is in the midst of a serious recession, economists have focused on understanding the factors that caused the recession. The most recent recession was associated with a number of factors, including the dramatic fall in house prices and sales, rising foreclosures of homes, a banking crisis that made it difficult for firms and consumers to obtain credit, and dramatic increases in fuel prices during the early part of 2008. Economists do not always agree on what the factors causing a recession were. The factors to which the 2001 recession has been ascribed include a fall in spending on equipment and buildings by firms and a sharp decline in the stock market. The first month of the 1990–1991 recession occurred just after Iraq invaded Kuwait, causing a disruption in the oil fields and a jump in world oil prices, so some argue that this jump in oil prices was a factor in the recession.

A Recession's Aftermath
After a recession, the economy usually takes several years to return to its prerecession state. Thus, a period of bad economic times always follows a recession while the economy recovers. Technically, economists define recessions as periods in which real GDP is declining, and recoveries as periods in which real GDP is rising

again. However, despite this technical distinction between bad economic times when things are getting worse (recession) and bad economic times when things are improving (recovery), many people still associate the word *recession* with bad economic times in general. Furthermore, not all economic indicators move in lockstep with real GDP. For example, although the 2008–2009 recession ended in June of 2009, the unemployment rate kept rising for five more months and did not fall below the levels reached at the end of the recession until another year had passed. Technically speaking, though, the recession was over in June 2009 when economic activity (including real GDP) began to pick up again—long before the effects of an improving economy were felt by most people. Conversely, when this recession began in December 2007, real GDP kept rising for another six months even though other indicators of economic activity showed a downturn much earlier.

Recessions versus Depressions Fortunately, we have not experienced a depression in the United States for a long time, and we all hope that it stays that way. Figure 5-4 shows the history of real GDP for about 100 years. The most noticeable

Figure 5-4

Growth and Fluctuations Since the Early Twentieth Century

Economic growth has been steady in the United States from the beginning of the twentieth century. The frequency and size of economic fluctuations, however, has diminished remarkably since the end of World War II. The most recent economic downturn was one of the more severe recessions that the economy had seen in the postwar period but still remained small in comparison with the Great Depression.

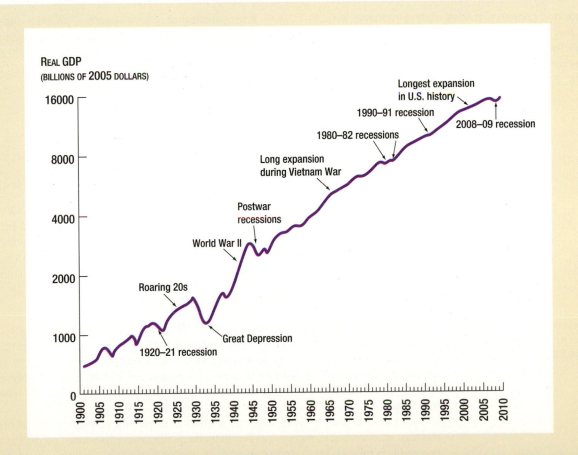

decline in real GDP occurred in the 1929–1933 recession. Real GDP fell by 32.6 percent in this period. This decline in real GDP was so large that it was given its own designation by economists and historians—the Great Depression.

Table 5-1 shows how much real GDP fell in each of the 17 recessions since the 1920s. The 1920–1921 recession and the 1937–1938 recession were big enough to be classified as depressions, but both were small compared with the Great Depression. Real GDP also declined substantially after World War II, when war production declined.

The postwar recessions are not remotely comparable in severity to the Great Depression or the other huge recessions of the 1920s and 1930s. The 2008–2009 recession, sometimes referred to as the Great Recession, was a significant slowdown in comparison to postwar recessions, both in terms of severity and length. But it had only one-eighth the decline in real GDP that occurred during the Great Depression, which was a downturn of a more significant scale. But because any recession rivets attention on people's hardship and suffering, the tendency always is to view a current recession as being worse than most previous recessions.

REVIEW

- The behavior of real GDP in the United States is characterized by a long-term upward trend (economic growth) and more transient increases and decreases around that trend (economic fluctuations).

- Economic growth provides lasting improvements in the well-being of people. Small differences in economic growth, sustained over long time spans, can transform societies.

- Periodically, economic activity stops increasing and begins to decline. A decline in economic activity that lasts for at least six months is known as a recession. Recessions vary in length and intensity, but have become less severe since the 1980s.

- A recession that is very severe is called a depression. The Great Depression of the 1930s was about eight times more severe than the 2008–2009 recession when measured by the decline in real GDP.

Unemployment, Inflation, and Interest Rates

As real GDP changes over time, so do other economic variables, such as unemployment, inflation, and interest rates. Looking at these other economic variables gives us a better understanding of the human story behind the changes in real GDP. They also provide additional information about the economy's performance—just as a person's pulse rate or cholesterol level gives information different from the body temperature. No one variable is sufficient.

Unemployment during Recessions

unemployment rate
the percentage of the labor force that is unemployed.

Unemployment fluctuates just as real GDP fluctuates. The **unemployment rate** is the number of unemployed people as a percentage of the labor force; the labor force consists of those who either are working or looking for work. Every time the economy goes into a recession, the unemployment rate rises because people are laid off and new jobs are difficult to find. The individual stories behind the unemployment numbers frequently represent frustration and distress.

Figure 5-5 shows what happens to the unemployment rate as the economy goes through recessions and recoveries. The increase in the unemployment rate during a recession eventually is followed by a decline in unemployment during the recovery. Note, for example,

Figure 5-5

The Unemployment Rate

The number of unemployed workers as a percentage of the labor force—the unemployment rate—increases during recessions because people are laid off and it is difficult to find work. Sometimes the unemployment rate continues to increase for a while after the recession is over, as in 1991 and 2001. But eventually unemployment declines during the economic recovery.

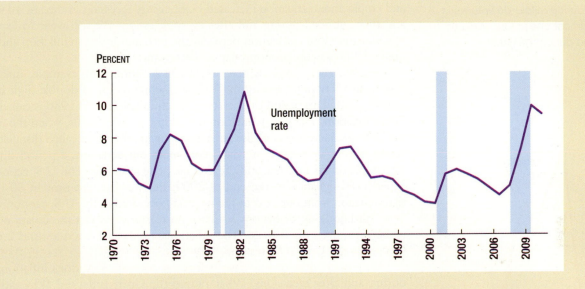

Source: Bureau of Labor Statistics, "Unemployment Rate—Civilian Labor Force."

how rapidly unemployment rose as the economy moved into recession in 2008, with the unemployment rate rising by more than 2.5 percentage points in 2008. Similar sharp increases in unemployment were seen during the recessions of 1973–1975 and 1981–1982.

Figure 5-6 shows how high the unemployment rate got during the Great Depression. It rose to nearly 25 percent; one in four workers was out of work. Fortunately, recent increases in unemployment during recessions have been much smaller. The unemployment rate reached 10.4 percent in the early 1980s, the highest level since World War II.

The highest unemployment level reached in the most recent recession was 10.1 percent in October 2008, a figure that pales in comparison to the levels reached in the Great Depression. It also is slightly lower than the peak levels reached in the 1982 recession. However, unemployment was much lower in the period leading into the recent recession (around 5 percent) than it was in the period leading up to the 1982 recession (7.5 percent). The extremely rapid rise in the unemployment rate clearly shows that this is a downturn whose impact will be felt for years to come. Figure 5-7 illustrates how rapidly unemployment rose during the calendar years of 2008 and 2009. During these two years, the unemployment rate increased from 4.9 percent to 9.9 percent. To put this number in more human terms, the number of unemployed workers across the country doubled from 7.6 million to 15.2 million.

Inflation

Just as output and unemployment have fluctuated over time, so too has inflation. The **inflation rate** is the percentage increase in the average price of all goods and services

inflation rate
the percentage increase in the overall price level over a given period of time, usually one year.

Figure 5-6

Unemployment during the Great Depression

The increase in unemployment in the United States during the Great Depression was huge compared with the increases in unemployment during milder downturns in the economy. Almost one in four workers was unemployed during the Great Depression.

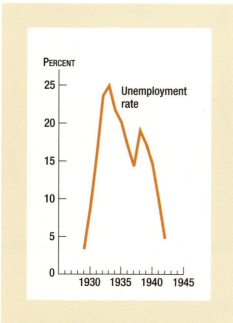

Source: Robert Van Giezeu and Albert E. Schwenk, ''Compensation from before World War I Through the Great Depression'' (Bureau of Labor Statistics).

interest rate
the amount received per dollar loaned per year, usually expressed as a percentage (for example, 6 percent) of the loan.

from one year to the next. Figure 5-8 shows the inflation rate for the same 40-year period we have focused on in our examination of real GDP and unemployment. Clearly, a low and stable inflation rate has not been a feature of the United States during this period. We can note several useful facts about the behavior of inflation.

First, inflation is closely correlated with the ups and downs in real GDP and employment: Inflation increased before every recession in the last 40 years and then subsided during and after every recession. We will want to explore whether this close correlation between the ups and downs in inflation and the ups and downs in the economy explains economic fluctuations.

Second, there are long-term trends in inflation. For example, inflation rose from a low point during the 1970s to a high point of double-digit inflation in 1980. This period of persistently high inflation until 1980 is called the Great Inflation. The Great Inflation ended in the early 1980s, when the inflation rate declined substantially. Such a decline in inflation is called disinflation. A much rarer occurrence is what economists call deflation, a period during which inflation is negative and the average price level falls. The U.S. economy experienced deflation at the end of 2009; this was the first time in 50 years that deflation from one year to the next had occurred in the U.S. economy.

Third, judging by history, we have no reason to expect the inflation rate to be zero, even on average. The inflation rate has averaged around 2 or 3 percent in the United States since 1990.

Why does inflation increase before recessions? Why does inflation fall during and after recessions? What caused the Great Inflation? Why did the economy move into deflation for the first time in 50 years? Why is inflation not equal to zero even in more normal times, when the economy is neither in recession nor in a boom? What can economic policy do to keep inflation low and stable? These are some of the questions and policy issues about inflation addressed by macroeconomics.

Interest Rates

The **interest rate** is the amount that lenders charge when they lend money, expressed as a percentage of the amount loaned. For example, if you borrow $100 for a year from a friend and the interest rate on the loan is 6 percent, then at the end of the year you must pay your friend back $6 in interest in addition to the $100 you borrowed. The interest rate is another key economic variable that is related to the growth and change in real GDP over time.

Different Types of Interest Rates and Their Behavior The economy includes many different interest rates: The *mortgage interest rate* is the rate on loans to buy a house; the *savings deposit interest rate* is the rate people get on their savings deposits at banks; the *Treasury bill rate* is the interest rate the government pays when it borrows money from people for a year or less; the *federal funds rate* is the interest rate banks charge each other on short-term loans. Interest rates influence people's economic behavior. When interest rates rise, for example, it is more expensive to borrow funds to buy a house or a car, so many people postpone such purchases.

Figure 5-9 shows the behavior of a typical interest rate, the federal funds rate, during the last 40 years. First, note how closely the ups and downs in the interest rate are correlated with the ups and downs in the economy. Interest rates rise before each recession and then decline during and after each recession. Second, as with the inflation rate, there are long-term trends in the interest rate. The interest rate rose in the 1970s and early

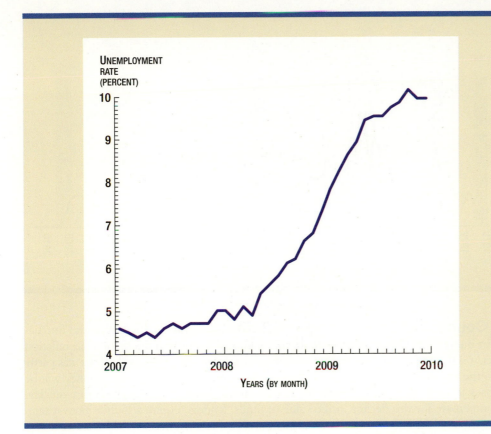

Figure 5-7

The Rapid Rise of Unemployment in 2008/09

When the economy moves from expansion into recession, unemployment can climb rapidly over a period of a few months, as we saw during the most recent recession.

Source: Bureau of Labor Statistics.

Figure 5-8

The Ups and Downs in Inflation

Inflation has increased before each recession and then declined during and immediately after each recession. In addition, a longer-term upward trend in inflation reached a peak in 1980. Since 1981, America has experienced a disinflation—a decline in the rate of inflation.

Source: Bureau of Labor Statistics, "Percent Change in CPI for All Urban Consumers."

1980s. Each fluctuation in interest rates during this period brought forth a higher peak in interest rates. Then, in the 1980s, the interest rate began a downward trend; each peak was lower than the previous peak. During the most recent recession, the federal funds rate fell to close to 0 percent, which is the lowest it can go.

Figure 5-9

The Ups and Downs in Interest Rates

Interest rates generally rise just before a recession and then decline during and just after the recession. There was also a longer-term trend upward in interest rates in the 1970s and a downward trend after the 1980s. (The interest rate shown here is the federal funds interest rate.)

Source: Board of Governors of the Federal Reserve, "Selected Interest Rates—Federal Funds Rate."

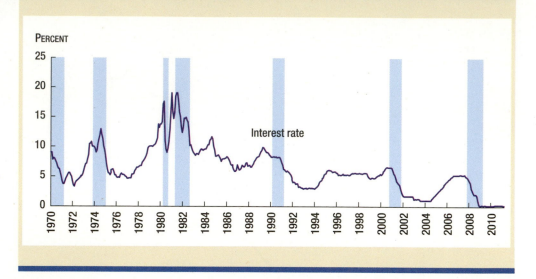

real interest rate
the interest rate minus the expected rate of inflation; it adjusts the nominal interest rate for inflation.

nominal interest rate
the interest rate uncorrected for inflation.

The Concept of the Real Interest Rate

As we will see, the trends and fluctuations in interest rates are intimately connected with the trends and fluctuations in inflation and real GDP. In fact, the long-term rise in interest rates in the 1960s and 1970s was partly due to the rise in the rate of inflation. When inflation rises, people who lend money will be paid back in funds that are worth less because the average price of goods rises more quickly. To compensate for this decline in the value of funds, lenders require a higher interest rate. For example, if the inflation rate is 20 percent and you lend someone $100 for a year at 6 percent, then you get back $106 at the end of the year. However, the *average* price of the goods you can buy with your $106 is now 20 percent higher. Thus, your 6 percent gain in interest has been offset by a 20 percent loss. It is as if you receive *negative* 14 percent interest: 6 percent interest less 20 percent inflation. The difference between the stated interest rate and the inflation rate is thus a better measure of the real interest rate. Economists define the **real interest rate** as the interest rate less the inflation rate that people expect. The term **nominal interest rate** is used to refer to the interest rate on a loan, making no adjustment for inflation. For example, the real interest rate is 2 percent if the nominal interest rate is 5 percent and inflation is expected to be 3 percent $(5 - 3 = 2)$. To keep the real interest rate from changing by a large amount as inflation rises, the nominal interest rate has to increase with inflation. Thus, the concept of the real interest rate helps us understand why inflation and interest rates have moved together. We will make much more use of the real interest rate in later chapters.

REVIEW

- The unemployment rate rises during recessions and falls during recoveries.

- Inflation and interest rates rise before recessions and then fall during and just after recessions.

- There was a long-term increase in interest rates and inflation in the 1970s. Interest rates and inflation were lower in the 1990s and into the 2000s.

- Two unusual features of the U.S. economy in recent times have been the negative rate of inflation, also known as deflation, and the nominal interest rate falling to a level of zero, which is the lowest it can go.

Macroeconomic Theory and Policy

Because strong economic growth raises the living standards of people in an economy, and because increases in unemployment during recessions cause hardship, two goals of economic policy are to raise long-term growth and to reduce the size of short-term economic fluctuations. However, the facts—summarized above—about economic growth and fluctuations do not give economists a basis for making recommendations about economic policy. Before one can be confident about recommending a policy, one needs a coherent theory to explain the facts.

Macroeconomic theory is divided into two branches. *Economic growth theory* aims to explain the long-term upward rise of real GDP over time. *Economic fluctuations theory* tries to explain the short-term fluctuations in real GDP. Economic growth theory and economic fluctuations theory combine to form *macroeconomic theory*, which explains why the economy both grows and fluctuates over time.

The Theory of Long-Term Economic Growth

Economic growth theory starts by distinguishing the longer-term economic growth trend from the short-term fluctuations in the economy. This distinction is not as easy to make as it may seem because the long-term growth trend itself may change.

It will be useful to give a name to the upward trend line in real GDP shown in Figure 5-1. We will call it **potential GDP**. Potential GDP represents the long-run tendency of the economy to grow. Real GDP fluctuates around potential GDP. No one knows exactly where potential GDP lies and exactly what its growth rate is, but any trend line that has the same long-term increase as real GDP and intersects real GDP in several places is probably a good estimate.

Potential GDP as defined here and as used by most macroeconomists is not the maximum amount of real GDP. As Figure 5-1 shows, real GDP sometimes goes above potential GDP. Thus, potential GDP is more like the average or trend level of real GDP.

Economic growth theory postulates that the potential GDP of an economy is given by its **aggregate supply**. *Aggregate* means total. Aggregate supply is all goods and services produced by all the firms in the economy using the available labor, capital, and technology. **Labor** is the total number of hours workers are available to work in producing

potential GDP
the economy's long-term growth trend for real GDP, determined by the available supply of capital, labor, and technology. Real GDP fluctuates above and below potential GDP.

aggregate supply
the total value of all goods and services produced in the economy by the available supply of capital, labor, and technology (also called potential gross domestic product [GDP]).

labor
the number of hours people are available to work in producing goods and services.

Aggregate Supply and the Production Function

The theory of economic growth is based on the production function, which is a model of how labor, capital, and technology jointly determine the aggregate supply of output in the economy. In these photos, the workers at the automobile plant are part of the economy's **labor** (left), the tools that the workers are using to assemble the cars are the economy's **capital** (middle), and computer programming skills are part of the economy's **technology** (right), which raises the value of output for a given amount of labor and capital.

capital
the factories, improvements to cultivated land, machinery and other tools, equipment, and structures used to produce goods and services.

technology
anything that raises the amount of output that can be produced with a given amount of labor and capital.

production function
the relationship that describes output as a function of labor, capital, and technology.

real GDP. **Capital** is the total number of factories, cultivated plots of land, machines, computers, and other tools available for the workers to use to produce real GDP. **Technology** is all the available know-how—from organizational schemes to improved telecommunications to better computer programming skills—that workers and firms can use when they produce real GDP. Labor, capital, and technology jointly determine aggregate supply.

The Production Function
We can summarize the relationship between the three determinants and the aggregate supply of real GDP as

$$\text{Real GDP} = F \text{ (labor, capital, technology)}$$

which we say in words as "real GDP is a function, F, of labor, capital, and technology." The function F means that some general relationship exists between these variables. For this relationship, we assume that higher capital, higher labor, and higher technology all mean higher real GDP; and lower capital, lower labor, and lower technology all mean less real GDP. We call this relationship the **production function** because it tells us how much production (real GDP) of goods and services can be obtained from a certain amount of labor, capital, and technology inputs. A higher long-term economic growth rate for the economy requires a higher growth rate for one or more of these three determinants. A lower long-term economic growth rate may be due to a slower growth rate for one or more of these three determinants.

The production function applies to the entire economy, but we also have production functions for individual firms in the economy. For example, consider the production of cars. The car factory and the machines in the factory are the capital. The workers who work in the factory are the labor. The assembly-line production method is the technology. The cars coming out of the factory are the output. The production function for the economy as a whole has real GDP as output, not just cars, and all available labor, capital, and technology as inputs, not just those producing cars.

Government Policy and Economic Growth

Most governments have been interested in finding ways to increase economic growth. Economic policies that aim to increase long-term economic growth are sometimes called *supply-side policies* because they concentrate on increasing the growth of potential GDP, which is the aggregate supply of the economy.

Fiscal Policy
Our preview of growth theory already tells us that policies to increase growth should focus on increasing the available supply of labor, capital, and technology. The growth rate of capital depends on how much businesses invest in new capital each year. The amount that businesses choose to invest depends in part on the incentives they have to invest. We will see that the incentive to invest depends on the amount of taxing, spending, and borrowing by government. Hence, government policy can affect the incentive to invest and thereby stimulate long-term economic growth. Government policy concerning taxing, spending, and borrowing is called *fiscal policy*.

Labor supply also depends on incentives. In the case of labor, it is the incentive for firms to hire workers, for people to work harder or longer, for workers who are not in the labor force to come into the labor force, or for people to retire later in life. Again, government policy toward taxing, spending, and borrowing affects these incentives.

Finally, technology growth also can be affected by government policy if the government gives incentives for researchers to invent new technologies or provides funds for education so that workers can improve their skills and know-how.

ECONOMICS *IN ACTION*

The Economic Impact of Japan's Triple Shock

Just as September 11, 2001, is a date seared into the American psyche, March 11, 2011, will be a date that Japan will never forget. On that day, Japan was hit by an earthquake, which in turn unleashed a devastating tsunami that decimated several coastal areas, which in turn created all the problems at the Fukushima nuclear power plant that left people across Japan and Asia worried about a nuclear accident second in severity only to Chernobyl. In the days and months following March 11, people throughout Japan tried to assess the human toll of the events of that fateful day. Macroeconomists were given the task of calculating the economic impact of the events of March 11 for the Japanese economy. As the economist Paul Krugman, who is a regular columnist for the *New York Times,* said in his op-ed column a few days after the September 11 attacks on the United States, "It seems almost in bad taste to talk about dollars and cents after an act of mass murder. Nonetheless, we must ask about the economic aftershocks from Tuesday's horror." Macroeconomic theory can help us understand the long- and short-term economic impact of tragedies caused by man or by nature.

In the case of the Japanese earthquake, the most obvious short-term costs were the destruction of life and property in the areas hit by the tsunami; the lost productivity that resulted from the relocation of so many people from the areas surrounding the nuclear power plant; the destruction of factories, equipment, and infrastructure in the affected areas; and the disruption caused to many multinational firms doing business in Tokyo when their foreign workers left Japan following the advice of their home governments. The preliminary estimates suggested that the direct effects would be small, relatively speaking, because the worst affected regions from the tsunami produced only about 2 or 3 percent of Japanese GDP. In fact, some analysts predicted that GDP may even rise in Japan in the short run because of the reconstruction work needed in the affected areas.

The theory of economic fluctuations (presented in Chapters 11 and 12) tells us that spending shocks have feedback effects that aggravate the initial direct effects. In the case of Japan, the disruption to the economy may be substantially greater than the destruction of property and cleanup costs would indicate. Because many Japanese companies are important providers of parts for manufacturing around the world, global trade in cars and electronics markets could be affected by the destruction of key manufacturing plants in the affected areas. Increasing worries about the safety of nuclear energy could slow down the pace of reactor construction and put upward pressure on other sources of energy like coal. The Japanese government, already struggling under high levels of debt, would have to borrow more money to invest in reconstruction efforts.

© Robert Gilhooly/Alamy

About 10 days after the tragedy, Justin Lin, the chief economist of the World Bank, predicted a loss of between 2.5 percent to 4 percent of Japanese GDP, a figure that would be in the $150–$200 billion range. These estimates could be worse if the nuclear plant crisis did not get resolved satisfactorily, and they could be reduced by good policy making by the Japanese government and the Japanese central bank. The theory of economic fluctuations states that when faced with an economic shock that reduces spending, policy makers can respond by putting into place specific measures designed not only to stop the fall in spending, but also to restore both confidence and spending by consumers and firms. Already the Japanese government has announced plans to rebuild the affected areas, and the Japanese central bank announced a substantial increase in the money supply to ensure that banks and financial markets functioned smoothly during the aftermath.

The theory of economic growth tells us that the long-term growth of an economy depends on its ability to produce goods and services, which in turn depends on the economy's stocks of labor, capital, and technology. Although the destruction of life and property in Japan was substantial on a human scale, the destruction was small relative to the size of the entire Japanese population and the entire Japanese capital stock. The long-term impacts to the Japanese economy may be more significant, however, particularly if the tragedy reduced the nation's ability to use nuclear power plants for energy production. As a relatively densely populated, manufacturing-intensive economy with relatively few resources for generating power, the Japanese economy and the Japanese people desperately need access to nuclear power. Whether such power plants can be safely constructed and operated on an earthquake-prone island with millions of people living in proximity to those power plants is the key question that only time can answer.

Monetary Policy Keeping inflation low and stable is another part of government policy to stimulate long-term economic growth. We will see that the government has an important role to play in determining the inflation rate, especially over the long term, because the inflation rate in the long term depends on the growth rate of the money supply, which can be controlled by the government. Government policy concerning the money supply and the control of inflation is called *monetary policy*. The government institution assigned to conduct monetary policy is the central bank. In the United States, the central bank is the Federal Reserve System.

Why should low and stable inflation be part of an economic growth policy? An examination of inflation and economic growth in a number of countries indicates that inflation is negatively correlated with long-term economic growth. The reason for this negative correlation over the long term may be that inflation raises uncertainty and thereby reduces incentives to invest in capital or improve technology. The theory of economic growth tells us that lower capital growth and lower technological growth reduce economic growth.

The Theory of Economic Fluctuations

Our review of the performance of the economy showed some of the hardships that come from economic fluctuations, especially recessions and unemployment. Can government economic policy improve economic performance by reducing the size of these fluctuations? To answer these questions, we need a theory to interpret the facts of economic fluctuations.

Aggregate Demand and Economic Fluctuations
The theory of economic fluctuations emphasizes fluctuations in the demand for goods and services as the reason for the ups and downs in the economy. Because the focus is on the sum of the demand for all goods and services in the economy—not just the demand for peanuts or bicycles—we use the term *aggregate demand*. More precisely, **aggregate demand** is the sum of the demands from the four groups that contribute to demand in the whole economy: consumers, business firms, government, and foreigners.

> **aggregate demand**
> the total demand for goods and services by consumers, businesses, government, and foreigners.

According to this theory, the declines in real GDP below potential GDP during recessions are caused by declines in aggregate demand, and the increases in real GDP above potential GDP are caused by increases in aggregate demand. For example, the decrease in real GDP in the recession that began in 2008 was driven by lower spending by consumers who were affected adversely by the collapse in the housing market, the dramatic declines in the stock market, and the rapidly rising gasoline prices in the early part of 2008, and by firms that were affected adversely by the lack of access to credit following the turmoil in the banking sector.

Thus, a key assumption of the theory of economic fluctuations is that real GDP fluctuates around potential GDP. Why is this a good assumption? How do we know that the fluctuations in the economy are not due solely to fluctuations in potential GDP, that is, in the economy's aggregate supply? The rationale for the assumption is that most of the determinants of potential GDP usually change rather smoothly. Clearly, population grows relatively smoothly. We do not have a sudden drop in the U.S. population every few years, nor do huge numbers of people migrate from the United States during recessions. The same is true with factories and equipment in the economy. Unless we have a major war at home, we do not suddenly lose equipment or factories in the economy on a massive scale. Even such disasters as the 1994 earthquake in California, the terrorist attacks of September 11, 2001, or the deadly Gulf Coast hurricanes of 2005 (Katrina and Rita), although devastating for affected individuals, take only a tiny fraction out of the potential GDP of the entire U.S. economy. Finally, technological know-how does not suddenly decline; we do not suddenly forget how to produce things. The steady upward movement of potential GDP thus represents gradual accumulations—growth of population, growth of capital, and growth of technology. Although many economists place greater emphasis on the role of aggregate demand in short-run economic fluctuations than on fluctuations in potential GDP, it is too extreme to insist that there are absolutely no fluctuations in potential GDP.

Macroeconomic Policy and Economic Fluctuations

Macroeconomic policy can have substantial effects on economic fluctuations. Many governments would like to implement policies that either help to avoid recessions or minimize the impact of recessions when they do occur. Monetary policy makers typically prefer to implement policies that minimize fluctuations in GDP. Policies used to influence economic fluctuations are sometimes called *demand-side policies* because they aim to influence aggregate demand in the economy.

Fiscal Policy On the fiscal side, the primary tools that the government uses to influence demand are government purchases and taxes. If the economy shows signs of entering a recession, the government can try to increase demand by implementing tax cuts or spending increases. Examples include the stimulus packages of 2008 and 2009, which were enacted to help bring the economy out of recession. These policies often are intended to mitigate the negative impact on aggregate demand of other factors, such as a fall in consumer or investor confidence or a fall in exports because of a recession in one of the countries among major U.S. trading partners. Economists debate the effectiveness of such policies.

Monetary Policy To keep inflation low and stable, the Federal Reserve also will implement policies that influence demand. The primary tools that the Federal Reserve uses to influence demand are changes in interest rates and the money supply. If signs indicate that inflation is on the rise because aggregate demand is growing faster than potential output, the Federal Reserve may step in and raise interest rates, which will slow down spending, as you will soon learn in Chapter 7. In addition to keeping inflation low and stable, the Federal Reserve also is concerned with minimizing the adverse impact of recessions. When the economy goes into recession, the Federal Reserve will try to increase demand by lowering interest rates. Again, 2008 was a good example of this type of behavior, as the Federal Reserve lowered interest rates dramatically—going from an interest rate of 4.25 percent to an interest rate of zero percent.

REVIEW

- Economic growth theory concentrates on explaining the long-term upward path of the economy.

- Economic growth depends on three factors: the growth of capital, labor, and technology.

- Government policy can influence long-term economic growth by affecting these three factors. To raise long-term economic growth, government policies can provide incentives for investment in capital, for research and development of new technologies, for education, and for increased labor supply. A monetary policy of low and stable inflation can have a positive effect on economic growth.

- Economic fluctuations theory assumes that fluctuations in GDP are due to fluctuations in aggregate demand.

- Monetary policy and fiscal policy can reduce the fluctuations in real GDP. Finding good policies is a major task of macroeconomics.

CONCLUSION

This chapter started with a brief review of the facts of economic growth and fluctuations. The key facts are that economic growth provides impressive gains in the well-being of individuals over the long term, that economic growth is temporarily interrupted by recessions, that unemployment rises in recessions, and that inflation and interest rates rise before recessions and decline during and after recessions. These are the facts on which macroeconomic theory is based and about which macroeconomic policy is concerned. Remembering these facts helps you understand theory and make judgments about government policy.

After showing how we measure real GDP and inflation in Chapter 6, we will look at explanations for the facts and proposals for macroeconomic policies in Chapters 7 through 15.

KEY POINTS

1. Macroeconomics is concerned with economic growth and fluctuations in the whole economy.
2. China, India, the Republic of Korea, and many other economies have grown dramatically in recent years.
3. Economic growth occurs because of increases in labor, capital, and technological know-how.
4. Economic policies that provide incentives to increase capital and resources devoted to improving technology can increase growth rates.
5. Economic fluctuations consist of recessions (when economic activity falls) followed by recoveries (when economic activity picks up again).
6. Recent recessions have been much less severe than the Great Depression of the 1930s, when real GDP fell by more than 30 percent.
7. Inflation and interest rates rise before recession and fall in the aftermath.
8. The most popular theory of economic fluctuations is that they occur because of fluctuations in aggregate demand.
9. Macroeconomic policies include monetary and fiscal policies that are aimed at keeping business cycles small and inflation low.
10. Economic growth theory and economic fluctuations theory combine to form macroeconomic theory, which explains why the economy grows and fluctuates over time.

KEY TERMS

aggregate demand, 122
aggregate supply, 119
capital, 120
compound growth, 471
economic fluctuations, 108
economic growth, 108
expansion, 111
inflation rate, 115
interest rate, 116
labor, 119
nominal interest rate, 118

peak, 111
potential GDP, 119
production function, 120
real gross domestic product (real GDP), 108
real interest rate, 118
recession, 111
recovery, 111
technology, 120
trough, 111
unemployment rate, 114

QUESTIONS FOR REVIEW

1. What are the two broad branches of macroeconomic theory?
2. What is the difference between economic growth and economic fluctuations?
3. What is the difference between a recession period and a recovery period?
4. How do unemployment, inflation, and interest rates behave during recessions?
5. How many recessions have there been since the Great Depression?
6. How do the two most recent recessions compare to past recessions?
7. What is potential gross domestic product (GDP)?
8. What is aggregate demand?
9. What are the primary determinants of economic growth?
10. Describe how monetary policy and fiscal policy can affect economic growth and economic fluctuations.

PROBLEMS

1. The following graph shows a period of back-to-back recessions that occurred in the United States in the 1980s. Show the peaks, recessions, troughs, and recovery phases of this unusual period.

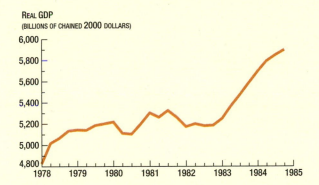

REAL GDP
(BILLIONS OF CHAINED 2000 DOLLARS)

2. What determines potential GDP? What factors could cause the growth rate of potential GDP to slow down? What economic policies can the government use to affect potential GDP?

3. Suppose the U.S. economy is at the trough of a business cycle.
   a. What is the relationship between real and potential GDP?
   b. Is it likely that real GDP will stay in this position relative to potential GDP for a long period of time (say, 10 years)? Explain briefly.

4. Suppose people start retiring at a later age because of improved medical technology.
   a. How will this affect the economy's potential GDP?
   b. Why might the government want to encourage later retirement?

5. Using the data from Canada and Britain shown in the following table, plot the unemployment rate on the vertical axis. How do these unemployment rates compare with the U.S. rate shown in Figure 5-5?

Rate of Unemployment (percent)

Year	Canada	Britain
1990	7.7	6.9
1991	9.8	8.8
1992	10.6	10.1
1993	10.8	10.5
1994	9.5	9.6
1995	8.6	8.7
1996	8.8	8.1
1997	8.4	7.0
1998	7.7	6.3
1999	7.0	6.0
2000	6.1	5.5

6. Compare Figure 5-5, showing unemployment, with Figure 5-8, showing the inflation rate for the same period in the United States. Describe how unemployment and inflation are correlated over the long term and over the short term.

7. Suppose that you had savings deposited in an account at an interest rate of 5 percent and your father told you that he earned 10 percent interest 20 years ago.
   a. Which of you was getting the better return?
   b. How would your answer change if you were told that the inflation rate in the United States was 12 percent 20 years ago and is 3 percent now?

8. Suppose you have $1,000, which you can put in two different types of accounts at a bank. One account pays interest of 8 percent per year; the other pays interest of 2 percent per year plus the rate of inflation.

a. Calculate the real return you will receive after one year if the inflation rate is 5 percent.

b. Which account will you choose if you expect the rate of inflation to be 8 percent? Why?

Compound growth explains why small differences in the annual economic growth rate make such huge differences in real gross domestic product (GDP) over time. Here we explain this compounding effect, show how to compute growth rates, and discuss alternative ways to plot growing variables over time.

How Compound Growth Works

Compound growth works just like compound interest on a savings account. Compound interest is defined as the "interest on the interest" you earned in earlier periods. For example, suppose you have a savings account in a bank that pays 6 percent per year in interest. That is, if you put $100 in the account, then after one year you will get $100 times 0.06, or $6 in interest. If you leave the original $100 plus the $6—that is, $106—in the bank for a second year, then at the end of the second year you will get $106 times 0.06, or $6.36 in interest. The $0.36 is the "interest on the interest," that is, $6 times 0.06.

At the end of the second year, you have $100 + $6 + $6.36 = $112.36. If you leave that in the bank for a third year, you will get $6.74 in interest, of which $0.74 is "interest on the interest" earned in the first two years. Note how the "interest on the interest" rises from $0.36 in the second year to $0.74 in the third year. Following the same calculations, the "interest on the interest" in the fourth year would be $1.15. After 13 years, the "interest on the interest" is greater than the $6 interest on the original $100. As a result of this compound interest, the size of your account grows rapidly. At the end of 20 years, it is $320.71; after 40 years, your $100 has grown to $1,028.57.

Compound growth applies the idea of compound interest to the economy. Consider, for example, a country in which real GDP is $100 billion and the growth rate is 6 percent per year. After one year, real GDP would increase by $100 billion times 0.06, or by $6 billion. Real GDP rises from $100 billion to $106 billion. In the second year, real GDP increases by $106 billion times 0.06, or by $6.36 billion. Real GDP rises from $106 billion to $112.36 billion. Table A.5-1

Table A.5-1

Example of Compound Growth

	Real GDP (billions)		Real GDP (billions)
Year 0	$100.0	Year 20	$ 320.7
Year 1	$106.0	Year 30	$ 574.3
Year 2	$112.4	Year 40	$ 1,028.6
Year 3	$119.1	Year 50	$ 1,842.0
Year 4	$126.2	Year 60	$ 3,298.8
Year 5	$133.3	Year 70	$ 5,907.6
Year 10	$179.1		

shows how, continuing this way, real GDP grows, rounding to the nearest $0.1 billion.

Thus, in one person's lifetime, real GDP would increase by about 60 times.

Exponential Effects

A convenient way to compute these changes is to multiply the initial level by 1.06 year after year. For example, the level of real GDP after one year is $100 billion times 0.06 plus $100 billion, or $100 billion times 1.06. After two years, it is $106 billion times 1.06, or $100 billion times $(1.06)^2$. Thus, for n years, we have

$$\text{(Initial level)} \times (1.06)^n = \text{level at end of } n \text{ years}$$

where the initial level could be $100 in a bank, the $100 billion level of real GDP, or anything else. For example, real GDP at the end of 70 years in Table A.5-1 is $100 billion times $(1.06)^n$ = $100 billion times 59.076 = $5,907.6 billion, with $n = 70$. Here the growth rate (or the interest rate) is 6 percent. In general, we have:

$$\text{(Initial level)} \times (1 + g)^n = \text{level at end of } n \text{ years}$$

where g is the annual growth rate, stated as a decimal; that is, 6 percent is 0.06. If you have a hand calculator with a key that does y^x, it is fairly easy to make these calculations, and if you try it you will see the power of compound growth. The term *exponential growth* is sometimes used because the number of years (n) appears as an exponent in the above expression.

When economists refer to average annual growth over time, they include this compounding effect. The growth rate is found by solving for g. That is, the growth rate, stated as a decimal fraction, between some initial level and a level n years later is given by

$$g = \left(\frac{\text{level at end of } n \text{ years}}{\text{initial level}}\right)^{1/n} - 1$$

For example, the average annual growth rate from year zero to year 20 in the table is

$$g = \left(\frac{320.7}{100}\right)^{1/20} - 1$$
$$= (1.06) - 1$$
$$= 0.06$$

or 6 percent. Again, if your calculator has a key for y^x, you can make these calculations easily.

To get the annual growth rate for one year, you simply divide the level in the second year by the level in the first year and subtract one to get the growth rate.

Rule of 72

You also can find how long it takes something to increase by a certain percentage. For example, to calculate how many years it takes something that grows at rate g to double, you solve $(1 + g)^n = 2$ for n. The answer is approximately $n = 0.72/g$. In other words, if you divide 72 by the growth rate in percent, you get the number of years it takes to double the amount. This is called the *rule of 72*. If your bank account pays 6 percent interest, it will double in 12 years.

Plotting Growing Variables

You may have noticed that some time-series charts have vertical scales that shrink as the economic variable being plotted gets bigger. Look, for example, at the scale in Figures 5-1 and 5-4 for real GDP. Financial analysts

Figure A.5-1

Comparison of Two Different Scales: Regular versus Ratio

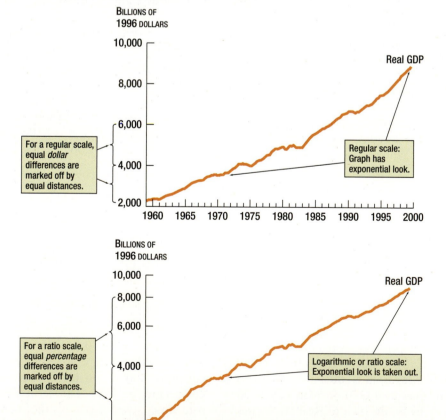

and economists use this type of scale, which is called a *ratio scale* (or sometimes a proportional scale or logarithmic scale), to present variables that grow over time. The purpose of a ratio scale is to make equal percentage changes in the variable have the same vertical distance.

If you plot a variable that grows at a constant rate on a ratio scale, it looks like a straight line, even though it would look as if it were exploding on a standard scale. To show what ratio scales do, real GDP for the past 40 years is plotted in Figure A.5-1 using a regular scale and a ratio scale. Note how the fluctuations in real GDP in the 1960s look smaller on a regular scale compared with the ratio scale, and how the ratio scale tends to take out the exponential look. This difference is one reason to look carefully at the scales of graphs. (The reason that ratio scales sometimes are called logarithmic scales is that plotting the logarithm of a variable is the same as plotting the variable on a ratio scale.)

KEY POINTS

1. Compound growth is similar to compound interest. Rather than applying the interest rate to the interest from earlier periods, one applies the growth rate to the growth from the previous period.
2. With compound growth, seemingly small differences in growth rates result in huge differences in real GDP.
3. When you see a diagram with the scale shrunk for the higher values, it is a logarithmic or ratio scale.
4. A ratio or logarithmic scale is more useful than a regular scale when a variable is growing over time.

KEY TERMS AND DEFINITIONS

compound growth: applying the growth rate to growth from the previous period; similar to compound interest.

QUESTIONS FOR REVIEW

1. What is the rule of 72?
2. What is a ratio scale?

PROBLEMS

1. Suppose that the annual rate of growth of gross domestic product (GDP) per capita is 2 percent. How much will real GDP per capita increase in 10 years? How much will it increase in 50 years? Answer the same questions for a growth rate of 1 percent and for a growth rate of 4 percent.
2. According to recent data, China's per capita GDP is growing at about 9 percent a year. How long will it take for China's per capita GDP to double? If China can grow at 9 percent a year for the next 16 years and at 6 percent a year for the following 24 years, how large will China's per capita GDP in 40 years be relative to its per capita GDP today?
3. Plot the data for the example economy in the table in this appendix on a graph at 10-year intervals from year 20 to year 60 on a regular scale. Now create a new graph with a ratio scale by first marking off 300, 600, 1,200, 2,400, and 4,800 at equal distances on the vertical axis. Plot the same data on this graph. Compare the two graphs.

6 Measuring the Production, Income, and Spending of Nations

Imagine, if you will, that you were one of a small group of subsistence farmers eking out a living on a small island where the only thing that grew was coconut trees. If you were asked to calculate the production of this economy, all you would have to do was count the number of coconuts that the people living on the island plucked from the trees. But suppose the island also had an abundance of banana plants. Then calculating the production of the economy would require that you count both coconuts and bananas. Understanding whether production had increased over time would be a challenge—would the 500 pounds of bananas and 1,000 coconuts produced this year be considered an increase in production compared with last year's crop of 750 pounds of bananas and 750 coconuts? You would have to figure out how to compare bananas to coconuts—perhaps not as impossible a task as comparing apples to oranges, but a challenge nonetheless.

Now imagine, if you will, being asked to calculate the production of the economy of the United States.

You would have to add up not just apples and oranges, but millions of other goods. You also would have to think about how to measure the output of doctors, lawyers, teachers, and economists. Some of the goods being produced in the economy would be shipped to other countries. Other goods that people were buying had been shipped to the United States from abroad. Some goods, like bicycle tires, were being used as inputs into the production of other goods, like bicycles. Measuring the production of a nation is indeed a challenge.

In the United States, that challenge has been assigned to the Bureau of Economic Analysis (BEA), an agency of the U.S. Department of Commerce. The BEA states its mission as being to promote "a better understanding of the U.S. economy by providing the most timely, relevant, and accurate economic accounts data in an objective and cost-effective manner." Every quarter, the BEA releases the official government statistics on real gross domestic product (GDP), the most widely used measure of production in the U.S. economy. BEA releases are eagerly awaited throughout the economy. Top officials at the White House (including the president) find these data so important that they ensure that they get them the night before they are released to the public. Because measuring the economy in a timely and accurate manner is essential for people in financial markets and other lines of business, bond and stock traders in New York, Tokyo, London, and everywhere else keep their eyes glued to their computer terminals when a new government statistic measuring the course of the economy is about to be released. By buying or selling quickly in response to the new information, they can make millions or avoid losing millions.

To economists, measurement of the economy is interesting in its own right, involving clever solutions to intriguing problems. One of the first Nobel Prizes in economics was given to Simon Kuznets for solving some of these measurement problems. As economics students, you cannot help but learn a little about how the economy works when you study how to measure it, just as geology students cannot help but learn a little about earthquakes when they study how the Richter scale measures them. Understanding economic problems, designing possible policy solutions to these problems, and understanding whether the policy solutions did in fact work all require access to reliable data.

The purpose of this chapter is not to train you to work in the BEA. Instead, the goals are to give you a general understanding of what measures the BEA uses, to help you better grasp the strengths and weaknesses of these measures, and to make you more familiar with some key macroeconomic relationships that exist in the economy.

Measuring GDP

To use GDP as a measure of production, we must be precise about *what* is included in production, *where* production takes place, and *when* production takes place.

A Precise Definition of GDP

GDP is a measure of the value of all the newly produced goods and services in a country during some period of time. Let us dissect this definition to determine what is in GDP and what is not, as well as where and when GDP is produced.

- *What?* Both *goods*—such as automobiles and new houses—and *services*—such as bus rides or a college education—are included in GDP. However, only *newly produced* goods and services are included. A ten-year-old baby carriage that is being sold at a garage sale is not included in this year's GDP; it was included in GDP ten years ago, when it was produced.
- *Where?* Only goods and services produced *within the borders* of a country are included in that country's GDP. Goods produced by Americans working in another country are not part of U.S. GDP; they are part of the other country's GDP. Goods and services produced by foreigners working in the United States are part of U.S. GDP.

- *When?* Only goods and services produced during some specified period of time are included in GDP. We always need to specify the period during which we are measuring GDP. For example, GDP in 2010 is the production during 2010. GDP for the third quarter of 2010 is the production between July 1 and September 30 of 2010. Rounded off to the nearest billion, GDP, or total production, was $14,660 billion in the United States in 2010. Rounded off to the nearest trillion, GDP was $15 trillion. That is an average production of about $40 billion worth of goods and services a day for each of the 365 days of the year.

Prices Determine the Importance of Goods and Services in GDP

GDP is a single number, but it measures the production of many different things, from apples to oranges, from car insurance to life insurance, from audio CDs to DVDs. How can we add up such different products? Is a CD more important than a DVD? Does a coconut count more toward GDP than a banana does?

Each good is given a weight when we compute GDP, and that weight is its *price*. If the price of a DVD is greater than that of a CD, then the DVD will count more in GDP. To see this, imagine that production consists entirely of CDs and DVDs. If a DVD costs $15 and a CD costs $10, then producing three DVDs will add $45 to GDP, and producing five CDs will add $50 to GDP. Thus, producing three DVDs plus five CDs adds $95 to GDP, as shown in Table 6-1.

Although this method of weighting by price might not appeal to you personally— you might like CDs more than DVDs—it is hard to imagine anything more workable. In a market system, prices tend to reflect the cost and value of the goods and services produced. One of the great problems of measuring GDP in centrally planned economies such as the former Soviet Union was that the price of goods was set by the government; thus, the weight given each item may have had little to do with either its cost or its value to individuals. Without market prices, measuring GDP in the Soviet Union was difficult.

Intermediate Goods versus Final Goods When measuring GDP, it is important not to count the same item more than once. Consider bicycle tires. When you buy a $150 bicycle, the tires are considered part of the bicycle. Suppose the tires are worth $20. It would be a mistake to count both the $20 value of the tires and the $150 value of the bicycle, for a total value of $170. That would count the tires twice, which is called *double counting*. When a tire is part of a new bicycle, it is an example of an **intermediate good**. Intermediate goods are part of **final goods**, which by definition are goods that undergo no further processing—in this case, the bicycle. *To avoid double counting, we never count intermediate goods; only final goods are part of the GDP.* If in a few years you buy a new $25 bicycle tire, then the tire will be a final good.

intermediate good
a good that undergoes further processing before it is sold to consumers.

final good
a new good that undergoes no further processing before it is sold to consumers.

Table 6-1

Adding Up Unlike Products: CDs and DVDs

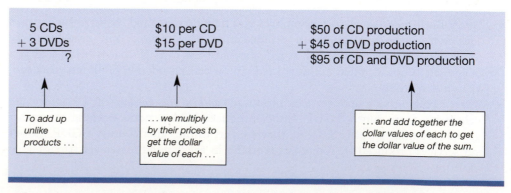

5 CDs	$10 per CD	$50 of CD production
+ 3 DVDs	$15 per DVD	+ $45 of DVD production
?		$95 of CD and DVD production

To add up unlike products ...   ... we multiply by their prices to get the dollar value of each ...   ... and add together the dollar values of each to get the dollar value of the sum.

ECONOMICS *IN ACTION*

Distinguishing between Stocks and Flows

The economist's distinction between stocks and flows can be illustrated by picturing water flowing into and out of a lake—for example, the Colorado River flowing into and out of Lake Powell behind Glen Canyon Dam. When more water flows in than flows out, the stock of water in Lake Powell rises. Similarly, a positive flow of inventory investment raises the stock of inventory at a firm. And just as the stock of water falls when more water flows out than flows in, negative inventory investment lowers the stock of inventory.

The distinction between stocks and flows is useful in other economic applications as well. The factories in America on December 31, 2010, are a stock. The number of factories built during 2010 is a flow. The funds in your checking account are a stock. The deposit you made last week is a flow.

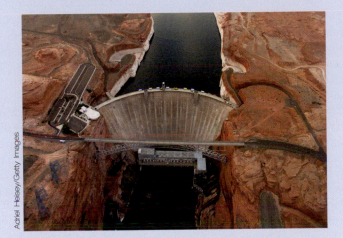
Adriel Heisey/Getty Images

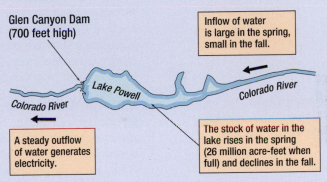

Glen Canyon Dam (700 feet high)

Inflow of water is large in the spring, small in the fall.

Lake Powell

Colorado River

Colorado River

A steady outflow of water generates electricity.

The stock of water in the lake rises in the spring (26 million acre-feet when full) and declines in the fall.

Stocks versus Flows The distinction between *stocks* and *flows* is one of the most useful concepts in economics, and it is especially important in understanding GDP. GDP is a measure of the flow of new goods and services—it measures the value of all the newly produced goods and services in the economy. GDP is not a measure of the stock of goods and services in the economy—it does not tell us the value of all the goods and services that exist in the economy.

For example, the number of new cars produced in the United States during a given time period is a flow measure, while the number of cars in the United States is a stock measure. Therefore, only the former will count toward GDP. Similarly, U.S. GDP for 2010 will count the value of new houses built in the United States in 2010 (a flow measure), but it will not count the value of all homes in the United States (a stock measure).

The economist's distinction between stocks and flows can be illustrated by picturing water flowing into a bathtub from a tap. The water coming from the tap is a flow measure, while the water that is in the bathtub is a stock measure. GDP in essence is measuring the flow from the tap (the new goods and services added to the economy) and not the water in the tub (all the goods and services that already exist).

Three Ways to Measure GDP Economists measure GDP in three ways. All three give the same answer, but they refer to conceptually different activities in the economy and provide different ways to think about GDP. All three are reported in the national income and product accounts, the official U.S. government tabulation of GDP put together by economists and statisticians at the U.S. Department of Commerce's BEA.

The first way measures the total amount that people *spend* on goods and services made in the United States. This is the *spending* approach. The second way measures the total income that is earned by all the workers and businesses that produce American goods and services. This is the *income* approach. In this approach, your income is a measure of what you produce. The third way measures the total of all the goods and services as they are *produced*, or as they are shipped out of the factory. This is the *production* approach. Note that each of the approaches considers the whole economy, and thus we frequently refer to them as aggregate spending, aggregate income, and aggregate production, in which case the word *aggregate* means total. Let us consider each of the three approaches in turn.

The Spending Approach

Typically, total spending in the economy is divided into four components: *consumption, investment, government purchases*, and *net exports*, which equal exports minus imports. Each of the four components corresponds closely to one of four groups into which the economy is divided: consumers, businesses, governments, and foreigners. Before considering each component, look at Table 6-2, which shows how the $14,660 billion of GDP in the United States in 2010 was divided into the four categories.

consumption
purchases of final goods and services by individuals.

Consumption   The first component, **consumption**, is purchases of final goods and services by individuals. Government statisticians, who collect the data in most countries, survey department stores, discount stores, car dealers, and other sellers to see how much consumers purchase each year ($10,349 billion in 2010, as given in Table 6-2). They count anything purchased by consumers as consumption. Consumption does not include spending by business or government. Consumer purchases may be big-ticket items, such as a new convertible, an operation to remove a cancerous tumor, a new stereo, a weekend vacation, or college tuition, or smaller-ticket items, such as an oil change, a medical checkup, a bus ride, or a driver's education class. Consumption accounts for a whopping 71 percent of GDP in the United States (see Figure 6-1).

investment
purchases of final goods by firms plus purchases of newly produced residences by households.

Investment   The second component, **investment**, consists of purchases of final goods by business firms and of newly produced residences by households. When a business such as a pizza delivery firm buys a new car, economists consider that purchase as part of investment rather than as consumption. The firm uses the car to make deliveries, which contributes to its production of delivered pizzas. Included in investment are all the new machines, new factories, and other tools used to produce goods and services. Purchases of intermediate goods that go directly into a manufactured product—such as a tire on a bicycle—are not counted as investment. These items are part of the finished

Table 6-2

Components of Spending in 2010 (billions of dollars)

Gross domestic product (GDP)	$14,660
Consumption	10,349
Investment	1,827
Government purchases	3,000
Net exports	–516

Source: U.S. Department of Commerce, Bureau of Economic Analysis.

product—the bicycle, in this case—purchased by consumers. We do not want to count such items twice.

The new machines, factories, and other tools that are part of investment in any year are sometimes called *business fixed investment;* this amounted to $1,415 billion in 2010. Government statisticians include two other items as part of investment: inventory investment and residential investment.

Inventory investment is defined as the change in *inventories,* which are the goods on store shelves, on showroom floors, or in warehouses that have not yet been sold or assembled into a final form for sale. For example, cars on the lot of a car dealer are part of inventories. When inventory investment is positive, then inventories are rising. When inventory investment is negative, then inventories are falling.

For example, if a car dealer had an inventory of 50 cars on December 31, 2009, got 35 new cars shipped from the factory during 2010, and sold 20 cars to consumers during the year, then the dealer's inventory will be 65 cars on December 31, 2010. The contribution of the car dealer to inventory investment for the year is positive 15 cars because the dealer's inventory rose from 50 cars to 65 cars.

If, instead, the dealer had an inventory of 50 cars on December 31, 2009, got 35 new cars shipped from the factory during 2010, and sold 45 cars to consumers during the year, then the dealer's inventory will be 40 cars on December 31, 2010. The contribution of the car dealer to inventory investment for the year is negative 10 cars because the dealer's inventory fell from 50 cars to 40 cars.

Inventory investment is included as a spending item when we compute GDP because we want an accurate measure of production. Consider the first car example again. If we looked only at consumption, then we would have concluded that only 20 cars were produced in the economy, even though 35 cars actually were produced. We need to add the 15 cars of inventory investment to the 20 cars of consumption to get an accurate measure of production.

What happens when consumers eventually purchase the cars that the dealer has in inventory? Suppose, in 2011, consumers buy 25 of the cars that were in the dealer's inventory. For 2011, consumption will rise by 25 cars, whereas inventory investment will be negative 25 cars, reflecting the fall in the dealer's inventory. Adding 25 cars of consumption to negative 25 cars of inventory investment gives zero cars added to overall GDP in 2011, which is just what we want because none of these cars were produced in 2011; we already had counted them as production for 2010.

In 2010, inventory investment throughout the economy was $72 billion. Some firms reduced inventories, but others added a greater amount. Inventory investment tends to fluctuate up and down and therefore plays a big role in the business cycle.

The other part of investment that is not business fixed investment is *residential investment,* the purchase of new houses and apartment buildings. About $340 billion worth of housing and apartments were constructed in 2010. This was a dramatic decline from $757 billion in 2006. Although much of this was purchased by consumers rather than businesses, it is included in investment because it produces services: shelter and, in some cases, a place to relax and enjoy life.

Combining the three parts of investment, we find that investment was $1,827 billion in 2010: $1,415 billion of business fixed investment, $340 billion of residential investment, and $72 billion of inventory investment. Investment was about 12 percent of GDP in 2010 (see Figure 6-2).

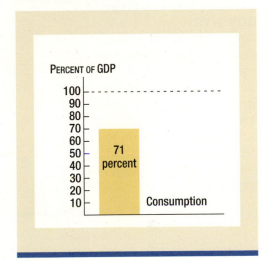

Figure 6-1

Consumption as a Share of GDP
Consumption was 71 percent of GDP in the United States in 2010.

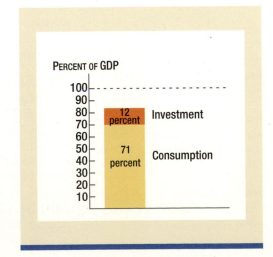

Figure 6-2

Investment and Consumption as a Share of GDP in 2010
Investment is a much smaller share of GDP than is consumption.

Figure 6-3

Government Purchases, Investment, and Consumption as a Share of GDP in 2010

Government purchases as a share of GDP are greater than investment but less than consumption. When the stacked bar goes above the 100 percent line, negative net exports result (a trade deficit), as shown here. If the stacked bar stops below the 100 percent line, a trade surplus results.

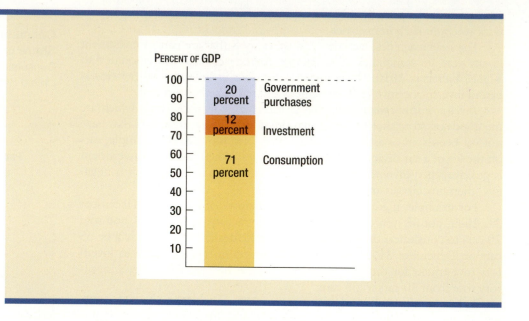

Note the special way the term *investment* is used in this discussion. To an economist, investment means the purchase of new factories, houses, or equipment. In everyday language, however, investment usually refers to an individual's putting away some funds for the future, perhaps in the stock market, such as "I'll invest in the stock market." Be sure to stay aware of this distinction.

government purchases
purchases by federal, state, and local governments of new goods and services.

Government Purchases The third component of spending, **government purchases**, is spending by federal, state, and local governments on new goods and services. Most U.S. government purchases are for the military. At the state and local levels, education, roads, and police dominate government purchases. Government purchases of goods and services were equal to $3,000 billion in 2010 (see Figure 6-3).

Not all government outlays are included in government purchases. A government welfare payment or retirement payment to an individual is not a purchase of a good or service; it is a *transfer payment* of income from the government to an individual. Transfer payments do not represent new production of anything, unlike the purchase of a weapon or a new road or a new building. Because GDP measures the production of new goods and services, government outlays on transfer payments like social security, unemployment compensation, and welfare payments are excluded. Only purchases are counted because only these items represent something produced. Government *outlays* are purchases plus transfer payments.

net exports
the value of exports minus the value of imports.

exports
the total value of the goods and services that people in one country sell to people in other countries.

imports
the total value of the goods and services that people in one country buy from people in other countries.

trade balance
the value of exports minus the value of imports.

Net Exports The final spending component is **net exports**, the difference between exports and imports. American **exports** are what Americans sell to foreigners, whether pharmaceuticals, computers, grain, or a vacation in Florida. American **imports** are what Americans buy from foreigners, whether cars, plasma televisions, shirts, or a vacation in France. Net exports are defined as exports minus imports. Net exports are a measure of how much more we sell to foreigners than we buy from foreigners. Another term for net exports is the **trade balance**. If net exports are positive, we have a trade surplus. If net exports are negative, we have a trade deficit. By these calculations, the United States had a trade deficit in 2010: $1,838 billion in exports and $2,354 billion in imports. Hence, net exports were a negative $516 billion, and appear in Table 6-2 as −$516 billion.

Net exports are added in when computing GDP by the spending approach for two reasons. First, we included foreign goods in consumption and investment spending. For example, an imported Toyota purchased at a car dealer in the United States is included in consumption even though it is not produced in the United States. To measure what is produced in the United States, that Toyota must be deducted. Thus, imports must be subtracted to get a measure of total production in the economy. The second reason is that the exports that Americans sell abroad are produced in the United States, but they are not counted in consumption or investment or government purchases in the United States. Thus, exports need to be added in to get a measure of production. Because, by definition, net exports are exports minus imports, adding net exports to spending is the same as adding in exports and subtracting out imports. Adding net exports to total spending kills two birds with one stone.

In 2010, the United States imported more than it exported, so the sum of consumption plus investment plus government purchases overstated what was produced in America. The sum of these three items exceeds GDP, as shown in Figure 6-3. In other words, GDP was $516 billion less than the sum of consumption plus investment plus government purchases.

Algebraic Summary The notion that we can measure production by adding up consumption, investment, government purchases, and net exports is important enough to herald with some algebra.

Let the symbol C stand for consumption, I for investment, G for government spending, and X for net exports. Let Y stand for GDP because we use G for government purchases. We will use these symbols many times again. The idea that production equals spending can then be written as

$$Y = C + I + G + X$$

> This is a key equation stating that production equals spending.

This equation states, using algebraic symbols, that production, Y, equals spending: consumption, C, plus investment, I, plus government purchases, G, plus net exports, X (meaning exports minus imports). In 2010, the values of these items (in billions of dollars) were as follows:

$$14{,}660 = 10{,}349 + 1{,}827 + 3{,}000 + (-516)$$

This simple algebraic relationship plays a key role in later chapters.

The Income Approach

The income that people earn producing GDP in a country provides another measure of GDP. To see why, first consider a simple example of a single business firm.

Suppose you start a wedding planning business. Your production and sales of wedding planning services in your first year is $50,000; this is the amount you are paid in total by 50 people for the $1,000 service. To produce these services, you pay a catering consultant and a florist consultant $20,000 each, or a total of $40,000, which is your total cost. Your profits are defined as the difference between sales and costs, or $50,000 − $40,000 = $10,000. Now, if you add the total amount of income earned in the production of your wedding planning service—the amount earned by the two consultants plus the profits you earn—you get $20,000 + $20,000 + $10,000. This sum of incomes is exactly equal to $50,000, which is the same as the amount produced. Thus, by adding up the income of the people who produce the output of the firm, you get a measure of the output. The same idea is true for the country as a whole, which consists of many such businesses and workers.

Table 6-3

Aggregate Income and GDP in 2010 (billions of dollars)

Aggregate income	
Labor income (wages, salaries, fringe benefits)	$ 7,991
Capital income (profits, interest, rents)	3,719
Depreciation	1,869
Taxes, subsidies, and transfers	1,118
Net income of foreigners	−188
Statistical discrepancy	151
Equals GDP	14,660

Source: U.S. Department of Commerce.

To show how this works, we look at each of the income items in Table 6-3. We first describe each of these items and then show that when we add the items up, we get GDP.

labor income
the sum of wages, salaries, and fringe benefits paid to workers.

Labor Income Economists classify wages, salaries, and fringe benefits paid to workers as **labor income**, or payments to people for their labor. *Wages* refers to payments to workers paid by the hour; *salaries* refers to payments to workers paid by the month or year; and *fringe benefits* refers to retirement, health, and other benefits paid by firms on behalf of workers. As shown in Table 6-3, labor income was $7,991 billion in 2010.

capital income
the sum of profits, rental payments, and interest payments.

Capital Income Economists classify profits, rental payments, and interest payments as **capital income**. *Profits* include the profits of large corporations like General Motors or Exxon and also the income of small businesses and farms. The royalties that an independent screenwriter receives from selling a movie script also are part of profits. *Rental payments* are income to persons who own buildings and rent them out. The rents they receive from their tenants are rental payments. *Interest payments* are income received from lending to business firms. Interest payments are included in capital income because they represent part of the income generated by the firms' production. Because many individuals pay interest (on mortgages, car loans, and so on) as well as receive interest (on deposits at a bank and so on), interest payments are defined as the difference between receipts and payments. Table 6-3 shows that capital income was $3,719 billion in 2010, much less than labor income. Capital income is about 45 percent of labor income.

depreciation
the decrease in an asset's value over time; for capital, it is the amount by which physical capital wears out over a given period of time. (Ch. 16)

Depreciation **Depreciation** is the amount by which factories and machines wear out each year. A remarkably large part of the investment that is part of GDP each year goes to replace worn-out factories and machines. Businesses need to replace depreciated equipment with investment in new equipment just to maintain productive capacity—the number of factories and machines available for use.

The difference between investment, the purchases of final goods by firms, and depreciation is called *net investment,* a measure of how much investment is new each year after depreciation is subtracted. Net investment was −$42 billion ($1,827 billion − $1,869 billion) in 2010. This implies that the stock of physical capital actually fell in the United States in 2010. More machines wore out than were added to the economy. Sometimes the $1,827 billion of investment, including depreciation, is called *gross investment.* The reason for the term *gross* in gross domestic product is that it includes gross investment, not just net investment.

When profits and the other parts of capital income are reported to government statisticians, depreciation has been subtracted out. But depreciation must be included as part of GDP because the new equipment that replaces old equipment must be produced by someone. Thus, when we use the income approach, it is necessary to add in depreciation if we are to have a measure of GDP.

Taxes, Subsidies, and Transfers When you buy a good, you often will pay a sales tax in addition to the price of the good; sales taxes are collected by businesses and sent directly to the government, either local, state, or federal. For example, the price of gasoline at the pump includes a tax that people who buy gasoline pay as part of the price and that the gasoline station sends to the government. When we tabulate total production by adding up the value of what people spend, we use the prices that businesses charge for a specific good—such as gasoline. That price includes the sales tax that is sent to the government. When we tabulate production by adding up income of consumers and profits of firms, however, the sales tax is not included in firms' profits. Thus, capital income does not include the sales taxes paid by businesses to the government. But those taxes are part of the income generated in producing GDP; the income happens to go to the government. We therefore must add such taxes to capital and labor income. Similarly, some subsidies from the government to firms are included in profits but do not represent income generated in producing GDP. Subsidies need to be subtracted. Similarly, transfer payments, which are payments between parties that do not involve goods or services being exchanged (for example, a charitable contribution to a museum by a corporation), also need to be removed from calculations because they do not represent income generated in producing GDP. Transfers and subsidies are considerably smaller in magnitude than taxes.

Net Income of Foreigners Foreigners produce part of the GDP in the United States. Their income, however, is not included in labor income or capital income. For example, the salary of a Canadian hockey player who plays for the Pittsburgh Penguins and keeps his official residence as Canada would not be included in U.S. labor income. But that income represents payment for services produced in the United States and so is part of U.S. GDP. We must add such income payments to foreigners for production in the United States because that production is part of GDP. Moreover, some of the U.S. labor and capital income is earned producing GDP in other countries, and to get a measure of income generated in producing U.S. GDP, we must subtract that amount. For example, the salary of a U.S. baseball player who plays for the Toronto Blue Jays and keeps his official residence as the United States represents payment for services produced in Canada and so is not part of U.S. GDP. We must exclude such income payments for production in other countries. To account for both of these effects, we must add *net* income earned by foreigners in the United States—that is, the income earned by foreigners in the United States less what Americans earned abroad—to get GDP. [In 2010, Americans earned more abroad ($706 billion) than foreigners earned in the United States ($518 billion); hence, in 2010, *net* income of foreigners was –$188 billion, as shown in Table 6-3.]

Table 6-3 shows the effects of adding up these five items. The sum is close but not quite equal to GDP. The discrepancy reflects errors made in collecting data on income or spending. This discrepancy has a formal name: the *statistical discrepancy*. In percentage terms the amount is small, less than 1 percent of GDP, considering the different ways the data on income and spending are collected. If we add in the statistical discrepancy, then we have a measure of *aggregate income* that equals GDP. From now on we can use the same symbol (Y) to refer to GDP and to aggregate income, because GDP and aggregate income amount to the same thing.

The circular flow diagram in Figure 6-4 illustrates the link between aggregate income and aggregate spending. People earn income from producing goods and services, and they spend this income (Y) to buy goods and services (C, I, G, and X).

The Production Approach

The third measure of GDP adds up the production of each firm or industry in the economy. To make this method work, we must avoid the "double counting" problem discussed earlier. For example, if you try to compute GDP by adding new automobiles to new steel to new tires, you will count the steel and the tires that go into producing the new automobiles twice. Thus, when we measure GDP by production, it is necessary to count only the **value added** by each manufacturer. Value added is the value of a firm's production less the value of the intermediate goods used in production. In other words, it is the value the firm adds to the intermediate inputs to get the final output. An automobile manufacturer buys steel, tires, and other inputs and adds value by assembling the car. When we measure GDP by production, we count only the value added at each level of production. Figure 6-5 shows how adding up the value added for each firm involved in producing a cup of espresso in the economy will automatically avoid double counting and give a measure of the final value of the cup of espresso when it is purchased at a coffeehouse or cafe. The same is true for the economy as a whole.

value added
the value of a firm's production minus the value of the intermediate goods used in production.

Figure 6-4

The Circular Flow of Income and Expenditure

This figure illustrates how aggregate expenditures equal aggregate income. Starting at the bottom right part of the figure, consumption (C) is joined by government purchases (G), investment (I), and net exports (X) to sum to aggregate expenditures (C + I + G + X) on the left. At the top of the figure, this aggregate spending is received by firms that produce the goods, and they pay out aggregate income (Y) to households in the form of wages and salaries as well as rents, interest, and profits. The government takes in taxes and makes transfer payments and government purchases.

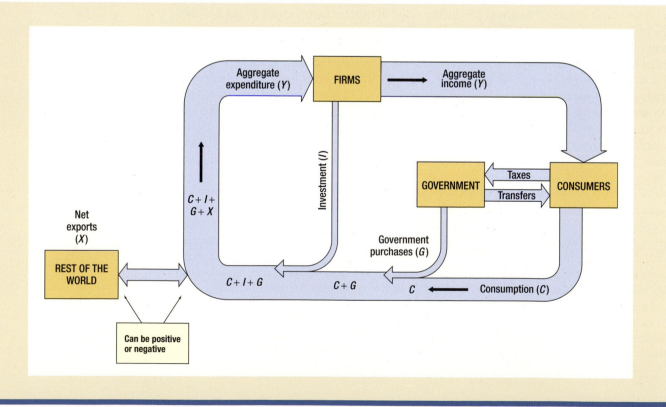

Figure 6-5

Value Added in Coffee: From Beans to Espresso

By adding up the value added at each stage of production, from coffee bean growing to espresso making, we get a measure of the value of a cup of espresso. Double counting is avoided. Using the same procedure for the whole economy permits us to compute GDP by adding up production.

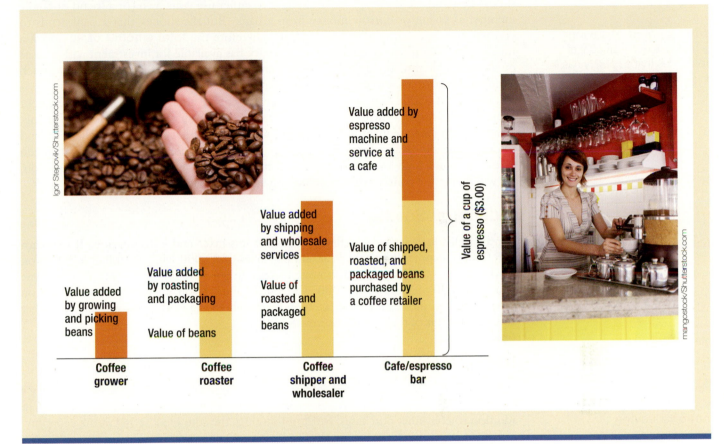

REVIEW

- GDP is a measure of all the goods and services newly produced in the economy during some period of time. GDP is a flow measure—how many new goods and services are being produced in the economy. It is not a stock measure—how many goods and services exist in the economy.

- GDP can be measured in three ways: by adding up all the spending in the economy, by adding up all the income in the economy, and by adding up all the production in the economy. All three give the same answer.

- Spending in the economy can be placed in one of four categories—consumption,

- investment, government purchases, and net exports.

- The sum of labor income; capital income; depreciation; taxes, subsidies, and transfers; and net income paid to foreigners gives another way to measure GDP.

- GDP also can be measured by adding up production, but with this method we must be careful not to double count. By adding up only the value added by each firm or industry, we automatically prevent double counting. Value added is the difference between a firm's sales and its payments for intermediate inputs to production.

Saving

Another important macroeconomic measure is the total amount of saving undertaken by an economy. Investment and saving have an important symbiotic relationship. To see why this is, consider what would happen if you wanted to build a factory that makes shoes. To build the factory, you would have to either use your own (or a friend or family member's) saving or borrow money from a bank. But the money that a bank lends to you will be some other individual's saving. Therefore the **total amount of saving** is a measure of the amount of resources the country has available for investment, either in its own country or abroad. Similarly, the total amount of investment depends on how much saving is available from that country and from other countries.

total amount of saving a measure of the amount of resources that a country has for investment, either in its own country or abroad.

Countries with a high level of saving have a greater ability to undertake investment projects than countries with a low level of saving. A country with a low level of saving, however, can increase investment if people and firms in other nations are willing to lend to or invest their own saving in that country. The U.S. economy in recent years has been able to sustain a high level of investment even when U.S. saving was low. In this section, we will define the concept of national saving and show how it is calculated.

Individual Saving

For an individual, saving is defined as income less taxes and consumption. If you earn $25,000 in income during the year and pay taxes of $5,000 while spending $18,000 on consumption—food, rent, and movies, for example—by definition, your saving for the year is $2,000 ($25,000 – $5,000 – $18,000). But if you instead spend $23,000 on food, rent, and movies for the year, then your saving is –$3,000; you will have to either take $3,000 out of the bank or borrow $3,000.

National Saving

For a country, saving is defined in a similar manner: by subtracting from a country's economy what is consumed. We subtract government purchases of goods and services in addition to consumer purchases. **National saving**, the sum of all saving in the economy, is defined as income less consumption and government purchases. That is,

national saving aggregate income minus consumption minus government purchases.

$$\text{National saving} = \text{income} - \text{consumption} - \text{government purchases}$$

Using the symbol S for national saving and the symbols already introduced for income (Y), consumption (C), and government purchases (G), we define national saving as follows:

Algebraic definition of national saving. →

$$S = Y - C - G$$

Using the numbers from Table 6-2, national saving in 2010 was $1,311 billion ($14,660 billion – $10,349 billion – $3,000 billion).

The major component of national saving is private saving: the sum of all savings by individuals in the economy. Some people save a lot, some do not save at all, and some are *dissaving*—that is, they have negative saving. For example, when people retire, they usually consume a lot more than their income—they are dissaving. When people are middle aged, their income is usually greater than their consumption—they are saving. Most young people either save very little or, if they are able to borrow, dissave. We define private savings using the symbol T for taxes, as follows:

$$\text{Private saving} = Y - C - T$$

A country, however, also has a government, and so we need to include government saving in our calculation of national saving. What do we mean by saving by the

REVIEW

- National saving is an important macroeconomic variable because it is a measure of the resources that a country has available for investment, either in its own economy or abroad.

- A country with a high level of national saving can have a high level of investment if it desires. A country with a low level of national saving can have a high level of investment only if people in other countries are willing to lend their savings to or invest them in the low-saving country.

- National saving is defined as income minus consumption minus government purchases. It can be decomposed into the sum of private saving and government saving.

- Private saving equals income minus consumption minus taxes. Government saving is the difference between government tax receipts and government expenditures, also known as the budget balance.

government? The difference between the government's receipts from taxes and the government's expenditures, the budget balance, is called government saving. When the balance is positive, a budget surplus results—that is, the government is saving. When the balance is negative, a budget deficit results—that is, the government is dissaving. Algebraically, we define government saving as follows:

$$\text{Government saving} = T - G$$

Combining private and government saving, we see that

$$\text{Private saving} + \text{government saving} = (Y - C - T) + (T - G) = (Y - C - G)$$
$$\text{Private saving} + \text{government saving} = \text{national saving}$$

Measuring Real GDP

Economists also are interested in assessing how the economy is changing over time. For example, they might want to know how rapidly the production of goods and services in India has grown over the last decade, and how that increase compares with the change in China's economy. However, the value of goods and services in an economy, as measured by GDP, is determined by both the quantity of goods and services produced and the price of these goods and services. Thus, an increase in the prices of all goods and services will make measured GDP grow, even if the amount of production in the economy does not increase.

Suppose, for example, that the prices of all goods in the economy double and that the number of items produced of every good remains the same. The dollar value of these items then will double even though physical production does not change. A $10,000 car will become a $20,000 car, a $10 CD will become a $20 CD, and so on. Thus, GDP will double as well. Clearly, GDP is not useful for comparing production at different dates when all prices increase. Although the example of doubling all prices is extreme, we do know from Chapter 5 that prices on the average tend to rise over time—a tendency that we have called inflation. Thus, when inflation exists, GDP becomes an unreliable measure of the changes in production over time.

Adjusting GDP for Inflation

Real GDP is a measure of production that corrects for inflation. To emphasize the difference between GDP and real GDP, we will use the term **nominal GDP** to refer to what previously has been defined as GDP.

real GDP
a measure of the value of all the goods and services newly produced in a country during some period of time, adjusted for changes in prices over time. (Ch. 5)

nominal GDP
gross domestic product without any correction for inflation; the same as GDP; the value of all the goods and services newly produced in a country during some period of time, usually a year.

Calculating Real GDP Growth To see how real GDP is calculated, consider an example. Suppose that total production consists entirely of the production of audio CDs and DVDs and that we want to compare total production in two different years: 2008 and 2009.

	2008		2009	
	Price	*Quantity*	*Price*	*Quantity*
DVDs	$15	1,000	$20	1,200
CDs	$10	2,000	$15	2,200

Notice that the number of DVDs produced increases by 20 percent and the number of CDs produced increases by 10 percent from 2008 to 2009. Notice also that the price of DVDs is greater than the price of CDs, but both increase between the two years because of inflation. Nominal GDP is equal to the dollar amount spent on CDs plus the dollar amount spent on DVDs, which is $35,000 in 2008 and $57,000 in 2009, a substantial 63 percent increase.

$$\text{Nominal GDP in 2008} = \$15 \times 1{,}000 + \$10 \times 2{,}000 = \$35{,}000$$
$$\text{Nominal GDP in 2009} = \$20 \times 1{,}200 + \$15 \times 2{,}200 = \$57{,}000$$

Clearly, nominal GDP is not a good measure of the increase in production: Nominal GDP increases by 63 percent, a much greater increase than the increase in either DVD production (20 percent) or CD production (10 percent). Thus, failing to correct for inflation gives a misleading estimate.

To calculate real GDP, we must use the *same* price for both years and, thereby, adjust for inflation. That is, the number of CDs and DVDs produced in the two years must be evaluated at the same prices. For example, production could be calculated in both years using 2008 prices. That is,

$$\text{Using 2008 prices, production in 2008} = \$15 \times 1{,}000 + \$10 \times 2{,}000 = \$35{,}000$$
$$\text{Using 2008 prices, production in 2009} = \$15 \times 1{,}200 + \$10 \times 2{,}200 = \$40{,}000$$

Keeping prices constant at 2008 levels, we see that the increase in production is from $35,000 in 2008 to $40,000 in 2009, an increase of 14.3 percent.

Production, however, also can be calculated in both years using 2009 prices. That is,

$$\text{Using 2009 prices, production in 2008} = \$20 \times 1{,}000 + \$15 \times 2{,}000 = \$50{,}000$$
$$\text{Using 2009 prices, production in 2009} = \$20 \times 1{,}200 + \$15 \times 2{,}200 = \$57{,}000$$

Keeping prices constant at 2009 levels, we see that the increase in production is from $50,000 in 2008 to $57,000 in 2009, an increase of 14.0 percent.

Observe that the percentage increase in production varies (14.3 percent versus 14 percent) depending on whether 2008 or 2009 prices are used. Such differences are inevitable, because we have no reason to prefer the prices in one year to those of another year when controlling for inflation. Economists arrive at a single percentage by simply *averaging* the two percentages.[1] In this example, they would conclude that the *increase in real GDP from 2008 to 2009 is 14.15 percent*, the average of 14.3 percent and 14 percent.

This 14.15 percent increase in real GDP is much lower than the 63 percent increase in nominal GDP and much closer to the actual increase in the number of CDs and tapes produced. By adjusting for inflation in this way, real GDP gives a better picture of the increase in actual production in the economy.

---

[1] A "geometric" average is used. The geometric average of two numbers is the square root of the product of the two numbers.

A Year-to-Year Chain This example shows how the growth rate of real GDP between the two years 2008 and 2009 is calculated in the case of two goods. The same approach is used for any other two years and more than two goods. To correct for inflation across more than two years, economists simply do a series of these two-year corrections and then "chain" them together. Each year is a link in the chain. For example, if the growth rate from 2007 to 2008 was 12.15 percent, then chaining this together with the 14.15 percent from 2008 to 2009 would imply an average annual growth rate of 13.15 percent for the two years from 2007 to 2009. That is,

2007   2008   2009

12.15   14.15

13.15

> Observe that 12.15 percent and 14.15 percent are chained together to get a 13.15 percent average for two years.

By chaining other years together, link by link, the chain can be made as long as we want.

Obtaining the Values of Real GDP To obtain real GDP in any one year, we start with a *base year* and then use the growth rates to compute GDP in another year. The base year is a year in which real GDP is equal to nominal GDP because GDP is valued using that year's price. Currently, 2005 is the base year for government statistical calculations of GDP in the United States. Thus, real GDP in 2005 and nominal GDP in 2005 are the same: $12,638 billion.

To get real GDP in other years, economists start with the base year and use the real GDP growth rates to find GDP in any other year. Consider 2006. The growth rate of real GDP in 2006—calculated using the methods just described for the entire economy—was 2.7 percent. Thus, real GDP in 2006 was $12,976 billion, or 2.7 percent greater than $12,638 billion. The $12,976 billion is 2006 real GDP measured in 2005 dollars. To emphasize that this number is calculated by chaining years together with growth rates, government statisticians say that real GDP is measured in "chained 2005 dollars."

Real GDP versus Nominal GDP over Time Figure 6-6 compares real and nominal GDP from 1990 to 2010. Observe that for the 2005 base year, real GDP and nominal GDP are equal. However, by 2010, real GDP had reached about $13.2 trillion, whereas nominal GDP was at $14.7 trillion. Thus, just as in the example, real GDP increased less than nominal GDP. For the years prior to 2005, real GDP is more than nominal GDP because 2005 prices were higher than prices in earlier years. From Figure 6-6 we can see that nominal GDP would give a misleading picture of the U.S. economy.

The GDP Deflator

Nominal GDP grows faster than real GDP because of inflation. The greater the difference between nominal GDP growth and real GDP growth, the greater the rate of inflation. In the case of deflation, with prices falling, nominal GDP would increase less than real GDP. Hence, a by-product of computing real GDP is a measure of the rate of inflation.

More precisely, if we divide nominal GDP by real GDP, we get the **GDP deflator**, a measure of the **price level**, which is the level of all the prices of the items in real GDP. That is,

$$\text{GDP deflator} = \frac{\text{nominal GDP}}{\text{real GDP}}$$

GDP deflator
nominal GDP divided by real GDP; it measures the level of prices of goods and services included in real GDP relative to a given base year.

price level
the average level of prices in the economy.

Figure 6-6

Real GDP versus Nominal GDP

Real GDP increases less than nominal GDP because real GDP takes out the effect of rising prices. The chart shows that for the 2005 base year, real GDP and nominal GDP are equal. Nominal GDP is below real GDP in earlier years because prices were generally lower before 2005.

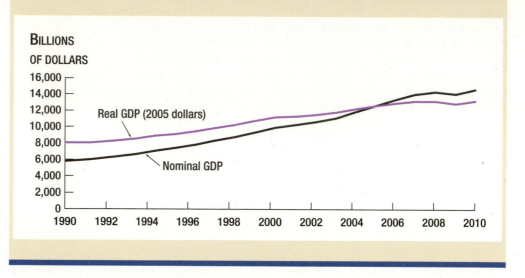

Here the GDP deflator is defined so that its value in the base year, such as 2005, is 1.00. (Sometimes it is scaled to equal 100 in the base year by multiplying by 100.)

The reason for the term *deflator* is that to get real GDP, we can deflate nominal GDP by dividing it by the GDP deflator. That is,

$$\text{Real GDP} = \frac{\text{nominal GDP}}{\text{GDP deflator}}$$

The percentage change in the GDP deflator from one year to the next is a measure of the rate of inflation.

Alternative Inflation Measures

The percentage change in the GDP deflator is not the most widely used measure of inflation. A much more frequently cited measure of inflation is based on the percentage change in the **consumer price index (CPI)**, which is the price of a fixed collection—a "market basket"—of consumer goods and services in a given year divided by the price of the same collection in some base year. For example, if the market basket consists of one DVD and two CDs, then the CPI for 2009 compared with the base year 2008 in the previous example would be

consumer price index (CPI)
a price index equivalent that calculates current price of a fixed market basket of consumer goods and services relative to a base year.

$$\frac{\$20 \times 1 + \$15 \times 2}{\$15 \times 1 + \$10 \times 2} = \frac{50}{35} = 1.43$$

The CPI inflation rate is the percent change in the CPI; it measures how fast the prices of the items in the basket increase. What are the differences between inflation measured using the CPI and inflation measured using the GDP deflator? The first difference is that the GDP deflator is measuring the price level of all domestically produced goods and services. This includes goods that affect the day-to-day life of consumers, such as the price of milk, the price of orange juice, and the cost of airplane tickets, but it also includes goods that individuals never purchase directly, such as the price of heavy machinery and the price of truck engines. Thus the CPI, as its name suggests, may be a more relevant measure of the price level that consumers care about.

The second difference is that CPI measures the price of a fixed collection of goods and services—the price of the basket—whereas the goods and services that make up

GDP, and hence are measured by the GDP deflator, change from year to year. The use of a fixed collection of goods and services in the CPI is one of the reasons economists think the CPI overstates inflation. When the price of goods rises, the quantity demanded should decline; when the price falls, the quantity demanded should rise. Thus, by not allowing the quantities to change when the price changes, the CPI puts too much weight on items with rising prices and too little weight on items with declining prices. The result is an overstatement of inflation; in other words, by assuming that people buy no less of the goods and services that have increased in price and buy no more of the goods and services that have decreased in price, the CPI tends to indicate that prices have gone up by more than they really have. During the 1990s, a group of economists appointed by the U.S. Senate and chaired by Michael Boskin of Stanford University found that the government, by adjusting expenditures according to this overstated CPI, was spending billions of dollars more than it would with a correct CPI. Hence, getting the economic statistics right makes a big difference.

The third difference between the CPI and the GDP deflator is that the CPI market basket can include goods and services that are produced in other countries, whereas the GDP deflator, by definition, will measure the price of domestically produced goods and services. In countries where imported goods lack good domestic substitutes, inflation measured using the CPI may be a better measure of the difficulties that both people and businesses in the economy face.

Figure 6-7 shows how measures of inflation using the GDP deflator and the CPI compare. The general inflation movements are similar, but the CPI is more volatile. The GDP deflator and the CPI each have strengths and weaknesses relative to the other. So you should think of them as alternative ways of measuring price levels and inflation rates, rather than as competing measurements.

Yet another measure of inflation is the producer price index (PPI), which measures the prices of raw materials and intermediate goods as well as the prices of final goods sold by producers. Prices of raw materials—oil, wheat, and copper—sometimes are watched carefully because they give early warning signs of increases in inflation.

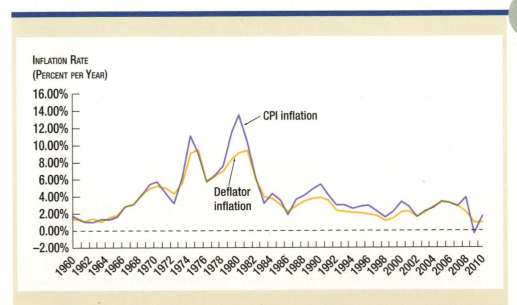

Figure 6-7

Comparison of Measures of Inflation

Measuring inflation with either the CPI or the GDP deflator shows the rise in inflation in the 1960s and 1970s and the lower inflation in the 1980s and 1990s. The CPI is more volatile: It bounces around more. (The inflation rate is based on yearly percent changes in the stated variable.)

REVIEW

- Nominal GDP changes when either the quantity of goods and services changes or the prices of those goods and services change. Therefore the change in nominal GDP is not a good measure of how the physical amount of production in the economy is changing over time.

- Economists use real GDP when they want to compare production over time. Real GDP corrects nominal GDP for inflation by measuring the production of goods and services in the dollars of a given base year, such as 2005.

- The GDP deflator is a measure of the price level in the economy. It is defined as the ratio of nominal GDP to real GDP. The percentage change in the GDP deflator from year to year is a measure of the inflation rate.

- The CPI is the most widely used measure of the price level in the economy. It is defined as the price of a representative market basket of goods and services, relative to the price of that basket in a base year. The percentage change in the CPI from year to year is the most widely used measure of the inflation rate.

- Some important differences exist between the CPI and the GDP deflator. Each has strengths and weaknesses compared with the other. You should think of them as alternative ways of measuring price levels and inflation rates.

Shortcomings of the GDP Measure

Although nominal GDP is the best measure of overall production that we have, it is deficient in several ways. You need to understand what these limitations are, so that you can make informed judgments about what is really happening in the economy. Nominal GDP has three main types of limitations: (1) revisions to GDP can change the assessment of the economy; (2) some types of production are omitted from GDP; and (3) the production of goods and services is only part of what affects the quality of life. When you compare two countries, the one with a higher level of GDP is not necessarily better off than the one with a lower level of GDP.

Revisions to GDP

Government statisticians obtain data on GDP from surveys of stores and businesses, and even from income tax data from the Internal Revenue Service. Not all of these data are collected quickly. Data on sales at stores and large firms come in within a month; however, data on exports and imports take several months. Some income tax data are reported only once a year. Information about small firms comes in even more slowly.

For this reason, the statistics on GDP frequently are revised as new data come in. For those who use the GDP data to make decisions, either in business or in government, faulty data on GDP, which are apparent only when the data are revised, can lead to mistakes. Revisions of GDP are inevitable and occur in all countries. These revisions can be quite large in magnitude. For example, in January 2006, the first estimate for GDP for the fourth quarter of 2005 was given as $12.735 trillion. In March 2006, the "final revision" of that number was given as $12.766 trillion, a difference of almost $30 billion.

Omissions from GDP

Given the description of how GDP is calculated, you will hardly be surprised to hear that production that does not occur in a formal market is difficult for government statisticians to measure. Examples include work done in the home and illegal commerce. The other principal difficulty in calculating GDP is how to deal with quality improvements in goods. Both of these problems are explained in more detail.

Home Work and Production Much of the production that people do at home—making dinner or a sweater, changing the car oil or a baby's diapers, cutting the grass or the kids' hair—is productive activity, but it is not included in GDP because the transactions are not recorded in the markets in which statisticians measure spending. Such production would be included in GDP if people hired and paid someone else to do any of these things. So if you look after your young siblings after school while your parents are at work, that typically will not count toward GDP, whereas if your parents were to take your siblings to a day-care center and pay for child-care services, that would count toward GDP. Some home production is included in GDP. If you run a mail order or telemarketing business out of your home and pay taxes on your income, for example, then this production likely will be counted in GDP.

Leisure Activity Much leisure activity is not included in GDP even though it may be enjoyable. Going to the beach or hiking in the mountains more often and working less might be something you decide to do as your income increases. If people start taking Friday afternoons off, GDP will go down, but the level of well-being may increase. The consumption of leisure is omitted from GDP unless it involves a purchase in the market, such as a ticket to a movie or a ballgame.

The Underground Economy A large amount of production is not counted in GDP because it is purposely hidden from the view of the government. Illegal activity—growing marijuana in the California coastal range, selling pharmaceuticals not yet approved by the Food and Drug Administration—is excluded from GDP because no one wants to report this activity to the government. People who get cash payments—perhaps in the form of tips at hotels or restaurants, or babysitting money from a neighbor—may not report this income, perhaps to avoid taxes, and thus it also is not counted. If people do not report interest on a loan to a friend or relative, this, too, is omitted from GDP.

The sum of all the missing items is referred to as the *underground economy*. Estimates of the size of the underground economy are understandably uncertain. They range from about 10 percent of GDP in the United States to about 25 percent in Italy to more than 40 percent in Peru.

The underground economy makes GDP a less useful measure of the size of an economy, and we should be aware of this fact when we use GDP. But the underground economy does not render GDP useless. It is unlikely that the underground economy grows much more or much less rapidly than the rest of the economy. Changes in laws can increase or decrease the incentives to produce outside the legal market economy, but these changes are unlikely to be large enough to affect the estimated growth rates of GDP by much.

Quality Improvements Our measure of GDP sometimes misses improvements in the quality of goods and services. For example, a $1,000 notebook computer purchased in 2010 may be of substantially better quality than a $2,000 notebook computer purchased in 2005. So the price of the notebook computer not only has fallen by 50 percent, but in fact the quality-adjusted price also has fallen by even more. Government statisticians, especially in industrial countries like the United States, have developed sophisticated techniques to measure the quality-adjusted price change of a good accurately. These techniques, however, do not always work perfectly, especially when the improvements are in hard-to-measure attributes. So, for example, the government statisticians can look at the amount of memory, the speed of the processor, and the storage capacity of the hard drive to gauge how much the quality of the notebook computer has improved; however, they may not be able to gauge as effectively the quality improvements that make a new model car more comfortable and better able to absorb shocks than the old model.

ECONOMICS *IN ACTION*

Measuring the Quality of Life Across Nations

By now, you are familiar with the idea that real GDP is not the only measure of a nation's well-being: Other factors, including the health of the country's people, the quality of its environment, peace, and security, are important determinants. Can we come up with an alternative measure of well-being that encompasses a broader range of indicators than just real GDP? How closely would such an indicator track real GDP—in other words, would the richest countries in the world also turn out to be the countries that have the best health, education, environmental, and stability outcomes?

The *Human Development Index (HDI)* calculated by the United Nations is one of the most significant attempts to measure the overall quality of life by examining a variety of indicators.

According to the *Human Development Report,* the HDI score covers three areas: living a long and healthy life, being educated, and having a decent material standard of living. Although the HDI is a broader measure than GDP, it does not cover a lot of areas. The most prominent of these, according to the report, are respect for human rights, inequality, and democracy. Recognizing these limitations, let's take a look at what the rankings look like. The five countries with the highest HDI scores are Norway, Iceland, Australia, Ireland, and Sweden. The five countries with the lowest HDIs are Niger, Sierra Leone, Mali, Burkina Faso, and Guinea Bissau.

An excerpt from the *Human Development Report* for a select group of countries is given below.

Notice that countries like Norway and the United States have both very high levels of real GDP per capita and high HDI scores. These countries are not just materially rich; they have also been able to use these resources to improve health and education outcomes for their citizens. At the other extreme is Niger—a desperately poor country that suffers from abysmally low levels of education and health, factors that are related to the overall lack of financial resources. The real insights of the HDI do not lie with these extremes, though. The interesting cases are countries like Cuba, China, and Sri Lanka, which have been able to achieve impressive life expectancy and literacy levels despite being substantially poorer than Norway and the United States.

If these are the overachievers, then there are also the underachievers, countries like Swaziland and Equatorial Guinea. Even though the people of Swaziland enjoy almost a third more GDP per capita than the people of Sri Lanka do, their life expectancy is only 31.3 years. Swaziland is a country that has been hard hit by the AIDS pandemic, and material wealth can do little to improve the lives of its people at this point given the spread of the disease. Another interesting case is Equatorial Guinea, which, despite having a GDP per capita that is three times China's, also suffers from low levels of life expectancy and education. The wealth of Equatorial Guinea comes from oil drilling. Clearly, that wealth has not made its way into the hands of the population at large— Equatorial Guinea seems to be a country where inequality is keeping the quality of life much lower than it needs to be.

The HDI is a useful reminder of the old adage that money does not always buy happiness. But also keep in mind that as far as countries go, it is a lot easier for a rich country to buy what happiness can be bought than it is for a poor country.

	HDI Score	Life Expectancy	Literacy	School Enrollment	Real GDP per Capita
Norway	0.965	79.6	>99%	100%	$38,500
United States	0.948	77.5	>99%	93%	$39,676
Cuba	0.826	77.6	>99%	80%	$ 5,700
China	0.768	71.9	91%	70%	$ 5,896
Sri Lanka	0.755	74.3	91%	63%	$ 4,390
Equatorial Guinea	0.653	42.8	87%	58%	$20,510
India	0.611	63.6	61%	62%	$ 3,139
Swaziland	0.500	31.3	80%	51%	$ 5,638
Niger	0.311	44.6	29%	21%	$ 711

Other Measures of Well-Being

Even if real GDP did include the underground economy and all the improvements in goods and services, it would not serve as the only measure of well-being. The well-being of an individual has many other important aspects, including, for example, a long and healthy life expectancy; a clean environment; and a small chance of war, crime, or the death of a child. The production of goods and services in a country can affect these other things, and indeed be affected by them, but it is not a measure of them.

Consider what has happened to some other measures of well-being as real GDP per capita has grown. Life expectancy in the United States has increased from about 69 years in the 1950s to 78 years in 2004. This compares with a life expectancy of only 47 years in the early part of the last century. Infant mortality also has declined, from about 26 infant deaths per 1,000 live births in the mid-1950s to 6.9 in 2000. In the early part of the twentieth century, infant mortality in the United States was 10 deaths for every 100 live births. The fraction of women who die in childbirth also has declined. So by some of these important measures, the quality of life has improved along with real GDP per capita.

But serious problems and room for gains still remain; as death rates from car accidents, heart disease, and stroke have decreased, death rates among young people from AIDS, suicide, and murder have been rising. Also of serious concern is the increasing percentage of children who live in poverty. Thus, the impressive gain in real GDP per capita has been correlated with both gains and losses in other measures of well-being.

A clean and safe environment is also a factor in the quality of life. But GDP itself does not provide an indication of whether pollution or many of the other measures of the quality of life are improving or getting worse. If a factory produces a lot of output while also putting out a considerable amount of airborne and waterborne pollutants, its production of goods is all that counts toward GDP. No mechanism is being used to subtract the damage to the environment.

REVIEW

- Real GDP per capita is not without its shortcomings as an indicator of well-being in a society. Certain items are omitted—home production, leisure, the underground economy, and some quality improvements.

- Other indicators of the quality of life, including vital statistics on mortality and the environment, can be affected by GDP per capita, but these indicators are conceptually distinct and independently useful.

CONCLUSION

In this chapter, we have shown how to measure the size of an economy in terms of its GDP. In the process, we have explained that income, spending, and production in a country are all equal and that GDP can be adjusted to make comparisons over time.

It is important to recall that aggregate income (or production or spending), the subject of our study, tells us much about the quality of life of the people in a country, but it does not tell us everything. As the economist-philosopher John Stuart Mill said in his *Principles of Political Economy,* first published in 1848: "All know that it is one thing to be rich, another to be enlightened, brave or humane ... those things, indeed, are all indirectly connected, and react upon one another."[2]

---

[2] John Stuart Mill, *Principles of Political Economy* (New York: Bookseller, 1965), pp. 1–2.

KEY POINTS

1. Gross domestic product (GDP), also known as nominal GDP, is the total production of new goods and services in an economy during a particular period.
2. GDP can be measured in three ways: by adding all spending on new goods and services in the economy, by adding all income earned in the domestic economy, and by adding all the value of goods and services produced in the economy.
3. The spending method of calculating GDP requires adding up expenditures on consumption goods, investment goods (machines, factories, housing, and inventories), government purchases, and net exports (exports–imports).
4. In the income method, GDP is calculated by adding labor income; capital income; depreciation; taxes, subsidies, and transfers; and net income of foreigners. Except for a small statistical discrepancy, the income approach gives us the same answer as the spending approach.
5. Value added is used to calculate GDP under the production method. Value added is defined as the difference between the value of the production sold and the cost of inputs to production.
6. Real GDP is a measure of production adjusted for inflation. It is the best overall measure of changes in the production of goods and services over time.
7. The GDP deflator, or the ratio of nominal GDP to real GDP, is a measure of the price level in the economy. The percentage change in the GDP deflator is a measure of inflation.
8. An alternative measure of the price level is the consumer price index (CPI), which is a measure of the price of a basket of representative goods and services in a particular year relative to the price of that basket in a base year. The change in the CPI is an alternative measure of inflation in the economy.
9. National saving is defined as income less consumption less government purchases. Countries that have a high level of national saving have more resources to use for investment in their own economy or abroad. Countries with low levels of national saving need other countries to be willing to lend to or invest their savings in those countries if they are to sustain high levels of investment.
10. GDP is not without its shortcomings. It does not include production in the underground economy or much work done in the home. And it is only one of many measures of well-being.

KEY TERMS

capital income, 138
consumer price index (CPI), 146
consumption, 134
depreciation, 138
exports, 136
final good, 132
GDP deflator, 145
government purchases, 136
imports, 136
intermediate good, 132

investment, 134
labor income, 138
national saving, 142
net exports, 136
nominal GDP, 143
price level, 145
real GDP, 143
total amount of saving, 142
trade balance, 136
value added, 140

QUESTIONS FOR REVIEW

1. Why do we add up total spending to compute GDP when GDP is supposed to be a measure of production?
2. Approximately what are the percentages of consumption, investment, government purchases, and net exports in GDP in the United States?
3. What is the significance of value added, and how does one measure it for a single item?
4. Why is the sum of all income equal to GDP?
5. Why is the purchase of a used car not included in GDP? Should it be?

6. Why do we add inventory investment to spending when computing GDP?
7. Why are increases in nominal GDP not a good measure of economic growth?
8. What is national saving?
9. Why does national saving equal the sum of private and government saving?
10. Why is the production of meals in the home not included in GDP? Should it be?

PROBLEMS

1. Determine whether each of the following would be included in GDP, and explain why or why not.
   a. You buy a used CD from a friend.
   b. You purchase a song from an online music provider like iTunes.
   c. You cook a romantic dinner for two on Valentine's Day.
   d. You buy a nice bottle of French wine to serve with dinner.
   e. You take your mom out to brunch on Mother's Day.
   f. The restaurant where you intend to go for brunch purchases strawberries, which it intends to serve at the brunch, from a local vendor.

2. Determine whether each of the following is consumption, investment, or neither. Explain your answer.
   a. A landscaping company buys a new four-wheel-drive vehicle to carry fertilizer and flowers.
   b. A doctor buys a new four-wheel-drive vehicle to use on vacation.
   c. A family puts a new kitchen in their house.
   d. The campus bookstore increases its inventory of textbooks.
   e. Your parents purchase their dream home, newly built to their specification by a local contractor.
   f. Your parents buy a vacation home from a friend who had owned that home for years.

3. A phenomenon of the twentieth-century U.S. economy was the replacement of home production by production purchased through markets.
   a. Give an example of a food item that was widely produced by family members in 1900 and that was widely purchased from businesses by 2000.
   b. Give an example of a clothing item that was widely produced by family members in 1900 and that was widely purchased from businesses by 2000.
   c. Give an example of a service that was widely produced by family members in 1900 and that was widely purchased from businesses by 2000.
   d. How does the replacement of home production with production purchased through markets affect real GDP? How does it affect the usefulness of comparisons of real GDP per capita at the end of the twentieth century with the same measure at the beginning of the twentieth century?
   e. The economies of some countries in the twenty-first century are more similar to the U.S. economy in 1900 than to the U.S. economy in 2000. How useful are comparisons between real GDP in the United States and in these economies?

4. Recognizing that both positive and negative effects may occur, how will GDP be affected by
   a. The legalization of drugs
   b. A law making the standard workweek 35 hours
   c. The replacement of checks by online banking
   d. A program granting legal status to previously undocumented immigrants working in the United States

5. Suppose the economy has only the following three goods:

Year	Good	Price	Quantity
2009	Ice cream cones	$2.50	1,000
	Hot dogs	$1.25	500
	Surfboards	$100.00	10
2010	Ice cream cones	$3.50	800
	Hot dogs	$2.25	400
	Surfboards	$100.00	14

   a. Calculate nominal GDP for 2009 and 2010.
   b. Calculate the percentage change in GDP from 2009 to 2010, first using 2009 prices and then using 2010 prices.

c. Calculate the percentage change in real GDP from 2009 to 2010, using your answers from part (b).

d. What is the GDP deflator for 2010 if it equals 1.0 in 2009?

6. Given the information in the following table for three consecutive years in the U.S. economy, calculate the missing data.

Year	Nominal GDP (in billions of U.S. dollars)	Real GDP (in billions of 2005 dollars)	GDP Deflator (2005 = 100)	Inflation (percent change in GDP deflator)	Real GDP per Capita (in 2005 dollars)	Population (in millions)
2005	12,623		100.0	3.3		297.4
2006		12,959		3.2		300.3
2007			106.2		43,542	303.3

7. Look at two scenarios, details of which are provided below, for monthly inventories and sales for a company producing cereal. In both scenarios, the company's sales are the same.

a. Calculate the inventory investment during each month and the resulting stock of inventory at the beginning of the following month for both scenarios.

b. Does maintaining constant production lead to greater or lesser fluctuations in the stock of inventory? Explain.

Scenario A

Month	Start-of-the-Month Inventory Stock	Production	Sales	Inventory Investment
Jan.	50	50	45	
Feb.		50	55	
Mar.		50	80	
Apr.		50	50	
May		50	40	

Scenario B

Month	Start-of-the-Month Inventory Stock	Production	Sales	Inventory Investment
Jan.	50	45	45	
Feb.		55	55	
Mar.		80	80	
Apr.		50	50	
May		40	40	

8. Suppose General Motors buys $50 million worth of tires from Goodyear in November of 2008 for use in its Chevrolet line of cars. Of these tires, $20 million are put into cars that are sold to consumers in December of 2008, and $10 million are put into cars that are produced in December but will not be sold to consumers until February of 2009. The remaining $20 million will be put into cars manufactured and sold in 2009. Describe how each of these tire-related transactions enters into inventory investment calculations in 2008 and 2009.

9. Use the following data for a South Dakota wheat farm.

Revenue	$1,000
Costs	
Wages and salaries	$ 700
Rent on land	$ 50
Rental fee for tractor	$ 100
Seed, fertilizer	$ 100
Pesticides, irrigation	$ 50

a. Calculate the value added by this farm.

b. Profits are revenue minus costs. Capital income consists of profits, rents, and interest. Show that value added equals capital income plus labor income paid by the farm.

c. Suppose that, because of flooding in Kansas, wheat prices increase suddenly and revenues rise to $1,100, but the prices of intermediate inputs do not change. What happens to value added and profits in this case?

10. Suppose the data in the following table describe the economic activity in a country for 2008. Given these data, calculate the following:

a. Inventory investment

b. Net exports

c. Gross domestic product
d. Statistical discrepancy
e. National saving

Verify that national saving equals investment plus net exports.

Component of Spending	Value (billions of dollars)
Consumption	$140
Business fixed and residential investment	$ 27
Inventory stock at the end of 2007	$ 10
Inventory stock at the end of 2008	$ 5
Depreciation	$ 12
Government outlays	$ 80
Government purchases	$ 65
Exports	$ 21
Imports	$ 17
Labor income	$126
Capital income	$ 70
Net income of foreigners	$ 5
Taxes, subsidies, and transfers	$ 28

The Spending Allocation Model

George Osborne became one of the most powerful men in the United Kingdom before reaching his fortieth birthday. The youngest man to become chancellor of the exchequer (the British equivalent of the secretary of treasury) since the beginning of the twentieth century, Mr. Osborne immediately captured everyone's attention with his first budget, which proposed a drastic series of cuts to government expenditures and increases to taxes to reduce the United Kingdom's budget deficit. In his speech to the House of Commons, Mr. Osborne said,

This Budget is needed to deal with our country's debts. This Budget is needed to give confidence to our economy. This is the unavoidable Budget. I am not going to hide hard choices from the British people or bury them in the small print of the Budget documents. You're going to hear them straight from me, here in this speech. Our policy is to raise from the ruins of an economy built on debt a new, balanced economy where we save, invest and export. An economy where the state does not take almost half of all our national income, crowding out private endeavour. An economy not overly reliant on the success of one industry, financial services—important as they are—but where all industries grow. An economy where prosperity is shared among all sections of society and all parts of the country.

On the other side of the Atlantic, Ben Bernanke, the chairman of the Federal Reserve, in a speech before the National Press Club in February 2011, expressed concerns about the long-run path of budget deficits in the United States. Mr. Bernanke predicted that

One way or the other, fiscal adjustments sufficient to stabilize the federal budget must occur at some point. The question is whether these adjustments will take place through a careful and deliberative process that weighs priorities and gives people adequate time to adjust to changes in government programs or tax policies, or whether the needed fiscal adjustments will be a rapid and painful response to a looming or actual fiscal crisis. Acting now to develop a credible program to reduce future deficits would not only enhance economic growth and stability in the long run, but could also yield substantial near-term benefits in terms of lower long-term interest rates and increased consumer and business confidence.

Both Mr. Osborne and Mr. Bernanke seem to be predicting that, over time, increases in government spending and higher budget deficits would result in less investment and less accumulation of capital in the economy. In this section, we develop an economic model that will help you better understand how lower budget deficits and decreasing the share of government purchases in gross domestic product (GDP) would result in lower interest rates, and, in turn, how lower interest rates would raise the share of investment in GDP.

The model we develop is called the *spending allocation model* because of its use in determining how GDP is allocated among the major components of spending: consumption, investment, government purchases, and net exports. Because each share of spending must compete for the scarce resources in GDP, an increase in the share of one of the components will lead to a reduction in the share of another component. Our model shows that real interest rates are a key factor that both influences and is influenced by spending. By explaining how real interest rates are determined in the long run, our model helps us predict how much of GDP in the long run goes to each of the four components.

The spending allocation model has some useful applications. You can use it to understand why the aging of the population of the United States, coupled with the increases in spending that will be required for programs like Medicare and social security, poses a threat to U.S. citizens. The increased costs of these programs makes it difficult to invest and grow in the decades ahead, and also difficult to understand how a reduction in government purchases in the early 1990s could have led to a boom in investment in the United States.

As you study the spending allocation model, it is imperative that you keep in mind that this model applies more to the long run than to the short run. Therefore, it is most useful in thinking about economic developments that occur over a period of years instead of months. For example, Mr. Bernanke was careful to talk about implications that were decades into the future instead of implications for the state of the economy in 2011.

The Spending Shares

We know that GDP is divided into four components: consumption, investment, government purchases, and net exports. Symbolically,

$$Y = C + I + G + X$$

where Y equals GDP, C equals consumption, I equals investment, G equals government purchases, and X equals net exports. This equation is the starting point for determining how large a share of GDP is allocated to each spending component.

Defining the Spending Shares

We define the spending shares by looking at how GDP is allocated among its various components. The **consumption share** of GDP is the proportion of GDP that is used

consumption share
the proportion of GDP that is used for consumption; equals consumption divided by GDP, or C/Y.

investment share
the proportion of GDP that is used for investment; equals investment divided by GDP, or I/Y. Sometimes called investment rate.

net exports share
the proportion of GDP that is equal to net exports; equals net exports divided by GDP, or X/Y.

government purchases share
the proportion of GDP that is used for government purchases; equals government purchases divided by GDP, or G/Y.

for consumption. The consumption share of GDP is defined as consumption (C) divided by GDP, or C/Y. For example, if $C = \$6$ trillion and $Y = \$10$ trillion, then the consumption share is $C/Y = 0.6$, or 60 percent. We can define the other shares of GDP analogously: I/Y is the **investment share**, X/Y is the **net exports share**, and G/Y is the **government purchases share**. Sometimes the investment share is called the *investment rate*.

We can establish a simple relationship between the shares of spending in GDP by taking the equation $Y = C + I + G + X$ and dividing both sides by Y. This simple division gives us a relationship that says that the sum of the shares of spending in GDP must equal one. Writing that algebraically yields the following:

$$1 = \frac{C}{Y} + \frac{I}{Y} + \frac{G}{Y} + \frac{X}{Y}$$

If we use the shares that existed in 2010 (see Table 6-2 in Chapter 6), we get

$$1 = \frac{10{,}352}{14{,}660} + \frac{1{,}821}{14{,}660} + \frac{3{,}002}{14{,}660} + \frac{-515}{14{,}660}$$
$$= .706 + .124 + .205 + (-0.035)$$

In other words, consumption accounted for around 70.6 percent of GDP, investment for 12.4 percent of GDP, government purchases for 20.5 percent of GDP, and net exports, in deficit at negative \$515 billion, for negative 3.5 percent of GDP. The negative share for net exports occurs because Americans imported more than they exported in 2010. In this example, the sum of the four shares on the right equals one, or, in percentage terms, 100 percent. And, of course, this must be true for any year.

Figure 7-1 shows the four shares of spending in GDP for the last 75 or so years in the United States. A huge temporary fluctuation in the shares of spending in GDP occurred in World War II, when government spending on the military rose sharply. Government purchases reached almost 50 percent of GDP, and the other three shares declined. Since World War II, the shares have been much steadier, but the movements

Figure 7-1

History of Spending Shares in GDP

The government purchases share rose sharply during World War II, and the other three shares declined. The government purchases share fell in the late 1990s before rising again in recent years.

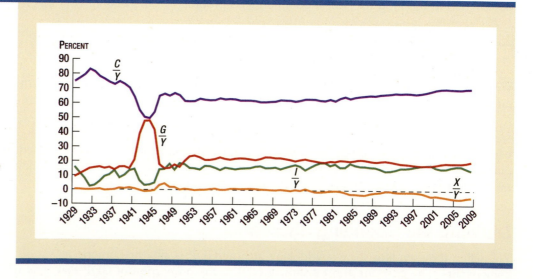

in government spending as a share of GDP seem to be related to the movements in the investment share of GDP. Between 1990 and 2000, the government purchases share decreased from about 20 percent to 17.5 percent, while the investment share increased from 14.8 percent to 17.7 percent. Between 2000 and 2010, however, the government purchases share of GDP increased from 17.5 percent to 20.5 percent, while the investment share decreased from 17.7 percent to 12.4 percent. The other two shares have shown more sustained patterns: The consumption share generally has been rising during the 30-year period 1980–2010, while the net exports share has been negative over that period, as the United States ran trade deficits that got progressively larger in the period leading up to the 2009 recession. (Recall that when net exports are negative, there is a trade deficit.)

If One Share Goes Up, Another Must Go Down

The shares of spending equation demonstrates a simple but important point: A change in one of the shares implies a change in one or more of the other shares. That the shares must sum to one means that an increase in any of the shares must entail a reduction in one of the other shares. For example, an increase in the share of spending going to government purchases must result in a decrease in the share going to one or more of the other components of spending. Similarly, a decrease in the government purchases share must result in an increase in some other share, such as the investment share. One cannot have an increase in government purchases as a share of GDP (going from, say, 20 percent to 25 percent) without a decline in the share of either consumption or investment or net exports.

What determines how the shares of GDP are allocated? What is the mechanism through which a change in one share—such as the government share of GDP—brings about a change in one of the other shares? Is it only the investment share that changes in response to a rise in the government share of GDP? Or do the consumption and net exports shares change as well? Which share would change by more as a result of the increase in the government share? To answer these questions, we develop the spending allocation model. At the heart of the spending model lies the real interest rate, which plays an important role in relating changes in one share to changes in another. We begin the derivation of the spending allocation model by taking a closer look at how real interest rates influence the various shares of GDP.

Before beginning this derivation of the spending allocation model, it is important to remember that the spending allocation model relates changes in one spending share to changes in the other spending shares *in the long run*. Recall from Chapter 5 that potential GDP is the economy's long-term trend level of GDP. We will refer to potential GDP as Y^*, to distinguish it from GDP. In the short run, actual GDP can (and does) fluctuate around potential GDP, but in the long run, we know that GDP is equal to potential GDP ($Y = Y^*$).

We will modify the equation that relates the shares to one another to represent a long-run relationship among the values of the spending shares. Because $Y = Y^*$ in the long run, this relationship can easily be written as follows:

$$1 = \frac{C}{Y^*} + \frac{I}{Y^*} + \frac{G}{Y^*} + \frac{X}{Y^*}$$

The intuition is unchanged—an increase in the long-run share of one of the components of GDP implies a decrease in the long-run share of one or more of the other components.

REVIEW

- GDP is divided into four components: consumption, investment, government purchases, and net exports. Expressing each as a share of GDP is a convenient way to describe how spending is allocated among the components.

- Simple arithmetic tells us that the sum of all the shares of spending in GDP must equal one. Thus, an increase in the share of GDP going to government purchases, for example, must be accompanied by a reduction in one or more of the other three shares—consumption, investment, or net exports.

- Several interesting patterns emerge when we look at data on these shares for the past 75 years. The government share of GDP rose sharply during World

War II, resulting in substantial falls in the other three shares.

- Changes in the government share of GDP seem to be inversely related to changes in the investment share of GDP over the last 25 years. During that period, the consumption share of GDP has been rising, while the net exports share of GDP has remained negative.

- The real interest rate plays a critical role in how changes in one share affect the other shares in the economy over the long run. To develop this relationship further, we redefine the spending shares in terms of potential GDP, because we know that in the long run, GDP will equal potential GDP.

The Effect of Interest Rates on Spending Shares

In this section, we show that the interest rate affects the three shares of spending by the private sector: consumption, investment, and net exports. Each private-sector spending component competes for a share of GDP along with government purchases, and the interest rate is a key factor in determining how the spending is allocated.

Consumption

In the long run, the value of the consumption share of GDP (C/Y^*) depends on people's decisions to consume, which are like any other choice with scarce resources, as defined in Chapter 1. If people decide to consume a larger fraction of their income, then the consumption share of GDP will increase. Conversely, if people decide to lower the fraction of income that they consume, then the consumption share of GDP will decrease.

Consumption and the Real Interest Rate
Keep in mind that people's decisions to consume more or less of their income today have implications for their consumption decisions tomorrow. Individuals who consume *more* today save *less,* and therefore have less to consume tomorrow. On the other hand, individuals who consume *less* today save *more,* and therefore have more to consume tomorrow. A person's choice between consuming today and consuming tomorrow depends on a relative price, just like any other economic decision. The price of consumption today relative to the price of consumption tomorrow is the real interest rate.

Why is the real interest rate the relative price of current consumption? If the real interest rate is high, then any saving you do today will deliver more funds in the future, which then can be used for future consumption (a larger home or more college education, for example). Conversely, when the real interest rate is high, increasing current consumption will reduce your saving and result in your passing up opportunities for future consumption.

We can better illustrate this link between the real interest rate and consumption with a numerical example. Suppose you earned enough to buy $1,000 worth of goods, but you were buying only $900 worth of goods and saving the remainder. If the real interest rate was 2 percent, your saving plus the interest you earned would allow you to consume $102 worth of goods next year. In other words, by consuming $100 less in goods today, you get to consume $102 more in goods tomorrow. But if the real interest rate instead were 6 percent, you would be able to consume $106 worth of goods in a year by consuming $100 less in goods today. The increase in the real interest rate from 2 percent to 6 percent raises the price of consuming $100 worth of goods today by $4 worth of goods in the future.

Even though this may seem like a small amount, keep in mind that small differences in interest rates can add up when you consider saving large sums of money to finance a college education or to save for retirement. So a higher real interest rate gives people more incentive to consume less and save for the future, whereas a lower real interest rate gives people more incentive to consume today instead of saving for the future. We therefore can conclude that consumption is negatively related to the real interest rate.

What is true for individuals on average also will be true for the economy as a whole. Figure 7-2 describes an economy in which the consumption share is negatively related to the real interest rate. For this example, when the real interest rate is 4 percent, the share of consumption in GDP will be about 65 percent. If the real interest rate increases to 8 percent, then the share declines to 64 percent. Alternatively, if the real interest rate declines, the consumption share increases.

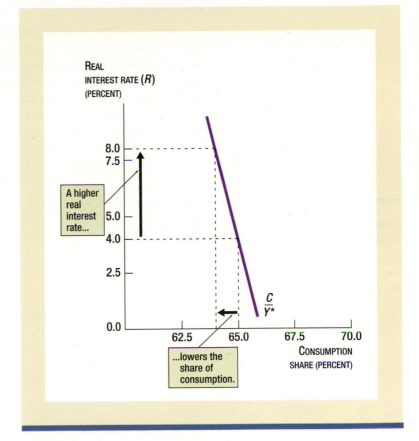

Figure 7-2

The Consumption Share and the Real Interest Rate

A higher real interest rate discourages consumption and encourages saving. Therefore, the share of GDP allocated to consumption will decrease in the long run.

Movements Along versus Shifts of the Consumption Share Line

Observe that the relationship between the real interest rate and consumption as a share of GDP in Figure 7-2 looks like a demand curve. Like a demand curve, it is downward sloping. And like a demand curve, it shows the quantity that consumers are willing to consume at each price, where the price is the real interest rate. A higher price—that is, a higher real interest rate—reduces the amount of goods and services that people will consume, and a lower price—that is, a lower real interest rate—increases the amount that they will consume. As with demand curves, when a change in the price (in this case, the real interest rate) leads to a change in the quantity demanded (in this case, the consumption share), we see a *movement along* the consumption share line, as shown in Figure 7-2.

As with a demand curve, it is also important to distinguish such movements along the consumption share line from *shifts of* the consumption share line. The real interest rate is not the only thing that affects consumption as a share of GDP. When a factor other than the real interest rate changes the consumption share of GDP, the consumption share line in Figure 7-2 shifts. For example, an increase in taxes on consumption—such as a national sales tax—would reduce the quantity of goods people would consume relative to their income. In other words, an increase in taxes on consumption would shift the consumption share line in Figure 7-2 to the left: Less would be consumed relative to GDP at every interest rate. Conversely, a decrease in taxes on consumption would shift the consumption share line in Figure 7-2 to the right.

Investment

A similar inverse, or negative, relationship exists between investment and the real interest rate. When businesses decide to invest, by buying new machines and equipment or by building a new factory, they need funds. Typically, they acquire these funds by borrowing. Higher real interest rates raise the cost of borrowing—the firm would need to produce enough additional output to pay back the loan plus interest, which implies that it would be willing to borrow only if it were confident about the success of the investment project. Another way of stating this is that investment projects undertaken at lower real interest rates may be postponed or canceled when interest rates rise because of the higher costs of borrowing.

Therefore, when real interest rates rise, firms are less likely to spend on investment, fewer new equipment purchases will be made, and fewer new factories will be built. Conversely, when real interest rates fall, firms are encouraged to spend more on investment, more equipment will be purchased, and more new factories will be built. This relationship holds even if firms use their own funds to finance their investment projects. Higher real interest rates increase the opportunity cost of using their own funds for investment: Firms are tempted to leave their money in the bank earning the higher interest rate, instead of putting those funds into investment projects.

Recall that investment also includes the purchases of new houses by individuals. Most people need to take out loans (mortgages) to purchase houses. When the real interest rate on mortgages rises, people purchase fewer or smaller houses because they would have to give up too much consumption to repay their mortgage plus interest; when the real interest rate falls, people purchase more or larger houses because they are more easily able to repay their mortgage plus interest. The story would be similar even if individuals used their savings to pay for their new home. A higher real interest rate increases the opportunity cost of taking the money out of the bank account and using it to buy a house.

Combining the behavior of firms that borrow or use their own funds to finance investment projects with that of individuals who take out mortgages or use their own funds to buy houses, the negative relationship between investment as a share of GDP and the interest rate that has been observed in the economy for many years makes sense: A higher real interest rate discourages investment, and a lower real interest rate encourages investment. Figure 7-3

Figure 7-3

The Investment Share and the Real Interest Rate

A higher real interest rate lowers the share of investment. The sensitivity of investment to the interest rate is greater than that of consumption to the interest rate, as shown in Figure 7-2.

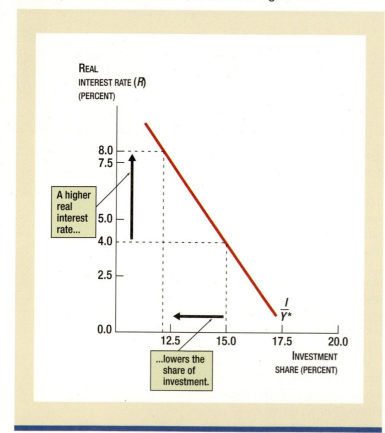

shows this negative relationship between the interest rate and the investment share. For this example, when the interest rate rises from 4 percent to 8 percent, the investment share decreases from 15 percent to 12 percent. Economists have observed that investment is more sensitive to interest rates than consumption is. Therefore, the line for I/Y^* in Figure 7-3 is flatter than the line for C/Y^* in Figure 7-2. As before, when a change in the real interest rate leads to a change in the investment share, this is reflected as a *movement along* the consumption share line. An example is shown in Figure 7-3.

Other factors besides the interest rate also affect investment; when these factors change, the investment share line in Figure 7-3 will *shift*. For example, an investment tax credit, which lowers a firm's taxes if the firm buys new equipment, would increase the amount that firms would invest at each interest rate. An investment tax credit would shift the investment share line in Figure 7-3 to the right: The investment that firms are willing to do as a share of GDP at a given interest rate would rise. A change in firms' expectations of the future also could shift the investment share line: If firms feel that new computing or telecommunications equipment will lower their costs in the future, they will purchase the equipment, thereby increasing their investment at a given interest rate; the investment share line will shift to the right. Conversely, pessimism on the part of firms about the benefits of investment could shift the line to the left.

Net Exports

Net exports also are negatively related to the real interest rate. The explanation behind this relationship is somewhat more involved than that for investment or for consumption. The **exchange rate**—the rate at which one country's currency can be exchanged for another—plays an integral role in this relationship. This explanation has three parts. First, we need to understand the relationship between the real interest rate and the exchange rate. Second, we need to understand the relationship between the exchange rate and exports and imports. Third, we will combine these two parts to obtain a relationship between the real interest rate and net exports.

exchange rate
the price of one currency in terms of another in the foreign exchange market. We express the exchange rate as the number of units of foreign currency that can be purchased with one unit of domestic currency.

The Interest Rate and the Exchange Rate Let us start with the relationship between the interest rate and the *exchange rate*. We will express the exchange rate in terms of the number of units of foreign currency that are needed to purchase one unit of domestic currency, or, in other words, as the price of a unit of domestic currency in terms of foreign currency. Thus, the exchange rates for the dollar for various international currencies will be expressed in the form of euros per dollar, yen per dollar, pounds per dollar, and so on.

A substantial influence on exchange rates is exerted by international investors, who must decide whether to put their funds in assets denominated in dollars—such as an account at a U.S. bank in New York City—or in assets denominated in foreign currencies—such as an account at a Japanese bank in Tokyo. If real interest rates rise in the United States, but not elsewhere, then international investors will put more funds in dollar-denominated assets because they can earn more by doing so. As international investors shift their funds from London, Frankfurt, Tokyo, and other financial centers to New York to take advantage of the higher interest rate in the United States, the demand for dollars will rise. This increased demand puts upward pressure on the dollar exchange rate, so that more units of foreign currency will be needed to buy $1 in the foreign exchange market. For example, an increase in the interest rate in the United States might cause the U.S. dollar to increase from 100 yen per dollar to 120 yen per dollar. Conversely, a lower interest rate in the United States brings about a lower exchange rate for the dollar. Thus, the interest rate and the exchange rate are positively related.

The Exchange Rate and Net Exports The next part of the relationship deals with how the exchange rate affects net exports. When the dollar becomes less valuable—that is, the dollar exchange rate becomes lower—foreign goods imported into the United States become less attractive to U.S. consumers because they are more expensive. For example, at the end of 2010, the dollar exchange rate against the euro was 0.75 euro (€) per dollar compared with the exchange rate at the end of 2005, which was €0.80 per dollar. In 2005, an American consumer could have bought a German-made Audi costing €40,000 for $50,000 (40,000/0.8). In 2010, when the exchange rate was €0.75 per dollar, the Audi would be much more expensive; it would cost around $53,333 (40,000/0.75). Thus, a lower exchange rate decreases the quantity demanded of imported goods.

Conversely, the lower exchange rate makes U.S. exports more attractive to foreign consumers. For example, a $20,000 Jeep Grand Cherokee would have cost a German consumer €16,000 in 2005 but would cost only €15,000 in 2010. Thus, a lower exchange rate increases U.S. exports. We have shown that a lower exchange rate will raise exports and lower imports. Because net exports is the difference between exports and imports, a lower exchange rate must mean an increase in net exports. Conversely, a higher exchange rate will mean a decrease in net exports.

Combining the Two Relationships Finally, we can combine these two relationships—one that relates the real interest rate to the exchange rate, and the other that relates the exchange rate to net exports—to obtain the desired relationship between the real interest rate and net exports:

Interest Rate		Exchange Rate		Net Exports
up	$\longrightarrow$	up	$\longrightarrow$	down
down	$\longrightarrow$	down	$\longrightarrow$	up

If the interest rate goes up, then net exports go down. The link is the exchange rate. The dollar increases in value (the exchange rate rises) as a result of the higher interest rate, which, in turn, makes net exports fall. Of course, all of this works in reverse, too. If the interest rate goes down, then the dollar decreases in value (the exchange rate goes down) and net exports go up.

The relationship between net exports as a share of GDP and the interest rate is shown in Figure 7-4. Like the consumption share line and the investment share line, the net exports share line is downward sloping. For this example, when the interest rate goes up from 4 percent to 8 percent, net exports go from zero to about −4 percent of GDP. Remember that when net exports are negative, there is a trade deficit. Changes in the interest rate lead to movements along the net exports line in Figure 7-4. Changes in other factors—such as a shift in foreign demand for U.S. products—may cause the line to shift.

Figure 7-4

The Net Exports Share and the Real Interest Rate

A higher real interest rate lowers the share of net exports because it tends to raise the exchange rate. The higher exchange rate lowers exports and raises imports, thereby lowering net exports. When net exports are negative, there is a trade deficit. When net exports are positive, there is a trade surplus.

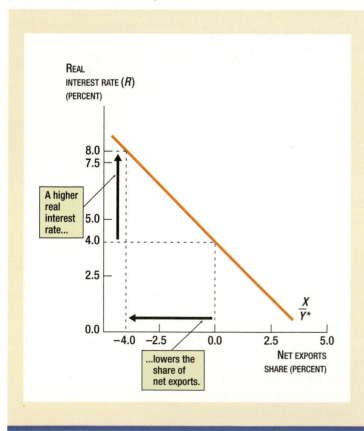

Putting the Three Shares Together

We have shown that the consumption, investment, and net exports shares are all negatively related to the interest rate. The three diagrams—Figures 7-2, 7-3, and 7-4—summarize this key idea. Our next task is to determine the interest rate, which then will enable us to determine the particular value of each share.

REVIEW

- Consumption, investment, and net exports are all negatively related to the real interest rate.

- The real interest rate is the price of consumption this year relative to next year. When the real interest rate rises, consumers will be more inclined to forgo current consumption and save so that they can consume more in the future. Accordingly, the share of consumption will rise when the real interest rate falls and will fall when the real interest rate rises.

- Changes in the real interest rate affect investment because they change the borrowing costs (and also the opportunity cost of using one's own money) for firms looking to invest in machines and factories and for individuals looking to buy and build homes. Business firms and individuals will spend less on investment when the real interest rate rises. Accordingly, the share of investment will rise when the real interest rate falls and will fall when the real interest rate rises.

- Changes in the real interest rate affect net exports through their effects on the exchange rate. A higher real interest rate raises the value of the domestic currency (a higher exchange rate) and thereby discourages exports and encourages imports, while a lower real interest rate results in a fall in the value of the domestic currency (a lower exchange rate), which encourages exports and discourages imports. Accordingly, the share of net exports will rise when the real interest rate falls and fall when the real interest rate rises.

- A downward-sloping relationship exists between the real interest rate and each of these three shares. Changes in the real interest rate are reflected as movements along these curves. Other factors besides the interest rate may also affect consumption, investment, and net exports. When one of these factors changes, the relationship between the interest rate and consumption, investment, or net exports shifts.

Determining the Equilibrium Interest Rate

Because the interest rate affects each of the three shares (consumption, investment, and net exports), it also affects the *sum* of the three shares. We will refer to the sum of the three shares as the nongovernment share of GDP, or NG/Y, because the fourth component of GDP is the government share. The collective impact is shown by the downward-sloping line in diagram (d) of Figure 7-5. As before, we are focusing on the shares in the long run, so the diagram shows the sum of consumption, investment, and net exports as a share of potential output (NG/Y^*).

The Nongovernment Share of GDP

Note carefully how Figure 7-5 is put together and how the downward-sloping line in diagram (d) is derived. We have taken the graphs from Figures 7-2, 7-3, and 7-4 and assembled them horizontally in diagrams (a), (b), and (c) of Figure 7-5. The downward-sloping blue line in diagram (d) is the sum of the three downward-sloping lines in

Figure 7-5

Summing Up Consumption, Investment, and Net Exports Shares

Diagrams (a), (b), and (c) are reproductions of Figures 7-2, 7-3, and 7-4. For each interest rate, the three shares are added together to get the sum of shares shown in diagram (d). For example, when the real interest rate is 4 percent, we get 65 percent for consumption share, 15 percent for investment share, and 0 percent for net exports, summing to 80 percent. The sum of the three nongovernment shares is negatively related to the real interest rate (R).

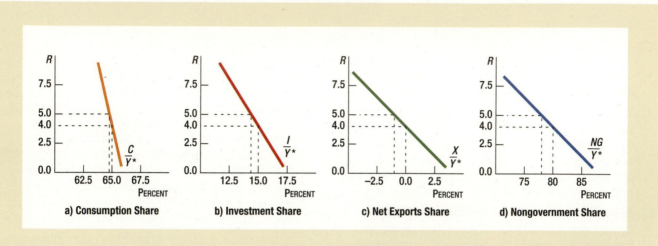

a) Consumption Share   b) Investment Share   c) Net Exports Share   d) Nongovernment Share

diagrams (a), (b), and (c). For example, when the interest rate is 4 percent, the line in diagram (d) shows that the nongovernment share—the sum of investment, consumption, and net exports as a share of GDP—is 80 percent; this is the sum of 65 percent for the consumption share, 15 percent for the investment share, and 0 percent for the net exports share. Similarly, the other points in diagram (d) are obtained by adding up the three shares at other interest rate levels. For example, at an interest rate of 5 percent, we see that the sum of the shares of consumption, investment, and net exports is down to about 78 percent.

The Government's Share of GDP and the Share of GDP Available for Nongovernment Use

We have determined that the real interest rate has a negative effect on the consumption, investment, and net exports shares of GDP. What about the impact of real interest rates on government purchases? We will assume that government purchases do not depend on the real interest rate; instead, they likely will be affected by the decisions made by elected representatives on behalf of the voters who elected them to office. So the share of government purchases (G/Y) will not be affected by fluctuations in interest rates. For example, if the decisions made by elected officials result in a government purchases share that is 22 percent of GDP, then that share will not be affected by changes in the real interest rate. This is shown by the vertical line in diagram (a) of Figure 7-6.

The government share determines how much is available for nongovernment use, that is, for either consumption, investment, or net exports. The share available for non-government use is easily defined as follows:

$$\text{Share available for nongovernment use} = 1 - \frac{G}{Y}$$

Figure 7-6

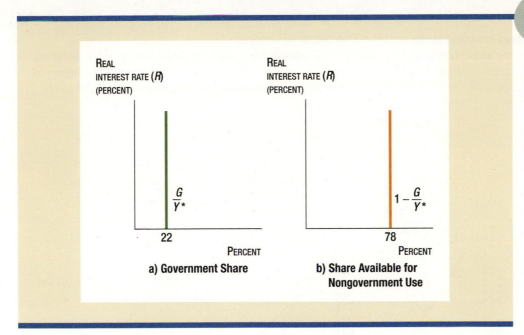

a) Government Share

b) Share Available for Nongovernment Use

Finding the Share Available for Nongovernment Use
If the government share of GDP is known, then the remaining share of GDP is what is available for nongovernment use. In this example, a 22 percent share of government purchases means that 78 percent of GDP is available for nongovernment use. Because the share G/Y* is not dependent on R, the share available for nongovernment use is also a vertical line, not dependent on R.

If the government share is not affected by changes in the real interest rate, the share that is available for nongovernment use also will not be affected. For the case shown in diagram (a) of Figure 7-6, with a share of government purchases of 22 percent, the share available for nongovernment use must equal 78 percent. The share of GDP available for nongovernment use is shown in diagram (b) of Figure 7-6. As always, we are looking at the long run, so the diagram shows the share of potential output available for nongovernment use.

Finding the Equilibrium Interest Rate

In equilibrium, the nongovernment share of GDP should equal the share of GDP available for nongovernment use. In mathematical terms, we can describe this equilibrium relationship in the long run as follows:

$$\frac{NG}{Y^*} = 1 - \frac{G}{Y^*}$$

What brings this equality about is the real interest rate, which is the key to the spending allocation model. Figure 7-7 illustrates how the interest rate brings about this equality. Look first at diagram (d). In diagram (d), the share available for nongovernment use $(1 - G/Y^*)$ is indicated by the vertical line at 78 percent. The nongovernment share of GDP (NG/Y^*), which is the sum of the consumption, investment, and net export shares, is shown by the downward-sloping line in Figure 7-7(d). This is the same line we derived in Figure 7-5(d). The equilibrium is the point at which the nongovernment share equals the share available for nongovernment use. Graphically, this is the intersection of the downward-sloping line and the vertical line. We see in diagram (d) of Figure 7-7 that the point of intersection for that economy occurs when the interest rate is 5 percent. This is the **equilibrium interest rate**, that is, the interest rate that makes the nongovernment share equal to the share available for nongovernment use.

equilibrium interest rate
the interest rate that equates the sum of the consumption, investment, and net exports shares to the share of GDP available for nongovernment use.

Figure 7-7

Determining the Equilibrium Real Interest Rate and the Shares of Spending

In this case, government purchases are assumed to be 22 percent of GDP. Mark the implied share available for nongovernment uses, 78 percent, in diagram (d). The equilibrium real interest rate is determined at the intersection of the two lines in diagram (d). Given this real interest rate, we can compute the consumption, investment, and net exports shares of spending in GDP using diagrams (a), (b), and (c).

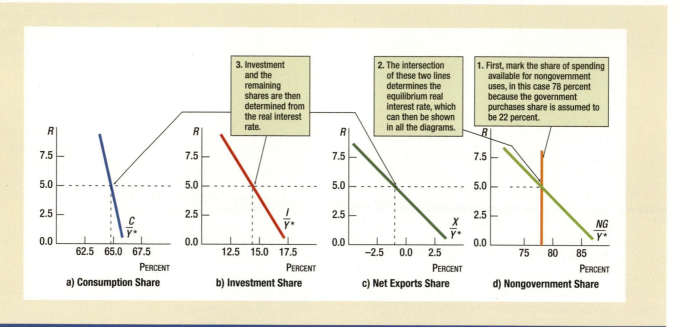

Once we determine the equilibrium interest rate, we can find the investment, consumption, and net exports shares. Each of these shares depends on the interest rate, as shown in diagrams (a), (b), and (c) of Figure 7-7. To determine each of the shares, simply draw a line across the three diagrams at the equilibrium interest rate. Then in diagram (a) we find the consumption share, in diagram (b) the investment share, and in diagram (c) the net exports share.

What happens if consumption, investment, or net exports increases? Then the nongovernment share will begin to rise above the share of GDP available after the government takes its share. This rise in spending will be reflected as a rightward shift of the downward-sloping nongovernment share line, which causes the equilibrium interest rate in the economy to increase. Conversely, if consumption, investment, or net exports decreases, then the nongovernment share will begin to fall below the share of GDP available after the government takes its share. This will be reflected as a leftward shift of the downward-sloping nongovernment share line, which causes the equilibrium interest rate in the economy to decrease.

What happens if the share of government purchases increases? Then the share available for nongovernment use will fall, which will be reflected in a leftward shift of the vertical line indicating the share available for nongovernment use. This causes the equilibrium interest rate in the economy to increase. Conversely, if the share of government purchases decreases, then the share available for nongovernment use will rise, which will be reflected in a rightward shift of the vertical line that indicates the share available for nongovernment use. This causes the equilibrium interest rate in the economy to decrease.

The following Economics in Action box traces through this analogy in more detail, showing you how you can find the impact of a change in one of these shares on the other shares and working through the change in the real interest rate.

ECONOMICS *IN ACTION*

Using the Spending Allocation Model to Analyze the Long-Run Implications of a Shift in Government Purchases

In this case study, you will see how the spending allocation model can be used to predict the effects of actual changes in the economy. We focus on a shift in government purchases to understand how we can use this model to examine what happens to the other components of GDP. We know as a matter of arithmetic that some other share must move in a direction opposite to that of the government share.

Suppose that the government share of GDP decreases by 2 percent, as happened in the 1990s as a result of a decrease in defense spending and other budget cuts. The effects of this change are shown in Figure 7-8. If government purchases as a share of GDP decrease by 2 percent, then we know that the share available for nongovernment use must *increase* by 2 percent. Thus, in diagram (d) of Figure 7-8, we shift the

vertical line marking the available nongovernment share to the right by 2 percentage points. As Figure 7-8(d) shows, there is now a new intersection of the two lines and a new, lower equilibrium real interest rate. The new real interest rate is 4 percent rather than 5 percent, a decrease of 1 percentage point.

The decrease in the real interest rate is the market mechanism that brings about an increase in the shares of consumption plus investment plus net exports. To see the effect on the consumption, investment, and net exports shares, we draw a horizontal line at a real interest rate of 4 percent, as shown in Figure 7-8, and read off the implied shares. According to the diagram, the share of consumption increases, the share of investment increases, and the share of net exports increases.

Figure 7-8

A Decrease in the Share of Government Purchases

If the government purchases share of GDP falls, then the share available for nongovernment use must rise by the same amount. This causes a fall in real interest rates, which increases the consumption, investment, and net exports share.

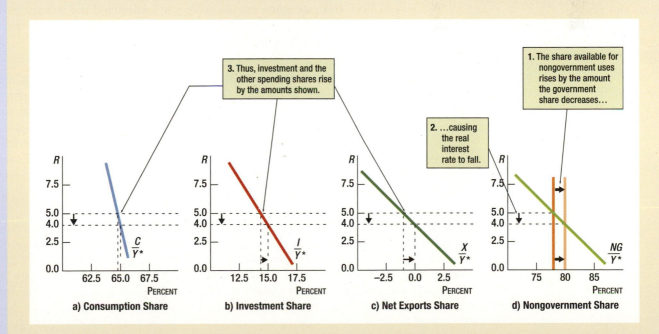

a) Consumption Share b) Investment Share c) Net Exports Share d) Nongovernment Share

(Continued)

ECONOMICS *IN ACTION*

Table 7-1 allows us to compare the predictions of the model with what really happened when the government purchases share was reduced by 2.2 percent between 1989 and 1997. During that period, all of the other shares increased as a result of the decline in the real interest rate. Although the precise magnitudes may not be exactly the same, the model explains the direction of movement well.

The same process would work in reverse if we *increased* the share of government purchases. In Figure 7-8, the real interest rate would have to rise. To find out the effect on the other components of spending, we would draw a horizontal line at a higher real interest rate. That would show us that the shares of investment, net exports, and consumption would fall.

Sometimes a decline in the investment share due to an increase in government purchases is called **crowding out** because investment is "crowded out" by the government purchases. Thus, we have shown that an increase in the share of government purchases causes a crowding out of investment in the long run. However, because the shares of net exports and consumption also fall, the crowding out of investment is not as large as it otherwise would be.

Table 7-1

Change in Spending Shares: 1989–1997 (percent)

Consumption share	+1.0
Investment share	+0.8
Net exports share	+0.4
Government purchases share	−2.2

A big shift in the government purchases share is assumed to cause changes in the other shares in this case study.

crowding out
the decline in private investment owing to an increase in government purchases.

The lessons from this case study can also help you understand the statements made by the chancellor of the exchequer and the chairman of the Federal Reserve that were described in this chapter's introduction.

Analogy with Supply and Demand Observe that the intersection of the two lines in diagram (d) of Figure 7-7 is much like the intersection of a demand curve and a supply curve. The green downward-sloping line—showing how the sum of investment, consumption, and net exports is negatively related to the interest rate—looks just like a demand curve. The orange vertical line—showing the share of GDP available for consumption, investment, and net exports—looks like a vertical supply curve. The intersection of the two curves determines the equilibrium price—in this case, the equilibrium interest rate in the economy as a whole.

The Real Interest Rate in the Long Run Having determined the equilibrium interest rate, it is important to mention once more two key features of this model. First, this analysis applies to the *long run*—perhaps three years or more—rather than to short-run economic fluctuations. Moreover, the interest rate in the analysis is the *real* interest rate, which, as defined in Chapter 5, is the nominal interest rate less the expected inflation rate. If the inflation rate is low, there is little difference between the real interest rate and the nominal interest rate; but if inflation is high, there is a big difference, and the real interest rate is a much better measure of the incentives affecting consumers and firms. An interest rate of 50 percent would seem high but actually would be quite low—2 percent in real terms—if people expected inflation to be 48 percent.

REVIEW

- The sum of the consumption, investment, and net exports shares of GDP is called the nongovernment share of GDP. It is negatively related to the interest rate because each of the individual components is negatively related to the interest rate.

- The government share of GDP is assumed to be unaffected by the real interest rate, being determined by the preferences of voters expressed through their elected representatives. The share of GDP available for nongovernment use then can be defined as one minus the government share of GDP. This, too, is unaffected by the real interest rate.

- The equilibrium interest rate is determined by the condition that the nongovernment share equals the share available for nongovernment use. Graphically, this is the interest rate at the intersection of the downward-sloping nongovernment share of GDP line and the vertical share of GDP available for nongovernment use line.

- Once we find the equilibrium interest rate, we then can find the shares of consumption, investment, and net exports by looking at the graphs of those relationships.

- We also can use the model to analyze what would happen to the equilibrium interest rate when there is a change in the government share or in one of the three nongovernment shares.

- Once we know the equilibrium interest rate, we also can find out how exactly the other shares in the economy respond to a change in one of the shares. This is helpful in understanding how a change in government purchases affects investment, for example.

The Relationship between Saving and Investment

By now you should be able to use the spending allocation model to illustrate how changes in the share of spending in one component of GDP affect the other components. In particular, we were able to use it to show how an increase in the consumption share of GDP or an increase in the government purchases share of GDP leads to a decrease in the investment share of GDP. In this section, we derive a similar relationship between the changes in the shares of GDP that are being *saved* and the share that is being invested. This alternative viewpoint is important to complete your understanding of how one sector of the economy can affect the others. For instance, we will show that the investment share of GDP will decrease when the government's budget deficit as a percentage of GDP rises, all else equal. The rise in the government budget deficit can be caused either by an increase in government spending or by a decrease in tax revenue. The latter effect is much better understood by looking at the economy from the saving side rather than the spending side.

In Chapter 6, we defined national saving (S) as GDP minus consumption minus government purchases, or

$$S = Y - C - G$$

national saving rate
the proportion of GDP that is saved, neither consumed nor spent on government purchases; equals national saving (S) divided by GDP, or S/Y.

The ratio of national saving to GDP, or S/Y, is the **national saving rate**. For example, in 2010, national saving was $1,306 billion and GDP was $14,660 billion, so the national saving rate was $1,306/14,660 = 0.089$ or 8.9 percent. If we divide each term in the definition of national saving by Y, we can write the national saving rate as one minus the shares of consumption and government purchases in GDP. That is,

National saving rate = 1 – consumption share – government purchases share,

or

$$\frac{S}{Y} = 1 - \frac{C}{Y} - \frac{G}{Y}$$

This equation tells us that a change in the economy will affect the national saving rate through its effect on the consumption share and the government purchases share. We once again will express everything in the long run, so the national saving rate in the long run is

$$\frac{S}{Y^*} = 1 - \frac{C}{Y^*} - \frac{G}{Y^*}$$

Note also that the equations tell us that the national saving rate depends on the interest rate. Because the consumption share of GDP is negatively related to the real interest rate and the government share of GDP is unrelated to the real interest rate, you easily can show that the national saving rate is positively related to the real interest rate. When the real interest rate rises, the consumption share of GDP falls, implying that the national saving rate rises. On the other hand, when the real interest rate falls, the consumption share of GDP rises, implying that the national saving rate falls.

Because we know that

$$1 = \frac{C}{Y^*} + \frac{I}{Y^*} + \frac{G}{Y^*} + \frac{X}{Y^*}$$

we can use the above definition of the national saving rate in the long run to write

$$\frac{S}{Y^*} = \frac{I}{Y^*} + \frac{X}{Y^*}$$

or, in other words, the national saving rate equals the investment share plus the net exports share. Both sides of this equation depend on the interest rate, as shown in Figure 7-9. The upward-sloping line in Figure 7-9 shows the national saving rate. An increase in the real interest rate causes the saving rate to rise. The downward-sloping line shows the sum of the investment and net exports shares; this sum is negatively related to the real interest rate because both the investment share and the net exports share are negatively related to the real interest rate.

The intersection of the two lines in Figure 7-9 determines the equilibrium interest rate. The interest rate is exactly the same as that in Figure 7-7. The only difference is that we are looking at the economy from a government and individual saving perspective rather than from a spending perspective.

Consider the same increase in the consumption share considered in the case study. An upward shift in the consumption share is equivalent to a downward shift in the saving rate. Thus, we shift the interest rate–saving rate relationship to the left in Figure 7-10, representing a downshift in the national saving rate. As shown in the figure, this leads to a higher interest rate and lower shares for investment and net exports. Similarly, an increase in the government expenditure share is also equivalent to a downward shift in the saving rate. This will lead to a shift in the interest rate–saving rate relationship to the left in Figure 7-10, resulting in a higher interest rate and lower shares for investment and net exports.

Obviously, we would not want to derive this alternative way of looking at the economy merely to replicate predictions that we were already able to make. We can make this model adaptable to more situations if we go back to another relationship we derived in Chapter 6, namely, that

$$S = (Y - C - T) + (T - G)$$

Figure 7-9

Determining the Interest Rate Using the Saving Rate Relationship

The saving rate (orange line) depends positively on the real interest rate. The sum (green line) of the investment share and the net exports share depends negatively on the real interest rate. The equilibrium interest rate is determined at the point at which national saving equals investment plus net exports, or the intersection of the two lines.

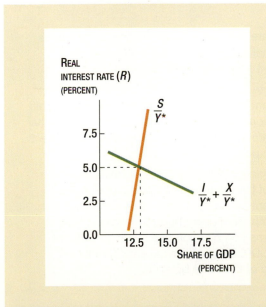

Figure 7-10

The Effect of a Downward Shift in the Saving Rate

The lower national saving rate raises real interest rates and lowers the investment share and the net exports share.

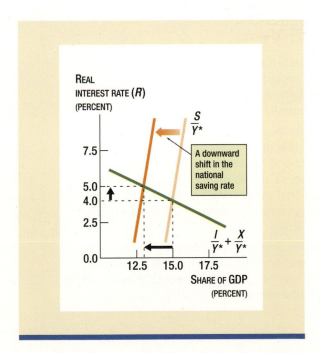

where T denotes taxes. This relationship states that national saving is equal to the sum of private and government saving. Therefore, the national saving rate will be the sum of the private saving rate and the government saving rate. The government saving rate is simply the budget balance as a percentage of GDP; when there is a budget deficit, this will be negative. We can express the relationship between saving, investment, and net exports in the economy in more detail then as

$$\text{Private saving rate} + \text{government saving rate} = \frac{I}{Y*} + \frac{X}{Y*}$$

This equation has powerful implications for the economy. If the government budget deficit increases (the government saving rate decreases), then the investment share of GDP will fall, assuming that the private saving rate or the net exports share of GDP does not change. If the economy is to keep its investment share unchanged in the face of rising budget deficits, then either private saving will have to increase to offset the fall in government saving, or the share of net exports will have to decrease. Practically speaking, if the rising demands of an aging society cause budget deficits as a percentage of GDP in the United States to increase (thus reducing the government saving rate), then one or more of the following outcomes will occur:

1. The private saving rate will have to increase, meaning that consumers most likely will have to cut back on spending.
2. The investment rate will decrease, which means less capital accumulation and the likelihood for slower economic growth in the future.
3. The trade balance will worsen, and we will buy more foreign goods while foreigners will buy fewer U.S. goods.

REVIEW

- We can apply the concepts used to derive the spending allocation model to examine how changes in saving behavior by consumers and the government affect other sectors of the economy.

- Because national saving is defined as $Y - C - G$, we can show that national saving is equal to the sum of investment and net exports. Expressing this relationship as shares of GDP in the long run, we can show that the national saving rate equals the sum of the investment share and the net exports share of GDP.

- The national saving rate is positively related to the interest rate, whereas the sum of the investment share and the net exports share of GDP is negatively related to the interest rate. The equilibrium real interest rate can be found as the rate that equates the national saving rate and the sum of the investment and net exports shares.

- An increase in the consumption share or the government share is equivalent to a downward shift in the national saving rate. This will result in a higher interest rate and will lower the shares of investment and net exports.

- We can disaggregate the national saving rate into the sum of the private saving rate and the government saving rate. This allows us to illustrate that the impact of rising budget deficits will be to create some combination of a lower investment share of GDP, a higher private saving rate, or a worsening of the trade balance.

CONCLUSION

In this chapter, we have developed a model that determines the equilibrium interest rate and explains how the shares of spending are allocated in the whole economy. The model can be used to analyze the impact of a change in government purchases or a shift in consumption or saving behavior.

The model has introduced an important macroeconomic factor to consider when assessing the appropriate size of government. Private investment is affected by the size of government in the economy. Private investment is greater when government purchases are less, even though government spending is needed to provide the roads, education, and legal system that help produce economic growth. What the model shows is that even when government spending does these good things, it reduces the share of GDP available for private investment.

The model also has strong predictions about the appropriate budget policy for the government to follow. In the long run, private investment is affected by the size of government saving in the economy. Private

investment is greater when the government saving rate is high. So once the government figures out the appropriate amount of spending to do on the roads, education, and legal system that help produce economic growth, it needs to ensure that it sets the tax rates appropriate for collecting the revenue needed to pay for that expenditure.

To the extent that consumption and net exports also shrink as government purchases increase, the effect on private investment of an increase in the share of government purchases is smaller. This also can be stated as to the extent that private savings increase and net exports shrink (the trade balance worsens), the effect on private investment of a decrease in the government saving rate is smaller.

Thus, there is a need for balance between government purchases and private investment. The mix ultimately will be determined in the political debate. This chapter provides some economic analysis that is useful in that debate.

KEY POINTS

1. Over the long term, consumption, investment, net exports, and government purchases compete for a share of gross domestic product (GDP). The four spending shares must sum to one.

2. Higher real interest rates raise the price of consumption and lead to a reduction of consumption as a share of GDP.

3. Higher real interest rates also reduce investment by raising the cost of borrowing and by raising the opportunity cost of using one's own funds.

4. Higher real interest rates lower the share of net exports by causing the exchange rate to rise, which reduces exports and raises imports.

5. The combined effect is a downward-sloping relationship between the real interest rate and the nongovernment share of GDP.

6. The government share of GDP is not dependent on the real interest rate. Accordingly, the share of GDP available for nongovernment use, which is one minus the government share of GDP, is not dependent on the real interest rate and is shown as a vertical line.

7. The equilibrium interest rate is found by equating the nongovernment share of GDP—the sum of the consumption, investment, and net

exports shares—to the share of GDP available for nongovernment use.

8. An increase in the share of government purchases crowds out the investment share of GDP by raising interest rates. The consumption and net exports shares also fall, crowding out the investment less severely. A decrease in the share of government purchases will lead to a lower real interest rate and an increase in all the other shares of spending.

9. The national saving rate is equal to the sum of the investment and net exports shares of GDP. The national saving rate, which equals the sum of private and government saving, is positively related to the real interest rate, while the sum of the investment and net exports shares of GDP is negatively related to the real interest rate.

10. An increase in consumption (a decrease in private saving) or an increase in government purchases (a decrease in government saving) will reduce national saving and shift the national saving curve inward. This will raise the equilibrium real interest rate and lower the investment share of GDP or lower the net exports share of GDP (worsen the trade balance).

KEY TERMS

consumption share, 157

crowding out, 170

equilibrium interest rate, 167

exchange rate, 163

government purchases share, 158

investment share, 158

national saving rate, 172

net exports share, 158

QUESTIONS FOR REVIEW

1. Why does an increase in the share of one component of gross domestic product (GDP) require a decrease in some other share?
2. What is the relationship between the consumption share and the real interest rate?
3. What is the relationship between the investment share and the real interest rate?
4. Explain carefully all the steps that relate the share of net exports to the real interest rate.
5. How do we indicate that the model in this chapter applies much more to the long run than to the short run?
6. Describe the following five relationships: (a) the government share of GDP and the real interest rate, (b) the government share of GDP and the share of GDP available for nongovernment use, (c) the real interest rate and the share of GDP available for nongovernment use, (d) the real interest rate and the nongovernment share of GDP, and (e) the share of GDP available for nongovernment use and the nongovernment share of GDP.
7. What determines the equilibrium interest rate?
8. What is crowding out? Graphically illustrate how it works, using the spending allocation model.
9. Describe the relationships that exist among the following: the national saving rate, the private saving rate, the government saving rate, the net exports share of GDP, and the investment share of GDP.
10. What are the long-term implications of a rise in the government budget deficit as a percentage of GDP (also known as a fall in the government saving rate)?

PROBLEMS

1. Suppose $C = 700$, $I = 200$, $G = 100$, and $X = 0$.
   a. What is gross domestic product (GDP)? Calculate each component's share of GDP.
   b. Suppose government spending increases to 150, but the other components of GDP do not change. What is government spending's share of GDP now? What is the new nongovernment share?
   c. Suppose that the level of potential GDP (Y^*) is 1,000 and is unaffected by the increase in government spending described previously. Without doing any calculations, explain in general terms what happens to C/Y^*, X/Y^*, and I/Y^* after the government spending increase in (b).
   d. Describe the mechanism by which each of these changes happens.

2. Suppose the following equations describe the relationship between the long-run shares of spending in GDP and the interest rate (R), measured in decimal fractions (that is, $R = 0.05$ means that the interest rate is 5 percent).

$$\frac{C}{Y^*} = 0.7 - 0.2(R - 0.05) \quad \frac{I}{Y^*} = 0.2 - 0.8(R - 0.05)$$

$$\frac{X}{Y^*} = 0 - 0.95(R - 0.05) \quad \frac{G}{Y^*} = 0.2$$

   a. Use algebra to determine the values of the interest rate and the long-run shares of spending in GDP.
   b. Do the calculations again for a long-run government share of 17 percent rather than 20 percent (that is, $G/Y^* = 0.17$).
   c. Suppose that the share of government purchases changes from 20 percent to 17 percent. Describe, in words, the mechanism by which each of the other shares changes.

3. Graph the relationships defined in Problem 2 to scale in a four-part diagram like Figure 7-7. Use the diagram to analyze each of the following situations:

   a. Suppose an increase in the foreign demand for U.S. goods changes the coefficient in the net exports share equation from 0 to 0.05. What happens to the interest rate and the consumption, investment, net exports, and government purchases shares in the United States in the long run?

   b. Determine how an increase in taxes that reduces the coefficient in the consumption share equation from 0.7 to 0.68 would affect the interest rate and the consumption, investment, net exports, and government purchases shares in the long run.

   c. Suppose firms are willing to invest 30 percent rather than 20 percent of GDP at an interest rate of 5 percent. How would this affect the interest rate and the shares of spending in GDP in the long run?

4. Using the diagram below, find the equilibrium interest rate when the share of government purchases in the long run is 20 percent. Show what happens to all the variables if there is an increase in investment because of a new tax policy that encourages investment.

5. Describe the long-run impact of a decline in defense spending by 1 percent of GDP on interest rates and on consumption, investment, and net exports as a share of GDP. Consider two different cases:

   a. No other changes in policy accompany the defense cut.

   b. The funds saved from the defense cut are used to increase government expenditures on roads and bridges.

6. Suppose personal income tax rates are cut and government spending is increased. Using a diagram, show what will happen to real interest rates. What will happen to the spending shares of GDP in the long run?

7. Draw two sets of diagrams like Figure 7-7 to depict two situations. In one set, draw investment and net exports as sensitive to interest rates—that is, the I/Y and X/Y curves are very flat. In the other set, draw investment and net exports as insensitive to interest rates—that is, the I/Y and X/Y curves are nearly vertical. For the same increase in government's share of GDP, in which set of diagrams will interest rates rise more? Why?

8. If China increases the value of its currency relative to the dollar, what will happen to interest rates in the United States? Explain your answer.

9. Many people believe that the U.S. saving rate is too low. Suppose all private citizens save at a higher rate. Show what happens to investment in this case, using the saving and investment diagram, where the S/Y^* curve shifts. Now show what happens to investment in the same situation using the spending share diagrams.

10. Suppose that the government imposes a consumption tax to discourage consumption and increase saving. Suppose that the impact of the consumption tax is a leftward shift in the C/Y^* line over time. Describe graphically how this affects each of the shares of GDP, using a saving and investment diagram. How would your answer change if the government used the tax money to increase its spending?

Problem 4

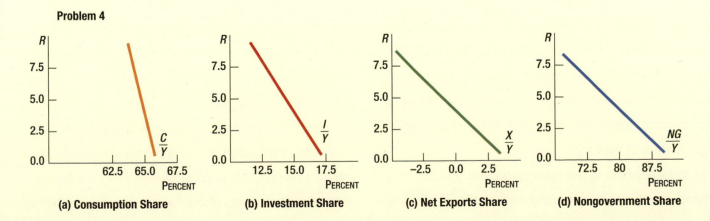

(a) Consumption Share   (b) Investment Share   (c) Net Exports Share   (d) Nongovernment Share

8 Unemployment and Employment

The first Friday of every month, the Bureau of Labor Statistics releases its summary of the Employment Situation of the economy, a report eagerly awaited by those who study the economy closely for a living. The report that came out in March 2008, two months into the beginning of the recession, painted a picture that seemed distressing at the time—the unemployment rate had risen from 4.8 percent to 5.1 percent and the number of unemployed workers had increased by 434,000 to a total of 7.8 million unemployed. Three full years later, the March 2011 jobs report painted a picture of an economy that made the March 2008 portrait seem like an unattainable dream—the unemployment rate had risen to 8.8 percent, and the number of unemployed workers was 13.5 million. Between the time this recession began (December 2007) and ended (June 2009), the number of unemployed workers rose by 7.1 million. How to get all those millions of people back to work had become the fundamental economic challenge of the twenty-first century.

Unemployment is the macroeconomic variable that affects people most personally. When the economy is booming and unemployment is low, it is easier for individuals to find jobs that are satisfying to them and that pay well. In contrast, when the economy is in recession and unemployment is high, jobs are harder to find, and people will settle for jobs that do not closely match their skills and do not pay very much money. Unemployment has painful economic consequences. Those who are unemployed experience the obvious hardships of income loss, loss of self-esteem, and an increasing toll on family life. Young people who live in a world of persistent unemployment fail to acquire job skills that will help them become productive citizens in the future. Beyond these individual and family hardships, unemployment has macroeconomic consequences as well. When more workers are unemployed, the production of goods and services is lower than it would be if more of those workers were employed. In other words, the economy is underutilizing its productive resources.

Even though college students are less likely than the general population to feel the immediate economic impact of a layoff, economic climates like we've seen in 2011 are extremely discouraging to college seniors.

Poor labor market conditions would make it more difficult for new college graduates to find a job in which they could put their knowledge and learning to use. They may have to move hundreds of miles to cities that offer more plentiful job opportunities, taking them far from friends and family. Some start making plans to head to graduate school, hoping to acquire more skills, and to delay their entry into the labor market. Day-to-day interactions among friends become a real challenge when some of them have found good jobs and others wonder whether they will ever be employed.

Historically, college graduates seem to have little reason to worry beyond the short run. Unemployment rates can, and do, vary among groups of individuals of different gender, age, race, and education, with the unemployment rate for college graduates being much lower than it is for the general population. They also vary dramatically across countries, even to the extent that the United States in a recession may have a lower unemployment rate than other economies that are booming. The current unemployment rate of 8.9 percent is well above what the United States economy has been experiencing in recent times. As the economy recovers, firms typically start hiring more workers and the number of unemployed workers will begin to fall; however, for some reason, the labor market has been slow to recover after this most recent recession. In the eighteen months between June 2009 (when the recession ended) and December 2010, the number of unemployed fell by fewer than 300,000. This uncertainty about the sluggish recovery of the labor market has added to the stress and uncertainty of college graduates as well as other workers.

It is essential for aspiring macroeconomists to learn more about unemployment and how to reduce it. This chapter examines the nature and causes of unemployment and teaches you how to use a simple model that will help answer such questions as the following: Why does unemployment rise in a recession? Why do people become unemployed, and how long do they remain unemployed? Why has the unemployment rate stayed so high even after the recession has ended? Why do unemployment rates differ so much among countries? Is it because of differences in education levels? Is it because of differences in attitudes toward work? Or, is it because of differences in the economic policies implemented by the different countries' governments?

Unemployment and Other Labor Market Indicators

In this section, we show how unemployment is defined and measured, and we discuss the various causes of unemployment.

How Is Unemployment Measured?

To understand what the data on unemployment mean, one must understand how unemployment is measured. Each month, the U.S. Census Bureau surveys a sample of

Current Population Survey
a monthly survey of a sample of U.S. households done by the U.S. Census Bureau; it measures employment, unemployment, the labor force, and other characteristics of the U.S. population.

unemployed person
an individual who does not have a job and is looking for work.

labor force
all those who are either employed or unemployed.

working-age population
persons over 16 years of age who are not in an institution, such as a jail or a hospital.

about 60,000 households in the United States. This survey is called the ***Current Population Survey***. By asking the people in the survey a number of questions, the U.S. Census Bureau determines whether each person 16 years of age or over is employed or unemployed.

Who Is Employed and Who Is Unemployed? To be counted as **unemployed**, a person must be looking for work but not have a job. To be counted as employed, a person must have a job, either a job outside the home—as in the case of a teaching job at a high school or a welding job at a factory—or a *paid* job inside the home—as in the case of a freelance editor or a telemarketer who works for pay at home. A person who has an *unpaid* job at home—for example, caring for children or working on the house—is not counted as employed.

The **labor force** consists of all people 16 years of age and older who are either employed or unemployed. If a person is not counted as either unemployed or employed, then that person is not in the labor force. For example, a person who is working at home without pay and who is not looking for a paid job is considered not in the labor force.

Figure 8-1 illustrates the definitions of employment, unemployment, and the labor force. Using December 2010 as an example, it shows that out of a **working-age population** of 238.9 million, 139.2 million were employed and 14.5 million were unemployed. The remaining 85.2 million were of working age but were not in the labor force.

The Labor Force and Discouraged Workers It is difficult to judge who should be counted as being in the labor force and who should not be counted. For example, consider two retired people. One decided to retire at age 65 and is now enjoying retirement in Florida. The other was laid off from a job at age 55 and, after looking for a job for two years, got discouraged and stopped looking, feeling forced into retirement. You may feel that the second person, but not the first, should be counted as unemployed. According to the official statistics, however, neither is unemployed; they are not in the labor force because they are not looking for work. In general, workers, such as the second retired worker, who have left the labor force after not being able to find a job are called *discouraged workers*.

Defining and measuring the labor force is the most difficult part of measuring the amount of unemployment. When a change was made in the way the questions in the *Current Population Survey* were phrased, it revealed that many women who were working at home without pay actually were looking for a paid job; as a result of the change in the question, these women are now counted as unemployed rather than as out of the labor force.

Part-Time Work A person is counted as employed in the *Current Population Survey* if he or she has worked at all during the week of the survey. Thus, part-time workers are counted as employed. The official definition of a *part-time worker* is one who works between one and 34 hours per week. About 26 percent of U.S. workers are employed part-time.

A big difference exists between the percentage of men who work part-time and the percentage of women who work part-time. In 2010, about 32 percent of employed women worked part-time, while only about 20 percent of employed men did so. Women give personal choice rather than unavailability of full-time jobs as a reason for part-time work more frequently than men do. About one-third of employed women who have children under age 3 work part time. Because of part-time work, the average number of hours of work per worker each week is about 34 hours, less than the typical 40 hours a week.

Figure 8-1

How to Find Labor Market Indicators

As shown at the top of this diagram, the working-age population (16 years of age and older) is divided into three groups: employed, unemployed, and not in the labor force. Three key labor market indicators are then computed from these categories. For example, the unemployment rate is the number of people unemployed divided by the number of people in the labor force. (The numbers in parentheses are in millions and are the statistics for December 2010.)

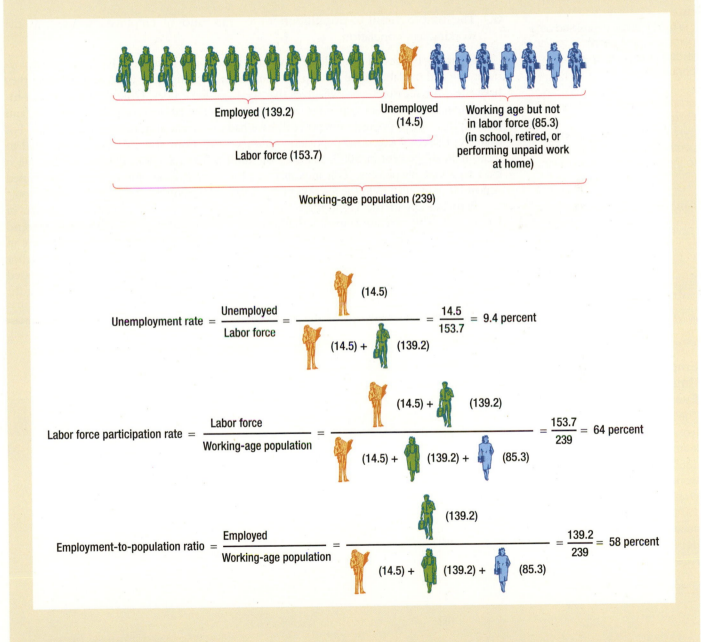

Source: Bureau of Labor Statistics.

Comparing Three Key Indicators

Now let us examine the three key indicators of conditions in the labor market. These are

unemployment rate
the percentage of the labor force that is unemployed. (Ch. 5)

1. The **unemployment rate**, the percentage of the labor force that is unemployed.

2. The **labor force participation rate**, the ratio of people in the labor force to the working-age population.

labor force participation rate
the ratio (usually expressed as a percentage) of people in the labor force to the working-age population.

3. The **employment-to-population ratio**, the ratio of employed workers to the working-age population.

employment-to-population ratio
the ratio (usually expressed as a percentage) of employed workers to the working-age population.

Figure 8-1 gives an example of how each indicator is calculated. Both the unemployment rate and the labor force participation rate depend on the labor force, and therefore they have the same measurement difficulties that the labor force does. Only the employment-to-population ratio does not depend on the labor force. The labor force participation rate and the employment-to-population ratio both have had important long-term upward trends. For example, the employment-to-population ratio increased from about 57 percent in 1950 to more than 64 percent in 2000, but after the most recent recession, this number has fallen back to about 58 percent. This indicates that the current economic downturn has erased almost 50 years of gains in the fraction of the employed among the working-age population.

Participation in the labor force has also changed over the decades, as shown in Figure 8-2. This increase is mainly due to more women entering the labor force, a trend that has been going on since the 1950s. In 1950, about 34 percent of women were in the labor force, but in 2010, 60 years later, about 58 percent of women are in the labor force. Possible explanations for this trend include reduced discrimination, increased opportunities and pay for women, the favorable experience of many women working for

Figure 8-2

Employment-to-Population Ratio for Men, Women, and Everyone

The percentage of working-age women who are employed has increased steadily since the 1950s. The percentage of working-age men who are employed declined until the late 1970s. After the mid-1990s, both series leveled off before declining during the current recession.

Source: Bureau of Labor Statistics.

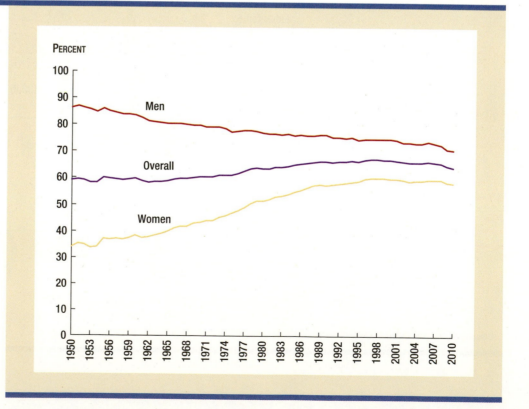

pay during World War II, and the women's movement, which emphasized the attractiveness of paid work outside the home. In recent years, this number has not grown by very much—in fact over the two decades from 1990 to 2010, the labor force participation rate of women has changed very little.

Aggregate Hours of Labor Input

As we have seen, some people work part time, others work full time, and some work overtime. For these reasons, the number of people employed is not a good measure of the labor input to production in the economy. For example, consider two bank tellers who both work half-time: One works four hours in the morning, the other works four hours in the afternoon, and both work five days a week. Even though they are two workers, together they work only as much as one full-time bank teller. So to count the labor input of these two part-time tellers as being twice as much as the labor input of one full-time teller would be an obvious mistake. Instead of the number of employed people, economists use hours worked to measure labor input. In the example of the bank tellers, the combined labor input of the two part-time tellers is the same as that of the one full-time teller: 40 hours a week.

Thus, the most comprehensive measure of labor input to the production of real gross domestic product (GDP) is the total number of hours worked by all workers, or **aggregate hours**. The number of aggregate hours of labor input depends on the number of hours of work for each person and the number of people working.

The growth of aggregate labor hours in the United States is slowing down. It grew by about 2 percent per year in the two decades between 1975 and 1995, but it increased by only 1 percent a year between 1995 and 2005 and has declined by about 1 percent per year over the past five years. This slowdown can be attributed to a reduction in the growth of the working-age population.

aggregate hours
the total number of hours worked by all workers in the economy in a given period of time.

Cyclical, Frictional, and Structural Unemployment

The unemployment rate fluctuates over time, sometimes fairly dramatically. Recall from Chapter 5 that the unemployment rate rises when the economy goes into a recession and falls when the economy expands. For example, as shown in Figure 8-3, when the economy expanded rapidly in the mid- to late 1990s, the unemployment rate was cut in half, falling from a peak of 7.8 percent in mid-1992 to a value of 3.9 percent by the end of 2000. When the U.S. economy went into recession in 2001, the unemployment rate rose back to above 6 percent. As the economy expanded again, the unemployment rate fell back down, reaching 4.5 percent by the end of 2006. The recession that began at the end of 2007 brought a dramatic increase in unemployment, peaking at 10.1 percent in October of 2009, and declining only slightly to 8.9 percent by the end of 2010.

Because the unemployment rate fluctuates so much depending on whether the economy is in a recession or a boom, economists always are interested in understanding what the unemployment rate would have been in the absence of these economic fluctuations. Economists use the term **natural unemployment rate** to refer to the unemployment rate that exists when the economy is not in a recession or a boom and real GDP is equal to potential GDP. The increase in unemployment above the natural rate during recessions is called **cyclical unemployment** because it is related to the short-term cyclical fluctuations in the economy. For example, the increase in the unemployment rate during the last recession was cyclical. The natural unemployment rate is caused by a combination of **frictional unemployment** and **structural unemployment**. Frictional unemployment occurs when new workers enter the labor force and must look for work,

natural unemployment rate
the unemployment rate that exists in the absence of a recession and a boom and real GDP is equal to potential GDP.

cyclical unemployment
unemployment resulting from a recession, when the rate of unemployment is above the natural rate of unemployment.

frictional unemployment
unemployment arising from normal turnover in the labor market, such as when people change occupations or locations, or are new entrants.

structural unemployment
unemployment resulting from structural problems, such as poor skills, long-term changes in demand, or insufficient work incentives.

Figure 8-3

The Unemployment Rate

The unemployment rate fluctuates around the natural unemployment rate, rising during recessions and falling when the economy grows rapidly during expansions.

Source: Bureau of Labor Statistics (unemployment rate); authors' calculation (natural rate).

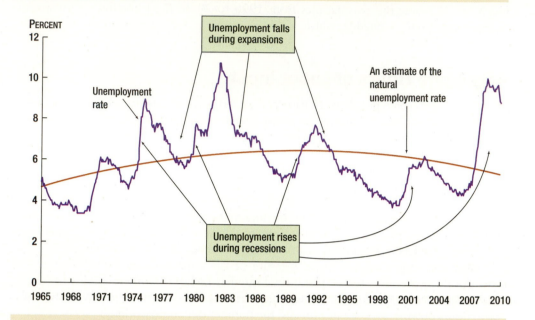

or when workers change jobs for one reason or another and need some time to find another job. Most frictional unemployment is short-lived. In contrast, some workers are unemployed for a long time, six months or more. These workers may have trouble finding work because they have insufficient skills or because their skills are no longer in demand as a result of a technological change or a shift in people's tastes toward new products. Such unemployment is called structural unemployment. The amount of frictional unemployment and structural unemployment in the economy is not constant, so the natural unemployment rate changes over time. But such changes are gradual and are not related to short-term economic fluctuations.

An estimate of the natural unemployment rate is shown in Figure 8-3. The natural rate of unemployment increased in the 1970s. One possible reason for the increase was the influx of young baby-boom workers into the labor force in the 1970s. Young people tend to have higher unemployment rates than older people. The natural unemployment rate declined in the 1990s as the labor force aged. The natural unemployment rate is not a constant and economists do not know its value precisely.

When economists use the term *natural unemployment rate,* they do not mean to say that this is "okay" or "just fine." They simply mean that whenever the operation of the overall macroeconomy is close to normal in the sense that real GDP is near potential GDP, the unemployment rate hovers around this natural rate. All else equal, having a low natural rate of unemployment is preferable because it means that, in normal times, fewer workers who are looking for work are unable to find it.

REVIEW

- Unemployment and employment in the United States are measured by the *Current Population Survey*.

- An unemployed individual is someone who does not have a job but is looking for work. An employed individual is someone who has a paid job. The labor force consists of all those who are either employed or unemployed.

- Because not all workers work full time, economists consider the aggregate number of hours worked to be the most comprehensive measure of labor input.

- The unemployment rate is the percentage of the labor force that is unemployed. The unemployment rate in the United States fluctuates cyclically, rising in times of recession and falling in times of expansion.

- The unemployment rate in the absence of cyclical increases or decreases is called the natural rate of unemployment. The natural rate of unemployment is caused by a combination of frictional unemployment (people changing jobs or occupations) and structural unemployment (unemployment caused by poor skills or changes in the types of goods produced in the economy).

- Two other important measures are the labor force participation rate (what fraction of the working-age population is in the labor force) and the employment-to-population ratio (what fraction of the working-age population has a job). Both ratios rose in the period from the 1960s to the 1990s because of more women entering the labor force.

ECONOMICS *IN ACTION*

The Employment Situation: February 2010

The U.S. Bureau of Labor Statistics reported in February 2010 that nonfarm payroll employment increased by 192,000, and the unemployment rate was little changed at 8.9 percent. Job gains occurred in manufacturing, construction, professional and business services, health care, and transportation and warehousing.

Unemployment (Household Survey Data)

The number of unemployed persons (13.7 million) and the unemployment rate (8.9 percent) changed little in February. The labor force was about unchanged over the month. The jobless rate was down by 0.9 since November 2010. Among the major worker groups, the unemployment rates for adult men (8.7 percent), adult women (8.0 percent), teenagers (23.9 percent), whites (8 percent), blacks (15.3 percent), and Hispanics (11.6 percent) showed little or no change in February. The jobless rate for Asians was 6.8 percent, not seasonally adjusted. The number of long-term unemployed (those jobless for 27 weeks or more) was 6 million and accounted for 43.9 percent of the unemployed.

Total Employment and the Labor Force (Household Survey Data)

Both the civilian labor force participation rate, at 64.2 percent, and the employment-population ratio, at 58.4 percent, were unchanged in February. The number of persons employed part time for economic reasons (sometimes referred to as involuntary part-time workers) was essentially unchanged at 8.3 million in February. These individuals were working part time because their hours had been cut back or because they were unable to find a full-time job.

Persons Not in the Labor Force (Household Survey Data)

In February, 2.7 million persons were marginally attached to the labor force, up from 2.5 million a year earlier. These individuals were not in the labor force, wanted and were available for work, and had looked for a job sometime in the prior 12 months. They were not counted as unemployed because they had not searched for work in the four weeks preceding the survey. Among the marginally attached, there were 1 million discouraged workers in February, a decrease of 184,000 from a year earlier. Discouraged workers are persons not currently looking for work because they believe no jobs are available for them. The remaining 1.7 million persons marginally attached to the labor force in February had not searched for work in the four weeks preceding the survey for reasons such as school attendance or family responsibilities.

The Nature of Unemployment

Having examined the aggregate data, let us now look at the circumstances of people who are unemployed. People become unemployed for many reasons, and people's experiences with unemployment vary widely.

Reasons People Are Unemployed

We can divide the many reasons people become unemployed into four broad categories. People are unemployed because they have either lost their previous job (*job losers*), quit their previous job (*job leavers*), entered the labor force to look for work for the first time (*new entrants*), or re-entered the labor force after being out of it for a while (*re-entrants*). Figure 8-4 shows how the 9.4 percent unemployment rate in December 2010 was divided into these four categories.

Job Losers   Among the people who lost their jobs in a typical recent year was a vice president of a large bank in Chicago. When the vice president's financial services marketing department was eliminated, she lost her job. After three months of unemployment, which she spent searching for work and waiting for responses to her letters and telephone calls, the former vice president took a freelance job, using her expertise to advise clients on financial planning matters. Within a year, she was making three times her former salary.

The vice president's unemployment experience, although surely trying for her at the time, had a happy ending. In fact, you might say that the labor market worked pretty well. At least judging by her salary, she is more productive in her new job. Although one job was destroyed, another one—a better one, in this case—was created.

Figure 8-4

Job Losers, Job Leavers, New Entrants, and Re-entrants (December 2010)
A significant part of the unemployment rate consists of people who lost their jobs. The rest consists of people who left their jobs to look for another job or who have just entered or re-entered the labor force.

Source: Bureau of Labor Statistics.

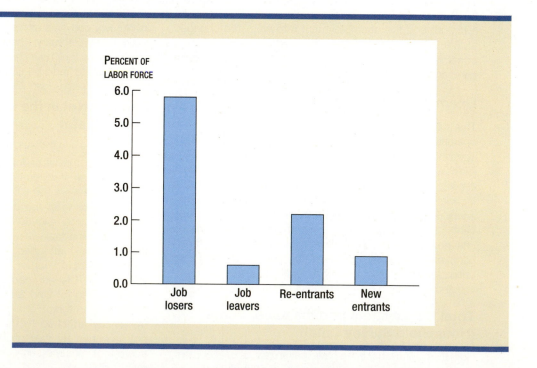

This transition from one job to another is part of the dynamism of any free market economy. The economist Joseph Schumpeter called this dynamism *creative destruction,* referring to the loss of whole business firms as well as jobs when new ideas and techniques replace the old. Creative destruction means that something better is created as something else is destroyed. In this case, a better job was created when one job was destroyed. The labor market in the United States is extremely fluid, with a large number of jobs being created and destroyed every month. In December 2010 alone, 3 million workers found jobs while 2.9 million workers lost jobs.

In an economy with growing employment, more jobs are created than are destroyed. In times of recession, however, when employment is likely to fall, more jobs are destroyed than are created. So the bank manager was lucky to have lost her job during a period when finding a comparable job was relatively easy, but many people who lose their jobs are not as lucky as the woman in our story.

On average, about half of all unemployed workers are unemployed because they lost their jobs for one reason or another. This number typically will rise in a recession. People may lose their jobs even when the economy is not in a recession. The economy is always in a state of flux, with some firms going out of business or shrinking and other firms starting up or expanding. Tastes change, new discoveries are made, and competition improves productivity and changes the relative fortunes of firms and workers.

Among the unemployed in recent years were real estate agents let go by realtors who were seeing drastic slumps in new home sales; construction workers unable to find jobs in the formerly booming housing markets of Nevada, Florida, Arizona, and California; managers laid off by banks that had been acquired by other banks because of financial difficulties; and workers in service sector firms who were struggling to survive turbulent times. Finding a comparable job was difficult for such workers: Most other firms at which they could have worked also were facing financial difficulties and therefore were laying off workers instead of hiring them, or they were undergoing the same type of structural changes that led to the workers being laid off from their previous firms.

The loss of a job not only has disastrous effects on income, but also can have psychological effects. It may mean that a worker's children cannot go to college or that the worker must sell his or her house. Unemployment compensation provides some relief—perhaps about $200 a week until it runs out. In many cases, however, this is well below what these workers were earning. Until they find a new job, they are part of the millions of unemployed. Some may wait until a comparable job comes along; others may accept a

Reasons People Are Unemployed

People are unemployed for different reasons: Some lost their job and are looking for another job (left), others quit their previous job and still are looking for a new job (middle), and yet others just entered or re-entered the labor force and are unemployed while looking for work (right).

job vacancies
positions that firms are trying to fill, but for which they have yet to find suitable workers.

lower-paying job. For example, a laid-off software programmer may take a job as a community college instructor for a much lower salary.

At the same time that unemployed workers are looking for jobs, many firms have jobs that have not been filled; these are called **job vacancies**. Job vacancies and unemployment exist simultaneously. You might think that these two should not coexist because the unemployed workers should be able to take the unfilled jobs, but unfortunately, that is not always possible. Many job vacancies require different skills from those of unemployed workers, are located in another part of the country, or offer lower wages than these workers' former salaries.

Job Leavers   On average, American workers change jobs every three or four years. Many of these job changes occur when people are young: Young workers are finding out what they are good at or what they enjoy or are rapidly accumulating skills that give them greater opportunities. A small part of unemployment—less than one-fourth—consists of people who quit their previous job to look for another job. While they are looking for work, they are counted as unemployed. Unemployment increases very little as a result of quits during recessions. In a recession, when unemployment is high, fewer workers quit their jobs because they fear being unemployed for a long period of time.

New Entrants and Re-entrants   Figure 8-4 also shows that a large number of the unemployed workers have just entered the workforce. If Jennifer, the college student we talked about at the beginning of this chapter, does not have a job lined up before she graduates, then she will be counted as an unemployed worker for the period of time while she looks for work. In fact, unemployment increases significantly each June as millions of students enter the labor force for the first time. This is called *seasonal unemployment* because it occurs each graduation "season." In contrast, unemployment is relatively low around the holiday season, when many businesses hire extra employees. Government statisticians smooth out this seasonal unemployment to identify other trends in unemployment, so newspaper reports on the unemployment rate rarely mention this phenomenon.

Some unemployed workers are re-entering the labor force. For example, a young person may decide to go back to school to improve her skills and then re-enter the labor force afterward. Others might drop out of the labor force for several years to take care of small children at home—a job that is not counted in the unemployment statistics.

Some new entrants and some re-entrants into the labor force find it difficult to get a job and therefore remain unemployed for long periods of time. In fact, although the hardships of people who lose their jobs are severe, the hardships for many young people, especially for those who dropped out of high school and who seem to be endlessly looking for work, also are severe. Similarly, re-entrants who have been away from the labor market for a long time, perhaps for as long as a couple of decades to raise children, will not find it easy to find work in a labor market that is quite different from the one in which they were last employed.

The Duration of Unemployment

The hardships associated with unemployment depend on its duration. Figure 8-5 shows how the unemployment rate is divided according to how long the unemployed workers have been unemployed. A significant fraction of unemployment is short term. A market economy with millions of people exercising free choice could not possibly function without some short-term unemployment as people changed jobs or looked for new opportunities.

As of December 2010, 44 percent of unemployed workers had been unemployed for more than six months—the truly long-term unemployed. Although the number of short-

Figure 8-5

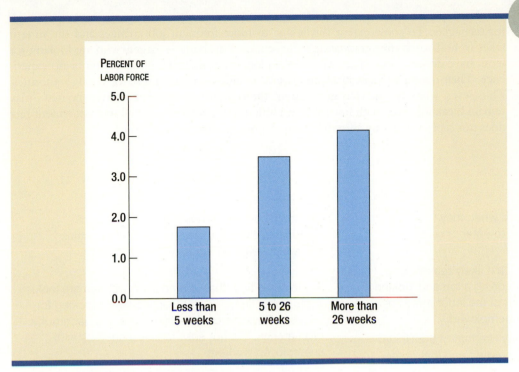

Unemployment by Duration (December 2010)
The overall unemployment rate was 9.4 percent in December 2010. A staggering 44 percent of this unemployment was long term—more than 26 weeks.

Source: Current Employment Survey (Washington, DC: Bureau of Labor Statistics).

term unemployed does not vary much over the business cycle, the number of long-term unemployed increases dramatically in recessions.

Unemployment for Different Groups

Regardless of how one interprets the numbers, certain groups of workers experience very long spells of unemployment and suffer great hardships as a result of the difficulty they have in finding work. Table 8-1 shows the unemployment rates for several different demographic groups in the United States in three time periods: 1994, 2004, and 2010. During all three of these time periods, the economy was a couple of years into the beginning of economic recovery from a recession.

Table 8-1

Unemployment Rates for Different Demographic Groups (percent of labor force for each group)

	1994	2004	2010
All persons	5.5	5.4	9.4
All females	5.5	5.2	10.1
All males	5.5	5.6	10.2
All whites	4.8	4.6	8.5
All blacks	9.9	10.8	15.8
All Hispanics	9.3	6.6	13.0
All females 20 years and older	4.8	4.7	9.4
All males 20 years and older	4.7	4.9	8.1
All teens 16–19	17.0	17.6	25.4

Source: Bureau of Labor Statistics.

Unemployment is lowest for adult men and women. But unemployment is quite high for teenagers. To some extent this is due to more frequent job changes and the time it takes to find work after graduating from school. But many teenagers who are looking for work have dropped out of school and therefore are unskilled and have little or no experience. Their unemployment rates are extremely high, especially those for young minorities. Thus, even when the news is good about the overall unemployment rate, the news may remain bleak for those with low skills and little experience. The overall unemployment rate does not capture the long-term hardships experienced by certain groups.

REVIEW

- People become unemployed when they lose their job, quit their job, or decide to enter or re-enter the labor force to look for a job.

- Being a new entrant is the least likely reason for a person to be unemployed. Losing a job and looking for work after some time out of the labor force are more likely reasons to be unemployed.

- In a large, dynamic economy like that of the United States, millions of jobs are created and lost during each month. In times of recession, more jobs are lost than are created.

- Many unemployed people are able to find a job fairly quickly. On average, only about one-sixth of unemployed people have been unemployed for

six months or more. These workers often lack appropriate skills or were employed in industries that are undergoing fundamental structural changes.

- At the same time that unemployed workers are looking for jobs, firms with job vacancies are looking for workers. Because of skill differences and geographic mismatches, it is not easy to fill vacant jobs with unemployed workers.

- Unemployment rates vary across different groups. Teenagers and minorities in the United States have very high unemployment rates, even in boom years, and often are the first to suffer in times of recession.

Modeling the Labor Market

Thus far in this chapter, we have introduced key labor market variables, like the unemployment rate and the labor force participation rate; looked at data on both the current values and past trends of these variables; and discussed why people become (and stay) unemployed. In this section, we change our focus from data and definitions to theory, and discuss how to construct a model of the labor market. If we are able to come up with a model that provides a good explanation of the labor market trends we discussed earlier, then we can use this model to identify policy changes, as well as other economic changes, that can help reduce the rate of unemployment in the economy. Lowering the rate of unemployment, especially the natural rate of unemployment, will give individuals the opportunity to earn a living and allow a country to make full use of its labor resources.

Labor Demand and Labor Supply

We begin with the basic supply and demand framework developed in Chapter 3. Figure 8-6 shows a labor demand curve and a labor supply curve. On the vertical axis is the price of labor (wage), and on the horizontal axis is the quantity of labor supplied or demanded. In a labor market, the **labor demand curve** describes the behavior of firms, indicating how much labor they would demand at a given wage. The **labor supply curve** describes the behavior

labor demand curve
a downward-sloping relationship showing the quantity of labor firms are willing to hire at each wage.

labor supply curve
upward sloping relationship showing the quantity of labor workers are willing to supply at each wage.

of workers, showing how much labor they would supply at a given wage. The *wage*, usually measured in dollars per hour of work, is the price of labor. To explain employment in the whole economy, it is best to think of the wage relative to the average price of goods. In other words, the wage on the vertical axis is the **real wage**, which we define as follows:

$$\text{Real wage} = \frac{\text{wage}}{\text{price level}}$$

Firms consider the wages they must pay their workers in comparison with the price of the products they sell. The workers consider the wage in comparison with the price of the goods they buy. Thus, in the whole economy, it is the real wage that affects the quantity of labor supplied and demanded.

The labor demand curve slopes downward because a lower real wage implies that the wage that the firm has to pay to hire a worker is falling relative to the price of the goods that the firm is selling. This reduced wage gives firms an incentive to hire more workers and pay existing workers to work more hours—the now-familiar result that the quantity demanded of labor rises as the price of labor (the real wage) falls. The labor supply curve slopes upward, because a higher real wage implies that the wage that the worker receives is rising compared with the price of the goods that the worker buys. This increased wage gives people greater incentive to work and gives those who are working an incentive to work more hours—another familiar result that the quantity supplied of labor rises as the price of labor (the real wage) rises.

As in any market, we would predict that the equilibrium quantity (hours of work) and the equilibrium price (the real wage) should occur at the intersection of the labor demand curve and the labor supply curve, as shown in Figure 8-6.

real wage
the wage or price of labor adjusted for inflation; in contrast, the nominal wage has not been adjusted for inflation.

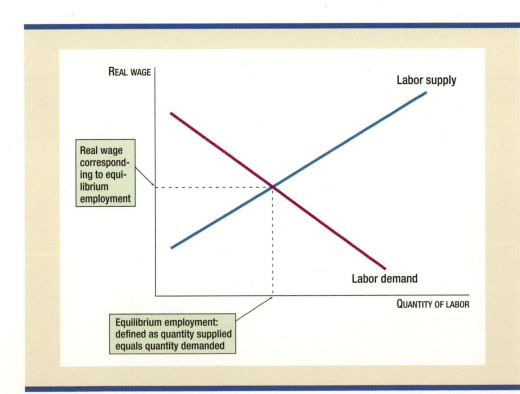

Figure 8-6

Labor Supply, Labor Demand, and Equilibrium Employment
The intersection of the labor supply curve and the labor demand curve determines equilibrium employment and the real wage.

Explaining Labor Market Trends

Let's use this basic supply and demand framework to analyze labor market behavior. Suppose the economy enters a boom period during which firms are facing an increasing demand from consumers for the goods and services they produce. Firms will be eager to hire more workers to produce the goods and services that their consumers are clamoring for, resulting in an increase in the demand for labor. As the labor demand curve shifts to the right, as shown in Figure 8-7, both the equilibrium price and the equilibrium quantity of labor will rise. In other words, during an economic expansion, the model predicts an increase in the real wage and an increase in employment. Suppose instead that the economy had tumbled into a recession, during which time firms were cutting back on their production and did not need to hire as many workers. Then the demand for labor would shift to the left, and the real wage and employment would decrease.

The prediction of the model that wages and employment should rise in expansions and fall in recessions seems intuitive. The simple model as depicted in Figure 8-7, however, has a glaring weakness. Notice that the economy is at the intersection of the supply curve and the demand curve, regardless of whether it is in an expansion or a recession. In other words, the real wage always adjusts so that the quantity of labor demanded is equal to the quantity of labor supplied. Given the definition of an unemployed worker as someone who is looking for work but unable to find a job, the model implies that unemployment is always zero, no matter what state the economy is in. The simple model, which predicts that the economy will be at the intersection of the supply and demand curves, is inconsistent with the facts. We need to modify the model before we can use it for analysis.

Why Is the Unemployment Rate Always Greater Than Zero?

Economists have developed two different explanations that adapt the standard labor supply and demand analysis to account for unemployment. Although quite different,

Figure 8-7

Modeling the Labor Market during an Economic Expansion

When the economy enters an expansion period, firms produce more output and thus need more workers. The demand for labor increases, shifting the demand curve to the right. Equilibrium real wages and equilibrium employment rise.

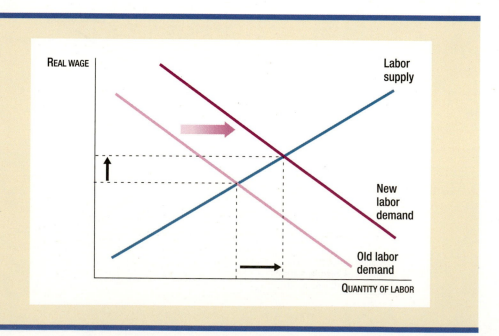

the explanations are complementary. In fact, it is essential for us to use both simultane-ously if we are to understand unemployment. We will refer to the two explanations as **job rationing** and **job search**.

Job Rationing The job-rationing story has two parts. One is an assumption that *the wage is higher than what would equate the quantity of labor supplied with the quantity of labor demanded*. This assumption may be true for several reasons, but first consider the consequences for the labor supply and demand diagram. Figure 8-8 shows the same labor supply and demand curves as Figure 8-6. In Figure 8-8, however, the wage is higher than the wage that would equate the quantity of labor supplied with the quantity of labor demanded. At this wage, the number of workers demanded by firms is smaller than the number of workers willing to supply their labor.

The other part of the job-rationing story tells us how to determine the number of workers who are unemployed. This part of the story assumes that the number of workers employed equals the quantity of labor demanded by business firms. When the wage is too high, firms hire a smaller number of workers, and workers supply whatever the firms demand. Figure 8-8 shows the resulting amount of employment at the given wage as point *A* on the labor demand curve. With employment equal to the number of workers demanded, we see that the number of workers willing to supply their labor is greater than the number of workers employed; the excess supply therefore results in unemployment. In the diagram, the amount of unemployment is measured in the horizontal direction.

This is a situation in which workers would be willing to take a job at the wage that firms are paying, but the job offers at that wage are insufficient. In effect, the available jobs are rationed—for example, by a first-come-first-served rule or by seniority. When enough workers have been hired, the firms essentially close their hiring offices, and the

job rationing
a reason for unemployment in which the quantity of labor supplied is greater than the quantity demanded because the real wage is too high.

job search
a reason for unemployment in which uncertainty in the labor market and workers' limited information require people to spend time searching for a job.

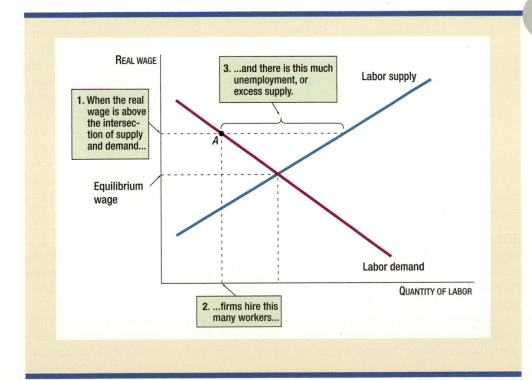

Figure 8-8

Excess Supply of Labor and Unemployment
The supply and demand curves are exactly as in Figure 8-6, except that the horizontal axis is interpreted as employment here. However, the real wage is too high to bring the quantity supplied into equality with the quantity demanded. The number of workers employed is given by point *A* on the demand curve, at which point the real wage is above the equilibrium wage. At this higher real wage, the quantity supplied is greater than the quantity demanded—a situation that we think of as unemployment.

remaining workers stay unemployed. If the wage were lower, then the firms would hire more workers, but the wage is not lower.

In most markets, a situation of excess supply brings about a reduction in the price—in this case, the wage. Thus, if this explanation of unemployment is to work in practice, a force has to be at work that prevents the wage from falling. If the theory is to be helpful in explaining unemployment, then the force has to be permanently at work, not just in a recession. Why doesn't the wage fall when there is an excess supply of workers? Three reasons explain why the wage always might be too high to bring the quantity of labor demanded into balance with the quantity of labor supplied.

minimum wage
a wage per hour below which it is illegal to pay workers. (Ch. 4)

1. *Minimum wages.* Most countries have a legal **minimum wage**, or lowest possible wage, that employers can pay their employees. A minimum wage can cause unemployment to be higher than it otherwise would be, as shown on the diagram in Figure 8-8: Employers would move down and to the right along their labor demand curve and hire more workers if the wage were lower.

    One of the reasons teenage unemployment is high (as shown in Table 8-1) may be related to the minimum wage. Because many teenagers are unskilled, the wage that firms would be willing to pay them is low. A minimum wage, therefore, may price them out of the market and cause them to be unemployed.

insider
a person who already works for a firm and has some influence over wage and hiring policy.

outsider
someone who is not working for a particular firm, making it difficult for him or her to get a job with that firm even though he or she is willing to work for a lower wage.

2. *Insiders versus outsiders.* Sometimes groups of workers—**insiders**, who have jobs—can prevent the wage from declining. If these workers have developed skills that are unique to the job, or if legislation prevents their being fired without significant legal costs, then they have some power to keep wages up. Labor unions may help these workers keep the wage higher than it otherwise would be. One consequence of the higher wage is to prevent the firm from hiring unemployed workers—the **outsiders**—who would be willing to work at a lower wage. This is a common explanation for the very high unemployment in Europe, and the theory has been developed and applied to Europe by the Swedish economist Assar Lindbeck and the British economist Dennis Snower.

efficiency wage
a wage higher than that which would equate quantity supplied and quantity demanded, set by employers to increase worker efficiency—for example, by decreasing shirking by workers.

3. *Efficiency wages.* Firms may choose to pay workers an **efficiency wage**—an extra amount to encourage them to be more efficient. Workers' efficiency or productivity might increase with the wage for many reasons. Turnover will be lower with a higher wage because workers will have less reason to look for another job: They are unlikely to find a position paying more than their current wage. Lower turnover means lower training costs for employers. Moreover, workers might not avoid work as much with a higher wage. This is particularly important to the firm when jobs are difficult to monitor. With efficiency wages, workers who are working are paid more than the wage that equates the quantity supplied with the quantity demanded. When workers are paid efficiency wages, unemployment will be greater than zero. Unemployed workers are eager to work at the prevailing wage, but they may be unable to obtain those jobs because existing workers value the high-paying jobs and are loath to give them up.

Job Search We now turn to the second explanation that modifies the standard labor supply and demand analysis. The labor market is constantly in a state of flux, with jobs being created and destroyed and people moving from one job to another. The demand for one type of work falls, and the demand for another type of work increases. Labor supply curves also shift.

In other words, the labor market is never truly in the state of rest conveyed by the fixed supply and demand curves shown in Figure 8-6. But how can we change the picture? Imagine labor demand and labor supply curves that constantly bounce around.

The demand for labor, the supply of labor, and the wage will be different during every period. Figure 8-6 will be in perpetual motion. Mathematicians use the adjective *stochastic* to describe this constant bouncing around. Economists apply the term *stochastic* to models of the labor market that are in perpetual motion. Rather than a fixed equilibrium of quantity and a fixed wage, a *stochastic equilibrium* exists. This stochastic equilibrium in the labor market characterizes the constant job creation and job destruction that exist in the economy. People enter the workforce, move from one job to another, lose their jobs, or drop out of the labor force. Wages change, inducing people to enter or re-enter the market. Figure 8-9 is a schematic representation of the flows of workers into and out of the labor market.

In a stochastic equilibrium, at any point in time people will be searching for a job. Many who do so will be unemployed for some time. They lost their job, quit their job, or came back to the job market after an absence from work. One of the reasons they remain unemployed for a while is that they find it to their advantage not to accept the first job that comes along. Rather, they wait for a possibly higher-paying job. While they wait, they are unemployed.

Figure 8-9

Labor Market Flows
The labor market is constantly in a state of flux, as people lose jobs, quit jobs, find jobs, and move into and out of the labor force. Most people pass through the unemployment box for a short period, but among the unemployed, some have not held jobs for a long time.

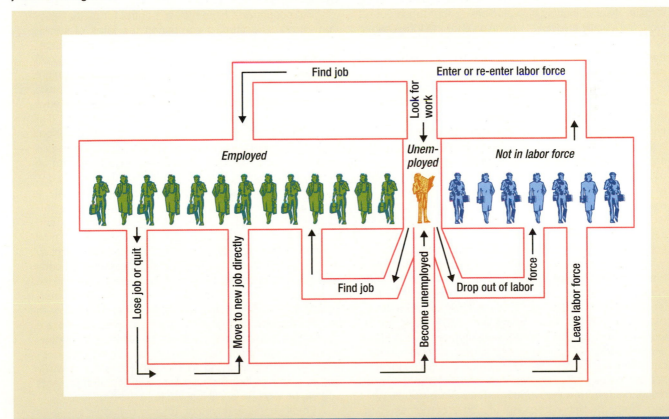

ECONOMICS *IN ACTION*

How Long is Too Long, for the Unemployed?

One of the worrying features of the most recent recession, and the sluggish recovery, has been the rapid increase in the number of workers who have been unemployed for 27 weeks or longer. The following *New York Times* article takes a closer look at some of those workers, and offers a glimpse into how cyclical unemployment can become structural unemployment after a year or so passes by.

Unemployed, and Likely to Stay That Way

BY Catherine Rampell, *The New York Times*, Dec. 2, 2010

The longer people stay out of work, the more trouble they have finding new work. That is a fact of life that much of Europe, with its underclass of permanently idle workers, knows all too well. But it is a lesson that the United States seems to be just learning. This country has some of the highest levels of long-term unemployment—out of work longer than six months—it has ever recorded. Meanwhile, job growth has been, and looks to remain, disappointingly slow, indicating that those out of work for a while are likely to remain so for the foreseeable future. Even if the government report on Friday shows the expected improvement in hiring by business, it will not be enough to make a real dent in those totals.

So the legions of long-term unemployed will probably be idle for significantly longer than their counterparts in past recessions, reducing their chances of eventually finding a job even when the economy becomes more robust. "I am so worried somebody will look at me and say, 'Oh, he's probably lost his edge,'" said Tim Smyth, 51, a New York television producer who has been unable to find work since 2008, despite having two decades of experience at places like Nickelodeon and the Food Network. "I mean, I know it's not true, but I'm afraid I might say the same thing if I were interviewing someone I didn't know very well who's been out of work this long."

Mr. Smyth's anxieties are not unfounded. New data from the Labor Department, provided to *The New York Times*, shows that people out of work fewer than five weeks are more than three times as likely to find a job in the coming month than people who have been out of work for over a year, with a re-employment rate of 30.7 percent versus 8.7 percent, respectively. Likewise, previous economic studies, many based on Europe's job market struggles, have shown that people who become disconnected from the workforce have more trouble getting hired, probably because of some combination of stigma, discouragement and deterioration of their skills.

This is one of the biggest challenges facing policy makers in the United States as they seek to address unemployment. Its underlying tenet—that time exacerbates the problem—means that the longer Congress squabbles about how to increase job growth, the more intractable the situation becomes. This, in turn, means Washington would need to pursue more aggressive (and, perversely, more politically difficult) job-creating policies in order to succeed. Even reaching an agreement over whether to extend benefits yet again has proved contentious.

Several factors lead to this downward spiral of the unemployed. In some cases, the long-term unemployed were poor performers in their previous positions and among the first to be terminated when the recession began. These people are weak job candidates with less impressive résumés and references. In other instances, those who lost jobs may have been good workers but were laid off from occupations or industries that are in permanent decline, like manufacturing.

But economists have tried to control for these selection issues, and studies comparing the fates of similar workers have also shown that the experience of unemployment itself damages job prospects. If jobless workers had been in sales, for instance, their customers might have moved on. Or perhaps the list of contacts they could turn to for leads is obsolete. Mr. Smyth, for example, says that so many of his former co-workers have been displaced that he is no longer sure whom to call on about openings. In particularly dynamic industries, like software engineering, unemployed workers might also miss out on new developments and fail to develop the skills required.

Still, this explanation probably applies to only a small slice of the country's 6.2 million long-term unemployed. "I can't imagine very many occupations and industries are of the type that if you're out for nine months, the world passes you by," said Heidi Shierholz, an economist at the Economic Policy Institute, a liberal research organization. "I think this erosion-of-skills idea is way overplayed. It's probably much more about marketability." Many unemployed workers fret about how to explain the yawning gaps on their résumés. Some are calling themselves independent "consultants" or "entrepreneurs." Mr. Smyth has been working on his own documentary film and trying to develop ideas for new TV shows with a friend. But with financing for such projects scarce, he says he is still looking for a full-time job.

Employers are reluctant to acknowledge any bias against the jobless, and many say they try to take broader economic circumstances into consideration. "Generally speaking, when the economy's good and someone's been out of work for a year, you might look at them funny," said Jay Goltz, who owns five small businesses in Chicago and contributes to a small-business blog for *The Times*. "These days I don't know if you can hold it against somebody."

Even so, old habits die hard, especially because unemployment has been unusually concentrated among a smaller group of workers in this recent recession than in previous ones, meaning that fewer workers bear the scarlet "U" of unemployment.

"From what I've seen, employers do tend to get suspicious when there's a long-term gap in people's résumés," said James Whelly, deputy director of workforce development at the San Francisco Human Services Agency. "Even though everyone on an intellectual level knows that this is a unique time in the economy, those old habits are hard to break with hiring managers and H.R. departments who are doing the screening."

It does not help when job seekers are repeatedly rejected—or worse, ignored. Constant rejection not only discourages workers from job-hunting as intensively, but also makes people less confident when they do land interviews. A Pew Social Trends report found that the long-term unemployed were significantly more likely to say they had lost some of their self-respect than their counterparts with shorter spells of joblessness. "People don't have money to keep up appearances important for job hunting," said Katherine S. Newman, a sociology professor at Princeton. "They can't go to the dentist. They can't get new clothes. They gain weight and look out of shape, since unemployment is such a stressful experience. All that is held against them when there is such an enormous range of workers to choose from."

The real threat, economists say, is that America, like some of its Old World peers, may simply become accustomed to a large class of idled workers. "After a while, a lot of European countries just got used to having 8 or 9 percent unemployment, where they just said, 'Hey, that's about good enough,'" said Gary Burtless, a senior fellow at the Brookings Institution. "If the unemployment rates here stay high but remain relatively stable, people may not worry so much that that'll be their fate this month or next year. And all these unemployed people will fall from the front of their mind, and that's it for them."

Policies to Reduce Unemployment Both the job-rationing model and the job-search model have implications for how public policy can reduce both the rate of unemployment and the natural rate of unemployment. The job-rationing model predicts that high minimum wages, rigid insider-outsider arrangements, and a greater need to pay efficiency wages can lead to more unemployment. This implies that public policies that reduce minimum wages or encourage more flexible union-employer relationships can reduce unemployment. Similarly, economic changes and policy changes that make it easier for firms to monitor shirking workers and cheaper to train new workers will enable firms to hire more workers at a reduced efficiency wage. As with any case of rationing, those who are lucky enough to have access to the commodity (in this case, jobs) are better off as a result of the restriction. Policies that remove the constraint and allow the market to reach equilibrium benefit those who now are able to obtain jobs while hurting those who previously had jobs but now earn a lower wage.

The job-search model implies that improved job-placement programs, retraining of unemployed workers, increasing the incentives of unemployed workers to look for work, and decreasing the costs of hiring new workers all will help reduce unemployment. In an economy in which unemployment compensation—money paid to workers who have been laid off from their job—is high, workers are likely to spend more time looking for a job or to hold out for a higher-paying job. Reducing unemployment compensation will provide more incentives for workers to look for work and increase the likelihood that they will find a good job match. Here too, you have to consider the trade-offs before implementing a policy change. Unemployment compensation mitigates the hardships associated with unemployment and allows people more time to search. But the more generous unemployment compensation is, the less incentive a worker has to actually take a job. If workers continue a perfunctory search for jobs, unemployment will remain high.

The challenge is to design an unemployment compensation system that supports workers who lose their jobs without increasing unemployment by a lot.

What about the natural rate of unemployment? If you take a closer look at the labor market flows in Figure 8-9, you will see that the rate of unemployment that usually prevails in an economy will depend on two things: (1) how great the flows into the group of employed workers are (these flows come from those who were unemployed and those who were already employed), and (2) how great the flows into the group of unemployed workers are (these flows come from both previously employed workers and those who previously were out of the labor force). Economies in which the flows into employment are relatively low or the flows into unemployment are relatively high (or both) will have a high natural rate of unemployment. Similarly, economies in which the flows into employment are high or the flows into unemployment are low (or both) will have a low natural rate of unemployment.

In the United States, lots of workers lose their jobs in a given month, but many of them are able to find new jobs easily, because firms face relatively few restrictions in their ability to hire workers. In addition, unemployment compensation in most of the United States typically runs out after 26 weeks; the evidence shows that many people stop searching and take a job just when their unemployment compensation runs out. Furthermore, new entrants to the labor market, like college students, typically are not eligible for unemployment compensation; these young workers are likely to find a job quickly, even if it is a lower-paying position than they ideally would like to have.

In contrast, in an economy like Spain's, workers who lose their jobs may find it difficult to move to another job because stronger unions restrict the quantity of labor demanded by firms or because generous long-term unemployment benefits, available to those without much work experience, discourage unemployed workers and new entrants from intensively searching for work. As a result, the natural rate for unemployment in Spain is likely to be higher than the natural rate in the United States. Furthermore, this can explain why a U.S. college student would be much more likely to find a job after graduation than the graduate's Spanish counterpart would.

REVIEW

- The supply and demand for labor is the starting point for modeling the labor market. The quantity demanded of labor falls as the real wage rises, whereas the quantity supplied of labor rises. The intersection of the labor supply and demand curves determines the amount of employment and the equilibrium real wage.

- The basic supply and demand framework predicts that employment and wages will rise during economic expansions and fall during recessions. Because the economy is always at the intersection of the supply and demand curves, the model seems to predict that unemployment is zero—the quantity of labor supplied is always equal to the quantity of labor demanded, and no one is looking for but unable to find work.

- The basic supply and demand theory needs to be modified to account for unemployment. Economists use two approaches, job rationing and job search, to explain why unemployment occurs.

- Job rationing occurs when the wage is too high. Unemployment can be interpreted as the difference between the quantity supplied and the quantity demanded at that high wage. Wages can be too high because of minimum-wage laws, insiders, or efficiency wages.

- Job search is another reason for unemployment. It takes time to find a job, and people have an incentive to wait for a good job.

- Policies that reduce the amount of rationing or lower the cost of job search can reduce unemployment.

CONCLUSION

This chapter provided two important lessons about labor markets. The first lesson introduced key concepts, such as the unemployment rate and the labor force participation rate. Understanding who the unemployed are, how long they stay unemployed, and how unemployment rates vary across time and across countries is a critical prerequisite for designing policies that can reduce unemployment.

The second lesson constructed a model of the labor market that would replicate the patterns observed in the labor market. That model then could be used to come up with policy recommendations that could help workers obtain jobs and help economies make better use of one of their most important productive resources. We showed that the simple supply and demand model could not realistically describe the labor market, but that augmenting that model to take into account job rationing and job search provides insight into possible policy interventions. Lower minimum wages, less rigid unions, better job training, and less generous unemployment benefits all can increase the rate at which people who are either unemployed or out of the labor force move into employment, as well as decrease the rate at which employed workers or workers who are out of the labor force move into the ranks of the unemployed. The challenge for policy makers is how to carry out these reforms to balance the benefits to currently unemployed workers with the costs to currently employed workers.

KEY POINTS

1. Unemployment and employment data are collected by the Bureau of Labor Statistics and are made available in the monthly *Current Population Survey*.

2. A person is unemployed if he or she is old enough to work and is looking for work, but does not have a job. The unemployment rate is the number of unemployed as a percentage of the labor force, which consists of all the employed and unemployed in the economy.

3. Two other widely used measures of the labor market are the employment-to-population ratio (the number of people employed as a percentage of the working-age population) and the labor force participation rate (the labor force as a percentage of the working-age population). Both of these indicators rose in the United States following the end of World War II as more women entered the workforce.

4. Not all workers work full time; many work part time, or fewer than 35 hours a week. This part-time work is especially common among women with young children. Because of part-time work, economists use aggregate hours worked, rather than aggregate employment, to measure the quantity of labor engaged in production.

5. The unemployment rate tends to rise during recessions and fall during expansion. The unemployment rate when the economy is neither in recession nor in an expansion is called the natural rate of unemployment.

6. People are unemployed for four reasons: They have lost their job, they have quit their job, they have entered the labor force for the first time, or they have re-entered the labor force.

7. The simple labor supply and demand model can predict some aspects of the behavior of labor markets but cannot explain the existence of unemployment in the economy.

8. To explain the behavior of unemployment, the simple model needs to be modified to take into account both job rationing, in which the wage is too high to equate supply and demand, and job search, in which unemployed people look for work but are unable to find work if an appropriate job opportunity does not come along.

9. Countries that have low natural rates of unemployment tend to be the ones in which it is relatively easy for the unemployed or those out of the labor force to find jobs and/or relatively more unlikely that people who do lose their job will be unable to find another job.

10. Economic policies such as exemptions for teenagers from the minimum-wage laws, time limits on unemployment compensation, or the provision of information about job openings to reduce job-search time can reduce the natural unemployment rate.

KEY TERMS

aggregate hours, 183

cyclical unemployment, 183

efficiency wage, 194

employment-to-population ratio, 182

frictional unemployment, 183

insider, 194

job rationing, 193

job search, 193

job vacancies, 188

labor demand curve, 190

labor force, 180

labor force participation rate, 182

labor supply curve, 190

minimum wage, 194

natural unemployment rate, 183

outsider, 194

real wage, 191

structural unemployment, 183

unemployed person, 180

unemployment rate, 182

working-age population, 180

QUESTIONS FOR REVIEW

1. How do economists define unemployment, and how do they measure how many people are unemployed?
2. How is the working-age population defined?
3. What is the definition of the labor force?
4. What has happened to the employment-to-population ratio for men and women since the 1950s?

5. What is the difference between frictional and structural unemployment?
6. Why isn't the unemployment rate equal to zero?
7. What is the difference between unemployment resulting from job rationing and unemployment resulting from job search?
8. What economic policies would reduce the natural rate of unemployment?

PROBLEMS

1. Which of the following people would be unemployed according to official statistics? Which ones would *you* define as unemployed? Why?

    a. A person who is home painting the house while seeking a permanent position as an electrician.

    b. A full-time student.

    c. A recent graduate who is looking for a job.

    d. A parent who decides to stay home taking care of children full time.

    e. A worker who quits his job because he thinks the pay is insufficient.

    f. A teenager who gets discouraged looking for work and stops looking.

2. The Problem 2 table contains some information about employment, labor force, and population levels in the United States at the turn of each decade.

    a. Using the data, fill in the table.

    b. Suppose the projection for the working-age population in the year 2020 for the United States is 265 million. If the unemployment rate and the labor force participation rate are the same in 2020 as they were in 2000, how much employment will there be?

    c. Using the same projection of 265 million for the working-age population in 2020, calculate employment with an unemployment rate of 5 percent and a labor force participation rate of 60 percent.

    d. Calculate the same for a labor force participation rate of 70 percent. Which of these estimates do you think is more realistic? Why?

3. What effect would a decline in part-time employment have on average weekly hours per

Problem 2

Year	Total Employment (millions)	Unemployment Rate (percent)	Labor Force Participation Rate (percent)	Working-Age Population (millions)
1980		7.2	63.6	168.9
1990		6.3	66.4	190.0
2000		3.9	67.0	213.7

Source: U.S. Department of Labor.

worker in the United States? If the employment-to-population ratio increases, what will happen to total hours of work in the United States?

4. Job search and advertising now are available on the Internet. Using e-mail, job applicants can submit résumés to prospective employers. One popular website of this kind is www.monster.com

   a. How should this service affect the unemployment rate?

   b. Suppose everybody in the working-age population has access to www.monster.com. Would you expect unemployment to be eliminated? Explain.

5. The age distribution of the population changes over time—in the United States, better health care (longer lives) and lower fertility (fewer kids) in recent years mean that the proportion of people over age 16 is increasingly larger. At the same time, the labor force participation rate is likely to decline as baby boomers retire. Using the same method as in the previous problem, calculate total employment and the employment-to-population ratio based on the scenario in the Problem 5 table.

   a. Describe what happens to total employment and the employment-to-population ratio in this scenario.

   b. Is it possible that labor force participation would fall so much that total employment would fall? How low would the labor force

participation rate have to be in 2020 for total employment to be lower than in 2000?

6. The Problem 6 table shows the demand for and supply of skilled labor at different hourly wages.

Problem 6

Demand for Labor		Supply of Labor	
Wage/Hour	Quantity	Wage/Hour	Quantity
$12	75	$12	47
14	68	14	54
16	61	16	61
18	54	18	68
20	47	20	75
22	40	22	82

   a. Draw the supply and demand curves for labor.

   b. What are the wage and quantity of labor at equilibrium?

   c. Suppose a law is passed forbidding employers to pay wages less than $20 per hour. What will the new quantity of labor in the market be? Who gains and who loses from this law?

7. Use a supply and demand diagram to show the possible reduction in teenage unemployment

Problem 5

Year	Unemployment Rate (percent)	Labor Force Participation Rate (percent)	Working-Age Population (millions)	Total Employment (millions)	Employment-to-Working-Age-Population Ratio
2000	3.9	67.0	214		
2010	5.0	64.0	240		
2020	5.0	62.0	265		

Source: U.S. Department of Labor.

from a lower minimum "training" wage for workers younger than 20 years old. For what reasons might older unskilled workers complain about such a policy?

8. Use the theories of job rationing and job search to explain why the natural rate of unemployment in the United States is lower than that in France. What can the French government do to try to remedy this situation? Might these remedies be politically unpopular?

9. Why do young workers have higher unemployment rates than older workers? Is labor productivity different? Why?

10. Why do some firms pay efficiency wages? What would you expect to be true in regions or industries for which the payment of efficiency wages is widespread?

9 Productivity and Economic Growth

For most of human history, there was no economic growth. True, kings and queens amassed vast quantities of wealth through conquest and exploitation; millions of slaves constructed coliseums, pyramids, and great walls; and talented individuals on all continents produced great works of art. But output per hour of work—the productive power of labor that determines the well-being of most people—hardly grew for thousands of years. Except for the ruling classes, people lived in extreme poverty.

This situation changed dramatically around the eighteenth century. Figure 9-1 shows the growth rates of *output per hour of work,* or **productivity**, for different periods during the last three centuries. Observe that almost no growth in output per hour of work occurred for most of the 1700s, much as in the thousands of years before. Then, in the late 1700s and early 1800s—the period historians call the Industrial Revolution—economic growth began to pick up, first in Europe and then in the United States. Productivity growth accelerated in the early 1800s and then rose to historically unprecedented levels in the twentieth century. And, as productivity rose, people's incomes also rose and poverty declined.

Just as productivity growth raised standards of living and reduced poverty in Europe and the United States in the 200 years since the Industrial Revolution, in the twenty-first century it is spreading around the world to China, India, and many other countries. In fact, differences in productivity growth among countries explain why some countries are poor and some are rich. Simply put, if productivity in a country is high, then that country is rich; if productivity in a country is low, then that country is poor. If you want to reduce the number of poor countries, then you have no choice but to increase productivity in poor countries. The ticket out of poverty is higher productivity.

Why did the growth of real gross domestic product (GDP) per hour of work begin to increase and then take off in the eighteenth century? Why is productivity growth high in some countries and low in other countries? The purpose of this chapter is to develop a theory of economic growth that helps answer these and many other questions. The theory of economic

growth tells us that increases in hours worked can increase the growth of real GDP, but not the growth of real GDP per hour of work. To explain the growth of productivity, we must focus on the two other factors: capital and technology. Capital raises real GDP per hour of work by giving workers more tools and equipment to work with. As we will show in this chapter, however, capital alone is not sufficient to achieve the growth we have seen over the past 200 years. Technology—the knowledge and methods that underlie the production process—also has played a big role.

Understanding the role of capital and technology enables economists to better evaluate the advantages and disadvantages of various economic policies to improve economic growth. For example, should economic policies designed to stimulate economic growth focus more on capital or more on technology? The U.S. economy has benefited from yet another resurgence of productivity growth in the past 10 years. What economic policy will best maintain this high rate of productivity growth?

Figure 9-1

Productivity Growth during the Past 300 Years

Productivity is defined as output per hour of work. Productivity *growth* is defined as the percentage increase in productivity from one year to the next. The bars indicate the average productivity growth during the years stated. The data are collected from Europe and the United States.

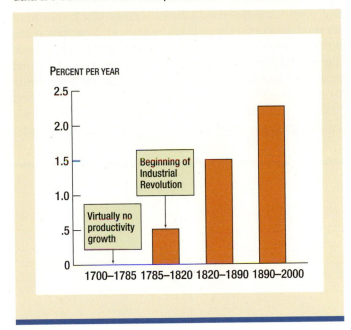

Labor and Capital without Technology

productivity
output per hour of work.

To better understand the important role played by technology in driving economic growth, we begin with a simplified theory in which economic growth depends only on labor and then consider a theory in which it depends on labor and capital.

Labor Alone

Suppose real GDP depends only on labor. That is, the amount of output in the economy can be described by the production function $Y = F(L)$, where Y is real GDP and L is labor input. When labor input increases, real GDP increases.

To understand this production function for the whole economy, it helps to consider the production of a single good. Imagine workers on a one-acre vineyard planting, maintaining, and harvesting grapes, and suppose that the only input that can be varied is labor. With more workers, the vineyard can produce more grapes, but according to the simple story that output depends only on labor, the vineyard cannot increase capital because there is no capital. For example, the vineyard cannot buy wagons or wheelbarrows to haul fertilizer around. The only way the vineyard can increase output is by hiring more workers to haul the fertilizer.

Now, suppose all this is true for the economy as a whole. The firms in the economy can produce more output by hiring more workers, but they cannot increase capital. The situation is shown for the entire economy in Figure 9-2. On the vertical axis is output. On the horizontal axis is labor input. The curve shows that more labor can produce more output. The curve is a graphical plot of the aggregate production function $Y = F(L)$ for the whole economy.

Diminishing Returns to Labor

The shape of the curve in Figure 9-2 is important. The flattening out of the curve shows **diminishing returns** to labor: The greater the number of workers used in producing output, the less the additional output that comes from each additional worker. Consider production of a single good again, such as grapes at the vineyard. Increasing employment at the one-acre vineyard from one to two workers raises production more than increasing employment from 1,001 to 1,002 workers. A second worker could take charge of irrigation or inspect the vines for insects while the first worker harvested grapes. But with 1,001 workers on the vineyard, the 1,002nd worker could find little to do to raise production. Diminishing returns to labor exist because labor is the only input to production that we are changing. As more workers are employed on the same

diminishing returns
a situation in which successive increases in the use of an input, holding other inputs constant, eventually will cause a decline in the additional production derived from one more unit of that input.

Figure 9-2

Only Changes in Labor Can Change Output

The curve shows the production function $Y = F(L)$, where Y is output and L is labor input (hours of work). In this theory, capital and technology are out of the picture. With more labor working on a fixed supply of land, there are diminishing returns, as shown by the curvature of the production function.

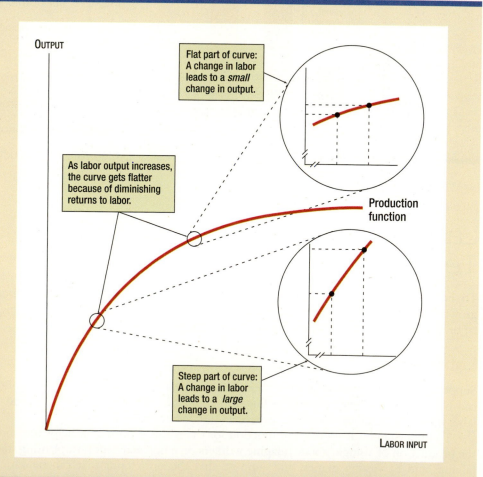

one-acre plot, the contribution that each additional worker makes goes down. Adding one worker when only one worker is employed can increase production by a large amount. But adding one worker when 1,001 already are working on the one-acre plot cannot add as much. For the same reasons, diminishing returns to labor exist for the whole economy.

Adding Capital

Now let us add capital to the production function. The total amount of capital in the economy increases each year by the amount of net investment during the year. More precisely,

$$\frac{\text{Capital at the end}}{\text{of this year}} = \frac{\text{net investment}}{\text{during this year}} + \frac{\text{capital at the end}}{\text{of last year}}$$

For example, if $10,000 billion is the value of all capital in the economy at the end of last year, then $100 billion of net investment during this year would raise the capital stock to $10,100 billion by the end of this year. This is a 1 percent increase in the capital stock.

With capital as an input to production, the production function becomes $Y = F(L, K)$, where K stands for capital. Output can be increased by using more capital, even if the amount of labor is not increased. Consider the vineyard example again. If a wheelbarrow is bought to haul the fertilizer around the vineyard, the vineyard can produce more grapes with the same number of workers. More capital at the vineyard increases output. The same is true for the economy as a whole. By increasing the amount of capital in the economy, more real GDP can be produced with the same number of workers.

Figure 9-3 illustrates how more capital raises output. The axes are the same as those in Figure 9-2, and the curve again shows that more output can be produced by

> Recall that net investment is equal to gross investment less depreciation (p. 482). Depreciation is the amount of capital that wears out each year.

Figure 9-3

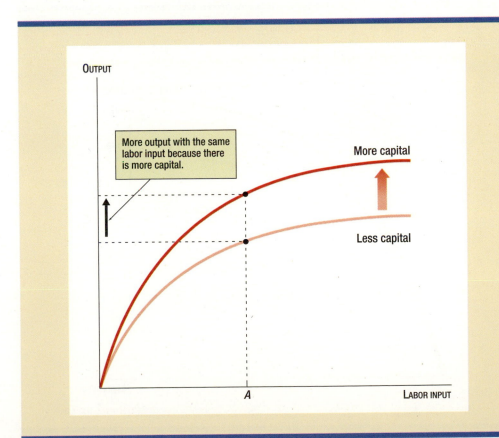

OUTPUT

More output with the same labor input because there is more capital.

More capital

Less capital

A   **LABOR INPUT**

Capital Is Also a Factor of Production

The axes in this figure are just like those in Figure 9-2, but now if more capital is added to production, more output can be produced with the same labor input. For example, when labor input is at Point *A*, more output can be produced with more capital.

more labor. But, in addition, Figure 9-3 shows that if we add capital to the economy—by investing a certain amount each year—the relationship between output and labor shifts up: More capital provides more output at any level of labor input. To see this, pick a point on the horizontal axis, say, Point *A,* to designate a certain amount of labor input. Then draw a vertical line up from this point, such as the dashed line shown in Figure 9-3. The vertical distance between the curve marked "Less capital" and the curve marked "More capital" shows that additional capital raises production.

Diminishing Returns to Capital   Figure 9-4 also shows *diminishing returns to capital.* Each additional amount of capital—another wheelbarrow or another hoe—results in a smaller addition to output. Hence, the gaps between the several production functions in Figure 9-4 get smaller and smaller as more capital is added. As more capital is added, the ability to increase output per worker reduces. Compare adding one wheelbarrow to the vineyard without any wheelbarrows with adding one wheelbarrow to the vineyard that already has 50 wheelbarrows. Clearly, the 51st wheelbarrow would increase farm output by only a minuscule amount, certainly much less than the first wheelbarrow. A one-acre vineyard would not even have much room for the 51st wheelbarrow.

Diminishing returns to capital also occur for the economy as a whole. Thus, adding more capital per worker cannot raise real GDP per worker above some limit, and even getting close to that limit will require an enormous amount of capital. Eventually, growth in output per hour of work will stop.

Thus, labor and capital alone cannot explain the phenomenal growth in real GDP during the last 200 years.

Figure 9-4

Capital Has Diminishing Returns Also

As capital per worker increases, each additional unit of capital produces less output. Thus, there is a limit to how much growth per worker additional capital per worker can bring.

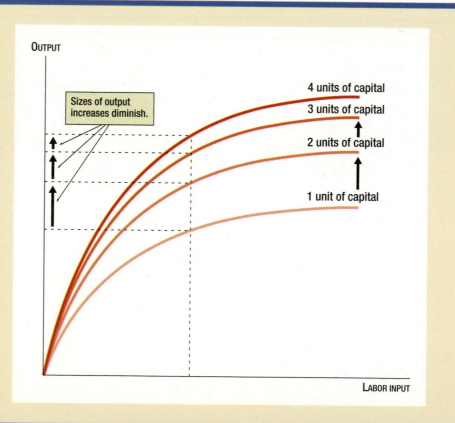

Technology: The Engine of Growth

We have seen that growth driven by increases in capital and labor, although important, is not sustainable. Diminishing returns imply that the additional output obtained by increasing these inputs becomes smaller and smaller, eventually leading to no further economic growth. For output to grow over the very long run, we need not just to *increase* inputs, but also to get more output from *existing* inputs. Technology is what enables us to get more output from a given quantity of inputs.

What Is Technology?

Technology is difficult to define, envision, and measure. A broad definition of **technology** is that it is anything that raises the amount of output that can be produced with a given

technology
anything that raises the amount of output that can be produced with a given amount of labor and capital. (Ch. 5)

ECONOMICS IN ACTION

The Role of Technology in Economic Growth

In the twenty-first century's highly automated world, the image (left) of women in long skirts packing fruit delicacies into glass jars in the mid- to late 1800s seems quaint beside the image (right) of robotic arms in an assembly line at this modern-day car plant. Yet both represent huge leaps in industrial productivity at different periods of history. Capital and technology played critical roles in the development of each of these increasingly more efficient methods of production.

ECONOMICS *IN ACTION*

Examples of Changes in Technology That Increased Productivity

Replacing horse-drawn tractors (on the left) with steam-powered tractors (in the center) is an example of a change in technology that increased output per hour of work. Another example is the introduction of computer technology for maintenance scheduling or ordering spare tractor parts on the Internet. What other advances in technology have increased farm output?

amount of inputs (labor and capital). In essence, technology is the stock of knowledge or ideas that exist in an economy: the ideas that help produce goods and services such as baby clothes, wine, and television shows; the ideas that help save lives, such as penicillin, vaccines, and heart transplants; and the ideas that help us communicate around the world, such as cell phones and the Internet.

When we add technology to capital and labor, we have the modern theory of economic growth. The theory can be summarized by the now familiar aggregate production function

$$Y = F(L, K, T)$$

where T stands for technology. Increases in technology therefore will increase output. Such increases in technology are termed *technological progress*. We sometimes use the term **technological change** instead of technological progress.

Invention, Innovation, and Diffusion
Technological change occurs when new ideas are developed into new products that increase production, such as the steel plow, the harvester, the combine, the automobile, radar, the telephone, the computer, the airplane, lasers, and fiber-optic cable. Economists distinguish between an **invention**, which is the

technological change
improvement in technology over time.

invention
a discovery of new knowledge.

discovery of new knowledge or a new principle, such as electricity, and **innovation**, in which the new knowledge is brought into application with a new product, such as the electric light-bulb. Economists also distinguish between the innovation itself and the **diffusion** of the innovation throughout the economy, a process that involves advertising, marketing, and spreading the innovation to new uses, such as the use of the electric lightbulb to create night shifts in factories.

The sewing machine is a good illustration of invention, innovation, and diffusion. By 1847, inventors had built 17 different machines capable of mechanically forming a stitch. But only one of these, Elias Howe's sewing machine, developed into a commercially successful innovation. As Howe tried to sell his invention to consumers, he discovered how to modify it to make it more useful and attractive. Soon the invention turned into a popular innovation that was used widely. Wide diffusion of the innovation occurred as others produced household versions of the sewing machine, like the one marketed by the Singer Company. This example also illustrates that innovation and diffusion require the work of an entrepreneur who recognizes the potential of the invention.

Technology depends in part on scientific knowledge, and many people feel that science will become more and more important in driving future technological change. But technology is much more than scientific knowledge. The discovery of DNA did not improve technology until it was applied to genetic engineering. The knowledge of mathematics made the invention and development of computers possible, a technology that obviously has improved productivity.

Organization and Specialization Technology also includes the way firms are organized. Better organization schemes can mean a smaller bureaucracy and more output per hour of work without the addition of capital. More efficient organization can improve the flow of information within a firm and thereby affect labor productivity. Better incentive programs that encourage workers to communicate their ideas to management, for example, increase productivity.

Henry Ford's idea of the assembly line greatly increased the productivity of workers. The assembly line enabled the car to come to the worker rather than having the worker go to the car. Thus, each worker could specialize in a certain type of activity; through specialization, productivity increased. The assembly line alone is estimated to have reduced the time it took a group of workers to produce a car from 12.5 hours to 0.5 hours. Productivity increased, and so too did wages.

New technology can affect how labor and capital are used at a firm. Economists distinguish between *labor-saving* and *capital-saving* technological change. *Labor-saving technological change* means that fewer workers are needed to produce the same amount of output; *capital-saving technological change* means that fewer machines are needed to produce the same amount of output. An example of a labor-saving technological change would be a steam-powered tractor replacing a horse-drawn plow, and later gasoline power replacing steam power, enabling the same worker to plow many more acres. An example of a capital-saving technological change is the night shift. Adding two crews of workers—one working in a steel mill from 4 P.M. to midnight and another working from midnight to 8 A.M.—makes the same steel-making furnaces three times as productive as when the working hours are only from 8 A.M. to 4 P.M.

Specialization of workers at a firm adds to productivity. Adam Smith emphasized the importance of specialization in his *Wealth of Nations;* his term *division of labor* refers to the way a manufacturing task could be divided among a group of workers, each of whom would specialize in a part of the job.

Because specialization permits workers to repeat the same task many times, their productivity increases, as in the old adage "practice makes perfect." Each time the task is repeated, the worker becomes more proficient—a phenomenon that economists call

innovation
application of new knowledge in a way that creates new products or significantly changes old ones.

diffusion
the spreading of an innovation throughout the economy.

learning by doing
a situation in which workers become more proficient by doing a particular task many times.

learning by doing. The commonsense principle of learning by doing is that the more one does something, the more one learns about how to do it. For example, as the number of airplanes produced of a particular type—say, a Boeing 777—increases, the workers become more and more skilled at producing that type of airplane. Careful studies of aircraft production have shown that productivity increases by 20 percent for each 100 percent increase in output of a particular type of plane. This relationship between learning and the amount of production is commonly called the "learning curve." Learning is a type of technological progress.

Human Capital

Many firms provide training courses for workers to increase their skills and their productivity. *On-the-job training* is a catchall term for any education, training, or skills a worker receives while at work.

Most workers receive much of their education and training before they begin working, whether in grade school, high school, college, or professional schools. Because increases in education and training can raise workers' productivity, such increases are considered another source of technological change.

human capital
a person's accumulated knowledge and skills.

The education and training of workers, called **human capital** by economists, is similar to physical capital—factories and equipment. To accumulate human capital—to become more educated or better trained—people must devote time and resources, much as a firm must devote resources to investment if physical capital is to increase.

The decision to invest in human capital is influenced by considerations similar to those that motivate a firm to invest in physical capital: the cost of the investment versus the expected return. For example, investing in a college education may require that one borrow the money for tuition; if the interest rate on the loan rises, then people will be less likely to invest in a college education. Thus, investment in education may be negatively related to the interest rate, much as physical investment is. Thus, to encourage more education and thereby increase economic growth and productivity, the U.S. government provides low-interest loans to college students, making an investment in college more attractive. We will return to the government's role in education as part of its broader policy to increase economic growth later in the chapter.

The Production of Technology: The Invention Factory

Technology sometimes is discovered by chance by a lone inventor and sometimes by trial and error by an individual worker. A secretary who experiments with several different filing systems to reduce search time or with different locations for the computer, the printer, the telephone, and the photocopier is engaged in improving technology around the office. Frequently, technological progress is a continuous process in which a small adjustment here and a small adjustment there add up to major improvements over time.

But more and more technological change is the result of huge expenditures of research and development funds by industry and government. Thomas Edison's "invention factory" in Menlo Park, New Jersey, was one of the first examples of a large industrial laboratory devoted to the production of technology. It in turn influenced the development of many other labs, such as the David Sarnoff research lab of RCA. Merck & Co., a drug company, spends nearly $1 billion per year on research and development for the production of new technology.

Edison's Menlo Park laboratory had about 25 technicians working in three or four different buildings. In the six years from 1876 to 1882, the laboratory invented the lightbulb, the phonograph, the telephone transmitter, and electrical generators. Each of these inventions turned out to be a successful innovation that was diffused widely.

ECONOMICS *IN ACTION*

Two Invention Factories: Past and Present

A large amount of technology was produced at Thomas Edison's invention factory (left); still more technology is being developed, such as a new paint recycling technique developed by paint chemist Keith Harrison (right). The amount of new technology can be explained by the laws of supply and demand. For example, a tax credit for expenditures on research will increase the supply of technology. But how is technology different from most other goods? If one person uses more technology, is there just as much available for others to use?

For each innovation, the Federal government granted a *patent*. A patent indicates that the invention is original and gives the inventor the exclusive right to use it until the patent expires. To obtain a patent on the rights to an invention, an inventor must apply to the Patent and Trademark Office of the Federal government. Patents give inventors an inducement to invent. The number of patents granted is an indicator of how much technological progress is going on. Edison obtained patents at a pace of about 67 a year at his lab.

Edison's invention factory required both labor and capital input, much like factories producing other commodities. The workers in such laboratories are highly skilled, with knowledge obtained through formal schooling or on-the-job training—human capital. A highly trained workforce is an important prerequisite to the production of technology.

The supply of technology—the output of Edison's invention factory, for example—depends on the cost of producing the new technology, which must include the great risk that little or nothing will be invented, and the benefits from the new technology: how much Edison can charge for the rights to use his techniques for making lightbulbs. Inventive activity often has changed as a result of shifts in the economy that change the costs and benefits. For example, increases in textile workers' wages stimulated the invention of textile machines, because such machines yielded greater profits by enabling the production of more output with fewer workers.

Special Features of Technology

Technology has two special qualities. The first is *nonrivalry*. This means that one person's use of the technology does not reduce the amount that another person can use. If one university uses the same student registration system as another university, that does not reduce the quality of the first university's system. In contrast, most goods are rivals in consumption: If you drink a bottle of Coke, one fewer bottle of Coke is available for other people to drink.

The second feature of technology is *nonexcludability*. This occurs when the inventor or the owner of the technology cannot exclude other people from using it (see the Economics in Action box on p. 553). For example, the system software for Apple computers shows a series of logos and pull-down menus that can be moved around the screen with a mouse. The idea easily could be adapted for use in other software programs by other companies. In fact, the Windows program of Microsoft has features similar to those of the Apple software, but according to the court that ruled on Apple's complaint that Microsoft was illegally copying, the features were not so similar that Microsoft could not use them. If the court had ruled in favor of Apple, then Apple could have excluded Microsoft from using the Apple features.

As the example of Apple and Microsoft shows, the legal system determines in part the degree of nonexcludability. Trademarks, copyrights, and patents help inventors exclude others from using their inventions without compensation. But it is impossible to exclude others from using much technology.

Thus, technology may *spill over* from one activity to another. If your economics teacher invents a new way to teach economics on a computer, it might spill over to your chemistry teacher, who sees how the technology can be applied to a different subject. Spillovers sometimes occur because research personnel move from one firm to another. Henry Ford knew Thomas Edison and was motivated to experiment on internal-combustion engines by Edison. Hence, Edison's research spilled over to another industry, but Edison would have found it difficult to receive compensation from Henry Ford even if he had wanted to.

Because inventors cannot be fully compensated for the benefits their ideas provide to others, they may produce too little technology. The private incentives to invent are less than the gain to society from the inventions. If the incentives were higher—say, through government subsidies to research and development—more inventions might be produced. Thus, the government has a potential role to play in providing funds for research and development, both in industry and at universities.

REVIEW

- Technological change has a broad definition. It is anything that increases production for a given level of labor and capital. Technological change has been an essential ingredient in the increase in the growth of real GDP per hour of work in the last 200 years.

- Technology can be improved by the education and training of workers—investment in human capital. Technology also can be improved through inventions produced in industrial research laboratories, as well as by trial and error. In any case, the level of technology is determined by market forces.

- But technology exhibits nonrivalry in consumption and a high degree of nonexcludability. These are precisely the conditions in which an underproduction of technology will occur.

Fundamental Causes of Economic Growth

Thus far we have seen the roles that labor, capital, and technology play in the production function of the economy, and thus in driving economic growth. In his recent treatise *Modern Economic Growth,* the MIT Economist Daron Acemoglu poses the question "If [labor, capital and technology] are so important in generating cross-country income differences and causing the takeoff into modern economic growth, why do certain societies fail to improve their technologies, invest more in physical capital, and accumulate more human capital?" to argue that it is too limiting to focus only on what he calls the proximate causes of economic growth, the things that directly lead to increased output from the production function. Instead, Acemoglu asks students of economic growth to dig deeper and find out the fundamental causes of economic growth, the factors that led different economies to acquire different levels of labor, capital, and technology. As Acemoglu puts it eloquently in his book,

> If physical capital accumulation is so important, why did Nigeria fail to invest more in physical capital? If education is so important, why are education levels in Nigeria still so low, and why is existing human capital not being used more effectively? The answer to these questions is related to the fundamental causes of economic growth—the factors potentially affecting why societies make different technology and accumulation choices.

What are some of the fundamental causes of economic growth? One possible candidate, that Acemoglu himself has studied extensively, is the role played by institutions. Institutions are systems that the people in the country have created or adopted to govern themselves. Institutions include the legal system, the political system, and the regulatory system, for example. Institutions can lend themselves to more labor, capital, and technology accumulation in a variety of ways. For instance, a system of strong property rights is an institution that encourages people to make investments and use resources wisely. Without property rights, slash-and-burn agriculture, overexploitation of natural resources, and urban shantytowns with no access to clean water, sewer or electricity services are common. Good governance is a key institution because corruption and red tape can prohibit the ability of entrepreneurs to engage in economic activity. A functioning legal system that protects the sanctity of contracts encourages more economic activity among firms and individuals, and allows the creation of credit markets that investors can tap into. Protection of patents and copyrights in the legal system can encourage innovative activity within the country. Democracy can be an important political institution because, without the right to vote, the existing elite will be able to run the country for their own welfare as the examples of Mobutu in Zaire, Marcos in the Philippines, and Duvalier in Haiti have shown.

Geography is another fundamental cause of economic growth. Two of the best-known public advocates of the importance of geography are the anthropologist Jared Diamond and the economist Jeffrey Sachs. Both have written compellingly about the importance of diseases that thrive in tropical but not temperate regions and the role these diseases can play in shaping the destiny of those regions. Diamond argues that the shape of a continent can influence its destiny—because agricultural crops vary by latitude, technological advances in one area of the extremely wide Eurasian or North American continents could be adopted by other areas in those continents far more easily than a similar adaptation could occur in the more elongated continents of Africa and South America. Similarly, whether or not a country is landlocked, whether or not it has navigable rivers, and how vulnerable it is to natural disasters all are geography-related explanations for why countries could end up with different endowments of capital, labor, and technology.

A third fundamental cause of economic growth is the willingness of a country to be open to interactions with the rest of the world. Openness can affect the pool of labor that is available in the economy through immigration policies that can address shortfalls of either skilled or unskilled labor. These policies have played an enormous role in the economic fortunes of countries like the United States, Australia, Brazil, and South Africa. Openness also can help an economy expand its access to capital because domestic investment does not have to be constrained by the availability of domestic saving. In an open economy, foreign investors can provide us with access to capital for investment projects. We also can look at the links between openness and technology. The development of new ideas is a difficult task: Creating the right environment requires financial resources for research, skilled scientists and engineers, and a strong system of intellectual property rights that allows incentives for firms who develop new technologies. Many developing countries will find it difficult to develop these new technologies by themselves mostly because they lack scientists and engineers or the resources to devote to research. Through economic, education, and scientific interactions with other countries, these developing countries can have access to a base of ideas and knowledge that is far greater than what they would have been able to access on their own.

REVIEW

- Labor, capital, and technology are proximate factors that help an economy directly produce more output. Students interested in better understanding the process of economic growth also may be interested in the fundamental causes, that is, the factors that led the economy to adopt a certain level of capital, labor, or technology.

- Institutions such as a well-functioning legal system or a strong system of property rights or intellectual property rights can encourage people to make long-term investments, engage in the costly process of innovation, and encourage more labor, capital, and technology accumulation.

- Fundamental causes could result from nature rather than the actions of man. Geography is one such example. The local disease climate, access to waterways, and vulnerability to natural disasters are all factors that can influence how much labor, capital, or technology an economy has.

Measuring Technology

Both technology and capital cause productivity—real GDP per hour of work—to grow. Perhaps surprisingly, it possible to determine how much productivity growth is due to technology, as distinct from capital. Robert Solow of MIT first showed how to do this and won the Nobel Prize for his innovation. In 1957, he published a paper that contained a simple mathematical formula. It is this formula—called the **growth accounting formula**—that enables economists to estimate the relative contributions of capital and technology.

growth accounting formula
an equation stating that the growth rate of productivity equals capital's share of income times the growth rate of capital per hour of work plus the growth rate of technology.

The Formula

The growth accounting formula is remarkably simple. It can be written as follows:

$$\text{Growth rate of productivity} = \frac{1}{3}\left(\text{growth rate of capital per hour of work}\right) + \text{growth rate of technology}$$

It is important to know why the growth rate of capital per hour of work is multiplied by a coefficient that is less than one, or only one-third in the formula. The reason is that economists view the production function for the economy as one in which output rises by only one-third of the percentage by which capital increases. For example, a vineyard owner can estimate by what percent grape output will rise if the workers have more wheelbarrows. If the number of wheelbarrows at the vineyard is increased by 100 percent and if the one-third coefficient applies to the vineyard, then grape production per hour of work will increase by 33 percent. In other words, this growth rate is a property of the grape production function. Statistical studies suggest that the one-third coefficient seems to apply to the production function for the economy as a whole.

We should not give the impression, however, that economists know the coefficient on capital growth in the growth accounting formula with much precision. Uncertainty exists about its size. It could be one-fourth or even five-twelfths. In any case, the growth accounting formula is a rule of thumb to help policy makers decide what emphasis to place on capital versus technology when developing programs to stimulate economic growth.[1]

Using the Formula

Here is how the formula works. The growth rates of productivity and capital per hour of work are readily determined from available data sources in most countries. Using the formula, we can express the growth rate of technology.

$$\begin{pmatrix} \text{Growth rate of} \\ \text{technology} \end{pmatrix} = \begin{pmatrix} \text{growth rate of} \\ \text{productivity} \end{pmatrix} - \frac{1}{3} \begin{pmatrix} \text{growth rate of capital} \\ \text{per hour of work} \end{pmatrix}$$

Thus, the growth rate of technology can be determined by subtracting one-third times the growth rate of capital per hour of work from the growth rate of real GDP per hour of work.

Consider an example. Suppose the growth rate of real GDP per hour of work is 2 percent per year. Suppose also that the growth rate of capital per hour of work is 3 percent per year. Then the growth rate of technology must be 1 percent per year: $2 - (1/3 \times 3) = 1$. Thus, one-half of the growth of productivity is due to technological change, and one-half is due to growth of capital per hour of work.

REVIEW

- The growth accounting formula shows explicitly how productivity growth depends on the growth of capital per hour of work and on the growth of technology.

- Using the growth accounting formula along with data on productivity and capital, one can calculate the contribution of technology to economic growth.

Technology Policy

The growth accounting formula tells us that if economic policy is to help maintain or increase productivity growth, it must provide incentives for, or remove disincentives to, technological progress. What policies might improve technological progress?

---

[1] A graphic derivation of the growth accounting formula is found in the appendix to this chapter.

ECONOMICS IN ACTION

Growth Accounting in Practice

Let us consider two practical cases in which the growth accounting formula tells us about the importance of technology for economic growth.

A Productivity Growth Slowdown

Table 9-1 shows productivity growth in the United States for three different periods. It also shows the amount of this productivity growth that is due to the growth of capital and the growth of technology. The table was computed using the growth accounting formula.

If you compare the first two rows of the table, you can see that productivity growth slowed down in the 1970s, from 2.5 percent per year to only 1.2 percent per year. This slowdown was a major concern of policy makers during this period. At first, policy makers were slow to recognize it. When statisticians at the Bureau of Labor Statistics first reported the slowdown in the mid-1970s, many people thought that it probably was temporary and that productivity growth would soon rebound. Instead, productivity continued to grow slowly for nearly 20 years.

What was the reason for the slowdown? The growth accounting formula helps answer this question. According to the formula, both the growth of capital and the growth of technology slowed down. But the slowdown in the growth of technology was larger. Technology growth fell by 0.8 percentage point from the 1956–1975 period to the 1976–1995 period, while capital growth fell by 0.5 percentage point. This decrease in growth suggested that a greater focus on policies to stimulate technological change and education would be appropriate.

A Productivity Growth Rebound

After remaining low for nearly a generation, productivity growth finally started to pick up again in the mid-1990s. The last row of Table 9-1 shows this rebound in productivity growth. In the second half of the 1990s and the first half of the 2000s, productivity growth rose to 2.9 percent—more than it was before the slowdown. Was capital or technology the main reason for the rebound? According to the growth accounting formula, technology growth surged from 1996 to 2006, contributing twice as much as capital.

Check the numbers in the table to ensure that the formula was used correctly:

$2.5 = 1.1 + 1.4$
$1.2 = 0.6 + 0.6$
$2.9 = 0.9 + 2.0$

So they check.

Table 9-1

Accounting for the 1970s Productivity Slowdown and the 1990s Productivity Rebound

Period	(1) Productivity Growth	(2) 1/3 Growth Rate of Capital per Hour of Work	(3) Technology Growth
1956–1975	2.5	1.1	1.4
1976–1995	1.2	0.6	0.6
1996–2006	2.9	0.9	2.0

Policy to Encourage Investment in Human Capital

One policy to encourage investment in human capital is to improve education. A more highly trained workforce is more productive. Better-educated workers are more able to make technological improvements. Hence, education reform (higher standards, incentives for good teaching) and increased funding would be ways to increase technological change. Some studies have shown that the U.S. education system is falling behind other countries, especially in mathematics and science in the kindergarten through 12th grade schools; hence, additional support seems warranted to increase economic growth.

Policy to Encourage Research and Innovation

In the twenty-first century, the United States and other industrial countries spend huge amounts of money on *research and development (R&D)*. Some of the research supports pure science, but much of it is applied research in engineering and medical technology. About 2.6 percent of U.S. GDP goes to R&D. The government provides much of its R&D funds through research grants and contracts to private firms and universities through the National Science Foundation and the National Institutes of Health and through its own research labs. Private firms, however, use most of the research funds.

The United States spends less on R&D as a share of GDP than other countries, but more in total. Total spending on research is a better measure of the usefulness of the spending than spending as a share of GDP if the benefits spill over to the whole economy.

Increased government support for R&D regardless of industry can be achieved through tax credits. A *tax credit for research* allows firms to deduct a certain fraction of their research expenditures from their taxes to reduce their tax bill. This increases the incentive to engage in R&D. Another way to increase the incentive for inventors and innovators is to give them a more certain claim to the property rights from their inventions. The government has a role to play in defining and enforcing property rights through patent laws, trademarks, and copyrights.

Technology Embodied in New Capital

Although we have emphasized that capital and technology have two distinct effects on the growth rate of productivity, it is not always possible to separate them in practice. To take advantage of a new technology, it may be necessary to invest in new capital. Consider the Thompson Bagel Machine, invented by Dan Thompson, which automatically can roll and shape bagels. Before the machine was invented, bakers rolled and shaped the bagels by hand. According to Dan Thompson, who in 1993 was running the Thompson Bagel Machine Manufacturing Corporation, headquartered in Los Angeles, "You used to have two guys handshaping and boiling and baking who could turn out maybe 120 bagels an hour. With the machine and now the new ovens, I have one baker putting out 400 bagels an hour."[2] That is a productivity increase of more than 500 percent. But the new technology is inseparable from the capital. To take advantage of the technology, bagel producers have to buy the machine and the new ovens to go with it.

Economists call this *embodied technological change* because it is embodied in the capital. An example of *disembodied technological change* would be the discovery of a new way to forecast the demand for bagels at the shop each morning so that fewer people would be disappointed when bagels run out on popular days and fewer bagels would be wasted on slack days. Taking advantage of this technology might not require any new capital.

The relationship between capital and technology has implications for technology policies. For example, policies that provide incentives for firms to invest might indirectly improve technology as they encourage investment in new, more productive equipment.

Is Government Intervention Appropriate?

Any time a question arises about whether government should intervene in the economy, such as with the technology policies just discussed, the operation of the private market should be examined carefully. For example, we noted that incentives for technology

---

[2] *New York Times*, April 25, 1993.

production may be too low without government intervention. Certainly, some of the research a business firm undertakes can be kept secret from others. In such cases, the firm may have sufficient incentive to do the research. But many research results are hard to keep secret. In that case, government intervention has a role to play in subsidizing the research. In general, policies to increase economic growth should be given the test for whether government intervention in the economy is necessary: Is the private market providing the right incentives? If not, can the government do better without a large risk of government failure? If the answers are "no" and "yes," respectively, then government intervention is appropriate.

REVIEW

- Policy proposals to increase productivity growth by providing incentives to increase technology include educational reform, tax credits for research, increased funding for research, moving government support toward areas that have significant spillovers, and improving intellectual property laws to better

define the property rights of inventors and extend them globally.

- Many technologies are embodied in new capital. Hence, policies to stimulate capital formation could also increase technology.

CONCLUSION: THE IMPORTANCE OF PRODUCTIVITY GROWTH

No concept in economics is more important to people's economic well-being than productivity growth, and economists widely agree about this essential principle. For example, William Baumol and his colleagues at New York University wrote in *Productivity and American Leadership:* "It can be said without exaggeration that in the long run probably nothing is as important for economic welfare as the rate of productivity growth."

Paul Krugman, the Nobel Prize–winning economist and columnist for the *New York Times*, wrote in his *Age of Diminished Expectations*: "Compared with the problem of slow productivity growth, all our other long-term economic concerns—foreign competition, the industrial base, lagging technology, deteriorating infrastructure and so on—are minor issues."

And Edward Lazear, chair of President Bush's Council of Economic Advisers, said, "Productivity growth is important and it's key, because it means that firms can pay workers higher wages. Indeed, real wage growth over any significant period of time is directly linked to productivity growth. For that reason, we must keep productivity growth strong."

In this chapter, we defined productivity growth and discussed how capital and technology are its essential determinants. We also pointed out that capital, like labor, is subject to

diminishing returns, so that technological progress must be an essential part of productivity growth in the long run. Even though labor, capital, and technology are what proximately determine an economy's ability to produce goods and services, we also discussed the need to look at the fundamental causes of economic growth, such as a country's institutions, geography, and culture of openness. These causes provide us with important insight about why some countries have an easier time accumulating capital, labor, or technology.

If economic policy makers want to increase people's income and reduce poverty—whether in the United States or in other countries—they must focus on increasing and maintaining productivity growth. Economists differ about the best way to accomplish this goal. For example, they debate whether policy should focus more on stimulating technology by subsidizing research or on increasing incentives for investment by keeping taxes on investment low. The growth accounting formula helps resolve some of these differences by determining the relative importance of capital and technology. In recent years in the United States, technology and capital both have contributed substantially to productivity growth, suggesting that policy should not focus solely on one determinant at the expense of the other.

KEY POINTS

1. The productivity growth rate—the percentage increase in output per hour of work—determines the economic well-being of people in the long run.

2. Along with labor and capital, technology determines economic growth. Technological progress explains much of the productivity growth wave that started in the late 1700s and enabled industrial countries to get rich.

3. Technology as defined by economists is much broader than high-technology products or inventions. Technology includes such things as better organizational structure for a firm and better education for workers as well as innovations like fiber-optic cables.

4. As a commodity, technology has the special features of nonexcludability and nonrivalry. Patent laws attempt to make technology more excludable and thereby increase the incentives to invest.

5. In studying economic growth, we should not just focus on the proximate factors, such as labor, capital, and technology, which directly determine an economy's ability to produce goods and services. We also should look to more fundamental causes of economic growth for important insights about how difficult it is to add more capital, labor, or technology

6. Examples of fundamental causes could include a country's institutions, geography, and culture of openness all of which can play an important role in driving economic growth.

7. The growth accounting formula is a great invention that has enabled economists to better understand the role of technology in the economy.

8. Technology policy has the goal of offsetting disincentives to invest and innovate that exist in the private market.

9. Policy proposals to increase technology include education reform, tax credits for research, increased funding for research, and improving intellectual property laws.

10. Government support for education and research is a key part of a modern technology policy.

KEY TERMS

diffusion, 211

diminishing returns, 206

growth accounting formula, 216

human capital, 212

innovation, 211

invention, 210

learning by doing, 212

productivity, 204

productivity curve, 223

technological change, 210

technology, 209

QUESTIONS FOR REVIEW

1. What is the essential difference between economic growth in the last 200 years and in the 2,000 years before that?

2. Why do capital and labor have diminishing returns?

3. Why are economists so sure that technology played a big role in economic growth during the last 200 years?

4. Why does technology include different ways to organize a business firm?

5. How is technology produced?

6. What is the importance of nonrivalry and nonexcludability for technology?

7. Of what practical use is the growth accounting formula?

8. What is wrong with a growth policy that focuses on capital formation but not on technology?

9. What do patents have to do with economic growth?

10. What is the rationale for government intervention in the production of technology?

PROBLEMS

1. The following table shows how output (shaded) depends on capital and labor.

	Labor				
	50	**100**	**150**	**200**	**250**
50	200	324	432	528	618
100	246	400	532	650	760
150	278	452	600	734	858
200	304	492	654	800	936
250	324	526	700	856	1,000

(left side label: **Capital**)

   a. Using the table, draw the production function $Y = F(L)$ when the capital stock (K) is 50. What do you observe about the shape of the production function?
   b. Now draw three similar curves that correspond to a capital stock of 100, 150, and 200. What happens to the production function?
   c. Using the diagrams you drew above, indicate the diminishing returns to labor and to capital.

2. Name one way in which use of the following technologies has made you more productive:
   a. ATM Machine
   b. Cell Phone
   c. The Internet
   d. Laptop computer

3. Identify each of the following as either a capital-saving or a labor-saving technological change:
   a. A public library installs an electronic machine that can automatically scan books for library patrons.
   b. A university upgrades its email system to be accessible by users with smartphones.
   c. A university reorganizes its departments to cut back on administrative costs.

4. Consider a country in which capital per hour of work from 1950 to 1973 grew by 3 percent per year and output per hour of work grew by about 3 percent per year. Suppose that from 1973 to 1991, capital per hour of work did not grow at all and output per hour of work grew by about 1 percent per year. How much of the slowdown in productivity (output per hour of work) growth was due to technological change? Explain. (Assume that the coefficient on capital in the growth accounting formula is one-third.)

5. If we estimate the share of capital in income incorrectly, it can affect our estimation of how large technological growth has been. Rework Problem 4 assuming that capital's share is one-fourth. Explain intuitively the difference in the importance of technology.

6. According to the spending allocation model in Chapter 7, a decrease in government spending results in, among other things, an increase in investment in the long run. Suppose the capital stock is $1 trillion and a fall in government spending causes a $50 billion rise in investment. Determine the effect of the change in government purchases on long-run per capita output growth, using the growth accounting formula. (Assume that the coefficient on capital in the growth accounting formula is one-third.)

   a. Suppose that a country has no growth in technology, and that capital and labor hours are growing at the same rate. What is the growth rate of real GDP per hour of work? Explain.
   b. Suppose that capital in the country described in part (a) continues to grow at its previous rate and technology growth is still zero, but growth in labor hours falls to half its previous rate. What happens to growth in real GDP per hour of work?

7. Which of the following types of government spending are likely to help economic growth? Why?
   a. Military spending on advertising for recruits
   b. Military spending on laser research
   c. Funding for a nationwide computer network
   d. Subsidies for a national opera company
   e. Extra funding for education programs

8. Many U.S. companies in the software, music, and movie industries have been asking the Chinese government to better enforce intellectual property rights. Discuss the impact of this enforcement on
   a. Chinese firms
   b. U.S. firms
   c. Chinese consumers

9. Suppose that Lesotho, an extremely poor African country, announces that it will ignore patents held by companies in the Western Hemisphere on HIV/AIDS-related pharmaceuticals and instead will buy copies of the drugs produced by Indian firms.
   a. Would you support such a decision? Why?
   b. Would your answer change if, instead of Lesotho, it was a richer country like Thailand or Brazil that was threatening to break the patent? Why?

The growth accounting formula states that

$$\text{Growth rate of productivity} = \frac{1}{3}\left(\begin{array}{c}\text{growth rate}\\\text{capital}\\\text{per hour}\\\text{of work}\end{array}\right) + \begin{array}{c}\text{growth rate}\\\text{of technology}\end{array}$$

To derive the formula, we start with the relationship between productivity (Y/L) and capital per hour of work (K/L) shown in Figure A.9-1. Because of diminishing returns to capital, the line is curved: As capital per hour of work increases, the increased productivity that comes from the additional capital per hour diminishes.

The curve in Figure A.9-1 is called a **productivity curve**; it can be represented in symbols as $(Y/L) = f(K/L)$, or productivity is a function of capital per hour of work.

Figure A.9-1

Productivity Curve
Productivity, or output per hour of work, is shown to increase with the amount of capital that workers have, as measured by capital per hour of work. The productivity curve gets flatter as output per hour of work increases because of diminishing returns to capital.

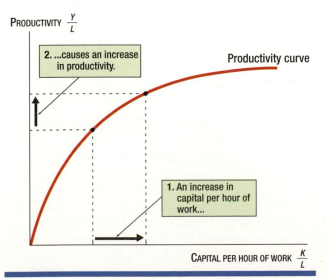

An upward shift in the productivity curve due to an increase in technological change is shown in Figure A.9-2. For example, with capital per hour constant at Point A in the figure, more technology leads to more productivity.

Figure A.9-2

A Shift in the Productivity Curve Due to Technology
An increase in technology permits an increase in productivity even if capital per hour of work does not change. For example, if capital per hour of work stays at A, productivity increases when the productivity curve shifts up.

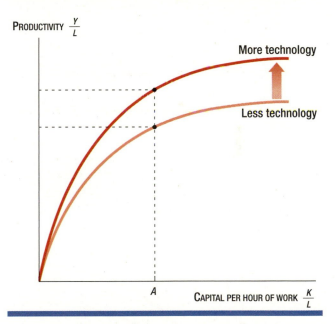

Productivity increases in the economy are due to a combination of *movements along* the productivity curve because of more capital per hour and *shifts of* the productivity curve because of technological change. The growth accounting formula is derived by translating the *movements along* and the *shifts of* the curve into two algebraic terms.

In Figure A.9-3, productivity and capital per hour in two different years (year one and year two) are shown. These could be 2003 and 2004 or any other two years. In this example, the growth rate of productivity is given by the increase in productivity $(C - A)$ divided by the initial level of productivity (A), or $(C - A)/A$. (The definition of the growth rate of a variable is the change divided by the initial level.)

Observe in Figure A.9-3 how the increase in productivity can be divided into the part resulting from higher capital per hour of work $(C - B)$ and the part resulting from technology $(B - A)$. Thus, we have

$$\underbrace{(C - A)/A}_{\substack{\text{Growth rate of} \\ \text{productivity}}} = \underbrace{(C - B)/A}_{\substack{\text{term related to} \\ \text{capital per hour}}} + \underbrace{(B - A)/A}_{\substack{\text{growth rate} \\ \text{of technology}}}$$

which is close to the growth accounting formula.

To finish the derivation, we need to examine the first term on the right. How does this term relate to capital per hour of work? The numbered boxes in Figure A.9-3 show that $C - B$ equals the *change* in capital per hour of work $\Delta(K/L)$ times the *slope* of the productivity curve. (The slope times the change along the horizontal axis gives the changes along the vertical axis.) Let the symbol r be the slope, which measures

how much additional capital increases output. Thus, $(C - B)/A$ is given by

$$\frac{\Delta(K/L)r}{(K/L)} = \frac{\Delta(K/L)r(K/Y)}{(Y/L)(K/Y)} = \frac{\Delta(K/L)r(K/Y)}{(K/L)}$$

The expression on the right is obtained by multiplying the numerator and the denominator of the expression on the left by (K/Y). Now the term on the right is simply the growth rate of capital per hour times $r(K/Y)$. The amount of income paid to capital is r times K if capital is paid according to how much additional capital increases output. Aggregate income is given by Y. Thus, the term $r(K/Y)$ is the share of capital income in aggregate income. This share is approximately one-third. Thus, the expression $(C - B)/A$ is the growth rate of capital per hour of work times one-third. Thus, the growth accounting formula is derived.

KEY POINTS

1. The productivity curve describes how more capital per hour of work increases productivity, or output per hour of work.
2. The productivity curve shifts up if technology increases.
3. The growth accounting formula is derived by dividing an increase in productivity into (1) a shift in the productivity curve resulting from more technology and (2) a movement along the productivity curve resulting from more capital per worker.

KEY TERMS AND DEFINITIONS

productivity curve: a relationship stating the output per hour of work for each amount of capital per hour of work in the economy.

QUESTIONS FOR REVIEW

1. What is the difference between the productivity curve and the production function?
2. What is the difference between a shift of the productivity curve and a movement along the curve?
3. Why does the share of capital income in total income appear in the growth accounting formula?

Figure A.9-3

Growth Accounting with Capital per Hour and Technology Increasing

Here a shift in the productivity curve and a movement along the productivity curve due to more capital per hour of work are combined. Productivity increases. The part of the increase due to capital and the part due to technological change are shown in the diagram.

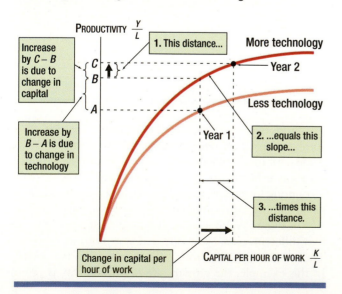

PROBLEMS

1. Consider the following relation between productivity and capital per hour for the economy.

Capital per Hour of Work (K/L)	Output per Hour of Work (Y/L)
$ 20	$ 40
$ 40	$ 80
$ 60	$110
$ 80	$130
$100	$140

a. Plot the productivity curve.
b. Suppose that in Year 1, $K/L = 40$ and $Y/L = 80$, but in Year 2, $K/L = 60$ and $Y/L = 110$. How much has technology contributed to the increase in productivity between the two years?

c. Suppose that between Year 2 and Year 3, the productivity curve shifts up by $20 at each level of capital per hour of work. If $K/L = 80$ and $Y/L = 150$ in Year 3, how many dollars did capital contribute to productivity growth between Year 2 and Year 3? How much was the contribution as a fraction of the growth rate of capital per worker?

2. Suppose the production function $Y = F(K, L)$ is such that Y equals the square root of the product (K times L). Plot the production function with Y on the vertical axis and L on the horizontal axis for the case in which $K = 100$. Plot the productivity curve with Y/L on the vertical axis and K/L on the horizontal axis.

10 Money and Inflation

Money provides an essential foundation for the economy, so if you want to understand how the economy works, you have to learn about money. Historians trace the origins of money to the very origins of civilization. As Babylon, Ur, and other ancient cities of Mesopotamia were being built 5,000 years ago, primitive forms of money, such as silver rings or even scraps of silver, were used to buy and sell in the street markets thousands of different goods—mortar, bricks, sandals for workers—that were needed for construction. The term *shekel*, which meant one-third of an ounce of silver, came into use at that time. Years later, images of kings or goddesses would be impressed on round pieces of silver, giving coins the look they still have in the twenty-first century. Without money, it is doubtful that these first large-scale civilizations could have arisen.

If the economy is working smoothly, you hardly notice the importance of money. Of course, you can see money being exchanged at the market—just as the Mesopotamians did—but this is hardly worth a comment. But occasionally the monetary foundation of an economy breaks down, and then you really notice the importance of money. After World War I, the government of Germany printed way too much money, and the price of everything rose by millions of percent, causing havoc in the economy and helping sow the seeds for World War II. In the 1970s, the U.S. government also created too much money. Although less pronounced than in Germany, inflation rose for more than a decade, and the U.S. economy went through one of its roughest periods, with one recession after another. Through much of the 1980s and 1990s, money was managed much better in the United States; inflation was low, and economic growth far steadier. In 2008 and 2009, the money supply in the United States increased sharply as actions were taken to deal with the financial crisis. This sharp increase raised concerns in some people's minds about whether inflation would start to rise after the financial crisis was over.

Sometimes government control of money completely breaks down. In 2001, 12 different provinces of Argentina started printing their own monies, causing great confusion. In Iraq under Saddam Hussein, the northern provinces used a different money from the southern provinces. After Saddam Hussein fell from power in 2003, a new currency had to be printed and flown into the country to prevent a financial collapse. This was no minor undertaking, as twenty-seven 747 planeloads of new currency were shipped into the country—a noticeable reminder of the importance of money. In Zimbabwe, the government of Robert Mugabe engaged in a desperate, but failing, race to print money faster than prices were rising to pay for all the government's expenditures. The economist Steve Hanke calculated that inflation in Zimbabwe had reached 89.7 sextillion percent (89.7×10^{21}) in later 2008. By early 2009, the people of Zimbabwe had abandoned the Zimbabwe dollar and were using foreign currencies—U.S. dollars, British pounds, and South African rand to conduct economic transactions.

The purpose of this chapter is to examine the role of money in the economy. After defining money, we show that commercial banks play a key role in providing money in a modern economy. We then examine how central banks—such as the Fed (the Federal Reserve) in the United States or the ECB (European Central Bank) in Europe—can control the supply of money. We also show why *excessive increases in the supply of money cause inflation*—one of the most important principles of macroeconomics.

What Is Money?

In a broad sense, money performs three functions in the economy: It can serve as a medium of exchange, a unit of account, and a store of value. More details about the three functions are given in the following sections. Economists emphasize the medium of exchange dimension in defining money. They define **money** as the part of a person's wealth that can be used readily for transactions, such as buying a sandwich or a bicycle. This definition differs from the more typical usage, in which the term is used to describe someone's wealth or income—as when we say, "she makes a lot of money" or "he has a lot of money." To an economist, money does not include what a person earns in a year or the total assets that she has, but it does include the portion of that person's wealth—such as the notes and coins in her purse—that can be used easily for transactions.

money
that part of a person's wealth that can be used readily for transactions; money also serves as a store of value and a unit of account.

Three Functions of Money

Medium of Exchange Money is a **medium of exchange** in that it is an item that people are willing to accept as payment for what they are selling because they in turn can use it to pay for something else they want. For example, in ancient times, people received coins for their agricultural produce, such as grain, and then used these coins to buy clothing.

medium of exchange
something that generally is accepted as a means of payment.

The use of coins was a great technological improvement over *barter*, in which goods are exchanged only for other goods. A barter system does not have a single medium of exchange. Thus, under a barter system, if you make shoes and want to buy apples, you have to find an apple seller who needs new shoes. The disadvantage of a barter system is that it requires a rare *coincidence of wants* in which the person who wants to consume what you want to sell (shoes, for example) has exactly what you want to consume (apples, for example).

Store of Value Money also is a **store of value** from one period to another. For example, in ancient times, people could sell their produce in September for gold coins and then use the coins to buy staples in January. In other words, they could store their purchasing power from one season to another.

store of value
something that will allow purchasing power to be carried from one period to the next.

Coins are not the only thing that can serve as a store of value. For example, rice and corn also can be stored from one season to the next; therefore, they also can serve as a store of value. But if you are not a farmer with a large storage bin, coins are much more likely to be used as money.

Unit of Account Money also has a third function: providing a **unit of account**. The prices of goods usually are stated in units of money. For example, prices of shoes or apples in ancient Greece were stated in a certain number of tetradrachmas—silver coins that had the goddess Athena on one side and her sacred animal, the owl, on the other— because people using these coins were familiar with that unit. Originally, units of money were determined by the weight of the metal. The British pound, for example, was originally a pound of silver. That terminology stuck even though, as we will see, modern money is unrelated to silver or any other metal.

To better understand the difference between the unit of account and the medium of exchange, it is helpful to find examples in which they are based on different monies. For example, when inflation got very high in Argentina in the early 1990s, the prices of many goods were quoted in U.S. dollars rather than Argentine pesos, but people usually exchanged pesos when they bought or sold goods. Thus, the U.S. dollar was the unit of account, while the medium of exchange was still the peso. But such cases are the exception; the unit of account and the medium of exchange are usually the same money.

Commodity Money

Many items have been used for money throughout history. Salt, cattle, furs, tobacco, shells, and arrowheads have been used as money. Traces of their former use still can be found in our vocabulary. The word *salary* comes from the Latin word for salt, and the word *pecuniary* comes from the Latin word for cattle. In World War II prisoner-of-war camps, cigarettes were used for money. On the island of Yap in the Pacific Ocean, huge stones weighing several tons were used for money.

Tourist standing next to traditional Stone Money of Yap Island, Micronesia.

Silver Coins of Ancient Greece.

Throughout history, the most common form of money has been metallic coins, usually made of gold, silver, or bronze. Gold coins were used as early as the seventh century B.C. in Lydia (now western Turkey); the Chinese were issuing bronze coins with a hole in the middle in the fifth century B.C.; and, in the fourth century, the Greeks issued the tetradrachmas. All these examples of money are commodities and therefore are called *commodity money*. Metals proved to be the most common form of commodity money because they could be divided easily into smaller units, are durable, and could be carried around.

When gold, silver, and other commodities were used as money, changes in the supply of these commodities would change their price relative to all other goods. An increase in the supply of gold, all else equal, would increase the number of gold coins that people were willing to pay to purchase other goods and services. In other words, the price of all other goods in the economy would rise relative to that of gold. Such an increase in the price of all goods in the economy is called inflation, as you may recall from the definitions of key economic concepts given in Chapter 6. Thus, increases in the supply of gold or any other commodity used as money would cause inflation. Whenever huge gold discoveries were made, the price of gold fell and inflation increased in countries that used gold as money. Thus, inflation was determined largely by the supply of precious metals. This relationship between the supply of money and inflation, which seems so clear in the case of commodity money, has persisted into modern times, even though now we use many other forms of money.

From Coins to Paper Money to Deposits

Although coins and other commodity monies are improvements over barter, other forms of money are more efficient. Starting in the late eighteenth and early nineteenth centuries, *paper money* began to be used widely and supplemented or replaced coins as a form of money. Although in a few examples paper money was used earlier, at this time, paper money generally was recognized as easier to use and it could save greatly on the use of precious metals.

Originally, the amount of paper currency was linked by law or convention to the supply of commodities. One reason for this link was the recognition that more money would cause inflation and that limiting the amount of paper money to the amount of some commodity like gold would limit the amount of paper money. Irving Fisher of Yale University, perhaps the most prolific and influential American economist of the early twentieth century, argued for linking paper money to commodities for precisely this reason. Many countries of the world linked their paper money to gold in the nineteenth and early twentieth centuries. They were on a *gold standard,* which meant that the price of gold in terms of paper money was fixed by the government. The government fixed the price by agreeing to buy and sell gold at that price. In the twenty-first century, the United States and other countries have severed all links between their money and gold. They are no longer on the gold standard and apparently have no intention of returning. Governments now supply virtually all the coin and paper money—the two together are called **currency**.

Although paper money was much easier to make and to use than coins, it too has been surpassed by a more efficient form of money. Many people now have **checking deposits** at banks or other financial institutions. These are deposits of funds on which an individual can write a check to make payment for goods and services. The deposits serve as money because people can write checks on them or use a debit card linked to that checking account. For example, when a student pays $100 for books with a debit card or a check, the student's checking deposit at the bank goes down by $100, and the bookstore's checking deposit at the bank goes up by $100. Checking deposits are used in much the same way as when a student pays with a $100 bill, which then is placed in the store's cash register. The student's holding of money goes down by $100, and the store's goes up by $100.

currency
money in its physical form: coin and paper money.

checking deposit
an account at a financial institution on which checks can be written; also called a checkable deposit.

ECONOMICS *IN ACTION*

Funny Money

Recall from our discussion that many improbable items have been used as money at various points in history. Few could match the medium of exchange described in the following article, excerpted from the *Wall Street Journal*: plastic and foil pouches of mackerel, which have caught on as money inside the prison system. In reading the article, think about the reasons why these pouches are valued as money within the prisons but would not be a successful medium of exchange outside of the prison system.

Mackerel Economics in Prison Leads to Appreciation for Oily Fillets

Packs of Fish Catch On as Currency, Former Inmates Say; Officials Carp

By Justin Scheck, *Wall Street Journal,* October 2, 2008

When Larry Levine helped prepare divorce papers for a client a few years ago, he got paid in mackerel. Once the case ended, he says, "I had a stack of macks." Mr. Levine and his client were prisoners in California's Lompoc Federal Correctional Complex. Like other federal inmates around the country, they found a can of mackerel—the "mack" in prison lingo—was the standard currency.

"It's the coin of the realm," says Mark Bailey, who paid Mr. Levine in fish. Mr. Bailey was serving a two-year tax-fraud sentence in connection with a chain of strip clubs he owned. Mr. Levine was serving a nine-year term for drug dealing. Mr. Levine says he used his macks to get his beard trimmed, his clothes pressed and his shoes shined by other prisoners. "A haircut is two macks," he says, as an expected tip for inmates who work in the prison barber shop.

There's been a mackerel economy in federal prisons since about 2004, former inmates and some prison consultants say. That's when federal prisons prohibited smoking and, by default, the cigarette pack, which was the earlier gold standard.

Prisoners need a proxy for the dollar because they're not allowed to possess cash. Money they get from prison jobs (which pay a maximum of 40 cents an hour, according to the Federal Bureau of Prisons) or family members goes into commissary accounts that let them buy things such as food and toiletries. After the smokes disappeared, inmates turned to other items on the commissary menu to use as currency.

Books of stamps were one easy alternative. "It was like half a book for a piece of fruit," says Tony Serra, a well-known San Francisco criminal-defense attorney who last year finished nine months in Lompoc on tax charges. Elsewhere in the West, prisoners use PowerBars or cans of tuna, says Ed Bales, a consultant who advises people who are headed to prison. But in much of the federal prison system, he says, mackerel has become the currency of choice.

Mackerel supplier Global Source Marketing Inc. says demand from prisons has grown since 2004. In recent years, demand has switched from cans—which wardens don't like because inmates can turn them into makeshift knives—to plastic-and-foil pouches of mackerel fillets, says Jon Linder, a vice president at supplier Power Commissary Inc., in Bohemia, N.Y.

Mackerel is hot in prisons in the U.S., but not so much anywhere else, says Mark Muntz, president of Global Source, which imports fillets of the oily, dark-fleshed fish from Asian canneries. Mr. Muntz says he's tried marketing mackerel to discount retailers. "We've even tried 99-cent stores," he says. "It never has done very well at all, regardless of the retailer, but it's very popular in the prisons."

Mr. Muntz says he sold more than $1 million of mackerel for federal prison commissaries last year. It accounted for about half his commissary sales, he says, outstripping the canned tuna, crab, chicken and oysters he offers.

Unlike those more expensive delicacies, former prisoners say, the mack is a good stand-in for the greenback because each can (or pouch) costs about $1 and few—other than weight-lifters craving protein—want to eat it.

So inmates stash macks in lockers provided by the prison and use them to buy goods, including illicit ones such as stolen food and home-brewed "prison hooch," as well as services, such as shoeshines and cell cleaning.

The Bureau of Prisons views any bartering among prisoners as fishy. "We are aware that inmates attempt to trade amongst themselves items that are purchased from the commissary," says bureau spokeswoman Felicia Ponce in an email. She says guards respond by limiting the amount of goods prisoners can stockpile. Those who are caught bartering can end up in the "Special Housing Unit"—an isolation area also known as the "hole"—and could lose credit they get for good behavior.

For that reason—and since communications between inmates and nonprisoners are monitored by prison officials—current inmates can't discuss mackerel transactions without risking discipline, say several lawyers and consultants who represent incarcerated clients.

Ethan Roberts knows about mackerel discipline first hand. Mr. Roberts, who was released in 2007 after serving eight years on a methamphetamine charge at prisons including the La Tuna Federal Correctional Institution in Texas, says he got busted for various piscine transactions. "I paid gambling debts" with mackerel, he says. "One time I bought cigarettes for a friend who was in the hole."

Mr. Roberts and other ex-inmates say some prisoners make specially prepared food with items from the prison kitchen and sell it for mackerel. "I knew a guy who would buy ingredients and use the microwaves to cook meals. Then people used mack to buy it from him," says Jonson Miller, an adjunct history professor at Drexel University in Philadelphia who spent two months in federal prison after being arrested at a protest on federal property. Mr. Miller was released in 2003, when prisoners were getting ready for cigarettes to be phased out, and says inmates then were already moving to mackerel.

Since the Pensacola Federal Prison Camp commissary in Florida was only open one day a week, some inmates would run a "prison 7-Eleven" out of their lockers, reselling commissary items at a premium in exchange for mackerel, says Bill Bailey, who served three months last year on a computer-hacking charge. "I knew one guy who would actually pay rent to use half of another guy's locker because his locker wasn't large enough to store all his inventory," he says.

Big Haul

The Pensacola lockers, at about 4 feet high, could store plenty of macks, he says, a good thing for inmates who played poker, since a winning hand could result in a big haul. A spokeswoman for Pensacola said prison authorities discipline inmates who are caught bartering. At Lompoc, says spokeswoman Katie Shinn, guards "are not aware of such a problem with mackerel." When officials do catch inmates bartering, she says, punishments can include a loss of commissary privileges or moving to a less desirable cell.

There are other threats to the mackerel economy, says Mr. Linder, of Power Commissary. "There are shortages world-wide, in terms of the catch," he says. Combined with the weak dollar, that's led to a surging mack. Now, he says, a pouch of mackerel sells for more than $1 in most commissaries.

Another problem with mackerel is that once a prisoner's sentence is up, there's little to do with it—the fish can't be redeemed for cash, and has little value on the outside. As a result, says Mr. Levine, prisoners approaching their release must either barter or give away their stockpiles.

That's what Mr. Levine did when he got out of prison last year. Since then, he's set up a consulting business offering advice to inmates and soon-to-be prisoners. He consults on various matters, such as how to request facility transfers and how to file grievances against wardens. It's similar to the work he provided fellow inmates when he was in prison. But now, he says, "I get paid in American dollars."

Measures of the Money Supply

In the twenty-first century, economists define the **money supply** as the sum of currency (coin and paper money) and deposits at banks. But opinions vary about what types of deposits should be included.

The narrowest measure of the money supply is called *M1*. The M1 measure consists mainly of currency plus checking deposits (travelers checks are also part of M1 but constitute less than 1 percent of total M1). The items in M1 have a great degree of *liquidity*, which means that they can be quickly and easily used to purchase goods and services.

Many things that people would consider money, however, are not included in M1. For example, if you had no cash but you wanted to buy a birthday gift for a relative, you could withdraw cash from your savings deposit. A *savings deposit* is a deposit that pays interest and from which funds normally can be withdrawn at any time. In other words, a savings deposit is also liquid, but not quite as liquid as a checking deposit. Similarly, *time deposits*—which require the depositor to keep the money at the bank for a certain amount of time or else lose interest—are not as liquid as checking deposits, but it is possible to withdraw funds from them. Economists have created a broader measure of the money supply, called *M2,* that includes everything that is in M1 plus savings deposits, time deposits, and certain accounts on which check writing is limited. Still broader concepts of the money supply can be defined, but M1 and M2 are the most important ones. Table 10-1 shows the total amounts of different definitions of the money supply for the whole U.S.

money supply
the sum of currency (coin and paper money) and deposits at banks.

Table 10-1

Measures of Money in the United States, January 2008 and 2011 (billions of dollars)

	2008	2011
Currency	757	920
M1: Currency plus checking deposits	1,368	1,832
M2: M1 plus time deposits, savings deposits, and other deposits on which check writing is limited or not allowed	7,498	8,808

Source: Federal Reserve Board.

economy in January 2008 and January 2011. All three measures of the money supply grew rapidly during the downturn that began in 2008 and the ensuing recovery.

Only about one-half of the M1 definition of the money supply is currency, and only about one-tenth of the M2 definition is currency. Economists disagree as to whether the more narrowly defined M1 or the more broadly defined M2 or something else is the best definition of the money supply. There is probably no best definition for all times and all purposes. For simplicity, in the rest of this chapter, we make no distinction between the M1 and M2 but simply refer to the money supply, M, as currency plus deposits.

REVIEW

- Commodity money—usually gold, silver, or bronze coins—originally served as the main type of money in most societies. Increases in the supply of these commodities would reduce their price relative to those of all other commodities and thereby cause inflation.

- Later, paper currency and deposits at banks became forms of money.

- Money has three roles: a medium of exchange, a store of value, and a unit of account.

The Fed, the Banks, and the Link from Reserves to Deposits

Federal Reserve System (the Fed)
the central bank of the United States, which oversees the creation of money in the United States.

bank
a firm that channels funds from savers to investors by accepting deposits and making loans.

We have seen that increases in the supply of commodity money such as gold would increase inflation. So would the excessive printing of paper money (currency) by governments. But in the twenty-first century, money consists of both currency and deposits. Nevertheless, it is possible for governments—usually through a central bank—to control the supply of money. In the United States, the central bank is the **Federal Reserve System**, nicknamed the "Fed." To understand how the Fed can control the supply of money, we must first look at how the Fed can control the amount of deposits at banks.

A **bank**—such as Bank of America or Citibank—is a firm that channels funds from savers to investors by accepting deposits and making loans. Figure 10-1 illustrates this function of banks. Banks are a type of *financial intermediary* because they "intermediate"

Figure 10-1

Channeling Funds from Savers to Investors

Savers, those whose income is greater than their consumption, can supply funds to investors in two ways: through banks (and other types of financial intermediaries) or by making direct loans, perhaps by buying bonds issued by a business firm. The banks earn profits by charging a higher interest rate on their loans than they pay on their deposits.

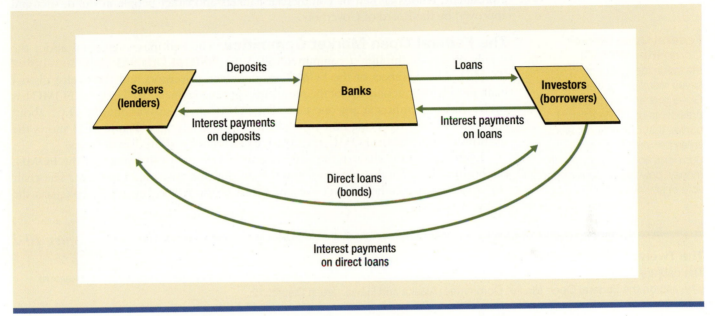

between savers and investors. Other examples of financial intermediaries are credit unions and savings and loan institutions. Banks are sometimes called *commercial banks* because many of their loans are to business firms engaged in commerce. Banks accept deposits from people who have funds and who want to earn interest and then lend the funds to other individuals who want to borrow and who are willing to pay interest. A bank earns profits by charging a higher interest rate to the borrowers than it pays to the depositors.

The Fed

The *central bank* of a country serves as a bank to other banks. In other words, commercial banks deposit funds at the central bank, and the central bank in turn makes loans to other commercial banks. We will see that the deposits of the commercial banks at the central bank are important for controlling the money supply. The Fed was established as the central bank for the United States in 1913 and now has more than 25,000 employees spread across the country.

Board of Governors At the core of the Fed is the *Federal Reserve Board*, or Board of Governors, consisting of seven people appointed to nonrenewable fourteen-year terms by the president of the United States and confirmed by the Senate. The Federal Reserve Board is located in Washington, D.C.

One of the governors is appointed by the president as chairman of the board; this appointment also requires Senate confirmation and can be renewed for additional terms. Alan Greenspan was first appointed chairman by President Reagan in 1987 and served until 2006, when Ben Bernanke was appointed by President George W. Bush. Chairman Bernanke's term was renewed by President Obama in 2010.

The District Federal Reserve Banks The Federal Reserve System includes not only the Federal Reserve Board in Washington but also twelve Federal Reserve Banks in different districts around the country (see Figure 10-2).

The term *Fed* refers to the whole Federal Reserve System, including the Board of Governors in Washington and the twelve district banks. Each district bank is headed by a president, who is chosen by commercial bankers and other people in the district and approved by the Board of Governors.

The Federal Open Market Committee The Fed makes decisions about the supply of money through a committee called the **Federal Open Market Committee (FOMC)**. The members of the FOMC are the seven governors and the twelve district bank presidents, but only five of the presidents vote at any one time. Thus, the FOMC has twelve voting members at any one time. The FOMC meets in Washington, D.C., about eight times a year to decide how to implement monetary policy. Figure 10-3 shows the relationship between the FOMC, the Board of Governors, and the district banks.

Even though the chair of the Fed has only one of the twelve votes on the FOMC, the position has considerably more power than this one vote might indicate. The chair also has executive authority over the operations of the whole Federal Reserve, sets the

Federal Open Market Committee (FOMC)

the committee, consisting of the seven members of the Board of Governors and the twelve presidents of the Fed district banks, that meets about eight times per year and makes decisions about the supply of money; only five of the presidents vote at any one time.

Figure 10-2

The Twelve Districts of the Fed

The country is divided into 12 districts, each with a district Federal Reserve Bank. Each district bank is headed by a president, who sits on the Federal Open Market Committee. Alaska and Hawaii are in District 12.

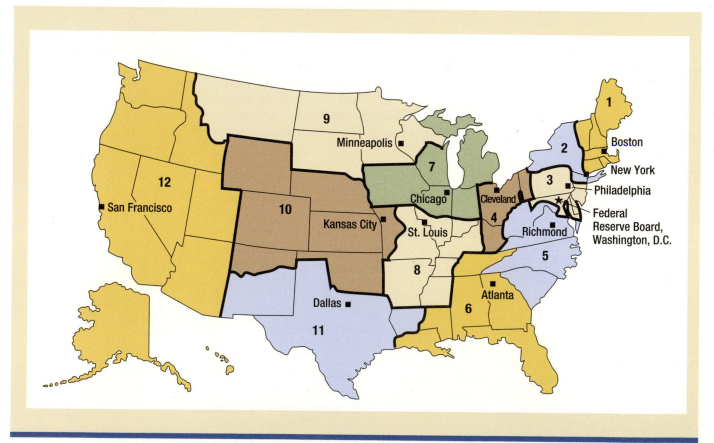

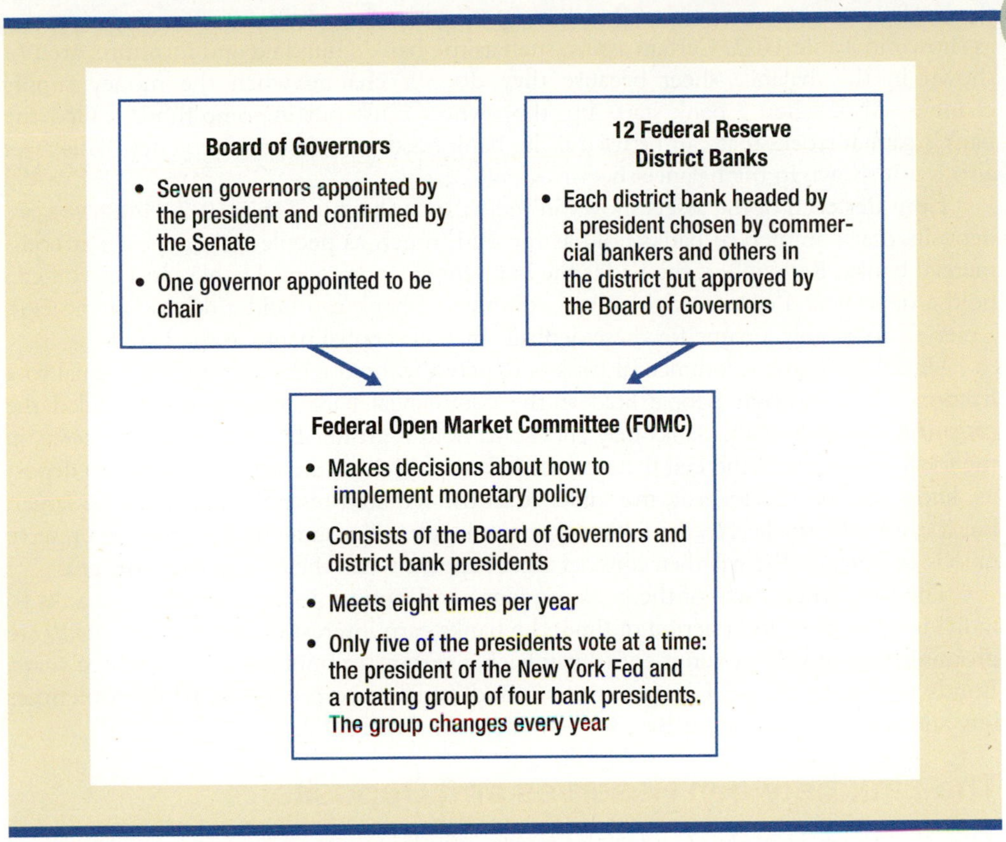

Figure 10-3

Board of Governors

- Seven governors appointed by the president and confirmed by the Senate
- One governor appointed to be chair

12 Federal Reserve District Banks

- Each district bank headed by a president chosen by commercial bankers and others in the district but approved by the Board of Governors

Federal Open Market Committee (FOMC)

- Makes decisions about how to implement monetary policy
- Consists of the Board of Governors and district bank presidents
- Meets eight times per year
- Only five of the presidents vote at a time: the president of the New York Fed and a rotating group of four bank presidents. The group changes every year

The Structure of the Fed
Decisions about monetary policy are made by the FOMC, which consists of the Fed governors and district Fed presidents.

agenda at FOMC meetings, and represents the Fed in testimony before Congress. When journalists in the popular press write about the Fed, they usually talk as if the chair has almost complete power over Fed decisions. Now that we have described the Fed, let us examine the operation of banks and how they, along with the Fed, create money.

The Banks

A commercial bank accepts deposits from individuals and makes loans to others. To understand how a bank functions, it is necessary to look at its balance sheet, which shows these deposits and loans. Table 10-2 is an example of a balance sheet for a bank, called BankOne.

The different items are divided into *assets* and *liabilities*. An **asset** is something of value owned by a person or a firm. A **liability** is something of value that a person or a firm owes, such as a debt, to someone else. Thus a bank's assets are anything the bank owns and any sum owed to the bank by someone else. A bank's liabilities are anything

asset
something of value owned by a person or a firm.

liability
something of value that a person or a firm owes to someone else.

Table 10-2

Balance Sheet of BankOne (millions of dollars)

Assets		Liabilities	
Loans	70	Deposits	100
Bonds	20		
Reserves	10		

This table shows the initial situation. The ratio of reserves to deposits is 0.1.

the bank owes to someone else. People's *deposits* at banks are the main liability of banks, as shown in Table 10-2. Certain assets, such as the bank's building and furniture, are not shown in this balance sheet because they do not change when the money supply changes. Also, when a bank starts up, the owners must put in some funds, called the bank's capital stock, that can be used if the bank needs cash in an emergency. This asset also is not shown in the balance sheet.

Consider each of the assets shown in the balance sheet in Table 10-2. **Reserves** are deposits that commercial banks hold at the Fed, much as people hold deposits at commercial banks. Remember, the Fed is the bank for the commercial banks. Just as you can hold a deposit at a commercial bank, a commercial bank can hold a deposit at the Fed. Reserves are simply a name for these deposits by commercial banks at the Fed.

Under U.S. law, a commercial bank is required to hold reserves at the Fed equal to a fraction of the deposits people hold at the commercial bank; this fraction is called the **required reserve ratio**. Banks may choose to hold a greater fraction of their deposits in the form of reserves at the Fed than required. In reality, then, the ratio of reserves to deposits, known as the *reserve ratio,* may differ from the required reserve ratio: It can be larger, but it cannot be smaller. In the following example, we will assume that the required reserve ratio is 10 percent. We will then consider what happens when the reserve ratio changes.

The two other assets of the bank are loans and bonds. *Loans* are made by banks to individuals or firms for a period of time; the banks earn interest on these loans. *Bonds* are promises of a firm or government to pay back a certain amount after a number of years. Bonds are issued by the U.S. government and by large corporations. Banks sometimes buy and hold such bonds, as BankOne has done in Table 10-2.

The Link between Reserves and Deposits

Because deposits at banks are a form of money, the Fed must be able to control the total amount of these deposits if it is to control the money supply. The link between the deposits at banks and the reserves at the Fed provides the key mechanism by which the Fed can exert control over the amount of deposits at the commercial banks. To see this control, we first look at some examples to show how this link between reserves and deposits works in the whole economy. To make the story simpler, we assume that everyone uses deposits rather than currency for their money. (We will take up currency again in the next section.)

A Formula Linking Reserves to Deposits
To see how the Fed can change the amount of deposits in the economy, let us assume that the Fed increases the amount of reserves that banks hold at the Fed. The Fed can cause such an increase in reserves simply by buying something from a bank and paying for it by increasing that bank's reserves at the Fed. The Fed typically has purchased bonds when it wants to increase reserves. So we will start there.

When the Fed buys bonds, it has to pay for them with something. It pays for them with bank reserves—the deposits banks have with the Fed. For example, if the Fed wants to buy bonds held by Citibank, it says, "We want $10 million worth of bonds, and we will pay for them by increasing Citibank's account with us by $10 million." This purchase is an electronic transaction. Citibank's deposits at the Fed (reserves) have increased by $10 million, and the Fed gets the bonds. It has exchanged bank reserves for the bonds. The buying or selling of bonds by the Federal Reserve is called an **open market operation**.

So next assume that the Fed buys $10 million of bonds from BankOne and pays for the bonds by increasing BankOne's reserves by $10 million. Thus, reserves rise at banks in the economy. Now, with the reserve ratio the same (in this example, equal to 0.1) for each bank in the economy, a formula links reserves and deposits for the whole economy. It is given by

$$\text{Reserves} = (\text{reserve ratio}) \times \text{deposits}$$

reserves
deposits that commercial banks hold at the Fed.

required reserve ratio
the fraction of a bank's deposits that it is required to hold at the Fed.

open market operation
the buying or selling of bonds by the central bank.

where reserves and deposits refer to the amounts in the whole economy. If we divide both sides of this expression by the reserve ratio, we get

$$\text{Deposits} = \left(\frac{1}{\text{reserve ratio}}\right) \times \text{reserves}$$

Thus, any increase in reserves is multiplied by the inverse of the reserve ratio to get the increase in deposits. For example, if the $10 million change in reserves is multiplied by $(1/0.1) = 10$, we get $100 million change in deposits.

One could have started the example by assuming that the Fed bought $10 million in bonds from some person other than a bank. That person would deposit the check from the Fed in a bank, and in the end, the answer would be exactly the same: A $10 million increase in reserves leads to a $100 million increase in deposits.

One also could analyze the effects of a decrease in reserves using the same formula linking reserves and deposits. A decrease in reserves occurs when the Fed sells bonds. For example, a decrease in reserves of $10 million would lead to a decrease in deposits of $100 million.

Bank-by-Bank Deposit Expansion Now let's look at the details of what is going on in the banks. In our example, when the Fed buys bonds, BankOne's holdings of bonds decline by $10 million, from $20 million to $10 million, and BankOne's reserves at the Fed increase by $10 million, from $10 million to $20 million. The balance sheet would then look like Table 10-3, a change from Table 10-2. The key point is that now $10 million more reserves are in the economy than before the Fed purchased the bonds from BankOne. The reserves are held by BankOne, but they will not be held for long.

Recall that in this example we are assuming that banks hold reserves equal to 10 percent of their deposits. But now, after the Fed's actions, BankOne has 20 percent of its deposits as reserves, or more than the 10 percent. Because banks can earn more by making loans or buying bonds than by holding reserves, the bank will have an incentive to reduce its reserves and make more loans or buy more bonds.

Suppose BankOne decreases its reserves by making more loans; with the reserve ratio of 0.1, the bank can loan $10 million. Suppose the bank loans $10 million to UNO, a small oil company, which uses the funds to buy an oil tanker from DOS, a shipbuilding firm. UNO pays DOS with a check from BankOne, and DOS deposits the check in its checking account at its own bank, BankTwo. Now BankTwo must ask BankOne for payment; BankOne will make the payment by lowering its reserve account at the Fed and increasing BankTwo's reserve account at the Fed by $10 million. BankOne's balance sheet at the end of these transactions is shown in Table 10-4.

Hence, after BankOne makes the loan and transfers its reserves to BankTwo, its reserves are back to 10 percent of its deposits. The story ends here for BankOne, but not for the economy as a whole because BankTwo now has $10 million more in reserves, and this addition will affect BankTwo's decisions. Let us see how.

Table 10-3

Balance Sheet of BankOne after Reserves Increase (millions of dollars)

Assets		Liabilities		
Loans	70	Deposits	100	*Note the effect of the Fed's purchase of bonds: Compared with Table 10–2, bonds are lower and reserves are higher in Table 10–3. The ratio of reserves to deposits is 0.2.*
Bonds	10			
Reserves	20			

Table 10-4

Balance Sheet of BankOne after It Makes Loans

Assets		Liabilities	
Loans	80	Deposits	100
Bonds	10		
Reserves	10		

By making more loans, the bank reduces the ratio of reserves to deposits back to 0.1.

Now BankTwo finds itself with $10 million in additional deposits and $10 million in additional reserves at the Fed. (Remember that deposits are a liability to BankTwo and the reserves are an asset; thus, assets and liabilities each have risen by $10 million.) Continuing with the 10 percent reserve ratio assumption, however, BankTwo needs to hold only $1 million in reserves for the additional $10 million in deposits. Thus, BankTwo will want to make more loans until its reserves equal 10 percent of its deposits. It will lend to other people an amount equal to 90 percent of the $10 million, or $9 million. The first row of Table 10-5 shows the increase in deposits, loans, and reserves at BankTwo. The story ends here for BankTwo, but not for the economy as a whole.

The people who get loans from BankTwo will use these loans to pay others. Thus, the funds probably will end up in yet another bank, called BankThree. Then, BankThree will find it has $9 million in additional deposits and $9 million in additional reserves. BankThree then will lend 90 percent of the $9 million, or $8.1 million, as shown in the second row of Table 10-5. This process will continue from bank to bank. We begin to see that the initial increase in reserves is leading to a much bigger expansion of deposits. The whole process is shown in Table 10-5. Each row shows what happens at one of the banks. The sums of the columns show the change for the whole economy. If we sum the columns through the end of the process, we will see that deposits, and thus the money supply, increase by $100 million as a result of the $10 million increase in reserves. The increase in deposits is 10 times the actual increase in reserves—exactly what the formula predicted. Usually, the whole process takes a short period of time (days rather than weeks) because banks quickly adjust their loans and reserves.

Table 10-5

Deposit Expansion (millions of dollars)

	Deposits	Loans	Reserves
BankTwo	10.00	9.00	1.000
BankThree	9.00	8.10	0.900
BankFour	8.10	7.29	0.810
BankFive	7.29	6.56	0.729
BankSix	6.56	5.90	0.656
BankSeven	5.90	5.31	0.590
BankEight	5.31	4.78	0.531
BankNine	4.78	4.30	0.478
BankTen	4.30	3.87	0.430
.	.	.	.
.	.	.	.
.	.	.	.
Final sum	100.00	90.00	10.000

The numbers in each column get smaller and smaller; if we add up the numbers for all the banks, even those beyond BankTen, we get the sum at the bottom.

The Explosion of Reserves and the Reserve Ratio in 2008

Banks sometimes hold more than the required amount of reserves at the Fed, and the reserve ratio can rise above the required reserve ratio. In our examples so far, we have assumed that the reserve ratio is constant. In this section, we explain what can happen when the reserve ratio changes. We focus on a particularly interesting real-world example.

In the fall of 2008, reserves at the Fed started increasing at a rapid rate. As in our examples in the previous section, the Fed increased reserves by purchasing bonds and paying for them by creating deposits. In this case, however, the Fed purchased large amounts of bonds and other securities issued by private firms rather than the federal government as it usually does. It also made *loans* to private financial firms to contain the financial crisis. The Fed reasoned that by buying the bonds it could drive the interest rate on those bonds down, which would ease the financial crisis, and that making loans to certain financial firms would help those firms avoid bankruptcy and reduce risks to the financial system.

When the Fed purchased these bonds and made the loans, it paid for them by creating reserves—crediting banks with deposits at the Fed. The increase in reserves was unprecedented. Figure 10-4 shows how large, sudden, and unusual the increase was. After remaining relatively steady, reserves exploded in the fall of 2008. They increased from $44 billion in August 2008 to $858 billion in January 2009, almost a 20-fold increase.

Demand deposits at banks also increased as a result of this increase in reserves, which is not surprising, given the connection between deposits and reserves explained in the previous section. The increase in demand deposits at banks also is shown in Figure 10-4. Note that the increase in demand deposits was not as large as one would expect if the reserve ratio were constant. In fact, as shown in Figure 10-5, the reserve ratio was not constant. It was nearly constant for a number of years, but then it increased sharply in the fall of 2008 as banks held some of the large increase in reserves as **excess reserves** over the amount they were required to hold. In other words, they did not lend out all the reserves. Banks did not lend out all the reserves because demand was insufficient for loans and because they were concerned about risks.

excess reserves
the amount of reserves over and above required reserves.

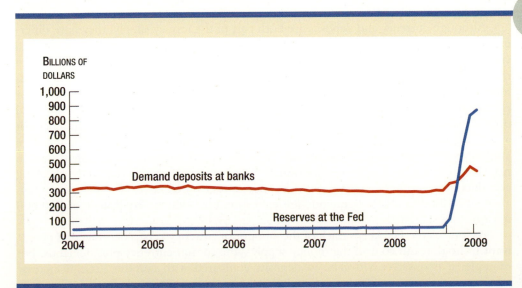

Figure 10-4

The Great Expansion of Reserves and Deposits in 2008

This chart shows bank reserves (deposits of banks at the Fed) and demand deposits at banks. The explosion of reserves occurred in the fall of 2008. Reserves increased as the Fed bought bonds and made loans, in an attempt to contain the financial crisis, and paid for them by crediting banks with deposits at the Fed.

Figure 10-5

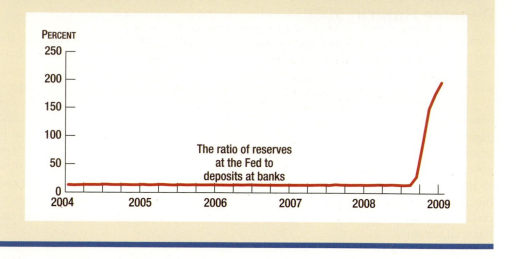

The Great Increase in the Reserve Ratio
After remaining steady for several years, the reserve ratio jumped in the fall of 2008 as the Fed increased the supply of reserves to the banking system.

The increase in demand deposits, in turn, increased the money supply, because demand deposits are part of the money supply. Recalling earlier periods of high money growth, some people became concerned that the increase in the money supply would cause inflation, and they criticized the Fed for increasing the money supply by such a large amount. The Fed, however, indicated that it did not see inflation as a problem. Policy officials were more concerned about the financial crisis. These officials indicated that if inflation picked up, they would be able to reduce the amount of reserves and reduce deposits and the money supply.

How the Fed Controls the Money Supply: Currency plus Deposits

We now have seen how an increase in reserves will increase the amount of deposits or a decrease in reserves will reduce the amount of deposits. But the money supply includes currency as well as deposits. With currency in the picture, the Fed must keep track of whether people want to hold more currency or less currency compared with deposits.

Although currency and deposits are both part of the money supply, they have different characteristics. For some purposes, people prefer currency to checking deposits, and vice versa. These preferences determine the amount of currency and checking deposits in the economy. If you want to hold more currency in your wallet because you find it is more convenient than a checking deposit, you just go to the bank and reduce your checking deposit and carry around more currency. If you are worried about crime and do not want to have much currency in your wallet, then you go to the bank and deposit a larger amount in your checking account. Thus, people decide on the amount of currency versus deposits in the economy. In Japan, where crime is less prevalent than in many other countries, people use much more currency compared with checking accounts than in other countries. Even Japanese business executives who earn the equivalent of $120,000 a year frequently are paid monthly with the equivalent of $10,000 in cash.

As long as the Fed keeps track of the amount of currency versus deposits that people want to hold, it can control the money supply—the sum of currency plus demands. For example, if it observes a decline in deposits compared with currency, it can increase reserves, thereby increasing deposits and preventing the money supply from declining.

How a Credit Crunch Affects Deposit Expansion

Earlier, we saw how the Fed can influence the money supply in the economy through an increase in reserves, which is transformed into a much larger increase in deposits by way of the banking sector. Occasionally, the economy suffers from a **credit crunch**, a period during which banks become cautious about making new loans. A credit crunch greatly reduces the amount by which deposits respond to an increase in reserves initiated by the Fed. An extreme version of this can be demonstrated using the balance sheet for Bank-One, shown in Table 10-3. Once the Fed increases BankOne's reserves by $10 million through an open market operation, if BankOne holds onto $20 million in reserves (even though they are required to hold only $10 million), or if they buy $10 million worth of safe U.S. government bonds instead of making $10 million worth of new loans, then no further expansion of deposits will occur through the banking sector.

Why might banks become more cautious about making loans? One possibility is that they perceive an increased risk of lending to all of their clients. For example, in late 2008, with house prices falling and many borrowers defaulting on their mortgages, banks may have become extremely cautious about the creditworthiness of clients. Another possibility is that bank balance sheets have suffered because an existing asset has lost value. For example, if some of the bonds that BankOne was holding in Table 10-3 were mortgage-linked bonds whose value declined sharply in 2008, then BankOne may decide to use the expanded reserves to fortify their other assets instead of to make new loans. To overcome the credit crunch, the central bank may have to dramatically increase the amount of new reserves to increase the money supply by the desired amount.

credit crunch
a period when banks become cautious in making new loans.

REVIEW

- Banks serve two important functions: They channel funds from savers to investors, and their deposits can be used as money.

- Commercial banks hold deposits, called reserves, at the Fed.

- The Fed increases reserves by buying bonds and reduces reserves by selling bonds.

- The deposits at banks expand by a multiple of any increase in reserves. Thus, a connection exists between reserves and deposits in the overall economy. The reserve ratio is not a constant, however, as observed in 2008.

- By keeping track of currency, the Fed can control the total money supply, which is the sum of currency and deposits.

Money Growth and Inflation

Early in this chapter, in the section "Commodity Money," we showed that when gold, silver, or other commodities were the primary form of money, increases in the supply of money would cause inflation. Even though paper currency and deposits are now the main forms of money, the same principle holds in the twenty-first century. That is, *all other things being equal,* an increase in the supply of money will cause inflation. In this section, we examine this principle by looking at some important episodes of inflation during the twentieth century. Before we do so, we introduce a famous equation that can help us test the principle that an increase in the supply of money eventually causes inflation.

Consider first a simple example. Suppose that all of your transactions are in a video game arcade with food-vending machines and video game machines. You will need money in your pocket to carry out your transactions each day. If you use the vending and video game machines 10 times a day, you will need 10 times more money in your pocket than if you use the machines once a day. Hence, 10 times more transactions means 10 times more money. If the prices for vending machine items and minutes on a video game machine double, then you will need twice as much money for each day's activities, assuming that the higher price does not cure your habit. Hence, whether the value of transactions increases because the number of items purchased increases or because the price of each item increases, the amount of money used for transactions will rise.

What is true for you and the machines is true for the whole population and the whole economy. For the whole economy, real gross domestic product (GDP) is like the number of transactions with the machines, and the GDP deflator (a measure of the average price in the economy) is like the average price of the vending and game machines. Just as the amount of money you use for transactions in the game arcade is related to the number of transactions and the price of each transaction, so too is the supply of money in the economy related to real GDP and the GDP deflator.

The Quantity Equation of Money

quantity equation of money
the equation relating the price level and real GDP to the quantity of money and the velocity of money: The quantity of money times its velocity equals the price level times real GDP.

This relationship between money, real GDP, and the GDP deflator can be summarized by the **quantity equation of money**, which is written

$$\text{Money supply} \times \text{velocity} = \text{GDP deflator} \times \text{real GDP}$$

or

$$MV = PY$$

where V is velocity, P is the GDP deflator, and Y is real GDP. For example, if the money supply was $1,000 billion, real GDP was $8,000 billion, and the GDP deflator was 1.1, then a value of 8.8 for velocity would satisfy the quantity equation ($1,000 \times 8.8 = 1.1 \times 8,000$).

velocity
a measure of how frequently money is turned over in the economy.

The term **velocity** measures how frequently money is turned over. It is the number of times a dollar is used on average each period to make purchases. To see this, suppose an automatic teller machine (ATM) is installed in the room with the vending machines and video games from the preceding example. Each morning, you withdraw cash from the ATM for your morning games, and each day at midday, an employee takes the cash from the vending and game machines and restocks the ATM. You then replenish your cash from the ATM to pay for your afternoon use of the games and vending machines; you now need to carry only half as much currency in your pocket as before the ATM was installed, when you had to bring enough cash to last all day. From your perspective, therefore, the velocity of money doubles. Money turns over twice as fast. As this example shows, velocity in the economy depends on technology and, in particular, on how efficient we are at using money.

Now, let's use the quantity equation to show how an increase in the money supply is related to inflation. If you look carefully at the quantity equation of money, you can see that if velocity and real GDP are not affected by a change in money, then an increase in the money supply will increase the GDP deflator (the average level of prices in the economy). A higher percentage increase in money—that is, *higher money growth*—will lead to a higher percentage increase in prices—that is, *higher inflation*. Thus, the quantity equation of money shows that higher rates of money growth lead to higher inflation, just as in the case of commodity money early in the chapter.

A restatement of the quantity equation using growth rates leads to a convenient relationship between money growth, inflation, real GDP growth, and velocity growth. In particular,

$$\text{Money growth} + \text{velocity growth} = \text{inflation} + \text{real GDP growth}$$

For example, if the money supply growth is 5 percent per year, velocity growth is 0 percent per year, and real GDP growth is 3 percent per year, then this equation says that inflation is 2 percent per year. (This growth rate form of the quantity equation follows directly from the quantity equation itself; in general, the rate of growth of a product of two terms is approximately equal to the sum of the growth rates of the two terms. Thus,

ECONOMICS *IN ACTION*

Hyperinflation and Too Much Money

So much money was printed during the period of German hyperinflation that it became cheaper to burn several million German marks to cook breakfast—as this woman was doing in 1923—than to buy kindling wood with the nearly worthless money. Inflation rose to more than 100 percent per week. Shop owners closed their shops at lunchtime to change the prices. Workers were paid twice weekly. People would rush to the stores and buy everything they needed for the next few days. Firms also set up barter systems with their workers, exchanging consumer goods directly for labor.

Almost three quarters of a century later, a similar story prevailed in Zimbabwe. At the very peak of the inflation, prices were doubling overnight, which meant that a daily laborer's real purchasing power was being cut in half every day. Even the most mundane transaction required carrying unimaginable quantities of money around, as the picture of the one hundred trillion dollar note shows.

In both countries, the hyperinflation initially was caused by the huge increase in money growth resulting from misguided government policies. However, once it started, everyone tried to get rid of cash as soon as possible, accelerating the inflationary process. Also, by the time the government received its tax revenue, it was not worth much because prices had risen sharply. So the government had to print even more money to pay its bills. In the last months of hyperinflation in Germany, more than 30 paper mills worked at full capacity to deliver paper currency. Even though 150 printing firms had 2,000 presses running 24 hours a day to print German marks, they could not keep up with the need for new notes.

Hyperinflations can be stopped only by a substantial break in the policy behavior of the government or central bank. On November 15, 1923, an economic reform stabilized the inflation rate. By then, the German prices were 100 billion times higher than they had been before the hyperinflation. In Zimbabwe, people stopped using Zimbabwean dollars and the government gave in to the inevitable and sanctioned the use of foreign currency. So the hyperinflation ended once the people decided that a different medium of exchange was needed and switched to using currency notes that could no longer be printed by the government of Zimbabwe.

© Bettmann/CORBIS

AP Photo/Tsvangirayi Mukwazhi

An unidentified woman holds an old one hundred trillion Zimbabwean dollar note. These old notes sell at an average of $3 to western collectors.

the growth rate of M times V equals the growth rate of M plus the growth rate of V, and the growth rate of P times Y equals the growth rate of P plus the growth rate of Y.)

According to the quantity equation, along a long-run economic growth path in which real GDP growth is equal to potential GDP growth, an increase in money growth by a certain number of percentage points in the long run will result in an increase in inflation of the same number of percentage points unless velocity growth changes. Thus, higher money growth will lead to higher inflation in the long run. If velocity growth remains at zero, as in the previous example, and real GDP growth remains at 3 percent per year, then an increase in money growth by 10 percentage points, from 5 to 15 percent, will increase inflation by 10 percentage points, from 2 to 12 percent.

Evidence

What evidence do we have that higher money growth leads to more inflation? The quantity equation tells us that we should look for evidence during periods when changes in real GDP and velocity were small compared with changes in money growth and inflation. During such periods, the change in money growth and inflation will be the dominant terms in the quantity equation.

Figure 10-6

The Relation between Money Growth and Inflation

As the data for these several countries show, higher money growth is associated with higher inflation. The data pertain to the period 1973–1991, when inflation differed greatly among the countries. Inflation and money growth are now lower in all these countries.

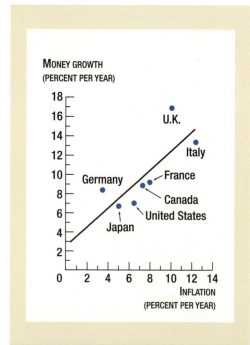

Worldwide Inflation in the 1970s and 1980s Figure 10-6 shows such a period: the years from 1973 to 1991, when many economies had big inflations, some much bigger than others. Money growth is plotted on the vertical axis, and inflation on the horizontal axis. In Figure 10-6, each point represents a country. For countries with higher money growth, inflation was higher. Hence, the quantity equation works well during this period. During the 1990s, inflation was low in all these countries, so the difference was insufficient to test how well the equation works. This period of high inflation is sometimes called the Great Inflation.

Hyperinflations An even more dramatic type of evidence showing that high money growth can cause inflation is hyperinflation. A hyperinflation is simply a period of very high inflation. The inflation in Germany in 1923 is one of the most famous examples of a hyperinflation. The German government had incurred huge expenses during World War I, and huge demands for war reparations from the victors in World War I compounded the problem. Because the government could not raise enough taxes to pay its expenses, it started printing huge amounts of money, which caused the hyperinflation of 1923. Figure 10-7 shows the *weekly* increase in German prices.

The German hyperinflation of 1923 was not a unique historic episode, and hyperinflation is not necessarily linked to war. Until recently, hyperinflations were common in Latin America. The size of the Latin American inflations is hard to imagine. The inflation rate in Brazil averaged 43.6 percent per year from 1912 to 1996. A Brazilian good that cost one dollar in 1912 would cost a quadrillion dollars (1,000 trillion) in the 1990s. Inflation in Chile was also very high—about 90 percent throughout the 1970s.

Figure 10-8 shows the price level in Brazil and Chile as well as the money supply in both countries. Clearly, money and prices are closely related. Fortunately, inflation in Chile has been much lower since the 1990s, and inflation in Brazil also has been declining. Not surprisingly, money growth is much lower now too. Money growth has been the cause of all hyperinflations. The most recent hyperinflation occurred in Zimbabwe starting in February 2007 when inflation exceeded 50 percent per month. By late 2009 the inflation rate was 98 percent a day. Prices doubled overnight and the currency became worthless. The Zimbabwean inflation was the second worst in history after Hungary in 1946.

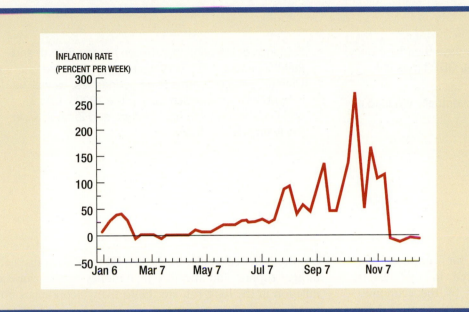

Figure 10-7

German Hyperinflation of 1923

The chart shows the weekly percent change in the price level in Germany in 1923. Inflation rose to truly astronomical levels for several months.

Figure 10-8

Money and Prices in Brazil and Chile during the Twentieth Century

The close relationship between money and the price level is obvious during this period of very high inflation. So far in the twenty-first century, inflation and money growth have been much lower in both countries.

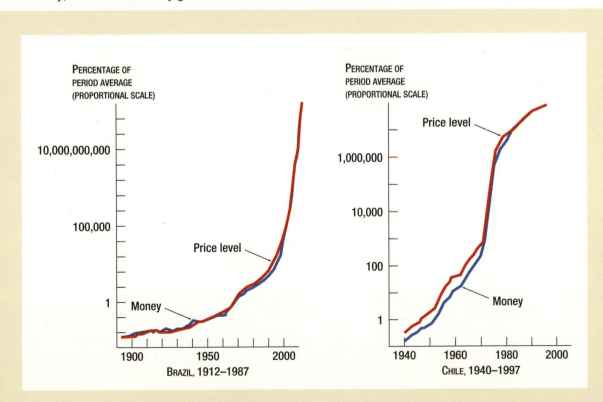

Source: Gerald Dwyer and Rik Hafer, "Are Money Growth and Inflation Still Related?" (Federal Reserve Bank of Atlanta, *Review,* Second Quarter 1999).

REVIEW

- The quantity equation of money says that the money supply times velocity equals real GDP times the GDP deflator.
- Higher rates of money growth eventually will lead to higher inflation.

- Evidence of the relation between money growth and inflation is found in the 1970s and 1980s in the United States and other large economies, as well as in hyperinflations in Germany in the 1920s, Brazil and Chile in the twentieth century, and Zimbabwe in the twenty-first century.

CONCLUSION

Money has fascinated economists for centuries. The famous quantity equation introduced in this chapter predates Adam Smith and was used by the economist-philosopher David Hume in the eighteenth century. Adam Smith placed money second in importance only to the division of labor in the first chapters of the *Wealth of Nations.*

Although the role of money appears mysterious and has caused some great debates in economics and politics, the ideas presented in this chapter are not controversial. The three functions of money, the deposit expansion proc-

ess, the technical ability of the central bank to control the money supply, and the fact that money is the cause of inflation in the long run are things many economists now agree on.

Many of the controversies about money pertain to the short-run fluctuations in the economy and revolve around the effects the Fed has on real GDP in the short run. After considering the reasons why real GDP may depart from potential GDP in the short run in Chapters 11 and 12, we will return to the effects the Fed has on short-run fluctuations in the economy.

KEY POINTS

1. Money has three roles: a medium of exchange, a store of value, and a unit of account.
2. Commodity money, ranging from salt to gold coins, has been used in place of barter for many centuries. Now paper money and deposits are also part of money.
3. Commercial banks are financial intermediaries; their deposits are part of the money supply.
4. Commercial banks hold reserves at the central bank.
5. The central bank changes reserves by buying and selling bonds.

6. The central bank can control the money supply by buying and selling bonds.
7. The central bank in the United States is the Federal Reserve System (the Fed).
8. When stated in terms of growth rates, the quantity equation of money describes the relationship between money growth, real GDP growth, and inflation.
9. Higher money growth eventually leads to higher inflation.

KEY TERMS

asset, 235

bank, 232

checking deposits, 229

credit crunch, 241

currency, 229

excess reserves, 239

Federal Open Market Committee (FOMC), 234

Federal Reserve System (the Fed), 232

liability, 235

medium of exchange, 227

money, 227

money supply, 231

QUESTIONS FOR REVIEW

1. What are the differences between the medium of exchange, store of value, and unit of account roles of money?
2. What are some examples of commodity money?
3. Why is currency a part of money even though an expensive purse to put the currency in is not?
4. What is a bank?
5. What is the Fed, and how is the FOMC organized?
6. What happens to bank reserves when the Fed buys bonds?
7. Why does higher money growth cause inflation?
8. What is the quantity equation of money?

PROBLEMS

1. Which of the following are money and which are not?
   a. A credit card
   b. A debit card
   c. A check in your checkbook
   d. A dollar bill
   e. A necklace containing 8 ounces of gold

2. Cigarettes were a popular form of currency in prisoner-of-war (POW) camps in World War II, and still are a valuable form of currency in prisons in many countries. Why would cigarettes be likely to serve as currency in such settings?

3. Who are the current members of the Board of Governors of the Federal Reserve? What positions did they hold previously that made them well suited for a position on the board?

4. State whether each of the following statements is true or false. Explain your answers in one or two sentences.
   a. When commodity money is the only type of money, a decrease in the price of the commodity serving as money is inflation.
   b. The same money is always used as both a unit of account and a medium of exchange at any one time in any one country.
   c. The smaller the reserve ratio at banks, the larger the money multiplier.
   d. The Federal Reserve reduces reserves by buying government bonds.

5. Assume that required reserves are 7 percent of deposits and that people hold no currency—all money is held in the form of checking deposits.

   a. Suppose that the Federal Reserve purchases $30,000 worth of government bonds from Ellen (a private citizen), and that Ellen deposits all of the proceeds from the sale into her checking account at Z Bank. Construct a balance sheet, with assets on the left and liabilities on the right, to show how Ellen's deposit creates new assets and liabilities for Z Bank.
   b. How much of this new deposit can Z Bank lend out? Assume that it lends this amount to George, who then deposits the entire amount into his account at Y Bank. Show this on Y Bank's balance sheet.
   c. How much of this new deposit can Y Bank lend out? Suppose Joe takes out a loan for this amount from Y Bank and deposits the money into his account at X Bank. Show this on X Bank's balance sheet.
   d. The process of lending and relending creates money throughout the banking system. As a result of Ellen's deposit, how much money, in the form of deposits, has been created so far? If this process resulting from Ellen's deposit continues forever, how much money will be created?

6. Why are credit cards not included in the money supply even though they can be used easily for transactions? (*Hint:* What do you think happens when you use a credit card to purchase an item at a store?)

7. According to the quantity equation, changes in the money supply will lead directly to changes in the price level if velocity and real GDP are unaffected

by the change in the money supply. Will velocity change over time? What factors might lead to changes in velocity? Are those changes related to changes in the money supply?

8. Consider the following table:

Year	Quantity of Money (billions of $)	Velocity	Real GDP (billions of $)	GDP Deflator
2004	$1,375	7.113	$10,703	
2005	$1,373	7.138	$11,049	
2006	$1,366	7.200	$11,415	

a. Fill in the missing data, using the quantity equation of money.
b. Why might velocity change in this way?
c. Calculate the inflation rate for 2005 and for 2006.
d. If money growth had been 5 percent per year in 2004 and 2005, what would inflation have been, assuming real GDP and velocity as in the table?

part three

ECONOMIC FLUCTUATIONS AND MACROECONOMIC POLICY

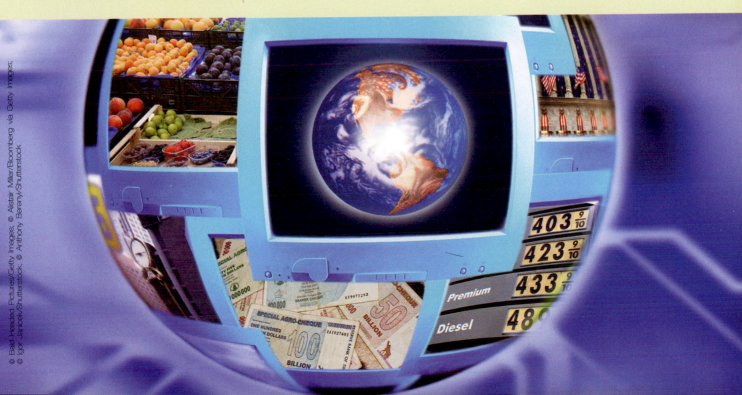

11 The Nature and Causes of Economic Fluctuations

Studying economic fluctuations is important because recessions bring unemployment and hardship to many people. Although the importance of long-run economic growth cannot be overstated, fluctuations around the growth trend affect the livelihood of millions of people. As John Maynard Keynes put it, "Economists set themselves too easy, too useless a task if in tempestuous seasons they can only tell us that when the storm is long past the ocean is flat again." Hence, the study of economic fluctuations is vital to understanding economics.

Economic fluctuations have been common for at least 200 years, but they have changed over time. One notable change was that recessions diminished in frequency and moderated in severity in the United States, and many other countries, during the 25-year period from 1982 to 2007, a phenomenon that many economists call the Great Moderation. The only recession that occurred in the United States during this period was the 2001 recession, which lasted only eight months, starting in March 2001 and ending in November 2001. Between 2001 and 2007 the economy then grew and 7.1 million jobs were created until the peak in December 2007. A key purpose of studying economic fluctuations is to explain why this Great Moderation occurred and to determine whether economic policies were responsible for it.

In December 2007, this period of Great Moderation came to an end when the economy entered a severe recession. Employment steadily declined all through 2008 as the recession worsened because of panic in the financial markets in the fall of 2008. By the time the recession officially ended in June of 2009, 7.8 million jobs in the U.S. economy had been lost. Even after

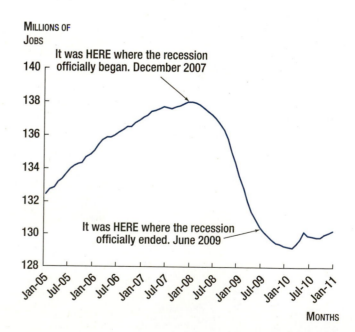

the economy began growing again, employment continued to decline with almost 1 million more jobs being lost until the number of jobs finally started growing again in early 2010. Recessions cause obvious harm to individuals who lose their job, and they make it much more difficult to find a job if you are looking for one. A person who entered the labor force in the summer of 2008 had a much greater difficulty finding a job than a person who entered the labor force in the summer of 2007 when the economy was near a peak. Understanding why the most recent recession was so severe in comparison with the 2001 recession will be an important first step in devising policies that could prevent millions of people from experiencing the hardship caused by job loss.

The recession that began in 2007, and ended 18 months later, is one of many economic fluctuations that the United States and other economies have experienced over the years. In this chapter, we take a closer look at economic fluctuations, which are defined as departures of the economy from its long-term growth trend. These departures include recessions, which are periods in which gross domestic product (GDP) declines sharply, moving the economy below its long-term trend. Another type of departure occurs when GDP rises rapidly, moving the economy above its long-term trend.

Changes in Aggregate Demand Lead to Changes in Production

Figure 11-1 illustrates the nature of economic fluctuations with particular reference to the recessions starting in 2001 and 2007. As shown in the upper left portion of Figure 11-1, real GDP clearly was above potential GDP in 1999 and 2000, but in mid-2001, as the recession took hold, real GDP fell below potential GDP. A recovery then started that brought real GDP back to potential GDP by 2004.

You also can see the 2007 recession in greater detail in the upper right portion of Figure 11-1. Following the return to potential output in 2004, the economy stayed at or above potential output until the recession began in December 2007. Real GDP fell sharply below potential GDP, and it continued to decline until the recession officially ended in June 2009. Since then real GDP has grown, but the initial decline was so dramatic that 18 months after the recession officially ended, real GDP remains well below potential.

Economic fluctuations occur simultaneously with long-term growth, as shown by the longer history in Figure 11-1. Real GDP has fluctuated around what otherwise might have been a steady upward-moving trend. Although no two economic fluctuations are alike—some are long, some are short; some are deep, some are shallow—they do have common features. Perhaps the most important one is that after a departure of real GDP from potential GDP, the economy eventually returns to a more normal long-run growth path.

We begin by looking at the first steps the economy takes as it moves away from potential GDP. In other words, we examine the initial, or short-run, increase or decrease of real GDP above or below potential GDP as in 2001 and 2008. We will show that the first steps of real GDP away from potential GDP are caused by changes in aggregate demand. Aggregate demand is the total amount that consumers, businesses, government, and foreigners are willing to spend on all goods and services in the economy. In contrast, the growth of potential GDP is caused by increases in the available supply of inputs to production: labor, capital, and technology.

Figure 11-1

Narrowing the Focus on Economic Fluctuations

The two magnified economic fluctuations center on the recessions that began in 2001 and 2007. We begin here with the 2001 recession because a full cycle is completed with a return to potential GDP by 2004.

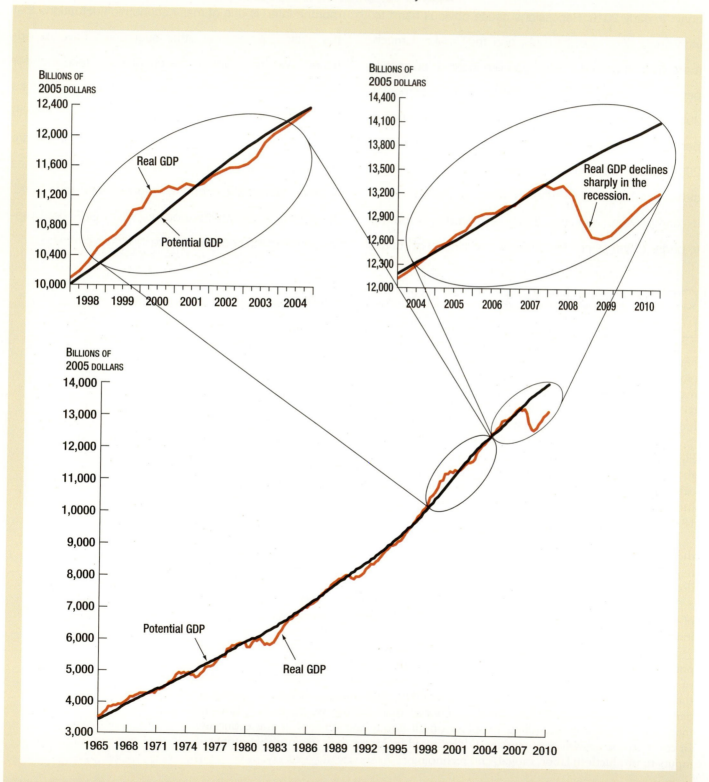

Figure 11-2 illustrates the essential idea used to explain economic fluctuations: Increases or decreases in real GDP to levels above or below potential GDP occur largely because of increases or decreases in aggregate demand in the economy. Changes in aggregate demand occur when consumers, business firms, government, or foreigners expand or cut back their spending. Potential GDP in three years is represented by points *a*, *b*, and *c* in Figure 11-2. These three values of potential GDP are part of the long-term steady increase in potential GDP over time resulting from increases in the supply of labor and capital and improvements in technology. Potential GDP represents what firms would want to produce in "normal times," when the economy is not in a recession. In normal times, real GDP is equal to potential GDP. Years 1 and 2 in Figure 11-2 are assumed to be normal years. Year 3, however, is not a normal year. Point *d* in the left panel of the figure shows a recession because real GDP has declined from Point *b*. Real GDP is below potential GDP at Point *d*. Firms produce less and lay off workers.

Figure 11-2

The First Step of an Economic Fluctuation

Potential GDP is shown by the black upward-sloping line in both diagrams. Points *a*, *b*, and *c* represent three different levels of potential GDP in three years. A downward departure of real GDP (shown in orange) from potential GDP is illustrated by point *d* on the left. Because real GDP falls, this is a recession. An upward departure of real GDP from potential GDP is illustrated by point *e* on the right. The departures are explained by changes in aggregate demand. The line at the bottom shows the percent deviation of real GDP from potential GDP.

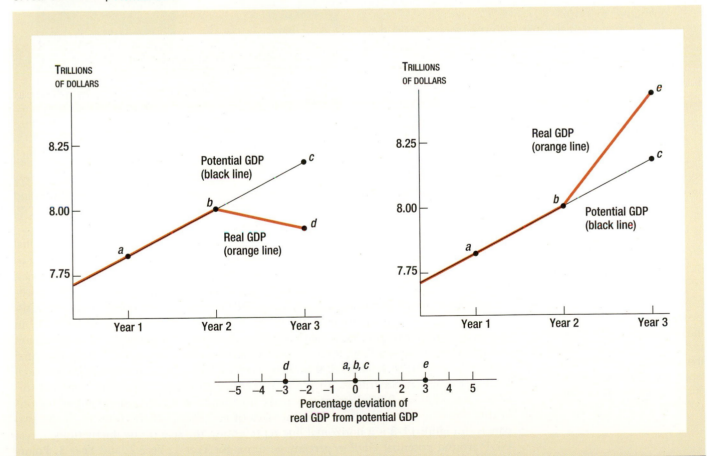

ECONOMICS *IN ACTION*

Real-Life Examples of How Firms Respond to Demand

Cummins, Inc. is a manufacturing firm headquartered in Columbus, Ohio. Cummins is not a household name, but it is a large company with about $1 billion per month in sales of engines and power generation equipment. The recession that began in 2007 had an adverse impact on automobile manufacturers, some of whom, like Dodge, bought engines from Cummins. In early 2009, Cummins announced that they were laying off 600 workers at a plant that made engines for Dodge and another 800 white-collar workers. Shares of Cummins were trading at around $20 per share at the time. But as the economy slowly recovered, and the recession came to an end in June of 2009, Cummins rebounded strongly. According to new reports, Cummins began hiring temporary workers to help with the increased production demand and even began to re-hire some of the workers they laid off. Cummins announced that 2010 was its best year of sales ever—at about $16 billion—and its stock price more than quintupled to $110.

Another company that has experienced similar fluctuations in demand is Toll Brothers, a firm that builds and sells houses to upper middle-income families. At the height of the housing boom, according to an article on Portfolio.com, profiling the company, the firm was selling almost $5 billion per year worth of new houses. But when the economy went into recession, the firm sold almost 50 percent fewer houses and laid off almost half their workforce—several thousand employees. Toll Brothers' fortunes have improved as the economy recovered, but it will be a long time before new house construction reaches the frenzied levels of the period leading up to the 2007 onset of the recession, and it will take a long time before most of the workers that were laid off are hired back.

Justin Sullivan/Getty Images

Unemployment rises. Eventually—this part of the story comes in later chapters—if demand stays low, firms begin to cut their prices, and real GDP moves back toward potential GDP. Thus, in recessions, changes in aggregate demand cause fluctuations in real GDP.

Point e in the right panel represents another departure of real GDP from potential GDP. In this case, real GDP rises above potential GDP. Firms produce more in response to the increase in aggregate demand; they employ more workers, and unemployment declines. Eventually—again, this part of the story comes in later chapters—if demand for their product stays high, firms raise their prices, and real GDP goes back down toward potential GDP.

potential GDP
the economy's long-term growth trend for real GDP, determined by the available supply of capital, labor, and technology. Real GDP fluctuates above and below potential GDP. (Ch. 5)

Economists frequently measure the departures of real GDP from **potential GDP** in percentages rather than in dollar amounts. For example, if potential GDP is $8 trillion and real GDP is $8.4 trillion, then the percentage departure of real GDP from potential GDP is 5 percent: $(8.4 - 8.0)/8.0 = 0.05$. If real GDP were $7.6 trillion and potential GDP remained at $8 trillion, then the percentage departure would be -5 percent: $(7.6 - 8.0)/8.0 = -0.05$. Percentages make it easier to compare economic fluctuations in different countries that have different sizes of real GDP. At the bottom of the two panels in Figure 11-2 is a horizontal line representing the size of the fluctuations in real GDP around potential GDP in percentage terms for Year 1, Year 2, and Year 3. Points d and e in Figure 11-2 represent the first steps of an economic fluctuation.

Production and Demand at Individual Firms

Why do firms produce more—bringing real GDP above *potential GDP*—when the demand for their products rises? Why do firms produce less—bringing real GDP below potential GDP—when the demand for their products falls? These questions probably have occupied more of economists' time than any other question in macroeconomics. Although more work still needs to be done, substantial improvements in economists' understanding of the issues have been made in the last 20 years.

The Unemployment Rate and the Deviations of Real GDP from Potential GDP
First consider some simple facts about how firms operate. In normal times, when real GDP is equal to potential GDP, most firms operate with some excess capacity so that they can expand production without major bottlenecks. Small retail service businesses from taxi companies to dry cleaners usually can increase production when customer demand increases. Another taxi is added to a busy route and one of the drivers is asked to work overtime. One of the dry cleaning employees who has been working part time is happy to work full time. The same is true for large manufacturing firms. When asked what percent of capacity their production is in normal times, manufacturing firms typically answer about 80 percent. Thus, firms normally have room to expand production: Capacity utilization sometimes goes up to 90 percent or higher. If firms need more labor to expand production, they can ask workers to work overtime, call workers back from previous layoffs, or hire additional workers. *The unemployment rate drops below the natural unemployment rate when real GDP rises above potential GDP.*

In recessions, when demand declines, these same firms clearly have the capability to reduce production, and they do. In recessions, capacity utilization goes down to 70 percent or lower. Firms ask workers to stop working overtime, they move some workers to part time, or they lay off some workers. Some firms institute hiring freezes to ensure that the personnel office does not keep hiring workers. *The unemployment rate rises above the natural unemployment rate when real GDP falls below potential GDP.* For example, the unemployment rate rose to more than 7 percent when the 1990–1991 recession brought real GDP below potential GDP. The relationship between the unemployment rate and the movements of real GDP relative to potential GDP is illustrated at right.

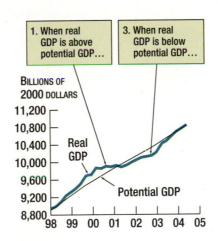

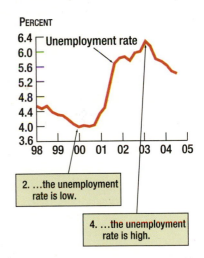

Could Economic Fluctuations Also Be Due to Changes in Potential GDP?

Our discussion thus far of the production decisions of individual firms has shown why it is natural to identify fluctuations in real GDP with fluctuations in aggregate demand. To be sure, economic fluctuations also occur because of changes in potential GDP. For example, when agriculture was a much larger fraction of real GDP, droughts and floods had more noticeable effects on real GDP. Although agriculture currently accounts for a very small fraction of total production, the possibility that increases or decreases in potential GDP may still play a large role in economic fluctuations currently is being

REMINDER

Recall from Chapter 5 that potential *GDP* depends on the economy's *aggregate supply*, which is determined by the available *capital*, *labor*, and *technology*. A drought or a flood would reduce aggregate supply.

ECONOMICS *IN ACTION*

Assessing the Prospects for Economic Recovery

One of the striking features of the recession that began at the end of 2007 and lasted for almost 18 months has been the sluggishness of the recovery process. The economy remains well below potential output and unemployment remained well above 9 percent almost a year and a half after the recession ended. Economists and policy makers eagerly await economic developments that would signal a robust and accelerating recovery, but such signs have remained frustratingly elusive, as the following newspaper article about President Obama's State of the Union address in 2011 indicates.

Uncertainty Over Economy Clouds Obama Speech

By Motoko Rich, *New York Times,* January 24, 2011

A year ago, the economy looked as if it were speeding down the runway, only to stall out in the spring.

Now tentative signs of a pickup are emerging across the country again. Factory production, retail sales and existing-home sales are rising, while unemployment claims are trending down. Companies like General Motors and Macy's have recently announced hiring plans, and bank lending to businesses is starting to expand. Investor sentiment is strengthening, as major stock market indexes climb to their highest levels since mid-2008.

This time, though, economists and business leaders are more measured in their optimism about the recovery. Growth is real, they say, though they remain unconvinced it will accelerate all that much. As President Obama prepares to tackle the economy in his State of the Union address Tuesday night, economists and industry executives are likewise sifting through the data.

The darkest clouds that marred the economic landscape last summer and fall have indeed lifted, but expectations have also been reined in. Many of the factors that have restrained growth, including heavy household debt and strained state and local budgets, remain. Parts of Europe are still unstable, and higher food and energy prices could crimp household spending. The construction industry has not yet staged a comeback.

The unemployment rate, stubbornly high at 9.4 percent, could climb higher as more people who stopped looking for work return to the job search. And few see enough jobs being created over the next year to help more than a small portion of the eight million people who lost work during the recession. So even if the economy is picking up steam, and the president is hoping to ride its momentum, making a significant dent in joblessness will

probably remain frustratingly difficult for him and his new economic advisers. "It's really a muddle-through economy," said David Rosenberg, chief economist and strategist for the investment firm Gluskin Sheff & Associates.

Part of what has changed is simply a growing belief that unlike in previous recoveries, the economy will not suddenly ignite. "After a normal recession, once the economy starts growing again, within six months, you're back to where you started," said Kenneth S. Rogoff, a professor at Harvard and co-author, with Carmen M. Reinhart, of "This Time Is Different," a history of financial crises. "We're still just crawling back to where we started." He added, "It's going to take a few more years, really, before we're back at whatever normal is."

One reason that hope was crushed last spring was that debt crises in Europe's weak countries destabilized the stock markets, in turn unnerving consumers. And when fiscal stimulus measures expired, like the tax credit for first-time homebuyers, the housing market sagged. Unlike last year, hardly anyone is expecting skyrocketing growth in coming months. Industry leaders instead talk of stable improvement.

"We don't expect a big upswing in sales," said Tom Henderson, a spokesman for General Motors. "It's just slow and steady, which is tracking along what we're seeing in the economy." The automaker announced on Monday that it was beginning a third shift at its pickup truck assembly plant in Flint, adding 750 jobs. Most of those slots will be filled by people who were laid off in recent years.

Overall sales are starting to improve, and bank lending to businesses rose in the fourth quarter of last year

A woman works on a GM truck on the assembly line of the General Motors Flint Assembly Plant. January 24, 2011.

for the first time since the end of 2008, according to an analysis of Federal Reserve data by Mark Zandi of Moody's Analytics. Small businesses—which represented about two-thirds of job growth in the last recovery—are still cautious. "It's not that sales haven't been improving, but it's improving from a really horrible level of a year ago," said William C. Dunkelberg, chief economist for the National Federation of Independent Business. "We still haven't got Main Street firing on many pistons."

Some small businesses are having trouble getting bank loans because they do not have the collateral. Ami Kassar, chief executive of MultiFunding, a small-business lending broker in Plymouth Meeting, Pa., said that many of his clients had seen the values of their homes, office buildings and warehouses fall so much that banks would not accept them as security. Mr. Kassar said that when his clients did procure loans, they often used the money to cover payrolls rather than to hire new workers, in part because many of their largest customers were taking longer to pay their bills.

Other small businesses are concerned about what they view as onerous regulation. Jason W. Speer, vice president of Quality Float Works, a small manufacturer of parts that are used in valves and pumps in the agricultural and oil industries, said the company hired six people last year, after letting four workers go during the recession. Mr. Speer said the company, in Schaumburg, Ill., northwest of Chicago, was ready to hire two more people, but was hesitating in part because of fear of new regulations and the burden of increased corporate taxes in Illinois. "Every little bit helps or hurts in a small company," said Mr. Speer. "There's a lot of agencies now that are coming out with new rulings and regulations, and it's hard to keep up with that. So instead of hiring or giving bonuses or buying new equipment, we're paying to cover us for regulation issues."

President Obama recently announced plans to initiate a government wide review of corporate regulation, vowing to "remove outdated regulations that stifle job creation." That measure, along with the one-year cut in the payroll tax, could spur consumer and business spending, said Mr. Dunkelberg. Time, too, tends to generate spending, as washing machines, boilers, industrial machinery and cars eventually wear out.

Mr. Henderson of G.M. said that part of the reason the company was adding a shift in Flint was that it had seen a surge in demand from small businesses like heating and air-conditioning companies, plumbers and carpenters who were buying trucks and vans. "In the fourth quarter, our sales to this segment were up 36 percent," he said.

Another sign of hope is in the jobs data. Last year, job growth was relatively strong in the first quarter as measured by the government, but other indicators—like the number of people filing for unemployment insurance each week and surveys of business hiring intentions—were still weak. Now, the average weekly jobless claims have fallen and several key surveys have indicated that companies are planning to hire this year. "There is supporting evidence that the market has turned decisively," said Joshua Shapiro, chief United States economist at MFR Inc. "If you look at all the evidence that surrounds the labor market, it's pretty compelling that we're on the cusp of further improvements here."

Another encouraging sign is that federally withheld employment taxes have been rising, according to an analysis of Treasury Department data by James F. O'Sullivan, chief economist at MF Global. Once hiring picks up, it feeds many corners of the economy, including housing. As people get jobs, Mr. O'Sullivan said, they move out of their parents' homes or split with roommates and rent new apartments. Eventually, some of them will start buying homes. At Toll Brothers, a higher-end home builder, the chief executive, Douglas C. Yearley Jr., hesitates to predict robust growth after disappointment last year. "I think we're just more guarded," he said.

examined by economists. Economic theories that emphasize changes in potential GDP as a source of economic fluctuations are called **real business cycle theories**. Most frequently, changes in technology are assumed to be the reason for changes in potential GDP in real business cycle theories.

The factors that underlie potential GDP growth—population, capital, technological know-how—tend to evolve relatively smoothly. Population growth, for example, is much steadier than real GDP growth. We do not have a drop in the population every few years and a sudden spurt the next year. Slowdowns in population growth occur gradually over time as birth rates and death rates change. Similarly, although individual factories or machines may be lost in a hurricane or flood, such losses do not happen in such a massive way across the whole country that they would show up as a recession or a boom in the whole economy. Thus, the amount of capital changes slowly over time. Even technological change does not seem capable of explaining most fluctuations. It is true that

real business cycle theory
a theory of macroeconomics that stresses that shifts in potential GDP are a primary cause of fluctuations in real GDP; the shifts in potential GDP usually are assumed to be caused by changes in technology.

some inventions and innovations raise productivity substantially in certain sectors of the economy over short periods of time. The impact on the whole economy is more spread out and gradual, however. Moreover, people do not suddenly forget how to use a technology. Technological know-how does not seem to decrease suddenly. For these reasons, potential GDP usually tends to grow relatively smoothly over time, compared with the fluctuations in aggregate demand.

REVIEW

- Economic fluctuations are largely a result of fluctuations in aggregate demand.

- When aggregate demand decreases, firms produce less; real GDP falls below potential GDP. Unemployment rises. When aggregate demand increases, firms first produce more; real GDP rises

above potential GDP. Firms also hire more workers, and the unemployment rate falls.

- Short-run fluctuations in potential GDP also occur, but in reality, most of the larger fluctuations in real GDP seem to be due to fluctuations of real GDP around a more steadily growing potential GDP.

Forecasting Real GDP

To illustrate how we use the idea that changes in aggregate demand lead to short-run fluctuations in real GDP, we will focus on an important macroeconomic task: short-term economic forecasting of real GDP about one year ahead. To *forecast* real GDP, economic forecasters divide aggregate demand into its four key components: consumption, investment, government purchases, and net exports. Remember that real GDP can be measured by adding together the four types of spending: what people *consume*, what firms *invest*, what *governments purchase*, and what *foreigners purchase* net of what they sell in the United States. In symbols, we have

$$Y = C + I + G + X$$

In other words, real GDP (Y) is the sum of consumption (C), investment (I), government purchases (G), and net exports (X).

A Forecast for Next Year

Suppose that it is December 2011 and a forecast of real GDP (Y) is being prepared for the year 2012. Using the preceding equation, a reasonable way to proceed would be to forecast consumption for the next year, then forecast investment, then forecast government purchases, and, finally, forecast net exports. When forecasting each item, the forecaster would consider a range of issues: Consumer confidence might affect consumption; business confidence might be a factor in investment; the electoral prospects of the political party controlling Congress might be a factor in government purchases; and developments in foreign countries might affect the forecast for net exports. In any case, adding these four spending items together would give a forecast for real GDP for the year 2012. For example, one economist may forecast that $C = \$9,600$ billion, $I = \$1,900$ billion, $X = -\$500$ billion, and $G = \$2,500$ billion. Then, that economist's forecast for real GDP is $\$13,500$ billion. Forecasts typically are expressed as growth rates of real GDP from one year to the next. If real GDP in 2011 is $\$13,250$ billion then the forecast would be for 1.9 percent growth for the year 2012.

Impact of a Change in Government Purchases

The preceding forecast is prepared by making one's best assumption about what is likely for government purchases and the other three components of spending. Another type of forecast—called a *conditional forecast*—describes what real GDP will be under alternative assumptions about the components of spending. For example, the U.S. president or Congress might want an estimate of the effect of a proposal to change government purchases on the economy in 2012. A conditional forecast would be a forecast of real GDP conditional on this change in government purchases.

Suppose the proposal is to raise federal government purchases by $500 billion in real terms in one year. What is the effect of such a change in government purchases on aggregate demand in the short run? If the government demands $500 billion more, then firms will produce $500 billion more. A forecast conditional on a $500 billion spending increase would be $500 billion more for real GDP, or $14,000 billion. Again, we just add up $9,600 billion, $1,900 billion, –$500 billion, and now $3,000 billion. Real GDP growth for the year is now forecast to be 5.7 percent, conditional on the policy proposal.

The forecast is based on the equation $Y = C + I + G + X$ and the idea that changes in aggregate demand cause real GDP fluctuations. Although simple, it is specific and substantive. According to this method of forecasting, changes in aggregate demand are responsible for most of the short-run ups and downs in the economy. It is this explanation that most economic forecasters use when they forecast real GDP for one year ahead.

REVIEW

- The four components of spending can be added to make a forecast for real GDP. Making such a forecast is an important application of macroeconomics.

- Forecasts may be conditional on a particular event, such as a change in government purchases or a change in taxes.

The Response of Consumption to Income

In the forecasting example, we assumed that none of the other components—consumption, investment, or net exports—change in response to the increase in government purchases. For example, consumption (C) was unchanged at $9,600 billion when we altered G in our conditional forecast. But these components of spending are likely to change. Thus, something important is missing from the procedure for forecasting real GDP. To improve the forecast, we must describe how the other components of aggregate demand—consumption, investment, and net exports—might change in response to other developments in the economy. We eventually will consider the response of consumption, investment, and net exports to many factors, including interest rates, exchange rates, and income. Bringing all these factors into consideration at once is complicated, however, and we must start with a simplifying assumption. Here the *simplifying assumption* is that consumption is the only component of expenditures that responds to income and that income is the only influence on consumption. Consumption is a good place to begin because it is by far the largest component of real GDP. Before we finish developing a complete theory

ECONOMICS *IN ACTION*

The Professional Forecasters

Short-term forecasting of real GDP—usually one year ahead—has become a major industry employing thousands of economists, statisticians, and computer programmers. Each month the *Blue Chip Economic Indicators* tabulates the forecasts of the top forecasting firms, such as Econoclast, Macroeconomic Advisors, and UCLA Business Forecasting. The average of all these forecasters is called the Blue Chip Consensus. If a government forecast differs much from this forecast, it frequently is criticized.

Consider, for example, the forecast for real GDP growth in the United States in 2010, as the economy was recovering from the 2008–2009 recession. The consensus forecast—the average of the economists surveyed in January 2010 by the Blue Chip Service—was that U.S. real GDP growth would be 3 percent in 2010 and 4.3 percent in 2011.

What was the growth in 2010? According to the preliminary estimate of the Bureau of Economic Analysis, which does the calculations of national income accounts, real GDP increased by 2.9 percent in 2010. The forecasters were almost exactly right in their prediction. This is not always the case, though. In 2001, when the economy was hit by unforeseeable negative shocks, the actual growth rate turned out to be 1.2 percent, whereas the prediction had been for a growth rate of 3.4 percent. Furthermore,

predictions of economic variables that are further out into the future are more likely to be wrong. For example, by the end of 2010, the Blue Chip service was predicting 2.5 percent growth for 2011, almost 1.8 percentage points less in growth than they had predicted a year prior.

"These projected figures are a figment of our imagination. We hope you like them."

of economic fluctuations, we will consider the other components and the other influences. Let us begin by examining why consumption may be affected by income.

The Consumption Function

consumption function
the positive relationship between consumption and income.

The **consumption function** describes how consumption depends on income. The notion of a consumption function originated with John Maynard Keynes, who wrote about it during the 1930s. Research on the consumption function has been intense ever since. For each individual, the consumption function says that the more income one has, the more one consumes. For the national economy as a whole, it says that the more income Americans have, the more Americans consume. For the world economy as a whole, it says that the more income the world has, the more the people in the world consume. Table 11-1 gives a simple example of how consumption depends on income in the U.S. economy.

As you can see from the table, as income increases from $1,000 billion to $2,000 billion, consumption increases as well, from $2,000 billion to $2,600 billion, and as income increases from $3,000 billion to $4,000 billion, consumption increases from $3,200 billion to $3,800 billion. More income means more consumption, but the consumption function also tells us *how much* consumption increases when income increases. Each change in income of $1,000 billion causes an increase in consumption of $600 billion. The changes in consumption are smaller than the changes in income. Notice that, in this example, at very low levels of income, consumption is greater than income. If consumption were greater than income for a particular individual, that individual would have to borrow. At higher levels of income, when consumption is less than income, the individual would be able to save.

The consumption function is supposed to describe the behavior of individuals because the economy is made up of individuals. Consequently, it summarizes the behavior of all people in the economy with respect to consumption. The simple consumption function is not meant to be the complete explanation of consumption. Recall that it is based on a simplifying assumption.

The Marginal Propensity to Consume A concept related to the consumption function is the **marginal propensity to consume (MPC)**. The MPC measures how much consumption changes for a given change in income. The term *marginal* refers to the additional amount of consumption that is due to a change in income. The term *propensity* refers to the inclination to consume. By definition,

$$\text{Marginal Propensity to Consume (MPC)} = \frac{\text{change in consumption}}{\text{change in income}}$$

What is the MPC for the consumption function in Table 11-1? Observe that the change in consumption from row to row is 600. The change in income from row to row is 1,000; thus, the MPC = 600/1,000 = 0.6. Although this is only a simple example, the MPC for the U.S. economy is around that magnitude.

Figure 11-3 graphs the consumption function by putting income on the horizontal axis and consumption on the vertical axis. We get the upward-sloping line by plotting the pairs of observations on consumption and income in Table 11-1 and connecting them with a line. This line, which demonstrates that consumption rises with income, is the consumption function. Its slope is equal to the MPC. For this example, the

Table 11-1

An Example of the Consumption Function (billions of dollars)

Consumption	Income
2,000	1,000
2,600	2,000
3,200	3,000
3,800	4,000
4,400	5,000
5,000	6,000
5,600	7,000
6,200	8,000
6,800	9,000
7,400	10,000
8,000	11,000
8,600	12,000
9,200	13,000
9,800	14,000

marginal propensity to consume (MPC)

the slope of the consumption function, showing the change in consumption that is due to a given change in income.

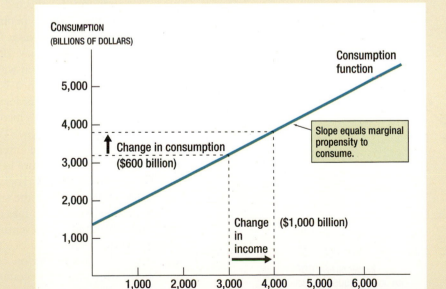

Figure 11-3

The Consumption Function
For the economy as a whole, more income leads to more consumption, as shown by the example of an upward-sloping consumption function in the figure. This represents the sum of all the individuals in the economy, many of whom consume more when their income rises. The graph is based on the numbers in Table 11-1.

MPC = 0.6. The graph shows that at low levels of income, consumption is greater than income, but at high levels of income, consumption is less than income.

Which Measure of Income? The consumption function is a straight-line relationship between consumption and income. Income in the relationship is sometimes measured by *aggregate income* (*Y*), which also is equal to real GDP, and sometimes by disposable income. *Disposable income* is the income that households receive in wages, dividends, and interest payments plus transfers they may receive from the government minus any taxes they pay to the government. Disposable income is the preferred measure of income when one is interested in household consumption because this is what households have available to spend. But the consumption function for the whole economy for aggregate income and that for disposable income look similar because aggregate income and disposable income fluctuate and grow together. In the United States and most other countries, taxes and transfers are nearly proportional to aggregate income.

For the rest of this chapter, we will use aggregate income, or real GDP, as the measure of income in the consumption function. We put real GDP, or income (we drop the word *aggregate* in *aggregate income*), on the horizontal axis of the consumption function diagram, because real GDP and income always are equal. Figure 11-4 shows the actual relationship between consumption and income, or real GDP. Note, however, that when we consider an explicit change in taxes, we must take into account the difference between disposable income and income.

Figure 11-4

Consumption versus Aggregate Income

The graph shows the close relationship between consumption and aggregate income, or real GDP, in the U.S. economy. The points fall close to the straight line drawn in the diagram.

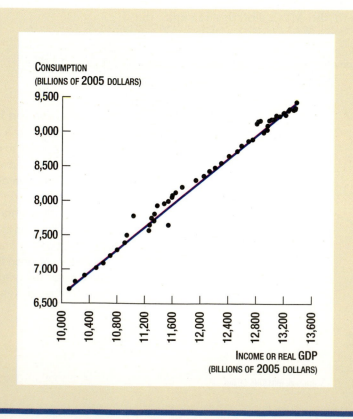

What about Interest Rates and Other Influences on Consumption?

Other factors besides income affect consumption. For example, you may recall from Chapter 7 that people's consumption is affected by the interest rate. Also, people's wealth—including their savings in a bank and their house—may affect their consumption. A person with a large amount of savings in a bank might consume a considerable amount even if the person's income in any one year is very low. Why have we not brought the interest rate or wealth into the picture here?

The answer is simple. To keep the analysis manageable at the start, we are putting the interest rate and other influences aside. We eventually return to consider the effects of interest rates and other factors on consumption. But during economic fluctuations, the effects of changes in income on consumption are most important, and we focus on these now.

ECONOMICS IN ACTION

Making *Time*'s Top 100

John Maynard Keynes was chosen by *Time* magazine as one of the 100 most influential people in the twentieth century. Keynes was the inventor of the marginal propensity to consume and of the broader idea emphasized in this chapter that a decline in aggregate demand could bring the economy below its potential.

Keynes was always active in bringing economics into practice. He gained notoriety in his thirties for a best-selling book called *The Economic Consequences of the Peace,* written in only two months during the summer of 1919. Keynes was an economic adviser to the British government, and he accompanied the prime minister to the Versailles peace conference in 1919 at the end of World War I. At that peace conference, the victors demanded heavy reparations from Germany, harming the German economy and thereby helping Hitler in his rise to power. In his 1919 book, Keynes predicted serious harm from the stiff reparations and ridiculed the heads of government at the conference, including his own prime minister, David Lloyd George, and the American president, Woodrow Wilson.

Keynes's most influential book, however, was *The General Theory of Employment, Interest and Money.* He wrote it in the midst of the Great Depression, providing an explanation for a worldwide tragedy that prevailing economic theory—with its microeconomic emphasis—hardly addressed. Much of the *General Theory* is difficult to read unless you are an economist, because as Keynes put it, his book is chiefly addressed to "my fellow economists." But Keynes's well-developed writing skills emerge in some of the less technical passages, especially those on speculation and expectations in financial markets. Keynes's ideas, such as the marginal propensity to consume and the importance of aggregate demand, spread rapidly and had a lasting influence: Referring to these ideas as the "Keynesian revolution" is no exaggeration.

Keynes's *Tract on Monetary Reform,* written in 1923, focused more on inflation than did the *General Theory.* His earlier writings suggest that if he had lived longer, he might have explained the high inflation of the 1970s as effectively as he explained the Great Depression of the 1930s.

Keynes appeared on the cover of *Time* magazine in 1965, when the influence of his economics was at its peak in Washington. However, in the 1970s, when inflation was rising and economic growth was slowing, Keynes's theory was criticized because it did not deal with inflation and with long-run economic growth. More-over, by emphasizing aggregate demand so much, Keynes's theory suggested to some policy makers that increases in government spending could increase real GDP almost without limit, regardless of supply constraints. Any thoughts that Keynes had waned in influence after the 1970s disappeared during the current recession. As economists and policy makers worried about whether the 2008–2009 recession would turn into another economic depression, Keynesian ideas and policies once again began to play a major role in policy circles and the news. Debates about the appropriate size of a fiscal stimulus program and the effectiveness of that stimulus program revolved around the concept of the Keynesian multiplier, an idea that you will learn about later in this chapter.

Walter Sanders//Time Life Pictures/Getty Images

John Maynard Keynes, 1883–1946

Born: Cambridge, England, 1883
Education: Cambridge University, graduated 1906
Jobs: India Office, London, 1906–1909; Cambridge University, 1909–1915; British Treasury, 1915–1919; Cambridge University, 1919–1946
Major Publications: *The Economic Consequences of the Peace,* 1919; *A Tract on Monetary Reform,* 1923; *A Treatise on Money,* 1930; *The General Theory of Employment, Interest and Money,* 1936

REVIEW

- The consumption function describes the response of consumption to changes in income. The elementary consumption function ignores the effects of interest rates and wealth on consumption.

- The MPC tells us *how much* consumption changes in response to a change in income.

- For the economy as a whole, the consumption function can be expressed in terms of aggregate income or disposable income. Aggregate income is always equal to real GDP.

Finding Real GDP When Consumption and Income Move Together

Now let us use the consumption function to get a better prediction of what happens to real GDP in the short run when government purchases change. In other words, we want to improve the conditional forecast of real GDP when government purchases change by taking the consumption function into account. Again, as in the earlier example of forecasting, let us assume that government spending will increase by $500 billion next year. Our goal is to find out what happens to real GDP in the short run.

Our first attempt at forecasting proposed that an increase in government spending would increase real GDP. But now we see that something else must happen, because consumption depends on income, and real GDP is equal to income. An increase in government spending will increase income. The consumption function tells us that an increase in income must increase consumption, which further increases GDP.

Here is the chain of logic in brief:

1. An increase in government spending increases real GDP.
2. Real GDP equals income; thus income increases.
3. Consumption depends on income; thus consumption increases.
4. An increase in consumption further increase real GDP.

In sum, consumption will increase when we raise government spending.

For example, when the government increases spending on new highway construction, the firms that produce materials and services for highway construction find demand rising and produce more. Existing workers work more hours and new workers find jobs working on highway construction. Therefore, they will receive a higher income than before. In addition, the profits at the construction firms will increase; thus, the income of the owners of the firms will rise as well. With more income, the workers and the owners will spend more; that is, their consumption will rise. This is the connection between government spending and consumption about which we are concerned: The increase in government purchases raises construction workers' income, which results in more consumption.

The process can work in reverse as well. This type of logic was applied by economists to estimate the impact of closing Fort Ord, the military base near Monterey Bay in California, on the Monterey economy. When the estimates were made, the base employed 3,000 civilians and 14,000 military personnel. Payroll was $558 million. Thus, closing the base would reduce incomes by as much as $558 million as these workers were laid off or retired. Although some workers might quickly find jobs elsewhere, the decline in income would result in a reduction in consumption by those workers. Using an MPC of 0.6, consumption would decline by $335 million (0.6 times 558) if income was reduced by $558 million. This reduced income would tend to throw others in the Monterey area out of work as spending in retail and service stores declined. This would further reduce consumption, and so on. Although this case study refers to a small region of the entire country, the same logic applies to the economy as a whole.

The 45-Degree Line

We can use a convenient graph to calculate how much income and consumption change in the whole economy and thereby project what will happen to real GDP. A line in Figure 11-5 shows graphically that income in the economy is equal to spending. In Figure 11-5, income is on the horizontal axis and spending is on the vertical axis. All the points at which spending equals income are on the upward-sloping line in Figure 11-5. The line has a slope of 1, or an angle of 45 degrees with the horizontal axis, because the distances from any point on the line to the horizontal axis and the vertical axis are equal. Along that line—which is called the 45-degree line—spending and income are equal.

The Expenditure Line

Figure 11-6 shows another relationship called the **expenditure line**. As in Figure 11-5, income, or real GDP, is on the horizontal axis, and spending is on the vertical axis. The top line in Figure 11-6 is the expenditure line. It is called the expenditure line because it shows how expenditure, or spending, depends on income. The four components that make up the expenditure line are consumption, investment, government purchases, and net exports. The expenditure line, however, shows how these four components depend on income. It is this dependency of spending on income that is the defining characteristic of the expenditure line. The next paragraph explains how the expenditure line is derived.

The consumption function is shown as the lowest line in Figure 11-6. It is the consumption function from Figure 11-3, which says that the higher income is, the more people want to consume. The next line above the consumption function in Figure 11-6 is parallel to the consumption function. This line represents the addition of investment to consumption at each level of income. It says that investment is so many billions of

45-degree line
the line showing that expenditure equals aggregate income.

expenditure line
the relation between the sum of the four components of spending $(C + I + G + X)$ and aggregate income.

Figure 11-5

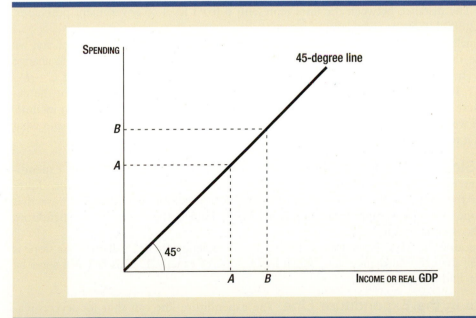

The 45-Degree Line
This simple line is a graphical representation of the income equals spending identity. The pairs of points on the 45-degree line have the same level of spending and income. For example, the level of spending at A is the same dollar amount as the level of income at A. Moreover, because income equals real GDP, we can put either income or real GDP on the horizontal axis.

Figure 11-6

The Expenditure Line
By adding investment (*I*),
government purchases (*G*), and
net exports (*X*) to the
consumption function, we build
the expenditure line.

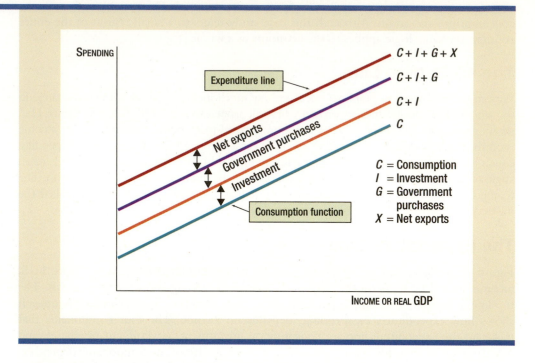

dollars in the U.S. economy, and the distance between the lines is this amount of investment. For example, if investment equals $800 billion, the distance between the consumption function and this next line is $800 billion.

The reason the line is parallel to the consumption line is that we are starting our explanation by saying that investment does not depend on income. This simplifying assumption means that investment is a constant number, and the distance between the lines is the same regardless of income. We just add the same amount at each point.

The next line in Figure 11-6 adds in a constant level of government purchases. This line is also parallel to the other lines because the increase at every level of income is the same. The distance between the lines represents a fixed level of government purchases, say, $2,500 billion, at every level of income.

Finally, to get the top line in Figure 11-6, we add in net exports. For simplicity, we assume that net exports do not depend on income, an assumption that we will change soon. Thus, the top line is parallel to all the other lines. The top line is the sum of $C + I + G + X$. It is the expenditure line. The most important thing to remember about the expenditure line is that it shows how the sum of the four components depends on income. Before we can use the expenditure line, we must know what determines its slope and what causes it to shift.

The Slope of the Expenditure Line   Observe in Figure 11-6 that the expenditure line is parallel to the consumption function. Therefore, the slope of the expenditure line is the same as the slope of the consumption function. We already know that the slope of the consumption function is the MPC. Hence, the slope of the expenditure line also is equal to the MPC.

Because the MPC is less than 1, the aggregate expenditure line is flatter (the slope is smaller) than the 45-degree line, which has a slope of exactly 1. This fact will soon be used to find real GDP.

Shifts in the Expenditure Line   The expenditure line can shift for several reasons. Consider first what happens to the expenditure line if government purchases fall

Figure 11-7

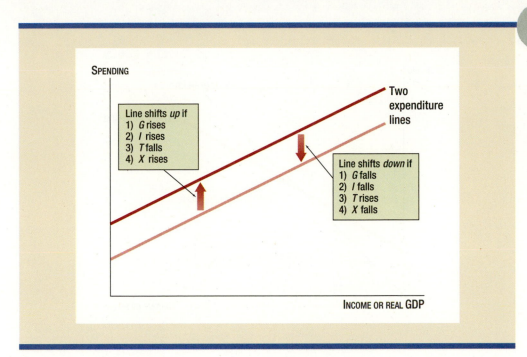

Shifts in the Expenditure Line

The expenditure line shifts down if (1) government purchases (G) fall, (2) investment (I) falls, (3) taxes (T) increase, or (4) net exports (X) fall. The expenditure line shifts up if (1) government purchases rise, (2) investment rises, (3) taxes are cut, or (4) net exports rise.

because of a cut in defense spending. As shown in Figure 11-7, the expenditure line shifts downward in a parallel fashion. The expenditure line is simply the sum $C + I + G + X$. Because G is less at all income levels, the line shifts down. The expenditure line is lowered because the distance between the consumption function and the other lines declines (see Figure 11-6). The reverse of this, an increase in government purchases, will cause the expenditure line to shift up.

What happens to the expenditure line if investment falls? Investment, remember, is the gap between the first and second lines in Figure 11-6. If investment declines (as might happen if businesses become pessimistic about the future and invest less), then the expenditure line shifts downward. With less investment, the gap between the lines shrinks. The reverse of this, an increase in investment, will cause the expenditure line to shift up, as shown in Figure 11-7.

A change in net exports, perhaps because of a change in the demand for U.S. exports to other countries, also will shift the expenditure line. A downward shift in net exports lowers the expenditure line, and an upward shift in net exports raises the expenditure line.

Finally, the expenditure line also can be shifted by changes in taxes. At any given level of income, an increase in taxes means that people have less to spend, and this will cause people to consume less. Hence, the expenditure line shifts down when taxes rise. The reverse of this, a cut in taxes, causes the expenditure line to shift up. We will use the symbol T to refer to taxes. For example, if $T = \$1,500$ billion, then people pay and the government receives $1,500 billion in taxes.

Determining Real GDP through Spending Balance

Having derived the expenditure line and the 45-degree line, we can combine the two to find real GDP. Figure 11-8 shows the expenditure line and the 45-degree line combined in one diagram. Observe that the two lines intersect. They must intersect because they have different slopes. Real GDP is found at the point of intersection of these two lines. Why?

Income and spending always are equal, and the 45-degree line is drawn to represent this equality. Therefore, at any point on the 45-degree line, income equals spending.

Figure 11-8

Spending Balance

Spending balance occurs when two relations are satisfied simultaneously: (1) income equals spending, and (2) spending equals consumption, which is a function of income, plus investment plus government purchases plus net exports. Only one level of income gives spending balance. That level of income is determined by the intersection of the 45-degree line and the expenditure line.

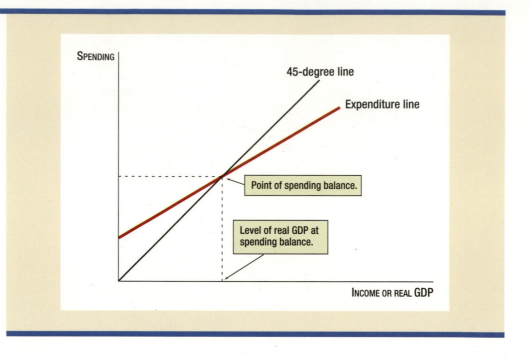

spending balance

the level of income or real GDP at which the 45-degree line and the expenditure line cross; also called equilibrium income.

Moreover, income and spending must be on the expenditure line, because only at points on that line do people consume according to the consumption function.

If both relationships hold—that is, income and spending are the same (we are on the 45-degree line) and people's consumption is described by the consumption function (we are on the expenditure line)—then, logically, we must be at the intersection of these two lines. We call that point of intersection **spending balance**. The level of income determined by that point is just the right level to cause people to purchase an amount of consumption that—when added to investment, government purchases, and net exports—gives exactly the same level of income. We would not have spending balance at either a higher or a lower level of income. The diagram in Figure 11-8 showing that the 45-degree line and the expenditure line cross is sometimes called the "Keynesian Cross" after John Maynard Keynes.

Table 11-2 provides an alternative way to determine spending balance. It uses a numerical tabulation of the consumption function rather than graphs. Total expenditure is obtained by adding the four columns on the right of Table 11-2. Consumption is shown to depend on income according to the same consumption function as in Table 11-1. Observe that income equals total expenditure in only one row. That row is where spending balance occurs. The row is shaded and corresponds to the point of intersection of the 45-degree line and the expenditure line in Figure 11-8.

Because the point of spending balance is at the intersection of two lines, we can think of it as an equilibrium, much as the intersection of a demand curve and a supply curve for wheat is an equilibrium. Because real GDP is not necessarily equal to potential GDP at this intersection, however, in a sense, the equilibrium is temporary; real GDP eventually will move back to potential GDP, as we will show in later chapters.

The point of spending balance is also an equilibrium in the sense that economic forces cause real GDP to be at that intersection. To see this, consider Table 11-2. As we noted, the shaded row corresponds to the intersection of the 45-degree line and the expenditure line: Income or real GDP equals expenditure. Suppose that income or real GDP were less than expenditure, as in one of the rows above the shaded row in Table 11-2. This would

Table 11-2

A Numerical Example of Spending Balance (billions of dollars)

Income or Real GDP	Total Expenditure	Consumption	Investment	Government Purchases	Net Exports
10,500	11,700	7,800	1,900	2,500	−500
11,500	12,300	8,400	1,900	2,500	−500
12,500	12,900	9,000	1,900	2,500	−500
13,500	13,500	9,600	1,900	2,500	−500
14,500	14,100	10,200	1,900	2,500	−500
15,500	14,700	10,800	1,900	2,500	−500
16,500	15,300	11,400	1,900	2,500	−500
17,500	15,900	12,000	1,900	2,500	−500
18,500	16,500	12,600	1,900	2,500	−500

not be an equilibrium because firms would not be producing enough goods and services (real GDP) to satisfy people's expenditure on goods and services. Firms would increase their production, and real GDP would rise until it equaled expenditure. Similarly, if real GDP were greater than expenditure, as in one of the rows below the shaded row in Table 11-2, firms would be producing more than people would be buying. Hence, firms would reduce their production, and real GDP would fall until it equaled expenditure.

A Better Forecast of Real GDP

Now let us return to forecasting real GDP using these new tools. Recall the example of making a forecast of real GDP for the year 2011 (from the vantage point of December 2010), conditional on a proposed increase in government purchases of $500 billion. Our new tools will enable us to take into account the effect of this increase on consumption, which we ignored in the simple forecast.

Figure 11-9 shows two expenditure lines. The bottom expenditure line is without the change in government purchases. In this case, $G = \$2,500$ billion, $C = \$9,600$ billion, $I = \$1,900$ billion, and $X = -\$500$ billion, yielding income, or real GDP, of $13,500 billion. For the conditional forecast, we assume that G is increased by $500 billion, to $3,000 billion. In Figure 11-9, that causes the expenditure line to shift up to the "new" line. Observe that the expenditure line shifts up by $500 billion—a parallel shift. This new expenditure line cuts the 45-degree line at a lower point.

Logic tells us that the economy will now operate at a different point of spending balance, the point at which the expenditure line and the 45-degree line now intersect. Thus, we move from one intersection to a new intersection as a result of the increase in the expenditure line. The new point of spending balance is at a higher level of GDP.

We now have a prediction that real GDP will rise if government spending increases. Observe in Figure 11-9 that the increase in real GDP is larger than the $500 billion increase in government purchases and, therefore, larger than the $500 billion decline in real GDP in the simple forecast. In addition to the increase in government purchases, consumption has risen because income has increased. The initial $500 billion is *multiplied* to create a larger than $500 billion change in real GDP because of the induced change in consumption. This multiplier phenomenon, which makes the change in real GDP larger than the change in government purchases, is called the *Keynesian multiplier* and applies to increases as well as to decreases in government purchases. In Figure 11-9, the multiplier looks quite large; the horizontal arrow is at least twice as large as the vertical arrow. It is certainly large enough to influence the government's decision to reduce government purchases. The example and the application illustrate that it is not just for fun that we have derived the expenditure line. It is an essential tool of the practicing macroeconomist.

Figure 11-9

From One Point of Spending Balance to Another

The expenditure line shifts up because of an increase in government purchases. This shifts up the forecast for real GDP. A forecast of real GDP conditional on the increase in government purchases therefore would be higher.

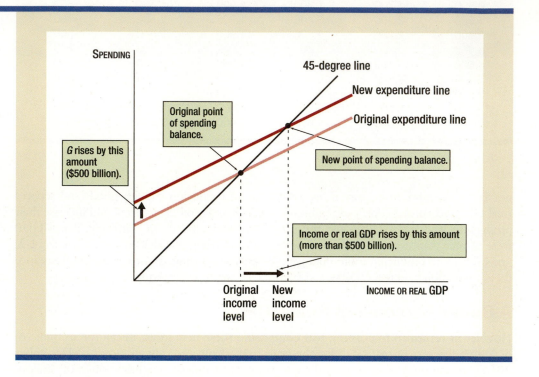

REVIEW

- Spending balance occurs when the identity $Y = C + I + G + X$ and the consumption function relating C to Y hold simultaneously.

- Spending balance can be shown on a graph with the 45-degree line and the expenditure line.

- The intersection of the two lines determines a level of income, or real GDP, that gives spending balance.

- A shift in the expenditure line brings about a new level of spending balance.

Spending Balance and Departures of Real GDP from Potential GDP

We have shown how to compute a level of real GDP for the purpose of making short-term forecasts. This level of real GDP is determined by aggregate demand—consumption, investment, government purchases, and net exports. It is not necessarily equal to potential GDP, which depends on the supply of labor, capital, and technology. Thus, we can have real GDP departing from potential GDP, as it does in recessions. Let's now show this graphically.

Stepping Away from Potential GDP

Figure 11-10 illustrates how the departures of real GDP from potential GDP can be explained by shifts in the expenditure line. The left panel of the figure shows three different expenditure lines. Each line corresponds to a different level of government purchases or a different level of net exports or investment. The right panel of Figure 11-10—which is much like Figure 11-2—shows real GDP and potential GDP during a three-year period. A close connection exists between the left and right panels of Figure 11-10. The vertical axes are identical, and the points c, d, and e represent the same level of spending in both panels.

Observe how the three expenditure lines intersect the 45-degree line at three different levels of real GDP. Let us suppose that the middle expenditure line intersects the 45-degree line at a level of real GDP that is the same as potential GDP in Year 3. This is Point c. The lower expenditure line represents a recession; real GDP at the intersection of this expenditure line and the 45-degree line (Point d) is at a level below potential GDP and also below the level of real GDP in Year 2. Thus, real GDP would decline from Year 2 to Year 3 with this expenditure line. On the other hand, the higher expenditure line corresponds to the case in which real GDP is above potential GDP in Year 3.

Figure 11-10

Spending Balance and Departures of Real GDP from Potential GDP

This figure shows how the levels of real GDP found through spending balance can explain the first steps of a recession or boom. The left panel shows spending balance for three expenditure curves; one (c) gives real GDP equal to potential GDP, a second (e) gives real GDP above potential GDP, and a third (d) gives real GDP below potential GDP. As shown in the right panel, two of these entail departures of real GDP from potential GDP.

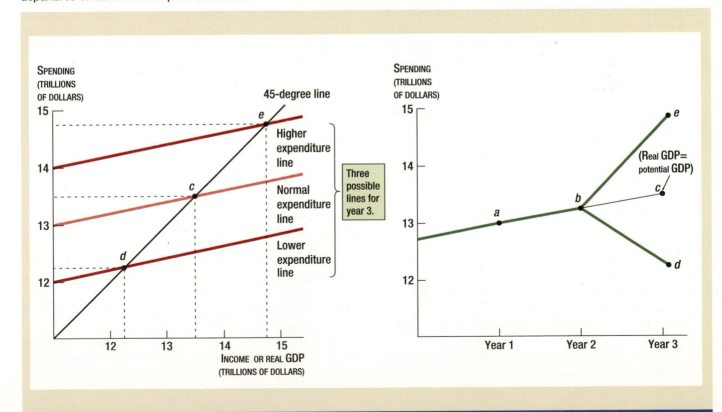

By referring to these values of real GDP as the *first* steps, we are emphasizing that they are not the end of the story. We will see that forces in the economy tend to bring real GDP back toward potential GDP. This calculation of real GDP gives only the short-run impact of changes in government spending, investment, net exports, or taxes.

REVIEW

- Shifts in the expenditure line can explain the departures of real GDP from potential GDP.

- When the expenditure line shifts down, real GDP declines, and, if it was previously equal to potential GDP, it will fall below potential GDP. Upward shifts in the expenditure line will bring real GDP above potential GDP.

- The expenditure line can shift for many reasons. Changes in taxes, government purchases, investment, and net exports will cause the expenditure line to shift.

CONCLUSION

With this chapter, we have begun to develop a theory of economic fluctuations. We have shown how economists explain departures of real GDP from potential GDP, using the idea that these fluctuations are due to changes in aggregate demand. A recession occurs when aggregate demand falls, bringing real GDP below potential GDP. We used this explanation to make short-term forecasts of real GDP. The expenditure line—showing how the demand for consumption, investment, and net exports depends on income—and the 45-degree line are key parts of the forecasting process. Thus far, however, our analysis has made several simplifying assumptions. For example, we assumed that the only thing people's consumption decisions respond to is a change in income.

In the next chapter, we show that consumption—as well as investment and net exports—responds to interest rates and inflation. The responses to interest rates and inflation will explain why real GDP returns to potential GDP in the long run.

KEY POINTS

1. Economic fluctuations are temporary deviations of real GDP from potential GDP.
2. Employment and unemployment fluctuate with real GDP. Unemployment increases in recessions and decreases in booms.
3. The fluctuations in real GDP and potential GDP are mainly due to fluctuations in aggregate demand.
4. The idea that fluctuations in real GDP are mainly due to aggregate demand is used to find real GDP when making a short-term forecast.
5. Real GDP can be predicted on the basis of forecasts of consumption, investment, net exports, and government purchases. But these items depend on income and, thus, on the forecast of real GDP itself.
6. The consumption function describes how consumption responds to income.
7. The expenditure line is built up from the consumption function.
8. The 45-degree line tells us that expenditures equal income.
9. Combining the expenditure line and the 45-degree line in a diagram enables us to determine the level of income, or real GDP.
10. The level of real GDP that gives spending balance changes when government spending changes. Real GDP will decline in the short run when government purchases are cut.

KEY TERMS

45-degree line, 265

consumption function, 260

consumption smoothing, 279

expenditure line, 265

forward-looking consumption model, 278

Keynesian multiplier, 275

life-cycle model, 278

liquidity constraint, 279

marginal propensity to consume (MPC), 261

marginal propensity to import (MPI), 278

permanent income model, 278

potential GDP, 254

real business cycle theories, 257

spending balance, 268

QUESTIONS FOR REVIEW

1. Why do theories of economic fluctuations focus on aggregate demand rather than potential GDP as the main source of short-run economic fluctuations?

2. Why do theories of economic growth focus on potential GDP (with its three determinants) rather than aggregate demand as the main source of economic growth?

3. Why does the unemployment rate rise when real GDP falls below potential GDP?

4. What is the normal rate of capacity utilization in manufacturing firms? What is the significance of this normal rate for explaining economic fluctuations?

5. What accounting identity does the 45-degree line represent?

6. Why does the expenditure line have a slope less than 1?

7. Why do economic forecasters have to take into account the consumption function?

8. Why is real GDP given by the intersection of the 45-degree line and the expenditure line?

PROBLEMS

1. In the latter part of 2008, the U.S. economy was hit by a sudden plunge in stock markets, accompanied by a slowdown in consumer and investor spending. Explain why these events would move real GDP below potential GDP.

2. Recall that aggregate demand is made up of consumption, investment, government purchases, and net exports. How would the terrorist attacks on September 11, 2001, affect the components of aggregate demand in the three-month period that immediately followed?

3. Suppose the information in the following table described the economic situation in the United States at the end of 2010.

Year	Real GDP (billions of 2005 dollars)	Potential GDP (billions of 2005 dollars)
2008	12,832	13,689
2009	13,139	13,928
2010	13,520	14,178
2011 (pessimistic forecast)	13,790	14,455
2011 (optimistic forecast)	13,925	14,455

a. Graph real GDP over time, placing the year on the horizontal axis. Calculate the growth rate of real GDP between 2008 and 2009, and between 2009 and 2010.

b. The optimistic forecast for the year 2011 is based on the possibility that businesses are optimistic about the economy. What will the growth rate of real GDP be if the optimistic forecast is true?

c. The pessimistic forecast is based on the possibility that businesses will be pessimistic about the economy. What will the growth rate of real GDP be if this forecast is correct?

d. What is the deviation (in terms of dollars and as a percentage) of real GDP from potential GDP in 2011 if the optimistic forecast is correct? What is the deviation (in terms of dollars and as a percentage) from potential GDP in 2011 if the pessimistic forecast is correct?

4. When a war begins, what happens to the relationship between GDP and potential GDP? Does your answer depend on the size of the war or its duration?

5. Sketch a diagram with a 45-degree line and an expenditure line that describes macroeconomic spending balance. What factors determine how steep the expenditure line is? Show on the diagram that, when government purchases increase, U.S. income increases by more than the upward shift in government purchases.

6. Suppose government purchases will increase by $100 billion, and a forecasting firm predicts that real GDP will rise in the short run by $100 billion as a result. Would you say that that forecast is accurate? Why? If you were running a business and you sub-scribed to that forecasting service, what questions would you ask about the forecast?

7. Suppose that business executives are very optimistic, and they raise their investment spending. What happens to the expenditure line? How will this affect real GDP? Sketch a diagram to demonstrate your answer.

8. Suppose that U.S. goods suddenly become unpop-ular in Europe. What happens to net exports? How will this shift the expenditure line? What happens to real GDP? Demonstrate this in a diagram.

9. The following table shows the relationship between income and consumption in an economy.

Income (Y) (in billions of dollars)	Consumption (C) (in billions of dollars)
0	5
10	11
20	17
30	23
40	29
50	35
60	41
70	47
80	53
90	59
100	65

Assume that investment (I) is $5 billion, government purchases (G) are $4 billion, and net exports (X) are $2 billion.

a. What is the numerical value of the MPC?

b. Construct a table that is analogous to Table 11-2 for this economy. What is the level of income at the point of spending balance?

c. For this level of income, calculate national saving. Is national saving equal to investment plus net exports?

d. Sketch a diagram with a 45-degree line and an expenditure curve that describes the preceding relationships. Show graphically what happens to income when the government lowers taxes.

10. In 2005, the Department of Defense announced its Base Realignment and Closure (BRAC) plan outlining which military bases were going to be shut down. This plan immediately caused great concern among the congressional representatives in whose districts the bases designated for closure were located. Suppose that a military base that employs 10,000 people was closed down. Describe the different sectors of the local economy that would be affected by the shutdown.

Deriving the Formula for the Keynesian Multiplier and the Forward-Looking Consumption Model

The Keynesian Multiplier

Here we derive a formula for the **Keynesian multiplier**, which gives the *short-run* impact on real gross domestic product (GDP) of things such as cuts in military purchases or a new federal program for road and bridge construction. We show how the multiplier depends on the marginal propensity to consume and on the marginal propensity to import.

A Graphical Review

Figure A.11-1 is a diagram like the one derived in Chapter 11, with income or real GDP on the horizontal axis and spending on the vertical axis. The 45-degree line equates spending and income. Figure A.11-1 has two expenditure lines. The "new" expenditure line is $500 billion higher than the "old" expenditure line, representing an upward shift resulting from an increase in government purchases, for example. Both expenditure lines show that expenditure in the economy—the sum of consumption plus investment plus government purchases plus net exports, or $C + I + G + X$—rises with income. We assume that the marginal propensity to consume (MPC) is equal to 0.6. Thus, the slope of both expenditure lines is 0.6.

Note that the "new" expenditure line intersects the 45-degree line at a different point from the "old" expenditure line. At this new intersection, the level of income, or real GDP, is higher than at the old intersection. On the horizontal axis, the black arrow pointing to the right shows this shift to a higher level of real GDP. Look carefully at the diagram to note the *size* of the change in real GDP along the horizontal axis and compare it with the change in the expenditure line. Observe that the horizontal change is *larger* than the vertical change. This is due to the multiplier. In fact, the term *multiplier* is used because the change in real GDP is a multiple of the shift in the aggregate expenditure line.

Figure A.11-1

Graphical Calculation of the Multiplier

An upward shift in the expenditure line raises real GDP in the short run by a multiple of the shift in the expenditure line. The multiplier can be found graphically. It is the ratio of the length of the black horizontal arrow to the length of the black vertical arrow.

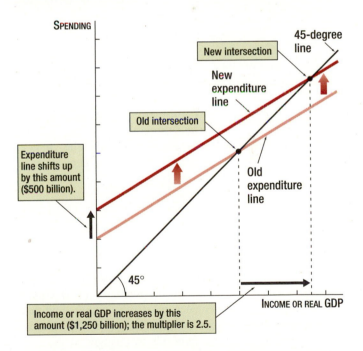

The multiplier is the ratio of the change in real GDP to the shift in the expenditure line, regardless of the reason for the shift in the expenditure line (whether it is due to a change in government purchases, a change in taxes, a change in investment, or a change in foreign demand). Thus, the multiplier is equal to the ratio of the length of the arrow along the horizontal axis to the length of the arrow along the vertical axis in Figure A.11-1. You can find the multiplier by measuring these lengths. If you do so, you will find that for the expenditure line with a slope of 0.6 in Figure A.11-1, the multiplier is 2.5.

The multiplier applies to anything that shifts the expenditure line. For example, an increase in government purchases of $500 billion would shift the expenditure line up by $500 billion. This would increase real GDP by $1,250 billion if the multiplier for government purchases is 2.5.

The Algebraic Derivation

We now want to derive a formula for the multiplier using algebra. Let us focus first on the case where the MPC is 0.6. To be specific, let us suppose that the particular reason for a change in the aggregate expenditure line is an increase in government purchases. Then the multiplier is the ratio of the change in real GDP to the change in government purchases.

The identity that income or real GDP (Y) equals consumption (C) plus investment (I) plus government purchases (G) plus net exports (X) can be written algebraically as

$$Y = C + I + G + X$$

To find the multiplier, we want to determine the impact of a *change* in government purchases on real GDP. That is, we want to find the change in Y that occurs when G changes. Any change in Y must come either directly from a change in G or indirectly from a change in C, I, or X, according to the preceding identity. Denote the change in any of these items by the Greek letter Δ. Then we can write the identity in terms of changes:

$$\Delta Y = \Delta C + \Delta I + \Delta G + \Delta X$$

That is, the *change* in real GDP is equal to the *change* in consumption plus the *change* in investment plus the *change* in government purchases plus the *change* in net exports. Now consider each of the four terms on the right.

The change in government purchases (ΔG) equals $100 billion. For convenience, we continue to assume that investment and net exports do not change. In other words, we assume that neither responds to changes in income. This is expressed in symbols as $\Delta I = 0$ and $\Delta X = 0$.

But we cannot assume that $\Delta C = 0$. The *consumption function* tells us that consumption changes when income changes. The consumption function we use for the algebraic calculation has an MPC of 0.6. Using algebra, we write $\Delta C = 0.6\Delta Y$. That is, the change in consumption equals 0.6 times the change in income; for example, if the change in income $\Delta Y = $10 billion, then the change in consumption $\Delta C = $6 billion if the MPC is 0.6.

Now let us take our ingredients:

1. $\Delta Y = \Delta C + \Delta I + \Delta G + \Delta X$.
2. The changes in investment and net exports are zero ($\Delta I = \Delta X = 0$).
3. The change in consumption is 0.6 times the change in income ($\Delta C = 0.6\Delta Y$).

Replacing ΔI with zero and ΔX with zero removes ΔI and ΔX from the right-hand side of the identity. Replacing ΔC with $0.6\Delta Y$ in the same identity results in

$$\Delta Y = 0.6\Delta Y + \Delta G$$

Note that the term ΔY appears on both sides of this equation. Gathering terms in ΔY on the left-hand side of the equation gives

$$(1 - 0.6)\,\Delta Y = \Delta G$$

Dividing both sides by ΔG and by $(1 - 0.6)$ results in

$$\Delta Y / \Delta G = 1/(1 - 0.6)$$
$$= 1/0.4$$
$$= 2.5$$

Thus, the change in income, or real GDP, that occurs when government purchases change, according to this calculation, is 2.5 times the change in government purchases. That is, $\Delta Y = 2.5\Delta G$. The number 2.5 is the multiplier. The algebraic calculation agrees with the graphical calculation.

You can perform this same calculation for *any value* of the MPC, not just 0.6. To see this, note that the change in consumption equals the MPC times the change in income, where the MPC is any number. Using the same approach as in the case of MPC = 0.6, we obtain a *formula for the multiplier*, which is

$$\frac{\Delta Y}{\Delta G} = \frac{1}{(1 - \text{MPC})}$$

The derivation of this formula is summarized in Table A.11-1.

Following the Multiplier through the Economy   To get a more complete understanding of the formula for the multiplier, it is useful to examine what happens as a change in government purchases winds its way through the economy.

Assume that the government increases its purchases, perhaps to build new highways. In this example, the government increases purchases of highway construction services and equipment at construction firms. The immediate impact of the change in government purchases is an increase in the production of this

Table A.11-1

Derivation of a Formula for the Keynesian Multiplier

Start with the identity
$$Y = C + I + G + X$$
and convert it to change form:
$$\Delta Y = \Delta C + \Delta I + \Delta G + \Delta X$$
Substitute $\Delta I = 0$, $\Delta X = 0$, and
$$\Delta C = MPC \times \Delta Y$$
into the change form of the identity to get
$$\Delta Y = MPC \times \Delta Y + \Delta G$$
Gather terms involving ΔY to get
$$(1 - MPC) \times \Delta Y = \Delta G$$
Divide both sides by ΔG and by $1 - MPC$ to get
$$\frac{\Delta Y}{\Delta G} = \frac{1}{1 - MPC}$$

Table A.11-2

A Numerical Illustration of the Multiplier at Work (billions of dollars)

Round	Change in Real GDP	Cumulative Change in Real GDP
First round	500.00	500.00
Second round	300.00	800.00
Third round	180.00	980.00
Fourth round	108.00	1,088.00
Fifth round	64.8	1,152.8
.	.	.
.	.	.
.	.	.
After an infinite number of rounds	0.00	1,250.00

equipment. With an increase in demand, construction firms produce more, and real GDP rises. The initial increase in real GDP from an increase in government purchases of $500 billion is that same $500 billion. If the government is purchasing more equipment, the production of equipment increases. We call this initial increase in real GDP the *first-round effect*, which includes only the initial change in government purchases.

The first round is not the end of the story. A further increase in real GDP occurs when the workers employed in highway construction start working more hours and new workers are hired. As a result, the workers' income rises, and the profits made by the firms increase. With both wage income and profit income rising, income in the economy as a whole rises by $100 billion. According to the consumption function, people will consume more. How much more? The consumption function tells us that 0.6 times the change in income, or $300 billion, will be the additional increase in consumption by the workers and owners of the construction firms. Real GDP rises by $300 billion, the increased production of the goods the workers and owners consume. This $300 billion increase in real GDP is the *second-round effect*. It is hard for anyone to know what the workers in the construction industry or the owners of the construction firms will start purchasing; presumably it will be an array of goods: clothes, movies, and restaurant meals. But with an MPC of 0.6, we do know that they will purchase $300 billion more of these goods. The increase in production spreads throughout the economy. After this second round, real GDP has increased by $800 billion, the sum of $500 billion on the first round and $300 billion on the second round. This is shown in the first and second rows of Table A.11-2.

The story continues. The workers who make the clothes and other goods and services for which there is $300 billion more in spending also have an increase in their income. Either they are no longer unemployed or they work more hours. Similarly, the profits of the owners of those firms increase. As a result, they consume more. How much more? According to the consumption function, 0.6 times the increase in their income. The increase in income outside of construction was $300 billion, so the increase in consumption must now be 0.6 times that, or a $180 billion increase. This increase is the *third-round effect*. As the increase permeates the economy, it is impossible to say what particular goods will increase in production, but we know that total production continues to increase. After three rounds, real GDP has increased by $980 billion, as shown in the third row of Table A.11-2.

The increase does not stop there. Another $180 billion more in consumption means that people somewhere in the economy have $180 billion more in income. This increases consumption further, by 0.6 times the $180 billion, or $108 billion. According to the column on the right of Table A.11-2, the cumulative effect on real GDP is now up to $1,088 billion after four rounds. Observe that each new entry in the first column is added to the previous total to get the cumulative effect on real GDP.

The story is now getting repetitive. We multiply 0.6 times $108 billion to get $64.8 billion. The total effect on real GDP is now $1,152.8 billion at the fifth round. In fact, we are already close to $1,250 billion. If we kept on going for more and more rounds, we would get closer and closer to the $1,250 billion amount obtained from the graphs and the formula for the multiplier.

What If Net Exports Depend on Income?

Thus far, we have made the simplifying assumption that net exports do not respond to income. When net exports do respond to income, the formula for the multiplier is a bit different. We now incorporate this response into our analysis.

We first need to consider how net exports respond to income. Recall that net exports are exports minus imports. To examine the effect of income on net exports, we look first at exports and then at imports.

Exports are goods and services that we sell to other countries, such as aircraft, pharmaceuticals, and telephones. Do U.S. exports depend on income in the United States? No, not much. If Americans earn a little more or a little less, the demand for U.S. exports is not going to increase or decrease. What is likely to make the demand for U.S. exports increase or decrease is a change in income abroad—changes in income in Japan, Europe, or Latin America will affect demand for U.S. exports. U.S. exports will not be affected even if the United States has a recession. Of course, if Japan or Europe has a recession, that is another story. In any case, we conclude that U.S. exports are unresponsive to the changes in U.S. income.

Imports are goods and services that people in the United States purchase from abroad, such as automobiles, sweaters, and vacations. Does the amount purchased of these goods and services change when our incomes change? Yes, because imports are part of consumption. Just as we argued that consumption responds to income, so must imports respond to income. Higher income will lead to higher consumption of both goods purchased in the United States and goods purchased abroad. That reasoning leads us to hypothesize that imports are related positively to income. The hypothesis is accurate when we look at observations on income and imports.

The **marginal propensity to import (MPI)** is the amount that imports change when income changes. Suppose the MPI is 0.2. The MPI is smaller than the MPC because most of the goods we consume when income rises are not imported.

If exports are unrelated to income and imports are positively related to income, then net exports—exports less imports—must be related negatively to income. Algebraically, we have

$$\Delta X = -\text{MPI} \times \Delta Y$$

Using this expression for ΔX, we can now follow the same algebraic steps we followed earlier to derive a formula for the multiplier. The multiplier now depends on the MPI along with the MPC. The derivation is summarized in Table A.11-3. The formula for the multiplier is

$$\frac{\Delta Y}{\Delta G} = \frac{1}{1 - \text{MPC} + \text{MPI}}$$

For example, if MPC = 0.6 and MPI = 0.2, the multiplier is 1.7.

The Forward-Looking Consumption Model

Although the consumption function introduced in Chapter 11 gives a good prediction of people's behavior in many situations, it sometimes works very poorly. For example, the MPC turned out to be quite small when taxes were cut in 1975; people saved almost the entire increase in disposable income that resulted from the tax cut. The MPC turned out to be quite large, however, for the tax cuts in 1982, only seven years later; in that case, people saved very little of the increase in disposable income. The forward-looking consumption model was designed to explain such changes in the MPC.

The **forward-looking consumption model** assumes that people anticipate their future income when making consumption decisions. The forward-looking consumption model was developed independently and in different ways by two Nobel Prize–winning economists, Milton Friedman and Franco Modigliani. Friedman's version is called the **permanent income model**, and Modigliani's version is called the **life-cycle model**. Both models improved on the idea that consumption depends only on current income.

Table **A.11-3**

Derivation of a Formula for the Keynesian Multiplier with Both the MPC and the MPI

Start with
$$\Delta Y = \Delta C + \Delta I + \Delta G + \Delta X$$
Assume that
$$\Delta I = 0$$
and that
$$\Delta C = \text{MPC} \times \Delta Y$$
and that
$$\Delta X = -\text{MPI} \times \Delta Y$$
Putting the above expressions together, we get
$$\Delta Y = (\text{MPC} \times \Delta Y) + \Delta G - (\text{MPI} \times \Delta Y)$$
and solving for the change in Y, we get
$$\frac{\Delta Y}{\Delta G} = \frac{1}{1 - \text{MPC} + \text{MPI}}$$

Forward-Looking People

The forward-looking model starts with the idea that people attempt to look ahead to the future. They do not simply consider their current income. For example, if a young medical doctor decides to take a year off from a high-paying suburban medical practice to do community service at little or no pay, that doctor's income will fall below the poverty line for a year. But the doctor is unlikely to cut consumption to a fraction of the poverty level of income. Even if the doctor were young enough to have little savings, borrowing would be a way to keep consumption high and even to buy an occasional luxury item. The doctor is basing consumption decisions on expected income for several years in the future—making an assessment of a more permanent income, or a life-cycle income—not just for one year.

We have many other examples of this model. Farmers in poor rural areas of Asia try to save something in good years so that they will be able to maintain their consumption in bad years. They try not to consume a fixed fraction of their income. In many cases, the saving is in storable farm goods like rice.

As these examples indicate, instead of allowing their consumption to vary with their income, which may be quite erratic, most people engage in **consumption smoothing** from year to year. Once people estimate their future income prospects, they try to maintain their consumption around the same level from year to year. If their income temporarily falls, they do not cut their consumption by much; *the MPC is very small—maybe about 0.05—in the case of a temporary change in income.* But if they find out that their income will increase permanently, they will increase their consumption a lot; *the MPC is very large—maybe 0.95—in the case of a permanent change in income.* For example, if a new fertilizer doubles the rice yield of a rice farmer's land permanently, we can expect that the farmer's consumption of other goods will about double because of higher permanent income.

The difference between the forward-looking consumption model and the simple consumption function in which consumption depends only on current income is illustrated in Figure A.11-2. In the right panel of Figure A.11-2, income is expected to follow a typical life-cycle pattern: lower when young, higher when middle-aged, and very low when retired. Consumption, however, does not follow these ups and downs; it is flat. The left panel shows the opposite extreme: the standard consumption function with a fixed MPC. In this case, people consume a lot when they are middle-aged, but they consume very little when they are young or old.

Occasionally, some people are prevented from completely smoothing their income because they have a **liquidity constraint**; that is, they cannot get a loan, and so they cannot consume more than their income. Such liquidity constraints do not appear to be important enough in the economy as a whole to negate the forward-looking model completely. Of course, not all people try to smooth their income; some people like to go on binges, spending everything, even if the binge is followed by a long lull.

Figure A.11-2

Two Extreme Forms of Consumption Behavior
The right panel shows the future outlook of a young person or family described by the forward-looking model of consumption. The left panel shows the outlook of a young family with a constant MPC. The path of income is the same in both cases.

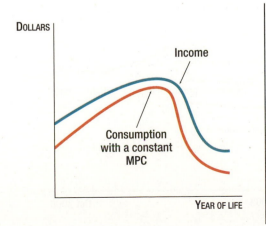

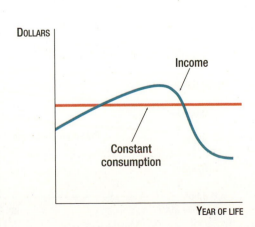

Tests and Applications of the Forward-Looking Model

Observations on consumption and income for the economy as a whole indicate that the forward-looking model significantly improves our understanding of observed changes in the MPC. For example, economists have demonstrated that the measured MPC for the economy as a whole is lower for the temporary changes in income that occur during recessions and booms than for the more permanent increases in income that occur as potential GDP grows over time. Studies of thousands of individual families over time show that the individual MPC for temporary changes in income is about one-third of the MPC for permanent changes in income.

Permanent versus Temporary Tax Cuts

The forward-looking model is also the most promising explanation for the low MPC during the tax cut of 2008. That tax cut was explicitly temporary—a one-time tax rebate, good for only one year. Figure A.11-3 shows that the impact was hard to notice in the data.

With a permanent tax cut, the MPC is high, so it has a big impact on real GDP. For a temporary tax cut, the MPC is low, so it has only a small impact on GDP. In estimating the effects of various tax proposals on the economy, economic forecasters try to take these changes in the MPC into account.

Anticipating Future Tax Cuts or Increases

The forward-looking model changes our estimate of the impact of changes in taxes that are expected to occur in the future. For example, if people are certain of tax cuts in the future, they may begin to increase their consumption right away, before the tax decreases. In this case, the MPC is technically huge, because consumption increases with little or no observed change in current income. Conversely, people may reduce their consumption in anticipation of a tax increase.

It is difficult to know how large these effects are because we do not observe people's expectations of the future. Estimates based on the assumption that people forecast the future no better and no worse than economic forecasters—this is the *rational expectations assumption*—suggest that the effects are large and significant.

In situations in which the expectations effects are obvious, we do see an impact. For example, in December 1992, after the 1992 presidential election, when a tax increase became more likely, it was evident that many people who could do so shifted their reported income for tax purposes from 1993 to 1992. But whether people held back their consumption in anticipation of future tax increases is difficult to say. In any case, because people's behavior is affected by their expectations of the future, attempts to estimate the impact of a policy proposal like a change in taxes need to take these expectations into account.

Figure A.11-3

Some Evidence from the 2008 Stimulus Act in Favor of the Permanent Income Hypothesis

Temporary rebate payments in May through August 2008 increased disposable personal income but had no noticeable effect on consumption.

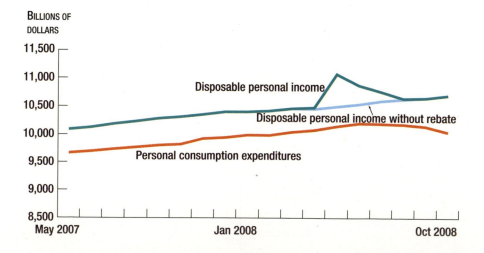

KEY POINTS

1. The multiplier can be found with graphs and with algebra. The algebraic approach results in a convenient formula.
2. The formula for the multiplier is $1/(1 - MPC)$ when net exports do not depend on income.
3. If net exports are negatively related to income, then the formula for the multiplier is $1/(1 - MPC + MPI)$.
4. The forward-looking consumption model explains why the MPC is low in some cases and high in others. It helps economists deal with the uncertainty in the multiplier.
5. The forward-looking consumption model also implies that anticipated changes in taxes affect consumption and are another reason for uncertainty about the MPC. Although such effects have been observed, it is difficult to estimate their size in advance.
6. The rational expectations assumption, which suggests that people forecast the future no better and no worse than economic forecasters, is one basis for making such estimates. With this assumption, the effects of anticipated tax changes on consumption are quite high.

KEY TERMS AND DEFINITIONS

Keynesian multiplier: the ratio of the change in real GDP to the shift in the expenditure line; the formula is $1/(1 - MPC)$, where MPC is the marginal propensity to consume.

marginal propensity to import (MPI): the change in imports because of a given change in income.

forward-looking consumption model: a model that explains consumer behavior by assuming that people anticipate future income when deciding on consumption spending today.

permanent income model: a type of forward-looking consumption model that assumes that people distinguish between temporary changes in their income and permanent changes in their income; the permanent changes have a larger effect on consumption.

life-cycle model: a type of forward-looking consumption model that assumes that people base their consumption decisions on their expected lifetime income rather than on their current income.

consumption smoothing: the idea that although their incomes fluctuate, people try to stabilize consumption spending from year to year.

liquidity constraint: the situation in which people cannot borrow to smooth their consumption spending when their income is low.

QUESTIONS FOR REVIEW

1. Why is the size of the multiplier positively related to the MPC?
2. Why is the size of the multiplier negatively related to the marginal propensity to import (MPI)?
3. How does the forward-looking consumption model differ from the consumption function with a fixed MPC?
4. Why is the MPC for a temporary tax cut less than the MPC for a permanent tax cut? What examples, if any, prove the point?
5. What is consumption smoothing?
6. Why do changes in future taxes that are anticipated in advance affect consumption?

PROBLEMS

1. Are the following statements true or false? Show using algebra.
    a. The multiplier is greater than one and rises if the marginal MPC rises.
    b. The multiplier for an economy in which net exports respond to income is smaller than the multiplier for an economy in which net exports do not respond to income.

2. The following table shows real GDP and imports (in billions of dollars) for an economy.

Real GDP or Income	Imports
2,000	400
3,000	500
4,000	600
5,000	700
6,000	800
7,000	900

Suppose that exports are equal to $700 billion.

a. Construct a graph showing how imports depend on income.

b. Construct a graph showing how net exports depend on income.

c. If the level of real GDP that occurs at spending balance is $6,000 billion, will a trade surplus or a trade deficit result? What type of policy regarding government purchases would bring the trade deficit or trade surplus closer to zero?

d. If the MPC is 0.6, what is the size of the multiplier?

3. a. Suppose Joe spends every additional dollar of income that he receives. What is Joe's MPC? What does his consumption function look like?

b. Suppose that Jane spends half of each additional dollar of income that she receives. What is Jane's MPC? What does her consumption function look like?

c. What differences in Joe's and Jane's incomes or jobs might explain the differences in their MPCs?

4. Suppose Uncle George sent you a check for $500 tomorrow because he is proud of your excellent grades and feels that you are a credit to the family. What would you do with the largest part of the money? Would you spend it, would you save it, or would you pay down your credit card debt (technically a form of saving)? Why? If Uncle George said that he would send you $500 every month while you are in college, would you allocate the funds among spending, saving, and debt reduction any differently? Why or why not?

5. Each month, a certain fraction of employees' pay is withheld and sent to the government as part of what is owed for personal income taxes. If the taxes owed for the year are less than the amount withheld, then a refund is sent early in the following year. If the taxes owed for the year exceed the amount withheld, then additional taxes must be paid by April 15. In 1992, the amount of income tax *withheld* was lowered by about $10 billion to increase consumption and real GDP and thereby speed recovery from the 1990–1991 recession. However, the amount of taxes owed was not changed. Discuss why the impact of this change would be smaller than that of an actual cut in taxes of $10 billion during that year.

12 The Economic Fluctuations Model

On February 17, 2009, newly elected President Barack Obama signed into law a $787 billion stimulus package that he claimed would "begin making the immediate investments necessary to put people back to work doing the work America needs done." The bill represented one of the most significant fiscal interventions in the history of the United States, yet it was enacted only 17 days after being proposed. Democrats and Republicans were bitterly divided on the bill, with Democratic leaders in Congress arguing that the bill would create millions of jobs, rebuild the nation's infrastructure, and give the economy a much-needed shot in the arm. On the other hand, not a single Republican member of the House and only three Republican senators voted for the bill. The Republican opponents argued that the bill was wasteful and would have little stimulative impact on the economy.

Eighteen months later, in the run up to the midterm Congressional elections, the debate raged on. The Council of Economic Advisers issued a report evaluating the American Recovery and Reinvestment Act (ARRA, the official name of the stimulus package) in which it concluded that the package had "raised the level of GDP [gross domestic product] as of the third quarter of 2010, relative to what it otherwise would have been, by 2.7 percent" and that "as of the third quarter of 2010, the ARRA has raised employment relative to what it otherwise would have been by between 2.7 and 3.7 million." Other economists disagreed with this assessment. In an article in the *Wall Street Journal*, the economists John Cogan and John Taylor (one of the authors of this text) argued that the stimulus package did not have much of an impact because it did not lead to an increase in the purchase of goods and services. They concluded that "[t]he bottom-line is the federal government borrowed funds from the public, transferred these funds to state and local governments, who then used the funds mainly to reduce borrowing from the public. The net impact on aggregate economic activity is zero."

Bitter political debates over economic issues, such as the 2009 stimulus bill, are a common sight in U.S. politics as well as in many other political systems around the world. As an observer of this debate, you should try to independently evaluate the validity of the underlying economic arguments made by the opposing parties and come to your own informed conclusion as to who has the more tenable position. This evaluation requires that you have a framework for understanding the fascinating, dynamic process through which a recession ends and a new expansion begins, and for deciding which government actions, if any, can cut the length of a recession or speed up the expansion. This chapter presents just such a framework in the form of a model of economic fluctuations—a simplified description of how the economy adjusts over time when it moves away from potential GDP, as in a recession.

Economic fluctuations models are used to make decisions about monetary policy at the Fed and at other central banks around the world. Private business analysts use the ideas to track the economy and predict central bank decisions. This model is much newer than the supply and demand model, which has been around for more than 100 years. It combines Keynes's idea, developed 75 years ago, that aggregate demand causes the departure of real GDP from potential GDP, with newer ideas, developed in the 1980s and 1990s, about how expectations and inflation adjust over time. Although newer, the economic fluctuations model is analogous to the supply and demand model (Chapter 3). Just as we presented the supply and demand model in a graph consisting of three elements:

- a demand curve,
- a supply curve, and
- an equilibrium at the intersection of the two curves.

We present the economic fluctuations model in a graph consisting of three elements:

- an aggregate demand (AD) curve,
- an inflation adjustment (IA) line, and
- an equilibrium at the intersection of the curve and the line.

We use the economic fluctuations model to explain fluctuations in real GDP and inflation in much the same way that we used supply and demand curves to explain quantity and price in the market for peanuts or other microeconomic markets. In the microeconomic supply and demand model, the intersection of the demand curve and the supply curve gives us a prediction of price and quantity. In the economic fluctuations model, the intersection of the aggregate demand (AD) curve and the inflation adjustment (IA) line gives us a prediction of real GDP and inflation.

We start our construction of the economic fluctuations model by deriving the aggregate demand curve and then the inflation adjustment line. We then will show how their intersection determines real GDP and inflation.

The Aggregate Demand Curve

The **aggregate demand (AD) curve** is a relationship between two economic variables: real GDP and the inflation rate. The inflation rate usually is measured as the annual percentage change in the overall price level from year to year. Figure 12-1 shows an aggregate demand curve for the United States. Observe that inflation is measured on the vertical axis, that real GDP is measured on the horizontal axis, and that we have drawn a vertical dashed line to mark the point at which real GDP equals potential GDP. The aggregate demand curve shows different combinations of real GDP and inflation. It is downward sloping from left to right because real GDP is related negatively to inflation

aggregate demand (AD) curve
a line showing a negative relationship between inflation and the aggregate quantity of goods and services demanded at that inflation rate.

Figure 12-1

The Aggregate Demand Curve

The aggregate demand curve shows that higher inflation and real GDP are negatively related.

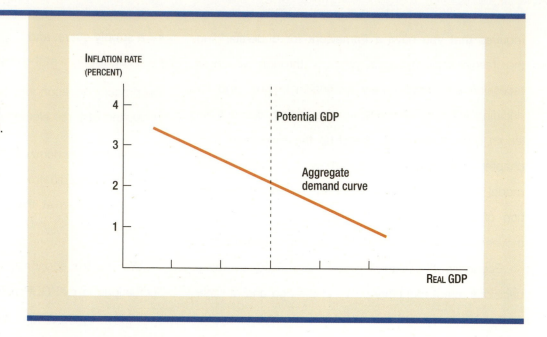

along the curve. The term *aggregate demand* is used because the movements of real GDP away from potential GDP are due to fluctuations in the sum (aggregate) of the demand for consumption, investment, net exports, and government purchases.

Why does the aggregate demand curve slope downward? We will answer this question and derive the curve in three stages. First, we show that a negative relationship exists between the real interest rate and real GDP. Second, we show that a positive relationship exists between inflation and the real interest rate. Third, we show that these two relationships imply a negative relationship between real GDP and inflation, and that that relationship is the aggregate demand curve. The following schematic chart shows how the three stages fit together.

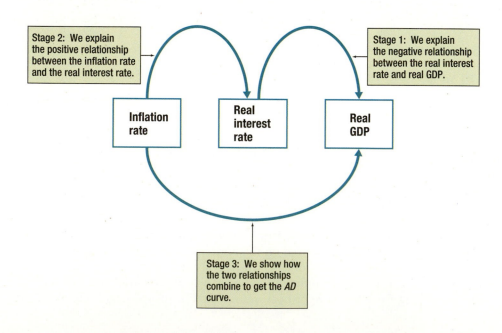

Interest Rates and Real GDP

Consumption, investment, and net exports each are related negatively to the interest rate. Combining these components provides an explanation of the negative relationship between real GDP and the interest rate. Keep in mind that the real interest rate is a better measure of the effects of interest rates on investment, consumption, and net exports because it corrects for inflation. Recall from Chapter 5 that the real interest rate equals the stated, or nominal, interest rate minus the inflation rate. The negative effect of the real interest rate on consumption, investment, and net exports is no different from that discussed in Chapter 7. If you already have studied that chapter, the next few pages will review that information.

Investment Investment is the component of expenditure that is probably most sensitive to the real interest rate. Recall that part of investment is the purchase of new equipment or a new factory by a business firm. Many firms must borrow funds to pay for such investments. Higher real interest rates make such borrowing more costly. The additional profits the firm might expect to earn from purchasing a photocopier or a truck are more likely to be lower than the interest costs on the loan if the real interest rate is high. Hence, businesses that are thinking about buying a new machine and need to borrow funds will be less inclined to purchase such an investment good if real interest rates are higher, and so higher real interest rates reduce investment spending by businesses. Also, remember that part of investment is the purchase of new houses. Most people need to take out a mortgage to buy a house. Like any loan, the mortgage has an interest rate, and higher interest rates make mortgages more costly. Hence, with higher real interest rates, fewer people take out mortgages and buy new houses. Spending for new housing declines.

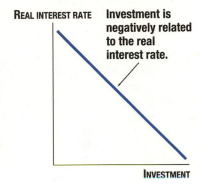

REAL INTEREST RATE   Investment is negatively related to the real interest rate.

INVESTMENT

The same reasoning works to show why lower real interest rates will increase investment spending: Lower real interest rates reduce the cost of borrowing and make investment more attractive to firms and households.

To summarize, both business investment and housing investment decline when the real interest rate rises, and they increase when the real interest rate falls. At any given time some firms or households are deciding whether to buy a new machine or a new house, and they are going to be less inclined to buy such things when the interest rate is higher.

Net Exports The negative relationship between net exports and the real interest rate requires a somewhat more involved explanation than the relationship between the real interest rate and investment. The relationship exists because higher real interest rates in the United States tend to lead to a higher dollar exchange rate and, in turn, a higher exchange rate reduces net exports.

A higher real interest rate in the United States compared with other countries increases the demand for U.S. dollar bank accounts and other assets that pay interest. That increased demand bids up the price of dollars; hence, the exchange rate—the price of dollars—rises. Now, with a higher exchange rate, net exports will be lower because U.S.-produced exports become more expensive to foreigners, who must pay a higher price for dollars, and imported foreign goods become cheaper for Americans, who can get more foreign goods for higher-priced dollars. With exports falling and imports rising, net exports—exports less imports—must fall. In sum, higher real interest rates reduce net exports.

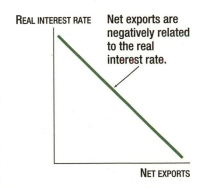

REAL INTEREST RATE   Net exports are negatively related to the real interest rate.

NET EXPORTS

The same reasoning works for lower real interest rates as well. If the real interest rate falls in the United States, then U.S. dollar bank accounts are less attractive compared with bank accounts in other currencies, such as those of Germany or Japan. This falling interest rate bids down the price of dollars, and the exchange rate falls. Now, with a lower exchange rate, net exports will be higher because U.S.-produced exports are less expensive to foreigners and imported foreign goods are more expensive for Americans. With exports rising and imports falling, net exports must rise. Thus, lower real interest rates increase net exports. To summarize, a negative relationship exists between the interest rate and the net exports that works through the exchange rate, as shown below.

Interest Rate		Value of the Domestic Currency		Net Exports
up	→	up	→	down
down	→	down	→	up

If the interest rate goes up, then the value of the domestic currency goes up, causing net exports to go down. If the interest rate goes down, then the value of the domestic currency goes down, causing net exports to go up.

Consumption   We have shown that two of the components of expenditure—investment and net exports—are sensitive to the real interest rate. What about consumption?

Although consumption probably is less sensitive to the real interest rate than the other components, some evidence indicates that higher real interest rates encourage people to save a larger fraction of their income. Higher real interest rates encourage people to save because they earn more on their savings. Because more saving means less consumption, this implies that consumption is related negatively to the interest rate. Most economists, however, feel that the effect of interest rates on consumption is much less than on investment and net exports.

The Overall Effect   To summarize the discussion thus far, investment, net exports, and consumption all are related negatively to the real interest rate. The overall effect of a change in real interest rates on real GDP now can be assessed.

Figure 12-2 shows the 45-degree line and two different expenditure lines corresponding to two different interest rates. Higher interest rates shift the expenditure line

REMINDER

Finished with Stage 1: Real GDP is related negatively to the real interest rate.

Why?

- Consumption (*C*) is negatively related to the *real interest rate*.
- Investment (*I*) is negatively related to the *real interest rate*.
- Net exports (*X*) are negatively related to the *real interest rate*.

Figure 12-2

The Interest Rate, Spending Balance, and Real GDP

A higher real interest rate shifts the expenditure line down because consumption, investment, and net exports depend negatively on the real interest rate. Thus, real GDP declines with a higher real interest rate. Conversely, a lower real interest rate raises real GDP.

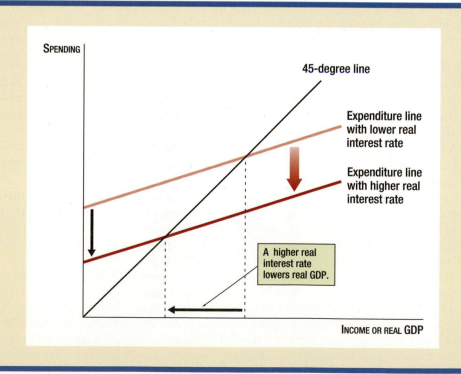

down because a higher interest rate lowers investment, net exports, and consumption, which all are part of expenditure.

Observe how the downward shift of the expenditure line leads to a new point of spending balance. The intersection of the expenditure line with the 45-degree line occurs at a lower level of real GDP. Note that real GDP is lower not only because the higher real interest rate lowers investment, net exports, and consumption, but also because a decline in income will lower consumption further. Real GDP declines by the amount shown on the horizontal axis, which is larger than the downward shift in the expenditure line. *Thus, an increase in the real interest rate lowers real GDP.*

What about a decline in the real interest rate? A lower real interest rate will raise the expenditure line. In that case, when the expenditure line shifts up, the point of spending balance at the intersection with the 45-degree line will be at a higher level of real GDP. *Thus, a decrease in the real interest rate raises real GDP.* In sum, we have shown that a negative relationship exists between the real interest rate and real GDP.

Interest Rates and Inflation

Now that we have seen why interest rates affect real GDP, let us proceed to the second stage in our analysis. We want to show why a rise in inflation will increase the real interest rate and thereby lower real GDP, or why a decline in inflation will decrease the real interest rate and thereby raise real GDP.

Central Bank Interest Rate Policy
The easiest way to see why the real interest rate rises when the inflation rate increases is to examine the behavior of the Fed. The Fed and central banks in other countries typically follow policies in which they respond to an increase in the inflation rate by raising the nominal interest rate. By far the most widely followed and analyzed decision by the Fed is its nominal interest rate decision.

Why do central banks raise the nominal interest rate when they think the inflation rate is rising? The inflation rate is ultimately the responsibility of the Fed, and the goal of controlling inflation requires that the central bank raise the nominal interest rate so that the real interest rate rises when the inflation rate rises. If the central bank raises the real interest rate successfully, then the higher real interest rate will reduce investment, consumption, and net exports. The reduced demand will then reduce inflationary pressures and bring inflation back down again.

The goal of controlling inflation also requires that the central bank lower the real interest rate when inflation falls. Suppose that the inflation rate starts to fall. If the central bank lowers the nominal interest rate so that the real interest rate falls, then the lower real interest rate will increase investment, consumption, and net exports. The increase in demand will put upward pressure on inflation.

Table 12-1 illustrates these actions of the Fed using a hypothetical example. For each inflation rate, a nominal interest rate decision by the Fed is shown. For example, when inflation is 2 percent, the nominal interest rate decision is 4 percent. When inflation rises to 4 percent, the nominal interest rate decision by the Fed is 7 percent. Thus, when inflation rises, the central bank raises the nominal interest rate, and when inflation falls, the central bank lowers the nominal interest rate.

Note that the nominal interest rate rises more than inflation rises in Table 12-1. The reason is that for an increase in the nominal interest rate to reduce demand, the real interest rate must rise because investment, consumption, and net exports depend negatively on the real interest rate, as described in the previous section. The nominal interest

Table 12-1

A Numerical Example of Central Bank Interest Rate Policy

(a) Inflation Rate	(b) Nominal Interest Rate Decision (made by the central bank)	Resulting Real Interest Rate (b) − (a)
0.0	1.0	1.0
1.0	2.5	1.5
2.0	4.0	2.0
3.0	5.5	2.5
4.0	7.0	3.0
5.0	8.5	3.5
6.0	10.0	4.0
7.0	11.5	4.5
8.0	13.0	5.0

monetary policy rule
a description of how much the interest rate or other instruments of monetary policy respond to inflation or other measures of the state of the economy.

federal funds rate
the interest rate on overnight loans between banks that the Federal Reserve influences by changing the supply of funds (bank reserves) in the market.

REMINDER

Actions the Fed takes:
To reduce the federal funds rate, the Fed increases the supply of reserves by buying bonds. To raise the federal funds rate, the Fed decreases the supply of reserves by selling bonds. The buying and selling of bonds are called open market operations.

rate has to rise by more than the inflation rate for the real interest rate to rise and demand to decline. If, instead, the nominal interest rate rose by less than the increase in the inflation rate, then the real interest rate would not rise; rather, it would fall. The behavior of the central bank illustrated in the third column of Table 12-1 is called a **monetary policy rule** because it describes the systematic response of the real interest rate to inflation as decided by the central bank.

How the Fed Changes the Interest Rate Keep in mind that the central bank does not set interest rates by decree or by direct control. Governments sometimes do control the price of goods; for example, some city governments control the rents on apartments. The central bank does not apply such controls to the interest rate. Rather, it enters the market in which short-term interest rates are determined by the usual forces of supply and demand. In the United States, the short-term interest rate the Fed focuses on is the interest rate on overnight loans between banks. This is called the **federal funds rate**, and the overnight loan market is called the federal funds market because reserves at the Fed are what are loaned or borrowed in this market. When the Fed wants to lower this interest rate, it supplies more reserves to this market. When it wants to raise the interest rate, it reduces reserves. Recall from Chapter 10 that the Fed can change the amount of reserves in the banking system through *open market operations*—that is, by buying and selling government bonds. If the Fed wants to increase reserves and thereby lower the federal funds rate, it buys government bonds. If the Fed wants to decrease reserves and thereby increase the federal funds rate, it sells government bonds.

A Graph of the Response of the Interest Rate to Inflation Figure 12-3 represents the monetary policy rule graphically, using the information in Table 12-1. When the inflation rate rises, the nominal interest rate rises along the blue upward-sloping line. When the inflation rate declines, the nominal interest rate declines. The nominal interest rate must rise by more than the inflation rate if the *real* interest rate is to rise when inflation rises; this requires that the slope of the monetary policy rule in Figure 12-3 be greater than 1. For example, if the slope is 1.5, then when the inflation rate increases by 1 percentage point, the interest rate rises by 1.5 percentage points, as in Table 12-1. In other words, the nominal interest rate rises by 0.5 percentage point *more* than the inflation rate rises, causing the *real* interest rate to rise by

0.5 percentage point. The resulting real interest rate decision of the Fed is indicated by the orange line: The real interest rate changes by 0.5 percentage point when the inflation rate changes by 1 percentage point. The real interest rate policy rule is shown in Figure 12-4.

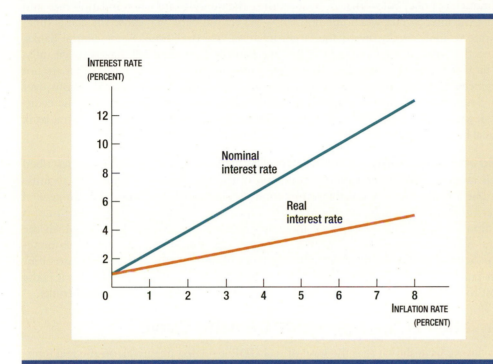

Figure 12-3

A Monetary Policy Rule

The monetary policy rule shows that the Fed raises the real interest rate when inflation rises and lowers the real interest rate when inflation falls. To accomplish this, the Fed has to move the nominal interest rate by more than 1 percentage point when the rate of inflation changes by 1 percentage point.

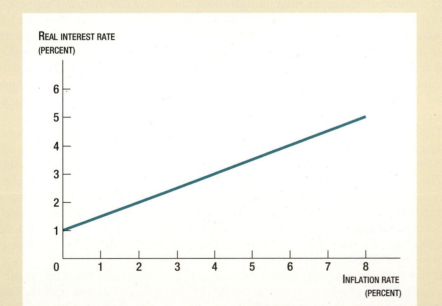

Figure 12-4

The Real Interest Rate is Positively Related to Inflation

From now on, the monetary policy rule of the Fed will be presented as a relationship between the inflation rate and the real interest rate. When inflation rises, the Fed raises the real interest rate (through a more than proportional increase in the nominal interest rate), whereas when inflation falls, the Fed lowers the real interest rate (by decreasing the nominal rate in a more than proportional manner).

target inflation rate
the central bank's goal for the average rate of inflation over the long run.

Most central banks have a **target inflation rate**, the inflation rate that the central bank tries to maintain on average over the long run. Because of various shocks to the economy, the central bank cannot control the inflation rate perfectly; sometimes the inflation rate will rise above the target inflation rate, and sometimes the inflation rate will fall below the target inflation rate. By reacting to these movements in inflation according to a monetary policy rule—that is, by increasing the interest rate when inflation rises and cutting the interest rate when inflation falls—the central bank will cause the actual inflation rate to move back toward the target inflation rate over time. Some central banks, such as the Bank of England and the Reserve Bank of New Zealand, have explicit inflation targets. Other central banks, like the Fed, have implicit inflation targets that are not announced explicitly, but that can be assessed by observing central bank decisions over time. The target inflation rate for many central banks is about 2 percent. For the economy described in Figure 12-3, at the target inflation rate of 2 percent, the central bank sets real interest rates at 2 percent by choosing a nominal rate of 4 percent.

A Good Simplifying Assumption The behavior of the central bank described in this section provides the easiest explanation of the response of interest rates to inflation, but it is not the only possible explanation. Economists have found that the general upward-sloping relationship in Figure 12-4, which we call the monetary policy rule, is common to many different types of monetary policies, including policies in which the central bank focuses on money growth. Although the position and shape of the monetary policy rule will differ for these different types of policies, the overall response of interest rates to inflation will be similar. We use this particular derivation because it is the easiest to explain and describes the actual behavior of the Fed and other central banks.

Derivation of the Aggregate Demand Curve

Thus far, we have shown that the level of real GDP is related negatively to the real interest rate and that the real interest rate is related positively to the inflation rate through the central bank's policy rule. We now combine these two concepts to derive the aggregate demand curve—the inverse relationship between the inflation rate and real GDP.

The chain of reasoning that brings about the aggregate demand curve can be explained by considering what would happen if the inflation rate rose. First, the interest rate would rise because the Fed would raise the real interest rate in response to the higher inflation rate. Next, the higher real interest rate would mean less investment spending, a decline in net exports, and a decline in consumption. Lower investment spending would occur because investment would be made more costly by the high real interest rate. U.S. goods would become more expensive, and foreign goods would become cheaper. Thus, net exports—exports minus imports—would decline.

The opposite chain of events would occur if inflation fell. First, the Fed would lower the real interest rate according to the monetary policy rule. The lower real interest rate, in turn, would cause investment, net exports, and consumption to rise. Hence, real GDP would rise.

Thus, we see that when the inflation rate rises, real GDP decreases, and when the inflation rate falls, real GDP increases. In other words, a negative relationship exists between inflation and real GDP. When we graph this relationship in a diagram with real GDP on the horizontal axis and inflation on the vertical axis, we get a downward-sloping curve like the one shown in Figure 12-1; this curve is the aggregate demand curve, which we have thus derived.

If you want to review the derivation, seeing all the paragraphs together on the same page, a self-guided graphic overview is provided in Figure 12-5. If you read the explanatory boxes in numerical order, you will be able to trace the chain of events following an increase in inflation, including the Fed's real interest rate increase according to its policy rule and the decline in real GDP.

Figure 12-5

A Self-Guided Graphic Overview

Follow the numbers to see an overview of the derivation of the aggregate demand curve. The black dots represent the situation *before* we increase the inflation rate. The pink dots represent the situation *after* we increase the inflation rate. When inflation rises, the central bank raises the real interest rate, and this lowers real GDP. Hence, we have the aggregate demand curve.

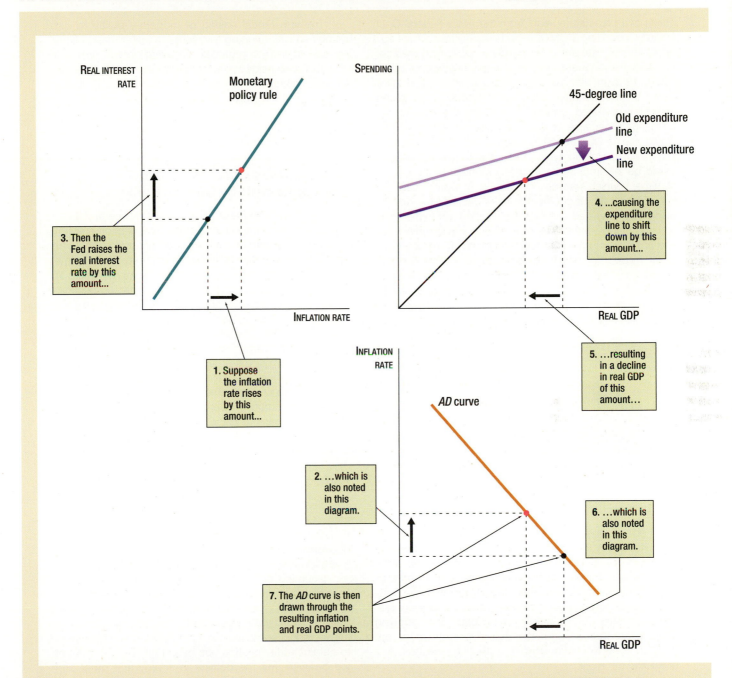

REAL INTEREST RATE

Monetary policy rule

3. Then the Fed raises the real interest rate by this amount...

INFLATION RATE

1. Suppose the inflation rate rises by this amount...

SPENDING

45-degree line

Old expenditure line

New expenditure line

4. ...causing the expenditure line to shift down by this amount...

REAL GDP

5. ...resulting in a decline in real GDP of this amount...

INFLATION RATE

AD curve

2. ...which is also noted in this diagram.

6. ...which is also noted in this diagram.

7. The *AD* curve is then drawn through the resulting inflation and real GDP points.

REAL GDP

ECONOMICS *IN ACTION*

The Fed Changes the Interest Rate

These two press statements from the Fed's Federal Open Market Committee (FOMC) show how changes in the Fed's target interest rate are determined by changes in the inflation rate, much as assumed by the monetary policy rule in Figure 12-3. In the first statement, issued in June 2008, about six months after the beginning of the most recent recession, the Fed explains that it left the interest rate unchanged because it was not clear whether inflation would rise (in which case the target interest rate would be increased) or fall (in which case the target interest rate would be lowered) in the next few months. In the second statement, which was issued a couple of months later, the Fed explains that it cut interest rates because the deteriorating economy had reduced the likelihood of higher inflation and made it more likely that inflation would move lower and not higher in the next few months. In an extremely unusual move, the policy decision made by the Fed was announced as a joint statement with leading central banks from the Euro area, Canada, Sweden, Switzerland and the United Kingdom, all of whom also were pledging to lower interest rates for similar reasons. With the benefit of hindsight, we now see what motivated the Federal Reserve and these other Central Banks to take such a dramatic step—the possibility that a full-blown financial crisis could trigger an extremely severe recession in the global economy.

© Bernhard Classen/Alamy
Headquarters for the European National Bank.

For Immediate Release: June 25, 2008

The Federal Open Market Committee decided today to keep its target for the federal funds rate at 2 percent. Recent information indicates that overall economic activity continues to expand, partly reflecting some firming in household spending. However, labor markets have softened further and financial markets remain under considerable stress. Tight credit conditions, the ongoing housing contraction, and the rise in energy prices are likely to weigh on economic growth over the next few quarters.

The Committee expects inflation to moderate later this year and next year. However, in light of the continued increases in the prices of energy and some other commodities and the elevated state of some indicators of inflation expectations, uncertainty about the inflation outlook remains high.

The substantial easing of monetary policy to date, combined with ongoing measures to foster market liquidity, should help to promote moderate growth over time. Although downside risks to growth remain, they appear to have diminished somewhat, and the upside risks to inflation and inflation expectations have increased. The Committee will continue to monitor economic and financial developments and will act as needed to promote sustainable economic growth and price stability.

Release Date: October 8, 2008
Joint Statement by Central Banks

Throughout the current financial crisis, central banks have engaged in continuous close consultation and have cooperated in unprecedented joint actions such as the provision of liquidity to reduce strains in financial markets. Inflationary pressures have started to moderate in a number of countries, partly reflecting a marked decline in energy and other commodity prices. Inflation expectations are diminishing and remain anchored to price stability. The recent intensification of the financial crisis has augmented the downside risks to growth and thus has diminished further the upside risks to price stability.

Some easing of global monetary conditions is therefore warranted. Accordingly, the Bank of Canada, the Bank of England, the European Central Bank, the Federal Reserve, Sveriges Riksbank, and the Swiss National Bank are today announcing reductions in policy interest rates. The Bank of Japan expresses its strong support of these policy actions.

Federal Reserve Actions

The Federal Open Market Committee has decided to lower its target for the federal funds rate 50 basis points to 1-1/2 percent. The Committee took this action in light of evidence pointing to a weakening of economic activity and a reduction in inflationary pressures.

Incoming economic data suggest that the pace of economic activity has slowed markedly in recent months. Moreover, the intensification of financial market turmoil is likely to exert additional restraint on spending, partly by further reducing the ability of households and businesses to obtain credit. Inflation has been high, but the Committee believes that the decline in energy and other commodity prices and the weaker prospects for economic activity have reduced the upside risks to inflation. The Committee will monitor economic and financial developments carefully and will act as needed to promote sustainable economic growth and price stability.

Movements along the Aggregate Demand Curve

Movements along the Aggregate Demand Curve Thus far, we have explained why the aggregate demand curve has a negative slope—that is, why higher inflation means a lower real GDP. A change in real GDP due to a change in inflation is thus a *movement along* the aggregate demand curve. In microeconomics, a similar movement along the demand curve occurs when a *change in the price* leads to a *change in quantity demanded*. When inflation rises, causing the Fed to raise the interest rate, and real GDP declines, a movement occurs up and to the left along the aggregate demand curve. When inflation declines and the Fed lowers the interest rate, causing GDP to rise, a movement occurs down and to the right along the aggregate demand curve.

Shifts of the Aggregate Demand Curve Now, the inflation rate is not the only thing that affects aggregate demand. Changes in government purchases, shifts in monetary policy, shifts in foreign demand for U.S. exports, changes in taxes, and changes in consumer confidence, among other things, affect aggregate demand. When any one of these factors changes aggregate demand, we call it a *shift* in the aggregate demand curve. Let us briefly consider some of those sources of shifts in the aggregate demand curve.

Government Purchases Imagine that government purchases rise. We know from our analysis of spending balance in Chapter 11 that an increase in government purchases will increase real GDP in the short run. This increase in real GDP occurs at any inflation rate: at 2 percent, at 4 percent, or at any other level. Now, if real GDP increases at a given inflation rate, the aggregate demand curve will shift to the right. This is shown in Figure 12-6. The new aggregate demand curve will be parallel to the original aggregate demand curve because no matter what the inflation rate is in the economy, the shift in government purchases is going to have the same effect on real GDP. The same reasoning implies that a decline in government spending shifts the aggregate demand curve to the left.

Changes in the Target Inflation Rate Suppose the Fed has an inflation target of 2 percent. Consider what happens when the Fed shifts its policy objectives. Suppose, for

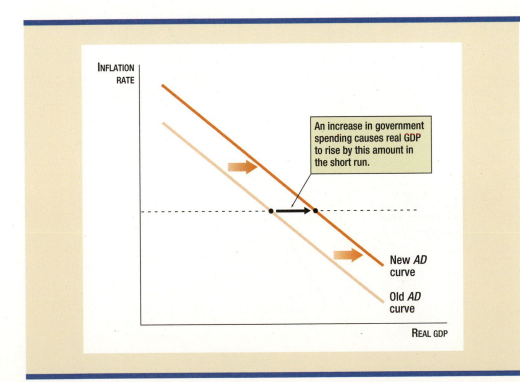

Figure 12-6

How Government Purchases Shift the Aggregate Demand Curve
An increase in government purchases shifts the *AD* curve to the right. Real GDP rises by the same amount at every level of inflation.

instance, that the Fed chair decides that a somewhat higher inflation rate, say, 3 percent, would be tolerable to achieve some other objective. One example of such a change would be if the Fed was concerned about credit market conditions because firms were curtailing investment, or because consumers were cutting back on spending because of the difficulty in obtaining loans at affordable rates—or because the Fed believed that the banking sector was in trouble with more banks needing to borrow money from one another to meet their obligations to depositors. In that case, the Fed immediately will try to increase spending by lowering the real interest rate. This move will enhance access to credit, stimulate greater spending, and affect real GDP regardless of the current inflation rate: The *AD* curve will shift to the right, as shown in Figure 12-7.

This type of action also could work in reverse—the Fed could decide that the current inflation target is too high and that it needs to act to lower the targeted rate of inflation. To get inflation to fall, the Fed immediately will try to lower spending by raising the real interest rate: The *AD* curve will shift to the left. In practice, such a shift to a lower targeted rate of inflation could happen for a variety of reasons, including changes in the preferences of policy makers. For instance, when Paul Volcker took over as chairman of the Federal Reserve, it was clear that he had a much greater dislike of inflation than his predecessors. Therefore, it was not a surprise when he raised interest rates substantially, shortly after taking office.

Other Changes Many other changes in the economy (other than a change in the inflation rate, which is a movement along the *AD* curve) will shift the *AD* curve. We

Figure 12-7

A Shift in the Monetary Policy Rule

A shift in the policy rule to higher inflation implies a decline in the real interest rate. The lower real interest rate increases real GDP in the short run. As a result, at a given inflation rate, the *AD* curve shifts to the right.

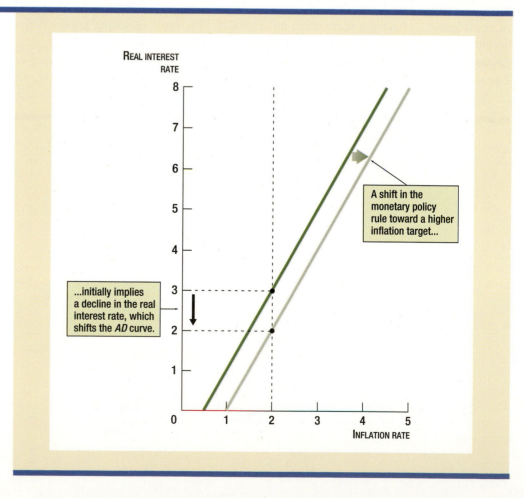

considered many such possibilities in Chapter 11; their effects on the aggregate demand curve are listed in Figure 12-8. For example, an increase in the foreign demand for U.S. products will increase net exports, raise real GDP, and shift the aggregate demand curve to the right. A drop in consumer confidence that reduces the amount of consumption at every level of income will shift the aggregate demand curve to the left. Finally, an increase in taxes shifts the aggregate demand curve to the left, whereas a decrease in taxes shifts the aggregate demand curve to the right.

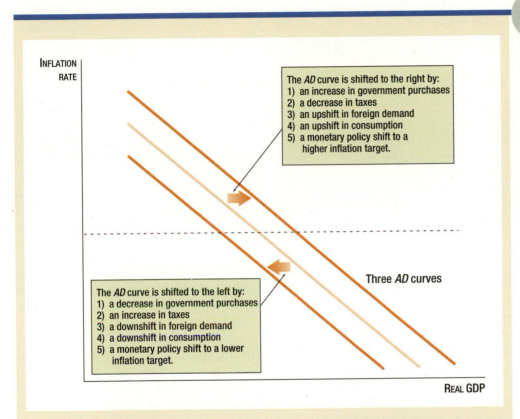

Figure 12-8

A List of Possible Shifts in the Aggregate Demand Curve

Many things shift the *AD* curve. An increase in government purchases shifts the AD curve to the right. A change in the monetary policy rule toward a higher inflation target shifts the AD curve to the right. A decline in government purchases and a change in the monetary policy rule toward a lower inflation target shift the curve to the left.

(Figure labels:)

The *AD* curve is shifted to the right by:
1) an increase in government purchases
2) a decrease in taxes
3) an upshift in foreign demand
4) an upshift in consumption
5) a monetary policy shift to a higher inflation target.

The *AD* curve is shifted to the left by:
1) a decrease in government purchases
2) an increase in taxes
3) a downshift in foreign demand
4) a downshift in consumption
5) a monetary policy shift to a lower inflation target.

Three *AD* curves

INFLATION RATE

REAL GDP

REVIEW

- The aggregate demand curve is an inverse relationship between inflation and real GDP.

- Investment, net exports, and consumption are negatively related to the real interest rate. Hence, real GDP falls when the real interest rate rises, and vice versa.

- When inflation increases, the central bank raises the real interest rate, and this lowers real GDP. Conversely, when inflation falls, the central bank lowers the real interest rate, and this raises real GDP. It does so by moving nominal interest rates by more

than 1 percentage point when inflation changes by 1 percentage point. These are movements along the aggregate demand curve.

- The aggregate demand curve shifts to the right when the central bank changes its monetary policy rule toward more inflation and shifts to the left when the central bank changes its policy rule toward less inflation.

- Higher government purchases shift the aggregate demand curve to the right. Lower government purchases shift the aggregate demand curve to the left.

The Inflation Adjustment Line

inflation adjustment (*IA*) line a flat line showing the level of inflation in the economy at a given point in time. It shifts up when real GDP is greater than potential GDP, and it shifts down when real GDP is less than potential GDP; it also shifts when expectations of inflation or raw materials prices change.

Having derived the aggregate demand curve and studied its properties, let us now look at the inflation adjustment line, the second element of the economic fluctuations model. The **inflation adjustment (*IA*) line** is a flat line showing the level of inflation in the economy at any point in time. Figure 12-9 shows an example of the inflation adjustment line in a diagram with inflation on the vertical axis and real GDP on the horizontal axis. For example, if the line touches 4 percent on the vertical axis, it tells us that inflation is 4 percent.

The inflation adjustment line describes the economic behavior of firms and workers setting prices and wages in the economy. Next, we discuss several important features about the slope and position of the inflation adjustment line.

The Inflation Adjustment Line Is Flat

That the inflation adjustment line is flat indicates that firms and workers adjust their prices and wages in such a way that the inflation rate remains steady in the short run as real GDP changes. Only over time does inflation change significantly and the line move. In the short run, inflation stays at 4 percent, or wherever the line happens to be when real GDP changes.

In interpreting the inflation adjustment line, it is helpful to remember that it is part of a *model* of the overall economy and thus is an approximation of reality. In fact, inflation does not remain *perfectly* steady, and the inflation adjustment line can have a small upward slope. But it is a good approximation to assume that the inflation adjustment line is flat.

Inflation does not change very much in the short run even if real GDP and the demand for firms' products changes for two good reasons: (1) expectations of continuing inflation and (2) staggered wage and price setting at different firms throughout the economy.

Expectations of Continuing Inflation
Expectations about the price and wage decisions of other firms throughout the economy influence a firm's price and wage decisions. For example, if the overall inflation rate in the economy has been hovering around 4 percent year after year, then a firm can expect that its competitors' prices probably will increase by about 4 percent per year, unless circumstances change. To keep prices near those of the competition, this firm will need to increase its price by about 4 percent each year. Thus, the inflation rate stays steady at 4 percent per year.

Wage adjustments also are influenced by expectations. If firms and workers expect that workers at other firms will be getting large wage increases, then meeting the competition will require similar large wage increases. A smaller wage increase would reduce the wage of the firm's workers relative to that received by other workers. Many firms base their wage decisions on the wages paid by other firms. If they see the wages at other firms rising, they will be more willing to increase wages.

Firms and workers also look to expectations of inflation when deciding on wage increases. In an economy with 4 percent inflation, wages will have to increase by 4 percent for workers just to keep up with the cost of living. Lower wage increases would result in a decline in workers' real wages.

Staggered Price and Wage Setting
Not all wages and prices are changed at the same time throughout the economy. Rather, price setting and wage setting are staggered over months and even years. For example, autoworkers might negotiate three-year

wage contracts in 1996, 1999, 2002, and so on. Dockworkers might negotiate three-year contracts in 1997, 2000, 2003, and so on. Bus companies and train companies do not adjust their prices at the same time, even though they may be competing for the same riders. On any given day, we can be sure that a wage or price is adjusting somewhere in the economy, but the vast majority of wages and prices do not change.

Staggered price and wage setting slows down the adjustment of prices in the economy. When considering what wage increases are likely in the next year, firms and workers know about the most recent wage increases. For example, an agreement made by another firm to increase wages by 4 percent per year for three years into the future will affect the expectations of wages paid to competing workers in the future. This wage agreement will not change unless the firm is on the edge of bankruptcy, and perhaps not even then. Hence, workers and firms deciding on wage increases tend to match the wage increases recently made at other firms. Thus, price and wage decisions made today are directly influenced by price and wage decisions made yesterday.

As with many things in life, when today's decisions are influenced by yesterday's decisions, inertia sets in. The staggering of the decisions makes it difficult to break the inertia. Unless policy makers have a reason to make a change—such as a persistent decline in demand or a change in expectations of inflation—the price increases or wage increases continue from year to year. The flat inflation adjustment line describes this inertia.

The Inflation Adjustment Line Shifts Gradually When Real GDP Departs from Potential GDP

The inflation adjustment line does not always stay put; rather, it may shift up or down from year to year. If real GDP stays above potential GDP, then inflation starts to rise. Firms see that the demand for their products is remaining high, and they begin adjusting their prices. If the inflation rate is 4 percent, then the firms will have to raise their prices by more than 4 percent if they want their relative prices to increase. Hence, inflation starts to rise. The inflation adjustment line is shifted upward to illustrate this rise in inflation; it will keep shifting upward as long as real GDP is above potential GDP.

If real GDP is below potential GDP, however, then firms will see that the demand for their products is falling off, and they will adjust their prices. If inflation is 4 percent, the firms will raise their prices by less than 4 percent—perhaps by 2 percent—if they want the relative price of their goods to fall. Hence, inflation will fall. The inflation adjustment line is shifted down to illustrate this fall in inflation. Figure 12-9 shows the direction of these shifts.

If real GDP stays at potential GDP, neither to the left nor to the right of the vertical potential GDP line in Figure 12-9, then inflation remains unchanged. This steady inflation is represented by an unmoving inflation adjustment line year after year.

Changes in Expectations or Commodity Prices Shift the Inflation Adjustment Line

Even if real GDP is at potential GDP, some special events in the economy can cause the inflation adjustment line to shift up or down. One important example is *shifts in expectations* of inflation. If firms and workers expect inflation to rise, they are likely to raise wages and prices by a large amount to keep pace with the expected inflation. Thus, an increase in expectations of inflation will cause the inflation adjustment line to shift up to a higher inflation rate. And a decrease in expectations of inflation will cause the inflation adjustment line to shift down.

REMINDER

The following is a brief summary of inflation adjustment in the economy as a whole:

- If real GDP = potential GDP, then the inflation rate does not change (*IA* line does not shift).

- If real GDP > potential GDP, then the inflation rate increases (*IA* line shifts up).

- If real GDP < potential GDP, then the inflation rate decreases (*IA* line shifts down).

Figure 12-9

Inflation Adjustment and Changes in Inflation

In the top panel, real GDP is above potential GDP and inflation is rising; the inflation adjustment line shifts up. In the bottom panel, real GDP is below potential GDP and inflation is falling; thus, the inflation adjustment line shifts down.

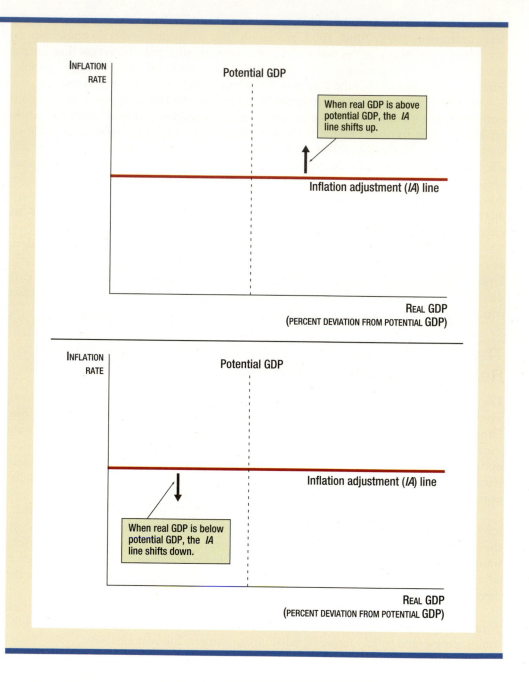

Another example is a change in commodity prices that affects firms' costs of production. For example, we will examine the effects on inflation of an oil price increase in Chapter 13. By raising firms' costs, such an oil price increase would lead firms to charge higher prices, and the inflation adjustment line would rise, at least temporarily.

Does the Inflation Adjustment Line Fit the Facts?

Are these assumptions about the inflation adjustment line accurate? Does inflation rise when real GDP is above potential GDP and fall when real GDP is below potential GDP?

Although there are exceptions, the answer is generally yes. Look back at Figure 5-8 in Chapter 5 for evidence.

One of the biggest declines in inflation occurred in the recession of 1982, when real GDP was far below potential GDP. Inflation also fell during the recessions of 1990–1991, 2001, and 2008 when real GDP fell below potential GDP. In 1998 and 1999, real GDP rose above potential GDP, but inflation did not immediately start to rise. This delay led some commentators to think that the inflation adjustment relationship was changing, but by late 1999 and 2000, inflation rose as predicted by the theory.

REVIEW

- The inflation adjustment (IA) line, the second element of the economic fluctuations model, is a flat line showing the level of inflation in the economy at any point in time. The inflation adjustment line describes the economic behavior of firms and workers setting prices and wages in the economy.

- Firms do not change their prices instantaneously when the demand for their product changes. Thus, when aggregate demand changes and real GDP departs from potential GDP, the inflation rate does not change immediately; the inflation adjustment line does not shift in response to such changes in the short run.

- Staggered wage and price setting tends to slow down the adjustment of inflation in the economy as a whole.

- Over time, inflation does respond to departures of real GDP from potential GDP. This response can be described by upward and downward shifts in the inflation adjustment line over time.

Combining the Aggregate Demand Curve and the Inflation Adjustment Line

We have now derived two relationships—the aggregate demand curve and the inflation adjustment line—that describe real GDP and inflation in the economy as a whole. The two relationships can be combined to make predictions about real GDP and inflation.

Along the aggregate demand curve in Figure 12-1, real GDP and inflation are negatively related. This curve describes the behavior of firms and consumers as they respond to a higher real interest rate caused by the Fed's response to higher inflation. They respond by lowering consumption, investment, and net exports. This line presents a range of possible values of real GDP and inflation.

The inflation adjustment line in Figure 12-9, on the other hand, tells us what the inflation rate is at any point in time. Thus, we can use the inflation adjustment line to determine exactly what inflation rate applies to the aggregate demand curve. For example, if the inflation adjustment line tells us that the inflation rate for 2007 is 3 percent, then we can go right to the aggregate demand curve to determine what the level of real GDP will be at that 3 percent inflation rate. The inflation adjustment line tells us the current location of inflation—and therefore real GDP—on the aggregate demand curve.

Figure 12-10 illustrates the determination of real GDP and inflation graphically. It combines the aggregate demand curve from Figure 12-1 with the inflation adjustment line from Figure 12-9. At any point in time, the inflation adjustment line is given, as shown in Figure 12-10. The inflation adjustment line intersects the aggregate demand curve at a single point. It is at this point of intersection that inflation and real GDP are determined. The intersection gives an *equilibrium* level of real

GDP and inflation. At that point, we can look down to the horizontal axis of the diagram to determine the level of real GDP corresponding to that level of inflation. For example, the point of intersection in the left panel of Figure 12-10 might be when inflation is 5 percent and real GDP is 2 percent below potential GDP. The point of intersection in the right panel is at a lower inflation rate when real GDP is above potential GDP. The point of intersection in the middle panel of Figure 12-10 has real GDP equal to potential GDP.

As Figure 12-10 makes clear, the intersection of the inflation adjustment line and the aggregate demand curve may give values of real GDP that are either above or below potential GDP. But if real GDP is not equal to potential GDP, then the economy has not fully recovered from a recession, as on the left of Figure 12-10, or returned to potential GDP after being above it, as on the right. To describe dynamic movements of inflation and real GDP, we must consider how the inflation adjustment line and the aggregate demand curve shift over time. That is the subject of Chapter 13.

Figure 12-10

Determining Real GDP and Inflation

Real GDP is determined at the intersection of the *AD* curve and the *IA* line. All three panels have the same *AD* curve and the same vertical line marking potential GDP. Three different levels of the *IA* line give three different levels of real GDP: less than, equal to, and greater than potential GDP.

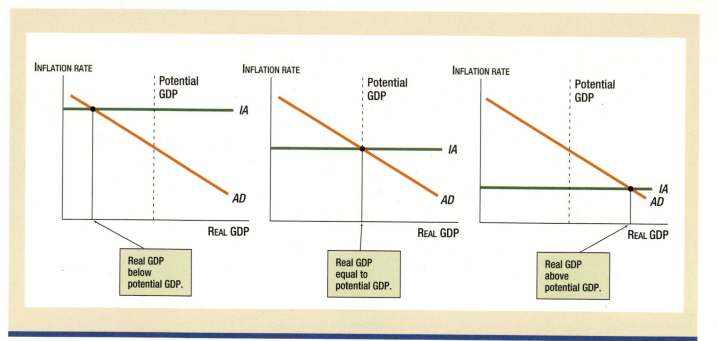

REVIEW

- In any year, the inflation adjustment line tells what the inflation rate is. Using the aggregate demand curve, we then can make a prediction about what real GDP is.

- The intersection of the aggregate demand curve and the inflation adjustment line gives a pair of observations on real GDP and inflation at any point in time.

CONCLUSION

With the three essential elements of the economic fluctuations model—the aggregate demand curve, the inflation adjustment line, and their intersection—put together, we now are ready to use the model to explain the fluctuations of real GDP and inflation. In reviewing the model, it is useful to consider the scissors analogy mentioned in our discussion of the supply and demand model in Chapter 3.

The aggregate demand curve is like one blade of the scissors. The inflation adjustment line is the other blade. Either blade alone is insufficient to explain economic fluctuations. Either blade alone is an incomplete story. But when the two blades of the scissors are put together to form a pair of scissors, they become a practical tool to explain the ups and downs in the economy. And compared with the complexity and vastness of the whole economy with millions of firms and consumers, this particular pair of scissors is amazingly simple.

KEY POINTS

1. Investment, net exports, and consumption depend negatively on the real interest rate. Hence, real gross domestic product (GDP), which includes investment, net exports, and consumption, depends negatively on the real interest rate.
2. Central banks' actions to adjust the nominal interest rate to maintain low inflation result in a relationship between the real interest rate and inflation. When inflation rises, the real interest rate rises. When inflation falls, the real interest rate falls.
3. The combined behavior of (1) the real interest rate response to inflation and (2) the private sector adjusting spending in response to the interest rate generates an inverse relationship between real GDP and inflation—the aggregate demand curve.
4. Movements along the aggregate demand curve occur when inflation rises, causing the real interest rate to rise and real GDP to fall. Such movements along the curve also occur when inflation falls, the interest rate declines, and real GDP rises.
5. The aggregate demand curve shifts for many reasons, including a change in government purchases and a change in monetary policy toward a higher inflation target.
6. When adjusting prices, firms respond slowly to changes in demand and take into account expectations of inflation. So do workers when wages are being adjusted. As a result, inflation tends to increase when real GDP is above potential GDP and tends to decrease when real GDP is below potential GDP.
7. The staggering of price and wage decisions tends to slow the adjustment of prices in the economy as a whole.
8. When combined with the aggregate demand curve, the inflation adjustment line provides us with a way to determine real GDP and inflation.

KEY TERMS

aggregate demand (AD) curve, 285
federal funds rate, 290
inflation adjustment (IA) line, 298

monetary policy rule, 290
target inflation rate, 292

QUESTIONS FOR REVIEW

1. Why are investment, net exports, and consumption inversely related to the real interest rate?
2. Why is real GDP inversely related to the real interest rate in the short run?
3. Why does the real interest rate rise when inflation begins to rise?
4. Why is real GDP inversely related to inflation in the short run? What is this relationship called?

5. What are examples of movements along the aggregate demand curve?
6. Why does a change in government purchases shift the aggregate demand curve to the right or left?
7. Why does a shift in monetary policy shift the aggregate demand curve to the right or left?

8. Why does inflation increase when real GDP is above potential GDP?
9. What is the significance of expectations of inflation for inflation adjustment?
10. Why does staggered price setting slow down price adjustment in the economy?

PROBLEMS

1. Compare and contrast the graphs used in the microeconomic supply and demand model with those used in the economic fluctuations model.
2. Which of the following statements are true, and which are false? Explain your answers in one or two sentences.

    a. An increase in the U.S. real interest rate will cause the dollar exchange rate to decline.
    b. The central bank typically raises the real interest rate when inflation rises.
    c. A higher real interest rate leads to greater net exports because the higher interest rate raises the value of the dollar.

3. Suppose the Fed is considering two different policy rules, shown in the following table. Graph the policy rules.

Inflation	Policy Rule 1 Interest Rate	Policy Rule 2 Interest Rate
0	1	3
2	3	5
4	5	7
6	7	9
8	9	11

    If the Fed currently is following Policy Rule 1 and then shifts to Policy Rule 2, which way will the aggregate demand curve shift? What reasons might the Fed have for changing its policy?

4. Suppose you have the following information on the Fed's and the European Central Bank's (ECB) policy rules:

    Fed real interest rate = 0.5(inflation rate − 2)
    ECB real interest rate = 0.2(inflation rate − 2) + 1

    a. Graph these policy rules. If the inflation rate is 2 percent in both countries, what will be the real interest rate in each country?

    b. Some argue that Europe has a much lower tolerance for inflation than the United States. Can you tell—either from the diagram or from the equations—whether this is true?

5. The table below gives a numerical example of an aggregate demand curve.

    a. Sketch the curve in a graph.
    b. What is the average rate of inflation in the long run?
    c. Suppose that the central bank shifts policy so that the average rate of inflation in the long run is 2 percentage points higher than in (b). Sketch a new aggregate demand curve corresponding to the higher inflation rate.

Real GDP (percent deviation from potential GDP)	Inflation (percent per year)
3.0	1.0
2.0	1.5
1.0	2.0
0.0	3.0
−1.0	4.0
−2.0	6.0
−3.0	9.0

6. State which of the following changes cause a shift in the aggregate demand curve and which ones are a movement along it. Also provide the direction of the change.

    a. A cut in government purchases.
    b. A crash in the U.S. stock market.
    c. A shift to a lower inflation target in the monetary policy rule.
    d. Being thrifty now becoming fashionable.
    e. An increase in the European interest rate.

7. The following table gives an example of an inflation adjustment line.

Real GDP (percent deviation from potential GDP)	Inflation (percent per year)
3.0	2.0
2.0	2.0
1.0	2.0
0.0	2.0
−1.0	2.0
−2.0	2.0
−3.0	2.0

a. Sketch the line in a graph.
b. If real GDP is above potential GDP, will the inflation adjustment line shift up or down? Explain.
c. In the same graph as part (a), sketch in the aggregate demand curve given in Problem 5. Find the equilibrium level of real GDP and inflation.
d. Show what happens to the inflation adjustment line if inflation expectations suddenly increase.

8. Suppose that a decline in unionization reduces the amount of wage contracts that are being signed and also brings about a reduction in the length of the typical wage contract that is signed. What would the impact on the *IA* line for that economy be? Explain.

9. Give three examples of goods and services that you buy whose prices change only periodically and therefore contribute to staggered pricing in the economy.

10. Suppose potential GDP is $5,000 billion. Use the data below to graph the aggregate demand curve.

Inflation (percent)	Real GDP (billions of dollars)
5	4,800
4	4,900
3	5,000
2	5,100
1	5,200

a. Suppose the current inflation rate is 2 percent. Draw the inflation adjustment line. What is the current value of real GDP?
b. In the long run, what will the inflation rate be if economic policy does not change? Explain how this adjustment takes place.

13 Using the Economic Fluctuations Model

For students and teachers of macroeconomics, the years 2008, 2009, and 2010 have a Dickensian feel to them. "It was the best of times, it was the worst of times, it was the age of wisdom, it was the age of foolishness."[1] On the one hand, it was the worst of times: to live in what President Barack Obama termed "the worst economic crisis since the Great Depression," consoling friends and family who had lost their jobs, studying at universities forced to make budget cuts and raise tuition, and facing a future with dwindling job prospects of one's own. Even after the recession ended in June 2009, the subsequent recovery was one of the most anemic recoveries the U.S. economy has experienced as unemployment remained well above 9 percent until the end of 2010. On the other (considerably less important) hand, it was the best of times to be studying macroeconomics, trying to understand how what began as a slowdown in housing prices in the United States ended up as a global economic recession that seemed to spare no country in its wake, and trying to understand the challenges that monetary and fiscal

policy makers would have in getting the economy back on track in a world in which uncertainty was rife, government budgets already were stretched to the limit, and central bankers had used up most of their conventional policy tools.

The goal of this chapter is to show you how you can use the economic fluctuations model to develop a good understanding of what causes recessions, expansions, and other vital developments in a modern dynamic economy. Indeed, economists around the world use such a model to study events in their own countries. The model also is extremely useful in determining the appropriate choices of economic policy—how a tax cut, a new spending program, or an interest rate cut is needed to stimulate the economy.

We begin by using the model in a general way to determine the path the economy takes after a shift in aggregate demand, whether that shift is due to a big change in government purchases, a shift in monetary policy, or some other factor. We trace the path of real gross domestic product (GDP) from the time of its initial departure from potential GDP—as in a recession—to its recovery. We explain why a recovery occurs and

---

[1] Charles Dickens, *A Tale of Two Cities*.

how long it takes. We also look at the effect of price shocks on the economy.

After we cover these general applications, we demonstrate the usefulness, and power, of the economic fluctuations model by applying it to understand the most recent recession experienced by the United States. Economists can provide invaluable contributions to society if they can use models like the economic fluctuations model to better understand economic developments and to formulate policies that can help the economy recover from a crisis or prevent such a serious crisis from occurring in the first place.

Changes in Government Purchases

We first use the economic fluctuations model to examine the forces leading to the return of real GDP to potential GDP. To do so, we focus on a particular example, a change in government purchases. In Chapter 11, we showed how a change in government purchases could push real GDP away from potential GDP in the short run. Now let's see the complete story.

Real GDP and Inflation over Time

Suppose the government cuts military purchases permanently. We want to examine the effects of this decrease in government purchases on the economy in the short run (about one year), the medium run (two to three years), and the long run (four to five years and beyond). The three lengths of time given in the parentheses are approximations; in reality, the times will not be exactly these lengths, but rather they will be somewhat longer or shorter. We use the term *short run* to refer to the initial departure of real GDP from potential GDP, *medium run* to refer to the recovery period, and *long run* to refer to the time at which real GDP is nearly back to potential GDP.

Figure 13-1 shows the aggregate demand curve and the inflation adjustment line on the same diagram. The intersection of the aggregate demand curve and the inflation adjustment line determines a level of inflation and real GDP. Let us assume that we began with real GDP equal to potential GDP. Thus, the initial intersection of the aggregate demand curve and the inflation adjustment line occurs at a level of real GDP equal to potential GDP.

Now, recall from Chapter 12 that a change in government purchases shifts the aggregate demand curve; in particular, a decline in government purchases shifts the aggregate demand curve to the left. Because the inflation adjustment line is flat, and because it does not move in the short run, a change in government purchases—shown by the shift from the "old" to the "new" aggregate demand curve in Figure 13-1—leads to a change in real GDP of the same amount as the shift in the aggregate demand curve. This is the short-run effect. The decrease in government purchases initially moves the aggregate demand curve to the left, and real GDP falls to the point indicated by the intersection of the inflation adjustment line and the new aggregate demand curve. At the new intersection, real GDP is below potential GDP.

As real GDP falls below potential GDP, employment falls because the decline in demand forces firms to cut back on production and lay off workers. The model predicts that unemployment rises, just as it does during actual declines in real GDP.

Now consider what happens over time. The tendency for inflation to adjust over time is represented by upward or downward shifts of the inflation adjustment line. Only in the short run does the inflation adjustment line stay put. What is likely to happen over time when real GDP is below potential GDP? Inflation should begin to decline, because firms will increase their prices by smaller amounts. We represent a decline in inflation by

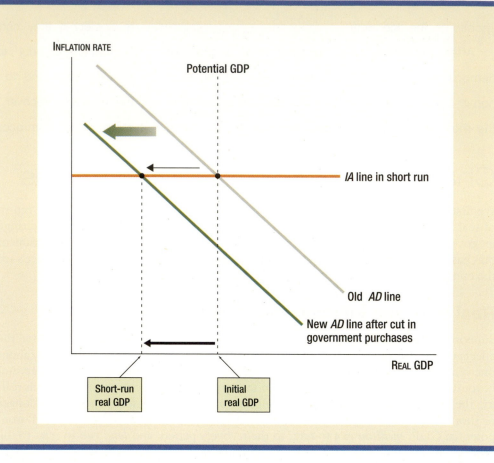

Figure 13-1

Short-Run Effects of a Reduction in Government Purchases

In the short run, the *IA* line does not move. Thus, in the short run, real GDP declines by the amount of the shift in the *AD* curve, as noted on the horizontal axis.

shifting the inflation adjustment line down, as shown in Figure 13-2. The initial impact of the change in government spending took us to the point we label *SR*, for short run, in Figure 13-2. At that point, real GDP is lower than potential GDP. Hence, inflation will fall and the inflation adjustment line shifts down, as shown in the diagram. Now we have a new point of intersection; we label that point *MR*, for medium run.

Note that real GDP has started to recover. At the point labeled *MR* in the diagram, real GDP is still below potential GDP, but it is higher than at the low (*SR*) point in the downturn. The reason real GDP starts to rise is that the lower inflation rate causes the central bank to lower the real interest rate. The lower real interest rate increases investment spending and causes net exports to rise. As a result, real GDP rises, and as it does, firms start to call back workers who were laid off. As more workers are employed, unemployment begins to fall.

Because real GDP is still below potential GDP, the tendency is for inflation to fall. Thus, the inflation adjustment line continues to shift downward until real GDP returns to potential GDP. Figure 13-2 shows a third intersection at the point marked *LR*, for long run, the point at which production has increased all the way back to potential GDP. At this point, real GDP has reached long-run equilibrium in the sense that real GDP equals potential GDP. With real GDP equal to potential GDP, the inflation adjustment line stops shifting down. Inflation is at a new lower level than before the decline in government purchases, but at the final point of intersection in the diagram, it is no longer falling. Thus, real GDP remains equal to potential GDP.

Note how successive downward shifts of the inflation adjustment line with intersections along the aggregate demand curve trace out values for real GDP and inflation as the economy first goes into recession and then recovers. In the short run, a decline in production comes about because of the decrease in government spending; that decline is followed by successive years of reversal as the economy recovers and real GDP returns to

Figure 13-2

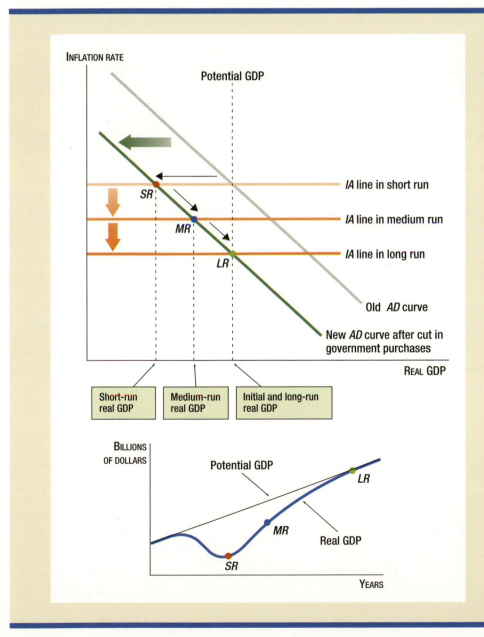

Dynamic Adjustment after a Reduction in Government Purchases

Initially, the reduction in government purchases shifts the *AD* curve to the left. This reduces real GDP to the point labeled *SR,* or the short run. Then the *IA* line begins to shift down because real GDP is less than potential GDP. The *IA* line keeps shifting down until real GDP is back to potential GDP.

potential GDP. This behavior is shown in the sketch in the lower part of Figure 13-2. Thus, we have achieved one of the major goals of this chapter: showing how real GDP returns to potential GDP after an initial departure because of a shift in aggregate demand. In the case in which the shift in aggregate demand is large enough to cause real GDP to decline, as in a recession, we have shown how recessions end and recoveries take the economy back to normal.

Details on the Components of Spending

It is possible to give a more detailed description of what happens to consumption, net exports, and investment during this temporary departure from, and return to, potential GDP.

Let's focus first on the short run and then on the long run. Figure 13-3 summarizes how each component of real GDP changes in the short run and the long run. The arrows in the table indicate what happens compared with what would have happened in the absence of the change in government purchases. The path of the economy in the absence of the hypothetical change is called the *baseline*. The term *baseline* is commonly used in public policy discussions to refer to what would happen if a contemplated policy action were not taken; the arrows in the table tell whether a variable is up or down relative to the baseline. In this case, the *baseline* for real GDP is potential GDP. Thus, a downward-pointing arrow in the real GDP column means that real GDP is below potential GDP; the sideways arrows indicate that real GDP is equal to the baseline or potential GDP; an upward-pointing arrow would mean that real GDP is above potential GDP.

Short Run   The decline in government spending gets things started, lowering aggregate demand and the level of real GDP. With lower real GDP, income is down, and so people consume less, as explained by the consumption function in Chapter 11. In the short run, investment does not change because interest rates have not yet changed. Net exports rise, however, because the lower level of income in the United States means that people will import less from abroad. Recall that *net exports is defined as exports minus imports*. Thus, if imports fall, then net exports must rise.

These short-run effects are shown in the first row in the table. Real GDP and consumption are down *relative to the baseline*. Net exports are up *relative to the baseline*.

Figure 13-3

More Detailed Analysis of a Reduction in Government Purchases

The arrows in the diagram keep track of the changes in the major variables relative to the baseline.

	Y	C	I	X	G
SR	↓	↓	↔	↑	↓
LR	↔	↑	↑	↑	↓

Long Run   Now consider the long run, approximately four to five years. By this time, real GDP has returned to potential GDP. Government spending is still lower than it was originally because we have assumed that this is a permanent decline in military spending. Because real GDP is equal to potential GDP, aggregate income in the economy—which equals real GDP—is back to normal. Because income is back to normal, the effects of income on consumption and net exports are just what they would have been in the absence of the change in government purchases.

What about interest rates and their effect on consumption, investment, and net exports? We know that the real interest rate would be lowered by the monetary policy maker when inflation declined. With a lower real interest rate, more real GDP will go to investment, net exports, and consumption to make up for the decline in the amount of real GDP going to the government. The diagram in Figure 13-3 shows that consumption, investment, and net exports are higher in the long run. We would expect the consumption effects to be small, however, because consumption is not sensitive to interest rates. Most of the long-run impact of the decline in government purchases is to raise investment and net exports.

A Higher Growth Path after a Recession To summarize, a decrease in government purchases has negative effects on the economy in the short run. Real GDP declines. Workers are laid off. Unemployment rises. In the long run, the economy is back to potential GDP, and consumption, investment, and net exports have gone up. Workers are called back, and unemployment declines to the point at which it was before the recession. In the long run, the decrease in government purchases permits greater private investment and more net exports. The increase in investment benefits long-run economic growth, as we know from Chapter 7; hence, the path of potential GDP over time has risen, and now real GDP is growing more quickly, as shown in Figure 13-4.

Observe also that the rate of inflation is lower in the long run than it was before the temporary decline in real GDP. Inflation declined during the period when real GDP was lower than potential GDP, and it did not increase again. This lower inflation rate means that the Fed implicitly has allowed the *target* rate of inflation—the average level of inflation over the long run—to drift down. If the Fed had wanted to keep the target rate of inflation from falling, it would have had to lower interest rates before the inflation rate started to fall. This decline in the interest rate would have pushed the aggregate demand curve back to the right and thereby kept the inflation rate from falling.

A good example occurred in the mid-1990s when government purchases were cut in an effort to reduce the federal budget deficit. Economists argued that the Fed should cut interest rates by an extra amount. They recognized that such action would cause the aggregate demand curve to shift to the right and prevent real GDP from declining in the short run while at the same time keeping the inflation rate from falling in the long run.

The Return to Potential GDP after an Increase in Government Spending

What if real GDP rises above potential GDP? Surprisingly, the adjustment of real GDP back to potential GDP can be explained using the same theory. For example, suppose an increase in real GDP above potential GDP is caused by an increase in government purchases for new highway construction. Starting from potential GDP, the aggregate demand curve would shift to the right. Real GDP would increase above potential GDP in the short run.

With real GDP above potential GDP, however, firms start to raise their prices more rapidly; inflation begins to rise. We would represent that as an upward shift in the inflation adjustment line. In the medium run, real GDP still would be

Figure 13-4

Increase in the Long-Term Growth after a Recession Caused by a Decrease in Government Purchases

The higher investment share of real GDP that results from the decline in government purchases leads to more capital and a higher growth of potential GDP. After the recession, real GDP will grow along, or fluctuate around, this higher growth path.

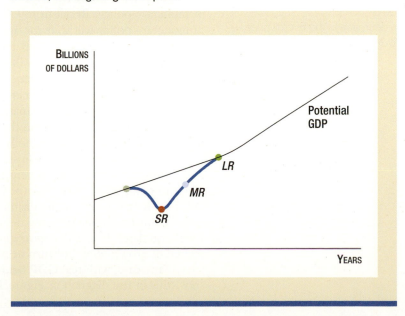

above potential GDP, and inflation would continue to rise. Eventually, real GDP would go back to potential GDP. Thus, we predict that real GDP goes back to potential GDP. In this case, however, because government purchases have risen, the new long-run equilibrium will have a higher interest rate, and the sum of consumption, investment, and net exports will be lower.

REVIEW

- Using the inflation adjustment line and the aggregate demand curve, we now can explain both the initial steps of real GDP away from potential GDP and the return to potential GDP.

- In the short run, a decline in government purchases shifts the aggregate demand curve to the left and causes real GDP to fall below potential GDP.

- In the medium run, when the interest rate starts to fall, real GDP begins to increase again. Investment and net exports start to rise and partly offset the decline in government purchases.

- In the long run, real GDP returns to potential GDP. Interest rates are lower, and consumption plus investment plus net exports has risen.

Changes in Monetary Policy

A large change in government spending, of course, is not the only thing that temporarily can push real GDP away from potential GDP. Changes in taxes, consumer confidence, or foreign demand also can cause recessions. But a particularly important factor is a change in monetary policy.

disinflation
a reduction in the inflation rate.

deflation
a decrease in the overall price level, or a negative inflation rate.

Consider, for example, a change in monetary policy that aims to lower the rate of inflation. Suppose that the inflation rate is too high, say 10 percent, as it was in the late 1970s, and the Fed decides to reduce the inflation rate to 3 percent. In effect, the central bank changes the target inflation rate from 10 percent to 3 percent. A reduction in the inflation rate is called **disinflation**. Declining prices, or a negative inflation rate is **deflation**, which is different from a declining inflation rate. The aim of the policy in this example is disinflation, not deflation.

Figure 13-5 shows the short-run, medium-run, and long-run impact of such a shift in monetary policy. Recall from Chapter 12 (see Figures 12-7 and 12-8) that a change in monetary policy will shift the aggregate demand curve. A change in monetary policy toward higher inflation will shift the *AD* curve to the right, and a change in monetary policy toward lower inflation will shift the *AD* curve to the left. In this case, we are examining a change in monetary policy that aims to lower the inflation rate, so the change shifts the aggregate demand curve to the left. This shift occurs because the Fed raises interest rates to curtail demand and thereby lower inflationary pressures.

One effect of the increase in the interest rate is to lower investment. In addition, the higher interest rate causes the dollar to appreciate, and this tends to reduce net exports. Because inflation is slow to adjust, we do not move the inflation adjustment line yet. Thus, inflation remains at 10 percent in the short run. At this time, things seem grim. The short-run effect of the change to a new monetary policy is to cause real GDP to fall below potential GDP. If the disinflation is large enough, this might mean a decline in real GDP, or a recession. If the disinflation is small and gradual, then the decline in real GDP could result in a *temporary growth slowdown*. In a temporary growth slowdown, real GDP growth does not turn negative, as it does in a recession.

In any case, with real GDP below potential GDP, inflation will begin to decline. We show this in the diagram in Figure 13-5 by moving the inflation adjustment line down.

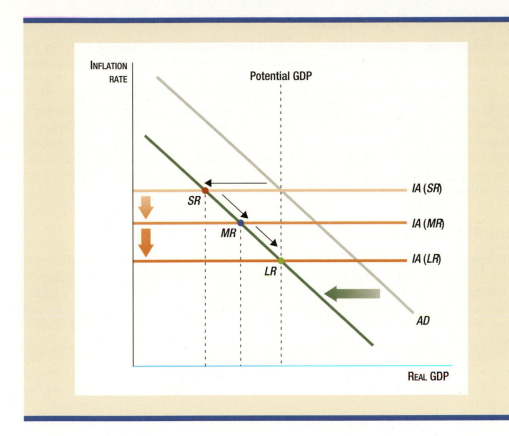

Figure 13-5

Disinflation: A Transition to Lower Inflation
The figure shows how a change in monetary policy to a lower target for inflation affects real GDP over time. In the end, inflation is lower and real GDP is back to potential GDP.

The lower inflation adjustment line, labeled *MR* for medium run, intersects the aggregate demand curve at a higher level of real GDP. Thus, the economy has begun to recover. The recovery starts because as inflation comes down, the Fed begins to lower the interest rate. As the interest rate declines, investment and net exports begin to rise again, and we move back along the aggregate demand curve.

At this medium-run situation, however, real GDP is still below potential GDP, so the inflation rate continues to decline. We show this in the diagram by shifting the inflation adjustment line down again. To make a long story short, we show the inflation adjustment line shifting all the way down to where it intersects the aggregate demand curve at potential GDP. Thus, in the long-run equilibrium, the economy has fully recovered, and the inflation rate is at its new lower target. The long-run equilibrium has consumption, investment, and net exports back to normal.

The overall dynamic impacts of this change in monetary policy are important. The initial impact of a monetary policy change is on real GDP. It is only later that the change shows up in inflation. Thus, the effect of monetary policy on inflation has a long lag.

Lower inflation, for example, 3 percent rather than 10 percent in this case, is likely to make potential GDP grow faster, perhaps because uncertainty is lower and productivity rises faster. If this is so, the return of real GDP to potential GDP will mean that real GDP is higher, and the long-run benefits of the disinflation to people in the economy may be great over the years. But such changes in the growth of real GDP will appear small in the span of years during which a disinflation takes place and will not change the basic story that a reduction in the rate of inflation, unless it is gradual, usually results in a recession.

The Volcker Disinflation

The scenario we just described is similar to the disinflation in the United States in the early 1980s under Paul Volcker, the head of the Fed from 1979 to 1987. First, interest rates skyrocketed as the disinflation began. The federal funds rate went to more than 20 percent. By any measure, real GDP fell well below potential GDP in the early 1980s. Workers were laid off, the unemployment rate rose to 10.8 percent, investment declined, and net exports fell. Eventually, pricing decisions began to adjust and inflation began to come down. As inflation came down, the Fed began to lower the interest rate. The economy eventually recovered: In 1982, the recovery was under way, and by 1985, the economy had returned to near its potential. The good news was that inflation was down from over 10 percent to about 4 percent.

Reinflation and the Great Inflation

reinflation

an increase in the inflation rate caused by a change in monetary policy.

The opposite of disinflation might be called **reinflation**, an increase in the inflation rate caused by a shift in monetary policy. This could be analyzed with our theory simply by reversing the preceding process, starting with a change in monetary policy to a higher inflation rate target. This higher target would cause the aggregate demand curve to shift right. Real GDP would rise above potential GDP, and unemployment would decline. But eventually inflation would rise and real GDP would return to potential.

Although it would be unusual for central bankers to explicitly admit they were raising the target inflation rate, there could be political pressures that would lead to less concern about inflation. In such a case, the target for inflation would rise implicitly.

Reinflation is one way to interpret the Great Inflation in the United States and other countries in the 1970s. In the late 1960s and 1970s, the Fed and other central banks around the world let the inflation rate increase. Other things were going on at that time, including a quadrupling of oil prices, but without the inflationary monetary policy, the decade-long inflation would not have been sustained for so long.

REVIEW

- Disinflation is a reduction in inflation. It occurs when the central bank shifts monetary policy in the direction of a lower inflation target.
- According to the theory of economic fluctuations, disinflation has either a temporary slowing of real GDP growth or a recession as a by-product. A higher interest rate at the start of a disinflation lowers investment spending and net exports. This lower spending causes real GDP to fall below potential GDP. Eventually the economy recovers. Inflation comes down, and so does the interest rate.
- The large disinflation in the early 1980s in the United States was accompanied by a recession, as predicted by the theory.

Price Shocks

demand shock

a shift in one of the components of aggregate demand that leads to a shift in the aggregate demand curve.

Shifts in the aggregate demand curve are called **demand shocks**. The change in government purchases and the shift in monetary policy described in the previous two sections of this chapter are examples of demand shocks. However, shifts in the aggregate demand curve are not the only things that can push real GDP away from potential GDP. In particular, the inflation adjustment line can shift.

ECONOMICS *IN ACTION*

Explaining the Recovery from the Great Depression

The Great Depression was the biggest economic downturn in American history. Simply no event in history has paralleled it either before or since. As shown in the figure, from 1929 to 1933, real GDP declined 35 percent. Between 1933 and 1937, real GDP rose 33 percent; it then declined 5 percent in a recession in 1938. Real GDP increased by a spectacular 49 percent between 1938 and 1942. By 1942, real GDP had caught up with potential GDP, as estimated in the figure.

Economists still disagree about what caused the Great Depression—that is, what caused the initial departure of real GDP from potential GDP. In their monetary history of the United States, Milton Friedman and Anna Schwartz argue that it was caused by an error in monetary policy that produced a massive leftward shift in the aggregate demand curve. Unfortunately, it took several years of continually declining real GDP, declining inflation, and even deflation before the errors in monetary policy were corrected.

Another explanation is that a downward shift in consumption and investment spending lowered total expenditures. Peter Temin of MIT has argued that such a spending shift was a cause of the Great Depression.

But whatever the initial cause, more consensus is shared that monetary policy eventually was responsible for the recovery from the Great Depression. Interest rates (in real terms) fell precipitously in 1933 and remained low or negative throughout most of the second half of the 1930s. These low interest rates led to an increase in investment and net exports. Christina Romer, head of President Obama's Council of Economic

Advisers until recently, and professor of economics at University of California at Berkeley, estimated that without the monetary response, "the U.S. economy in 1942 would have been 50 percent below its pre-Depression trend path, rather than back to its normal level." Could the recovery from the Great Depression have been associated with an increase in government purchases or a reduction in taxes? Evidently not. Romer shows that government purchases and tax policy basically were unchanged until 1941, when government spending increased sharply during World War II. By that time, the economy had already made up most of the Depression decline in real GDP relative to potential GDP.

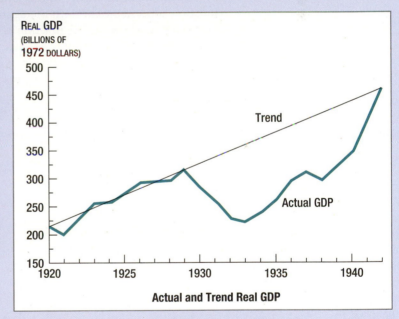

Actual and Trend Real GDP

What Is a Price Shock?

Shifts in the inflation adjustment line are called **price shocks**. A price shock usually occurs when a temporary shortage of a key commodity, or group of commodities, drives up prices by such a large amount that it has a noticeable effect on the rate of inflation. Oil price shocks have been common in the last 35 years. For example, oil prices rose sharply in 1974, in 1979, in 1990, in 2005, in 2007–2008 and then again in early 2011. After many of these shocks, but not all, real GDP usually has declined and unemployment has increased. Hence, such shocks appear to move real GDP significantly, though temporarily, away from potential GDP.

price shock
a change in the price of a key commodity such as oil, usually because of a shortage, that causes a shift in the inflation adjustment line; also sometimes called a supply shock.

Price shocks sometimes are called *supply shocks* to distinguish them from demand shocks resulting from changes in government spending or monetary policy. However, a shift in potential GDP—rather than a shift in the inflation adjustment line—is more appropriately called a supply shock. Shifts in potential GDP—such as a sudden spurt in productivity growth because of new inventions—can, of course, cause real GDP to fluctuate. Recall that **real business cycle theory** places great emphasis on shifts in potential GDP. Although a price shock might be accompanied by a shift in potential GDP, it need not be. In this case, we are looking at departures of real GDP from potential GDP and thus focusing on price shocks.

real business cycle theory
a theory of macroeconomics that stresses that shifts in potential GDP are a primary cause of fluctuations in real GDP; the shifts in potential GDP usually are assumed to be caused by changes in technology. (Ch. 11)

The Effect of Price Shocks

How does our theory of economic fluctuations allow us to predict the effect of price shocks? The impact of a price shock can be illustrated graphically, as shown in Figure 13-6. In the case of a large increase in oil prices, for example, the inflation adjustment line will shift up to a higher level of inflation. A large increase in oil prices at first will lead to an increase in the price of everything that uses oil in production: heating homes, gasoline, airplane fuel, airfares, plastic toys, and many other things. The overall inflation rate is affected. When the inflation rate rises, the inflation adjustment line must shift up.

The immediate impact of the shock is to lower real GDP, as the intersection of the inflation adjustment line with the aggregate demand curve moves to the left. This result occurs because the higher inflation rate causes the central bank to raise interest rates, reducing investment spending and net exports.

With real GDP below potential GDP, however, the reduction in spending will put pressure on firms to adjust their prices. The lower price increases bring about a lower

Figure 13-6

A Price Shock
Initially, inflation and the *IA* line rise because of a shock to oil or agricultural prices. This causes real GDP to fall. With real GDP below potential GDP, inflation begins to decline. As inflation declines, real GDP returns to potential GDP.

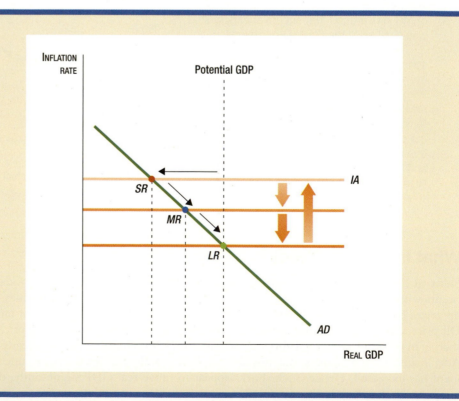

rate of inflation. Thus, in the period following the rise of inflation, we begin to see a reversal. Inflation starts to decline. As inflation falls, interest rates begin to decline, and the economy starts to recover again. The rate of inflation will return to where it was before the price shock.

Temporary Shifts in the Inflation Adjustment Line In this analysis of the price shock, the central bank raises interest rates, and the resulting decline in real GDP exerts a countervailing force to reduce inflation. It is possible for some price shocks to have only a temporary effect on inflation. Such a temporary effect can be shown graphically as a rise followed by a quick fall in the inflation adjustment line. In such a situation—in which case the price shock would be expected to automatically reverse itself—it would be wise for the central bank to delay raising the interest rate. Then if the price shock has only a temporary effect on inflation, the decline in real GDP can be avoided. In reality, whenever a price shock occurs, a great debate results about whether it will have a temporary or a permanent effect on inflation. The debate is rarely settled until after the fact.

Price shocks also can occur when commodity prices fall. In this case, the inflation adjustment line would shift downward—just the opposite of the case of an increase in commodity prices—and this would cause real GDP to rise as the Fed lowered interest rates. For example, in the later part of 2008, oil prices declined. This resulted in a temporary decrease in inflation and a rise in real GDP—exactly what would be predicted by the theory of economic fluctuations.

Stagflation An important difference between price shocks and demand shocks is that, in the case of a price shock, output declines while inflation rises. With demand shocks, inflation and output are positively related over the period of recession and recovery. The situation in which inflation is up and real GDP is down is called **stagflation**. As we have shown, price shocks can lead to stagflation.

stagflation
the situation in which high inflation and high unemployment occur simultaneously.

REVIEW

- A price shock is a large change in the price of some key commodity like oil. Such shocks can push real GDP below potential GDP.

- In the aftermath of a price shock, the interest rate rises. Eventually, with real GDP below potential GDP, inflation begins to come down, and the economy recovers.

Using the Economic Fluctuations Model to Understand the Recent Recession

By now you should be comfortable with using the economic fluctuations model in a general setting to examine the impact of particular economic events—changes in fiscal policy, monetary policy, consumer behavior, or price shocks—in isolation. What the economic fluctuations model is most useful for, however, is to understand actual economic developments in which many things change, often simultaneously, in the economy. In this section, we show how the model can explain what brought about the recession that began in late 2007. We also can show how the model could be used to understand the policies that were implemented to help the recovery phase that began when the recession ended in June 2009.

What Caused the Recession?

Historically, economists do not always agree on what factors triggered a particular recession; a good example is the recession that began at the end of 2007 and especially its subsequent worsening in 2008. Some of the factors mentioned include the following:

1. *Collapse of the Housing Bubble.* A long period of rapidly rising housing prices came to an end. The slowdown and a subsequent sharp fall in housing sales, starts, and prices led to rising foreclosures, lower consumer spending, and large-scale layoffs in housing and construction-related jobs.
2. *Financial Crisis.* Sharp falls in the value of mortgage loans had a negative impact on the financial health of banks, investment banks, and mortgage lenders, leading to the collapse of several leading financial institutions.
3. *Credit Crunch.* Substantial cutbacks in lending as the remaining banks and financial institutions became extremely cautious about making new loans to nongovernmental entities, leading to a sharp curtailment of economic activity because of the lack of credit.
4. *Commodity Price Inflation.* Substantial increases in commodity prices and, especially, the price of gasoline in 2007 and the early part of 2008 eating into consumer expenditure.
5. *Stock Market Collapse.* Sharp decreases in stock markets in the United States and worldwide, on the order of 30–50 percent in 2008, substantially eroding wealth and retirement portfolios of consumers.
6. *Greater Uncertainty.* A substantial rise in uncertainty, as consumers worried about their job security, retirement income, and ability to afford mortgage payments on their homes began to cut back on their purchases; firms concerned about access to credit, deteriorating sales conditions, and concerns about the sharp decline in stock prices cut back on investment projects; and state and local governments operating under balanced budget requirements faced shortfalls in tax revenue and rising demand for income support programs for the needy.

If we are to accurately understand the causes of the recession, we need to look at the period leading up to the onset of the recession to understand what might have precipitated these events. The classic explanation of financial crises, going back hundreds of years, is that they are caused by excesses—frequently monetary excesses—which lead to a boom and an inevitable bust. In the recent crisis, then, it was monetary excesses that created the conditions for the housing boom (although much of the responsibility of the subsequent spillover of that boom into the financial industry has to be shared with the decision makers at the firms that collapsed or suffered in the subsequent bust). In terms of the federal funds interest rate, from 2000 to 2006, the Federal Reserve lowered its inflation target in a manner that was inconsistent with the type of policy that it had followed fairly regularly during the previous 20-year period of good economic performance (see the Economics in Action box "How Much Did Monetary Policy Excesses Contribute to the Housing Bubble and Bust?").

Figure 13-7 provides a graphic analysis of how these factors can be represented using the economic fluctuations model. The boom in spending can be modeled as a rightward shift of the AD curve from AD_1 to AD_2. This first causes real GDP to rise above potential GDP, then leads to rising inflation as the IA line shifts up gradually. Two intersections of the AD curve and the IA line, labeled SR_1 and MR_1, show this movement. This is the period leading up to the onset of recession, when the U.S. economy still seemed to be doing well, with the main concern being signs of rising inflation.

Figure 13-7 then shows a shift in the AD curve to the left as the housing bubble collapses and consumers and firms cut back on their spending in the face of dwindling wealth, greater uncertainty, and lack of access to credit. The rise in commodity prices causes the *IA* line to shift up as well. The combination of these shifts causes a recession, with real GDP falling well below potential GDP, and this is shown on the diagram as SR_2.

The time-series sketches in the lower part of the figure show the movement in real GDP that is traced out by the combination of these shifts. If you compare these fluctuations in real GDP with what actually happened, you will see a close resemblance.

How to Recover from the Recession

The basic analysis we have done with the economic fluctuations model shows us that when an economy goes into recession, it eventually will recover on its own as inflation falls gradually over time and the Federal Reserve lowers real interest rates to facilitate the recovery. The recovery will be further aided if some of the factors that precipitated the initial downturn, such as a rise in commodity prices or cutbacks in consumer and firm spending driven by uncertainty, reverse themselves.

It is very likely, however, that policy makers would like to take steps to speed up this recovery process further, leading to substantial changes in fiscal and monetary policy designed to boost aggregate demand in the economy. This was indeed the case in the 2008–2009 recession, with the Fed lowering interest rates rapidly until the nominal interest rate reached zero, and the government implementing a $152 billion and a $787 billion stimulus package of spending increases and tax cuts in 2008 and 2009, respectively. In addition, the price of commodities decreased drastically in the fall of 2008, and the Fed, in conjunction with the U.S. Treasury Department, created a package to ease the woes of the banking sector and enable more credit to flow to support economic activity.

We can use the economic fluctuations model to show how a combination of lower commodity prices, increases in government spending and tax cuts, and a decision by the Federal Reserve to lower interest rates preemptively—that is, to tolerate a higher inflation target if it meant that the lack of credit in the economy would be eased by the lower interest rates—could help the economy return to potential output.

Figure 13-8 provides a graphic analysis of how these factors can be represented using the economic fluctuations model. The combination of falling commodity prices and the gradual fall in inflation over time as a result of the economy being below

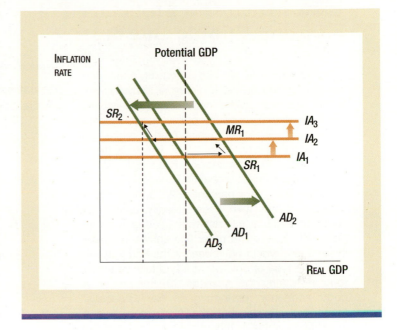

Figure 13-7

Explaining the Onset of the Recession

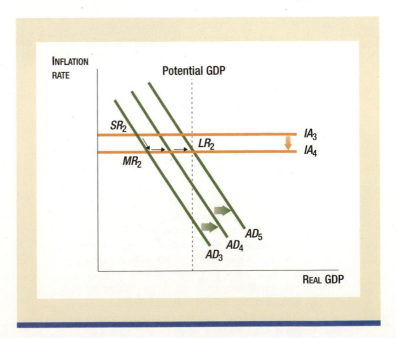

Figure 13-8

Recovering from the Recession

ECONOMICS *IN ACTION*

How Much Did Monetary Policy Excesses Contribute to the Housing Bubble and Bust?

In the recent crisis, we had a housing boom and bust, which in turn led to financial turmoil in the United States and other countries. Some economists argue that monetary policy excesses were the main cause of the housing market boom and the resulting bust. Figure 13-9, which is taken from *The Economist* magazine, is a simple way to illustrate the story of monetary excesses. The line that dips down to 1 percent in 2003, stays there into 2004, and then rises steadily until 2006 shows the actual interest rate decisions of the Federal Reserve. The other line shows what the interest rate would have been if the Fed had followed the type of policy that it had followed fairly regularly during the previous 20-year period of good economic performance. *The Economist* magazine calls this line the Taylor rule: It is a smoothed version of the interest rate one gets by plugging actual inflation and GDP into a policy rule that John Taylor proposed in 1992. According to Taylor, this rule is a good description of the policy that worked well during the Great Moderation beginning in the early 1980s.

Figure 13-9 shows that the actual interest rate decisions fell well below what historical experience would suggest policy should be. It thus provides empirical evidence of monetary excesses during the period leading up to the housing boom. The unusually low interest rate decisions were purposeful deviations by the Fed from the "regular" interest rate settings based on the usual macroeconomic variables. The Fed used transparent language to describe the decisions, saying, for example, that interest rates would be low for "a considerable period" and that they would rise slowly at a "measured pace," which were ways to clarify that the decisions were deviations from that rule in some sense.

The low interest rate environment is connected to the housing price boom. Figure 13-10 shows the number of new housing construction projects in the United States since 2000. The five-year period between 2001 and 2006, which showed the largest deviations of actual Fed policy from the ideal, is also the period when new U.S. housing construction projects rose extremely sharply, before eventually collapsing. The line labeled "Counterfactual" in Figure 13-10 shows what housing starts would have been had policy followed the historic ideal presented in Figure 13-9.

Figure 13-9

Deviations of Actual Fed Policy Decisions from Historical Ideal

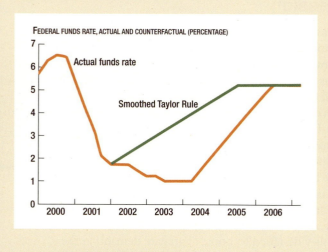

Source: The Economist, October 18, 2007.

Figure 13-10

The Boom and Bust in Housing Starts

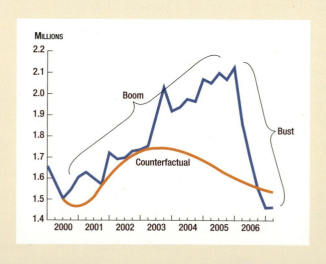

In periods of low interest rates, excessive risk taking is more likely. First, people are likely to take on bigger mortgages at the (temporarily) lower interest rates without full consideration about how to repay those mortgages, were rates to increase. Banks and other financial institutions encourage this behavior because credit is plentiful and even the low mortgage rates are much higher than the interest rates they could earn by lending money to other banks in the federal funds market. Finally, rising house prices create their own momentum as more and more people are drawn into the housing market by the prospect of owning something whose value is rising rapidly. Thus, an interaction exists between the monetary excesses and the risk-taking excesses. This example illustrates how unintended consequences can result when policy deviates from the norm.

potential output will move the *IA* line down from the intersection of the *AD* curve and the *IA* line, labeled SR_2 (where the analysis in Figure 13-7 left off) to the new intersection shown as MR_2. The figure then shows two shifts out of the *AD* curve to the right as the Fed resorts to a large preemptive cut of interest rates and the government implements a stimulus package. The combination of these shifts moves real GDP back to potential GDP, shown on the diagram as LR_2.

The portrait of recovery laid out in Figure 13-8 does not actually match the experience of the U.S. economy, which is still well below potential output almost 18 months after the recession ended. This sluggish recovery can be attributed to the complexity of the current macroeconomic situation facing the United States. Some of these complexities include the constraints imposed by the fact that nominal interest rates are zero, the doubts about the speed or extent of the economic impact of the nearly $1 trillion stimulus package, or the complexities of rescuing the banking sector without rewarding the bad behavior that led to the crisis in the first place. Others can be attributed to the fact that commodity prices started to rise again, that consumers and investors remain cautious even though the recession has ended and to the fact that problems in the banking sector and the housing market still have not sorted themselves out as large numbers of homes have been foreclosed on and remain unsold as property of the banks.

CONCLUSION

Using a diagram with the aggregate demand curve and the inflation adjustment line, we can explain not only the first steps toward recessions but also the economy's recovery. The model works well in explaining actual economic fluctuations and thus is useful for analyzing macroeconomic policy, as we do in Chapters 14 and 15.

This model implies that real GDP returns toward potential GDP in the long run, which is an attractive feature of the model because, in reality, all recessions have ended. Real GDP appears to fluctuate around potential GDP rather than getting stuck forever in a recession. The tendency for real GDP to return toward potential GDP allows us to use the theory of long-run growth when discussing long-run trends in the economy. As the economy fluctuates, potential GDP gradually increases over time.

KEY POINTS

1. Using the economic fluctuations model is much like using the supply and demand model in microeconomics. You need to understand whether a particular change in the economy is reflected in a shift of the aggregate demand curve or the inflation adjustment

line, as well as the direction in which the respective curves shift.

2. An increase in government purchases temporarily causes real GDP to rise, but eventually real GDP returns to potential GDP.
3. A decline in government purchases temporarily reduces real GDP, but over time, the economy recovers.
4. Shifts in monetary policy, including explicit attempts to disinflate or reinflate, cause real GDP to depart from potential GDP temporarily. Eventually, real GDP returns to potential GDP and only the inflation rate is changed.
5. Price shocks can cause recessions. A price shock that raises the inflation rate will cause the interest rate to rise and real GDP to fall.
6. If the Fed sets interest rates according to a monetary policy rule, then it will raise interest rates following a rise in inflation and eventually inflation will come back down.
7. If a price shock is clearly temporary, then the Fed should not change the interest rate.
8. Shifts of the aggregate demand curve and the inflation adjustment line trace out actual observations fairly closely. Thus, the economic fluctuations model works well, but, like most models in economics and elsewhere, it is not perfect.

KEY TERMS

deflation, 312
demand shocks, 314
disinflation, 312
price shocks, 315

real business cycle theory, 316
reinflation, 314
stagflation, 317

QUESTIONS FOR REVIEW

1. What causes the economy to recover after a recession?
2. What is the difference between the long-run and short-run effects of a change in government spending?
3. What is disinflation, and how does the central bank bring it about?
4. What is reinflation, and what impact does it have on real GDP in the short run and the long run?
5. What is a price shock, and why have price shocks frequently been followed by increases in unemployment?

6. What is the difference between a price shock and a supply shock?
7. Why do monetary policy errors lead to economic fluctuations?
8. In what way is the economic fluctuations model discussed in this chapter consistent with real-world observations?

PROBLEMS

1. Using the aggregate demand curve and the inflation adjustment line, describe what would happen to real GDP and inflation in the short run, in the medium run, and in the long run if the government increased spending permanently. Assume that the economy was initially at potential output before the increase. Be sure to provide an economic explanation for your results.
2. Consider an economy that is at potential output. Using the aggregate demand curve and the inflation adjustment line, describe what would

happen to real GDP and inflation in the short run, in the medium run, and in the long run if the government cut spending on defense. Be sure to provide an economic explanation for your results.
3. For each of the scenarios in Problems 1 and 2, describe what would happen to consumption, investment, and net exports in the short run and in the long run.
4. Suppose that an increase in government spending had the long-run effects that you described in Problem 1. If the central bank wants to return to

the original inflation rate that existed before the increase, how can it achieve its objective? Describe the proposed change in policy and its short-run, medium-run, and long-run effects on real GDP and inflation.

5. Suppose gasoline prices increase sharply when the time comes for you to graduate. Use the economic fluctuations model to explain why you might have difficulty in finding a job in the six months after you graduate.

6. The economy begins at potential GDP with an inflation rate of 2 percent. Suppose a price shock pushes inflation up to 6 percent in the short run, but the Fed views the effect on inflation as temporary. It expects the inflation adjustment line to shift back down to 2 percent the next year, and in fact, the inflation adjustment line does shift back down.

   a. If the Fed follows its usual policy rule, where will real GDP be in the short run? How does the economy adjust back to potential?

   b. Now suppose that because the Fed is sure that this inflationary shock is only temporary, it decides not to follow its typical policy rule, but instead maintains the interest rate at its previous level. What happens to real GDP? Why? What will the long-run adjustment be

in this case? Do you agree with the Fed's handling of the situation?

7. Suppose that two countries are similar except that one has a central bank with a higher target inflation rate. The two countries have identical potential GDP and are both at their long-run equilibrium. Explain this situation by using two diagrams with an aggregate demand curve and an inflation adjustment line. Explain how these different equilibrium levels of inflation are possible.

8. If U.S. productivity increases, what will happen to potential GDP? What will happen to the inflation rate?

9. Would an increase in government spending lead to a higher rate of inflation in the long run? Show that the answer depends on where the economy was, relative to potential GDP, before the increase.

10. China's economy has seen dramatic increases in investment, consumer spending, government expenditure on infrastructure, and exports to the United States and to Europe. Inflation in China, however, has remained fairly moderate. Explain why this may be the case using the aggregate demand curve and the inflation adjustment line.

14 Fiscal Policy

I n response to the recession that began in December 2007 and ended in June 2009, Presidents George W. Bush and Barack Obama both proposed—and convinced the Congress to enact—countercyclical fiscal policy legislation with the express purpose of stimulating the economy. In February 2008 President Bush signed the $152 billion Economic Stimulus Act, which included direct payments to individuals and families so that they would increase consumption and thereby jump-start the economy. A year later President Barack Obama signed the much larger $787 billion American Recovery and Reinvestment Act of 2009, which included not only payments to individuals and families but also grants to the state and local governments to finance increased infrastructure and other spending.

Even though ostensibly aimed at helping the economy recover from recession, these fiscal policy packages generated substantial policy disagreements and controversy. Critics of the 2008 stimulus bill argued that people used at best a small fraction of the stimulus funds to increase consumption. Critics of the 2009 stimulus argued that the funds sent to the states were not used to increase infrastructure spending and

thereby did not jump-start government purchases of goods and services. Proponents of the legislation argued that the recession would have been much worse without the fiscal policy actions.

Soon after these short-run stimulus packages were passed another fiscal policy issue took center stage: the large government budget deficits and growing federal debt. In part, because the payments to individuals or the grants to the states were financed by issuing more debt, the growing debt was caused by the stimulus packages. But the seeds of the debt problem were planted before the recession when legislation was passed that implied increased spending in the future. But here, too, controversy exists, with some claiming that the debt is not such a problem and others arguing that insufficient taxes rather than spending is the main cause of the deficit and debt.

In this chapter, we examine the economic theories and facts that bear on the controversies over short-term countercyclical fiscal policy and the problem of long-term debt. We begin by reviewing how federal government decisions are made whether about spending, tax revenues, the deficit, or the debt.

The Government Budget

The **federal budget** is the major document describing fiscal policy in the United States. The budget includes the estimates of the surplus or deficit that get so much attention as well as proposals for taxes and spending. Let's look at how the federal budget in the United States is put together.

federal budget
a summary of the federal government's proposals for spending, taxes, and the deficit.

Setting the Annual Budget

In the United States, the president submits a new budget to Congress each year for the following fiscal year. The fiscal year runs from October to October. For example, *The Budget of the United States: Fiscal Year 2012* applies to spending and taxes from October 1, 2011, through September 30, 2012. It was submitted to Congress by the president in February 2011. The president typically devotes part of the State of the Union address to describing the budget and fiscal policy. Also at the start of each year, the Council of Economic Advisers (CEA) prepares and releases the *Economic Report of the President*, providing the economic forecasts underlying the budget. The Congressional Budget Office (CBO) makes its own economic forecasts.

In putting together the federal budget, the president proposes specific spending programs that fit into an overall philosophy of what the government should be doing. In any one year, however, most of the spending in the budget is determined by ongoing programs, which the president usually can do little to change. For example, payments of social security benefits to retired people are a large item in the budget, but the amount of spending on social security depends on how many people are eligible. As more people retire, spending automatically goes up unless the social security law is changed. Thus, in reality, the president can change only a small part of the budget each year, unless new legislation is passed.

A Balanced Budget versus a Deficit or Surplus Taxes to pay for the spending programs also are included in the budget. As part of the budget, the president may propose an increase or a decrease in taxes. *Tax revenues* are the total dollar amount the government receives from taxpayers each year. When tax revenues are exactly equal to spending, there is a **balanced budget**. When tax revenues are greater than spending, there is a **budget surplus**. When spending is greater than tax revenues, there is a **budget deficit**, and the government must borrow to pay the difference.

balanced budget
a budget in which tax revenues equal spending.

budget surplus
the amount by which tax revenues exceed government spending.

Budget Deficit	Budget Balance	Budget Surplus
Tax revenues < spending	Tax revenues = spending	Tax revenues > spending

budget deficit
the amount by which government spending exceeds tax revenues.

The Proposed Budget versus the Actual Budget Keep in mind that the budget the president submits is only a *proposal*. The actual amounts of tax revenues and spending during the fiscal year are quite different from what is proposed. There are two main reasons for this difference.

First, Congress usually modifies the president's budget, adding programs and deleting others. Congress deliberates on the specific items in the president's budget proposal for months before the fiscal year actually starts. After the president's budget has been debated and modified, it is passed by Congress. Only when the president signs the legislation is the budget enacted into law. Because of this congressional modification, the enacted budget is always different from the proposed budget. Figure 14-1 shows the budget moving from a proposal to completion. The same *budget cycle* occurs every year, but it does not always progress smoothly. In many years the president and Congress do not settle on a budget until well into the fiscal year.

Second, because of changes in the economy and other unanticipated events such as wars and natural disasters, the actual amounts of spending and taxes will be different

REMINDER
Note the difference between tax rate and tax revenues. For the income tax, if the average tax rate is 20 percent and income is $3,000 billion, then tax revenues are $600 billion.

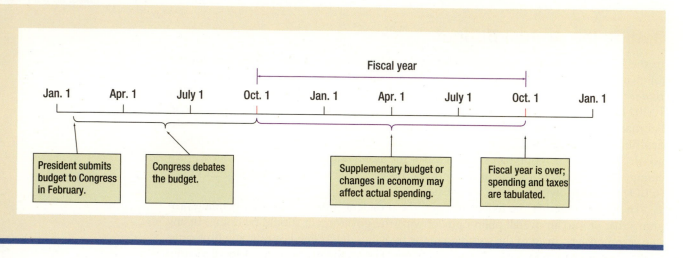

Figure 14-1

A Typical Budget Cycle

The budget cycle begins well before the fiscal year begins. After considering various spending and tax options, the president submits a budget proposal to the Congress in February. The cycle is not complete until the end of the fiscal year. By then, a new budget is being enacted.

from what is enacted. After the fiscal year has begun and the budget has been enacted, various *supplementals* are proposed and passed. A supplemental is a change in a spending program or a change in the tax law that affects the budget in the current fiscal year.

A Look at the Federal Budget

Table 14-1 contains a summary of tax revenues and expenditure for the federal budget for fiscal year 2011.

The Deficit Table 14-1 shows more expenditures than tax revenues, so there is a deficit. Budget deficits have been common in the United States for many years, although 1998 to 2001 were years of surplus. Deficits are projected to continue in the future unless government programs change. Figure 14-2 shows the deficit in recent years and projections into the future. It also shows tax revenue and spending.

Taxes and Spending Sources of tax revenue include *personal income taxes* paid by individuals on their total income, *corporate income taxes* paid by businesses on their profits, and *payroll taxes,* a percentage of wages paid by workers and their employers that supports government programs such as social security. Payroll taxes provide a large amount of revenues, nearly as much as personal income tax revenues.

On the expenditure side of the budget, one must distinguish between *purchases* of goods and services (such as defense), *transfer payments* (such as social security and Medicare and Medicaid), and *interest payments*. Only purchases are included in the symbol *G* that we have been using in the text. Purchases represent *new* production, whether of computers, federal courthouses, or food for military troops.

Interest payments are what the federal government pays every year on its debt. The government pays interest on its borrowings just like anyone

Table 14-1

FY 2011 Federal Tax Revenues and Expenditures
(billions of dollars)

Tax revenues	2,228	
Personal income		998
Corporate income		201
Payroll		819
Other		210
Expenditures	3,708	
Social security		727
Medicare and Medicaid		846
Defense		712
Interest		225
Other		1,198
Deficit	1,480	

Source: Office of Management and Budget.

Figure 14-2

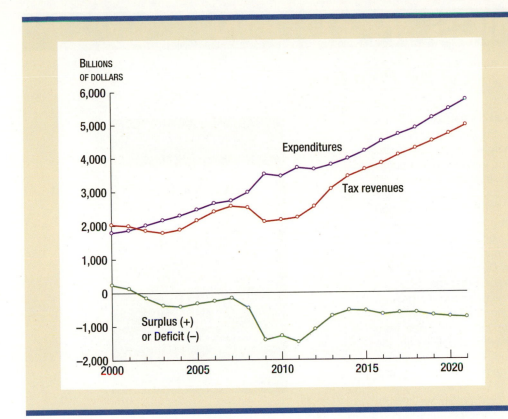

Federal Tax Revenues, Expenditures, and the Surplus or Deficit 2000–2021

The surplus turned to deficit in 2002 as tax revenues fell while spending continued to increase. After nearly reaching a surplus in 2007, the deficit then grew larger as spending rose and tax revenues fell in the 2007–2009 recession.

else. Total interest payments equal the interest rate multiplied by the amount of government debt outstanding. For example, if the interest rate on government debt is 5 percent and total outstanding debt held by the public is $5,000 billion, then interest payments would be $250 billion (0.05 × $5,000).

A significant part of the budget—nearly 50 percent—consists of social security, Medicare, and Medicaid. Social security and Medicare provide income and health care for the elderly, and Medicaid provides health care for people and families with very low incomes. Under current law, federal spending is projected to grow rapidly because of the increase in spending on these programs as the baby boomers retire and then live longer, and spending on health care increases. If Congress and the president do not change the law to either reduce the growth of spending or increase tax revenue, then the federal deficit will grow much larger in the future.

The Federal Debt

The **federal debt** is the total amount of outstanding loans that the federal government owes. If the government runs a surplus, the debt comes down by the amount of the surplus. If the government has a deficit, the debt goes up by the amount of the deficit.

Consider an example involving thousands of dollars rather than trillions of dollars. Think of a student, Sam, who graduates from college with a $14,000 outstanding loan. In other words, he has a debt of $14,000. Suppose that the first year he works, his income is $30,000, but he spends $35,000. Sam's deficit for that year is $5,000, and his debt rises to $19,000. Assume that in his second year of work, he has an income of $35,000 and spends $38,000; his deficit is $3,000, and his debt rises to $22,000. Each

federal debt
the total amount of outstanding loans owed by the federal government.

ECONOMICS IN ACTION

The *Economic Report of the President*

Early each year, the president of the United States issues an economic report, which contains the economic forecast for the year prepared by the president's CEA. Most economic reports are filled with interesting economic facts and applications to the pressing fiscal policy issues of the day.

President John Kennedy's 1963 *Economic Report* made the case for his tax cuts, arguing that "it is appropriate to reduce significantly the highest income tax rates at the same time that a more comprehensive tax base is provided." Nearly 20 years later, President Ronald Reagan's 1982 *Economic Report* argued that the lower tax rates he advocated would stimulate economic growth. President Bill Clinton's 1994 *Economic Report* presented the case for "shifting federal spending priorities from consumption to investment," a key fiscal policy principle of his administration. These and the latest economic reports are available online at fraser.stlouisfed.org and are worth reviewing.

The *Economic Report of the President* always attracts news attention and sometimes generates huge controversy. For example, the 2004 *Economic Report* explained, as part of an argument in favor of international trade, why distinguishing between a manufacturing job and a service job is difficult, saying that making a hamburger—a service job—was really a lot like manufacturing. The innocent comparison generated a tidal wave of ridicule because it sounded like the president's advisers were belittling the decline in manufacturing jobs in the United States. A CBS News report was headlined "Building Blue-Collar ... Burgers? Bush Report: Fast Food Work a Form of Manufacturing?" It said:

> The annual economic report—most of which consists of charts and statistics—has been the focus of unusual scrutiny this year, perhaps reflecting the presidential campaign and concern about the lack of job creation despite an ongoing recovery.... "When a good or service is produced at lower cost

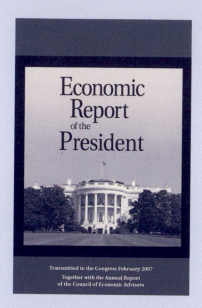

Economic Report of the President

Transmitted to the Congress February 2007
Together with the Annual Report
of the Council of Economic Advisers

in another country, it makes sense to import it rather than to produce it domestically. This allows the United States to devote its resources to more productive purposes," the report read. The statement, which reflects standard economic theory about the efficiencies of trade, was denounced by Democrats and Republicans alike. "These people, what planet do they live on?" asked Democratic presidential candidate and North Carolina Sen. John Edwards. Even Republican House Speaker Dennis Hastert wrote to the White House protesting the claim.

Not surprisingly all the reports since the 2004 *Economic Report* have been given extra scrutiny by the White House to prevent such embarrassing attention, but they continue to be a valuable resource in which you can read about economics being used in action.

year his debt rises by the amount of his deficit. In the third year, Sam earns $40,000 and spends $33,000; he has a surplus of $7,000. This would reduce his debt to $15,000.

The laws of accounting that we apply to Sam also apply to Uncle Sam. A federal government deficit of $1 trillion means that the outstanding government debt increases by $1 trillion. Figure 14-3 shows the debt along with the deficit in the United States for two decades. The first decade is history as tabulated by federal government economists. The years from 2012 to 2021 are forecasts made by government economists in 2011.

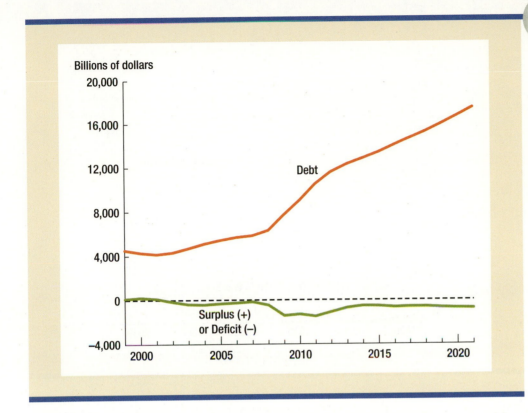

Figure 14-3

The Government Debt and Deficit

When there is a deficit, the debt increases. When there is a surplus, the debt falls. After a brief period in which government debt fell, the rate of increase has picked up significantly in the past few years.

For most of these years the debt increases because there are deficits. Observe, however, that the debt declined in 2000 and 2001 when there was a surplus. The debt then started increasing again. It rose particularly sharply during the 2007–2009 recession, but it is projected to continue increasing in the future long after that recession ended.

If Congress and the president do not change the law to either reduce the growth of spending or increase tax revenue, then the federal deficit will remain and the debt will continue to grow rapidly. As the debt grows, interest payments on the debt also will grow and absorb an ever larger share of the spending, leaving a smaller share for government to provide public goods and a social safety net.

As the government debt increases other problems occur. History shows that governments with high debt are prone to financial crises, which has been evident in Greece in recent years as many Americans have noticed. In fact, excessive debt in Greece, Ireland, Portugal, and Spain put the whole of Europe into a financial crisis. One concern is that holders of the debt lose confidence and refuse to continue financing the deficit. From the time of the first U.S. secretary of the treasury, Alexander Hamilton, the United States has established a strong reputation for paying its debts, but that credibility could decline if actions are not taken to control the growth of the debt. In addition, because foreign governments hold nearly one-half of the federal debt, people are concerned that they suddenly might sell the debt and cause an international crisis. Because of these concerns, interest has been renewed in dealing with the problem and politicians in Washington have begun to look for solutions.

The Debt-to-GDP Ratio When looking at the debt and the deficit over time, it is important to consider the size of the economy. For example, a $3 trillion debt may not be much of a problem for an economy with a gross domestic product (GDP) of $10 trillion but could be overwhelming for an economy with a GDP of $1 trillion. An easy way

Figure 14-4

Debt as a Percentage of GDP

The debt history since the founding of the United States is shown along with future projections by the CBO. Debt as a percentage of GDP normally has increased in major war periods, such as World War II, but then declined as the deficit is reduced and GDP grows. The projection is made under the assumption that the federal law for Medicare, social security, and taxes as of 2010 does not change. To prevent this disastrous scenario, budget reforms are required.

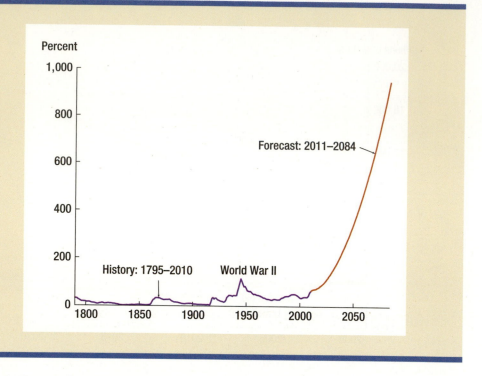

debt-to-GDP ratio

the total amount of outstanding loans the federal government owes divided by nominal GDP.

to compare the debt to the size of the economy is to measure the debt as a percentage of GDP—the **debt-to-GDP ratio**. It is appropriate to consider the ratio of debt to nominal GDP rather than real GDP because the debt is stated in current dollars, just as nominal GDP is.

Figure 14-4 shows the history of the debt as a percentage of GDP in the United States since 1795 and projections by the CBO into the future. Note that the debt was a high percentage of GDP at the end of World War II because the U.S. government had borrowed large amounts to finance its military expenditures during the war. The debt-to-GDP ratio rose in the 1980s and then leveled off and fell in the 1990s, but it began to increase again when deficits returned. Unless budget reforms are put in place, the debt will explode in the future.

State and Local Government Budgets

Much of the government spending and taxation in the United States occurs outside of the federal government, in state and local governments. Although fiscal policy usually refers to the plans of the federal government, it is the combined action of federal, state, and local governments that has an impact on the overall economy. For example, during the 2007–2009 recession, many states cut back on spending, which would tend to reduce real GDP in the short run, just as reduced spending at the federal level would. The 2009 stimulus bill included hundreds of billions in assistance to state or local government intended to ward off cuts. Taken as a whole, state and local governments are a large force in the economy. In 2004 state and local government expenditures were about two-thirds of federal government expenditures.

Most of the state and local government expenditures are for public schools, local police, fire services, and roads. Observe that state and local government *purchases* of goods and services are larger than federal government purchases, especially when national defense is excluded.

Like the federal government, the state and local governments, on average, have been running deficits after a few years of surpluses in the late 1990s. These deficits worsened dramatically during the 2008 recession.

Countercyclical Fiscal Policy

Government spending and taxes are called the *instruments* of fiscal policy. They are the variables that affect the economy. Now let's see how changes in the instruments of fiscal policy affect the size of economic fluctuations.

Impacts of the Instruments of Fiscal Policy

We first consider a change in government purchases and then go on to consider a change in taxes.

Changes in Government Purchases
We know that if a change occurs in government purchases, real GDP initially will change. If real GDP equaled potential GDP at the time of the change in government purchases, then real GDP would move away from potential GDP. Hence, a first lesson about fiscal policy is "do no harm." Erratic changes in government purchases can lead to fluctuations of real GDP away from potential GDP.

But suppose real GDP was already away from potential GDP. Then the change in government purchases could move real GDP closer to potential GDP. This is shown in Figure 14-5. In the top panel, real GDP starts out below potential GDP. An increase in government purchases shifts the aggregate demand curve to the right and moves real GDP back toward potential GDP. In the bottom panel, real GDP is above potential GDP, and a decrease in government purchases shifts the aggregate demand curve to the left, bringing real GDP back toward potential GDP. The important point is that a change in government purchases shifts the aggregate demand curve from wherever it happens to be at the time of the change.

Remember that these government purchases will make a difference for real GDP only in the short term. Had the government not intervened, prices eventually would have adjusted; consumption, investment, and net exports would have changed; and real GDP would have returned to potential GDP, albeit with a lower inflation rate in the top panel of Figure 14-5, and a higher inflation rate in the bottom panel. The short-term effect, however, may have partially offset a temporary decline in aggregate demand in a recession. So the short-run impacts of government purchases provide fiscal policy with the potential power to reduce the size of economic fluctuations.

Figure 14-5

Effect of a Change in Government Purchases

If real GDP is below potential GDP, as in the top panel, an increase in government purchases, which shifts the *AD* curve to the right, will move real GDP toward potential GDP. If real GDP is above potential GDP, as in the bottom panel, a decrease in government purchases will move real GDP toward potential GDP. These are short-run effects.

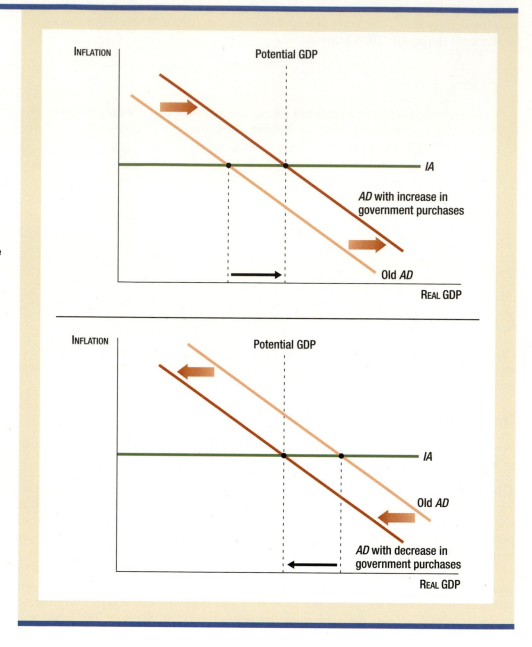

An increase in government purchases on roads and bridges is one example of how changes in government spending could affect investment and therefore impact potential GDP in the long run. But, for now, we focus on how the government can move the economy closer to potential GDP, rather than on how it can move potential GDP through fiscal policy changes.

Changes in Taxes A change in taxes also affects real GDP in the short run. At any given level of real GDP, people will consume less if taxes increase because they have less income to spend after taxes. They will consume more if taxes are cut. In either case, the aggregate demand curve will shift. The top panel of Figure 14-6 shows how a tax cut will shift the aggregate demand curve to the right and push real GDP closer to potential GDP if it is below potential GDP. The bottom panel shows a tax increase reducing real

GDP from a position above potential GDP. Again, these are short-term effects. Prices eventually will adjust and real GDP will return to potential GDP.

Both increases and decreases in taxes also can affect potential GDP. For example, if an increase in tax rates causes some people to work less, then the labor supply will not be as large and potential GDP will be lower. Again, our focus here is on the departures of real GDP from potential GDP.

Countercyclical Fiscal Policy

As the analysis in Figures 14-5 and 14-6 shows, fiscal policy, in principle, can offset the impact of shocks that push real GDP away from potential GDP because government

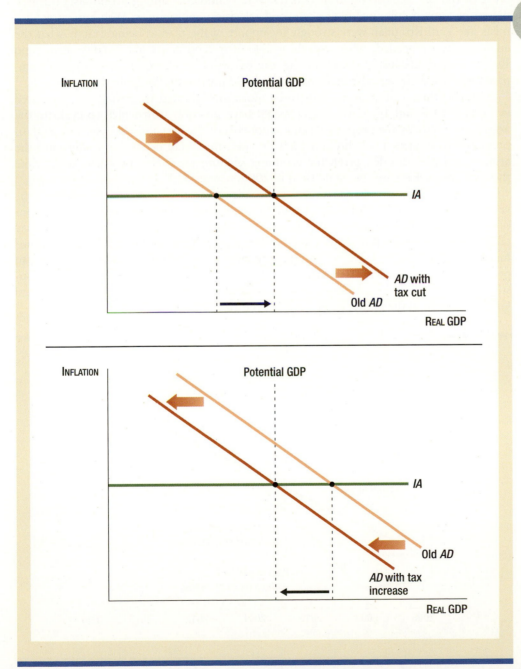

Figure 14-6

Effects of a Change in Taxes

A decrease in taxes shifts the *AD* curve to the right and can move real GDP toward potential GDP, as in the top panel. An increase in taxes moves real GDP toward potential GDP in the lower panel.

countercyclical policy
a policy designed to offset the fluctuations in the business cycle.

spending and taxes affect real GDP in the short run. Such use of fiscal policy is called **countercyclical policy**, because the cyclical movements in the economy are being "countered," or offset, by changes in government spending or taxes. Recessions can be countered by cuts in taxes or increases in spending. The stimulus package of 2009 was a good example of a countercyclical fiscal policy—a $787 billion package of government spending increases and tax cuts that aimed to help the U.S. economy recover from a deep recession by increasing real GDP and moving the economy closer to potential output.

But why would such an intervention be controversial? Clearly, Republicans and Democrats disagreed strongly about the 2009 stimulus package with only three Republican senators and no Republican members of the House of Representatives voting in favor of the bill. Similar vigorous debates were conducted among economists through newspaper op-ed columns, blog posts, and television appearances. Well-known economists like Paul Krugman were strongly in support of the plan as being exactly what the ailing economy needed, while equally well-known economists like Eugene Fama and Robert Barro were just as confident that the bill would do little for the economy compared with the long-term budgetary costs it would impose on the United States.

Clearly, then, our analysis needs to be more sophisticated than what was presented in Figures 14-5 and 14-6, or else we would have no tools with which to evaluate the arguments made by the proponents and opponents of the stimulus package. The analysis presented in Figures 14-7 through 14-9 provides the detail needed to understand the arguments on both sides, given the economic circumstances that prevailed at the time the stimulus package was being debated in 2009.

Figure 14-7 shows what a stimulus policy ideally would do. A deep recession in the year 2009 is shown. Without any change in government purchases or taxes, the economy would eventually recover, as shown in the figure, even though the recovery may take four or five years. But suppose the government implements the $787 billion stimulus plan with its mix of spending on infrastructure, aid to state governments so they can provide money to the poor to purchase food and utilities, and tax cuts that increase consumer spending. If these policies are put into place immediately, they will raise real GDP, as shown in the figure, and hasten the return to potential GDP.

Figure 14-7

Effect of a Well-Timed Countercyclical Fiscal Policy

The figure shows a likely path of recovery from a recession caused by a decline in demand for U.S. products. A well-timed cut in taxes or increase in government purchases can reduce the size of the recession and bring real GDP back to potential GDP more quickly. The size of the economic fluctuation is smaller. The analysis is shown in Figure 14-8.

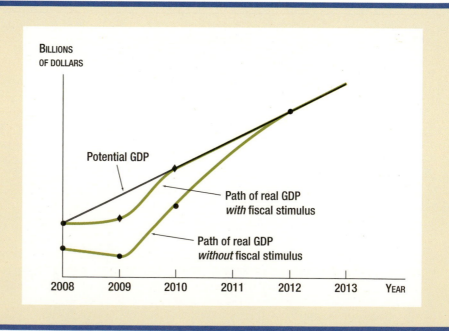

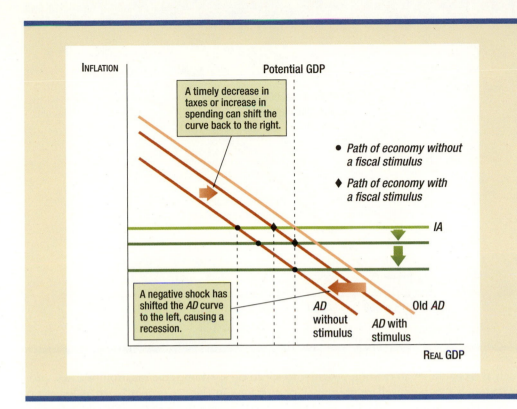

Figure 14-8

Analysis of a Well-Timed Countercyclical Fiscal Policy

A decline in demand shifts the *AD* curve to the left. Without a countercyclical fiscal policy, real GDP recovers back to potential GDP, but a timely cut in taxes or an increase in government purchases can offset the drop in demand and bring real GDP back to potential GDP more quickly.

How would this work when prices are adjusting and when the inflation rate is changing as well? Figure 14-8 provides the analysis. The recession is caused by the leftward shift in the aggregate demand curve. But the cut in taxes or increase in spending shifts the aggregate demand curve in the opposite direction. The aggregate demand curve shifts back to the right. If these countercyclical measures are timely enough and if they are of the appropriate magnitude—both big ifs—then the recession may be small and short-lived. The example shows real GDP falling only slightly below potential GDP.

Figure 14-9 shows a less ideal case that reflects the arguments of some of the critics. Critics argue that too few of the projects targeted by the stimulus bill are ready to be implemented immediately, so it will take a year or two before they are enacted. Furthermore, the critics argue that consumers will be reluctant to increase spending even if they receive tax cuts either because the cuts are temporary or because consumers are concerned about what will happen to their taxes in the future when the government has to repay the money it borrowed to implement the stimulus bill. If government purchases are increased, but the response is too late, and if consumer spending does not respond immediately to the tax cuts, the outcome in terms of real GDP may not be much better than in the absence of stimulus, as shown in Figure 14-9. Given the substantial budgetary cost, this would imply that the stimulus was a worse option than doing nothing at all in terms of countercyclical fiscal policy. It also is possible that if the bulk of the spending projects in the stimulus package kick in after the economy has begun to recover on its own, the excessive growth in aggregate demand will cause inflation to increase.

Disagreements about the usefulness of fiscal policy boil down to an assessment of whether the scenario in Figure 14-7 or in Figure 14-9 is more likely. Let's first consider some examples from recent history that may guide us in assessing which path is more likely.

Discretionary Change in the Instruments of Fiscal Policy Discretionary fiscal policy refers to specific changes in laws or administrative procedures,

discretionary fiscal policy
changes in tax or spending policy requiring legislative or administrative action by the president or Congress.

Figure 14-9

Effect of a Poorly Timed Fiscal Policy

Here, in contrast to Figure 14-7, the fiscal stimulus comes too late, when the economy is already recovering, possibly leading to an increase in inflation.

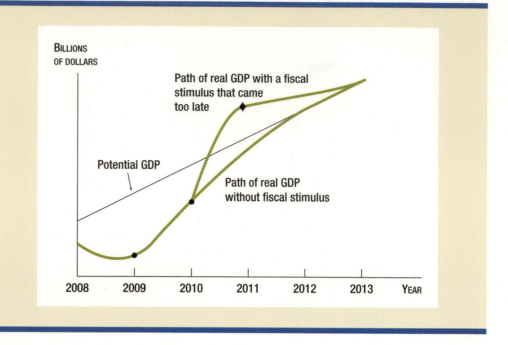

such as a change in an existing program to speed up spending, the creation of a new program (such as a new welfare program), or a change in the tax system (such as lower tax rates). These changes in the law are discretionary changes because they require action on the part of the Congress or the president.

One of the most significant post–World War II discretionary fiscal policy actions was the tax cut proposed by President John F. Kennedy in 1963 and enacted after his death when Lyndon Johnson was president. The early 1960s were a period when real GDP was below potential GDP, and this large discretionary tax cut was a factor in speeding the economic recovery. This cut in taxes probably also stimulated the growth of potential GDP and therefore was good for the long run.

More recent examples of discretionary fiscal policies include the Economic Growth and Tax Relief Reconciliation Act, enacted by Congress in June 2001. One part of the plan was a $300 ($600 for couples) rebate check that the government mailed to eligible taxpayers in the summer of 2001. Some economists argue that the tax cut was helpful in raising spending during the recession, although, because of its temporary nature, the extent to which it helped is the source of some debate among economists.

The tax component of the 2009 stimulus package signed into law by President Obama is similar to the tax cut–based stimulus bill signed into law early in 2008 by President Bush. As Figure 14-10 suggests, these temporary increases in disposable income did little or nothing to stimulate consumption demand, and thereby aggregate demand, or the economy.

Figure 14-10 illustrates the economic impact of the temporary payments in 2008 and in 2009. The upper line shows U.S. disposable personal income, which is income after taxes and government transfers; it therefore includes the temporary payments from the government. Notice the sharp increase in disposable personal income in May 2008, when checks were mailed or deposited in people's bank accounts. Disposable personal income then started to come down in June and July as total payments declined and by August had returned to the trend that was prevailing in April.

The lower line in Figure 14-10 is personal consumption expenditures over the same period. Observe that consumption shows no noticeable increase at the time of the

ECONOMICS *IN ACTION*

Was the Cash for Clunkers Program a Clunker?

In addition to the large macroeconomic stimulus programs of 2008 and 2009, a number of other discretionary fiscal policies were undertaken in sectors such as housing and automobiles. Economists have been evaluating these programs to determine whether they were effective. The evaluations will help determine whether such policies should be used in the future.

A particularly important policy to evaluate is the widely discussed $3 billion "Cash for Clunkers" program. Enacted in 2009, it offered subsidies from $3,500 to $4,500 to people who purchased new cars if they agreed to trade in their old gas-guzzling clunker when they bought a new car. The program was available in the summer of 2009. The hope was that this temporary incentive would jump-start automobile consumption and help get the economy moving again.

Economists Atif Mian of Berkeley and Amir Sufi of the University of Chicago studied the program carefully after it was completed. They compared regions of the United States that had differences in the number of clunkers to estimate the effects of the program on automobile consumption. They published their results in a research paper "The Effects of Fiscal Stimulus: Evidence from the 2009 'Cash for Clunkers' Program."

Mian and Sufi found an effect on consumption, but it mainly was to shift purchases forward a few months. Consumption was higher than it would have been without the program during the months when the program was available, but lower than it would have been after the program ended. Thus, no noticeable net increase in consumption resulted. Apparently, people who were planning to trade in their clunker simply did so a few months earlier than they would have without the program. This is what economic theory would suggest. It is like a clearance sale: If a business has a temporary period of discount prices, people will shift their purchases to the time of the sale.

The graph illustrates the Mian–Sufi results. It shows the effect of the changes in automobile purchases on total personal consumption expenditures. Observe that consumption first increased as people were encouraged to trade in their clunker and purchase new cars. It then declined because many of the trade-ins and purchases simply were brought forward. You can see that consumption rises above what it would have been without the program and then actually falls below what it would have been. One might argue that bringing forward purchases like this is exactly what such programs are supposed to do in a recession, but the graph makes it very clear that the offsetting secondary effects occur so quickly that the net result is an insignificant blip in the recovery. The impact is not sustainable.

Even if the blip in consumption were not offset, the graph raises questions about how such a temporary program could sustain a recovery. Suppose that there was not an offset. Then consumption would return to normal after the temporary purchases. But we still would see consumption growth picking up for a month or two and then slowing down. Again, that is not sustainability.

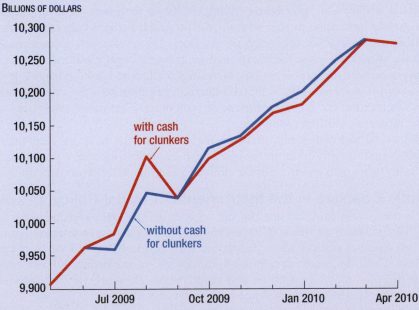

Personal Consumption Expenditures

BILLIONS OF DOLLARS

with cash for clunkers

without cash for clunkers

Figure **14-10**

Income and Consumption during the Two Discretionary Stimulus Programs

The 2008 and 2009 stimulus programs raised disposable personal income as checks were sent to people. The purpose was to jump-start consumption and stimulate aggregate demand. According to the data shown in this chart, consumption did not increase as a result of these programs. Economists who view the programs as effective argue that consumption would have declined more without the programs. See the Economics in Action box on the previous page for a discussion of the Cash for Clunkers program.

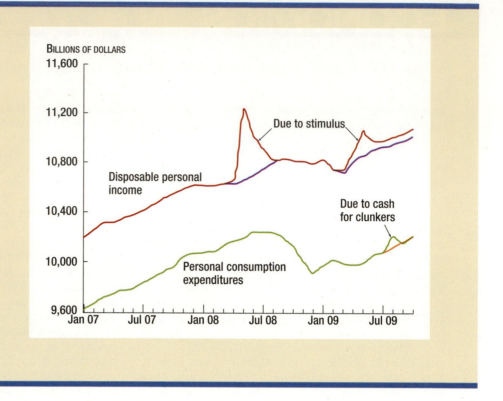

rebate. As the picture illustrates, the temporary rebate apparently did little to stimulate consumption demand, and thereby aggregate demand, or the economy.

What could explain this discrepancy between what was predicted by our model and the empirical reality? One possibility—though difficult to prove—is simply that consumption would have fallen further without the program, perhaps because of other factors such as an increase in the price of gasoline. The permanent income model of consumption model is a more likely explanation. It implies that consumers respond less to changes in income that are temporary compared with more lasting changes. If so, the magnitude of the outward shift of the *AD* curve in response to a tax cut depends very much on whether the tax cut is permanent or temporary. Temporary tax rebates would have little impact on consumer spending.

Figure 14-10 also casts some doubt on the success of the temporary tax provisions of the 2009 stimulus bill. Although the increase in disposable income was smaller, it was spread out for more than a year. Still, it is difficult to see an effect on consumption.

Automatic Changes in the Instruments of Fiscal Policy

Discretionary actions by the government are not the only way in which taxes and spending can be changed. In fact, many of the very large changes in taxes and spending are automatic. Income tax revenues expand when people are making more and fall when people are making less. Thus, tax revenues respond automatically to the economy. Tax payments rise when the economy is in a boom and more people are working. Tax revenues fall when the economy is in a slump and unemployment rises.

These changes in tax revenues are even larger with a progressive income tax. With a *progressive tax* system, individual tax payments *rise* as a proportion of income as income increases. With a progressive tax, a person earning $100,000 per year pays proportionately more in taxes than a person earning $20,000 per year. Because of this progressive tax system, as people earn more, they pay a higher tax rate, and when they earn less, they pay a lower tax rate.

Parts of government spending also change automatically. Unemployment compensation, through which the government makes payments to individuals who are unemployed, rises during a recession. When unemployment rises, so do payments to unemployed workers. Social security payments also increase in a recession because people may retire earlier if job prospects are bad. Welfare payments rise in a recession because people who are unemployed for a long period of time may qualify for welfare. As poverty rates rise in recessions, welfare payments increase.

These automatic tax and spending changes are called **automatic stabilizers** because they tend to stabilize the fluctuations of real GDP. How significant are these automatic stabilizers? Consider the 2001 recession, when discretionary fiscal stimulus was quite small. Real GDP in 1999 and 2000 was above potential GDP. But by late 2001 and 2002, real GDP was dropping below potential GDP. As this happened, government spending went up and taxes went down.

The magnitude of these effects was quite large. The difference between proposed and actual taxes and spending in the 2002 budget provides an estimate of the effect of the recession on taxes and spending. Tax revenue was $336 billion less than had been proposed before the recession. Thus, taxes were reduced automatically by this amount. Spending, however, was $50 billion more than had been proposed before the recession. Thus, spending rose by $50 billion in response to the recession. The combined effect of a $336 billion reduction in taxes and a $50 billion increase in spending was vital in keeping the recovery going. Because tax receipts went down in the recession and transfer payments went up, people's consumption was at a higher level than it otherwise would have been. These automatic changes in tax revenues and government spending tended to stabilize the economy and probably made the recession less severe than it otherwise would have been. These changes did not completely offset other factors, however, because there still was a recession.

The Discretion versus Rules Debate for Fiscal Policy

For many years, economists have debated the usefulness of discretionary and automatic fiscal policy. Automatic fiscal policy is an example of a fiscal policy rule describing how the instruments of fiscal policy respond to the state of the economy. Thus, the debate is sometimes called the "discretion versus rules" debate.

Proponents of discretionary fiscal policy argue that the automatic stabilizers will not be large enough or well timed enough to bring the economy out of a recession quickly. Critics of the discretionary policy emphasize that the effect of policy is uncertain and that the impact of policy has long lags. By the time spending increases and taxes are cut, a recession could be over; if so, the policy would only lead to an overshooting of potential GDP and an increase in inflation. Three types of lags are particularly problematic for discretionary fiscal policy: a recognition lag, the time between the need for the policy and the recognition of the need; an implementation lag, the time between the recognition of the need for the policy and its implementation; and an impact lag, the time between the implementation of the policy and its impact on real GDP.

Although lags and uncertainty continue to contribute to the discretion versus rules debate, other issues have become central. Many economists feel that policy rules are desirable because of their stability and reliability. A fiscal policy rule emphasizing the automatic stabilizers might make government plans to reduce the deficit more believable. Countercyclical fiscal policy raises the deficit or reduces the surplus during recessions. With discretionary policy, nothing guarantees that the surplus will return or increase after the recession. With an automatic policy rule, the expectation is that the deficit will decline after the recession is over.

automatic stabilizers
automatic tax and spending changes that occur over the course of the business cycle that tend to stabilize the fluctuations in real GDP.

The Structural versus the Cyclical Surplus

We noted earlier that taxes and spending change automatically in recessions and recoveries. These automatic changes affect the budget, so to analyze the budget, it is important to separate out these automatic effects. The *structural*, or *full-employment*, *surplus* was designed for this purpose. The **structural surplus** is what the surplus would be if real GDP equaled potential GDP.

Figure 14-11 introduces a graph to explain the structural surplus. On the horizontal axis is real GDP. On the vertical axis is the budget surplus: tax revenues less expenditures. The budget is balanced when the surplus is zero, which is marked by a horizontal line in the diagram. The region below zero represents a situation in which taxes are less than spending and the government has a deficit. The region above zero is a situation in which the government budget has a surplus. On the horizontal axis, *A*, *B*, and *C* represent three different levels of real GDP.

The upward-sloping line in Figure 14-11 indicates that as real GDP rises, the budget surplus gets larger. Why? The automatic stabilizers are the reason. When real GDP rises, tax revenues rise and spending on transfer programs falls. Because the surplus is the difference between tax revenues and spending, the surplus gets larger. Conversely, when real GDP falls, tax receipts decline and spending on transfer programs increases, so the surplus falls. The upward-sloping line in Figure 14-11 pertains to a particular set of government programs and tax laws. A change in these programs or laws would *shift* the line. For example, a decrease in tax rates would shift the line down.

Figure 14-12, a similar diagram, shows potential GDP and real GDP in a year when real GDP is below potential GDP. Imagine raising real GDP up to potential GDP. We would predict that the surplus would go up, because tax receipts would rise as the economy grew and transfer payments would go down because fewer people would be unemployed, fewer people would be retiring, and fewer people would be on welfare. As we move to the right in the diagram, the surplus gets larger. The structural surplus occurs when real GDP equals potential GDP. The structural surplus provides a way to separate out cyclical changes in the budget caused by cyclical changes in the economy.

structural surplus
the level of the government budget surplus under a scenario in which real GDP is equal to potential GDP; also called the full-employment surplus.

Figure 14-11

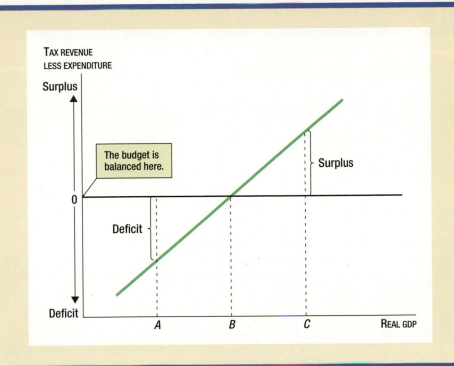

The Effect of Real GDP on the Budget

When real GDP falls, the budget moves toward deficit because spending rises and tax receipts fall. When real GDP is at point *A*, there is a deficit; at point *B*, the budget is balanced; and at point *C*, there is a budget surplus.

Figure 14-12

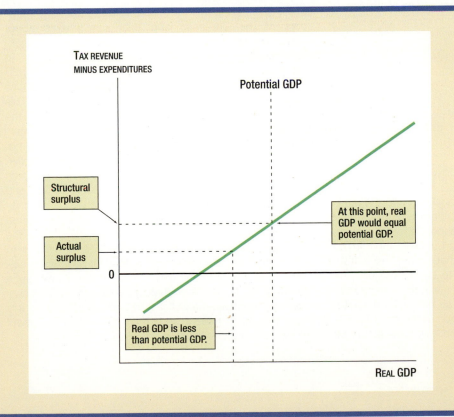

The Structural Surplus versus the Actual Surplus in a Recession Year

The surplus that occurs when real GDP is equal to potential GDP is called the structural surplus, as shown in the figure. The actual surplus falls below the structural surplus when real GDP falls below potential GDP. If the recession is big, an actual deficit could result even with a structural surplus.

ECONOMICS *IN ACTION*

The Case for Discretionary Fiscal Policy

The most influential economic case in support of the stimulus act of 2009 was made by Christina Romer, (then) the chair of the president's CEA, and Jared Bernstein, economic adviser to the vice president. In a white paper released in January 2009, they estimated that the stimulus bill would create more than 3 million jobs and keep unemployment from rising above 8 percent.

The first part of the Romer-Bernstein analysis focused on the aggregate demand effects of the package. They used multipliers of the type we discussed in Chapter 11 to assess the overall GDP impact of the tax cuts and spending increases contained in the package. The multipliers they used for each quarter are listed below. These multipliers, along with some assumptions about how aid to state governments would affect demand, were used to calculate the overall impact on GDP.

Tax and Spending Multipliers Used to Evaluate the Stimulus Bill

Quarter	Spending Multiplier	Tax Multiplier
1	1.05	0
2	1.24	0.49
3	1.35	0.58
4	1.44	0.66
5	1.51	0.75
6	1.53	0.84
7	1.54	0.93
8–15	1.57	0.99
16	1.55	0.98

The GDP effects were then translated into the number of jobs created using a reasonable rule of thumb that a "1 percent increase in GDP corresponds to an increase in employment of approximately 1 million jobs." The increase in the number of jobs that would result from the stimulus plan was estimated to be 3.7 million. The authors cautioned that this did not mean that the number of jobs in 2010 would necessarily be higher than what it was before the onset of the recession at the end of 2007. The estimated number of 3.7 million new jobs should be interpreted as the difference between the number of jobs that existed after the stimulus was implemented and the number of jobs that would have existed if no stimulus were implemented.

Romer and Bernstein recognized that the impact of temporary tax cuts might be small, saying, "Large proportions of temporary tax cuts are saved, blunting their stimulatory impact on output and employment." Because of the dire economic situation, however, they assumed that households would treat the tax cuts as essentially permanent in making their spending decision. If this assumption is not valid, then the estimated number of jobs would be substantially less.

Romer and Bernstein also estimated the time it would take to stimulate the economy. They argued that funds for food stamps, unemployment benefits, and welfare payments would be spent quickly, whereas the spending on infrastructure, education, health, and energy would take time. Overall, they estimated that job creation would peak in 2010.

These estimates of the economic impact of a fiscal policy package played a critical role in informing members of the Congress and their constituents about whether a vote for a policy was appropriate. For packages approaching $1 trillion including interest, as in 2009, the estimated economic impacts matter greatly.

In the end, the unemployment rate rose well above 8 percent, reaching 10.1 percent in October 2009. This high unemployment rate was, of course, at odds with the white paper and led people to criticize the Romer-Bernstein finding and argue that the stimulus was not effective because they overestimated the size of multiplier. For example, a National Bureau of Economic Research paper by John Cogan, Tobias Cwik, John Taylor, and Volker Wieland found much smaller multipliers.

But others, including Romer and Bernstein, argued that unemployment would have been worse without the stimulus, maybe rising to 12 percent. It is difficult to know for sure. Economics is not an experimental science. You cannot run an experiment over again without a stimulus package. Nevertheless, economics likely will continue to inform the policy and political debate, so it is important to do more research on the economic impact of the discretionary fiscal policy.

REVIEW

- Because tax revenues and spending fluctuate as the economy fluctuates, the surplus, or deficit, is cyclical. Deficits frequently arise or get bigger in recessions.

- The structural surplus adjusts the actual surplus for these cyclical changes in the economy.

CONCLUSION

Because the government is such a large player in the economy, its fiscal actions (spending, taxing, and borrowing) exert a powerful influence on real GDP and employment. Such actions can cause real GDP to depart from potential GDP and can alter the long-term growth rate of potential GDP.

A first principle of fiscal policy, therefore, is that the government should not take actions that would harm the economy. Avoiding erratic changes in fiscal policy and ensuring that taxes are not increased during recessions are part of this first principle.

A second principle is that fiscal policy in principle can smooth the fluctuations in the economy. Tax cuts and spending increases during recessions can help offset the declines in demand.

Economists debate about whether the government is capable of taking discretionary actions that will have these effects. Policy lags and uncertainty make discretionary fiscal policy difficult. Economists disagree little, however, about the importance of automatic stabilizers, under which tax and spending actions occur automatically without legislation. Automatic stabilizers cause the deficit to rise in recessions and fall during better times.

Another part of government policy that has powerful effects on the economy is monetary policy. We take up monetary policy in Chapter 15.

KEY POINTS

1. Fiscal policy consists of the government's plans for spending and taxes.
2. The government's budget is the primary document of fiscal policy. It gives the priorities for spending and taxes. In the United States, the president must submit a budget proposal to Congress.
3. The United States has had large federal budget deficits in recent years. These are increasing the debt and raising risks to the economy.
4. Because Congress modifies the proposals and because of unanticipated events, the actual budget differs considerably from the proposed budget.
5. Changes in spending and taxes can move real GDP away from potential GDP in the short run. But in the long run, real GDP returns to potential GDP.
6. Changes in taxes and spending can offset shocks to real GDP.
7. Lags and uncertainty make discretionary fiscal policy difficult.
8. Automatic stabilizers are an important part of fiscal policy. Tax revenues automatically decline in recessions. Transfer payments move in the reverse direction.

KEY TERMS

automatic stabilizers, 339
balanced budget, 325
budget deficit, 325
budget surplus, 325
countercyclical policy, 334

debt-to-GDP ratio, 330
discretionary fiscal policy, 335
federal budget, 325
federal debt, 327
structural surplus, 340

QUESTIONS FOR REVIEW

1. Why are actual expenditures and revenues always different from the president's proposals?
2. How is the government's debt affected by the government's budget surplus?
3. Why would a tax cut in a recession reduce the size of the recession?
4. Why might a proposal to cut taxes in a recession do little to mitigate the recession?
5. What is meant by the discretion versus rules debate?
6. What are automatic stabilizers, and how do they help mitigate economic fluctuations?
7. What is the difference between the structural surplus and the actual surplus?
8. What would happen to the actual surplus in a recession?

PROBLEMS

1. Suppose you have the following data on projected and actual figures for the U.S. budget for a given year (in billions of dollars).

	Projected Budget	Actual Budget
Taxes	2,286	2,407
Expenditures	2,709	2,655

    a. What was the projected budget surplus or deficit? What was the actual budget surplus or deficit? Why might this happen?

    b. If the government debt was $4,592 billion at the start of the year, what was the debt at the end of the year?

    c. If real GDP was $12,300 billion, what is the debt-to-GDP ratio?

2. Examine the hypothetical budget data, shown below, for calendar years 2012–2015 (in billions of dollars).

Year	Budget Surplus	Government Debt as of January 1	GDP
2012	−150	1,000	4,000
2013	−100	1,150	4,200
2014	100		4,800
2015	200		5,400

    a. Fill in the missing values in the table.

    b. What is the percentage change in debt and GDP from 2012 to 2013?

    c. Calculate the debt-to-GDP ratio for each year. How does this ratio change over time? Why?

3. Suppose you are in charge of deciding the appropriate fiscal policy for an economy in which real GDP is less than potential GDP. One of your economic advisers recommends a reduction in government spending. Using an *AD-IA* diagram, indicate the short-run, medium-run, and long-run effects of this plan. Did you receive good advice from your economic adviser?

4. Suppose the economy is currently $100 billion above potential GDP, and the government wants to pursue discretionary fiscal policy to cool off the economy. Show this situation using an *AD-IA* diagram.

5. Suppose Congress is considering a balanced budget amendment to the Constitution that requires that the budget be balanced every fiscal year. Explain how this law could make the economy more unstable.

6. Do you think that a zero national debt would be best for the country? Why or why not? Do you think that a zero level of debt would be best for you? Why or why not?

7. Suppose you get a summer job working in Congress and a recession begins while you are there. Write a memo to your boss, who is a member of Congress, on the pros and cons of a big highway- and bridge-building program to combat the recession.

8. Will projects such as Alaska's proposed "bridge to nowhere," a $300 million bridge that would connect two remote Alaskan communities, help the national economy avoid a recession? How would you reconcile this with your answer to Problem 7?

9. Suppose that real GDP has just fallen below potential GDP in a recession and the Council of Economic Advisers is trying to forecast the recovery from the recession. They are uncertain about whether Congress will pass the president's proposed tax cut right away or will delay it a year. Trace out two possible scenarios with an *AD-IA* diagram that describes the impact of the uncertainty.

10. Suppose the government surplus is 3 percent of real GDP, but economists say that the structural surplus is 2 percent. Is real GDP currently above or below potential GDP? Why? Draw the diagram showing this situation.

15 Monetary Policy

In earlier chapters, we explored the role of monetary policy in keeping inflation low and helping the economy grow more stably without large booms and busts. For example, if inflation starts to rise, the Federal Reserve (the Fed) typically increases the interest rate to bring inflation back down. If inflation starts to fall, the Fed typically lowers the interest rate to keep inflation from falling further and to prevent a deflation.

We also saw how monetary policy occasionally has led to inflation or instability, such as when the Fed kept interest rates too low in the 1970s, which likely led to the Great Inflation, or when it kept interest rates very low from 2003 to 2005, which may have accelerated the housing price boom and the resulting housing bust, which was a factor in the financial crisis of 2007 and 2008.

In this chapter, we delve deeper into the operations of monetary policy, considering five key policy issues. First, we look at how the Federal Reserve responded to the financial crisis by expanding the size of its balance sheet. Second, we examine the demand for money in terms of the interest rate, and consider what happens when the interest rate hits its lower bound of zero, as also occurred during the recent financial crisis. Third, we study how the Fed can avoid getting into such situations by responding in a systematic way to both inflation and to real gross domestic product (GDP). Fourth, we consider the rationale for central bank independence, and fifth, we look at the international role of monetary policy in affecting the exchange rate.

The Federal Reserve's Balance Sheet

At the time of the financial crisis in early 2009, the Fed released a statement saying that it planned to "stimulate the economy through open market operations and other measures that are likely to keep the size of the Federal Reserve's balance sheet at a high level." We already know what open market operations are from Chapter 10, but what are these "other measures" and what does it mean to keep the "the size of the Federal Reserve's balance sheet at a high level"? To answer these questions we first need to take a look at the Federal Reserve's balance sheet.

The Federal Reserve's Assets and Liabilities

Table 15-1 shows the basic form of the balance sheet of the Fed or other central banks. As with any balance sheet, we put assets on the left and liabilities on the right. The most important thing about a balance sheet is that any change in assets implies an equal change in liabilities.

Consider first the liability side of the Fed's balance sheet. The first item is *currency*, which is the amount of dollar bills and coins of various denominations in circulation. Recall that currency held by the public is part of the money supply.

The second item is *reserves*, which are deposits that banks hold at the Fed. When the Fed purchases bonds in an open market operation, it pays for the bonds by crediting banks with a deposit on itself. In Chapter 10, we showed that these reserves are an asset on the banks' balance sheets. From the perspective of the balance sheet of the Fed, we see that they are a liability.

Now consider the asset side of the balance sheet. This side has four major items: government securities, private securities, loans to banks, and loans to other financial institutions.

Government securities are mainly U.S. Treasury bonds with maturities over a year and U.S. Treasury bills with maturities less than a year. Buying and selling these securities is a traditional role of central banks as they go about doing open market operations. If the Fed buys $10 billion in government securities, then the left-hand asset side of the Fed's balance sheet increases by $10 billion. What adjusts on the right-hand liability side? If the Fed pays for the government securities by crediting the banks' deposit accounts, then reserves increase by $10 billion. So we see the basic principle at work: Changes in assets must always equal changes in liabilities. The balance sheet is a convenient way to keep track of the traditional open market operations.

Next consider *private securities*, which are bonds issued by firms. What types of securities are in this category? One example is commercial paper, which is a type of bond with a short-term maturity issued by a financial or nonfinancial firm. Another example is

Table 15-1

Major Items on the Balance Sheet of the Fed

Assets	Liabilities
Government Securities	Currency
Private Securities	Reserves
Loans to Banks	
Loans to Other Financial Institutions	

a mortgage-backed security (MBS), which is a collection of mortgages bunched together into one bond. These collections were put together by financial firms and government-sponsored enterprises, such as Fannie Mae and Freddie Mac, to make the mortgages more attractive to investors. Other examples in the private securities category are securities backed by student loans, automobile loans, or credit card debt.

During the financial crisis, the Fed bought these securities to prevent the financial crisis from worsening. For example, in March 2008, the Fed was concerned that Bear Stearns would fail and that this would cause other firms who had lent money to Bear Stearns to fail, harming the whole financial system and the economy. So it bought some of Bear Stearns's assets and arranged the sale of the rest of Bear Stearns to another financial firm, JP Morgan. Similarly, it bought some of the assets of AIG to prevent it from failing in September 2008. By the end of 2008, the Fed was buying MBS to reduce mortgage interest rates and thereby help stop the bust in housing markets. It bought commercial paper because few investors were buying it, and the Fed was concerned that the lack of credit availability would harm the economy.

The last two items on the asset side of the balance sheet are loans. Making *loans to banks* is one of the traditional roles of the Fed. It is part of the Fed's *lender of last resort* function. The Fed originally made loans to banks that take deposits from the public to prevent runs on the banks. A run occurs when many people simultaneously withdraw their deposits from the bank. In the nineteenth century and in the Great Depression of the 1930s, people would lose confidence in banks and withdraw their deposits. But simple rumors could cause such runs and ruin banks that otherwise were solvent. By acting as the lender of last resort, ready to lend in such circumstances, the Fed could prevent these runs and preserve financial stability. When the Fed makes loans to banks it charges an interest rate called the **discount rate**. During the financial crisis, many banks borrowed large amounts from the Fed, and the Fed made it easier by creating a special term auction facility (TAF) for which the interest rate could be less than the discount rate.

The final category on the Fed's balance sheet consists of loans to other financial institutions that are not banks. These other financial institutions include insurance companies, such as AIG. The Fed might lend to these institutions for reasons that are similar to its reason for buying private securities: It might be concerned that, without these loans, the firms would fail and that the failure would ripple through the economy.

Purchasing private securities and making loans to financial institutions other than banks are quite unusual actions for central banks. Economists debate about whether such actions have the intended effects, although the Fed has argued that they are effective. Economists also debate about the legality and appropriateness of the Fed taking on these responsibilities, which certainly are not in the traditional set of monetary policy tools. Economists generally agree, however, that the Fed eventually should revert to its traditional role after the effects of the crisis dissipate.

The Size of the Balance Sheet

What does the Fed mean by the size of the balance sheet? It simply means the sum of all the assets on the balance sheet or equivalently the sum of all the liabilities. When the Fed purchases assets, the size of the balance sheet increases.

Think about the size of the Fed's balance sheet using the liability side—currency plus reserves. Economists have another term for the sum of currency plus reserves. They call it the **monetary base**. Figure 15-1 shows how the Fed's balance sheet exploded at the time of the financial crisis.

discount rate
the interest rate that the Fed charges commercial banks when they borrow from the Fed.

monetary base
currency plus reserves.

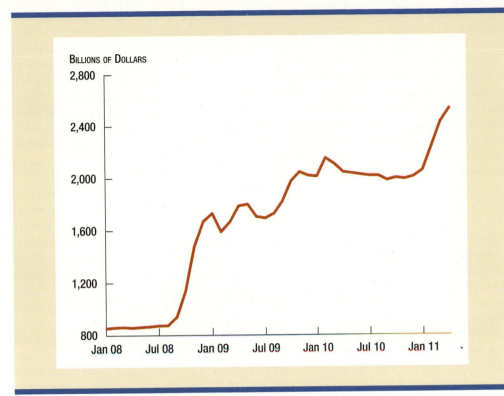

Figure 15-1

The Monetary Base and the Size of the Fed's Balance Sheet

The monetary base—currency plus reserves—is a measure of the size of the Fed's balance sheet. The monetary base increased substantially during the financial crisis at the end of 2008 and rose again during the second bout of quantitative easing in late 2010 and 2011.

REVIEW

- The size of the Fed's balance sheet is the sum of all the assets, or all the liabilities. The size of the balance sheet has expanded by a large amount during the financial crisis.

- The major items on the asset side of the Fed's balance sheet are securities and loans. The major items on the liability side are currency and reserves.

- Securities consist of government securities and private securities. Purchases and sales of government securities, commonly called open market operations, are a traditional role of monetary policy.

- Purchasing private securities is an unusual action taken to lessen the severity of financial crises.

- Loans consist of loans to banks and loans to other firms. Loans to banks are part of the traditional lender of last resort function of the Fed.

- Loans to other firms are also unusual. They are undertaken to prevent the firms from failing, which the Fed worries would disrupt the financial system.

Money Demand and Zero Interest Rate

Now that we have examined the balance sheet of the Fed and shown how changes in the Fed's purchases lead to changes in reserves, let us examine how changes in reserves affect the interest rate. We will show that (1) decreases in the money supply caused by decreases in reserves will increase the interest rate; (2) increases in the money supply created by increases in reserves will lower the interest rate; and (3) the interest rate cannot go below zero, so at some point increases in reserves will stop lowering the interest rate.

The Money Demand Curve **Money demand** is defined as a relationship between the interest rate and the quantity of money people are willing to hold at any given interest rate. As shown in Figure 15-2, the amount of money demanded is related negatively to the nominal interest rate. The scale for the nominal interest rate in Figure 15-2 starts at 0 percent and increases to 1 percent, 2 percent, 3 percent, and so on. One reason people hold money is to carry out transactions: to buy and sell goods and services. People will hold less money if the nominal interest rate is high. That is, a higher interest rate reduces the amount of money people want to carry around in their wallets or hold in their checking accounts. Conversely, a lower nominal interest rate will increase the amount of money people want to hold. Why is money demand negatively related to the nominal interest rate?

Money (currency plus checking deposits) is only part of the wealth of most individuals. People also hold some of their wealth in financial assets that pay interest. For example, some people have time deposits at banks. Others hold securities, such as Treasury bills. Holding money is different from holding time deposits or Treasury bills because currency does not pay interest and checking deposits pay low, or no, interest. If you hold all your money in the form of cash in your wallet, clearly you do not earn any interest. Thus, an individual's decision to hold money is best viewed as an alternative to holding some other financial asset, such as a Treasury bill. If you hold money, you get little or no interest; if you hold one of the alternatives, you earn interest.

The interest rate on the vertical axis in Figure 15-2 is the average nominal interest rate on these other interest-bearing assets that people hold as alternatives to money. Now, if the interest rate on these alternatives rises, people want to put more funds in the alternatives and hold less as money. If they hold the funds as currency, they get no interest on the funds. If they hold the funds in a checking account, they may get a small amount of interest, but certainly less than they would get from other financial assets. The quantity of money demanded is lower at higher interest rates because putting the funds in interest-bearing assets becomes more attractive compared with keeping the funds in a wallet.

Figure 15-2

The Demand for Money
The interest rate is the opportunity cost of holding money. A higher interest rate on U.S. Treasury bills or other interest-bearing assets raises the opportunity cost of holding money and lowers the quantity of money demanded.

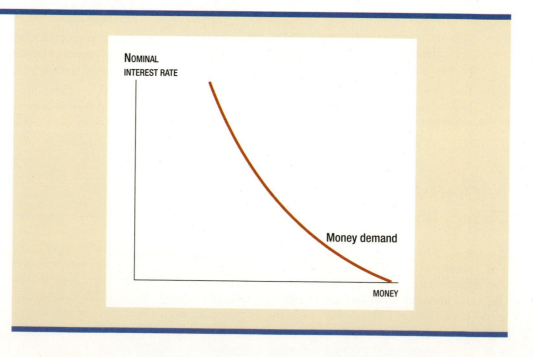

The interest rate on the alternatives to holding money is the *opportunity cost* of holding money. When the opportunity cost increases, people hold less money. When the opportunity cost decreases, people hold more money.

Figure 15-2 represents money demand in the economy as a whole. The curve is obtained by adding up the money demanded by all the individuals in the economy at each interest rate. The money held by businesses—in cash registers or in checking accounts—also should be added in.

The Interest Rate and the Quantity of Money

Using the money demand curve, it is possible to find the quantity of money in the economy that will be associated with any given nominal interest rate decision by the Fed. First, note that close correlation exists between the federal funds rate set by the Fed and interest rates on short-term Treasury bills and other interest-bearing assets that people can hold as an alternative to holding money. This close correlation is shown in Figure 15-3. Thus, when the Fed changes the federal funds rate, other interest rates tend to change in the same direction.

Now, for any given interest rate, one can use the money demand curve to find the quantity of money in the economy. This is illustrated in Figure 15-4. If the Fed lowers the federal funds rate, then the lower interest rate increases the quantity of money demanded and, as shown in the left graph, the quantity of money in the economy rises. Or, if the Fed raises the interest rate, the quantity of money in the economy decreases, as shown in the right graph of Figure 15-4.

What about Focusing on the Money *Supply*?

One question you might ask about Figure 15-4 is, "Where is the money *supply*?" Recall from Chapter 10 that the Fed affects the quantity of money supplied in the economy by open market operations. Does the quantity of money supplied equal the quantity of money demanded? Yes, of course it does. The demand and supply of money is no different from any other demand and supply model. As monetary policy now works in the United States and most other countries, the central bank adjusts the money supply so that it intersects the money demand curve at the nominal interest rate chosen by the central bank. For example, as the interest rate falls in the left graph of Figure 15-4, the money supply must be increased so that the intersection of money demand and money supply moves as shown. Figure 15-5 shows how the money supply shifts in both cases shown in Figure 15-4.

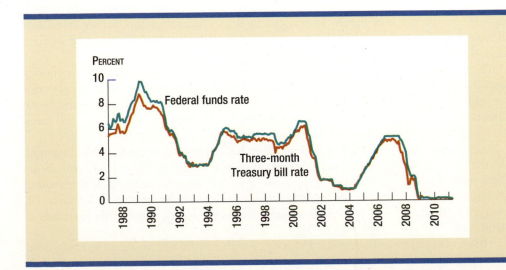

Figure 15-3

Short-Term Interest Rates

The federal funds rate (shown in blue) is the interest rate set by the Fed. Other short-term interest rates, such as the three-month Treasury bill rate (shown in orange), move up and down with the federal funds rate. Note how the interest rates reached zero in late 2008.

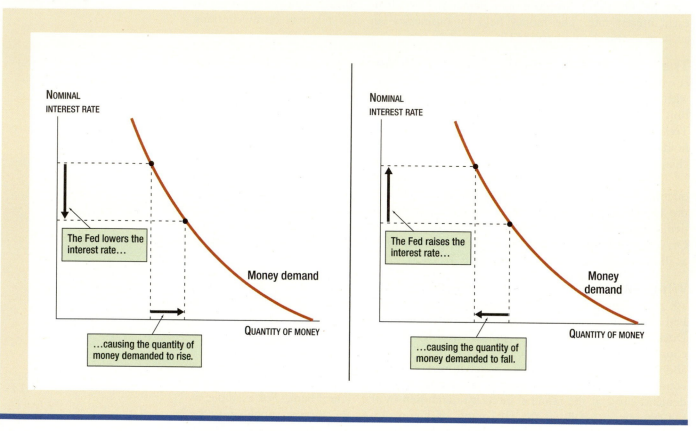

When the Fed Changes the Interest Rate, the Quantity of Money Changes

When the Fed lowers the interest rate, people want to hold more money. When the Fed raises the interest rate, people want to hold less money.

Figure 15-4

Such movements in the money supply occur as the Fed makes open market purchases or sales to change the interest rate. When the Fed decides to lower the interest rate, for example, it must increase reserves. And we know from Chapter 10 that when the Fed increases reserves, the money supply increases. Thus, the increase in the money supply in the left graph of Figure 15-5 is exactly what the analysis in Chapter 10 tells us will happen when the central bank increases reserves. Whether you focus on the interest rate or the money supply, the story is the same.

Then why doesn't the Fed simply focus on the money supply? Because the money demand curve tends to shift around a lot; if the Fed simply kept the money supply constant, the interest rate would fluctuate as money demand shifted back and forth. These fluctuations in the interest rate would cause fluctuations in real GDP—perhaps large enough to cause a recession—and thus would not be good policy.

Some economists, such as Milton Friedman, have argued that the Fed should simply hold the growth of the money supply constant, a policy that is called a *constant money growth rule*. Central banks, however, now feel that money demand shifts around too much for a constant money growth rule to work well. As we saw in Chapter 10, however, throughout history large increases in money growth cause large increases in inflation.

Those who object to the constant money growth rule do not object to keeping inflation low. They feel that a constant money growth rule will lead to more and larger

Figure 15-5

Money Supply Changes Implied by Interest Rate Changes
When the Fed decides to lower or raise the interest rate, the money supply must change. Increases in reserves raise the money supply and lower the interest rate. Decreases in reserves will lower the money supply and raise the interest rate.

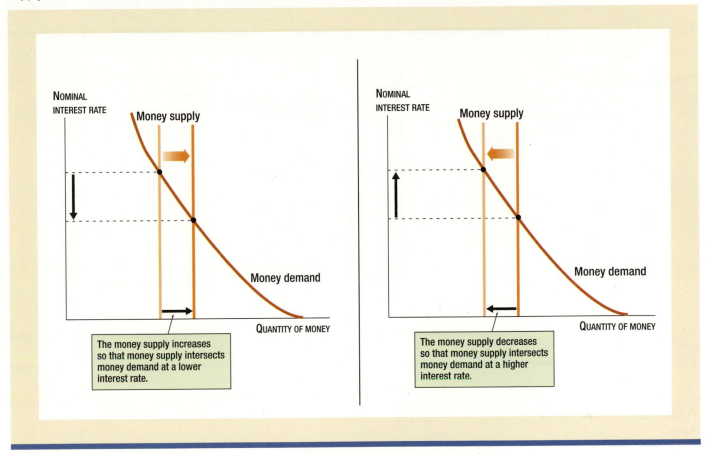

fluctuations in real GDP and inflation than other policies would. That is why they recommend that the Fed and other central banks focus more on interest rates.

When the Interest Rate Hits Zero

If you look carefully at Figures 15-4 and 15-5, you will notice that the money demand curve flattens out as it approaches the horizontal axis, which represents the zero interest rate. The curve does not cross the horizontal axis because the nominal interest rate cannot go negative. Why? Because a negative interest rate means that you would have to pay interest to people for loaning them your money instead of having them pay you. Rather than pay someone, you could simply hold onto your money in dollar bills, which would at least pay a zero interest rate, better than negative. So the interest rate does not go into zero territory. For this reason, we have drawn the money demand curve so that it flattens out rather than crosses the horizontal axis. (Technically, the interest rate can go very slightly negative on some assets because it serves as a storage fee for very large sums of money; but for all practical purposes, zero is the lower bound on the interest rate.)

Now suppose that the Fed continued increasing the money supply beyond the amount shown in Figure 15-5. For example, in Figure 15-6, we show in more detail how

liquidity trap
a situation in which increases in the money supply (liquidity) do not lower the interest rate any further; the interest rate is at or near zero.

the money demand curve flattens out as the interest rate approaches zero. When the interest rate gets to zero, we have reached what is called the **liquidity trap**, a situation in which increases in the money supply (liquidity) will not lower the interest rate any further.

As you can see in Figure 15-7, the interest rate did effectively reach zero in the United States in December 2008. The Federal Open Market Committee announced

Figure 15-6

The Liquidity Trap
Increases in the money supply result in smaller reductions in the interest rate until the interest rate approaches zero.

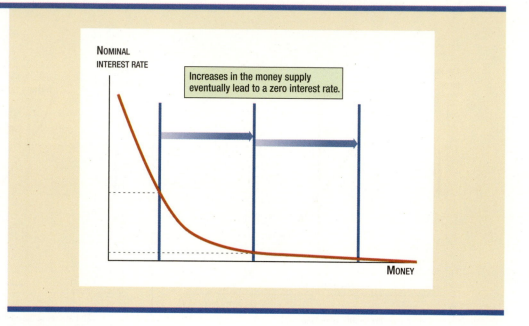

Figure 15-7

Toward the Zero Interest Rate
As the Fed increased reserves sharply in 2008, the federal funds interest rate declined toward zero. This result is what would be expected from the theory of the money demand curve, because the increase in reserves increased the money supply to some extent.

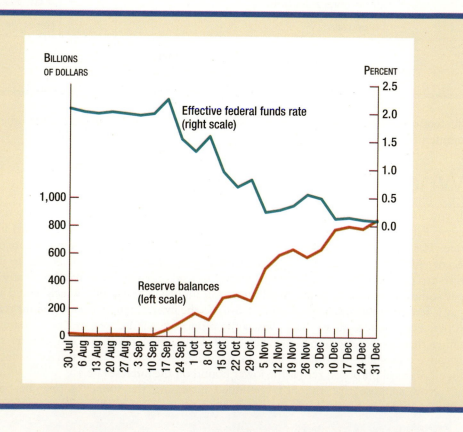

ECONOMICS IN ACTION

Quantitative Easing Explained

Quantitative easing refers to large increases in the monetary base and the Federal Reserve's balance sheet, as a result of the Fed buying large quantities of assets such as mortgage-backed securities (MBS) or long-term Treasury securities. Following the financial panic in 2008, the Federal Reserve undertook two large-scale purchases of such assets, commonly called Quantitative Easing 1 (QE1) and Quantitative Easing 2 (QE2).

QE1 consisted of the purchase of $1.25 trillion of MBS and $300 billion of long-term Treasury securities mostly in 2009. QE2 consisted of purchasing $600 billion of long-term Treasury securities in 2010 and 2011. Looking at Figure 15-1, you can see how these purchases greatly expanded the size of the Fed's balance sheet. Recall that the purchases were financed by increasing the monetary base, mainly in the form of reserves at the Fed, as the Fed credited banks' deposits at the Fed to pay for the purchases.

Quantitative easing became the subject of much criticism and controversy especially at the time that QE2 was rolled out in 2010. Some argued that the increase in the monetary base would cause inflation. Others argued that the large balance sheet would be hard to reduce in the future when the Fed wanted to increase the interest rate. Still others argued that it would do little good in terms of reducing long-term interest rates. Foreign central banks argued that it would cause inflation in their countries as the effects of the increased monetary base spread around the world.

A highly critical and not always accurate YouTube video "Quantitative Easing Explained" went viral, demonstrating the intensity of the debate and criticism.

that its target for the federal funds rate would be in the range of 0 to 0.25 percent. Figure 15-7 shows how the interest rate fell from 2 to about 0 as reserves at the Fed increased.

Quantitative Easing

What should central banks do when the interest rate hits zero? As shown in Figure 15-6 they can continue to increase the money supply by increasing reserves; even though that will not lower the interest rate, it can stimulate the economy. This is called *quantitative easing* because the emphasis is on increasing the quantity of reserves or money rather than reducing the interest rate.

Some economists argue that people might use the larger amount of reserves or money to purchase goods and services directly and thereby stimulate the economy. Others argue that more reserves or money will lower the interest rates on a range of securities. For example, in the recent financial crisis, the Federal Reserve argued that quantitative easing lowered interest rates on mortgages and long-term Treasury securities. It emphasized, however, that the lower rates were due to the direct purchases of these securities rather than the increase in the quantity of reserves.

REVIEW

- The Fed affects the short-term nominal interest rate by changing reserves through open market operations.

- Money demand depends negatively on the nominal interest rate.

- When the Fed changes the interest rate, the quantity of money changes.

- Changes in the quantity of money supplied lead to reductions in the interest rate. Changes in reserves lead to changes in the money supply.

- At some point, the interest rate hits zero. Then the central bank uses quantitative easing or credit easing.

Running Monetary Policy to Ward Off Crises

The best way to avoid the problems of the zero interest bound is to run monetary policy in a way that avoids hitting the bound in the first place. This means avoiding booms and busts which cause crises.

Aggregate Demand: Just Right, Too Hot, or Too Cold?

First consider Figure 15-8, which illustrates the problem monetary policy faces in trying to avoid booms and busts by keeping real GDP near to potential GDP. The three graphs in Figure 15-8 each illustrate a different situation.

The Goldilocks Economy: Just Right
In the middle graph, the aggregate demand curve intersects the inflation adjustment line at the point at which real GDP equals potential GDP and the inflation rate is equal to the target inflation rate. Because real GDP is equal to potential GDP, inflation does not have the tendency to rise or to fall. Thus, this graph represents an ideal point: The inflation rate is equal to the target inflation rate, and real GDP is equal to potential GDP. The aggregate demand curve is in the correct place, because it intersects the inflation adjustment line at the point at which real GDP equals potential GDP *and* at which the inflation rate equals the target inflation rate. Financial market analysts refer to this situation as a "Goldilocks economy": not too hot, not too cold, just right.

Misalignment: Aggregate Demand Is Too High
In contrast to the middle graph in Figure 15-8, the other two graphs represent misalignments of real GDP and potential GDP. In the right graph aggregate demand has increased too much—perhaps because of an expansionary shift in consumption, investment, or net exports. At this position, inflationary forces are in place that soon will cause the inflation adjustment line to rise. Unlike the short-run position in Figure 15-9 (the gain-then-pain scenario, in which the central bank intentionally has shifted monetary policy), the situation in the right graph of Figure 15-8 is unintentional. The task of monetary policy is to prevent such misalignments and to correct them once they occur.

How would the central bank correct this type of misalignment? It would raise the real interest rate above the level it would choose in the middle graph. The higher real interest rate would reduce aggregate demand and bring the *AD* curve back to a point at which it intersected the inflation adjustment line at potential GDP. Financial market analysts would say that the Fed was trying to "cool off the economy" by raising the interest rate in this way.

Another Type of Misalignment: Aggregate Demand Is Too Low
The left graph of Figure 15-8 represents the opposite, but no less undesirable, type of misalignment of real GDP and potential GDP. In this case, aggregate demand has gotten too low—perhaps because of a contractionary shift in consumption, investment, or net exports. With real GDP less than potential GDP, the inflation adjustment line soon will fall below the target inflation rate. Moreover, with real GDP below potential GDP,

Figure 15-8

Aligning the Aggregate Demand Curve

The aggregate demand curve is lined up correctly when real GDP equals potential GDP and the inflation rate is on target, as in the middle graph. Otherwise, aggregate demand is too high, and the Fed must raise the interest rate; or aggregate demand is too low, and the Fed must lower the interest rate.

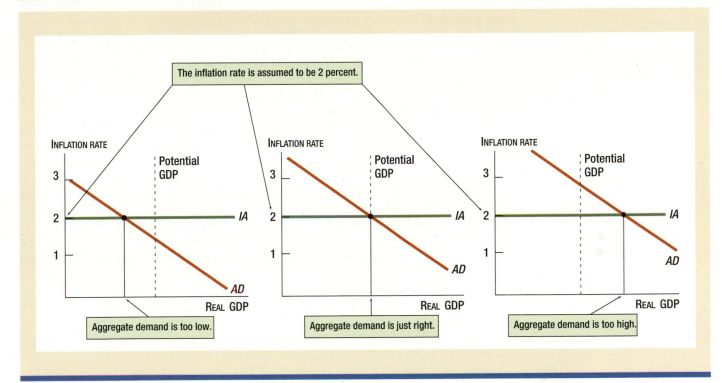

unemployment has increased. Monetary policy should try to prevent or correct this type of misalignment, too.

To correct such a misalignment, the central bank would lower the real interest rate below the level it would choose in the middle graph. The lower real interest rate would increase consumption, investment, and net exports and bring the *AD* curve back to the right.

The Inherent Uncertainty in Monetary Policy

This example also illustrates that, in practice, it is not easy for the Fed to keep real GDP near potential GDP by varying the interest rate. Although the Fed increased interest rates to rein in aggregate demand, economists were concerned that real GDP would not respond as quickly as in the past. At the time, it appeared that investment and consumption might be more responsive to the increase in the interest rate than the Fed thought they would be.

In general, how long it takes for a change in the interest rate to affect aggregate demand is uncertain. Other things affect aggregate demand, too, and some of those things might work in the opposite direction to the change in interest rates.

Moreover, potential GDP is difficult to estimate. Recall that potential GDP is determined by the underlying supply of labor, capital, and technological change. In many situations, central banks do not know for sure whether real GDP is or is not equal to potential GDP. Uncertainty about potential GDP is particularly high during periods when technology seems to be changing rapidly and the path of potential GDP is changing.

Increased Transparency and Predictability

To bring real GDP into alignment with potential GDP, the Fed reacts to the *gap*, or the *difference*, between real GDP and potential GDP. That is, it raised the real interest rate when real GDP rose above potential GDP. Similarly, if real GDP were to fall below potential GDP, as shown in the top left graph of Figure 15-8, the Fed would lower the real interest rate.

This type of interest rate reaction to the gap between real GDP and potential GDP is typical of the Fed and many other central banks. Just as responding promptly and by enough to an increase in inflation represents a good policy, so too does moving the aggregate demand curve in a way that brings real GDP back into equality with potential GDP.

Central banks have endeavored to be more transparent and predictable in their responses to inflation and real GDP. Some have formally announced a target for inflation. The increased predictability can be described using the concept of a monetary policy rule, as we discussed in Chapter 12. In fact, it is possible to combine the reaction to inflation and the reaction to the gap into one monetary policy rule, and thereby obtain a more accurate description of central bank behavior. Remember that a monetary policy rule is a description of a central bank's behavior in the same sense that a microeconomic demand curve is a description of a person's consumption behavior. Just as a person's purchase decisions may depend on two variables, (1) price and (2) income, so too may the central bank's real interest rate decisions depend on two variables, (1) the inflation rate and (2) the gap between real GDP and potential GDP.

Table 15-2 shows a numerical example of this type of policy rule. On the left is the inflation rate. On the top is the gap between real GDP and potential GDP. The entries in the shaded part of the table show the real interest rate. For example, the blue entry shows that when inflation is 2 percent and real GDP is equal to potential GDP (the percent gap between real GDP and potential GDP is zero), the real interest rate is 2 percent. When inflation rises to 4 percent, the real interest rate rises to 3 percent. Each column of Table 24-1 tells the same story: When inflation rises, the central bank raises

Table 15-2

Real Interest Rate Reaction to Inflation and to the Gap between Real GDP and Potential GDP (compare with Table 12-1 in Chapter 12 on page 290)

		Percent Gap between Real GDP and Potential GDP		
		−2	0	2
Inflation Rate (percent)	0	0	1	2
	2	1	2	3
	4	2	3	4
	6	3	4	5
	8	4	5	6

Note: The entries in the shaded area show the real interest rate for each inflation rate and the gap between real GDP and potential GDP.

the real interest rate. To raise the real interest rate, the nominal interest rate has to rise by more than inflation rises.

Now observe in Table 15-2 that the central bank's response also depends on what happens to real GDP. When real GDP rises above potential GDP—and the gap increases—the central bank raises the real interest rate. And when real GDP falls below potential GDP, the central bank lowers the real interest rate.

The monetary policy rule in Table 15-2 is a more accurate description of monetary policy than the rule in Chapter 12, Table 12-1, because central banks do react to the gap between real GDP and potential GDP, as the discussion of Fed policy makes clear. Hence, financial market analysts use monetary policy rules like this one to predict interest rate changes in many different countries.

REVIEW

- Monetary policy is a constant struggle to avoid booms and busts. The Fed carries out this policy by trying to keep the aggregate demand curve in a position at which real GDP is equal to potential GDP and the inflation rate is equal to the target inflation rate.

- The Fed and other central banks increase the real interest rate when real GDP grows above potential

GDP and lower the real interest rate when real GDP falls below potential GDP.

- The response of the real interest rate to the gap between real GDP and potential GDP can be combined with the response to inflation to get a monetary policy rule that accurately describes central bank behavior.

Central Bank Independence

Fed officials are appointed to long terms that may span several different presidents; the four-year term of the chair of the Fed does not necessarily coincide with the term of any

     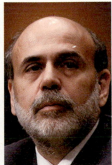

| William McChesney Martin 1951–1969 | Arthur Burns 1969–1978 | G. William Miller 1978–1979 | Paul Volcker 1979–1987 | Alan Greenspan 1987–2006 | Ben Bernanke 2006– |

Six Decades of Fed Chairs

The Federal Reserve Board has had six chairs during the past 60 years. Inflation was low during most of Martin's term but rose in the late 1960s and even more in the 1970s under Burns and Miller. Inflation fell dramatically under Volcker and remained low under Greenspan. Bernanke began his term with inflation pressures rising, but three years later, in early 2009, deflation seemed to be more of a problem.

ECONOMICS *IN ACTION*

Central Banks Sacrifice Independence as Crisis Grows

BY RICH MILLER AND SIMON KENNEDY

Feb. 9 (Bloomberg)—The global financial crisis is forcing the world's central bankers to surrender some of their prized independence. Regaining it won't be easy.

More than a principle is at stake. For longer than a quarter-century, independent central banks have been able to take painful and politically unpopular measures needed to restrain inflation. The worst economic calamity since the 1930s leaves Federal Reserve Chairman Ben S. Bernanke, Bank of England Governor Mervyn King, Bank of Japan Governor Masaaki Shirakawa and their colleagues under pressure to align policies with those of their nations' elected leaders.

"The lines between central banks and governments are becoming fuzzier," says Nouriel Roubini, a New York University economist. "Inflation is the path of least resistance for politicians, but it is dangerous."

The U.S. risks a deflationary economic decline—in which output, prices and wages all fall—even after repeated interest-rate cuts that have driven the overnight bank lending rate close to zero. In response, Bernanke has joined with the U.S. Treasury in unprecedented steps to revive credit.

Buying Up Securities

"Monetary authorities and the fiscal authorities are working hand-in-glove," Canadian Finance Minister Jim Flaherty said in an interview.

While that may be necessary now, it could turn into a problem later. Some Fed policy makers have already stressed the need to move quickly, once the crisis passes, to sop up all the money they have pumped into the financial system. Critics charge that the Fed and other central banks laid the groundwork for the current turmoil by not raising rates fast enough once the 2001 recession passed.

Inviting a Crisis

"The importance of doing this correctly cannot be overemphasized," Federal Reserve Bank of Kansas City President Thomas Hoenig said in a Jan. 7 speech. "We have sometimes been slow to remove our accommodative policy, and in doing so, we have invited the next round of inflation, excess and crisis."

Treasury Secretary Timothy Geithner has voiced the opposite concern, noting that Japan in the 1990s and the U.S. in the 1930s snuffed out incipient recoveries by prematurely tightening credit. He has vowed not to repeat that mistake.

His views carry considerable weight at the Fed. Not only is he a former New York Fed Bank president, but the Treasury is providing seed capital for many of the credit facilities the central bank will ultimately have to unwind—including $20 billion to cover any initial losses on the Fed's planned $200 billion program to promote loans to students, small businesses and auto buyers.

'First Loss'

"If you have Treasury taking the first loss, you may feel some responsibility to take their advice," says Vincent Reinhart, the Fed's former director of monetary affairs and now a resident scholar at the American Enterprise Institute in Washington.

What's more, the Treasury may end up playing a greater role in helping the Fed soak up the hundreds of billions of dollars of liquidity it has pushed into the financial system. That's because of changes in the size and makeup of the Fed's balance sheet.

In the past, the Fed has withdrawn money from the market by selling Treasury debt it holds to private investors. Those holdings have now dwindled, even as the balance sheet has ballooned, because the central bank has been swapping its Treasuries for riskier, harder-to-sell assets in an effort to revive the credit markets.

That means the Fed may need to rely on the Treasury to sell bills on its behalf when it wants to withdraw money from the economy. The Fed's flexibility "could be blocked by a Treasury decision," Reinhart says.

Short-Term Assets

Bernanke plays down the difficulty. "A significant shrinking of the balance sheet can be accomplished relatively quickly," he said in a Jan. 13 speech, in part because many assets the Fed holds are short-term and thus can be retired routinely as they come due.

Some of Bernanke's colleagues fret that the Fed has also opened itself up to political interference by allocating credit to certain sectors of the economy according to the types of securities it purchases. Stanford University Professor John Taylor dubs that strategy "mondustrial" policy—a hybrid of monetary and industrial policy.

In response to comments Taylor made during a Jan. 3 panel discussion in San Francisco, Federal Reserve Bank of St. Louis President James Bullard said he's "very concerned" about maintaining independence.

president. For example, Paul Volcker served through most of the Reagan years, even though he was appointed by President Carter. Alan Greenspan, originally appointed by President Reagan, served throughout the eight years of the Clinton presidency. Therefore, like Supreme Court justices in the United States, Fed officials develop an independence from government influence.

As the Economics in Action box "Central Banks Sacrifice Independence as Crisis Grows" shows, the unprecedented actions by the Fed during the financial crisis have raised questions about its independence. Some say that distinctions between the actions of the Fed and what usually would be done by other government agencies are getting fuzzier. For example, providing loans to individuals or firms usually is not done by independent agencies of government. Such loans are made by agencies like the Department of Housing and Urban Development or the Department of Commerce. These agencies must have their loans authorized by Congress; the cabinet members who head the departments are in no way independent of the president of the United States. They do not have fixed terms. To assess these challenges to central bank independence, one needs to understand the rationale for **central bank independence**. The main rationale is that an independent central bank can prevent the government in power from using monetary policy in ways that appear beneficial in the short run but that can harm the economy in the long run.

central bank independence
a description of the legal authority of central banks to make decisions on monetary policy with little interference by the government in power.

The Gain-Then-Pain Scenario

We showed in Chapter 13 that a shift in monetary policy toward a higher inflation target will temporarily raise real GDP above potential GDP, but that only inflation will be higher in the long run. Such a change in monetary policy would first entail a reduction in interest rates and would shift the aggregate demand (AD) curve to the right, as shown in Figure 15-9. Real GDP would rise along with investment, consumption, and net exports; unemployment would fall. In the short run, this change in GDP does not have an effect on inflation because of the slowness of firms to change their price decisions. The economic gain from the reduction in unemployment without an increase in inflation might help in a reelection campaign, or it might enable the government to push legislation for new programs through the political system. The economic pain—higher inflation in the long run, also shown in Figure 15-9—would not be seen until after the election or after the legislation is passed.

Thus, the political system has a natural tendency toward higher inflation. If the government in power had complete control over the decisions of the central bank, it could take actions to make the economy look good in the short run for political purposes and not worry that the economy might look bad in the long run. Removing the central bank from the direct control of the government reduces this politically induced bias toward higher inflation because then it is more difficult for the government to get the central bank to take such actions.

The Phillips Curve Observe that during the period of time when the IA line is shifting up in the gain-then-pain scenario, real GDP is above potential GDP, and the inflation rate is higher than at the start of the scenario. For example, inflation is higher and real GDP is higher at the point labeled MR in Figure 15-9 than they are at the starting point. And during this period, the unemployment rate is lower because the unemployment rate falls when real GDP rises. In sum, during the period of time between the initial shift of the AD curve and the end of the scenario, the unemployment rate is *down* and the inflation rate is *up*. Thus, unemployment and inflation have a negative correlation.

In fact, a negative correlation between unemployment and inflation has been observed for many years in the real world, because of such shifts in the AD curve. This negative correlation between inflation and unemployment is called the *Phillips curve*, after A. W. Phillips, the economist who first showed that such correlations existed in British data from 1861 to 1957. A replica of the original Phillips curve is shown in Figure 15-10.

The Phillips curve was used in the 1960s and 1970s to justify a monetary policy that included higher inflation. People argued that higher inflation would lead to lower unemployment. In other words, they argued that a long-run trade-off existed between inflation and unemployment.

Figure 15-9

The Gain-Then-Pain Scenario

The Fed can temporarily stimulate the economy in the short run—real GDP rises above potential GDP. But soon inflation starts to rise. In the long run, the inflation rate is higher and real GDP is back to potential GDP.

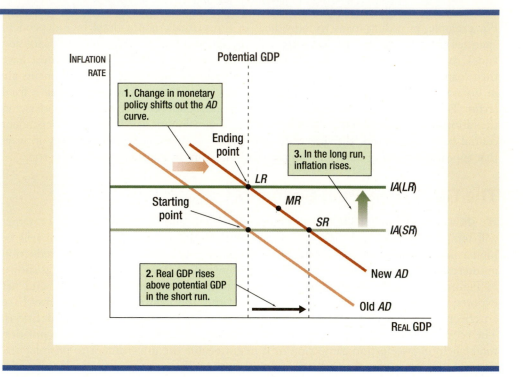

Figure 15-10

The Original Phillips Curve

A. W. Phillips first published this graph. Each point represents one year. The negatively sloped curve drawn through the scatter of points had enormous influence and led some to argue, mistakenly, that a long-run trade-off existed between inflation and unemployment.

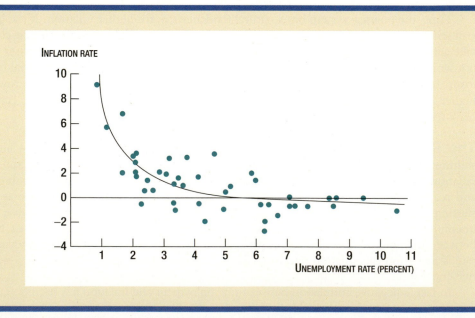

How did they use the Phillips curve to support this view? Look at the Phillips curve in Figure 15-10. You might think that a monetary policy that aimed for higher inflation could lead to a lower unemployment rate in the long run. That is what the curve seems to suggest. But the theory in the *AD-IA* diagram and, in particular, the gain-then-pain scenario shows that no such trade-off exists in the long run. If monetary policy raised inflation, real GDP eventually would return to potential GDP, the unemployment rate would return to the natural rate, and we would be left with only higher inflation, not lower unemployment.

It has become a basic principle of modern macroeconomics—implied by the *AD-IA* diagram—that no long-run trade-off exists between inflation and unemployment. The facts are consistent with the principle: In the 1950s and early 1960s, inflation was low; in the late 1960s and 1970s, inflation was high; and in the 1980s and 1990s, inflation was low again. But the average unemployment rate during these periods was roughly the same, around 5 or 6 percent. Furthermore, the lower unemployment rate in the late 1990s did not result in much higher inflation. Any tendency for unemployment and inflation to be correlated negatively will disappear in the long run. This does not mean that a higher-inflation monetary policy will not produce a short-run gain. It does mean, however, that it will result in long-run pain.

The Political Business Cycle

The **political business cycle** is the tendency of governments to use economic policy to cause real GDP to rise and unemployment to fall just before an election and then let the economy slow down right after the election. Many economic and political studies have shown that an incumbent's chances of being reelected are increased greatly if the economy is doing well. After the election, inflation may rise and cause a bust, but that would occur long before the next election.

Research in the 1970s by William Nordhaus of Yale University uncovered some evidence of a political business cycle in the United States. For example, the strong economy before the 1972 election may have been due to a monetary policy change that pushed real GDP above potential GDP. On the other hand, the U.S. economy was in a recession just before the 1980 and 1992 elections—the exact opposite of a political business cycle. Thus, the evidence for a political business cycle in the United States is no longer strong. In either case, political business cycles are harmful to the economy. Preventing political business cycles is another reason for having a central bank that has some independence from the politicians that are in power.

Time Inconsistency

It is difficult for governments to resist the temptation to use monetary policy for short-run gain despite the long-run pain. Even governments whose sole aim is to improve the well-being of the average citizen will say that they want low inflation but then will stimulate the economy to lower unemployment, even though they are fully aware of the inflationary consequences down the road.

This situation is known as **time inconsistency** because governments say they want low inflation but are later inconsistent by following policies that lead to higher inflation. They act like a teacher who tells the class that they will have to take an exam just to get the students to study, but then, on the day of the exam, announces that it is canceled. The students are happy to miss the exam, and the teacher does not have to grade it. Everyone appears better off in the short run.

Just as the teacher who cancels the exam will lose credibility with future classes, however, a central bank that tries the inconsistent policy will lose credibility. People will assume that the central bank actually will raise inflation even if it says it is aiming for low inflation.

Check your thinking about the implications of the gain-then-pain scenario for the relationship between unemployment and inflation.
In the short run, between the start and end of the scenario:
Inflation ↑
Real GDP > potential GDP
Unemployment rate <
                natural rate
So a negative correlation exists between inflation and unemployment, a Phillips curve.
In the long run:
Inflation ↑
Real GDP = potential GDP
Unemployment rate =
                natural rate
So, a long-run trade-off does not exist between inflation and unemployment.

political business cycle
a business cycle caused by politicians' use of economic policy to overstimulate the economy just before an election.

time inconsistency
the situation in which policy makers have the incentive to announce one economic policy but then change that policy after citizens have acted on the initial, stated policy.

Potential Disadvantages of Central Bank Independence

Central bank independence is no guarantee against monetary policy mistakes, however, and it could even lead to more mistakes. In principle, an independent central bank could cause more inflation than a central bank under government control. For example, those in charge of the central bank—after they are appointed—could succumb to arguments that high inflation is not so harmful after all. Or, at the other extreme, those in charge of the central bank become so focused on inflation that they are blinded to the effects of monetary policy on real GDP and employment and thus either cause a recession or make an existing recession deeper or longer. Therefore, a disadvantage of central bank independence is that it can be taken too far.

Whether independent or not, central banks need to be held *accountable* for their actions. If those in charge of the central bank do not perform their job well, it is appropriate that they not be reappointed. When the central bank of New Zealand was given greater independence in the 1980s, its accountability was formalized explicitly: If the head of the central bank does not achieve low inflation goals agreed to in advance, the head is fired. But the central bank has independence in determining how to achieve these goals.

Is there any evidence that independence has led to better inflation performance without any increase in the severity or frequency of recessions? If you look at Figure 15-11, you will see that central banks that have more independence have had lower inflation. This lower inflation has not been associated with more or longer recessions. The figure shows New Zealand *before* the central bank was given more independence; since then, it has moved down and to the right, toward lower inflation.

Figure **15-11**

Central Bank Independence and Inflation

The scatter plot shows that the more independent a central bank is, the lower the average inflation rate. The independence of the central bank is calculated by studying the laws of each country, including the length of the term of office of the head of the central bank (a longer term means more independence) and restrictions on the central bank lending to the government.

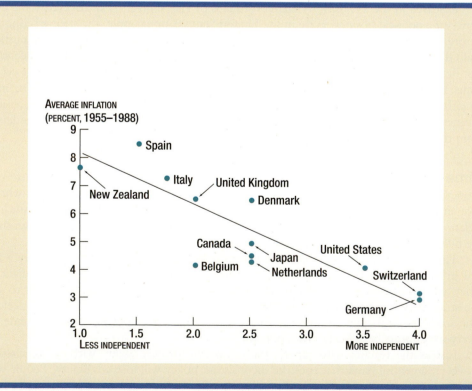

The Exchange Rate

Thus far in this chapter we have focused on the interest rate as the main consideration in conducting monetary policy. But the exchange rate is affected by changes in interest rates and also must be considered carefully in a full assessment. When the Fed cuts the interest rate, the value of the dollar declines because the lower interest rate makes dollar assets less attractive. And the lower value of the dollar makes exports cheaper and imports more expensive, which will add to the stimulus of the economy.

Some economists argue that the exchange rate is even more important when the interest rate hits zero, as in the recent crisis, because it can continue to fall, stimulating the economy by increasing exports and reducing imports. When much of the global economy is in recession or crisis, however, a depreciation of the dollar could make the recession worse in other countries by reducing those country's exports. Such changes in exchange rates are an essential part of the impact of monetary policy in the economic fluctuations model explained in Chapters 12 and 13, because the United States follows a **flexible exchange rate policy**, allowing the exchange rate to fluctuate in this way.

But what if the Fed did not want the exchange rate to change? Or what if the U.S. government and another country, such as Japan, agreed to fix the exchange rate? Such a policy is called a **fixed exchange rate policy**. How would that policy affect monetary policy?

Such questions are not simply hypothetical. Throughout history, governments have decided from time to time to adopt fixed exchange rate policies. The United States and most industrial countries were part of a fixed exchange rate system—called the Bretton Woods system—from the end of World War II until the early 1970s. Most recently, 12 countries in Europe have permanently fixed their exchange rates by forming a monetary union with a single currency, the euro. Until recently, Argentina fixed its exchange rate to the U.S. dollar. Other countries, like Ecuador, have adopted the U.S. dollar as their currency, and some people have suggested that the other countries in the Western Hemisphere join with the United States in a permanently fixed exchange rate system, with countries in Asia joining a fixed exchange rate system with Japan. This scenario would result in three large fixed exchange rate systems in the world—centered around the dollar, the euro, and the yen. Some have imagined a whole world with fixed exchange rates—with the dollar, the yen, and the euro fixed together. Thus, it is important to look at the implications of a fixed exchange rate for monetary policy, as we do in

Quick review: The *exchange rate* is the rate at which one country's currency is exchanged for another country's currency. For example, one U.S. dollar could be exchanged for 10.80 Mexican pesos on December 31, 2006. An *appreciation* of the dollar— say, from 11 to 12 pesos— means that it can be exchanged for more pesos.

flexible exchange rate policy
a policy in which exchange rates are determined in foreign exchange markets and governments do not agree to fix them.

fixed exchange rate policy
a policy in which a country maintains a fixed value of its currency in terms of other currencies.

this section, not only to understand what is happening in different countries in the twenty-first century, but also to understand proposals that would affect the United States and the whole world in the future.

The Effects of a Fixed Exchange Rate System on Monetary Policy

Suppose the United States decided to set up or join a fixed exchange rate system with Japan. Suppose also that after the United States joins the system, inflation starts to rise in the United States, and monetary policy makers want to raise the interest rate. Such an increase in the interest rate will tend to raise the value of the dollar relative to the Japanese currency. But if the dollar were fixed in value, as it would be with a fixed exchange rate policy, such a rise in the dollar would not be possible. Hence, if exchange rates were fixed, the Fed could not raise the interest rate in the United States relative to the interest rate in Japan. The fixed exchange rate would impose a serious restriction on U.S. monetary policy because interest rates in the United States could not be changed.

In general, if two countries have a fixed exchange rate and people are free to move funds back and forth between the two countries, then the interest rates in the two countries must move together. If, in the example of the United States and Japan, the Fed wanted to raise interest rates, then the Bank of Japan would have to raise interest rates by the same amount. But that might not be in the best interests of Japan, especially if the Japanese economy was in a recession. Like the two steering wheels of a driver's training car, which move in tandem, interest rates in any two countries with a fixed exchange rate must move together.

A Single European Currency and a Single Central Bank

The euro is the single currency used in the European Monetary Union. On January 1, 2002, euro notes and coins came into circulation in 12 European countries, replacing the national currencies of each of the countries, including Germany, where the European Central Bank (shown at right) is located. The seven banknote denominations have a common design in all the countries. In 2010, people began to worry that the euro would break apart because of the debt crisis in Greece and Ireland.

The connection between interest rates in different countries is visible to people in smaller countries that fix their currencies to the dollar, as Argentina painfully found out in 2001 and 2002. In 1991, Argentina chose to fix the value of the peso to the dollar, thus forcing its central bank to give up an independent monetary policy. When interest rates in the United States fell in the mid-1990s, this was beneficial to Argentina, as its interest rates fell as well. When U.S. rates rose rapidly in 2000 as the Fed battled inflation, however, Argentina was forced to raise its interest rates as well, pushing the weakened economy into a recession that lasted almost four years.

Ever since the 12 countries in the European Monetary Union permanently fixed their exchange rates with each other, there effectively has been only one overnight interest rate in Europe. The central banks of Germany, France, Italy, Spain, and other countries in the European Monetary Union have banded together into a new European Central Bank. The overnight interest rates in France, Germany, Italy, and the other countries move together, so in reality, the central bank makes decisions about only one interest rate. With the European Monetary Union, Germany and France cannot have separate monetary policies. They have only one monetary policy. If real GDP fell below potential GDP in France and remained equal to potential GDP in all the other countries, then a reduction in the interest rate by the European Central Bank, which would be right for France, would be wrong for Europe as a whole, so it probably would not occur. In such a circumstance, it might be necessary to use countercyclical *fiscal* policy in France—spending increases or tax cuts, as described in the previous chapter—because monetary policy would not be changed.

A real-life example of the effect of fixed exchange rates on monetary policy arose in Britain in 1992. At that time, interest rates were rising in Germany, because the German inflation rate was rising. But policy makers in Britain, which was facing hard economic times, did not want British interest rates to rise. The British faced a decision: Either they could raise their interest rates to keep them near Germany's, or they could let their interest rates fall below Germany's rate. In the latter case, their exchange rate would depreciate. For much of 1991 and 1992, the British kept their exchange rate stable, and this necessitated a rise in British interest rates. But by the end of 1992, increasingly poor economic conditions in Britain forced the British to give up the fixed exchange rate. Then interest rates in Britain could fall.

Interventions in the Exchange Market

Why wasn't it possible for the British government to go into the exchange market and buy and sell foreign exchange and thereby prevent these changes in the exchange rate? For example, if the British government purchases British pounds, this increases the demand for pounds and thereby raises the pound exchange rate. Thus, if the high interest rates in Germany were reducing the value of the British pound, why couldn't the British government buy pounds to offset these pressures? Such buying and selling of foreign currency by governments is called **exchange market intervention**. Such intervention does occur, and it can affect the exchange rate for short periods of time. The world currency markets are so huge and fast moving, however, that even governments do not have the funds to affect the exchange rate for long by buying and selling foreign exchange.

If one currency has a substantial interest rate advantage, funds will flow into that currency, driving up its value; exchange market intervention by governments cannot do much about this. Empirical studies have shown that exchange market intervention—if it is not matched by a change in interest rates by the central bank—can have only small effects on the exchange rate.

exchange market intervention

purchases and sales of foreign currency by a government in exchange markets with the intention to affect the exchange rate.

Another possibility is to prevent funds from flowing between the countries. If a law restricted the flow of funds into and out of a country, then that country could have both a fixed exchange rate and a separate interest rate policy. Such controls on the flow of capital were discussed intensely after the collapse of fixed exchange rates in Asia in 1997, and Malaysia did institute some restrictions on financial capital flows. Such restrictions have disadvantages, however. They are difficult to enforce, and they can reduce the amount of foreign capital a country needs for development.

The Rationale for Fixed Exchange Rates

If fixed exchange rates lead to the loss of a separate monetary policy, then why do countries form fixed exchange rate systems? One reason to adopt a fixed exchange rate is that exchange rate volatility can interfere with trade, which certainly is one of the reasons the European countries established the European Monetary Union. Firms may not develop long-term relationships and contacts with other countries if they are worried about big changes in the exchange rate.

Another, perhaps more important, reason to form a fixed exchange rate system is that some countries have had a history of poor monetary policies. For example, Italy had high inflation before it decided to join with the other countries of Europe in a monetary union. And Argentina had many years of hyperinflation before it fixed its exchange rate with the United States and abandoned its own monetary policy.

The goal of fixing the exchange rate in these cases is to adopt the good monetary policy of a country whose central bank has a history of good policy: the Fed in the case of Argentina, and the central banks of Germany and France in the case of Italy. In these cases, the benefits of a fixed exchange rate system may outweigh the loss of a separate monetary policy. The evidence, however, is mixed. In the case of Italy, the policy seems to have worked: Inflation has been in single digits for many years. Conversely, in Argentina, where the policy seemed to work well initially in bringing down inflation, restricting the hand of monetary policy makers seemed to make it tough for the country to recover from its recession of the late 1990s.

REVIEW

- Interest rates must move together in countries with fixed exchange rates and with a free flow of funds between the countries.

- With a fixed exchange rate, each country cannot have a separate monetary policy.

- By permanently fixing exchange rates, a country can adopt the monetary policy of another country.

CONCLUSION

Monetary policy making is a powerful, but difficult, job. It is especially difficult during a financial crisis, as this chapter has shown. Central bankers like to say that the job is like driving a car by looking only through the rear-view mirror. They have to take actions that greatly affect the economy without knowing where the economy is going, only where it has been.

In this chapter, we have seen exactly why the job is difficult. During an unprecedented financial crisis, it may be necessary to use unprecedented and untested tools. It is difficult to resist political pressure for short-term benefits at the expense of long-term costs. And even in normal times, it is difficult to keep aggregate demand in line with potential GDP in a world where potential GDP is hard to estimate and policy effects on aggregate demand are uncertain.

We also have learned that while monetary policy has a powerful effect, it cannot do everything. It cannot lower unemployment permanently, and trying to do so will only raise inflation. And a country cannot have both a fixed exchange rate and the ability to adjust interest rates to control inflation and prevent recessions.

All these ideas are useful for understanding the frequent headlines and news stories about the Fed. And they help take some of the mystique out of what many people feel is the most mysterious institution in the world.

KEY POINTS

1. The Fed's balance sheet shows the key actions of the Fed during the crisis and in normal times.
2. The Fed introduced credit easing during the financial crisis.
3. Central bank independence is a way to avoid political business cycles and the temptation to raise inflation for short-term gain.
4. The gain-then-pain scenario illustrates that a monetary policy shift to high inflation has short-run benefits but long-run costs.
5. An important task of monetary policy is to manage aggregate demand so that real GDP equals potential GDP.
6. A good monetary policy rule is responsive to real GDP as well as to inflation.
7. The demand for money is negatively related to the interest rate.
8. The Fed changes the quantity of money when it changes the interest rate.
9. Reserve requirements are rarely changed. The Fed also can increase the money supply by lowering the discount rate. This typically, but not always, is done in conjunction with lowering the federal funds rate.
10. Fixed exchange rates restrict monetary policy.

KEY TERMS

central bank independence, 361
discount rate, 348
exchange market intervention, 367
fixed exchange rate policy, 365
flexible exchange rate policy, 365

liquidity trap, 354
monetary base, 348
money demand, 350
political business cycle, 363
time inconsistency, 363

QUESTIONS FOR REVIEW

1. What is the size of the Fed's balance sheet?
2. What is credit easing?
3. What are some "other measures" taken by the Fed in the financial crisis?
4. What is the zero lower bound on the interest rate?
5. What are the advantages and disadvantages of central bank independence?
6. What is an example of a political business cycle?
7. Why would the Fed raise real interest rates if real GDP were above potential GDP?

8. What is the Phillips curve?
9. Why is the demand for money inversely related to the interest rate?
10. What is the opportunity cost of holding money?
11. Why is there a loss of monetary policy independence with fixed exchange rates?
12. Why would a country adopt a fixed exchange rate policy?

PROBLEMS

1. Why is an independent central bank more likely to put emphasis on price stability rather than on keeping unemployment low, compared with a central bank that is not independent?
2. The original Federal Reserve Act of 1913 allowed the secretary of the U.S. Treasury to be a member of the Federal Reserve Board, but a later amendment prohibited this. How would allowing the secretary of the U.S. Treasury to be a member affect the conduct of monetary policy?
3. What is the discount rate? How does it differ from the federal funds rate? Describe how the Fed affects each of these interest rates.
4. Banks can borrow from each other on the federal funds market or borrow from the Fed. Banks borrow far more on the federal funds market than from the Fed. You can borrow from your friends or from your parents. From whom are you more likely to borrow? Why do you think banks prefer to borrow from each other?
5. During the early 1990s, Japan experienced deflation and real GDP was below potential GDP. Draw a diagram showing the situation in Japan. Suppose the Japanese central bank decided that it had to reinflate and set a target inflation rate of 2 percent. How would it accomplish this? Show the short-run, medium-run, and long-run effects.
6. Using the aggregate demand curve and the inflation adjustment line, show what the Fed should do if real GDP is below potential GDP and the current inflation rate is equal to the target inflation rate, which is the ideal inflation rate from the Fed's perspective.

7. The Taylor Rule states that the central bank should set the short-term nominal interest rate (i) based on the inflation gap [the difference between inflation (π) and desired inflation (π^*)] and the output gap [the percentage difference between real GDP (Y) and potential GDP (Y^*)]. An example of a Taylor Rule would be the formula

$$i - \pi = 1.5 + 0.5(\pi - \pi^*) + 0.5\left(\frac{Y - Y^*}{Y^*}\right)$$

The term on the left-hand side is the real interest rate. Consider the following table:

	Base Scenario	Scenario B	Scenario C
Inflation rate (π), %	2.0	4.0	2.0
Target inflation rate (π^*), %	2.0	2.0	2.0
Output gap, %	0.0	0.0	2.0
Real interest rate			
Nominal interest rate			

a. Fill in the real and nominal interests rates chosen by the policy maker in the base scenario.
b. How does scenario B differ from the base scenario in terms of the inflation and output gaps? Calculate the real interest rate. Has the real interest rate moved in the direction that

would move the inflation rate toward its target?

c. How does scenario C differ from the base scenario in terms of the inflation and output gaps? Calculate the real interest rate. Has the real interest rate moved in the direction that would move output toward the potential level?

d. Suppose a new chair of the central bank is appointed and she switches to a new policy rule of the form given in the next equation. Recalculate the real and nominal interest rates for the three scenarios. What has been the effect of the change in weights?

$$i - \pi = 1.5 + 0.75(\pi - \pi^*) + 0.25\left(\frac{Y - Y^*}{Y^*}\right)$$

8. Suppose two countries are identical except for the fact that the central bank of one country lets interest rates rise sharply when real GDP rises above potential GDP and the other does not. Draw the aggregate demand curve for each country. What are the benefits and drawbacks of each country's policy?

9. Sweden and the United Kingdom chose not to join the European Monetary Union (EMU). Explain what a decision to join the EMU would imply for the monetary policy-making abilities of the central banks of these two countries.

10. Explain why restricting flows of funds into or out of a country can give that country's central bank the ability to conduct monetary policy even with a fixed exchange rate. What are some of the disadvantages of such a restriction?

16 Capital and Financial Markets

In this chapter we extend our analysis of markets to *financial markets,* such as the stock market and the bond market, as well as to *markets in physical capital,* such as housing, office buildings, and factories. These markets have a profound impact on people's lives, especially during times of economic and financial crisis when prices fluctuate wildly.

Figure 16-1 shows why. Each bar in the figure shows how much $1 invested in the stock market in 1987 would give back each year since then. For example, $1 invested in the stock market in 1987 would have given back $5.88 in 2008. That sounds good, but if you had sold the stocks one year earlier in 2007, before the huge drop in the stock market in 2008, you would have gotten much more, $9.33. And if you held on after the 2008 crash, you would have gotten back up to $8.35. As Figure 16-1 makes clear, although the long-term trend in the stock market investments is positive, the market experienced short-term setbacks as in 2008 and in other years such as 2001–2003. This volatility is what makes investing in the stock market risky, especially over shorter periods of time. Figure 16-1 shows the return on an average of 500 stocks. The returns on individual stocks can be even more volatile. For example, the price of the stock of the financial firm

JP Morgan Chase & Co. fell from $53 in April 2007 to a low of $16 in March 2008 and then bounced back to $47 in April 2011.

Markets in physical capital also can be volatile, as illustrated in Figure 16-2, which shows the median price of a house in the United States during the same period of time as Figure 16-1. Note that housing prices were stable through most of the 1990s, but they rose rapidly from 2000 to 2006 before coming back down rapidly. By the end of 2008, housing prices had returned to the levels of early 2004. As with the individual stock price, the prices of different houses rise or fall at rates different from the averages, depending on individual and local demand and supply factors. Prices in Michigan did not rise much during the national housing boom, whereas prices rose more rapidly than average in California and Florida. The bust in housing prices in California and Florida was also sharp.

We begin by defining physical and financial capital and describing how firms use them. We show that a firm's demand for physical capital can be analyzed in much the same way that we analyze a firm's demand for labor. We then consider the specific markets for financial capital, stocks, and bonds, while developing new tools to handle risk and uncertainty.

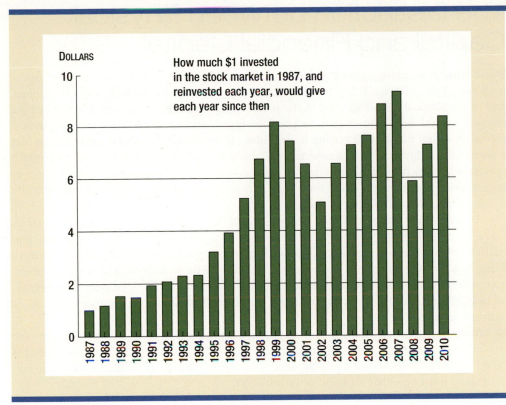

Figure 16-1

Returns from Investing in the Stock Market

Although the trend is up over several decades, the volatility over shorter periods of time can be dramatic and risky.

Source: Computed from S&P 500 Index.

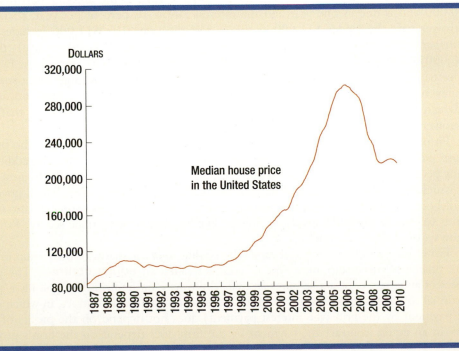

Figure 16-2

Housing Boom and Bust

House prices rose rapidly—a boom—until 2006, then fell rapidly—a bust—illustrating how prices in physical capital markets can be as volatile as financial markets.

Source: Computed from the Case-Shiller Price Index using median price in the year 2000.

The Distinction between Physical Capital and Financial Capital

Some basic terminology about physical and financial capital is useful in studying capital markets. *Physical capital* refers to all the machines, factories, oil tankers, office buildings, and other physical resources used in the production of goods or services. Firms combine physical capital with labor inputs to produce goods and services. They obtain physical capital by either building it, buying it, or renting it. For example, McDonald's might hire a construction firm to build a new facility near a highway, a local school district might purchase several hundred computers for use in classrooms, and a real estate developer might rent a construction crane for a year to help move building materials onto the site of a large apartment building project.

An important characteristic of physical capital is that it provides productive services for a number of years. Residential housing—single-family homes, apartments, and trailers—also is a form of physical capital. It provides productive services in the form of living space that people can enjoy year after year. Government-owned roads, schools, and military equipment also are physical capital. It is useful to think of government capital as helping to produce services, whether transportation services, education services, or national security.

Another important characteristic of physical capital is that it does not remain in new condition permanently. The gradual decline in the productive usefulness of capital is called **depreciation**. Trucks, trailers, roads, machines, and even buildings wear out and eventually must be either replaced or refurbished.

depreciation
the decrease in an asset's value over time; for capital, it is the amount by which physical capital wears out over a given period of time.

To purchase, rent, or build capital, a firm needs to obtain funds. These funds are an example of *financial capital*. Firms can obtain financial capital in two different ways: by issuing debt (borrowing) and by issuing equity (selling an ownership stake in the firm).

When a firm wants to borrow money, it can take out a bank loan. When a firm takes out a loan, it agrees to pay back the amount it borrowed plus interest at a future date. The amount of interest is determined by the *interest rate*. If the amount borrowed is $10,000 and is due in one year and the interest rate is 10 percent per year, then the borrower pays the lender $11,000 at the end of the year. The $11,000 includes the *principal* on the loan ($10,000) plus the *interest payment* ($1,000 = 0.1 times $10,000). Larger firms also can issue *corporate bonds*. A bond is an agreement by the issuer to make a specified number of payments in the future in exchange for a sum of money today. Both loans and bonds are a type of contract called a **debt contract** in which the lender agrees to provide funds today in exchange for a promise that the borrower will pay back the funds at a future date with interest.

debt contract
a contract in which a lender agrees to provide funds today in exchange for a promise from the borrower, who will repay that amount plus interest at some point in the future.

Firms are not the only entities that take out debt contracts. Most people who buy a house get a **mortgage**, which is a loan of funds to purchase real estate. In addition, many people get loans from banks to buy cars and consumer appliances. The biggest single issuer of bonds in the United States is the federal government. The federal government borrows funds by selling *government bonds*. State and local governments also issue bonds to finance physical capital investments like building a new public school, fixing a highway, or building a tunnel.

mortgage
a loan to purchase a house.

Firms also can obtain financial capital by issuing *stock*, or shares of ownership in the firm. Shares of ownership are a type of contract called an **equity contract**. The purchaser of an equity contract acquires an ownership share in the firm that typically is proportional to the size of the equity contract. In contrast to a debt contract, in which case the payment by the firm (the interest payment) does not depend on the profits of the firm, in an equity contract the payment by the firm does depend on the firm's profits.

equity contract
shares of ownership in a firm; payments to the owners of the shares depend on the firm's profits.

Firms that make lots of profits will pay out more in *dividends* to their shareholders. Shareholders also can benefit if the firm increases in value because their shares will be worth more when they are sold.

Once bonds or stocks have been issued, they can be exchanged or traded. Highly organized financial markets trade stocks and bonds. The government and corporate bond markets are located in New York City, London, Tokyo, and other large financial centers. The stock markets include the New York Stock Exchange, the Nasdaq, several regional stock exchanges in the United States, and many stock exchanges in other countries.

Having defined some key terms, we now proceed to discuss the different types of capital markets. We begin with markets for physical capital.

REVIEW

- Physical capital and financial capital are distinct but closely related. Physical capital refers to the machines, buildings, and physical resources needed to produce output. To expand their physical capital, firms need to raise funds in some way. These funds are known as financial capital.

- Firms can buy, build, or rent physical capital. They can acquire financial capital by means of debt contracts or equity contracts.

- Debt contracts, such as bonds or loans, allow borrowers access to a sum of money today in exchange for a promise to repay that sum of money plus interest in the future. Equity contracts allow firms to obtain money today in exchange for handing over an ownership stake in the firm.

- The bonds or stocks that firms issue can be traded. Organized markets for trading bonds and stocks are found in all the world's financial centers.

Markets for Physical Capital

The demand for physical capital is a relationship between the quantity of capital demanded by firms and the price of this capital. The demand for capital is a *derived demand* in the same sense that the demand for labor is a derived demand; that is, the demand for capital derives from the goods and services that firms produce with capital. In this section we show that just as the quantity of labor that the firm employs depends on the marginal revenue product of labor, the quantity of capital that the firm employs depends on the marginal revenue product of capital.

Rental Markets

The firm's capital decision is best understood if we first assume that the firm *rents* capital in a competitive rental market. In fact, it is common for firms to rent capital; many types of equipment have a rental market in which many rental firms specialize in renting the equipment to other firms. For example, a construction firm can rent a dump truck; a clothing store can rent a storefront at a mall; an airline can lease an airplane. The price in the rental market is called the **rental price of capital**. It is the amount that a rental firm charges for the use of capital equipment for a specified period of time, such as a month.

Consider a hypothetical construction company, called Lofts-R-Us, deciding whether to rent a dump truck from a rental company called Acme Rental. To show how much capital a firm like Lofts-R-Us would rent, we need to consider the effect of this capital on the firm's profits. The marginal revenue product of capital can be used to assess this effect on profits. The **marginal revenue product of capital** is defined as the change in total revenue as the firm increases its capital by one unit. We assume that the marginal

rental price of capital
the amount that a rental company charges for the use of capital equipment for a specified period of time.

marginal revenue product of capital
the change in total revenue because of a one-unit increase in capital.

revenue product of capital declines as more capital is employed at the firm. For example, suppose the marginal revenue product of capital is $3,000 as capital rises from zero trucks to one truck, $1,500 as capital rises from one truck to two trucks, and $500 as capital rises from two trucks to three trucks.

Suppose the rental price of a dump truck is $1,000 a month. This price is what Acme Rental charges, and all other rental firms in the area charge essentially the same price. Because the rental market is competitive, neither Acme Rental nor Lofts-R-Us has enough market power to affect the rental price. How many dump trucks would Lofts-R-Us use? With the marginal revenue product of capital from one dump truck equal to $3,000 a month, the firm will employ at least one dump truck. In other words, if the firm's total revenue increases by $3,000 and the rental price for the truck is $1,000, then it makes sense to rent the dump truck. With the marginal revenue product of capital from a second dump truck equal to $1,500, the firm will employ a second dump truck; by doing so, it can increase its profits by $500. With the marginal revenue product of capital from a third dump truck equal to only $500, however, the firm will lower its profits if it rents a third dump truck. Thus, if the rental price of the dump truck is $1,000, the firm will employ exactly two dump trucks. The firm rents the largest amount of capital for which the marginal revenue product of capital is greater than the rental price; if fractional units of capital were possible, then the firm would keep renting more capital until *the marginal revenue product of capital was exactly equal to the rental price.*

The Demand Curve for Capital To derive the demand curve for capital, we must determine the quantity of capital demanded by the firm as the rental price of capital changes. For example, if the rental price of dump trucks declines to $400, then the quantity of dump trucks demanded by the firm will increase; a third dump truck will be rented because the price is now below the marginal revenue product of capital. In other words, as the rental price of capital falls, the quantity of capital demanded increases. Similarly, as the rental price of capital rises, the quantity of capital demanded decreases.

Figure 16-3 illustrates this general principle. It shows the marginal revenue product of capital for any firm. As more capital is employed, the marginal revenue product

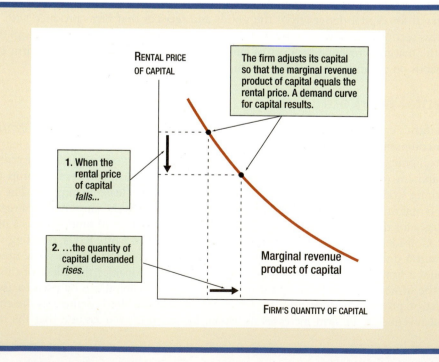

Figure 16-3

Demand for Physical Capital by One Firm

A profit-maximizing firm chooses a quantity of capital that gives a marginal revenue product of capital equal to the rental price. Because the marginal revenue product of capital declines as more capital is used, a lower rental price of capital results in a larger quantity of capital demanded.

RENTAL PRICE OF CAPITAL

The firm adjusts its capital so that the marginal revenue product of capital equals the rental price. A demand curve for capital results.

1. When the rental price of capital *falls...*

2. ...the quantity of capital demanded *rises.*

Marginal revenue product of capital

FIRM'S QUANTITY OF CAPITAL

declines. For profit maximization, the firm will rent capital to the point at which the marginal revenue product of capital equals the rental price. Thus, as we lower the rental price, the quantity of capital demanded increases. In other words, the demand curve for capital is downward sloping.

The demand curve for capital is determined by the marginal revenue product of capital. If the marginal revenue product changes, the demand curve for capital will shift. For example, if the marginal product of dump trucks rises, the demand for dump trucks by Lofts-R-Us will shift outward.

Demand for Factors of Production in General Here we showed that the marginal revenue product of capital equals the rental price. This same principle applies to any factor of production for which the market in that factor is competitive. *For any input to production, a profit-maximizing firm will choose a quantity of that input such that the marginal revenue product equals the price of that input.*

The Market Demand and Supply The market demand for physical capital is found by adding up the demand for physical capital by many firms. Figure 16-4 shows such a market demand curve.

On the same diagram, we show the market supply curve. It is the sum of the supply curves for all the firms in the industry providing capital for rent, such as Acme Rental. The higher the rental price of capital, the more likely Acme Rental is to buy new dump trucks and offer them as rentals to firms like Lofts-R-Us. If other rental firms behave the way that Acme Rental does, then the market supply of rental capital will be increasing with rental prices.

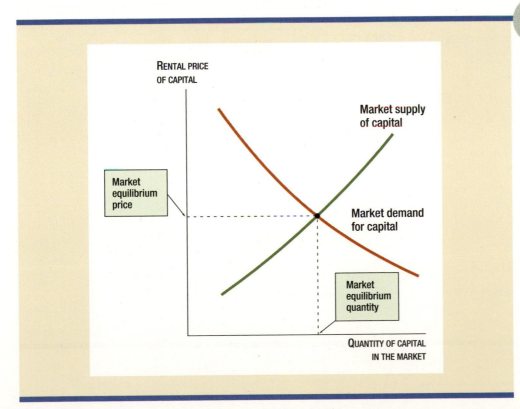

Figure 16-4

Market Supply and Demand for Physical Capital
The market demand for capital is the sum of the demands of the individual firms that use the equipment. The market supply is the sum of the supplies at the individual firms that provide the equipment. Market equilibrium occurs in cases in which the quantity of capital demanded equals the quantity of capital supplied.

The equilibrium rental price and the equilibrium quantity of capital rented are shown in the diagram. The supply and demand model for capital illustrated in Figure 16-4 then can be used to predict the effects of tax changes or other changes in the capital market in much the same way as any other supply and demand model. For example, if the government places a tax on construction firms like Lofts-R-Us proportional to the quantity of trucks they rent, perhaps because the heavy trucks damage city roads more than cars do, then the marginal revenue product of capital will decline and the demand curve for capital will shift down, or to the left. This shift in demand will lower the equilibrium rental price received by Acme and reduce the quantity of capital rented. Alternatively, if the city government is eager to have new apartment buildings in the city, it may offer a subsidy on the rental of capital by construction firms. This would shift the demand curve for capital up, or to the right, and increase the quantity of capital rented.

The Case of Fixed Supply: Economic Rents

An important special case of a market for physical capital occurs when the supply of physical capital is completely fixed. Alfred Marshall gave the following famous example of physical capital with a completely fixed supply: "Let us suppose that a meteoric shower of a few thousand large stones harder than diamonds fell all in one place, so that they were all picked up at once, and no amount of search could find any more. These stones, able to cut every material, would revolutionize many branches of industry."[1]

The important thing about Marshall's stones is that their supply cannot be increased or decreased regardless of the price of the stones. In other words, the supply curve for Marshall's stones is perfectly vertical, or perfectly inelastic, as shown in Figure 16-5.

Figure 16-5

The Case of a Fixed Supply of Capital

When the supply of capital is perfectly inelastic, a shift in demand changes the rental price but not the quantity supplied. Marshall's stones are a hypothetical example of capital with a perfectly inelastic supply.

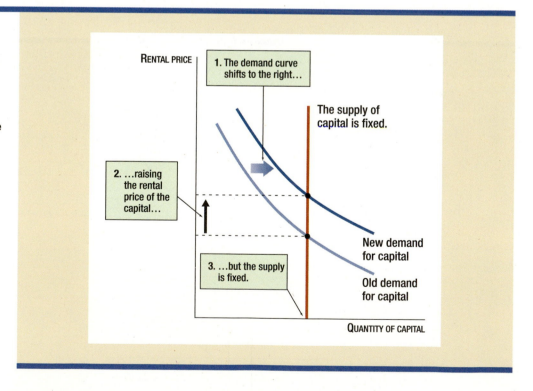

RENTAL PRICE

1. The demand curve shifts to the right…

The supply of capital is fixed.

2. …raising the rental price of the capital…

3. …but the supply is fixed.

New demand for capital

Old demand for capital

QUANTITY OF CAPITAL

---

[1] Alfred Marshall, *Principles of Economics*, 8th ed. (New York: Macmillan, 1920), 415.

Figure 16-5 shows what happens when the demand for capital that is in fixed supply shifts, such as Marshall's stones. A change in demand will change the price, but it will not change the quantity. Demand completely determines the price in this case because the quantity supplied cannot change.

Economists have a special terminology for the price in this circumstance: **Economic rent** is the price of anything that has a fixed supply. Economic rent is also sometimes called *pure rent*. Economic rent is a significant concept in economics precisely because the quantity supplied does not depend on the price. Thus, a tax on economic rents would not change the amount supplied; it would not affect economic efficiency or cause a deadweight loss. For example, if the government passed a tax (even a 99.9 percent tax) on the rental payments charged by the lucky owners of Marshall's stones, the quantity of stones supplied would not change.

Marshall's stones are of course a hypothetical example. In practice, certain types of land may come close to being an item in fixed supply, but it is always possible to improve land or clear land and thereby change its supply to some degree. The perfectly inelastic supply of Marshall's stones or the near perfectly inelastic supply of certain types of land is in sharp contrast to the higher elasticity of supply of most capital goods. The supply of dump trucks, apartment buildings, and other types of capital is sensitive to changes in the price. Increases in the price provide an incentive to increase the quantity supplied, and decreases in the price provide an incentive to decrease the quantity supplied. In reality, therefore, taxes on capital would be expected to change the quantity of capital supplied.

economic rent
the price of something that has a fixed supply.

The Ownership of Physical Capital

Rental markets for capital are common, but they are not the only way in which firms obtain capital. The same construction firm that rents dump trucks might choose to purchase and own a dump truck rather than rent one, especially if it expects to continually be engaged in projects for which a truck is required. The firm also may own the warehouse where it stores its building materials and the office where it keeps its books and meets prospective customers. Although legal and tax differences exist between renting and ownership, the economic principles are similar. In fact, even though owners of physical capital do not pay a rental price, economic considerations indicate that they pay an *implicit* rental price.

When a firm buys equipment, it must either borrow funds to pay for the equipment or use its own funds, funds that it could have put in an interest-earning account at a bank. If it borrows the funds, the monthly interest payment on the loan is like a rental payment. If it uses its own funds, the interest it would have received at the bank is an opportunity cost and is considered to be similar to a rental payment. In addition to these payments, the firm that owns the equipment must factor in the wear and tear, or depreciation, on the equipment. The amount by which the firm's equipment deteriorates is also a cost.

In sum, for a firm that chooses to purchase and own capital, the **implicit rental price** of capital for a year equals the interest payments for the year plus the amount of depreciation during the year. For example, suppose the interest rate is 10 percent, the purchase price of a dump truck is $40,000, and the dump truck depreciates $8,000 per year. Then the implicit rental price is $12,000 per year (0.10 times $40,000, plus $8,000), or $1,000 a month, the same as the rental price in our dump truck example. The implicit rental price depends on the interest rate. The higher the interest rate, the higher the interest payments during the year, and thus the higher the implicit rental price. When the interest rate rises, the implicit rental price rises. When the interest rate falls, the implicit rental price falls.

The concept of the implicit rental price makes the firm's decision to buy a dump truck, or any other piece of capital, analogous to the decision to rent. The demand curve looks the same as that in Figure 16-3, except that it is the implicit rental price rather than the actual rental price that is on the vertical axis.

implicit rental price
the cost of the funds used to buy the capital plus the depreciation of the capital over a given period of time.

The Housing Market

The model of the demand and supply of physical capital can be applied to the demand and supply for residential houses, which for many people is the largest capital item they rent or own. The application of the model to housing is straightforward because many people have had the experience of renting a house or an apartment.

Let's start with a market for rental housing. The rental price of a house is simply the rent on the house for a period of time, such as $500 per month. Rather than the marginal revenue product of a truck to a firm, think of the marginal benefit of a house to an individual. Then, applying the same reasoning, we conclude that an individual will rent a house if the rental price is less than the marginal benefit of the house to the individual. Because few people rent more than one house, we assume that marginal benefit decreases with the size of the house rather than with the number of houses. Thus, an individual will consume housing up until the marginal benefit of the housing is equal to the rental price. The implication is that the *quantity of housing demanded is related negatively to the rental price of housing.*

Finally, by adding up all the individual demand curves, we get a market demand for housing. In the housing market as a whole, the higher the rental price on houses, the lower the quantity of houses demanded. Hence, the *demand curve for housing is sloped negatively.* The supply curve of housing is analogous to the supply curve for other kinds of capital. Rather than the Acme Dump Truck Rental company, we might have the Acme Student Apartment Rental company. The concepts are similar.

To move from markets in which people rent their homes to markets in which people own their homes, we can use the *implicit rental price* concept. For a house owned by an individual or a family, the implicit rental price will equal the interest rate on the mortgage (the loan on the house) plus the amount of depreciation on the house during the year. The quantity of housing demanded depends negatively on the implicit rental price. Hence, we have a demand for housing that looks just like the demand curve in Figure 16-4.

Observe that because the quantity of housing demanded depends negatively on the implicit rental price, it also depends negatively on the mortgage interest rate. Hence, if mortgage interest rates decline, we would predict an increase in the demand for housing. Indeed, many experts think a major reason for the housing boom during the years leading up to the housing bust in 2006 was that mortgage interest rates were low. The theory thus explains important trends in housing markets.

REVIEW

- The demand for physical capital at a firm is a derived demand. What firms are willing to pay for capital depends on the value of the goods and services they can produce with that capital.

- Firms that rent capital will choose to rent capital up to the point at which the marginal revenue product of capital equals the rental price of capital.

- The marginal revenue product of capital decreases as the quantity of capital used by the firm increases. So when the rental price goes down, the firm will want to add extra machines until the marginal revenue product of capital equals the rental price.

- If capital is purchased rather than rented, the firm still faces an implicit rental price.

- The demand curve for purchased capital, then, looks similar to the demand curve for rental capital; the demand curve is downward sloping in the (implicit) rental price.

- The theory also implies a demand curve for housing and offers an explanation for the housing boom in 2002–2006.

Markets for Financial Capital

Having seen how markets for physical capital work, let us turn to the examination of markets for financial capital. As we discussed, firms that want to acquire physical capital need to obtain financial capital. They can obtain financial capital by issuing stocks and bonds. Stocks and bonds are traded on financial markets. Their prices are determined by the actions of buyers and sellers, like prices in any other market. Understanding what drives the prices of stocks and bonds is important for determining firms' ability to acquire financial capital. It is also important for investors who buy stocks and bonds as a way to save for their future retirement or simply as a way to make money.

Stock Prices and Rates of Return

Prices of the stocks of most large firms can be found in daily newspapers. Investors are interested in buying those stocks whose prices are likely to rise and that are more likely to pay back their profits to shareholders in the form of dividends. We can define the annual **return** from holding a stock as the *dividend* plus the *capital gain* during the year. The **capital gain** during the year is the increase in the price of the stock during the year. A **capital loss** is a negative capital gain: a decrease in the price. When comparing dividends across companies, we typically look at the **dividend yield**, that is, the dividend stated as a percentage of the price. Similarly, in comparing returns across companies, we typically look at the **rate of return**, that is, the return stated as a percentage of the price of the stock.

A simple example can illustrate these terms. For example, the dividend for Hewlett-Packard in 2006 was $0.32 per year. At its year-end stock price of $41.19, the dividend yield was 0.8 percent. During 2006, the price of Hewlett-Packard stock rose from $29.28 to $41.19, a capital gain of $11.91. Combined with the dividend, the total return was $12.23, a rate of return of 41.8 percent. In this example, the capital gain is a much bigger portion of the rate of return than the dividend.

But stock market returns are not always as good as in this example. Consider the same company two years later: Hewlett-Packard's stock price fell from $50.48 to $36.29 per share during 2008, a *negative* capital gain or a capital loss of $14.19. Including the $0.32 in dividends it paid during the year, Hewlett-Packard's total rate of return was negative 27.5 percent. 2008 was not a good year for stocks. The stock price of Caterpillar, the famous maker of large-scale construction equipment, fell from $72.56 to $44.67 during the year. Including a $1.56 dividend payout, its return was negative 36.3 percent. Indeed, the average stock price of all the 500 major U.S. companies—as measured by the Standard and Poor's (S&P) 500 Index—fell by 38.5 percent during 2008, which substantially cut into gains made in the previous two decades, as shown in Figure 16-1.

You can figure out which firms are the most profitable, and hence more likely to generate a high rate of return for their shareholders, by looking at firms' accounting profits, also known as **earnings**. Firms pay out some of their profits as dividends; the rest of the profits are retained and invested in physical capital or research. Stock tables list the **price-earnings ratio**: the price of the stock divided by the annual earnings per share. The price-earnings ratio for Hewlett-Packard in 2006 was 17.1. With the price of the stock at $41.19, this means that earnings for the year were $2.4088 per share ($41.19/$2.4088 = 17.1). A firm's earnings ultimately influence the return on the firm's stock, so the price-earnings ratio is watched closely.

Bond Prices and Rates of Return

Bond prices for both corporate and government bonds also can be found in the financial pages of the newspaper. The Economics In Action box in this chapter shows you how to read the prices of different types of bonds.

return
the income received from the ownership of an asset; for a stock, the return is the dividend plus the capital gain.

capital gain
the increase in the value of an asset through an increase in its price.

capital loss
the decrease in the value of an asset through a decrease in its price.

dividend yield
the dividend stated as a percentage of the price of the stock.

rate of return
the return on an asset stated as a percentage of the price of the asset.

> **Check the result.** The dividend was $0.32. The closing price was $41.19. Dividing 0.32 by 41.19 gives 0.008, or 0.8 percent.

earnings
the accounting profits of a firm.

price-earnings ratio
the price of a stock divided by its annual earnings per share.

coupon

the fixed amount that a borrower agrees to pay to the bondholder each year.

maturity date

the date when the principal on a loan is to be paid back.

face value

the principal that will be paid back when a bond matures.

yield

the annual rate of return on a bond if the bond were held to maturity.

> **Here is a typical quote on bond yields:**
>
> "The price of the 30-year Treasury bond rose less than 1/8 point, or less than $1.25 for a bond with $1,000 face value, to 84 4/32. Its yield, which moves in the opposite direction of its price, dropped to 7.60 percent from 7.61 percent on Thursday."

A bond has four key characteristics: *coupon, maturity date, face value,* and *yield*. The **coupon** is the fixed amount that the borrower agrees to pay the bondholder each year. The **maturity date** is the time when the coupon payments end and the principal is paid back. The **face value** is the amount of principal that will be paid back when the bond matures. The bond boldfaced in the box has a maturity date of February 2037 and a coupon equal to 4.75 percent of the face value of the bond. That is, 4.75 percent, or $47.50, a year on a bond with a face value of $1,000, will be paid until 2037, and in February 2037, the $1,000 face value will be paid back. (The coupon is called a "rate" because it is measured as a percentage of the face value.)

Once the government has issued bonds, they can be sold or bought in the bond market. In the bond market, bond traders make a living buying and selling bonds. The bond traders will *bid* a certain price at which they will buy, and they will *ask* a certain price at which they will sell. The bid price is slightly lower than the ask price, which enables the bond traders to earn a profit by buying at a price that is slightly lower than the price at which they sell.

The **yield**, or yield to maturity, is defined as the annual rate of return on the bond if the bond were bought at the current price and held to maturity. When people refer to the current interest rate on bonds, they are referring to the yield on the bond. Observe that the yield on the boldfaced bond maturing in February 2037 was 4.68 percent on March 1, 2007, slightly below the 4.75 percent coupon rate.

Why are bond yields different from the coupon rate? An inverse, or negative, relationship exists between the yield and the price. They have an inverse relationship because the payments of the bond are fixed—the borrower (bond issuer) agrees to pay back the lender (bondholder) the principal on the maturity date and make coupon payments in the interim—regardless of what the buyer paid for the bond. The higher the price you pay today to get this fixed stream of interest and principal payments in the future, the lower the rate of return (yield) you earn. So unlike the coupon rate, which stays fixed, the yield will fluctuate with price. Furthermore, as the price rises, the yield will fall, and vice versa.

Why do bond yields fluctuate? Consider a simple example. Suppose you just bought a one-year bond for $100 that says that the government will pay 5 percent of the face value, or $5, plus $100 at the end of the one-year period. Now suppose that just after you bought the bond, interest rates on bank deposits suddenly jumped to 10 percent. Your bond says that you earn 5 percent per year, so if you hold it for the entire year, your rate of return is less than you could get on a bank deposit. Suddenly the bond looks much less attractive. You probably would want to sell it, but everyone else knows the bond is less attractive, also. You would not be able to get $100 for the bond. The price would decline until the rate of return on the bond was close to the interest rate at the bank. For example, if the price fell to $95.45, then the payment of $105 at the end of the year would result in a 10 percent rate of return [that is, $0.10 = (105 - 95.45)/95.45$]. In other words, the yield on the bond would rise until it reached a value closer to 10 percent than to 5 percent.

If you look at the U.K. government bonds in the box, you will notice a bond maturing in 2017 with a coupon rate of 8.75 percent and a yield of 4.75. This bond must have been issued at a time when market interest rates were closer to 8.75 percent. As interest rates in the United Kingdom fell, people found that holding the bond was a more attractive proposition than keeping money in the bank, so they bid up the price of the bond, driving down the yield until it approached the new market interest rates in the United Kingdom. This implies that periods of falling interest rates are good for bondholders and bond issuers because the prices of their bonds rise, while periods of rising interest rates are bad for both bondholders and bond issuers.

On the basis of these considerations, we can use a formula to calculate the relationship between the price and the yield for bonds of any maturity. Let P be the price of the

Table 16-1

Bond Price Formula

One-year maturity:	$P = \dfrac{R}{1+i} + \dfrac{F}{1+i}$
Two-year maturity:	$P = \dfrac{R}{1+i} + \dfrac{R}{(1+i)^2} + \dfrac{F}{(1+i)^2}$
Three-year maturity:	$P = \dfrac{R}{1+i} + \dfrac{R}{(1+i)^2} + \dfrac{R}{(1+i)^3} + \dfrac{F}{(1+i)^3}$
For very long term:	$P = \dfrac{R}{i}$

P = price of bond
R = coupon
F = face value
i = yield

bond. Let R be the coupon. Let F be the face value. Let i be the yield. The formula relating to the price and the yield in the case of a one-year bond is indicated in the first row of Table 16-1.

For a one-year bond, a coupon payment of R is paid at the end of one year together with the face value of the bond. The price P is what you would be willing to pay *now, in the present,* for these future payments. It is the *present discounted value* of the coupon payment plus the face value at the end of the year. By looking at the formula in the first row of Table 16-1, you can see the negative relationship between the price (P) of the bond and the yield (i) on the bond. The higher the yield, the lower the price; and conversely, the lower the yield, the higher the price.

A two-year-maturity bond is similar. You get R at the end of the first year and R plus the face value at the end of the second year. Now you want to divide the first-year payment by $1 + i$ and the second-year payment by $(1 + i)^2$. The formula still shows the inverse relationship between the yield and the price. A bond with a three-year or longer maturity is similar. Computers do the calculation for the news reports, so even 30-year bond yields can easily be found from their price.

We can use a convenient and simple approximation method to determine the price or yield on bonds with very long maturity dates. It says that the price is equal to the coupon divided by the yield: $P = R/i$. This formula is the easiest way to remember the inverse relationship between the price and the yield. It is a close approximation for long-term bonds like the 30-year bond.

REVIEW

- Firms that want to purchase physical capital need financial capital to do so. They obtain financial capital by issuing stocks and bonds. Stocks and bonds are traded on financial markets.

- The return from holding stock is the dividend plus the change in the price. The rate of return is equal to the return measured as a percentage of the price of the stock.

- The return from holding bonds to maturity is the yield of the bond. Bond yields and bond prices move in opposite directions.

- Periods of falling interest rates are good for bondholders and bond issuers because the prices of bonds rise, while periods of rising interest rates are bad for both bondholders and bond issuers.

ECONOMICS *IN ACTION*

Understanding Stock and Bond Price Listings in Newspapers

Newspaper stock tables, such as this one from the *Financial Times* (March 1, 2007), summarize information about firms and the stocks that they issue. The table here is part of a much bigger table in which all the stocks traded on the New York Stock Exchange are listed in alphabetical order. Other tables provide information about stocks traded on other stock exchanges, such as the Nasdaq or the London Stock Exchange, in exactly the same way.

To understand how to read this table, focus on one company, such as the computer firm Hewlett-Packard, which was started in a garage by David Packard and

William Hewlett in the 1930s. The information in the table pertains to a single day, February 28, 2007 (which was why the data were reported on March 1, the following day). According to the table, the price of Hewlett-Packard stock decreased by $0.45 cents to $38.93 on that day. Key terms introduced in this chapter—such as dividend yield and price-earnings ratio—are highlighted. To check your understanding, see if you can find out each of the critical pieces of information for one of the other firms in the table, such as Hershey, the maker of Hershey's Kisses.

| 52 weeks | | | | | | | |
Hi	Lo	Stock	Yld (%)	PE	Vol 1,000s	Close	Net Chg
21.84	19.26	HealthMgmt	1.2	26.3	18,476	19.87	−0.09
47.69	37.35	Heinz	3.1	25.1	1,406	45.67	−0.20
57.00	49.34	Hershey	2.0	22.6	1,146	52.99	+.11
56.02	38.50	Hess Cp	0.8	8.7	2,378	53.19	+.14
43.53	**29.79**	**Hew.-Pack**	**0.8**	**17.1**	**10,833**	**38.93**	**−0.45**
37.53	23.00	HiltonHotl	0.5	25.4	2,900	34.90	−0.40
43.81	33.13	HomeDep	2.3	14.2	10,254	39.45	−0.15

| High and low for previous year | | Stock name | Dividend as a percent of price | Price-earnings ratio | Number of shares traded (in 1,000s) | Closing price | Change in price from previous day |

| 52 weeks | | | | | | | |
Hi	Lo	Stock	Yld (%)	PE	Vol 1,000s	Close	Net Chg
43.53	29.79	Hew.-Pack	0.8	17.1	10,833	38.93	−0.45

The *Financial Times* also reports the prices of bonds, which, once they have been issued by a firm or by a government, are actively traded in bond markets. The next table reports information on government-issued bonds from the United Kingdom and the United States. Focus on the highlighted bond; it has a coupon rate of 4.75 percent and matures in February 2037. Thus, in February 2007, this newly issued bond has 30 years left to maturity. Sometimes bond price tables report the price that is *bid* for bonds by bond traders and the price that is

asked for bonds by the traders. Only the bid price is given in this table, but the bid and ask are close to each other. (The difference is sufficient to give the traders some profit; note that the price asked by the trader is always greater than the price bid.)

Notice that the reported yield is different from the coupon rate for all the bonds listed. Also notice that this difference is especially pronounced for some of the U.K. bonds.

Mar 1	Redemption date	Coupon	Bid price	Bid yield	Day chg yield	Wk chg yield	Month chg yield	Year chg yield
U.K.	12/07	7.25	101.3200	5.45	−0.01	−0.07	−0.16	+1.07
	03/12	5.00	99.7300	5.06	−0.09	−0.19	−0.30	+0.78
	08/17	8.75	132.7290	4.75	−0.05	−0.19	−0.25	+0.58
	03/36	4.25	100.1500	4.24	−0.01	−0.15	−0.17	+0.40
U.S.	02/09	4.75	100.2344	4.63	−0.01	−0.24	−0.33	−0.08
	02/12	4.63	100.5391	4.50	−0.01	−0.23	−0.34	−0.13
	02/17	4.63	100.5313	4.56	—	−0.17	−0.28	−0.03
	02/37	**4.75**	**101.1406**	**4.68**	**+0.01**	**−0.15**	**−0.25**	**+0.12**

Source: Reuters.

| Date bond matures | Coupon as a percent of the face value | Bid price | Yield to maturity | Changes over time |

The Trade-off between Risk and Return

One of the hallmarks of financial markets is volatility. The prices of individual stocks and bonds rise and fall over time. Over the long run, stock prices show a positive trend, but there are periods of significant decline from time to time, and the prices of individual stocks traded in the financial markets are volatile. Similarly, even though you always can earn a rate of return equivalent to the yield by holding a bond issued by the U.S. government to maturity, in the interim, the price of the bond will vary.

In the example discussed earlier, the price of a share of Hewlett-Packard increased by almost 42 percent in 2006, but in 2008, the price fell by 27.5 percent. Even the broad S&P 500 Index fell by 38.5 percent in 2008. Because of such variability, buying stocks is a risky activity. The price of bonds can change by a large amount. For example, from mid-1996 to mid-1997, the price of government bonds rose by nearly 20 percent, but from mid-1993 to mid-1994, the price of government bonds *fell* by nearly 20 percent. Thus, government bonds are also a risky investment.

In this section, we show that the riskiness of stocks and bonds affects the decision of people to trade in financial markets. To do so, we first examine how individuals behave when they face risk.

Behavior under Uncertainty

Most people do not like uncertainty. They are *risk averse* in most of their activities. Given a choice between two jobs that pay the same wage, most people will be averse to choosing the riskier job where there is a good chance of being laid off. Similarly, given a choice between two investments that pay the same return, people will choose the less risky one.

Let us examine this idea of risk aversion further. To be more precise, suppose that Melissa has a choice between the two alternatives shown in Table 16-2. She must decide

Table 16-2

Two Options: Different Risks, Same Expected Return

Low-Risk Option	High-Risk Option
A bank deposit with	*A corporate stock with either*
5 percent interest (return = $500)	a. A 5 percent dividend and a 30 percent price decline ($500 − $3,000 = −$2,500)
	b. A 5 percent dividend and a 30 percent price increase ($500 + $3,000 = $3,500)

expected return

the return on an uncertain investment calculated by weighting the gains or losses by the probability that they will occur.

what to do with her life savings of $10,000 for the next year. At the end of the year, she plans to buy a house, and she will need some money for a down payment. She can put her $10,000 in a bank account, where the interest rate is 5 percent, or she can buy $10,000 worth of a stock that pays a dividend of 5 percent and will incur either a capital gain or a capital loss. In the bank, the value of her savings is safe, but if she buys the stock, she has a 50 percent chance that the price of the stock will fall by 30 percent and a 50 percent chance that the price of the stock will rise by 30 percent. In other words, the risky stock will leave Melissa with the possibility of a return of negative $2,500 (a loss) or a return of $3,500 (a gain). The bank account leaves her with a guaranteed $500 return.

Both of the options in Table 16-2 have the same **expected return**. The expected return on an investment weights the different gains or losses according to how probable they are. In the case of the safe bank account, there is a 100 percent chance that the return is $500, so the expected return is $500. In the case of the stock, the expected return would be negative $2,500 times the probability of this loss (1/2) plus $3,500 times the probability of this gain (also 1/2). Thus, the expected return is $500 (−2,500/2 + 3,500/2 = −1,250 + 1,750 = 500), the same as the return on the bank account.

The expected return is one way to measure how attractive an investment is. The word *expected* may appear misleading, because in the risky option $500 is not "expected" in the everyday use of the word. You do not expect $500; you expect either a loss of $2,500 or a gain of $3,500. If the term is confusing, think of the expected return as the average return that Melissa would get if she could take the second option year after year for many years. The losses of $2,500 and gains of $3,500 would average out to $500 per year after many years. (The term *expected return* has been carried over by economists and investment analysts from probability and statistics, in which case the term *expected value* is used to describe the mean, or the average, of a random variable.)

Given that the expected returns are the same, if Melissa is a risk-averse person (that is, if she would dread a capital loss more than she would cherish a capital gain of a similar magnitude), she will choose the less risky of these two options. Although it is clear that Melissa would choose the less risky of the two options in Table 16-2, perhaps Melissa would accept some compensation to offset her risk aversion. Although most people are averse to risk, they are willing to take on some risk if they are compensated for it. In the case of a risky financial investment, the compensation for higher risk could take the form of a higher expected return.

How could we make Melissa's expected return higher in the risky investment? Suppose Melissa had the choice between the same safe option as in Table 16-2 and a high-risk stock that paid a dividend of 20 percent. This new choice is shown in Table 16-3; the difference is that the risky stock now offers a dividend of 20 percent, much greater than the 5 percent in the first example and much greater than the 5 percent on the bank account. With the greater chance of a higher return on the stock, Melissa might be willing to buy the stock. Even in the worst situation, she loses just $1,000, which may still

Table 16-3

Two Options: Different Risks, Different Expected Returns

Low-Risk Option	High-Risk Option
A bank deposit with	*A corporate stock with either*
5 percent interest (return = $500)	a. A 20 percent dividend and a 30 percent price decline ($2,000 − $3,000 = −$1,000)
	b. A 20 percent dividend and a 30 percent price increase ($2,000 + $3,000 = $5,000)

leave her with enough for the down payment on her new house. The expected return for the high-risk option is now $2,000, much greater than the $500 for the bank account ($−1,000/2 + 5,000/2 = −500 + 2,500 = 2,000$).

In other words, Melissa probably would be willing to take on the risky investment. And if the 20 percent dividend in the example is not enough for her, some higher dividend (25 percent? 30 percent?) would be. This example illustrates the general point that risk-averse people are willing to take risks if they are paid for it.

Before we develop the implication of our analysis of individual behavior under uncertainty, we should pause to ask about the possibility that some people might be risk lovers rather than risk avoiders. The billions of dollars that are bet in state lotteries in the United States and in private gambling casinos in Las Vegas, Atlantic City, and Monte Carlo indicate that some people enjoy risk. With few exceptions, however, most of the gambling on lotteries, slot machines, and even roulette wheels represents a small portion of the income or wealth of the gambler. Thus, you might be willing to spend $0.50 or even $5 on lottery tickets or a slot machine for the chance of winning big, even if the odds are against you. Many people get enjoyment out of such wagers; but if the stakes are large compared with one's income or wealth, then few people want to play. For small sums, some people are risk lovers, but for large sums, virtually everybody becomes a risk avoider to some degree or another.

Playing It Safe?

Most people are risk-averse when it comes to large sums, but many are risk lovers when the stakes are low or when they can limit their potential losses—such as at casinos where people can choose to gamble a set amount or combine gambling with entertainment.

Risk and Rates of Return in Theory

What are the implications of our conclusion that investors will be willing to take risks if they are compensated with a higher return on the stock or bond? In the stock market, the prices of individual stocks are determined by the bidding of buyers and sellers. Suppose a stock, AOK, had a price that gave it the same expected rate of return as a bank account. Now AOK, being a common stock, clearly has more risk than a bank account because its price can change. Hence, no risk-averse investor will want to buy AOK. Just as Melissa will prefer to put her funds in a bank account in the example in Table 16-2 rather than into the risky option, investors will put their funds in a bank rather than buy AOK. People who own shares of AOK will sell and put their funds into a bank. With everybody wanting to sell AOK and no one wanting to buy it, the price of AOK will start to fall.

Now, the price and the expected rate of return are inversely related—recall that for a stock, the rate of return is the return divided by the price. Thus, if the price falls and the dividend does not change, the rate of return will rise. This fall in the price will drive up the expected rate of return on AOK. As the expected rate of return increases, it eventually will reach a point at which it is high enough to compensate risk-averse investors. In other words, when the expected rate of return rises far enough above the bank account rate to compensate people for the risk, the price fall will stop. We will have an equilibrium at which point the expected rate of return on the stock is higher than the interest rate on the safe bank account. The higher rate of return will be associated with the higher risk.

Now some stocks are more risky than others. For example, the risk on the stocks of small firms tends to be higher than the risk on the stocks of larger firms, because small firms tend to be those that are just starting up. Not having yet proved themselves, small firms have a higher risk. People like Melissa will sell the more risky stocks of smaller companies until the expected rate of return on those stocks is high enough compared with the less risky stocks of larger companies.

equilibrium risk-return relationship

the positive relationship between the risk and the expected rate of return on an asset, derived from the fact that, on average, risk-averse investors who take on more risk must be compensated with a higher return.

In equilibrium, we therefore expect to see a positive relationship between risk and the expected rate of return on securities. Securities with higher risks will have higher returns than securities with lower risks. Figure 16-6 shows the resulting **equilibrium risk-return relationship**.

There is probably no more important lesson about capital markets than this relationship. Individual investors should know it well. It says that to get a higher rate of return *on average over the long run,* you have to accept a higher risk. Again, the market forces at work are the same as the ones that led to the compensating wage differentials in the labor market. In the

---

Figure 16-6

The Equilibrium Relationship between Return and Risk

More risky securities tend to have higher returns on average over the long term. For example, bank deposits are low risk and have a low expected return. Corporate stocks are higher risk—their price fluctuates—but on average over the long term have a higher return. The higher return is like a compensating wage differential in the labor market. It compensates those who take on more risk.

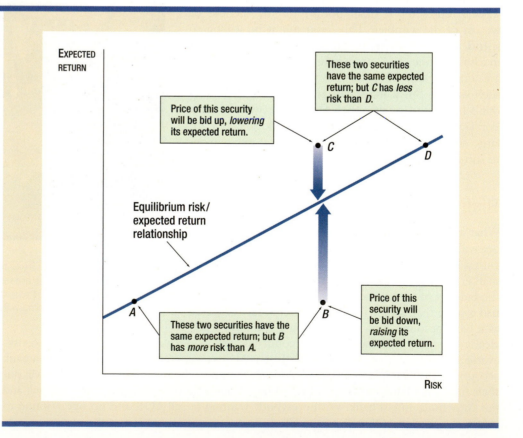

Table 16-4

Average Rates of Return for Different Risks

	Average Rate of Return per Year (percent)	Risk (average size of price fluctuations)
U.S. Treasury bills	3.7	3.1
Long-term government bonds	5.9	9.5
Large-company stocks	11.9	20.4
Small-company stocks	16.7	32.6

Source: © 2011 Morning Star. All Rights Reserved. Used with permission.
Note: These rates of return are for 1926–2010 and are not adjusted for inflation. The average rate of inflation was 3.1 percent, which can be subtracted from each of the average returns to get the real return. The risk is the "standard deviation," a measure of volatility commonly used in probability and statistics.

labor market, the higher wage in some jobs is the price that workers accept to take on the greater risk, or, more generally, the less pleasant aspects of the job.

Risk and Return in Reality

In reality, this theoretical relationship works very well. A tremendous amount of data over long periods of time on the financial markets support this relationship. The most widely cited evidence was compiled by Roger Ibbotson of Yale University who tabulated data, shown in Table 16-4, on the average return over many years for the four important types of securities we have mentioned in the theoretical discussion. The most risky of the four—the stocks of small firms—has the highest rate of return. The next highest in risk are the common stocks of large firms. The least risky—short-term U.S. Treasury bills that are as safe as bank deposits—has the smallest rate of return. Long-term bonds, for which price changes can be large, have a rate of return greater than that of U.S. Treasury bills. Although the relative risks of these four types of securities may seem obvious, a measure of the differences in the sizes of their price volatility is shown in the second column and confirms the intuitive risk rankings. In general, Table 16-4 is a striking confirmation of this fundamental result of financial markets that higher expected rates of return are associated with higher risk.

Diversification Reduces Risk

The familiar saying "Don't put all your eggs in one basket" is particularly relevant to stock markets. Rather than a basket of eggs, you have a portfolio of stocks. A *portfolio* is a collection of stocks. Putting your funds into a portfolio of two or more stocks, whose prices do not always move in the same direction, rather than one stock is called **portfolio diversification**. The risks from holding a single stock can be reduced significantly by putting half your funds in one stock and half in another. If one stock falls in price, the other stock may fall less, may not fall at all, or may even rise.

Holding two stocks in equal amounts is the most elementary form of diversification. With thousands of stocks to choose from, however, diversification is not limited to two. Figure 16-7 shows how sharply risk declines with diversification. By holding ten different stocks rather than one, you can reduce your risk to about 30 percent of what it would be with one stock. If you hold some international stocks, whose behavior will be even more different from that of any one U.S. stock, you can reduce the risk even further. Mutual fund companies provide a way for an investor with only limited funds to diversify by holding 500 or even 5,000 stocks along with other investors. Some mutual funds—called *index funds*—consist of all the stocks in an index like the S&P 500 Index.

portfolio diversification
spreading the collection of assets owned to limit exposure to risk.

Figure 16-7

Risk Declines Sharply with Diversification

By holding more than one stock, risk can be reduced. By holding 10 U.S. securities, the risk is reduced to 30 percent of the risk of holding one security. Diversifying internationally permits one to reduce risk further. (The risk is measured by the standard deviation.)

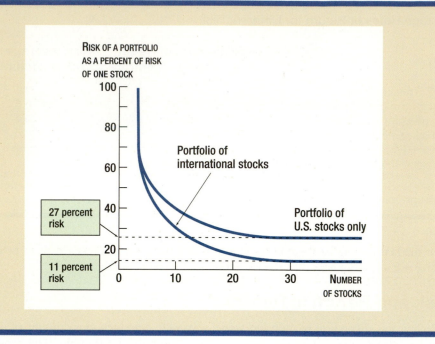

Efficient Market Theory

The shares of firms' stock on the market can be traded quickly at any time of day. For most large and medium-size companies, some people are always willing to buy and sell. If people hear that Intel has made a discovery that is expected to raise its profits, they rush to buy Intel stock. If people suddenly learn about a decline in a company's profits or about losses, then people rush to sell that company's stock. This rush to buy and sell changes prices instantaneously, so that the price adjusts rapidly to good news or bad news. The rapid adjustment means that unexploited profit opportunities are rare for regular investors without inside information or a special ability to anticipate news, whether good or bad. The **efficient market hypothesis** states that profit opportunities are eliminated in financial markets as stock prices adjust quickly to new information. Rates of return greater than those resulting from the price of risk disappear soon after any good news about a stock appears.

Many tests over the years have found the efficient market hypothesis to be a close approximation of security price determination. It has led to the growth in popularity of index funds, for which investors do not pay advisers to tell them when to buy and sell stock. They simply invest in a fund that includes a large number of stocks.

efficient market hypothesis the idea that markets adjust rapidly enough to eliminate profit opportunities immediately.

REVIEW

- Financial markets are volatile; both stock prices and bond prices tend to rise and fall over time. The riskiness of bonds and stocks affects the willingness of people to buy and sell these financial assets, and hence, affects their return.

- We can calculate the expected return of a risky asset by weighting the possible gains and losses by the probability that these gains or losses will occur. Given the choice between a risky asset and a safe asset that have the same expected return, an

- individual who is risk averse always will choose the safe asset.
- Risk-averse investors will hold risky assets only if they are compensated in the form of a higher expected return. Thus, when buyers and sellers trade stocks or bonds in the market, a relationship between return and risk emerges: Higher risk is associated with higher returns.

- Investors can reduce risk by diversifying their portfolio, that is, by holding many different stocks. Mutual funds and index funds offer diversification opportunities even to investors who have little money to put into the stock market.
- Earning stock returns in excess of those justified by the greater level of associated risk is difficult. The efficient market hypothesis predicts that stock prices adjust quickly to eliminate such lucrative return opportunities.

Corporate Governance Problems

When corporations issue stock to buy physical capital or to start up operations, a separation between the owners of the corporation—the stockholders—and the managers of the corporation is created. This separation leads to incentive problems—the manager might not act in the interest of the shareholder. Here we show how these problems can be analyzed with a theory called *asymmetric information theory*.

Asymmetric Information: Moral Hazard and Adverse Selection

Consider a start-up firm. When an entrepreneur at a start-up firm obtains financial capital by issuing stock, a special relationship is formed. Those who supplied the financial capital by buying the stock become owners or at least part owners of the company. If the entrepreneur does well and the company is successful, they reap large returns. But shareholders of a firm have less information than the managers about the firm. This difference in information, called **asymmetric information**, can cause several problems. First, the manager might not act in the interest of the owners. Taking unnecessary business trips on the company's aircraft to exotic places or not working hard to find the right employees is harmful to the shareholders' interests. This is sometimes called **moral hazard**, a term borrowed from research on the insurance industry, for which asymmetric information is also a problem. Moral hazard in insurance occurs when people are less careful about trying to prevent fires after they get fire insurance. In the case of the firm, the manager may be less careful about the firm after the shareholders' or investors' funds have been obtained.

Another problem is that those entrepreneurs who have more risky projects would seek equity financing—for which dividend payments to shareholders would be optional—rather than debt financing, for which interest payments are required. This is called **adverse selection**, yet another term borrowed from insurance. In insurance, adverse selection occurs, for example, when people who are unhealthy select health insurance while healthy people do not. In this case, managers who have more risky projects elect equity financing more often than those who have less risky projects. This makes potential shareholders or investors less willing to supply funds to equity markets.

Incentives to Overcome Adverse Selection and Moral Hazard Problems

One way in which problems of moral hazard and adverse selection can be limited is through the use of **profit-sharing** agreements, whereby managers are given a share of the profits earned by the firm. That way, the managers of the firms have a financial stake in the

asymmetric information
different levels of information available to different people in an economic interaction or exchange.

moral hazard
in insurance markets, a situation in which a person buys insurance against some risk and subsequently takes actions that increase the risk; analogous situations arise when other markets have asymmetric information.

adverse selection
in insurance markets, a situation in which the people who choose to buy insurance will be the riskiest group in the population; analogous situations apply in other markets.

profit sharing
programs in which managers and employees receive a share of profits earned by the firm.

A Shareholder Meeting: Principals, Agents, and Asymmetric Information

Theories of corporate governance view a firm's shareholders (shown in the crowd) as the *principals* and the managers (shown on the stage) as the agents. Management incentive plans such as profit sharing are seen as ways to foster good management performance when the principals have little information about what the *agents* actually do—a situation called *asymmetric information.*

firm's success, and hence, their interests are aligned with the shareholders' interests—agents gain when the principal gains and agents lose when the principal loses.

Another way to overcome the problems caused by moral hazard and adverse selection is for shareholders to get together and take over the company so that the problematic management team can be replaced. The mere threat of such a takeover can be an incentive for management to act in shareholders' interest rather than their own. *Private equity* firms like the Blackstone Group specialize in buying shares of a public company and taking it private, so that they can replace the existing management with managers who presumably can improve the firm's performance.

Such takeovers also have been criticized. Some say that the threat of being bought out by a hostile takeover firm or a private equity firm leads management to adopt a more short-sighted attitude toward the operation of the company's affairs than is ideal. Companies also expend considerable resources constructing "takeover defenses," which attempt to make it more difficult for outsiders to use a hostile takeover to take control of the firm.

REVIEW

- Managers of a firm usually know more about the firm than the shareholders. This asymmetric information causes moral hazard—in which the firm's managers may run the firm less efficiently than the shareholder would want.

- Profit sharing—in which the managers share in the profits of the firm or in the returns to holding the stock—is a way to prevent moral hazard.

The Role of Government in Financial Markets

Government policy has a role to play in financial markets. Poor governance which takes the extreme form of outright fraud is illegal under U.S. law. Indeed, managers who commit fraud against their shareholders are prosecuted and sent to jail if they are caught; the Federal Bureau of Investigation has a whole division on the lookout for such crimes.

One common type of fraud in financial markets—securities fraud—occurs when managers lie or misreport facts about the firm's financial statements or the firm's profitability to entice investors to buy or hold their stock. The Securities and Exchange Commission (SEC) has responsibilities for such securities violations. It also regulates certain investment management firms, such as mutual funds, under the Investment Act of 1940 to promote accurate financial reporting.

One glaring example of fraud arose in the case of Bernard Madoff, who ran an investment company with responsibility for managing billions of dollars of his clients' money. His fraudulent scheme cost his investors a reported $50 billion. It was called a *Ponzi scheme*, in which his existing investors' returns were paid using his new investors' funds rather than from legitimate investments in the stock or bond markets. Madoff was sentenced to prison for 150 years in June 2009. Some accused the SEC for failing in its responsibility to detect this fraud long before it became so big.

Examples from a Financial Crisis

Many examples of mismanagement and fraudulent action can be found during the financial crisis in 2007 and 2008. Indeed, some analysts think that such actions were in part responsible for the crisis. For example, mortgage loans were offered to high-risk individual homeowners who were unlikely to make the interest payments. The resulting high-risk mortgages were then sold to other financial institutions, whose managers apparently were unaware of the risks. When the homeowners with these mortgages stopped making their payments, the financial institutions found the mortgages were nearly worthless. In the meantime, the originators were far from the scene and no longer accountable. As a result, the risk at these financial institutions rose; they were reluctant to make more loans or they charged much higher interest rates on the loans, which added to the crisis.

Another possible role for government is to intervene to prevent the failure of large financial institutions and thereby prevent instability in the financial markets. Indeed, during 2008, the federal government intervened in several ways by loaning or investing funds to help some of these financial institutions. The expectation of such intervention can cause its own form of moral hazard, however, if investors expect the government always to rescue them. This expectation will reduce the incentives they have to manage risks themselves. Moreover, government intervention can cause uncertainty and perhaps make matters worse, an example of government failure.

Consider the financial panic of 2008. Although the financial crisis had been going on for more than a year, it suddenly worsened into a full-fledged sell-off in the fall of 2008. The S&P 500 Index fell from 1,255 on September 19 to 899 on October 10, a decline of 28 percent in three weeks, a staggering loss for many people.

Many argued that the panic was caused by the U.S. government's decision not to intervene to prevent the bankruptcy of a financial institution, Lehman Brothers, which then led to expectations of more failures and instability. An examination of the timing of stock price movements, however, shows that the answer is more complicated. Figure 16-8 focuses on a few key dates and events, including the panic itself, which is marked with the brackets.

Monday, September 15, is the day that Lehman declared bankruptcy after learning over the previous weekend that the government would not provide funds to pay its creditors and keep it open. You can see that the stock market moved down a bit, but it then bounced back up on September 16. By the end of the week, the S&P 500 was virtually the same as it was one week earlier, so the decision to let Lehman Brothers go bankrupt apparently was not what caused the panic. But if not, then what was the cause?

On Friday of that same week, the U.S. Treasury announced that it was going to propose a large rescue package for the entire U.S. banking system, although the size and details were not determined. During the weekend, the package was put together; on Tuesday, September 23, Federal Reserve Board Chairman Ben Bernanke and Treasury Secretary Henry Paulson testified in the Senate about the package, which they called the Troubled Assets Relief Program (TARP). They said it would be enormous, $700 billion, yet provided few details and made no mention of oversight or restrictions on the use. They were questioned intensely and the reaction was quite negative. Members of Congress received a large volume of critical mail.

As shown in Figure 16-8, following this poorly received testimony, the crisis seriously deepened, as measured by the sharp fall in the stock market for the next three weeks. It is plausible that events around September 23 increased risks and drove the markets down, including the realization by the public that the intervention plan had not been fully thought through and that conditions were much worse than many had been led to believe. A great deal of uncertainty about what the government would do to aid financial institutions, and under what circumstances, was revealed. Such uncertainty would have driven up risk and thereby driven down the market. Clarity about the TARP

Figure 16-8

Stock Prices during the Panic

The S&P 500 Index fell by nearly 30 percent, but was it the result of the Lehman bankruptcy or the government actions?

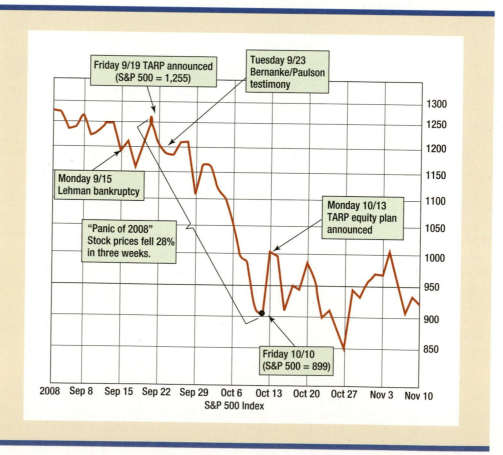

improved on October 13 when the government announced it would buy shares in banks with the TARP money. The panic ended at that time.

Government Regulation of Financial Institutions

Financial institutions—especially banks—are the most heavily regulated firms in the United States. The main rationale for the federal government to regulate banks is that the federal government guarantees the deposits that people hold at the banks. If the bank takes on too much risk and fails as a result, then the deposit holders will be paid off, subject to certain limits, by the government. Because taxpayer money is at risk, the government has responsibility for ensuring that the banks do not put too much risk on the taxpayers.

The government does this by issuing regulations that require that the banks' capital, including the dollar amount of shares held by shareholders, to be above a certain fraction of the bank's loans and other investments. This ensures that the shareholders will pay before the government in the case of large loan losses. The government also supervises the banks to ensure that the loans they hold do not exceed certain risk levels.

In the United States, the banks are regulated by the Office of the Comptroller of the Currency, the Federal Reserve System, and in some cases the state governments. It is now clear that many banks—including the large Citicorp, headquartered in New York City—took on too much risk in the years leading up to the financial crisis, and this has raised questions about the effectiveness of the regulation and supervision. People ask why hundreds of government regulators on the premises of banks like Citicorp did not see or report such risks or take actions to limit the risks. Because of these concerns, many of the regulations were changed in legislation passed in 2010 after the financial crisis. But economists and others debate whether the new legislation actually will improve the effectiveness of the regulation and supervision.

One concern is that the operations of the financial institutions are too complex for government regulators to monitor. Another concern is that government supervisors are too close to the management of the banks, a form of regulatory capture in which the regulators are "captured" by the banks and tend to overlook certain risky activities.

Indeed, a book published in 2011 by Gretchen Morgenson and Joshua Rosner, *Reckless Endangerment: How Outsized Ambition, Greed, and Corruption Led to Economic Armageddon,* argues that such cozy relationships were responsible for the risks taken leading up to the financial crisis. The authors give many examples of cases in which government officials took actions that benefited banks and other financial institutions and showed that these individuals in turn helped the government officials. This mutual support system thwarted good economic policies and encouraged reckless ones. It thereby brought on the crisis, sending the economy into a deep recession.

REVIEW

- The government has a role to play in the financial markets, including enforcing the law against securities fraud.

- The government also has a role to play in regulating and supervising financial firms that can cause a risk to taxpayers or the economy.

- In considering the role of government in financial markets, however, the possibility of government failure also must be considered.

CONCLUSION

This chapter has used some basic economic tools to analyze capital and financial markets. In reviewing the chapter, it is helpful to see how the key results apply to you personally.

First, by diversifying a portfolio of stocks, you can reduce risk substantially. Conversely, by holding an undiversified portfolio, you are needlessly incurring risk.

Second, remember the efficient market hypothesis that profit opportunity disappears quickly in financial markets. Instead of buying and selling securities frequently, you may be better off investing in a mutual fund.

Third, if you do try to pick your own portfolio rather than use a mutual fund, concentrate on areas with which you are familiar. If you go into a medical career, you may know more than even the best investors about the promise of a new medical device or drug.

Fourth, over the short run, holding corporate stocks is more risky than putting your funds in a bank account, but over the long term, the higher rate of return on stocks outweighs the risks for most people. If you need money in the short term—to pay next year's tuition, for example—stocks may not be worth the risk. Years like 2008 during which stocks fall by as much as 38 percent are a reminder of these risks.

KEY POINTS

1. Physical capital refers to the physical resources used to produce goods and services.
2. Financial capital, which includes stocks and bonds, is used by firms to obtain funds to invest in physical capital.
3. A firm's demand for physical capital is a derived demand. A firm will use capital up to the point at which the marginal revenue product of capital equals the rental price.
4. The supply and demand for capital determines the rental price or the implicit rental price. Tax and subsidy policies that affect the demand for capital goods will affect both the equilibrium rental price of capital and the equilibrium quantity of capital used by firms.
5. Firms raise money for investing in physical capital by issuing stocks and bonds. Once issued, the stocks and bonds trade on financial markets.
6. The rate of return on stocks is equal to the dividend plus the change in the price as a percentage of the price. The rate of return on bonds held to maturity is the yield of the bond.
7. The rate of return on stocks tends to rise when firms have higher earnings, which are either paid out in the form of dividends or reinvested in the company. The rate of return on bonds tends to rise in periods during which market interest rates are falling.
8. Stock markets and bond markets tend to be extremely volatile. To understand how the riskiness of these assets affects their return, we need to understand how investors behave. Risk-averse investors will buy more risky stocks or bonds only if the expected rate of return is higher.
9. In market equilibrium, a positive relationship exists between risk and rate of return. If you want to get a higher rate of return, you have to accept higher risk.
10. Diversification helps reduce risk. Even individuals with limited resources can diversify their portfolios by investing in mutual funds.

KEY TERMS

adverse selection, 391
asymmetric information, 391
capital gain, 381
capital loss, 381
coupon, 382

debt contract, 374
depreciation, 374
discount rate, 399
discounting, 399
dividend yield, 381

QUESTIONS FOR REVIEW

1. What is the difference between physical capital and financial capital?
2. How is the relationship between the marginal revenue product of capital and the rental price related to the firm's decision to rent additional units of physical capital?
3. Why is the quantity of physical capital demanded negatively related to the rental price of capital?
4. How does the implicit rental price of capital depend on the interest rate and depreciation?
5. What is the difference between a stock and a bond?
6. What determines the rate of return on stocks? On bonds?
7. What does it mean for an individual to be risk averse?
8. How do the actions of risk-averse individuals influence the relationship between risk and return in financial markets?
9. What is diversification? How does it affect risk?
10. What do economists mean when they say that financial markets are efficient?

PROBLEMS

1. Which of the following are physical capital, and which are financial capital?
   a. A Toyota Camry at Avis Car Rental.
   b. A loan you take out to start a newspaper business.
   c. New desktop publishing equipment.
   d. A bond issued by the U.S. government.
   e. A pizza oven at Pizza Hut.
2. Suppose that Marshall's stones were dropped all over the earth and finding them was difficult.
   a. Would the supply curve for capital still be perfectly inelastic?
   b. Would there be economic rent?
3. Suppose a company owns a computer that costs $5,000 and depreciates $1,000 per year.
   a. If the interest rate is 5 percent, what is the implicit rental price of the computer?
   b. Explain why the implicit rental price depends on the interest rate.
4. The U.S. government issues a one-year bond with a face value of $1,000 and a zero coupon.
   a. If the yield is 10 percent, what will the market price of the bond be?
   b. Now suppose you observe that the bond price falls by 5 percent. What happens to its yield?
5. Suppose a two-year bond has a 5 percent coupon and a $1,000 face value, and the current market interest rate is 5 percent.
   a. What is the price of the bond?
   b. Now suppose that you believe that the interest rate will remain 5 percent this year, but next year will fall to 3 percent. How much are you willing to pay for the two-year bond today? Why?

6. Consider the following possibilities for your stock market investment portfolio.

	Good Market	Bad Market	Disastrous Market
Probability	0.50	0.30	0.20
Rate of return	0.25	0.10	−0.25

a. What is the expected return of this stock market investment portfolio?

b. Would you choose this expected return or take a safe return of 7 percent from a savings deposit in your bank? Why?

c. Suppose your teacher chooses the safe return from the bank. Is your teacher risk averse? How can you tell?

7. You are considering the purchase of stocks of two firms: a biotechnology corporation and a supermarket chain. Because of the uncertainty in the biotechnology industry, you estimate that there is a 50–50 chance of your either earning an 80 percent return on your investment or losing 80 percent of your investment within a year. The food industry is more stable, so you estimate that you have a 50–50 chance of either earning 10 percent or losing 10 percent.

a. Which stock would you buy if you were a risk-averse individual? Why?

b. What do you think other investors (most of whom are risk averse) would do?

c. What would be the effect of these actions on the relative prices of the two stocks?

8. Graph the data on risk and expected return (in percent) for the following securities.

Asset	Expected Rate of Return	Risk
Bank deposit	3	0
U.S. Treasury bills	4	3
Goodcorp bonds	9	10
ABC stock	11	24
XYZ stock	13	24
Riskyco stock	16	39

Draw an equilibrium risk-return line through the points.

a. Which two assets should have changes in their prices in the near future?

b. In which direction will their prices change?

9. Suppose a study indicated that stock prices usually were lower during the holiday season than during the rest of the year. What would be the likely reaction of the market?

10. Suppose you have $10,000 and must choose between investing in your own human capital or investing in physical or financial capital.

a. What factors will enter into your decision-making process?

b. How much risk will be involved with each investment?

c. What would you do? Why?

Present Discounted Value

A dollar in the future is worth less than a dollar today. This principle underlies all economic decisions involving actions over time. Whether you put some dollars under the mattress to be spent next summer, borrow money from a friend or family member to be paid back next year, or are a sophisticated investor in stocks, bonds, or real estate, that same principle is essential to making good decisions. Here we explain why the principle is essential and derive a formula for determining exactly *how much* less a dollar in the future is worth than a dollar today. The formula is called the *present discounted value formula.*

Discounting the Future

First let's answer the question, why is the value of a dollar in the future less than the value of a dollar today? The simplest answer is that a dollar can earn interest over time. Suppose a person you trust completely to pay off a debt gives you an IOU promising to pay you $100 in one year: How much is that IOU worth to you today? How much would you be willing to pay for the IOU today? It would be less than $100, because you could put an amount less than $100 in a bank and get $100 at the end of a year. The exact amount depends on the interest rate. If the interest rate is 10 percent, the $100 should be worth $90.91. If you put $90.91 in a bank earning 10 percent per year, at the end of the year you will have exactly $100. That is, $90.91 plus interest payments of $9.09 ($90.91 times 0.1 rounded to the nearest penny) equals $100.

The process of translating a future payment into a value in the present is called **discounting**. The value in the present of a future payment is called the **present discounted value**. The interest rate used to do the discounting is called the **discount rate**. In the preceding example, a future payment of $100 has a present discounted value of $90.91, and the discount rate is 10 percent. If the discount rate were 20 percent, the present discounted value would be $83.33 (because if you put $83.33 in a bank for a year at a 20 percent interest rate, you would have, rounding to the nearest penny, $100 at the end of the year). The term *discount*

is used because the value in the present is *less* than the future payment; in other words, the payment is "discounted," much as a $100 bicycle on sale might be "discounted" to $83.33.

Finding the Present Discounted Value

The previous examples suggest that a formula can calculate present value, and indeed it can. Let

> the present discounted value be *PDV*
>
> the discount rate be *i*
>
> the future payment be *F*

The symbol i is measured as a decimal, but we speak of the discount rate in percentage terms; thus, we would say, "the discount rate is 10 percent" and write, $i = 0.1$.

Now, the present discounted value *PDV* is the amount for which, if you put it in a bank today at an interest rate i, you would get an amount in the future equal to the future payment *F*. For example, if the future date is one year from now, then if you put the amount *PDV* in a bank for one year, you would get *PDV* times $(1 + i)$ at the end of the year. Thus, the *PDV* should be such that

$$PDV \times (1 + i) = F$$

Now divide both sides by $(1 + i)$; you get

$$PDV = \frac{F}{1 + i}$$

which is the formula for the present discounted value in the case of a payment made one year in the future. That is,

$$\text{Present discounted value} = \frac{\text{payment in one year}}{(1 + \text{the discount rate})}$$

For example, if the payment in one year is $100 and the discount rate $i = 0.1$, then the present discounted value is $90.91 [$100/(1 + 0.1)], just as we reasoned previously.

To obtain the formula for the case for which the payment is made more than one year in the future, we must recognize that the amount in the present can be put in a bank and earn interest at the discount rate for more than one year. For example, if the interest rate is 10 percent, we could get $100 at the end of two years by investing $82.64 today. That is, putting $82.64 in the bank would give $82.64 times (1.1) at the end of one year; keeping all this in the bank for another year would give $82.64 times (1.1) times (1.1), or $82.64 times 1.21, or $100, again rounding off. Thus, in the case of a future payment in two years, we would have

$$PDV = \frac{F}{(1+i)^2}$$

Analogous reasoning implies that the present discounted value of a payment made N years in the future would be

$$PDV = \frac{F}{(1+i)^N}$$

For example, the present discounted value of a $100 payment to be made 20 years in the future is $14.86 if the discount rate is 10 percent. In other words, if you put $14.86 in the bank today at an interest rate of 10 percent, you would have about $100 at the end of 20 years. What is the present discounted value of a $100 payment to be made 100 years in the future? The above formula tells us that the PDV is only $0.00726, less than a penny. All of these examples indicate that the higher the discount rate or the further in the future the payment is to be received, the lower the present discounted value of a future payment.

In many cases, we need to find the present discounted value of a *series* of payments made in several different years. We can do this by combining the previous formulas. The present discounted value of payments F_1 made in one year and F_2 made in two years would be

$$PDV = \frac{F_1}{(1+i)} + \frac{F_2}{(1+i)^2}$$

For example, the present discounted value of $100 paid in one year and $100 paid in two years would be $90.91 plus $82.64, or $173.55. In general, the present discounted value of a series of future payments F_1, F_2, ..., F_N over N years is

$$PDV = \frac{F_1}{(1+i)} + \frac{F_2}{(1+i)^2} + \cdots + \frac{F_N}{(1+i)^N}$$

KEY POINTS

1. A dollar to be paid in the future is worth less than a dollar today.
2. The present discounted value of a future payment is the amount you would have to put in a bank today to get that same payment in the future.
3. The higher the discount rate, the lower the present discounted value of a future payment.

KEY TERMS AND DEFINITIONS

discounting: the process of translating a future payment into a value in the present.
present discounted value: the value in the present of future payments.
discount rate: an interest rate used to discount a future payment when computing present discounted value.

QUESTIONS FOR REVIEW

1. Why is the present discounted value of a future payment of $1 less than $1?
2. What is the relationship between the discount rate and the interest rate?
3. What happens to the present discounted value of a future payment as the payment date stretches into the future?
4. Why is discounting important for decisions involving actions at different dates?

PROBLEMS

1. Find the present discounted value of
   a. $100 to be paid at the end of three years.
   b. $1,000 to be paid at the end of one year plus $1,000 to be paid at the end of two years.
   c. $10 to be paid at the end of one year, $10 at the end of two years, and $100 at the end of three years.
2. Suppose you win $1 million in a lottery and your winnings are scheduled to be paid as follows: $300,000 at the end of one year, $300,000 at the end of two years, and $400,000 at the end of three

years. If the interest rate is 10 percent, what is the present discounted value of your winnings?

3. You are considering two job offers. You expect to work for the employer for five years. For simplicity, we assume that you will be paid at the end of each year. The two offers are summarized in the following table.

Year	Offer 1	Offer 2
1	$30,000	$40,000
2	$33,000	$30,000
3	$36,000	$33,000

Year	Offer 1	Offer 2
4	$39,000	$36,000
5	$42,000	$39,000

The primary difference between the two offers is a signing bonus of $10,000 paid under Offer 2. The annual salary paid in years two through five is higher under Offer 1 than under Offer 2. If the interest rate is 5 percent, which is the better offer? If the interest rate is 10 percent, which is better?

part four

TRADE AND
GLOBAL MARKETS

17 Economic Growth and Globalization

A front page article in the *New York Times* on February 14, 2009, began with these sobering words:

From lawyers in Paris to factory workers in China and bodyguards in Colombia, the ranks of the jobless are swelling rapidly across the globe.

Worldwide job losses from the recession that started in the United States in December 2007 could hit a staggering 50 million by the end of 2009.

The article pointed out what had been obvious for a while, how interconnected the economic fortunes of countries are. When the U.S. and European economies slumped, the reverberations were felt in semiconductor factories in Taiwan, China, and in garment factories in Sri Lanka. When U.S. stock markets slumped, large investment banks, mutual funds, and hedge funds began to pull money out of markets in India and Brazil. U.S. Treasury Secretary Tim Geithner quickly engaged himself in talks with his counterparts in Europe and Asia to come up with some type of coordinated response to the worldwide economic slowdown. This demonstrated the negative side of globalization—thanks to improvements in telecommunications, information networks, and computer technology, the events that affected one country, whether positive or negative, had repercussions in many nations across the globe.

This highly visible interconnectedness of nations raises some fundamental questions about economic theory, not just about why economic fluctuations spread from one country to another but also about more fundamental differences in economic growth across countries. Although economic growth theory tells us how technology and capital have provided people with the means to raise their productivity, something is disquieting about the theory when we look around the world. As we compare living standards, it is clear that people in some countries are much better off than people in other countries. Why has access to capital been so difficult for some poor countries who have spent decades stuck in poverty and not growing at all? Why hasn't the spread of technological information allowed poor countries to grow faster? Will acceleration of globalization change all this? In this chapter, we look for answers to these crucial questions about the uneven patterns of economic growth in different countries. We begin our quest for the answers by looking at economic growth performance in different parts of the world.

Catching Up or Not?

If technological advances can spread easily, as seems reasonable with modern communications, then poorer regions with low productivity and low income per capita will tend to catch up to richer regions by growing more rapidly. Why? If the spread of new technology is not difficult, then regions with lower productivity can adopt the more advanced technology of other regions to raise their productivity. Recall from the **growth accounting formula** that an increase in the growth of technology leads to an increase in productivity growth.

Investment in new capital also would tend to cause poor regions to catch up to the rich. Consider a relatively poor region in which both capital per worker and output per worker are low. Imagine several hundred workers constructing a road with only a little capital—perhaps only a few picks and shovels, not even a jackhammer. With such low levels of capital, the returns to increasing the amount of capital would be very high. The addition of a few trucks and some earthmoving equipment to the construction project would bring huge returns in higher output. Regions with relatively low levels of capital per worker therefore would attract a greater amount of investment, and capital would grow rapidly. The growth accounting formula tells us that productivity grows rapidly when capital per worker grows rapidly. Thus, productivity would grow rapidly in poorer regions where capital per worker is low.

A rich region in which the capital per worker is high, however, would gain relatively little from additional capital. Such a region would attract little investment, and the growth rate of capital would be lower; therefore, the growth of productivity also would be lower.

In summary, economic growth theory predicts that regions with low productivity will grow relatively more rapidly than regions with high productivity. Regions with low productivity will tend to catch up to the more advanced regions by adopting existing technology and attracting capital.

Figure 17-1 illustrates this catch-up phenomenon. It shows the level of productivity on the horizontal axis and the growth rate of productivity on the vertical axis. The downward-sloping line is the **catch-up line**. A country or region on the upper left-hand part of the line is poor—with low productivity and, therefore, low income per capita—but growing rapidly. A country on the lower right-hand part of the line is rich—with high productivity and, therefore, high income per capita—but its growth is relatively less rapid. That the catch-up line exists and is downward sloping is a prediction of growth theory.

Catch-up within the United States

Let us first see how the catch-up line works when the regions are the states within the United States. Figure 17-2 presents the data on real income per capita and the growth rate of real income per capita for each of the states. Because productivity and real income per capita move closely together, we can examine the accuracy of the catch-up line using the real income per capita data. (Again, the adjective *real* means that the income data are adjusted for inflation.) Real income per capita in 1880 is on the horizontal axis, and the growth rate of real income per capita from 1880 to 1980 is on the vertical axis. Each point on the scatter diagram represents a state, and a few of the states are labeled. If you pick a state (observe Nevada, for example, down and to the right), you can read its growth rate by looking over to the left scale, and you can read its 1880 income per capita level by looking down to the horizontal scale.

The diagram clearly shows a tendency for states with low real income per capita in 1880 to have had high growth rates since then. The state observations fall remarkably near a catch-up line. Southern states like Florida and Texas are in the high-growth

growth accounting formula
productivity growth rate =
$\frac{1}{3}\left(\begin{array}{c}\text{growth rate of capital}\\\text{per hour of work}\end{array}\right)+$
(growth rate of technology)
(Ch. 9).

catch-up line
the downward-sloping relation between the level of productivity and the growth of productivity predicted by growth theory.

Figure 17-1

The Catch-up Line

Growth theory with spreading technology and diminishing returns to capital and labor predicts that regions with lower productivity will have higher growth rates of productivity. The catch-up line illustrates this prediction. Because productivity is so closely related to income per capita, the catch-up line also can describe a relationship between income per capita and the growth rate of income per capita.

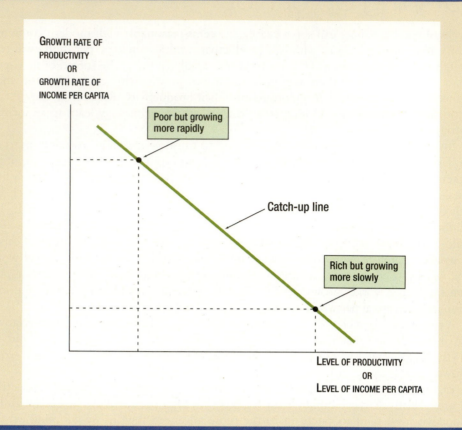

Figure 17-2

Evidence of Catch-up within the United States, 1880-1980

In the United States, those states that had low real income per capita in 1880 grew relatively rapidly compared to states that had high income per capita. The poor states tended to catch up to the richer states. A catch-up line is drawn through the dots.

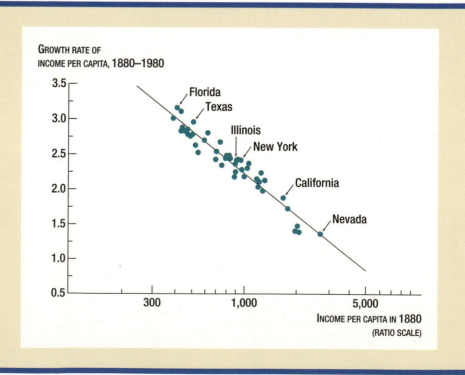

group. On the other hand, in states that had a relatively high income per capita in 1880, income per capita grew relatively slowly. This group includes California and Nevada.

Thus, the theory of growth works quite well in explaining the relative differences in growth rates in the U.S. states. The tendency is for relatively poor regions to grow more rapidly than relatively rich regions.

Catch-up in the Industrial Countries

What if we apply the same thinking to different countries? After all, communication is now global. Figure 17-3 is another scatter diagram with growth rate and income per capita combinations. It is like Figure 17-2 except that it plots real gross domestic product (GDP) per capita in 1960 against growth in real GDP per capita from 1960 to 2005 for several industrial countries.

Observe in Figure 17-3 that the richer countries, such as the United States, grew less rapidly. In contrast, relatively less rich countries, such as Japan, Ireland, and Spain, grew more rapidly. Canada and France are somewhere in between. These countries tend to display the catch-up behavior predicted by growth theory. Apparently, technological advances are spreading and capital-labor ratios are rising more rapidly in countries where they are low and returns to capital are high. So far, our look at the evidence confirms the predictions of growth theory.

Figure 17-3

Evidence of Catch-up in Industrial Countries, 1960–2005
For the industrial countries shown in the diagram, GDP per capita growth has been more rapid for those that started from a lower level of GDP per capita. Thus, there has been catching up, as shown by the catch-up line drawn through the points.

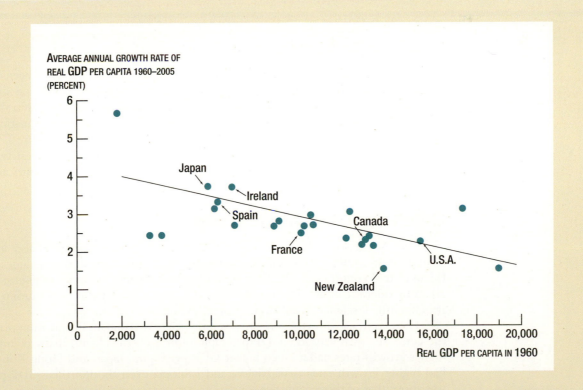

Figure 17-4

Evidence of Catch-up in East Asia, 1980–2005

Over the past quarter century, many East Asian economies have grown extremely rapidly. As a result, they have experienced dramatic improvements in per capita GDP and closed the gap between themselves and richer economies like the United States.

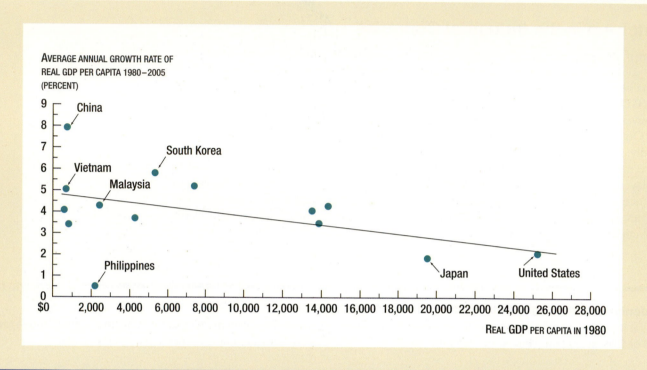

Catch-up in East Asia

One of the most remarkable success stories of the last half-century has been the rapid economic growth rates achieved by many East Asian economies. Beginning with countries like South Korea in the 1960s and picked up by countries like China in the 1980s, the East Asian economies have grown extremely rapidly, resulting in a dramatic transformation of their economies and of the living standards of their people. Figure 17-4 shows what the growth experience of East Asian economies has been over the last twenty-five years. As you can see, many economies grew extremely rapidly, with China and South Korea being the most striking examples.

Catch-up in the Whole World

However, so far we have not looked at whether the poorest economies also are experiencing catch-up. Figure 17-5 shows a broader group of countries that includes not only the industrial countries in Figure 17-3 and the East Asian economies in Figure 17-4 but also a broader set of developing countries. It is apparent that this larger group of countries has little tendency to fall along a catch-up line.

The countries with very low growth rates, such as Bangladesh and Ethiopia, are also the countries with very low GDP per capita. On the other hand, many countries with higher growth rates had a much higher GDP per capita. Japan and Hong Kong, China, had higher growth rates than Nigeria and Ethiopia even though their GDP per capita was above that of these countries.

Figure 17-5

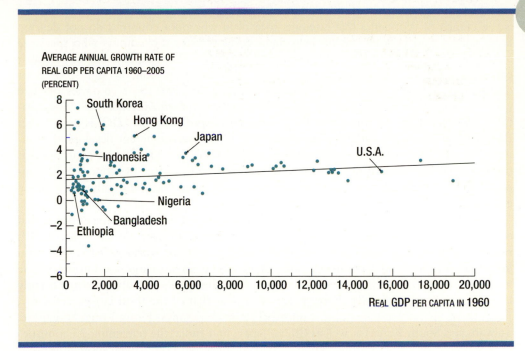

Average annual growth rate of real GDP per capita 1960–2005 (percent); labeled points: South Korea, Hong Kong, Japan, Indonesia, U.S.A., Nigeria, Bangladesh, Ethiopia. Horizontal axis: Real GDP per capita in 1960.

Lack of Catch-up for Developing Countries, 1960–2005

Unlike the U.S. states or the industrial countries, there has been little tendency for poor countries to grow more rapidly than rich countries. The gap between rich and poor has not closed.

Comparing countries like Indonesia and South Korea with countries like Bangladesh and Nigeria is striking. South Korea and Indonesia had about the same real GDP per capita as Nigeria and Bangladesh in 1960, but South Korea and Indonesia surged ahead with a more rapid growth rate over the next 45 years, leaving Bangladesh and Nigeria behind. And this is not the exception. Contrary to the predictions of economic growth theory, which says that technological advances should spread and capital per hour of work should rise from low levels, Figure 17-5 shows little tendency for relatively poor countries to grow relatively rapidly. It appears that something has been preventing either the spread and the adoption of new technology or the increase in investment needed to raise capital-labor ratios. We examine possible explanations as this chapter proceeds.

REVIEW

- Economic growth theory predicts that poorer regions will tend to catch up to richer ones. The flow of technology around the world and investment in new capital will bring this about.
- Data for the U.S. states and for the advanced countries show that such catch-up exists and is quite strong.

- However, little evidence indicates catch-up in the world as a whole. Many of the poor countries have fallen even further behind the industrial countries, whereas other poor countries, in particular those in East Asia, have grown rapidly.

Economic Development

As well as raising questions about economic growth theory, the lack of catch-up evidenced in Figure 17-5 presents a disturbing situation. Disparities are huge in world income distribution, and billions of people in low-income countries lack the necessities

economic development
the process of growth by which countries raise incomes per capita and become industrialized; also refers to the branch of economics that studies this process.

developing country
a country that is poor by world standards in terms of real GDP per capita.

that those in high-income countries frequently take for granted. **Economic development** is the branch of economics that attempts to explain why poor countries do not develop faster and to find policies that do help them develop faster. Economists who specialize in economic development frequently are experts on the problems experienced by particular countries—such as a poor education system, political repression, droughts, or poor distribution of food. The term **developing country** describes those countries that are relatively poor. In contrast, the term *industrial country* or *advanced economy* describes relatively well-off countries. Sometimes the term *less-developed country (LDC)* is used rather than *developing country*. Other terms also distinguish between different developing countries. For example, *emerging-market countries* such as Chile and Malaysia are countries that once were poor but have since grown rapidly and moved to a stage of economic development during which they are closer to advanced economies than most other developing economies.

Table 17-1 shows the shares of world GDP produced by advanced economies and developing countries. Thus, this table looks at aggregate income (which equals GDP) rather than at income per capita. More than 50 percent of world GDP comes from industrial countries. As the table shows, China is the second-largest economy in the world and a major force in the world economy even though its per capita income is fairly low. China's GDP is already almost twice as large as that of the third-largest economy, Japan. Note that if you take out the industrial Asian economies (Hong Kong; Singapore; Taiwan; and South Korea) as well as China, Japan, and India, the remaining 25 countries in developing Asia only produce about 5 percent of world GDP. Even more striking is

Table 17-1

Shares of World GDP Produced by Different Countries

	Number of Countries	Percent of World GDP
Advanced Economies	**34**	**53.4**
Major Industrial Countries	7	40.4
United States		20.1
Japan		5.9
Germany		4.0
United Kingdom		3.0
France		3.0
Italy		2.5
Canada		1.8
Rest of Euro Area	14	5.6
Industrialized Asia	4	3.8
Other Industrialized	9	3.6
Developing Countries	**150**	**46.6**
China		12.9
India		5.1
Rest of Developing Asia	25	4.9
Sub-Saharan Africa	44	3.0
Middle East/North Africa	20	5.0
Latin America/Caribbean	32	8.5
Central and Eastern Europe	27	7.5

Source: From *World Economic Outlook* April 2008, p. 235. Reprinted by permission of International Monetary Fund.

the fact that all 44 countries in Sub-Saharan Africa produce only about 3 percent of world GDP. As we soon will see, the distribution of the world population does not look like the distribution of world GDP because the majority of the world's people live in China, India and other developing economies.

Geographic Patterns

Figure 17-6 shows the location of the relatively rich and the relatively poor countries around the world. Notice that the higher-income countries tend to be in the northern part of the world. Exceptions to this rule are Australia and New Zealand, with relatively high income per capita. Aside from these exceptions, income disparity appears to have a geographic pattern—the North is relatively rich and the South is relatively poor. Often people use the term *North-South problem* to describe world income disparities.

But whether it is North versus South or not, many rich or many poor countries appear to be located together in large contiguous regions. The original increase in economic growth that occurred at the time of the Industrial Revolution started in northwestern Europe—England, France, and Germany. It then spread to America, which industrialized rapidly in the nineteenth and twentieth centuries. It also spread to Japan

Figure 17-6

Rich and Poor Countries around the World
The highest-income regions tend to be located in North America, Europe, Japan, Australia, and the Middle East.

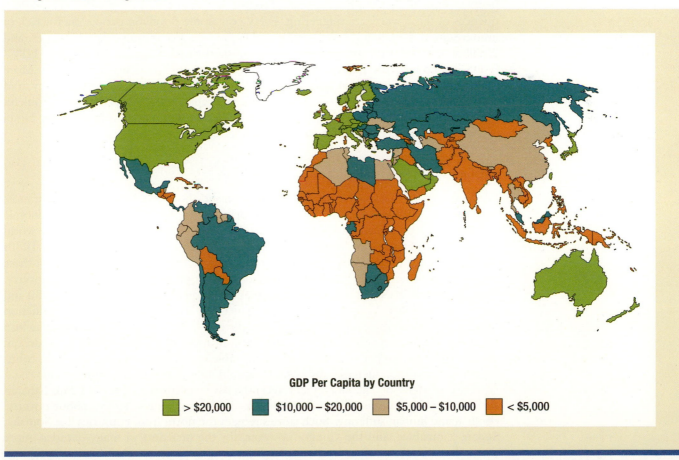

GDP Per Capita by Country

> $20,000 $10,000 – $20,000 $5,000 – $10,000   < $5,000

during the late-nineteenth-century Meiji Restoration, one of the main purposes of which was to import Western technology into the Japanese economy.

Billions Still in Poverty

The richest countries in the world, with more than $20,000 in GDP per capita (adjusted for differences in purchasing power across countries), account for about a billion people. The United States, with more than 300 million people, is among the richest, along with Japan and most of Western Europe. This group of countries, which accounted for more than 50 percent of world GDP, accounts for about one-sixth of the world's population.

Close to a billion people also live in emerging-market economies with a per capita GDP of between $10,000 and $15,000, many of them in the large economies of Brazil, Mexico, Turkey, and South Africa as well as in other Latin American and Eastern European economies. Another 1.7 billion people (400 million of them outside of China) live in countries that have an income per capita between $5,000 and $10,000. But the rest of the world's people—about 45 percent—live in countries with an income per capita of less than $5,000 per year. This amount is below the poverty level in advanced countries. Income per capita in Brazil and South Africa is about one-quarter of that in the United States. In China, it is about 15 percent of that in the United States. Income per capita for the poorest Sub-Saharan African countries like Ethiopia, Uganda, and Tanzania is a mere 2 percent to 3 percent of that in the United States.

The economists Shaohua Chen and Martin Ravallion calculated that in 2005 about 900 million people lived on less than US$1.00 a day and that close to 2.5 billion people—close to half the human race—lived on less than US$2.00 per day. The consequences of this poverty are staggering. Every year, some 3 million people die for lack of immunization, 1 million die from malaria, 3 million die from water-related diseases, and 2 million die from exposure to stove smoke inside their own homes. In addition, HIV/AIDS has ravaged the populations of developing nations, particularly in Africa. More than 1 billion people do not have safe water to drink, 2 billion have no electricity, and 2 billion lack adequate sanitation. Low income per capita is a serious economic problem, but the implications go well beyond economics. Large differences in income per capita and extensive poverty can lead to war, revolution, or regional conflicts.

Hope for the Future

We have plenty of reasons, however, to be optimistic about the future. One of the most encouraging developments of the last few decades has been the dramatic economic growth rates experienced by China and India, home to more than one-third of the world population. As Figure 17-7 shows, China grew extremely rapidly beginning in the 1980s and India began to grow more rapidly about a decade later. Economic growth in these two economies has lifted hundreds of millions of people out of a life of dire poverty. Chen and Ravallion's calculations indicate that in the quarter century between 1980 and 2005, the number of people living on less than US$1 a day was cut in half, a reduction of nearly 700 million people living in dire poverty with almost all of that reduction occurring in China. Even though the reduction in India was minuscule by comparison, the fact that the number of poor people held stable was an encouraging sign for a country whose population increased by several hundred million people over this period.

Further signs of encouragement recently have emerged in parts of Sub-Saharan Africa, a region that has long produced a steady stream of news stories about poverty, conflict, and human suffering. Such stories remain the norm from countries like Somalia, Sudan, Zimbabwe, and the Congo; however, for the first time in many decades, more than a handful of countries in the region seem to provide cause for genuine optimism.

Figure 17-7

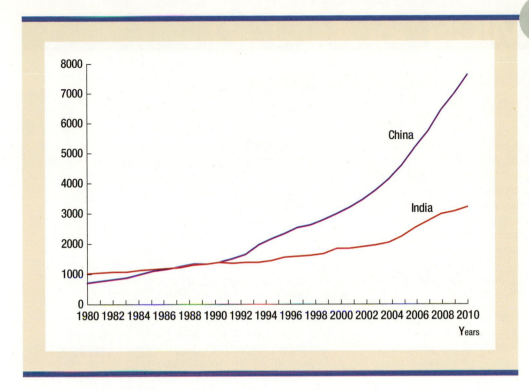

Rapid Growth in China and India

China and India are the two most populous nations in the world, home to more than 2.5 billion people. Rapid growth in these two economies has been one of the great success stories of the last quarter century for the world economy.

The economist Steven Radelet has been one of the most prominent chroniclers of this new "Emerging Africa," writing about how countries like Ghana, South Africa, Tanzania, and Zambia have demonstrated more than a decade-long trend of improved economic performance, thus lowering poverty and providing better prospects and more hope for the youth of the region.

Will these improvements persist? Is the lack of catch-up that has left so many behind finally a thing of the past? We next examine the reasons why some countries or regions have been unable to catch up to the rich countries in the way that the East Asian economies or China seems to have been able to do. Our examination will consider the two key determinants of increasing productivity—improvements in technology and higher capital per worker. We consider technology in the next section and then consider capital in the following section.

REVIEW

- The lack of catch-up experienced by poor countries has resulted in considerable income inequality around the world. The vast majority of the people in the world do not live in the rich industrial nations.

- With a few exceptions, most of the rich countries are in the northern regions of the globe and most of the poor countries are in the southern regions.

- Low income per capita is a serious economic problem for well-being. Millions of people die in poor countries from a lack of access to basic amenities

like childhood immunization, clean water, lack of sanitation, and environmental hazards.

- Economic growth in China and India has improved the lives of hundreds of millions of people and provided cause for optimism. More recent indicators suggest that some parts of Sub-Saharan Africa finally are beginning to experience economic development.

- More work needs to be done to understand why only a subset of the LDCs seem to have been able to catch up with the wealthier economies.

ECONOMICS *IN ACTION*

Empowering Entrepreneurs in the Nations That Are Catching Up

The rapid growth of China has been one of the most fascinating issues for economists. When a team of economists from the **International Monetary Fund (IMF)** began to study this issue a couple of decades after the growth spurt began, they wrote down their findings in a paper with the appropriately pithy title "Why Is China Growing So Fast?" They pinpointed the major program of economic reform that China undertook in 1978 as the critical policy change that set the Chinese economy on the path to rapid growth. In their paper, the authors describe this program of reform as follows:

> [In] an effort to awaken a dormant economic giant, it encouraged the formation of rural enterprises and private businesses, liberalized foreign trade and investment, relaxed state control over some prices, and invested in industrial production and the education of its workforce. By nearly all accounts, the strategy has worked spectacularly.

By freeing up Chinese workers and firms from having to meet state mandated targets on quantities and varieties of goods, and by providing them the freedom to set up their own businesses, Chinese firms now were able to earn as much as they could by selling whatever they wanted at whatever price the market determined. Just as in the industrial nations two centuries before, the entrepreneurs of China began to invent and develop products that were most beneficial to individuals and keep the profits. They no longer had to worry about the profits being confiscated by the modern-day ruler, the state, and transformed the Chinese economy as a result.

The IMF research team estimated that during the period from 1979–1994 "productivity gains accounted for more than 42 percent of China's growth and by the early 1990s had overtaken capital as the most significant source of that growth."

A similar story can be told about the rise of the Indian economy in the 1980s and 1990s as well. The economist Aravind Panagariya writes about the restrictive trade policies that India imposed in the 1960s and 1970s having disastrous consequences for the economy by suppressing productivity. He writes:

> When you play against the best in the world, not only does it make you work harder because you face tough competition, you also learn from your rivals. Competition also forces you to devise new techniques and strategies. The story with entrepreneurs is similar. If you are only going to compete domestically, you will not only miss out on the latest production and marketing techniques and products, but also the intense competition that forces you to be most efficient.

Beginning in the early 1990s, India made dramatic reductions in trade barriers, allowed domestic entrepreneurs the freedom to expand into sectors that they previously had not been allowed to, and removed government restrictions on the ability of firms to compete with state-owned monopolies in areas such as telecommunications. The result, as with the industrial nations and China, was a dramatic transformation of an economy in which productivity had been stifled for far too long.

International Monetary Fund (IMF)
an international agency, established after World War II, designed to help countries with balance of payments problems and to ensure the smooth functioning of the international monetary system.

The Spread and Use of Technology

You should remember two important facts about economic growth. First, a large and persistent increase in economic growth began during the Industrial Revolution about 200 years ago, and this increase in economic growth raised income per capita in some countries to levels experienced only by royalty throughout most of human history. Second, economic growth did not spread throughout much of the world, leaving people in many countries hardly better off than their ancestors. Could these two facts be linked? Could they have the same explanation? A number of ideas have been put forth to explain the increase in economic growth in the late 1700s, and some of these ideas may explain why growth has not accelerated in many developing countries.

Entrepreneurs in the Industrial Nations

Some economists and historians have pointed to developments in science as the explanation of the rapid increase in economic growth in Europe in the 1700s. But if that is the explanation, why did the Industrial Revolution not begin in China or in the Islamic nations, where scientific knowledge was far more advanced than in Europe? Others note the importance of natural resources, but these were available in many other countries that did not have an Industrial Revolution; also, growth in Japan has been high since the mid-nineteenth century, yet Japan has almost no natural resources. Still others have focused on exploitation, slavery, colonialism, and imperialism, but these evils existed long before the Industrial Revolution.

What, then, is the reason for this increase in economic growth that we associate with the Industrial Revolution? Historians of capitalist development from Karl Marx onward have stressed that, in the 1700s, for the first time in human history, entrepreneurs were gaining the freedom to start business enterprises. Economic historian Angus Maddison shows in an influential book, *Phases of Capitalist Development*, that the Dutch were the first to lead in productivity, with the British and then the United States soon catching up. He also shows that in the 1700s, many Dutch farmers owned their land, the feudal nobility was small and weak, and the potential power was in the hands of entrepreneurs. Hence, people had greater freedom to produce and sell manufactured and agricultural products. By the late 1700s and early 1800s, similar conditions existed in the United Kingdom and the United States. Firms could ship their products to market and hire workers without political restrictions.

Moreover, these firms were able to earn as much as they could by selling whatever they wanted at whatever price the market determined. They began to invent and develop products that were most beneficial to individuals. The business enterprises could keep the profits. Profits were no longer confiscated by nobles or kings. Individual property rights—including the right to earn and keep profits—were being established and recognized in the courts.

Karl Marx—although known more for his critique of capitalism—saw earlier than others that the unleashing of business enterprises and entrepreneurs was the key to economic growth. He credited the business and entrepreneurial class—what he called the bourgeois class—with the creation of more wealth than previously had been created throughout all of history.

The sudden increase in technology and productivity may have occurred when it did because of the increased freedom that entrepreneurs had to start businesses, to invent and apply new ideas, and to develop products for the mass of humanity in areas where the large markets existed.

Remaining Problems in Developing Countries

If true, the idea that an economic growth surge follows the removal of restrictions on business

This knitting cooperative in Ecuador opens up a market for women who traditionally knitted at home for their families. The freedom to start businesses and to produce and sell manufactured products without restriction is a critical piece of the economic growth puzzle for many developing countries.

enterprises may have lessons for economic development. Many developing countries, which have yet to experience rapid growth and catch-up, place restrictions on entrepreneurial activity and have weak enforcement of individual property rights.

Regulation and Legal Rights Good examples of these restrictions have been documented in the research of economist Hernando de Soto on the economy of Peru. De Soto showed that developing countries have a tremendous amount of regulation. This regulation has been so costly that a huge informal economy has emerged. The **informal economy** consists of large numbers of illegal businesses that can avoid the regulations. Remarkably, de Soto found that 61 percent of employment in Peru was in the informal, unregulated, illegal sector of the economy. In the city of Lima, around 33 percent of the houses were built by this informal sector. About 71,000 illegal vendors dominated retail trade, and 93 percent of urban transportation was in the informal sector.

This large informal sector exists because the costs of setting up a legal business are high. It takes 32 months—filling out forms, waiting for approval, getting permission from several agencies—for a person to start a retail business. It takes six years and 11 months to start a housing construction firm. Hence, it is essentially impossible for someone to try to start a small business in the legal sector. Therefore, the informal sector grows.

Why does it matter if the informal sector is large? How does this impede development? Precisely because the sector is informal, it lacks basic legal rights such as the enforcement of the laws of property rights and contracts. These laws cannot be enforced in a sector that is outside the law. Bringing new inventions to market requires the security of private property so that the inventor can capture the benefits from taking the risks. Without this, the earnings from the innovation might be taken away by the government or by firms that copy the idea illegally. For example, if a business in the informal sector finds that another firm has reneged on a contract to deliver a product, that business has no right to use the courts to enforce the contract because the business itself is illegal.

The explanation given earlier for why the Industrial Revolution occurred in Western Hemisphere countries seems to point to this as a reason. In Europe in the 1700s, a new freedom for businesses to operate in the emerging-market economy led to new products and technology. Laws to prevent theft or fraud gave people more certainty about reaping the returns from their entrepreneurship.

Lack of Human Capital For existing technology to be adopted—whether in the form of innovative organizational structures of firms or as new products—it is necessary to have well-trained and highly skilled workers. For example, it is hard to make use of sophisticated computers to increase productivity when few skilled computer programmers are available.

Recall that human capital refers to the education and training of workers. Low investment in human capital is a serious obstacle to increasing productivity because it hampers the ability of countries that are behind to use new technology.

In fact, economists have found that differences in human capital in different countries can explain why some countries have been more successful at catching up than others. The developing countries that have been catching up most rapidly—in particular, the newly industrialized countries like South Korea; Hong Kong; Taiwan; and Singapore—have strong education systems in grade school and high school. This result demonstrates the enormous importance of human capital for raising productivity.

---

informal economy
the portion of an economy characterized by illegal, unregulated businesses.

ECONOMICS *IN ACTION*

The Millennium Challenge Corporation

The Millennium Challenge Corporation (MCC) is a new foreign aid program through which the United States gives assistance to poor countries. It was established by an act of Congress in 2003, and its stated mission is to reduce poverty by promoting economic growth. In designing the MCC, the administration and Congress took account of the basic principles of economic development that have emerged from economic research in recent years. They are exactly the ones described in this chapter. Hence, the MCC is an excellent example of economics in action.

The basic idea is to give more aid to countries that are following progrowth policies. How do you determine which countries those are? Numerical indicators are used. Countries that rank high on the indicators receive assistance from the MCC. Countries that rank low do not. The MCC uses 16 indicators, including the following:

- *Open trade policy.* The numerical measure of openness is taken from the Heritage Foundation's Index of Economic Freedom. The index is based on average tariff rates and other barriers to trade. Open economies—those with low trade barriers—tend to grow faster than more closed economies.

- *Days to start a business.* This index comes from the World Bank. The shorter the time it takes to start a business, the more entrepreneurs are empowered. Bureaucratic barriers to business formation hinder entrepreneurship.

- *Regulatory quality rating.* The World Bank also measures the burden on business arising from licensing requirements and bureaucratic corruption. Excessive regulations and their arbitrary application deter investment and raise the cost of doing business, thereby reducing economic growth.

- *Rule of law.* This index comes from Freedom House. It attempts to measure the effectiveness and predictability of the judiciary and the enforceability of contracts.

- *Civil liberties.* This is another Freedom House indicator. It evaluates freedom of expression, association and organizational rights, rule of law and human rights, and personal autonomy and economic rights.

Of course, none of these indicators is a perfect measure of actual policies, but overall, they provide an excellent measure of the kinds of economic policies that promote economic growth. In fact, if you rank countries on these criteria, you will find that they correlate highly with the level of development.

Countries that have ranked relatively high on the list and have been awarded MCC grants thus far include Ghana, Madagascar, Georgia, and Honduras. It will take some time before a full evaluation of the effectiveness of this program can be made, but the preliminary results indicate that, at the least, it is encouraging better economic policies. If it works well, then more of this new type of foreign aid should follow.

REVIEW

- The removal of restrictions on private enterprise and enforcement of individual property rights may have been the key factors unleashing the growth of productivity at the time of the Industrial Revolution.

- In more recent times, both China and India saw dramatic economic transformations after policies that were designed to suppress private enterprise and create obstacles to entrepreneurship were lifted.

- Similar restrictions may explain why other developing countries have not been able to experience the kind of rapid economic growth that China and India have experienced in recent years.

- An educated workforce is needed to adopt technology. Better-educated and more highly skilled workers—those with human capital—also can use available capital more efficiently.

Increasing Capital per Worker

In addition to obstacles to the spread and adoption of new technology, obstacles to the increase in capital per worker can prevent poor countries from catching up.

Population Growth

For the capital-to-labor ratio to increase, it is necessary to invest in new capital. The amount of investment in new capital, however, must be larger than the increase in labor, or capital will increase by less than labor and the ratio of capital to labor—the factor influencing productivity—will fall. Thus, high population growth raises the amount of investment needed to increase, or even maintain, the level of capital per worker. High population growth rates, therefore, can slow down the increase in capital per worker.

Population growth rates have declined substantially in locations where income per capita has risen to high levels, such as Europe, Japan, and the United States. Economic analysis of the determinants of population indicates that the high income per capita and resulting greater life expectancy may be the reason for the decline in population growth. When countries reach a level of income per capita at which people can survive into their old age without the support of many children, or at which the chance is greater of children reaching working age, people choose to have fewer children.

Population growth rates also have declined in the fast-growing East Asian economies and in China and India. Fertility rates in India were cut in half during the latter part of the twentieth century and the decline in China may have been even more dramatic as a result of the controversial "one-child" policy. Other poor nations in the twenty-first century probably could follow the example of these countries and raise income per capita by lowering their rates of population growth.

National Saving

Capital accumulation requires investment, which requires saving. From our national income accounting equation, $Y = C + I + G + X$, we get the equation $Y - C - G = I + X$, which states that national saving is equal to the sum of investment plus net exports. Recall that national saving is the sum of private saving and government saving. In some developing countries where income per capita is barely above subsistence levels, the level of private saving—people's income less their consumption—is low. Government saving—tax receipts less expenditures—also is low, perhaps because there is little income to tax and because governments have trouble controlling expenditures. Saving rates in Africa are low compared with the higher saving rates in advanced economies and in Asia. This could explain why capital accumulation is low in these nations that have not experienced catch-up.

On the other hand, some of the economies that did experience catch-up, such as China or the East Asian economies, increased saving quite dramatically, which in turn meant that they had more resources that they could invest into the domestic economy. For many poor countries, however, it is natural for national saving to be less than investment and thus for imports to be greater than exports (net exports less than zero). In other words, a poor country naturally looks to investment from abroad as a source of capital formation for economic growth.

> National saving
> = investment + net exports
> $S = I + X$

Foreign Investment from the Advanced Economies

foreign direct investment (FDI)
investment by a foreign entity in at least a 10 percent direct ownership share in a firm.

Investment from abroad can come in the form of **foreign direct investment (FDI)**, such as when the U.S. firm Gap Inc. opens a store in Mexico. Technically, when a foreign firm invests in more than 10 percent of the ownership of a business in another country, that investment is defined as direct investment.

ECONOMICS *IN ACTION*

Emerging Africa

A 2011 study released by the African Development Bank got considerable publicity in the U.S. media because it contained good economic news about Sub-Saharan Africa. Good news has been a rarity for that region, but the early signs of what may be in store in the first half of the twenty-first century are exciting. The chief economist of the African Development Bank described a 200-million-strong middle class in Africa, composed of people who were willing to spend between $750 and $1,500 a year or $2 to $4 a day. The arrival of this middle class marks a momentous occasion because it allows entrepreneurs in these African nations the ability to sell their products to a thriving domestic market without having to continually seek out foreign buyers for their wares. A thriving middle class also will bolster the livelihood of those who provide services—such as teachers, drivers, cooks, nurses, and hairdressers—who previously would not be able to export their services to foreign markets.

The report highlights that even though many of the middle class are salaried workers who obtained jobs based on education achievements, they were "more likely to have values aligned with greater market competition and better governance, greater gender equality, more investment in higher education, science and technology." So the rise of this middle class is likely to serve as a catalyst for political and economic changes that will encourage more entrepreneurial freedom for Africans, remove government restrictions that stifle productivity, and encourage African nations to catch up over the first part of the twenty-first century much the same way that the East Asian economies did in the latter half of the twentieth century.

The economist Steve Radelet has been one of those writing most often about this rise of Africa in the last 15 years. In his book *Emerging Africa*, Radelet identifies 12 countries (Burkina Faso, Botswana, Ethiopia, Ghana, Lesotho, Mali, Mozambique, Namibia, South Africa, Tanzania, Uganda, and Zambia) that are leading the way and identifies five other countries that are likely to follow in their footsteps (Benin, Kenya, Liberia, Malawi, and Senegal). What does Steve Radelet think helped these 17 countries come to the cusp of finally being able to embark on a catch-up growth path? Increased democratization has made leaders more responsive to the conditions of their citizens, and better economic policies have sought to reduce the excessive controls that the state previously imposed on private enterprises. Technology has played a key role, according to Radelet, particularly the spread of Internet technology and cellular phones, which have connected people in ways that were almost impossible a generation ago and have created an entirely new class of entrepreneurs. Finally, Radelet emphasizes the role that international organizations and rich nations played in granting debt relief to many of these economies, enabling them to better harness national saving for productive investment in the future rather than to pay off for the debts and excesses of the past.

But perhaps the biggest transformation in Africa, and the one that makes many people optimistic about its future, has been the dynamism of the young people of Africa. In a world in which many industrial nations as well as East Asian countries face the problems of rapidly aging populations, Africa is a young continent. If it can continue to generate young workers, skilled and unskilled, it can play an increasingly major role in producing goods and services for the world economy. Educated young men and women in Africa finally are seeing what economic growth can provide—a life that is much better than the one their parents lived. They are breaking free of the past, and catching up to the future.

Foreign investment also occurs when foreigners buy smaller percentages (less than 10 percent) of firms in developing economies. For example, foreign investment in Mexico takes place when a German buys newly offered common stock in a Mexican firm. In that case, the foreign investment from abroad is defined as **portfolio investment**, that is, less than 10 percent of ownership in a company.

As you may have read about in the newspapers, FDI has played a substantial role in the rapid catch-up demonstrated by China over the last few years. China has leveraged the substantial amount of unskilled resources and manufacturing-friendly policies and regulations to become the "manufacturer to the world" in recent years. India has been

portfolio investment
investment by a foreign entity in less than a 10 percent ownership share in a firm.

Activists such as U2 star Bono have been effective proponents of efforts to improve the effectiveness of foreign aid. By working with the governments of the United States, the United Kingdom, and others, activists have helped improve and increase foreign aid through such programs as the MCC and 100 percent debt cancellation of World Bank loans to the poorest countries.

just as successful in attracting FDI in areas related to the provision of services as China has been in attracting FDI related to the production of manufactured goods. Indian call centers, software programmers, and information technology firms have attracted substantial foreign resources seeking to take advantage of the skilled English-speaking workforce that India is able to offer.

Another way investment can flow in from abroad is through borrowing. Firms in developing economies or their governments can borrow from commercial banks, such as Bank of America, Mizuho, or Crédit Lyonnais. Sometimes the governments of developing economies obtain loans directly from the governments of industrial economies. Borrowing from government-sponsored international financial institutions, such as the IMF and the World Bank, also can occur. Many emerging-market economies have expanded and improved their banking sectors and their financial markets to attract foreign investors. Although these liberalizations have greatly expanded access to capital for domestic firms, recent history suggests that a country can face negative effects from too much unregulated money entering, and then rapidly departing, the domestic economy.

Borrowing from International Agencies

World Bank

an international agency, established after World War II, designed to promote the economic development of poorer countries through lending channeled from industrial countries.

The **World Bank** and the International Monetary Fund (IMF) were established after World War II as part of a major reform of the international monetary system. Both institutions make loans to developing countries. They serve as intermediaries, channeling funds from the industrial countries to the developing countries.

Many of the World Bank's loans are for specific projects—such as building a $100 million dam for irrigation in Brazil and a $153 million highway in Poland. Although these project loans have been helpful, they are much smaller in total than private investment in these countries.

In recent years, the IMF has tried to use its loans to encourage countries to implement difficult economic reforms. Frequently, it tries to induce countries to make these reforms by making the loans conditional on the reforms; this is the idea of *conditionality*. Under conditionality, the IMF gives loans to countries only if the countries undertake economic reform—such as eliminating price controls or privatizing firms. This conditionality is viewed as a way to encourage reforms that are difficult to put into effect because of the various vested interests in each country.

The IMF has been criticized heavily in recent years for going too far with its conditions and actually giving bad economic advice to developing countries. For example, during the financial crisis in East Asia in 1997 and 1998, the IMF insisted that the countries in crisis implement politically controversial reforms before it would agree to make loans to deal with the crisis.

REVIEW

- High rates of population growth and low national saving rates are two of the obstacles to raising capital per worker in developing economies. Many of the economies that experienced catch-up were able to lower their population growth rates and increase national saving.

- Poor economies that are open can increase domestic investment by attracting FDI and portfolio investment. These policies can help raise capital per worker in the poor economies even in cases in which

they are unable to save more. Both China and India have been successful at attracting FDI inflows in recent years.

- Poor countries can accumulate capital per worker by borrowing money from international organizations. The IMF makes loans to developing countries that frequently are conditional on an economic reform program, a practice that came under heavy criticism in the Asian financial crisis of the 1990s. The World Bank makes loans mainly for specific projects.

CONCLUSION

In this chapter, we documented fundamental differences in economic growth across countries and demonstrated that these differences do not have a broad-based tendency to go away over time. The consequence of this lack of catch-up is that people in the industrial nations are much better off on average than the people in developing nations. Some developing countries have managed to catch up over the past half-century, most noticeably countries in East Asia, such as South Korea and Malaysia. These countries have either become industrial nations (for example, South Korea) or have been categorized as emerging-market economies (for example, Brazil, Russia, or China), closer in spirit to the industrial economies than to their poorer counterparts.

Over the past three decades, the most remarkable improvements in economic growth have come from China, and more recently from India. The consequence of this economic growth has been a remarkable reduction in poverty, especially in China. But many other countries have not been able to replicate the experiences of South Korea, China, and India and have spent decades stuck in poverty without any growth. This has been particularly true for countries in Africa, although a few African nations recently have shown some promising signs of growth.

How can we explain the lack of catch-up in the global economy? Among the possible explanations for the lack of catch-up are obstacles to the spread of technology, such as

government restrictions on entrepreneurs and a shortage of human capital, and obstacles to higher capital per worker, such as low saving rates and low foreign investment. The removal of similar obstacles in Western Europe in the eighteenth century may have been the cause of the Industrial Revolution. Their removal in China and India set the stage for the now almost three-decades-long boom in economic growth that has transformed the lives of people living in the two most populous nations of the world. Similar reforms in the other nations, yet to experience catch-up, may result in another great growth wave in the developing economies. If real GDP in all the other countries of the world grows at a rate that is even half of what a country like China has achieved, then the economic landscape of the world will be transformed in the rest of this century. These countries face many obstacles to such a transformation. One threat comes from the rise of terrorism and military conflicts that divide nations, disrupt progress, and divert resources from more productive uses. The increasing tendency for economic fluctuations, such as the recent U.S. recession, to be synchronized into a global economic slowdown may lead to a backlash in the form of increased protectionism and a more vocal anti-globalization movement. It is hardly an exaggeration to say that the progress of humankind in the twenty-first century may depend critically on whether increased globalization is a force for, or an obstacle to, global economic growth.

KEY POINTS

1. Economic growth theory pinpoints capital accumulation and technological change as the two key ingredients of productivity growth. In a world without obstacles to the spread of technology or to investment in new capital, growth theory predicts that poor regions will catch up to rich regions.

2. Catch-up has occurred in the U.S. states, among the industrial countries, and among some economies in East Asia but is distressingly absent from many developing countries.

3. Low incomes and poverty have persisted for the vast majority of the world's population while other countries have become richer.

4. Some countries may have poor growth performance because of restrictions on markets and a lack of property rights. The lifting of those restrictions in Europe in the 1700s was a cause of the economic growth associated with the Industrial Revolution.

5. Similarly, the removal of such restrictions was a key factor to the increased productivity and economic development in India and China and is likely to have a similar result for any other developing country that hopes to break free of economic stagnation and to catch up with the industrial nations

6. In many countries in the twenty-first century, especially in Latin America and Asia, the potential for higher economic growth is great, as the market system is being encouraged and restrictions on entrepreneurs are being removed.

7. High rates of population growth and low national saving rates are two of the obstacles to raising capital per worker in developing economies.

8. Poor economies can increase capital per worker by attracting foreign direct investment (FDI) and portfolio investment. Both China and India have been successful at attracting FDI inflows in recent years.

KEY TERMS

catch-up line, 405

developing country, 410

economic development, 410

foreign direct investment (FDI), 418

growth accounting formula, 405

informal economy, 416

International Monetary Fund (IMF), 414

portfolio investment, 419

World Bank, 420

QUESTIONS FOR REVIEW

1. Why does economic growth theory predict that productivity and real income per capita will grow relatively more rapidly in poor countries?

2. In what way does the catch-up line describe more rapid growth in poor countries?

3. Why is catch-up observed among the industrial economies but not for the whole world?

4. How did the removal of government restrictions on entrepreneurs lead to more economic growth, both historically in the industrial nations as well as in modern times in countries like China and India that experienced catch-up?

5. What role does human capital play in the adoption and spread of technology?

6. Why is the identity that investment plus net exports equals saving important for understanding the flow of capital around the world?

7. How did countries like China and India benefit from the flows of capital in a globalized world?

8. What is the difference between foreign direct investment and portfolio investment?

9. What role do international organizations like the International Monetary Fund and the World Bank play in promoting economic growth and economic development?

10. Why do we say that increased globalization occasionally can harm an economy as well as help the economy catch up?

PROBLEMS

1. Plot on a scatter diagram the data for the Asian countries that appear below. Does a catch-up line appear in the scatter diagram?

Country	Per Capita Real GDP in 1960 (2000 U.S. dollars)	Average Annual Rate of Growth from 1960 to 2000 (%)
Thailand	1,051	4.6
Pakistan	526	2.9
Philippines	1,581	1.3
China	746	4.3
Malaysia	1,918	3.9
Indonesia	403	3.4

2. The rule of 72 gives the approximate doubling time of a variable if you know its rate of growth. For example, if the population of a country is 200 million and the rate of growth of its population is 2 percent per year, then it will take approximately 36 years for the country's population to reach 400 million. Assume that per capita income in 2006 is $40,000 in the United States and $5,000 in China. If the per capita growth rate in China is 9 percent a year, how long will it take for China to reach a per capita income level that is equivalent to the United States' 2006 per capita income level?

3. Which of the following will increase the likelihood of poor countries catching up to rich countries, and which will decrease the likelihood? Explain.

   a. Industrial countries do not allow their technology to be bought or leased by firms in developing countries.
   b. Worldwide saving rates shift up.
   c. The legal system in developing countries is improved to protect property rights.
   d. Governments in developing countries make use of their international aid to buy armaments from developed countries.
   e. Investment in human capital increases in the developing countries.

4. The U.S. states have moved toward one another in real income per capita over the past 100 years, but the countries of the world have not. What differences between state borders and country borders might explain this problem?

5. Figure 17-2 shows that California and Nevada had very high levels of per capita income in 1880. What was the source of their high income? Identify some countries in the world that currently have relatively high per capita income for a similar reason.

6. Figure 17-6 identifies the countries with the highest GDP per capita in the world. What characteristics of the labor forces in these countries provide part of the explanation for their higher incomes?

7. Suppose a developing country does not allow foreign investment to flow into the country and, at the same time, has a very low saving rate. Use the fact that saving equals investment plus net exports and the growth accounting formula to explain why this country will have difficulty catching up with the industrial countries. What can the country do to improve its productivity if it does not allow capital in from outside the country?

8. Most developing countries have low saving rates and governments that run budget deficits. What will be required for such countries to have large increases in their capital stocks? What will happen if industrial countries' saving rates decline as well? How does this affect the developing countries' prospects for catching up?

Bangalore, an Indian city of about 6 million people, has undergone a remarkable economic transformation in recent times. Bangalore is now one of the leading cities in the production of computer software; according to India's National Association of Software and Service Companies, the value of software produced in Bangalore has increased 750-fold in the last 15 years. The rapid increase in jobs in the software and information technology industry has brought prosperity to an increasing number of workers in Bangalore. An article that appeared in *USA Today* on March 22, 2004, describes the transformation of the lives of Bangalore's software workers, who earn a salary doing work outsourced by U.S. companies and then spend their earnings on IBM computers, Hyundai cars, Domino's Pizza, and Stairmasters (to work off the pizza!).

Similar stories can be told about U.S. trade with many countries in the world. Every day, people in countries like China, Germany, Korea, Japan, and Sri Lanka buy U.S. products: Caterpillar tractors, Motorola cellular phones, Microsoft software, Boeing 747s, and Merck pharmaceuticals. At the same time, Americans drive cars made in Germany and Japan, listen to CDs and MP3s on electronic equipment made in China and Malaysia, play tennis wearing Nike shoes made in Korea, or go swimming in Ocean Pacific swimsuits made in Sri Lanka.

These stories about firms selling their products around the world and people consuming goods made in other countries illustrate reasons why people benefit from international trade. First, international trade allows different countries to specialize in what they are relatively efficient at producing, such as pharmaceuticals in the United States or electronic equipment in Malaysia. Second, international trade gives firms such as Merck access to a large world market, enabling them to invest heavily in research and reduce costs by concentrating production.

This chapter explores the reasons for these **gains from trade** and develops two models that can be used to measure the actual size of these gains. We also take a look at the difference between international trade *theory*, which describes the gains from trade, and international trade *policy*, which often seems to seek to restrict trade despite those gains. From David Ricardo working in the British parliament to repeal protectionist trade laws 150 years ago to the present-day debates over the "Buy American" clause in the 2009 stimulus bill, the goal is the same: to understand the gains from trade and achieve the economic gains from trade in practice in a democracy. We begin, however, with a brief look at recent trends in international trade.

Recent Trends in International Trade

International trade is trade between people or firms in different countries. Trade between people in Detroit and Ottawa, Canada, is international trade, whereas trade between Detroit and Chicago is trade within a country. Thus, international trade is just another kind of economic interaction; it is subject to the same basic economic principles as trade between people in the same country.

International trade differs from trade in domestic markets, however, because national governments frequently place restrictions, such as **tariffs** or **quotas**, on trade between countries that they do not place on trade within countries. For example, the Texas legislature cannot limit or put a tariff on the import of Florida oranges into Texas. The **commerce clause** of the U.S. Constitution forbids such restraint of trade between states. But the United States can restrict the import of oranges from Brazil. Similarly, Japan can restrict the import of rice from the United States, and Australia can restrict the import of Japanese automobiles.

International trade has grown much faster than trade within countries in recent years. Figure 18-1 shows the exports for all countries in the world as a percentage of the world gross domestic product (GDP). International trade has doubled as a proportion of the world GDP during the last 30 or so years. Why has international trade grown so rapidly? What economic or technological forces have led to this increase in globalization?

One reason that international trade has grown so rapidly can be attributed to the dramatic reduction in the cost of transportation and communication. The cost of air travel fell to $0.095 per mile in 2000 from $0.87 per mile in 1930, and the cost of a

gains from trade
improvements in income, production, or satisfaction owing to the exchange of goods or services. (Ch. 1)

international trade
the exchange of goods and services between people or firms in different nations. (Ch. 1)

tariff
a tax on imports.

quota
a governmental limit on the quantity of a good that may be imported or sold.

commerce clause
the clause in the U.S. Constitution that prohibits restraint of trade between states.

Figure 18-1

World Exports as a Share of GDP
The faster growth of exports compared with GDP is probably due to the reduction in trade restrictions and the lower cost of transportation, both characteristics of greater globalization.

Source: Maddison, A. (2001), *The World Economy: A Millennial Perspective*, Development Centre Studies, OECD Publishing, http://dx.doi.org/10.1787/9789264189980-en

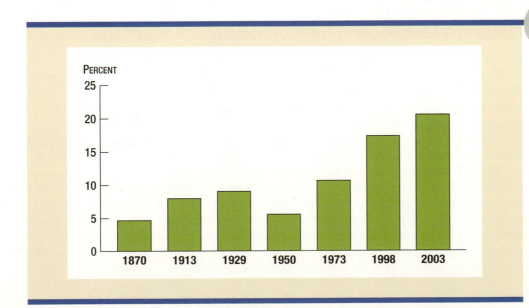

three-minute phone call from New York to London fell to $0.24 in 2002 from $315 in 1930 (adjusting the 1930 prices for general inflation). Use of e-mail and access to the Internet, unheard of in 1930, reduce costs even further.

The most important reason that trade has expanded so rapidly, however, is that government restrictions on trade between countries have come down. Western European countries are integrating into a single market. Canada, Mexico, and the United States have agreed to integrate their economies into a free trade area, where the term *free* indicates the elimination of restrictions on trade. Previously closed economies have opened themselves to world trade through major political and economic reforms. The formerly closed economies in Eastern Europe, the Russian Federation, and, especially, China have joined the world trading system. Export-oriented countries in Asia are growing rapidly, and governments in South America such as Argentina and Chile are opening their economies to competition and foreign trade. These countries are making these changes in an effort to help people. But how do people gain from international trade? Let us now consider that question.

REVIEW

- The basic principles of economics apply to international trade between people in different countries.

- Governments have a greater tendency to interfere with trade between countries than with trade within their own country.

- International trade has grown rapidly in recent years because of reduced transportation and communication costs and, especially, lower government barriers to trade.

Comparative Advantage

comparative advantage
a situation in which a person or country can produce one good at a lower opportunity cost than another person or country. (Ch. 1)

According to the theory of **comparative advantage**, a country can improve the income of its citizens by allowing them to trade with people in other countries, even if the people of the country are less efficient at producing all items.

Getting a Gut Feeling for Comparative Advantage

First, consider a parable that conveys the essence of comparative advantage. Rose is a highly skilled computer programmer who writes computer-assisted drawing programs. Rose owns a small firm that sells her programs to architects. She has hired an experienced salesman, Sam, to contact the architects and sell her software. Thus, Rose specializes in programming, and Sam specializes in sales.

You need to know a little more about Rose. Rose is a friendly, outgoing person, and because she knows her product better than Sam does, she is better than Sam at sales. We say that Rose has an **absolute advantage** over Sam in both programming and sales because she is better at both jobs. But it still makes sense for Rose to hire Sam because her efficiency at programming compared with Sam's is greater than her efficiency at sales compared with Sam's. We say that Rose has a *comparative advantage* over Sam in programming rather than in sales. If Rose sold her programs, then she would have to sacrifice her programming time, and her profits would fall. Thus, even though Rose is better at both programming and sales, she hires Sam to do the selling so that she can program full time.

All this seems sensible. One additional part of the terminology, however, may at first seem confusing but is important. We said that Rose has the comparative advantage in

absolute advantage
a situation in which a person or country is more efficient at producing a good in comparison with another person or country.

programming, not in sales. But who does have the comparative advantage in sales? Sam does. Even though Sam is less efficient at both sales and programming, we say that he has a comparative advantage in sales because, compared with Rose, he does relatively better at sales than he does at programming. A person cannot have a comparative advantage in both of only two activities.

Opportunity Cost, Relative Efficiency, and Comparative Advantage

The idea of comparative advantage also can be explained in terms of **opportunity cost**. The opportunity cost of Rose or Sam spending more time selling is that she or he can produce fewer programs. Similarly, the opportunity cost of Rose or Sam spending more time writing programs is that she or he can make fewer sales.

Observe that, in the example, Sam has a lower opportunity cost of spending his time selling than Rose does; thus, it makes sense for Sam to do the selling rather than Rose. In contrast, Rose has a lower opportunity cost of spending her time writing computer programs than Sam does; thus, it makes sense for Rose to write computer programs rather than Sam.

Opportunity costs give us a way to define comparative advantage. A person with a lower opportunity cost of producing a good than another person has a comparative advantage in that good. Thus, Rose has a comparative advantage in computer programming, and Sam has a comparative advantage in sales.

Comparative advantage also can be explained in terms of relative efficiency. A person who is relatively more efficient at producing good X than good Y, compared with another person, has a comparative advantage in good X. Thus, again, we see that Rose has a comparative advantage in computer programming because she is relatively more efficient at producing computer programs than at making sales compared with Sam.

From People to Countries
Why is this story about Rose and Sam a parable? Because we can think of Rose and Sam as two countries that differ in efficiency at producing one product versus another. In the parable, Rose has a comparative advantage over Sam in programming, and Sam has a comparative advantage over Rose in sales. In general, *country A has a comparative advantage over country B in the production of a good if the opportunity cost of producing the good in country A is less than in country B*, or, alternatively but equivalently stated, *if country A can produce the good relatively more efficiently than other goods compared with country B*. Thus, if you understand the Rose and Sam story, you should have no problem understanding comparative advantage in two countries, which we now examine in more detail.

Productivity in Two Countries

Consider the following two goods: (1) vaccines and (2) television sets. Different skills are required for the production of vaccines and television sets. Vaccine production requires knowledge of chemistry and biology, and the marketing of products for which doctors make most of the choices. Producing television sets requires knowledge of electrical engineering and microcircuitry, and the marketing of goods for which consumers make most of the choices.

Table 18-1 provides an example of productivity differences in the production of vaccines and television sets in two different countries, the United States and Korea. Productivity is measured by the amount of each good that can be produced by a worker per day of work. To be specific, let us suppose that the vaccines are measured in vials, that the televisions are measured in numbers of television sets, and that labor is the only factor of production in making vaccines and television sets. The theory of comparative advantage does not depend on any of these assumptions, but they make the exposition much easier.

opportunity cost
the value of the next-best forgone alternative that was not chosen because something else was chosen. (Ch. 1)

Electronics versus Pharmaceuticals

In the example used in this chapter, Korea has a comparative advantage in an electronic good (television sets), and the United States has a comparative advantage in a pharmaceutical (vaccines). Thus, with trade, the electronic good will be produced in Korea, as shown in the left-hand photo, and the pharmaceutical good will be produced in the United States, as shown in the right-hand photo.

According to Table 18-1, in the United States, it takes a worker one day of work to produce six vials of vaccine or three television sets. In Korea, one worker can produce one vial of vaccine or two television sets. Thus, the United States is more productive than Korea in producing both vaccines and television sets. We say that a country has an *absolute advantage* over another country in the production of a good if it is more efficient at producing that good. In this example, the United States has an absolute advantage in both vaccine and television set production.

The United States, however, has a comparative advantage over Korea in the production of vaccines rather than television sets. To see this, note that a worker in the United States can produce six times as many vials of vaccine as a worker in Korea but only 1.5 times as many television sets. In other words, the United States is relatively more efficient in vaccines than in television sets compared with Korea. Korea, being able to produce television sets relatively more efficiently than vaccines compared with the United States, has a comparative advantage in television sets.

Observe also how opportunity costs determine who has the comparative advantage. To produce three more television sets, the United States must sacrifice six vials of vaccine; in other words, *in the United States, the opportunity cost of one more television set is two vials of vaccine*. In Korea, to produce two more television sets, the Koreans must sacrifice one vial of vaccine; in other words, *in Korea, the opportunity cost of one more television set is only one-half vial of vaccine*. Thus, we see that the opportunity cost of producing television sets in Korea is lower than in the United States. By examining opportunity costs, we again see that Korea has a comparative advantage in television sets.

Table 18-1

Example of Productivity in the United States and Korea

	Output per Day of Work	
	Vials of Vaccine	*Number of Television Sets*
United States	6	3
Korea	1	2

An American Worker's View Because labor productivity in both goods is higher in the United States than in Korea, wages are higher in the United States than in Korea in the example. Now think about the situation from the point of view of U.S. workers who are paid more than Korean workers. They might wonder how they can compete with Korea. The Korean workers' wages seem very low compared with theirs. It does not seem fair. But as we will see, comparative advantage implies that U.S. workers can gain from trade with the Koreans.

A Korean Worker's View It is useful to think about Table 18-1 from the perspective of a Korean worker as well as that of a U.S. worker. From the Korean perspective, it might be noted that Korean workers are less productive in both goods. Korean workers might wonder how they can ever compete with the United States, which looks like a productive powerhouse. Again, it does not seem fair. As we will see, however, the Koreans also can gain from trade with the Americans.

Finding the Relative Price

To measure how much the Koreans and Americans can gain from trade, we need to consider the *relative price* of vaccines and televisions in Korea and the United States. The relative price determines how much vaccine can be traded for televisions and, therefore, how much each country can gain from trade. For example, suppose the price of a television set is $200 and the price of a vial of vaccine is $100. Then two vials of vaccine cost the same as one television set; we say the relative price is two vials of vaccine per television set.

Relative Price without Trade First, let us find the relative price with no trade between the countries. The relative price of two goods should depend on the relative costs of production. A good for which the cost of producing an additional quantity is relatively low will have a relatively low price.

Consider the United States. In this example, a day of work can produce either six vials of vaccine or three television sets. With labor as the only factor of production, six vials of vaccine cost the same to produce as three televisions sets; that is, two vials of vaccine cost the same to produce as one television set. Therefore, the relative price should be two vials of vaccine per television set.

Now consider Korea. Electronic goods should have a relatively low price in Korea because they are relatively cheap to produce. A day of work can produce either one vial of vaccine or two television sets; thus one vial of vaccine costs the same to produce as two television sets in Korea. Therefore, the relative price is one-half vial of vaccine per television set.

Relative Price with Trade Now consider what happens when the two countries trade without government restrictions. If transportation costs are negligible and markets are competitive, then the price of a good must be the same in the United States and Korea. Why? Because any difference in price would quickly be eliminated by trade; if the price of television sets is much less in Korea than in the United States, then traders will buy television sets in Korea and sell them in the United States and make a profit; by doing so, however, they reduce the supply of television sets in Korea and increase the supply in the United States. This will drive up the price in Korea and drive down the price in the United States until the price of television sets in the two countries is the same. Thus, with trade, the price of vaccines and the price of television sets will converge to the same levels in both countries. The relative price therefore will converge to the same value in both countries.

If the relative price is going to be the same in both countries, then we know the price must be somewhere between the prices in the two countries before trade. That is,

> **Another example of relative prices may be helpful:**
>
> Price of U2 concert = $45
> Price of U2 t-shirt = $15
> Relative price = three t-shirts per concert

Table 18-2

The Relative Price (The relative price—vials of vaccine per television set—must be the same in both countries with trade.)

	United States	Korea
Relative price before trade:	2 vials of vaccine per television set	1/2 vial of vaccine per television set
Relative price range after trade:	Between 1/2 and 2	Between 1/2 and 2
Relative price assumption:	1	1

the price must be between two vials of vaccine per television set (the U.S. relative price) and one-half vial of vaccine per television set (the Korean relative price). We do not know exactly where the price will fall between one-half and two. It depends on the *demand* for vaccines and television sets in Korea and the United States. *Let us assume that the relative price is one vial of vaccine per television set after trade*, which is between one-half and two and is a nice, easy number for making computations. The calculation of the price with trade is summarized in Table 18-2.

Measuring the Gains from Trade

How large are the *gains from trade* because of comparative advantage? First, consider some examples.

One Country's Gain Suppose that 10 U.S. workers move out of electronics production and begin producing pharmaceuticals. We know from Table 18-1 that these 10 U.S. workers can produce 60 vials of vaccine per day. Formerly, the 10 U.S. workers were producing 30 television sets per day. But their 60 vials of vaccine can be traded for television sets produced in Korea. With the relative price of one vial per television set, Americans will be able to exchange these 60 vials of vaccine for 60 television sets. Thus, Americans gain 30 more television sets by moving 10 more workers into vaccine production. This gain from trade is summarized in Table 18-3.

The Other Country's Gain The same thing can happen in Korea. A Korean manufacturer can now hire 30 workers who formerly were working in vaccine production to

Table 18-3

Changing Production and Gaining from Trade in the United States and Korea

	United States (10 workers)		
	Change in Production	**Amount Traded**	**Net Gain from Trade**
Vaccines	Up 60 vials	Export 60 vials	0
Television sets	Down 30 sets	Import 60 sets	30 sets
	Korea (30 workers)		
	Change in Production	**Amount Traded**	**Net Gain from Trade**
Vaccines	Down 30 vials	Import 60 vials	30 vials
Television sets	Up 60 sets	Export 60 sets	0

produce television sets. Vaccine production declines by 30 vials, but television production increases by 60 sets. These 60 television sets can be traded with Americans for 60 vials of vaccine. The reduction in the production of vaccine of 30 vials results in an import of vaccine of 60 vials; thus, the gain from trade is 30 vials of vaccine. The Koreans, by moving workers out of vaccine production and into television set production, are getting more vaccine. This gain from trade for Korea is summarized in Table 18-3. Observe that the exports of television sets from Korea equal the imports of television sets to the United States.

Just Like a New Discovery International trade is like the discovery of a new idea or technique that makes workers more productive. It is as if workers in the United States figured out how to produce more television sets with the same amount of effort. Their trick is that they actually produce vaccines, which then are traded for the television sets. Like any other new technique, international trade improves the well-being of Americans. International trade also improves the well-being of the Koreans; it is as if they discovered a new technique, too.

A Graphic Measure of the Gains from Trade

The gains from trade because of comparative advantage also can be found graphically with production possibilities curves, as shown in Figure 18-2. The figure has two graphs—one for the United States and the other for Korea. In both graphs, the horizontal axis has the number of television sets and the vertical axis has the number of vials of vaccine produced.

Production Possibilities Curves without Trade The solid lines in the two graphs show the production possibilities curves for vaccines and television sets in the United States and in Korea before trade. To derive them, we assume, for illustrative purposes, that the United States has 10,000 workers and Korea has 30,000 workers who can make either vaccines or television sets.

If all the available workers in the United States produce vaccines, then total production will be 60,000 vials of vaccine (6 × 10,000) and zero television sets. Alternatively, if 5,000 workers produce vaccines in the United States and 5,000 workers produce television sets, then total production will be 30,000 vials of vaccine (6 × 5,000) and 15,000 television sets (3 × 5,000). The solid line in the graph on the left of Figure 18-2 shows these possibilities and all other possibilities for producing vaccines and television sets. It is the production possibilities curve without trade.

Korea's production possibilities curve without trade is shown by the solid line in the graph on the right of Figure 18-2. For example, if all 30,000 Korean workers produce television sets, a total of 60,000 television sets can be produced (2 × 30,000). This and other possibilities are on the curve.

The slopes of the two production possibilities curves without trade in Figure 18-2 show how many vials of vaccine can be transformed into television sets in Korea and the United States. The production possibilities curve for the United States is steeper than that for Korea because an increase in production of one television set reduces vaccine production by two vials in the United States but by only one-half vial in Korea. The slope of the production possibilities curve is the opportunity cost; the opportunity cost of producing television sets in the United States is higher than it is in Korea.

Production Possibilities Curves with Trade The dashed lines in the two graphs in Figure 18-2 show the different combinations of vaccine and television sets available in Korea and the United States when trade exists between the two countries at a relative price of one vial of vaccine for one television set. These dashed lines are labeled

Figure 18-2

Comparative Advantage

On the left, Americans are better off with trade because the production possibilities curve shifts out with trade; thus, with trade, Americans reach a point like *C* rather than *A*. The gains from trade because of comparative advantage are equal to the distance between the two production possibilities curves—one with trade and the other without trade. On the right, Koreans also are better off because their production possibilities curve also shifts out; thus, Koreans can reach point *F*, which is better than point *D*. To reach this outcome, Americans specialize in producing at point *B* and Koreans specialize in producing at point *E*.

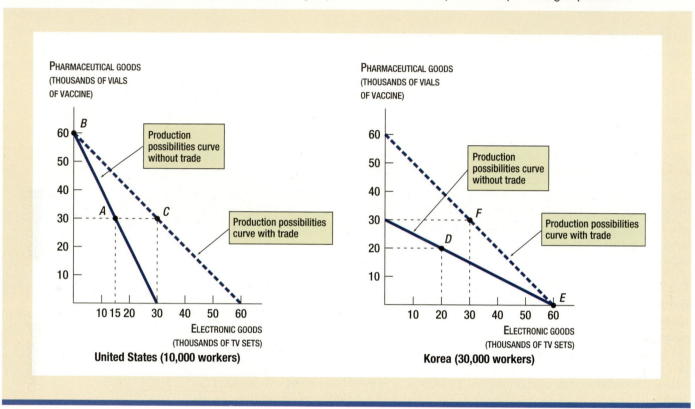

"production possibilities curve with trade" to contrast them with the "production possibilities curve without trade" label on the solid line. The diagram shows that the production possibilities curves with trade are shifted out compared with the curves without trade.

To see how the production possibilities curve with trade is derived, consider how the United States could move from point *A* to point *C* in Figure 18-2. At point *A*, without trade, Americans produce and consume 15,000 television sets and 30,000 vials of vaccine by having 5,000 workers in each industry. Now suppose all U.S. workers move out of television set production into vaccine production, shifting U.S. production to zero television sets and 60,000 vials of vaccine, as shown by point *B*. Then by trading some of the vaccine, Americans can obtain television sets. As they trade more vaccine away, they move down the production possibilities curve with trade: one less vial of vaccine means one more television set along the curve. If they move to point *C* in the diagram, they have traded 30,000 vials of vaccine for 30,000 television sets. Americans now have 30,000 television sets and are left with 30,000 vials of vaccine. By producing more vaccine, the Americans get to purchase more television sets. The distance from point *A* (before trade) to point *C* (after trade) in Figure 18-2 is the gain from trade: 15,000 more television sets.

It would be possible, of course, to choose any other point on the production possibilities curve with trade. If Americans prefer more television sets and fewer vials of

ECONOMICS *IN ACTION*

Doing Politics and Economics

David Ricardo was a man of action. He went to work as a stockbroker at age 14 and eventually accumulated a vast fortune, including a beautiful country estate. He then became one of the most influential economists of all time. He also ran for and won a seat in the British Parliament from which to argue his economic position.

As an economist, Ricardo continued the tradition of Adam Smith. In fact, he became interested in economics after reading Smith's *Wealth of Nations* during a vacation. But Ricardo greatly extended and improved on Smith's theories and made them more precise. Along with Smith and Thomas Robert Malthus—who was Ricardo's close friend but frequent intellectual opponent—Ricardo is considered by historians to be in the classical school, which argued for laissez-faire, free trade, and competitive markets in eighteenth- and nineteenth-century Britain.

Ricardo grappled with three of the most important policy issues in economics: inflation, taxes, and international trade. But Ricardo's most famous contribution is to international trade—in particular, his theory of comparative advantage. Ricardo used this theory when he was in Parliament to argue for repeal of the restrictions on agricultural imports known as the corn laws.

Ricardo's theory of comparative advantage is a good example of how he improved on the work of Adam Smith.

Smith used commonsense analogies to illustrate the gains from trade; one of his examples was "The tailor does not attempt to make his own shoes, but buys them from the shoemaker." As with this tailor and shoemaker example, Smith focused on cases in which one person had an absolute advantage in one good and the other person had an absolute advantage in the other good. But Ricardo showed how gains could be achieved from trade even if one person was better at producing both goods. Here is how Ricardo put it way back in 1817:

> Two men can both make shoes and hats, and one is superior to the other in both employments; but in making hats, he can only exceed his competitor by one-fifth or 20 per cent., and in making shoes he can excel him by one-third or 33 per cent.;—will it not be for the interest of both that the superior man should employ himself exclusively in making shoes, and the inferior man in making hats?

David Ricardo, 1772–1823

Born: London, 1772

Education: Never attended college

Jobs: Stockbroker, 1786–1815
Member of Parliament, 1819–1823

Major Publications: *The High Price of Bullion*, 1810; *On the Principles of Political Economy and Taxation*, 1817; *A Plan for a National Bank*, 1824

vaccine, they can move down along that dashed line, trading more of their vaccine for more television sets. In general, the production possibilities curve *with* trade is further out than the production possibilities curve *without* trade, indicating the gain from trade.

Observe that the slope of the production possibilities curve with trade is given by the relative price: the number of vials of vaccine that can be obtained for a television set.

When the relative price is one vial per television set, the slope is negative one because one less vial gives one more television set. If the relative price were one-half vial per television set, then the production possibilities curve with trade would be flatter.

The gains to Korea from trade are illustrated in the right-hand graph of Figure 18-2. For example, at point *D*, without trade, Koreans produce 20,000 television sets with 10,000 workers and, with the remaining 20,000 workers, produce 20,000 vials of vaccine. With trade, they shift all production into television sets, as at point *E* on the right graph. Then they trade the television sets for vaccine. Such trade allows more consumption of vaccine in Korea. At point *F* in the right diagram, the Koreans could consume 30,000 vials of vaccine and 30,000 television sets, which would be 10,000 more of each than before trade at point *D*. As in the case of the United States, the production possibilities curve shifts out with trade, and the size of the shift represents the gain from trade.

This example of Americans and Koreans consuming more than they were before trade illustrates the *principle of comparative advantage: By specializing in producing products in which they have a comparative advantage, countries can increase the amount of goods available for consumption.* Trade increases the amount of production in the world; it shifts out the production possibilities curves.

Increasing Opportunity Costs: Incomplete Specialization One of the special assumptions in the example we have used in Table 18-2 and Figure 18-2 to illustrate the theory of comparative advantage is that opportunity costs are constant rather than increasing. It is because of this assumption that the production possibilities curves without trade in Figure 18-2 are straight lines rather than the bowed-out lines that we studied in Chapter 1. With increasing opportunity costs, the curves would be bowed out.

The straight-line production possibilities curves are the reason for *complete* specialization, with Korea producing no vaccines and the United States producing no television sets. If opportunity costs were increasing, as in the more typical example of the production possibilities curve, then complete specialization would not occur. With increasing opportunity costs, as more and more workers are moved into the production of vaccine in the United States, the opportunity cost of producing more vaccine will rise. And as workers are moved out of vaccine production in Korea, the opportunity cost of vaccine production in Korea will fall. At some point, the U.S. opportunity cost of vaccine production may rise to equal Korea's, at which point further specialization in vaccine production would cease in the United States. Thus, with increasing opportunity costs and bowed-out production possibilities curves, specialization most likely will be incomplete. But increasing opportunity cost does not change the principle of comparative advantage. By specializing to some degree in the goods for which they have a comparative advantage, countries can increase world production. Substantial gains are realized from trade, whether between Rose and Sam or between America and Korea.

REVIEW

- Comparative advantage shows that a country can gain from trade even if it is more efficient at producing every product than another country. A country has a comparative advantage in a product if it is relatively more efficient at producing that product than the other country.

- The theory of comparative advantage predicts that gains from trade can be realized from increasing production of the good for which a country has a comparative advantage and from reducing production of the other good. By exporting the good for which it has a comparative advantage, a country can increase consumption of both goods.

- Comparative advantage is like a new technology in which the country effectively produces more by having some goods produced in another country.

Reasons for Comparative Advantage

What determines a country's comparative advantage? There are some obvious answers. For example, Central America has a comparative advantage over North America in producing tropical fruit because of weather conditions: Bananas will not grow in Kansas or Nebraska outside of greenhouses.

In most cases, however, comparative advantage does not result from differences in climate and natural resources. More frequently, comparative advantage is due to decisions made by individuals, by firms, or by the government in a given country. For example, a comparative advantage of the United States in pharmaceuticals might be due to investment in research and in physical and human capital in the areas of chemistry and biology. An enormous amount of research goes into developing technological know-how to produce pharmaceutical products.

In Korea, on the other hand, less capital may be available for such huge expenditures on research in the pharmaceutical area. A Korean comparative advantage in electronic goods might be due to a large, well-trained workforce that is well suited to electronics and small-scale assembly. For example, the excellent math and technical training in Korean high schools may provide a large labor force for the electronics industry.

Comparative advantages can change over time. In fact, the United States did have a comparative advantage in television sets in the 1950s and early 1960s, before the countries of East Asia developed skills and knowledge in these areas. A country may have a comparative advantage in a good it has developed recently, but then the technology spreads to other countries, which develop a comparative advantage, and the first country goes on to something else.

Perhaps the United States' comparative advantage in pharmaceuticals will go to other countries in the future, and the United States will develop a comparative advantage in other, yet unforeseen areas. The term *dynamic* comparative advantage describes changes in comparative advantage over time because of investment in physical and human capital and in technology.

Labor versus Capital Resources

To illustrate the importance of capital for comparative advantage, imagine a world in which all comparative advantage can be explained through differences between countries in the amount of physical capital that workers have to work with. It is such a world that is described by the Heckscher-Ohlin model, named after the two Swedish economists, Eli Heckscher and Bertil Ohlin, who developed it. Ohlin won a Nobel Prize for his work in international economics. The Heckscher-Ohlin model provides a particular explanation for comparative advantage.

Here is how comparative advantage develops in such a model. Suppose the United States has a higher level of capital per worker than Korea. In other words, the United States is **capital abundant** compared with Korea, and—what amounts to the same thing—Korea is **labor abundant** compared with the United States. Pharmaceutical production uses more capital per worker than electronics production; in other words, pharmaceutical production is relatively **capital intensive**, whereas electronics production is relatively **labor intensive**. Hence, it makes sense that the United States has a comparative advantage in pharmaceuticals: The United States is relatively capital abundant, and pharmaceuticals are relatively capital intensive. Conversely, Korea has a comparative advantage in electronics because Korea is relatively labor abundant, and electronics are relatively labor intensive. Thus, the Heckscher-Ohlin model predicts that if a country has a relative abundance of a factor (labor or capital), it will have a comparative advantage in those goods that require a greater amount of that factor.

capital abundant
a higher level of capital per worker in one country relative to another.

labor abundant
a lower level of capital per worker in one country relative to another.

capital intensive
production that uses a relatively high level of capital per worker.

labor intensive
production that uses a relatively low level of capital per worker.

The Effect of Trade on Wages

An important implication of the Heckscher-Ohlin model is that trade will tend to bring factor prices (the price of labor and the price of capital) in different countries into equality. In other words, if the comparative advantage between Korea and the United States was due only to differences in relative capital and labor abundance, then trade would tend to increase real wages in Korea and lower real wages in the United States.

More generally, trade tends to increase demand for the factor that is relatively abundant in a country and decrease demand for the factor that is relatively scarce. This raises the price of the relatively abundant factor and lowers the price of the relatively scarce factor. Suppose the United States is more capital abundant than Korea and has a comparative advantage in pharmaceuticals, which are more capital intensive than electronics. Then with trade, the price of capital will rise relative to the price of labor in the United States. The intuition behind this prediction—which is called **factor-price equalization**—is that demand for labor (the relatively scarce factor) shifts down with trade as the United States increases production of pharmaceuticals and reduces its production of electronic goods. Conversely, the demand for capital (the relatively abundant factor) shifts up with trade. Although no immigration occurs, it is as if foreign workers competed with workers in the labor-scarce country and bid down the wage.

Because technology also influences wages and productivity, it has been hard to detect such movements in wages because of factor-price equalization. The wages of workers in the industrial world with high productivity resulting from high levels of technology remain well above the wages of workers in the developing world with low productivity resulting from low levels of technology.

In other words, changes in technology can offset the effects of factor-price equalization on wages. If trade sufficiently raises technological know-how, then no one has to suffer from greater trade. In our example of comparative advantage, U.S. workers are paid more than Korean workers both before and after trade, because their overall level of productivity is higher. Workers with higher productivity will be paid more than workers with lower productivity even in countries that trade.

Factor-price equalization can explain another phenomenon—that is, the growing wage disparity in the United States during the past 25 years, in which the wages of high-skilled workers have risen relative to the wages of less-skilled workers. The United States is relatively abundant in high-skilled workers, and developing countries are relatively abundant in low-skilled workers. Thus, high-skilled workers' wages should rise and low-skilled workers' wages should fall in the United States, according to factor-price equalization. In this application of factor-price equalization, the two factors are high-skilled workers and low-skilled workers.

factor-price equalization the equalization of the price of labor and the price of capital across countries when they are engaging in free trade.

REVIEW

- Comparative advantage changes over time and depends on the actions of individuals in a country. Thus, comparative advantage is a dynamic concept.

- International trade will tend to equalize wages in different countries. Technological differences, however, can keep wages high in high-productivity countries.

Gains from Expanded Markets

In the introduction to this chapter, we mentioned the gains from trade that come from larger markets. Having discussed the principle of comparative advantage, we now examine this other source of the gains from trade.

An Example of Gains from Trade through Expanded Markets

Let us start with a simple example. Consider two countries that are similar in resources, capital, and skilled labor, such as the United States and Germany. Suppose Germany and the United States both have a market for two medical diagnostic products—magnetic resonance imaging (MRI) machines and ultrasound scanners. Suppose the technology for producing each type of diagnostic device is the same in each country. We assume that the technology is identical because we want to show that trade will take place without differences between the countries.

Figure 18-3 illustrates the situation. Without trade, Germany and the United States each produce 1,000 MRIs and 1,000 ultrasound scanners. This amount of production meets the demand in the two separate markets. The cost per unit of producing each MRI machine is $300,000, and the cost per unit of producing each ultrasound scanner is $200,000. Again, these costs are the same in each country.

Figure 18-3

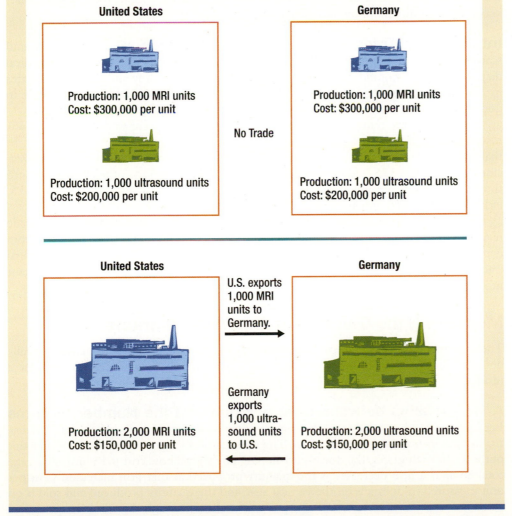

Gains from Global Markets In this example, the technology for producing MRI machines and ultrasound scanners is assumed to be the same in the United States and Germany. In the top panel, with no trade between the United States and Germany, the quantity produced in each country is low and the cost per unit is high. With trade, the U.S. firm increases its production of MRIs and exports to Germany; the German firm increases its production of ultrasound scanners and exports to the United States. As a result, cost per unit comes down significantly.

Effects of a Larger Market Now suppose that the two countries trade. Observe in Figure 18-3—and this is very important—that the *cost per unit* of producing MRIs and ultrasound scanners *declines as more are produced*. Trade increases the size of the market for each product. In this example, the market is twice as large with trade as without it: 2,000 MRIs rather than 1,000 and 2,000 ultrasound scanners rather than 1,000. The production of MRIs in the United States can expand, and the production of ultrasound scanners in the United States can contract. Similarly, the production of ultrasound scanners in Germany can expand, and the production of MRIs in Germany can contract. With the United States specializing in production of MRIs, the cost per unit of MRIs declines to $150,000. Similarly, the cost per unit of ultrasound scanners declines to $150,000. The United States exports MRIs to Germany so that the number of MRIs in Germany can be the same as without trade, and Germany exports ultrasound scanners to the United States. The gain from trade is the reduction in cost per unit. This gain from trade has occurred without any differences in the efficiency of production between the two countries.

Note that we could have set up the example differently. We could have had Germany specializing in MRI production and the United States specializing in ultrasound scanner production. Then the United States would have exported ultrasound scanners, and Germany would have exported MRIs. But the gains from trade would have been exactly the same. Unlike the comparative advantage motive for trade, the expanded markets motive alone cannot predict the direction of trade.

Intraindustry Trade versus Interindustry Trade MRIs and ultrasound scanners are similar products; they are considered to be in the same industry, the medical diagnostic equipment industry. Thus, the trade between Germany and the United States in MRIs and ultrasound scanners is called **intraindustry trade**, which means trade in goods in the same industry.

In contrast, the trade that took place in the example of comparative advantage was **interindustry trade**, because vaccines and television sets are in different industries. In that example, exports of vaccines from the United States greatly exceed imports of vaccines, producing a U.S. industry trade surplus in vaccines. Imports of television sets into the United States are much greater than exports of television sets, producing a U.S. industry trade deficit in television sets.

These examples convey an important message about international trade: Trade resulting from comparative advantage tends to be interindustry, and trade resulting from expanded markets tends to be intraindustry. In reality, a huge amount of international trade is intraindustry trade. This indicates that creating larger markets is an important motive for trade.

intraindustry trade
trade between countries in goods from the same or similar industries.

interindustry trade
trade between countries in goods from different industries.

Measuring the Gains from Expanded Markets

The medical equipment example illustrates how larger markets can reduce costs. To fully describe the gains from trade resulting from larger markets, we need to consider a model.

A Relationship between Cost per Unit and the Number of Firms

Let us examine the idea that *as the number of firms in a market of a given size increases, the cost per unit at each firm increases*. The two graphs in Figure 18-4 are useful for this purpose. In each graph, the downward-sloping line shows how cost per unit (or average total cost) at a firm decreases as the quantity produced at that firm increases. Cost per unit measured in dollars is on the vertical axis, and the quantity produced and sold is on the horizontal axis. Observe that cost per unit declines through the whole range shown

in Figure 18-5, the number of firms is on the horizontal axis. The curve in Figure 18-6 is downward sloping because a greater number of firms means a lower price.

Equilibrium Price and Number of Firms
In the long run, as firms either enter or exit an industry, price will tend to equal cost per unit. If the price for each unit were greater than the cost per unit, then new firms would have a profit opportunity, and the number of firms in the industry would rise. If the price were less than the cost per unit, then firms would exit the industry. Only when price equals cost per unit is a long-run equilibrium achieved. Because price equals cost per unit, the curves in Figure 18-5 and 18-6 can be combined to determine the price and the number of firms in long-run equilibrium. As shown in Figure 18-7, the industry arrives at a long-run equilibrium when the downward-sloping line for Figure 18-6 intersects the upward-sloping line (for the smaller market) from Figure 18-5. At this point, price equals cost per unit.

Corresponding to this long-run equilibrium is an equilibrium number of firms. More firms would lower the price below cost per unit, causing firms to leave the industry; fewer firms would raise the price above cost per unit, attracting new firms to the industry. Figure 18-7 shows how the possibility of entry and exit results in a long-run equilibrium with price equal to cost per unit.

Increasing the Size of the Market
Now let us see how the industry equilibrium changes when the size of the market increases because of international trade. In Figure 18-8, we show how an increase in the size of the market, perhaps resulting from the creation of a free trade area, reduces the price and increases the number of firms. The curve showing the cost per unit of each firm shifts down and out as the market expands; that is, for each number of firms, the cost per unit declines for each firm. This brings about a new intersection and a long-run equilibrium at a lower price. Moreover, the increase in the number of firms suggests that product variety will increase, which is another part of the gains from trade.

The North American Automobile Market
The gains from trade because of larger markets arise in many real-world examples. Trade in cars between Canada and the United States now occurs even though neither country has an obvious comparative advantage. Before 1964, trade in cars between Canada and the United States was restricted. Canadian factories thus had to limit their production to the Canadian market. This kept cost per unit high. When free trade in cars was permitted, the production in Canadian factories increased, and the Canadian factories began to export cars to the United States. With more cars produced, cost per unit declined.

Figure 18-6

The Relationship between the Price and the Number of Firms
As the number of firms increases, the market price declines. This curve summarizes this relationship.

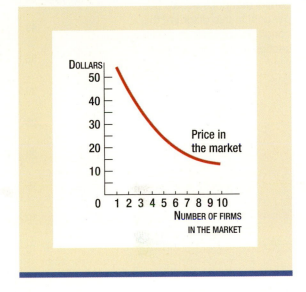

REVIEW
- Lowering cost per unit through the division of labor requires large markets. International trade creates large markets.

- A graphical model can be used to explain the gains from international trade; the model shows that a larger market reduces prices.

Figure 18-7

Long-Run Equilibrium Number of Firms and Cost per Unit

A condition for long-run equilibrium is that price equals cost per unit. In this diagram, this condition is shown at the intersection of the two curves.

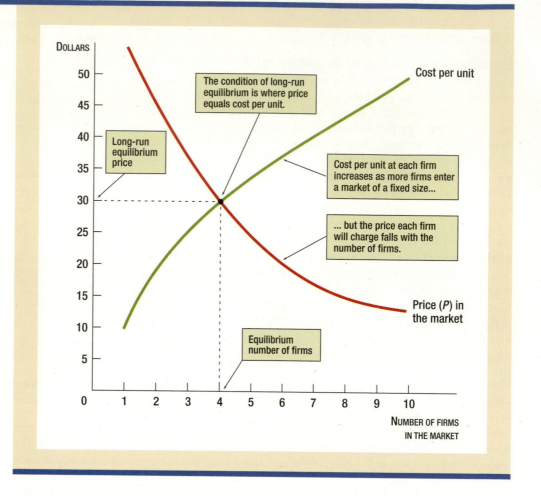

The condition of long-run equilibrium is where price equals cost per unit.

Long-run equilibrium price

Cost per unit at each firm increases as more firms enter a market of a fixed size...

... but the price each firm will charge falls with the number of firms.

Cost per unit

Price (*P*) in the market

Equilibrium number of firms

NUMBER OF FIRMS IN THE MARKET

Tariffs and Quotas

In a democracy, a big difference exists between having a good economic idea and implementing the idea in practice. Even if you have the greatest economic idea in the world, you have to spread the word, convince people, debate those in opposition, and even compromise if the idea is to be voted on favorably, is to be signed into law, or is to serve as the basis for an international agreement. In spite of all the benefits from international trade that we have discussed, governments use many methods to restrict international trade. Policies that restrict trade are called *protectionist policies* because the restrictions usually protect industries from foreign imports.

Examining the economic impact of trade restrictions helps you understand why some industries lobby for protectionist policies. As you delve into the economic analysis, think about whether a protectionist policy would help or hurt you. If the United States restricts trade in clothing, how would this restriction affect U.S. clothing producers, foreign clothing producers, U.S. retailers that sell clothing, and U.S. consumers who buy clothing? How would the restriction affect U.S. employment in clothing production and the price of clothing? We will see that trade restrictions create winners and losers, but that the gains for the winners will be smaller than the losses of the losers. That is, the losses from trade restrictions outweigh the gains, creating deadweight loss. You also can check your understanding by considering the removal of an existing trade restriction.

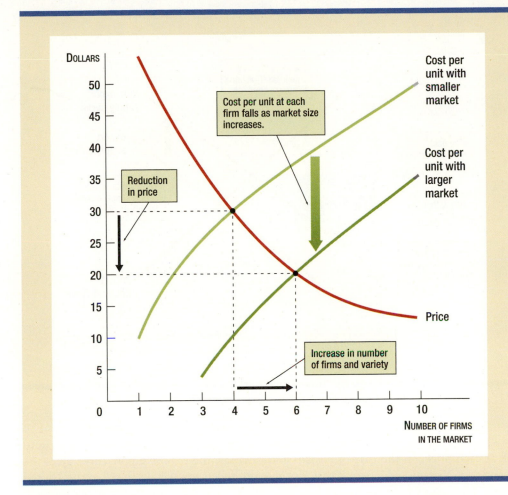

Figure 18-8

Gains from Trade Because of Larger Markets
When trade occurs, the market increases from the size of the market in one country to the combined size of the market in two or more countries. This larger market shifts the upward-sloping line down because cost per unit for each firm is lower when the market is bigger. In the long-run equilibrium at the intersection of the two new curves, the price is lower and more firms are in the market. With more firms, more variety is achieved. Lower price and more variety are the gains from trade.

Again, winners and losers will result from the removal of trade restrictions, but the gains for the winners will be larger than the losses for the losers. Removing trade restrictions therefore eliminates deadweight loss.

Tariffs

The oldest and most common method by which a government restricts trade is the *tariff*, a tax on goods imported into a country. The higher the tariff, the more trade is restricted. An **ad valorem tariff** is a tax equal to a certain percentage of the value of the good. For example, a 15 percent tariff on the value of goods imported is an ad valorem tariff. If $100,000 worth of goods is imported, the tariff revenue is $15,000. A **specific tariff** is a tax on the quantity sold, such as $0.50 for each kilogram of zinc.

The economic effects of a tariff are illustrated in Figure 18-9. We consider a particular good—automobiles, for example—that is exported from one country (Japan, for example) and imported by another country (the United States, for example). An *import demand curve* and an *export supply curve* are shown in Figure 18-9. The *import demand curve* gives the quantity of imported goods that will be demanded at each price. It shows that a higher price for imported goods will reduce the quantity of the goods demanded. A higher price for Nissans and Toyotas, for example, will lead to a smaller quantity of Nissans and Toyotas demanded by Americans. Like the standard demand curve, the import demand curve is downward sloping.

ad valorem tariff
a tax on imports evaluated as a percentage of the value of the import.

specific tariff
a tax on imports that is proportional to the number of units or items imported.

Figure 18-9

The Effects of a Tariff

A tariff shifts the export supply curve up by the amount of the tariff. Thus, the price paid for imports by consumers rises and the quantity imported declines. The price increase (upward-pointing black arrow) is less than the tariff (upward-pointing green arrow). The revenue to the government is shown by the shaded area; it is the tariff times the amount imported.

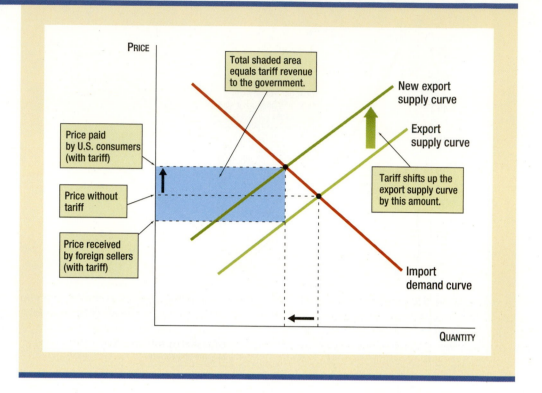

The *export supply curve* gives the quantity of exports that foreign firms are willing to sell at each price. In the case of Nissans and Toyotas, the export supply curve gives the quantity of Nissans and Toyotas that Japanese producers are willing to sell in the United States. The supply curve is upward sloping, just like any other supply curve, because foreign producers are willing to supply more cars when the price is higher.

In equilibrium, for any single type of good, the quantity of exports supplied must equal the quantity of imports demanded. Thus, the intersection of the export supply curve and the import demand curve gives the amount imported into the country and the price.

When the government imposes a tariff, the supply curve shifts up, as shown in Figure 18-9. The tariff increases the marginal cost of supplying cars to the United States. The amount of the tariff in dollars is the amount by which the supply curve shifts up; it is given by the length of the green arrow in Figure 18-9.

The tariff changes the intersection of the export supply curve and the import demand curve. At the new equilibrium, a lower quantity is imported at a higher price. The price consumers pay for cars rises, but the increase in the price is less than the tariff. In Figure 18-9, the upward-pointing black arrow shows the price increase. The green arrow, which shows the tariff increase, is longer than the black arrow along the vertical axis. The size of the price increase depends on the slopes of the demand curve and the supply curve.

The price received by suppliers equals the price paid by consumers less the tariff that must be paid to the government. Observe that the price received by the sellers declines as a result of the tariff.

The amount of revenue that the government collects is given by the quantity imported times the tariff, which is indicated by the shaded rectangle in Figure 18-9. For example, if the tariff is $1,000 per car and 1 million cars are imported, the revenue is $1 billion. Tariff revenues are called *duties* and are collected by customs.

ECONOMICS *IN ACTION*

From Steel to Shrimp: The Same Old Tariff Story

Consider the case for and against a tariff to protect two different industries—steel and shrimp. In 2002, an increasing amount of steel in the United States was being imported, and steel prices were low. Many U.S. steel-producing companies were in debt, and in the past five years, thirty steelmakers had sought bankruptcy protection. To avoid additional bankruptcies and loss of jobs, the steel industry lobbied for protection from imported steel. In March 2002, President Bush imposed tariffs on steel imports. The tariffs were as high as 30 percent and were to last three years.

We predicted that a tariff on steel would increase the price of steel in the United States, increasing the profits of steelmakers and hurting steel consumers. As predicted, steel prices increased, steelmakers profited, and the steel-consuming industry was hurt by the higher prices. Some manufacturers claimed that the tariffs jeopardized more jobs in the steel-consuming industry than they saved in the steel-producing industry. Steelmakers in the rest of the world filed complaints with the World Trade Organization (WTO). The WTO ruled that the U.S. tariffs on steel were illegal. In December 2003, President Bush reversed this protectionist policy, removing the tariffs on steel. If you were determining trade policy, how would you view the trade-off between U.S. steel jobs and the effects of the higher price of steel on the U.S. manufacturing industry?

Between 2000 and 2004, shrimp imports in the United States increased 70 percent. This increase in the supply of shrimp caused the price of shrimp to tumble. U.S. shrimp fishermen lobbied for tariffs on imported shrimp, claiming that foreign shrimp was being dumped on the U.S. market at prices below production costs. In July 2004, the United States proposed tariffs on shrimp imported from some countries.

U.S. consumers benefit from the increase in shrimp imports and the tumble in shrimp prices. Foreign shrimp producers profit from their sale of shrimp in the United States. U.S. shrimp producers are requesting protection from these low shrimp prices. With tariffs, we would expect profits for U.S. shrimp producers to increase, imports to fall, the price of shrimp to increase, and foreign producers' profits to fall. If you were determining trade policy, how would you view this trade-off between the health of the U.S. shrimp-producing industry and the price of shrimp for U.S. consumers? Does your answer to these questions about trade-offs depend on whether the protected industry is steel or shrimp?

The tariff also has an effect on U.S. car producers. Because the tariff reduces imports from abroad and raises their price, the demand for cars produced by import-competing companies in the United States—General Motors or Ford—increases. This increase in demand will raise the price of U.S. cars. Thus, consumers pay more for both imported cars and domestically produced cars.

Quotas

Another method of government restriction of international trade is the *quota*. A quota sets a limit, a maximum, on the amount of a given good that can be imported. The United States has quotas on the import of ice cream, sugar, cotton, peanuts, and other commodities. Foreigners can supply only a limited amount of these goods to the United States.

The economic effect of a quota is illustrated in Figure 18-10. The export supply curve and the import demand curve are identical to those in Figure 18-9. The quota, the maximum that foreign firms can export to the United States, is indicated in Figure 18-10 by the solid orange vertical line labeled "quota." Exporters cannot supply more goods than the quota, and, therefore, U.S. consumers cannot buy more than this amount. We have chosen the quota amount to equal the quantity imported with the tariff in Figure 18-9. This shows that if it wants to, the government can achieve the same effects on the quantity imported using either a quota or a tariff. Moreover, the price increase in Figure 18-10, represented by the black arrow along the vertical axis, is the

Seattle, 1999

The goal of the World Trade Organization (WTO) is to reduce trade barriers. But not everyone agrees with the goal, as the protest against the WTO meeting in Seattle reminded us. Although large antitrade protests have been less common in recent years, protectionist or isolationist sentiments continue to build as people worry about competition from China and other developing countries.

Figure **18-10**

The Effects of a Quota

A quota can be set to allow the same quantity of imports as a tariff. The quota in this figure and the tariff in Figure 18-9 allow the same quantity of imports into the country. The price increase is the same for the quota and the tariff. But, in the case of a quota, the revenue goes to quota holders, not to the U.S. government.

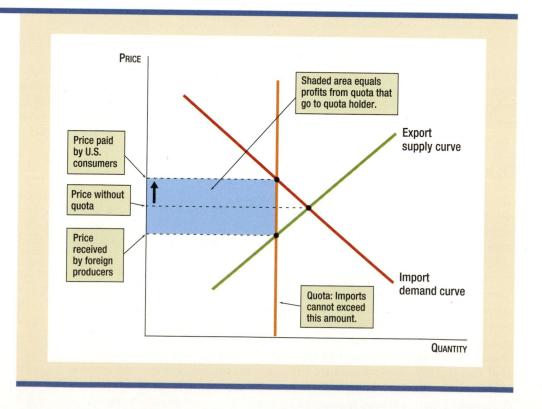

ECONOMICS IN ACTION

The End of the Multi-Fiber Agreement

This news story from the Associated Press discusses the economic impact of the termination of the Multi-Fiber Agreement (MFA) on the economy of Sri Lanka. In this particular case, the cost to Sri Lanka is the loss of the quota rents that the country had earned under the MFA. The winners will be the lower-cost producers in countries like Mexico, who no longer will be shut out of the U.S. market, as well as consumers in the U.S. market.

Sri Lanka's Revenue from Garment Exports to America Set to Drop 20 Percent as Trade Agreement Expires

November 15, 2004, Associated Press

Sri Lanka's revenue from garment and textile exports to the United States, its biggest customer, is expected to fall about 20 percent next year following the expiration of a preferential trade agreement, an industry official said Monday. The United States has purchased an annual average of about US$2.5 billion (€1.9 billion) garments and textiles from Sri Lanka since the two countries signed the Multi-Fiber Agreement in 1974. But the agreement is set to expire next month.

Tuli Cooray, who heads a committee of Sri Lankan business and government officials advising the industry, said American buyers will probably switch to lower cost manufacturers in China, Mexico and elsewhere in South Asia. As a result, he said Sri Lanka's shipments of garments and textiles to the United States will likely fall about 20 percent to about US$2 billion (€1.5 billion), in 2005.

Cooray said most small and medium garment manufacturers may need to downsize to stay in business, but added that the industry will bounce back by focusing on markets closer to home, such as India and Japan. "We don't envisage any serious shocks," Cooray told Dow Jones Newswires. "We have already initiated talks with Indian partners amid efforts to obtain a piece of that market," he said.

Overseas shipments of textiles and garments comprise 50 percent of Sri Lanka's total export earnings, and the United States has been the largest buyer of garments from Sri Lanka.

same as the price increase in Figure 18-9. Viewed from the domestic market, therefore, a quota and a tariff are equivalent. If the quota is set to allow in the same quantity of imports as the tariff, then the price increase will be the same. Consumers will pay more for imports in both cases, and the demand for domestically produced goods that are substitutes for imports will increase. The price of domestically produced cars also will increase if a quota is set on foreign cars.

Then what is the difference in the effects of a tariff and a quota? Unlike the situation with a tariff, no revenue goes to the government with a quota. The difference between the price that the foreign suppliers get and the higher price that the consumers pay goes to the holders of the quota—the ones who are allowed to import into the country. Foreign countries frequently hold the quotas. The revenue the quota holders get is indicated by the shaded rectangle in Figure 18-10. It is equal to the quantity imported times the difference between the price paid by the consumers and the price received by the producers. The size of that rectangle is identical to the size of the rectangle showing the revenue paid to the government in the case of the tariff in Figure 18-9.

On January 1, 2005, the 1973 Multi-Fiber Agreement, a set of quotas on textiles and apparel, expired. This system of global quotas restricting imports added an estimated 20 percent to the cost of clothing, while benefiting companies in places like the Philippines that specialized in supplying clothing under this quota system. The lifting of the quotas created widespread fears among U.S. and European Union clothing manufacturers about the flood of cheap Chinese apparel into these markets. A coalition of U.S. producers claimed that 650,000 jobs were at risk. Since then, the European Union and the United States have both struggled to find a solution that will work for China and for domestic manufacturers, retailers, and consumers.

Since the expiration of the quotas, exports from China have surged, adding to downward pressure on prices of clothing in the United States. In contrast, exports from countries like the Philippines and Sri Lanka, that previously had quotas, have suffered. The surge in exports from China has caused U.S. clothing producers to lobby for new quotas though U.S. clothing retailers are opposed to them. If you were determining trade policy, how would you view this trade-off between U.S. clothing prices and U.S. clothing production?

The Costs of Trade Restrictions

Trade barriers, such as tariffs and quotas, distort prices and reduce the quantity consumed, benefiting domestic producers at the expense of domestic consumers and foreign producers. For example, the United States imposes quotas on sugar to increase the price of domestic sugar beets and sugar cane. Producers receive $1 billion a year in additional surplus as a result of higher prices, but U.S. consumers lose $1.9 billion, for a net loss of $.9 billion to the United States.

The Multi-Fiber Agreement, which ended in January 2005, was another trade restriction that had substantial implications for U.S. consumers. The estimated loss to U.S. consumers was $24 billion a year, and the cost to the U.S. economy was around $10 billion a year.

REVIEW

- The most common ways for government to restrict foreign trade are tariffs and quotas. Each has the same effect on price and quantity.

- With a tariff, the revenue from the tariff goes to the government. With a quota, that revenue goes to quota holders.

- Trade restrictions alter the allocation of resources in the economy and are significant sources of deadweight loss.

The History of Trade Restrictions

revenue tariff
an import tax whose main purpose is to provide revenue to the government.

As discussed, tariffs are the oldest form of trade restriction. Throughout history, governments have used tariffs to raise revenue. **Revenue tariffs**, whose main purpose is raising revenue, were by far the most significant source of federal revenue in the United States before the income tax was made constitutional by the Sixteenth Amendment to the U.S. Constitution in 1913 (see Figure 18-11). Revenue tariffs are still common in developing countries because they are easy for the government to collect as the goods come through a port or one of a few checkpoints.

U.S. Tariffs

Tariffs are a big part of U.S. history. Even before the United States was a country, a tariff on tea imported into the colonies led to the Boston Tea Party. One of the first acts of the U.S. Congress placed tariffs on imports. Figure 18-12 summarizes the history of tariffs in the United States since the early 1800s.

From the Tariff of Abominations to Smoot-Hawley Tariffs were high throughout much of U.S. history, rarely going below 20 percent in the nineteenth century. In addition to raising revenue, these tariffs reduced imports of manufactured goods. The tariffs offered protection to manufacturers in the North but raised prices for consumers. Because the South was mainly agricultural and a consumer of manufactured goods, a constant dispute arose between the North and the South over these tariffs.

The highest of these tariffs was nicknamed the "tariff of abominations." This tariff, passed in 1828, brought the average tariff level in the United States to more than 60 percent. The tariff made purchases of farm equipment much more expensive in the southern states. It almost led to a civil war before the actual Civil War, as the southern states threatened to secede. Because the tariff was so high, however, it soon was repealed, and for the next 10 years tariffs were relatively low by nineteenth-century standards.

The most devastating increase in tariffs in U.S. history occurred during the Great Depression. The **Smoot-Hawley tariff** of 1930 raised average tariffs to 59 percent. Congress and President Hoover apparently hoped that raising tariffs would stimulate U.S. production and offset the Great Depression. But the increase had precisely the opposite effect. Other countries retaliated by raising their tariffs on U.S. goods. Each country tried to beat the others with higher tariffs, a phenomenon known as a **trade war**. The Smoot-Hawley tariff had terrible consequences. Figure 18-13 is a dramatic illustration of the decline in trade that occurred at the time of these tariff increases during the Great Depression. The Smoot-Hawley tariff made the Great Depression worse than it would have otherwise been.

Figure 18-11

Tariffs as a Share of Total Federal Revenue
The first tariff, passed in 1789, represented nearly all of the federal government's revenue; 200 years later, tariff revenues were only about 1 percent of the total.

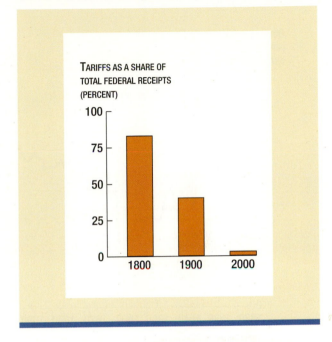

TARIFFS AS A SHARE OF TOTAL FEDERAL RECEIPTS (PERCENT)

From the Reciprocal Trade Agreement Act to the WTO
The only good thing about the Smoot-Hawley tariff was that it demonstrated to the whole world how harmful tariffs can be. To achieve lower tariffs, the Congress passed and President Roosevelt signed the *Reciprocal Trade Agreement Act* in 1934. This act was probably the most significant event in the history of U.S. trade policy. It authorized the president to cut U.S. tariffs by up to 50 percent if other countries would cut their tariffs on a reciprocating basis. The reciprocal trade agreements resulted in a remarkable reduction in tariffs. By the end of World War II, the average tariff level was down from a peak of 59 percent under Smoot-Hawley to 25 percent. The successful approach to tariff reduction under the Reciprocal Trade Agreement Act was made permanent in 1947 with the creation of a new international organization, the *General Agreement on Tariffs and Trade (GATT)*. GATT was set up to continue the process of tariff reduction. During the half-century since the end of World War II, tariffs have continued to decline on a reciprocating basis. By 1992, the average U.S. tariff level was down to 5.2 percent.

In 1993, GATT was transformed into the **World Trade Organization (WTO)**, which continues to promote reciprocal reductions in tariffs and other trade barriers. But the WTO also has authority to resolve trade disputes between countries. For example, if the United States complains that Europe is violating a trade agreement by restricting U.S. beef imports in some way, then the WTO determines whether the complaint has merit and what sanctions should be imposed on Europe. This dispute resolution authority has led to complaints, such as those made by the protesters in Seattle in 1999, that the WTO represents a loss of sovereignty for individual countries. On the other side of the argument, by resolving disputes, the WTO can avoid misunderstandings that otherwise can lead to trade wars between countries when trade disputes occur.

Smoot-Hawley tariff
a set of tariffs imposed in 1930 that raised the average tariff level to 59 percent by 1932.

trade war
a conflict among nations over trade policies caused by imposition of protectionist policies on the part of one country and subsequent retaliatory actions by other countries.

World Trade Organization (WTO)
an international organization that can mediate trade disputes.

Figure 18-12

History of Tariffs in the United States

This chart shows the ratio of tariff revenues to the value of imports subject to tariffs measured as a percentage. This percentage is a measure of the average tariff excluding goods not subject to any tariff.

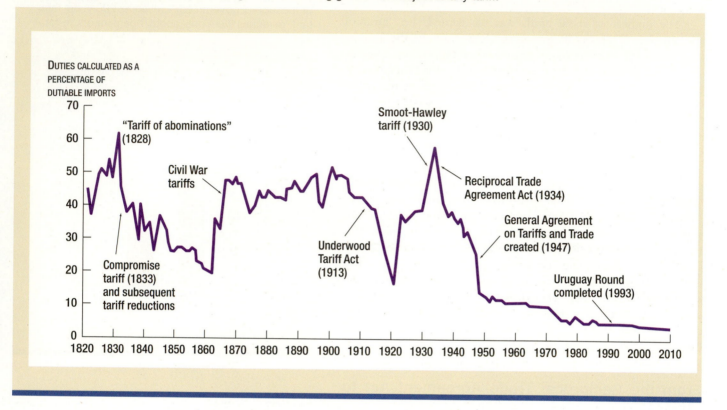

DUTIES CALCULATED AS A PERCENTAGE OF DUTIABLE IMPORTS

"Tariff of abominations" (1828)

Civil War tariffs

Smoot-Hawley tariff (1930)

Reciprocal Trade Agreement Act (1934)

General Agreement on Tariffs and Trade created (1947)

Uruguay Round completed (1993)

Underwood Tariff Act (1913)

Compromise tariff (1833) and subsequent tariff reductions

antidumping duty
a tariff imposed on a country as a penalty for dumping goods.

Antidumping Duties No history of U.S. tariffs would be complete without a discussion of antidumping duties. **Antidumping duties** are tariffs put on foreign firms as a penalty for dumping. When a firm sells products in another country at prices below average cost or below the price in the home country, it is called *dumping*. Dumping can occur for many reasons. For example, the firm might want to sell at a lower price in the foreign market than in the home market because the demand in the foreign market is more elastic. If so, consumers in the foreign market benefit. But some people argue that dumping is a way for firms in other countries to drive domestic firms out of business and thereby gain market share and market power. Regardless of motive, in the United States and other countries, dumping is illegal; the penalty is a high tariff—the antidumping duty—on the good that is being dumped. Steel is one of the industries protected with antidumping duties in the United States, at a cost to consumers of as much as $732,000 per job protected, about 10 times what a steelworker earns. President Bush's increase in steel tariffs in 2002 provoked retaliation by the European Union and Japan, adding to the deadweight loss caused by trade barriers.

Many economists are concerned that antidumping duties, or even the threat of such duties, place serious restrictions on trade. They reduce imports and raise consumer prices. Moreover, they frequently are used for protectionist purposes. Firms in industries that desire additional protection can file dumping charges and request that tariffs be raised. Frequently, they are successful. Thus, an important issue for the future is how to reduce the use of antidumping duties for restricting trade.

Figure 18-13

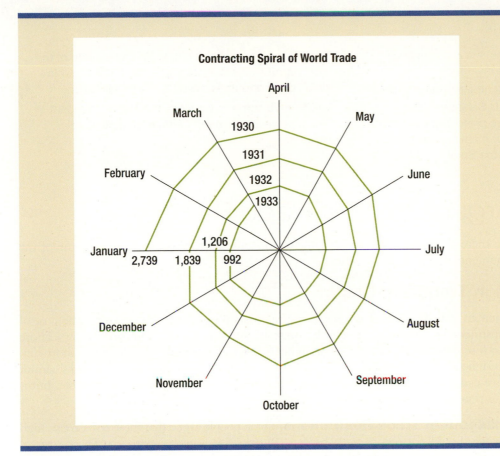

Contracting Spiral of World Trade

Decline in World Trade during the Great Depression
This circular graph, used by Charles Kindleberger of MIT, illustrates how world trade collapsed after tariffs increased during the Great Depression. The distance from the middle of the graph to the point on each spoke is the amount of trade (in millions of dollars) during each month.

The Rise of Nontariff Barriers As tariffs were being reduced in the post–World War II period, a conflicting trend began to emerge. Some of the other methods of restricting trade—called **nontariff barriers** to trade—grew in popularity. Nontariff barriers include anything from quotas to quality standards aimed at reducing the import of foreign products. Nontariff barriers may have arisen as a replacement for tariffs in response to political pressure for protection of certain industries.

Quality and performance standards sometimes are nothing more than barriers to trade. Some standards may have a good purpose, such as safety or compatibility with other products, but others do not. Consider the Canadian plywood standards for building construction, which keep out U.S. plywood. The Canadians argue that the standards are needed to satisfy building requirements in Canada, but Americans argue that plywood that does not meet the Canadian standards works just as well. A safety restriction against U.S.-made baseball bats in Japan during the 1980s is another example. Most Americans viewed the bats as perfectly safe and viewed the Japanese safety standard as a restriction on trade.

Quality and performance standards, therefore, are a tricky problem because governments can argue that they are imposed to improve economic conditions in their own country. The U.S. Food and Drug Administration (FDA) does not allow untested drugs into the United States even though foreign governments deem them safe. The FDA argues that the restriction is necessary to protect consumers, but foreign governments view it as a trade restriction. Although such a standard does seem like a trade barrier, in reality, it is a matter of dispute.

nontariff barrier
any government action other than a tariff that reduces imports, such as a quota or a standard.

Arguments for Trade Barriers

Are there any good economic arguments for trade barriers? Let's examine some of the arguments that typically are made.

High Transition Costs

When an industry shrinks as a result of the removal of restrictions on trade, the cost of adjustment in the short run may be quite large, even if other industries grow. Those who lose their jobs in the protected industry, even temporarily, suffer. In the short run, it is difficult to retrain workers. Workers who are laid off as the industry shrinks cannot move easily to another industry. Many have to retire early. Retraining is possible, but it takes time and is difficult for older workers.

Phaseout of Trade Restrictions
Some people argue that these costs are so high that we should not reduce trade barriers. But there is a better approach. These costs of adjustment are a reason for a slow phaseout of trade barriers. *Phaseout* means that trade barriers are reduced a little bit each year. A slow phaseout of trade barriers was part of the North American Free Trade Agreement (NAFTA) between Canada, Mexico, and the United States. This agreement called for a phaseout period of 10 to 15 years, depending on the product. For example, some tariffs were scheduled to be cut by 25 percent in the first year, 50 percent after five years, and 100 percent after 10 years. The purpose of the slow phaseout was to allow production to shift from one industry to another slowly. The intention was to adjust the workforce through attrition as workers normally retired.

Trade Adjustment Assistance
Another approach is to use *trade adjustment assistance*, which refers to transfer payments to workers who happen to be hurt because of a move to free trade. Unemployment insurance and other existing transfer programs may go a long way toward providing such assistance. Because society as a whole benefits from free trade, some increased resources can be used to help the workers who bear the brunt of the adjustment. In other words, the extra income that can be obtained by trade may be used to ease the adjustment.

Transition costs are not a reason to avoid free trade. They are a reason to phase out the restrictions on trade gradually and to provide trade adjustment assistance to workers as needed.

The Infant Industry Argument

infant industry argument
the view that a new industry may be helped by protectionist policies.

One of the earliest statements of the **infant industry argument** in favor of trade restrictions was put forth by Alexander Hamilton in 1791 in his *Report on Manufactures*. Hamilton argued that manufacturing firms in the newly created United States should be protected from imports. Once the industries were established, they could compete with foreign imports. But as they got started, they needed protection until they reached a certain scale.

A danger with the infant industry argument is that the protection may last long after it was initially justified. In Latin America, for example, infant industry arguments were used to justify import protection in the 1950s. These barriers to trade, however, lasted long after any kind of reasonable infant industry argument could be made.

The National Security Argument

A nation's security is another argument for trade restrictions. The national security argument is that the country needs to be able to produce certain goods, such as special metals, computers, ships, or aircraft, in time of war. If the country does not have an industry that produces them, it could be at a severe disadvantage.

Firms can use these national security arguments, however, to seek protection from foreign imports. Japanese rice farmers, for example, made national security arguments for protection from rice imports. In fact, the rice restriction has little to do with national security because rice can be imported from many different countries. In the United States, the textile industry has argued on national security grounds that it needs protection because it provides military uniforms made from U.S. textiles.

It is important to examine alternatives to trade restrictions before applying the national security argument and restricting trade. For example, rather than restricting rice imports, the Japanese could store a large amount of rice in case of a war emergency. Or if the United States really thought that uniforms were a national security issue, it could store millions of extra uniforms rather than restrict textile imports. In fact, the United States does have stockpiles of many rare minerals and metals needed for national defense production.

The Retaliation Argument

Threatening other countries or retaliating against them when they have trade restrictions is another possible reason to deviate from free trade. If the United States threatens the Japanese by saying that it will close U.S. markets, this may encourage Japan to open its markets to the United States. Thus, by retaliating or threatening, it is possible to increase international trade around the world.

Those seeking protection, however, also can use the retaliation argument. Those in the United States who are most vocal about retaliation against other countries frequently are those who want to protect an industry. Many economists worry about threats of retaliation because they fear that other countries will respond with further retaliation, and a trade war will occur.

The Foreign Subsidies Argument

If foreign governments subsidize their firms' exports, does this justify U.S. government subsidies to U.S. firms to help them compete against the foreign firms?

Foreign subsidies to foreign producers are a particularly difficult issue. If foreign subsidies lower the price of U.S. imports, then U.S. consumers benefit. If Europe wants to use taxpayer funds to subsidize aircraft manufacturers, then why not enjoy the lower-cost aircraft? Foreign subsidies enable industries to thrive more for political reasons than for economic ones. From a global perspective, such government intervention should be avoided, because it hurts consumers by encouraging less economically efficient production and, ultimately, higher prices.

Environment and Labor Standards Arguments

During the 1990s, a new type of argument against reducing trade barriers emerged: that tariffs or quotas should not be removed against countries with weak or poorly enforced environmental protection laws and labor standards, such as child labor laws and workplace safety laws. Because such laws and standards generally are weaker in developing countries than in industrial countries, this argument frequently opposes reducing trade barriers to the imports of goods from relatively poor countries. For example, this argument is made by people who are against reducing tariffs on imports of Brazilian oranges into the United States.

Environmental and labor standard arguments are of two main types. First, some people argue that holding back on the reduction of trade barriers until countries change their environmental and labor policies is a good way to persuade these countries to change. An important counterargument, however, is that low trade barriers lead to improvements in environmental and working conditions. History has shown that as their income grows, people become more concerned with the environment and their working conditions; people in deep poverty do not have the time or resources to deal with such issues. Thus, by raising income per capita, lower trade barriers can improve the environment and the workplace. Moreover, more effective and cheaper technologies to improve the environment or increase safety become available through trade.

A second type of argument is that it is difficult for workers and firms in the industrial countries to compete with those in the developing countries who do not have to pay the costs of complying with environmental protection laws. By keeping trade barriers high, however, income growth may not be sufficient to address the environmental problems in developing countries, so the differences in the law persist.

The Public Health Argument

In 2008, hundreds of Chinese infants reportedly were being poisoned by tainted milk products that contained an industrial chemical known as melamine. This led to the withdrawal of various types of food products that were made from Chinese milk and milk powder. The European Union banned the importation of Chinese-made soy-based products for infants, and the United States halted the import of all milk-based products from China. The public health scare came only a couple of years after disruptions to trade in chicken stemming from outbreaks of bird flu in countries like Brazil and Thailand.

Such episodes lead to calls for limits on imports of food and medicine from countries whose quality control standards may not be as stringent as in the importing country. But such episodes are not limited to food products from developing nations. The export of beef from the United Kingdom to Europe was banned after an outbreak of "mad cow disease" in the mid-1990s. The European Union restricts the importation of U.S. beef that comes from cattle injected with growth hormones. Many African nations have resisted importing genetically modified seeds and grain despite the promise of more drought-resistant, higher-yield varieties that can improve farm productivity.

The public health arguments for trade restrictions present a complicated issue. On the one hand, few people would argue against a temporary halt in food imports following a scandal like the melamine incident or after an outbreak of disease like the avian flu. Such bans, once put in place, often tend to linger on for years, long after the source of the problem has been identified and addressed. And, sometimes, the arguments seem motivated more by the desire to protect domestic firms than consumer health, an example being the need to protect U.S. consumers in Detroit from buying pharmaceuticals produced just across the border in Ontario, Canada.

The Political Economy of Protection

Firms seek protection from foreign competition simply because the protection raises their profits. But the firms may use any of the above arguments to justify their case. In a famous satire of firms seeking protection from foreign competitors, a French economist, Frédéric Bastiat, wrote more than 150 years ago about candlemakers complaining about a foreign rival—the sun. The candlemakers in Bastiat's satire petitioned French legislators to pass a law requiring the closing of all shutters, curtains, and blinds during the day to protect them from this competition. The behavior Bastiat described seems to apply to many modern producers who seek protection from competition.

Firms seeking protection frequently are successful in part because they spend a lot more time and money lobbying the U.S. Congress than do the people who would be hurt by the protection. Even though consumers *as a whole* benefit more from reducing trade barriers than firms in the protected industry are harmed, each consumer benefits relatively little, so spending a lot of time and money lobbying is not worthwhile. It is difficult to get enough votes to remove trade barriers when a few firms each have a lot to lose, even though millions of consumers have something to gain.

REVIEW

- Transition costs, environmental and labor standards, national security, infant industry, and retaliation are some of the arguments in favor of trade restrictions. Each has the possibility of being used by protectionists.

- Although many arguments in favor of trade barriers have been put forth over the years, in each case, we have better ways to deal with the problems raised. The case for free trade holds up well in the debates when the economic rationale for the gains from trade is applied correctly and understood.

How to Reduce Trade Barriers

Viewed in their entirety, the economic arguments against trade restrictions seem to overwhelm the economic arguments in favor of trade restrictions. The economic arguments in favor of free trade have been in existence for more than 200 years. The recommendation of early economists such as Adam Smith and David Ricardo was simple: Reduce trade barriers.

It was not until many years after Smith and Ricardo wrote their recommendations, however, that they were translated into a practical trade policy. Then, as now, political pressures favoring protection made the repeal of trade barriers difficult. Hence, a carefully formulated trade policy is needed to reduce trade barriers. Next we consider a variety of approaches.

Unilateral Disarmament

One approach to removing trade barriers in a country is simply to remove them unilaterally. Making an analogy with the arms race, we call this policy *unilateral disarmament*. When a country unilaterally reduces its arms, it does so without getting anything in arms reduction from other countries. With unilateral disarmament in trade policy, a country reduces its trade barriers without other countries also reducing their trade barriers. Unilateral disarmament is what Smith and Ricardo recommended for England.

ECONOMICS *IN ACTION*

How Health Scares Can Disrupt Trade

The following article describes how the United States halted imports of Chinese products that contained milk after the melamine scandal broke. It describes the process by which the restrictions on imports will be lifted, and it presents the voices of several critics who think that the United States was too slow to act on behalf of consumer interests.

F.D.A. Detains Chinese Imports for Testing

By Gardiner Harris and Andrew Martin

Candy, snacks, bakery products, pet food and other Chinese products that contain milk will be detained at the border until tests prove that they are not contaminated, the federal government announced Thursday.

The Food and Drug Administration said it issued the alert because of concern about such products being contaminated with the toxic chemical melamine. It was discovered in infant formula in September and has sickened more than 50,000 infants in China and killed at least four.

Since that time, melamine has been found in a wide range of other products, including milk, eggs and fish feed. As a result, companies in the United States have recalled several products generally sold in Asian specialty stores, including a nondairy creamer and Mr. Brown brands of instant coffee and tea. But to date, the contamination here was not thought to be widespread.

"We're taking this action because it's the right thing to do for the public health," said Dr. Steven Solomon, a deputy associate F.D.A. commissioner.

But consumer advocates said the agency's action was too little and too late.

"Although F.D.A.'s action today is a step in the right direction, it does not do enough to ensure consumer safety, especially since melamine contamination in Chinese products continues to broaden," said Wenonah Hauter, executive director of Food & Water Watch.

As a result of the latest alert, Chinese products that contain milk or milk powder will automatically be detained at the border until the manufacturer or its customer has the product tested and it is found to be free of contamination, or they show documentation indicating that the product does not contain milk or milk-derived ingredients.

"The burden shifts to the importer," Dr. Solomon said.

F.D.A. analyses have detected melamine and cyanuric acid, another contaminant, in "a number of products

that contain milk or milk-derived ingredients, including candy and beverages," according to an alert that the agency sent to field personnel. The alert also noted that inspectors in more than 13 other countries had discovered melamine in Chinese products including milk, yogurt, frozen desserts, biscuits, chocolates and cookies.

The agency routinely blocks imports of individual food products, but it is rare for it to block an entire category of one country's foods. Last year, the F.D.A. blocked five types of farm-raised seafood as well as vegetable protein from China because of repeated instances of contamination.

Unscrupulous food and feed dealers in China add melamine to their products because it increases nitrogen content to give the appearance in testing that protein levels are adequate. Because it dissolves poorly, melamine can block the body's filtering system, potentially leading to kidney failure and death.

Dr. Solomon said the alert was likely to apply mostly to specialty products sold in Asian markets. But Benjamin England, a former lawyer at the agency, described the latest alert as "massive" and said it could affect "a tremendous amount of goods."

"It's going to jam the ports up all the way up the supply chain," said Mr. England, who represents food supply companies.

As a result of the earlier alerts on seafood and vegetable protein, many private laboratories that perform product tests for F.D.A. review already have long waiting lists, Mr. England said. In addition, the agency takes three to four weeks to review submitted tests, Mr. England said, so delays in shipping will be significant.

The import alert could extend to Chinese shrimp, Mr. England said, because much of it is breaded and the breading could contain dairy products. China is also one of the world's biggest makers of supplements, and some protein powders and shakes are made largely with powdered milk.

The effect of the alert is likely to be long-lasting, Mr. England said, because importers must prove that each and every shipment is free of contamination.

"It's impossible to get off the alert list," Mr. England said.

China exports a relatively small but growing amount of dairy products to the United States, about $13 million in 2007, most of which was casein, a dairy ingredient. (By contrast, New Zealand exported $697 million to the United States.) But the figures do not include food products and dietary supplements that include milk or milk-derived ingredients, a potentially much larger universe.

"Today's F.D.A. Import Alert on dairy products from China should have little or no impact on the U.S. dairy industry," said Peggy Armstrong, a spokeswoman for the International Dairy Foods Association, a trade group. "Dairy imports from China account for less than 1 percent of total dairy products imported to this country annually."

Representative Rosa DeLauro, Democrat of Connecticut, criticized the agency's response, saying it should have acted sooner. The import alert should include egg and fish products "given that animal feed has been found to be contaminated with melamine," she said in a release.

"Clearly, the problems involving melamine in China are significantly deeper than F.D.A. would have us believe," Ms. DeLauro said.

The import detention order comes at a delicate time. Secretary of Health and Human Services Michael O. Leavitt and Dr. Andrew C. von Eschenbach, commissioner of the F.D.A., will travel next week to China to open agency offices in Beijing, Guangzhou and Shanghai. Months of negotiations were needed for it to gain permission to open offices there.

Michael Herndon, an agency spokesman, said the new import order "shouldn't affect the opening of F.D.A. offices."

The problem with unilateral disarmament is that some individuals are hurt, if only temporarily, and it is hard to compensate them. Of those who gain, each gains only a little. Of those who lose, each loses a lot. The political pressures that the losers exert are significant. As a result, unilateral disarmament is rarely successful in the industrial countries as a means of reducing trade barriers.

Multilateral Negotiations

An alternative to unilateral disarmament is **multilateral negotiations**, which involve simultaneous tariff reductions by many countries. With multilateral negotiations, opposing political interests can cancel each other out. For example, import-competing domestic industries that will be hurt by the reduction of trade barriers, such as textiles in the United States or agriculture in Europe and Japan, can be countered by export interests that will gain from the reduction in trade barriers. Because consumers will gain, they are also a potential counter to protectionism, but they are too diffuse to make a difference, as we just discussed. With multilateral negotiations, interested exporters who gain from the reduction in barriers will push the political process to get the reductions.

Multilateral negotiations also balance international interests. For example, to get developing countries to remove their barriers to imports of financial and telecommunications services, the United States had to agree to remove agricultural trade barriers in the United States.

Multilateral trade negotiations have taken place in a series of negotiating rounds, each of which has lasted several years. During each round, the countries try to come to agreement on a list of tariff reductions and the removal of other trade restrictions. Since 1947, eight rounds of negotiations have taken place. The most recently completed round was the **Uruguay Round**, named after the country where the first negotiations occurred in 1986. The Uruguay Round negotiations ended in 1993. Since 2002, the United States has been involved in negotiations for another global trade round, called the **Doha Development Round**. As with all such multilateral negotiations, this round is proving to be long and difficult and still is not finished.

The reduction in tariffs through multilateral negotiations under GATT has been dramatic. Tariffs have declined to below 3 percent on average in the United States with the

multilateral negotiations
simultaneous tariff reductions on the part of many countries.

Uruguay Round
the most recently completed round of multilateral negotiations, opened in 1986 and completed in 1993.

Doha Development Round
the latest round of multilateral negotiations, opened in November 2001 in Doha, Qatar.

implementation of the Uruguay Round agreement. Recall that this compares with nearly 60 percent in the mid-1930s.

Most-Favored-Nation Policy Multilateral negotiations almost always are conducted on a *most-favored-nation* (*MFN*) basis. MFN means that when the United States or any other country reduces its tariffs as part of a multilateral trade agreement, it reduces them for everyone. Since the late 1990s, the term *normal trade relations* (*NTR*) frequently has been used in place of MFN because it is a more accurate description of the policy. In the twenty-first century, if a country is not granted MFN or NTR status, the United States imposes very high tariffs on the country. For example, concern about human rights in China has led some to argue that the United States should not grant MFN or NTR status to China. Without MFN or NTR, tariffs on Chinese imports to the United States would be about 60 percent.

Regional Trading Areas

Creating regional trading areas is an increasingly popular approach to reducing trade barriers. For example, NAFTA, the free trade agreement between the United States, Canada, and Mexico, removes all trade restrictions among those countries. An even wider free trade area covering the whole Western Hemisphere has been proposed.

Regional trading areas have some advantages over multilateral approaches. First, fewer countries are involved, so the negotiations are easier. Second, regional political factors can offset protectionist pressures. For example, the political goal of European unity helped establish grassroots support to reduce trade barriers among the countries of Europe.

Trade Diversion versus Trade Creation Regional trading areas have disadvantages, however, in comparison with multilateral reductions in trade barriers under GATT. **Trade diversion** is one such disadvantage. Trade is diverted when low-cost firms from countries outside the trading area are replaced by high-cost firms within the trading area. For example, as a result of NAFTA, producers of electronic equipment in Southeast Asia have to pay a U.S. tariff, while producers of the same equipment in Mexico do not have to pay the tariff. As a result, some production will shift from Southeast Asia to Mexico; that is viewed as trade diversion from what might otherwise be a low-cost producer. The hope is that **trade creation**—the increase in trade resulting from the lower tariffs between the countries—will outweigh trade diversion.

Free Trade Areas versus Customs Unions An important difference exists between two types of regional trading areas: **free trade areas (FTAs)** and **customs unions**. In both, barriers to trade between countries in the area or the union are removed. But external tariffs are treated differently: Under a customs union, such as the European Union (EU), external tariffs are the same for all countries. For example, semiconductor tariffs are exactly the same in France, Germany, and the other members of the EU. Under an FTA, external tariffs can differ for the different countries in the FTA. For example, the United States' external tariffs on textiles are higher than Mexico's. These differences in external tariffs under an FTA cause complications because a good can be shipped into the country with the low tariff and then can be moved within the FTA to the country with the high tariff. To prevent such external tariff avoidance, *domestic content restrictions* must be incorporated into the agreement. These restrictions say that for a product to qualify for the zero tariffs between the countries, a certain fraction of the product must be made within the FTA. For example, under NAFTA, the majority of parts in television sets and automobiles must be manufactured in Canada, Mexico, or the United States for the television or car to qualify for a zero tariff.

trade diversion
the shifting of trade away from the low-cost producer toward a higher-cost producer because of a reduction in trade barriers with the country of the higher-cost producer.

trade creation
the increase in trade resulting from a decrease in trade barriers.

free trade area (FTA)
an area that has no trade barriers between the countries in the area.

customs union
a free trade area with a common external tariff.

ECONOMICS *IN ACTION*

Ending the Corn Laws

Corn laws, recorded as far back as the twelfth century, restricted imports of grains, including wheat, rye, and barley, into England. Adam Smith devoted an entire chapter of his 1776 *Wealth of Nations* to the corn laws, arguing that "the praises which have been bestowed upon the law ... are altogether unmerited."[1] But legislation introduced in 1791 raised the grain import tariff even further. The corn laws were unpopular with everyone except landowners and farmers.

The Anti-Corn League, founded in 1839 by Richard Cobden, was the most significant pressure group in nineteenth-century England. The Anti-Corn League used the economic arguments of Smith and Ricardo that the corn laws were an economic disaster and a moral tragedy: The laws impoverished and even starved the working class, constrained the growth of manufacturing, and provided government support to the wealthy. The catalyst was the Irish potato famine of 1845, which raised agricultural prices even further.

Robert Peel was the Tory prime minister from 1841 to 1846. Until 1845, he was against repeal of the corn laws, primarily because of strong support for them from landowners in the Tory party. But under pressure from Cobden and the Anti-Corn League, he changed his position after the potato famine and argued for the repeal of the corn laws.

In February 1846, Peel introduced a package of measures abolishing duties on imported corn over a three-year period. Only a minority of his party supported him, but the package passed. The split in the Tory party ended Peel's career, and the party did not win another election until 1868.

Thus, Peel paid a high political price for his policy of reducing trade protection, a policy that many feel helped make the British economy strong for the rest of the nineteenth century. How do you think he would have fared had he used one of the other methods (such as multilateral negotiations) to reduce protection rather than "unilaterally disarming"?

[1] Adam Smith, *Wealth of Nations* (New York: Modern Library, 1994), p. 560.

CONCLUSION

Few economists disagree with the proposition that tariffs, quotas, and other trade barriers reduce the economic well-being of a society. In fact, polls of economists show that they disagree less on this proposition than on virtually any other in economics. This unanimity among economists was reflected in the debate over the NAFTA in the United States. Every living Nobel Prize–winning economist endorsed the agreement to eliminate tariffs and quotas among Canada, Mexico, and the United States.

In this chapter, we first focused on the economic gains to the citizens of a country from international trade. We noted two reasons for such gains: comparative advantage and larger markets that reduce cost per unit. Both reasons apply to trade within a country as well as to international trade. We also showed how to measure the gains from trade because of comparative advantage and larger markets.

This chapter also shows that despite the benefits that come from trade, many restrictions on international trade still exist. Although few economists disagree with the proposition that tariffs, quotas, and other trade barriers reduce the economic well-being of a society, political pressure continues to erect new trade barriers or to prevent the existing ones from being removed.

It is important to point out that the benefits of international trade go well beyond economic gains. International trade sometimes puts competitive pressure on governments to deliver better policies. Within the United States, competition between states can make regulatory and tax policies more efficient. Similarly, competition can make regulatory policies in countries more efficient. International trade also can improve international relations. Trade enables Americans to learn more about Southeast Asians or Europeans or Latin Americans. This improves understanding and reduces the possibilities for international conflict. Developing international trade with China might even reduce the possibility of another cold war or new international conflict in the future. If many people have an economic stake in a relationship, they will not like a military action that threatens that relationship. Thus, the need for good trade policies to reduce trade barriers is likely to increase rather than decrease in the future. The challenge is to develop a means for conducting international trade policy in a world with many sovereign governments, each of which is free to formulate its own policy.

KEY POINTS

1. According to the principle of comparative advantage, countries that specialize in producing goods for which they have a comparative advantage can increase world production and raise consumption in their own country.

2. The gains from trade resulting from comparative advantage can be shown graphically by shifting out the production possibilities curve.

3. The relative price of two goods with trade is between the relative prices in the two countries without trade.

4. Comparative advantage is a dynamic concept. If people in one country improve their skills or develop low-cost production methods through research, they will alter the comparative advantage.

5. If differences in the relative abundance of capital and labor are the reason for differences in comparative advantage, then international trade will tend to equalize real wages.

6. Lower cost per unit in larger markets is another key reason for gains in trade. When the size of the market increases, the price declines, more firms enter the market, and product variety is greater.

7. Despite the economic arguments put forth in support of free trade, plenty of restrictions on trade still are in place in the world.

8. Tariffs and quotas are the two main methods of restricting international trade. They are equivalent in their effects on prices and imports.

9. Tariffs were originally a major source of government revenue but are relatively insignificant sources of revenue in the twenty-first century. Quotas do not generate any revenue for the government. The quota holders get all the revenue.

10. National security and infant industry are two of the main arguments frequently put forth in support of trade barriers. In most cases, they are overwhelmed by the arguments in favor of reduced trade barriers.

11. Eliminating restrictions on trade unilaterally is difficult because of the harm done to those who are protected by the restrictions. Regional trading areas and multilateral tariff reductions attempt to reduce trade barriers by balancing export interests against import-competing interests.

12. Free trade areas and customs unions both create trade and divert trade.

KEY TERMS

QUESTIONS FOR REVIEW

1. What is the difference between absolute advantage and comparative advantage?
2. What is the difference between the production possibilities curve before trade and after trade?
3. In what sense is comparative advantage a dynamic concept?
4. Why might costs per unit decline when the market increases in size?
5. What is the difference between interindustry trade and intraindustry trade?

6. In what sense are a tariff and a quota equivalent?
7. What is the infant industry argument in favor of trade protection?
8. Why is unilateral disarmament a difficult way to reduce trade barriers?
9. How do multilateral negotiations or regional trading areas make the reduction of trade barriers easier politically?
10. Why might a regional trade agreement cause trade diversion?

PROBLEMS

1. Bill and Hillary are two very smart lawyers who also have an active interest in public policy. Bill can write a law paper in three months or a policy paper in one month. Hillary can write a law paper or a policy paper in one month. Bill and Hillary like each other a lot and would like to get married. However, because the marriage of two lawyers often is fraught with difficulty, they decide that one of them should write law papers and the other should write policy papers.

   a. Draw a production possibilities curve for Bill and one for Hillary.
   b. Who has an absolute advantage in writing law papers? In writing policy papers?
   c. Who has a comparative advantage in writing law papers? In writing policy papers?
   d. Explain how to reconcile your answers to (b) and (c).

2. Suppose that the United States has 200 million units of labor and Mexico has 100 million units, and that the production of wheat and strawberries per unit of labor in the United States and Mexico is as follows:

	Wheat	Strawberries
Mexico	1 bushel	3 pints
United States	2 bushels	3 pints

   a. What is the shape of the production possibilities curves for each country? What does this shape imply about the nature of the trade-off between wheat and strawberries? Is this a realistic assumption? Explain.

   b. Which country has a comparative advantage in wheat production? Why?
   c. With free trade between the United States and Mexico, is it possible that 1 bushel of wheat will trade for 1 pint of strawberries? Why or why not?
   d. Suppose the free trade price is 1 bushel of wheat for 2 pints of strawberries. Draw a diagram indicating the production possibilities curve with and without trade.

3. Suppose there are two goods, wheat and clothing, and two countries, the United States and Brazil, in the world. The production of wheat and clothing requires only labor. In the United States, it takes one unit of labor to produce four bushels of wheat and one unit of labor to produce two items of clothing. In Brazil, it takes one unit of labor to produce one bushel of wheat and one unit of labor to produce one item of clothing. Suppose the United States has 100 units of labor and Brazil has 120.

   a. Draw the production possibilities curve for each country without trade. Which country has the absolute advantage in each good? Indicate each country's comparative advantage.
   b. In what range will the world trading price ratio lie when these countries open up to free trade? Will both countries be better off? Why? Show this on your diagram.

4. Comparative advantage explains interindustry trade in different goods between countries. How do economists explain intraindustry trade, that is, trade in the same industry between countries?

Why might people in the United States want to buy German cars, and Germans want to buy cars from the United States?

5. Suppose that each firm in an industry has the total costs shown below.

Quantity of Output	Total Costs (dollars)
1	50
2	54
3	60
4	68
5	80
6	90
7	105
8	112

a. Suppose that the quantity demanded in the market is fixed at four. Calculate the average total cost for each firm when one, two, and four firms are in the industry. Draw a diagram indicating the relationship between average total cost and number of firms.

b. Suppose the quantity demanded in the market expands because of an opening of trade and is now fixed at eight. Draw a diagram similar to the one in part (a) indicating the relationship between average total cost and the number of firms. Why does the opening of trade cause this shift in the curve?

6. The following relationship between price, cost per unit, and the number of firms describes an industry in an economy.

Number of Firms	Cost per Unit ($)	Price ($)
1	10	90
2	20	80
3	30	70
4	40	60
5	50	50
6	60	46
7	70	43
8	80	40
9	90	38
10	100	36

a. Graph (1) the relationship between cost per unit and number of firms and (2) the relationship between price and number of firms. Why does one slope up and the other slope down?

b. Find the long-run equilibrium price and number of firms.

c. Now suppose the country opens its borders to trade with other countries; as a result, the relationship between cost per unit and the number of firms becomes as follows:

Number of Firms	Cost per Unit ($)
1	5
2	10
3	15
4	20
5	25
6	30
7	35
8	40
9	45
10	50

Find the long-run equilibrium price and number of firms.

d. What are the gains from expanding the market through the reduction in trade barriers?

7. Suppose French wine suddenly becomes popular in the United States. How does this affect the price and quantity of imports of French wine? Suppose the U.S. wine industry lobbies for protection. If the government imposes a tariff to restore the original quantity of imports, what will happen to the price of French wine in the United States? Show how much tariff revenue the government will collect.

8. India has a 70 percent tariff on imported chocolate.

a. Sketch a diagram to show the impact of this tariff on the price of imported chocolate in India.

b. Suppose India cuts the tariff to zero but imposes a quota that results in the same high price for imported chocolate. Show this in a diagram.

c. From the government's perspective, is it better off with a tariff or with a quota? Explain.

9. Suppose the president of a nation proposes a switch from a system of import quotas to a system of tariffs, with the idea that the switch will not affect the quantity of goods imported. Who will be in favor of the switch? Who will oppose it?

10. Suppose the U.S. government has decided that for national security reasons, it must protect the

machine tools industry. Name two ways in which the government can accomplish this goal. Which policy would you recommend? Why?

11. Suppose the North American Free Trade Agreement causes the United States to import lumber from Canada instead of from Finland, even though Finland is a lower-cost producer than Canada. Identify and explain this phenomenon.

12. Assume that several hundred independent farmers in Argentina are the only producers of a rare plant that is used for medicinal purposes around the world. Imagine that you are an economic adviser to the Argentine government. The president asks you to find a way to capture some of the economic rents from the production of this rare plant, so that more profits stay in Argentina. Your job is to design a trade policy that accomplishes the president's goal. Explain verbally what your trade policy would be, how it would affect quantity and price in the market, and how it would affect all the players in this market.

Money serves a vital role as a medium of exchange in an economy. Money facilitates economic transactions within a country by eliminating the need for the double coincidence of wants. When it comes to transactions that take place across countries that use different moneys, however, a complication arises. When a supermarket chain in the United States wants to buy beef from Argentina or when a company in France wants to buy computers from the United States, for example, they typically have to exchange their own currency for the foreign currency before completing the transaction. The rate at which one currency can be exchanged for the other, also known as the **exchange rate**, plays an important part in deciding whether an economic transaction between countries will occur.

How are exchange rates set? For many countries, the value of their currency is determined by supply and demand conditions in the foreign exchange market. The foreign exchange market is a global market. Any time, day or night, the market in foreign currencies is open somewhere in the world. When the market closes for the day in Tokyo, it is just opening in London. When it closes in London, it is just open-

ing in San Francisco. When the market closes in San Francisco, it is getting ready to open again in Tokyo. The total sum of money being traded on the foreign exchange market over a period of one week exceeds the volume of global foreign trade for a year. In this chapter, we illustrate how the exchange rate, the price of foreign currency, is determined in the foreign exchange market. As you will soon see, some unusual features of the foreign exchange market lead exchange rates to be a volatile price.

Some countries have adopted a "fixed" exchange rate regime in which the country fixes its currency to another. We will demonstrate how a fixed exchange rate system works, and what the consequences are of choosing a fixed exchange rate that artificially favors either buyers of foreign goods or sellers of domestic goods. This explanation will help us understand the policy disputes between the United States and China regarding China's decision to limit the movements of its currency and keep the value of its currency low.

Finally, we will consider the European Economic and Monetary Union (EMU) where a group of countries replaced their own currencies with a new single currency. After more than a decade of successful operation, a financial crisis in several countries in 2010 and 2011, including Greece and Portugal, has led some economists to suggest that these countries leave the union and return to their own currency.

Knowing what happens to Greece or Portugal when they are part of a currency union or to China when it fixes its exchange rate is extremely important for understanding the world economy.

Exchange Rates

Important Definitions

Conceptually, an exchange rate between two currencies is a simple idea: It is the price of one country's currency in terms of another on the foreign exchange market. Confusion regarding exchange rates is common, and often stems from a lack of consistency regarding how the exchange rate is defined. For instance, some newspapers will report the exchange rate between the dollar and the euro as $1.25 per euro but report the exchange rate between the dollar and the yen as 120 yen per dollar. When you then read about the exchange rates going "up" or "down," the connotation of what "up" and "down" means differs depending on whether we are talking about an exchange rate written as dollars per foreign currency or foreign currency per dollar.

Here, we define the exchange rate as a number of units of foreign currency that are needed to purchase one unit of the domestic currency, or, in other words, the price of a unit of domestic currency in terms of foreign currency. If the United States is the domestic economy, then the exchange rate with the euro will be expressed as 0.80 euros per dollar rather than as $1.25 per euro.

An increase in the exchange rate signifies that the domestic currency has increased in value (and the foreign currency has decreased in value) because it takes more units of foreign currency to buy a unit of domestic currency. This is called an **appreciation** of the domestic currency. Conversely, a decrease in the exchange rate signifies that the domestic currency has decreased in value (and the foreign currency has increased in value) since it takes fewer units of foreign currency to buy a unit of domestic currency. This is called a **depreciation** of the domestic currency.

We can use the exchange rate to convert the price of goods from one currency to another. For example, if a BMW costs 40,000 euros and the exchange rate between Germany and the United States was 0.8 euros per dollar, then the price of the BMW to someone in the United States is (40,000 euros)/(0.8 euros per dollar) = $50,000. Similarly, the price of a $2,000 Apple computer to someone in Germany would be $2,000 × 0.8 euros per dollar = 1,600 euros.

Exchange Rates and Net Exports

As we discussed in Chapter 7, changes in the exchange rate change the price that people in one country have to pay for the other country's goods. Consider the example about the BMW and the Apple computer and suppose that the dollar appreciates from 0.8 euros per dollar to a value of 1 euro per dollar. Then, the price of the 40,000 euro BMW will now be $40,000 instead of $50,000. Similarly, the $2,000 Apple computer would now cost 2,000 euros in Germany instead of 1,600 euros.

All else equal, then an appreciation of the domestic currency makes foreign goods cheaper at home and domestic goods more expensive abroad, whereas a depreciation of the domestic currency makes foreign goods more expensive at home and domestic goods cheaper abroad. We can conclude, therefore, that an appreciation of the domestic

exchange rate
the price of one currency in terms of another in the foreign exchange market. We express the exchange rate as the number of units of foreign currency that can be purchased with one unit of domestic currency. (Ch. 7)

appreciation
an increase in value of a currency.

depreciation
a decrease in value of a currency.

currency leads to more imports and fewer exports, that is, it decreases net exports, whereas a depreciation of the domestic currency leads to more exports and fewer imports, that is, it increases net exports.

Changes in the exchange rate are not the only reason why domestic goods may be more or less expensive compared with foreign goods. So, even when the exchange rate does not change, a higher rate of inflation in the domestic economy than in the foreign economy will make domestic goods more expensive abroad, driving down net exports. Conversely, a higher rate of inflation in the foreign economy than in the domestic economy will make domestic goods cheaper abroad, increasing net exports.

REVIEW

- An exchange rate between two currencies is the price of one country's currency in terms of another on the foreign exchange market. The convention here is to define the exchange rate in terms of foreign currency units per unit of domestic currency.

- An increase in the exchange rate signifies that the domestic currency has increased in value, also called an appreciation of the domestic currency. A decrease in the exchange rate signifies that the domestic currency has decreased in value, also known as a depreciation of the domestic currency.

- All else equal, a depreciation of the domestic currency makes foreign goods more expensive at home and domestic goods cheaper abroad. This implies an increase in net exports. Conversely, an appreciation of the domestic currency leads to a decrease in net exports.

- Even when the exchange rate does not change, a higher rate of inflation in the domestic economy will make domestic goods more expensive abroad, driving down net exports. Conversely, a higher rate of inflation in the foreign economy will make domestic goods cheaper abroad, increasing net exports.

Exchange Rate Determination

Because the exchange rate as we defined it is simply the price of domestic currency (in terms of foreign currency), then we should be able to understand how that price is determined by analyzing the foreign exchange market using the familiar supply–demand framework.

Figure 19-1 demonstrates how to use a standard supply–demand framework to analyze the foreign exchange market. Because the exchange rate is simply the price of domestic currency, we can quickly draw a parallel with the regular supply–demand analysis. When the price of domestic currency is high (low), the quantity of domestic currency demanded will be low (high), resulting in a downward-sloping demand curve. Similarly, when the price of domestic currency is high (low), the quantity of domestic currency supplied will be high (low), resulting in an upward-sloping supply curve. The demand for domestic currency here is coming from those who have foreign currency that they wish to exchange into domestic currency, while the supply of domestic currency is coming from those who have domestic currency that they desire to convert into foreign currency.

When the demand for domestic currency rises or the supply of domestic currency falls, all else equal, domestic currency will appreciate—that is, the price of domestic currency rises. When the demand for domestic currency falls or the supply of domestic currency rises, all else equal, the domestic currency will depreciate—that is, the price of domestic currency falls. This simple supply–demand framework allows us to make two key predictions about what determines the behavior of exchange rates in the economy.

Figure 19-1

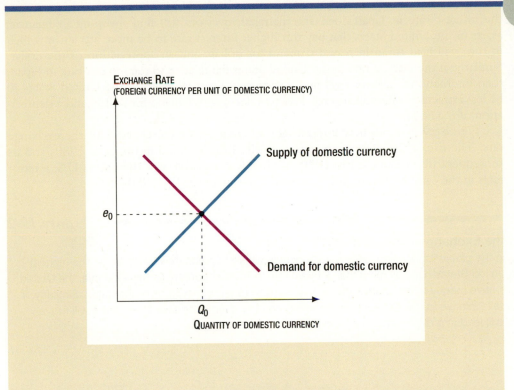

EXCHANGE RATE
(FOREIGN CURRENCY PER UNIT OF DOMESTIC CURRENCY)

Supply of domestic currency

e_0

Demand for domestic currency

Q_0
QUANTITY OF DOMESTIC CURRENCY

Supply and Demand Model of the Foreign Exchange Market

The exchange rate is the price of domestic currency (expressed in terms of foreign currency). The quantity of domestic currency demanded (in exchange for foreign currency) varies inversely with the price of domestic currency (the exchange rate). The quantity of domestic currency supplied (in exchange for foreign currency) varies directly with the price of domestic currency (the exchange rate). The resulting equilibrium exchange rate is given by e_0 and the quantity of domestic currency exchanged for foreign currency is given by Q_0

The two predictions are (1) that interest rate differentials affect the behavior of exchange rates in the short run and (2) that price differentials for goods determines the behavior of exchange rates in the long run.

In practice, you have to be careful in using a traditional supply–demand model to analyze the foreign exchange market. In a traditional goods market, like the market for oranges, the factors affecting demand, such as the income levels of consumers, the price of apples, or the health benefits of drinking orange juice, likely will be quite distinct from the factors affecting supply, such as the costs of transportation or winter weather conditions in Florida. This means that we can analyze the impact of a particular event on the orange juice market by considering whether it would shift the demand curve or the supply curve. In the foreign exchange market, however, the factors affecting demand and factors affecting supply are likely to be much less distinct. For instance if an economy experiences some political unrest, this unrest would lead to both a decrease in the demand for domestic currency as well as an increase in the supply of domestic currency.

Interest Rate Differentials and Short-Run Exchange Rate Movements

In the short run, investors operating in the global foreign exchange market decide where to place their funds to get the highest return. The funds they invest are highly mobile; tens of millions of dollars worth of foreign currency can be moved from one country to another in a matter of seconds by means of a few keystrokes or a mouse-click. The movement of funds around the world to receive the highest return creates a link between interest rate differentials and the behavior of the exchange rate.

For example, suppose that the interest rate in the United States rises by more than the interest rate in Japan does. International investors will find investing in financial assets in the United States that pay this higher interest rate to be more attractive, which in turn will lead to an increased demand for dollars and an appreciation of the dollar. Similarly, if the interest rate in the United States fell relative to the interest rate in Japan, then international investors will find investing in financial assets in the United States to be less attractive. This scenario will lead to a decreased demand for dollars and a depreciation of the dollar.

Figure 19-2 shows how interest rate differentials are correlated with the exchange rate. The rise of the dollar with respect to the British pound in the early 1980s and its subsequent decline in the late 1980s are highly correlated with the rise in U.S. interest rates in the early 1980s and the subsequent decline in the late 1980s.

Figure 19-2

Interest Rate Differentials and the Exchange Rate, 1980–2010

In the short run, investors operating in the global foreign exchange market decide where to place their funds to get the highest return. When the interest rate in the United States rises by more than interest rate in another country (in this example, the United Kingdom), international investors will move money to the United States; this will lead to an appreciation of the dollar. Similarly, if the interest rate in the United States falls relative to the interest rate in another country, then international investors will move money out of the United States; this will lead to a depreciation of the dollar.

Price Differentials and Long-Run Exchange Rate Movements

If transport costs are low, and people are not prevented from buying whatever they want, the same commodity in two countries will sell for about the same amount; this is called **the law of one price**. The idea that the law of one price will hold for many different products is what underlies the theory of **purchasing power parity (PPP)**, which states that the exchange rate will adjust to equalize the price levels of two economies. The intuition here is that if PPP did not hold, then people would buy goods and services in the country where they are cheap, transport them to the country where they are expensive, and make a profit. This can only happen if the transportation costs are low and the goods and services can in fact be shipped from one country to another. The cost of shipping some goods (cement, milk) can be very high, whereas other products, especially services such as a haircut, may not be tradable across countries. The more nontradable goods and services are, and the higher transportation costs are, the less likely it is that PPP will hold.

PPP works better over long periods of time than over short periods. PPP predicts that when the domestic inflation rate exceeds the foreign inflation rate for a long period of time, then the domestic currency must depreciate over that time period so that domestic goods prices do not rise faster than foreign goods prices, when measured in the same currency. Conversely, PPP predicts that when the foreign inflation rate exceeds the domestic inflation rate, then the domestic currency must appreciate over time to ensure that foreign goods prices do not rise faster than domestic goods prices, when measured in the same currency.

Figure 19-3 shows how inflation differentials are correlated with the exchange rate in the last twenty-five years for a group of the United States' largest trading partners as predicted by the theory.

law of one price
the notion that if transport costs are low, and people are not prevented from buying whatever they want, the same commodity in two countries will sell for about the same amount when measured in the same currency.

purchasing power parity (PPP)
a theory that states that the exchange rate will adjust to equalize the price levels of two countries.

Figure 19-3

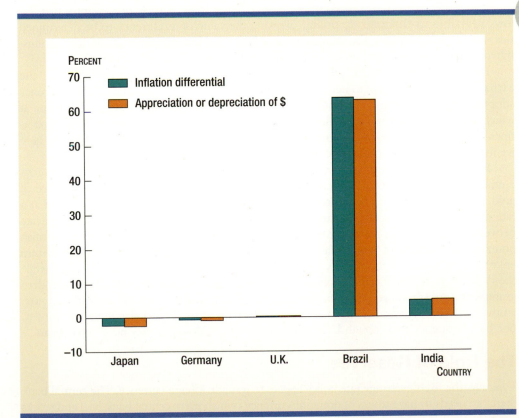

Purchasing Power Parity, 1980–2010
As predicted by PPP, the U.S. dollar has appreciated against countries with high inflation (Brazil, India) and depreciated against countries with low inflation (Germany, Japan) while remaining essentially unchanged against countries with similar inflation (the United Kingdom).

REVIEW

- Because the exchange rate is the price of domestic currency (in terms of foreign currency), we can use the supply–demand framework to understand how the exchange rate is determined.

- When the demand for domestic currency rises or the supply of domestic currency falls, all else equal, the domestic currency will appreciate. When the demand for domestic currency falls or the supply of domestic currency rises, all else equal, the domestic currency will depreciate.

- The supply–demand framework predicts that interest rate differentials affect exchange rates in the short run and that price differentials for goods affect exchange rates in the long run.

- International investors move their funds around the world to get the highest return. If the interest rate in the United States rose relative to the interest rate in Japan, then international investors would find financial assets in the United States more attractive, leading to an appreciation of the dollar. Conversely, a fall in U.S. interest rates would lead to a depreciation of the dollar.

- PPP states that the exchange rate will adjust to equalize the price levels of two economies. PPP predicts that the domestic currency will depreciate over time when the domestic inflation rate exceeds the foreign inflation rate so that domestic goods prices do not rise faster than foreign goods prices when measured in the same currency. Conversely, PPP predicts that the domestic currency will appreciate over time when the foreign inflation rate exceeds the domestic inflation rate.

Fixed Exchange Rates

In our analysis thus far, we assumed that a country's currency was freely traded on the foreign exchange market and that the exchange rate was freely determined by the actions of the buyers and sellers in that market. The United States is an example of a country that follows a **flexible exchange rate policy**, allowing the value of its currency to be determined this way. In such a system, the exchange rate is likely to fluctuate quite substantially, as illustrated in Figure 19-4 for the euro–dollar exchange rate between 2000 and 2010.

flexible exchange rate policy
a policy in which exchange rates are determined in foreign exchange markets and governments do not agree to fix them. (Ch. 15)

But throughout history, governments have exercised substantial control over the exchange rate system. Governments who want to tightly control the value of their currency adopt a **fixed exchange rate policy**, whereby the government announces a fixed rate at which the central bank will exchange domestic currency for foreign currency. The implications of a fixed exchange rate system for monetary policy were explored in Chapter 15; here we focus more on how such a system operates.

fixed exchange rate policy
a policy in which a country maintains a fixed value of its currency in terms of other currencies. (Ch. 15)

In the early nineteenth century, Britain adopted a gold standard under which the government pegged the price of gold at a fixed price of about 4 British pounds per ounce of gold. In 1879, the United States joined the gold standard, agreeing to buy or sell gold at a rate of about $20 an ounce. Because both currencies were tied to gold, the exchange rate between the pound and the dollar were also tied together at a rate of about $5 per British pound. From the end of World War II through the early 1970s, the Bretton-Woods system linked the currencies of the world's largest economies to the U.S. dollar at a set value, while the dollar in turn was linked to gold at a price of $35 per ounce of gold. A more modern example was in Argentina during the period from 1992 to 2002, when the Argentinean government set up a system that fixed the Argentinean peso to the U.S. dollar at a rate of one to one by agreeing to hold enough U.S. dollars to convert all peso currency notes into dollars.

The Role of Reserves

Typically, the fixed exchange rate policy applies to a single foreign currency. The central bank therefore needs to have stocks of domestic currency (which every central bank has) and stocks

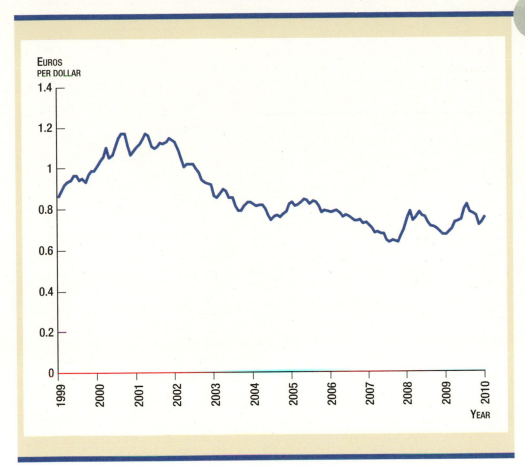

Figure 19-4

Fluctuations in the Euro–Dollar Exchange Rate
Since its introduction in 1999, the euro has fluctuated against the dollar, sometimes quite dramatically. After an initial period of depreciation, the euro underwent a sustained appreciation from 2002 until 2008. The dollar appreciated during the recession in the United States. Since the recession ended, the two currencies have continued to fluctuate against each other with no clear pattern of sustained appreciation or depreciation.

of the foreign currency (also known as foreign currency reserves). Although reserves could theoretically be held in the form of any currency, typically, most foreign exchange reserves are held in terms of the currency to which the country is fixing its currency.

When a participant in the foreign exchange market comes to the central bank and exchanges domestic currency for foreign currency, the central bank's holdings of foreign currency reserves go down and their holdings of domestic currency go up. Conversely, when a participant in the foreign exchange market comes to the central bank and exchanges foreign currency for domestic currency, the central bank's holdings of foreign currency reserves go down and their holdings of domestic currency go up.

Figure 19-5 shows the exchange rate between the U.S. dollar and the Chinese renminbi between 2000 and 2010. The Chinese exchange rate was pegged to the dollar until 2005 when it was allowed to appreciate. China then returned to a fixed exchange from 2008 to 2010, around the period of the financial crisis. Beginning in 2010, the Chinese government again ended the peg and let their currency appreciate, but it is clear that they still were exercising a great deal of control over the exchange rate, which is less volatile than euro–dollar rate shown in Figure 19-4.

Overvaluation and Undervaluation

A fixed exchange rate is unlikely to equal the rate that would prevail in a flexible exchange rate system without central bank involvement. Recall that in a flexible exchange rate

Figure 19-5

Lack of Fluctuations in the Yuan–Dollar Exchange Rate

In contrast to the euro–dollar exchange rate the yuan–dollar exchange rate looks much more tightly controlled. Between 1999 and 2005, the exchange rate was fixed at 8.28 yuan per dollar. After 2005, China agreed to let the yuan appreciate but controlled the pace of that appreciation quite tightly. When the recession of 2008/09 hit, China again kept the exchange rate from appreciating only to relax their control again and resume the slow appreciation after the crisis ended.

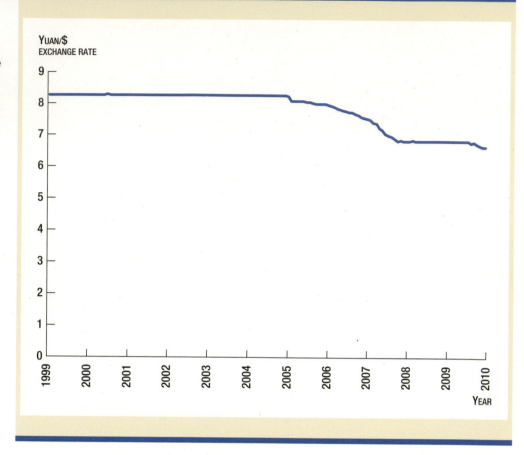

overvalued

a currency is said to be overvalued if the fixed exchange rate system makes the domestic currency artificially more valuable.

undervalued

a currency is said to be undervalued if the fixed exchange rate makes the domestic currency artificially less valuable.

system the prevailing exchange rate would be the rate at which the quantity supplied of domestic currency on the foreign exchange market equals the quantity demanded. Suppose that rate happens to be 20 units of foreign currency per unit of domestic currency, and consider what would happen in the two scenarios in which the government fixes the exchange rate (1) at a value that is higher than 20 or (2) at a value lower than 20.

First, consider the case in which the central bank wants to fix the value of the domestic currency at a value of 25 units of foreign currency per unit of domestic currency. As you can see in Figure 19-6, this implies an excess supply of domestic currency. The central bank will see its foreign exchange reserves decrease because more people want to hand in domestic currency to the central bank in exchange for foreign currency. Because the fixed exchange rate makes the domestic currency artificially more valuable, we say that the domestic currency is **overvalued**.

Why would a government want to overvalue its currency? Well, by making the domestic currency artificially more valuable, consumers and importers in the economy will benefit from having access to cheap foreign goods. Conversely, exporters will suffer because their goods will be artificially more expensive to foreign buyers.

Next, consider the case in which the central bank wants to fix the value of the domestic currency at a value of 15 units of foreign currency per unit of domestic currency. In this case, because the fixed exchange rate makes the domestic currency artificially less valuable, we say that the domestic currency is **undervalued**. As you can see in Figure 19-7, this implies an excess demand for domestic currency, and the central bank will see its foreign exchange reserves increase rather than decrease because more people want to exchange foreign currency for domestic currency.

A government would want to undervalue its currency because exporters in the economy will benefit from their goods being more attractive to foreign buyers, as a result of the domestic currency now artificially being less valuable. In contrast, consumers and importers would suffer because goods produced in other countries would cost more.

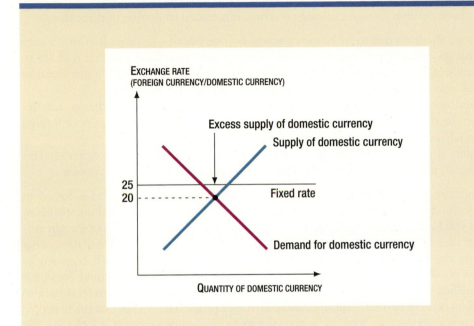

Figure 19-6

An Overvalued Fixed Exchange Rate

Suppose that the exchange rate that would prevail in the market under a flexible exchange rate regime was 20 units of foreign currency per unit of domestic currency. Now suppose that the central bank wants to fix the value of the domestic currency at a value of 25 units of foreign currency per unit of domestic currency. This implies that there is an excess supply of domestic currency (equivalent to an excess demand for foreign currency). The central bank's foreign exchange reserves will decrease as a result.

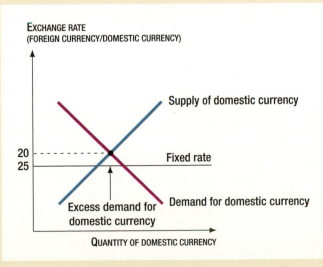

Figure 19-7

An Undervalued Fixed Exchange Rate

Suppose that the exchange rate that would prevail in the market under a flexible exchange rate regime was 20 units of foreign currency per unit of domestic currency. Now suppose that the central bank wants to fix the value of the domestic currency at a value of 15 units of foreign currency per unit of domestic currency. This implies that there is an excess demand for domestic currency (equivalent to an excess supply of foreign currency). The central bank's foreign exchange reserves will increase as a result.

Consequences of Sustained Overvaluation

So what happens when the overvaluation continues? The central bank will continue to run down its foreign exchange reserves and correspondingly increase its domestic currency holdings. Having too few foreign exchange reserves is a serious problem because it means that the fixed rate cannot be sustained—when the central bank runs out of reserves, it cannot maintain the fixed exchange rate anymore. When the central bank does not have enough foreign exchange reserves, it is forced to do one of three things:

1. Change the fixed rate to make the currency less overvalued—so move it from 25 units of foreign currency per unit of domestic currency to a new fixed rate that is closer to 20 units of foreign currency per unit of domestic currency. This is called a **devaluation** of the domestic currency, the fixed exchange rate analog to a depreciation.
2. Abandon the fixed exchange rate regime and move to a flexible exchange rate regime. In this case, the exchange rate will again move closer to 20 units of foreign currency per unit of domestic currency but will no longer be fixed.
3. Acquire more foreign exchange reserves sufficient to meet the excess demand. This approach usually is successful only if the underlying overvaluation is temporary.

> **devaluation**
> when a fixed exchange rate is adjusted so that the domestic currency is worth less than it used to be.

In practice the situation is often more drastic. Suppose the government is forced to devalue from say 25 to 20 in the above example. If you had money in the domestic economy and you knew that the exchange rate was going to jump from 25 units of foreign currency per unit of domestic currency to 20 units of foreign currency in a few days, what would you do? Well, you would try to get your money out of the domestic economy as quickly as possible—if you had 1 million units of domestic currency, you could convert it into 25 million units of foreign currency and then, after the devaluation, convert it back to 1.25 million units of domestic currency and earn a nice profit. This means that many people will be rushing to convert domestic currency into foreign currency when it looks like the central bank is running into difficulty with its foreign exchange reserves.

This type of a panic in which everyone stampedes to exit the domestic currency and acquire foreign currency was fairly common in the 1980s and 1990s, with the notable examples being the East Asian currency crisis of 1997, the European currency crisis of 1991–1992, and the Argentinean crisis of 2001.

Consequences of Sustained Undervaluation

Undervaluation creates a different set of problems than overvaluation. Undervaluation occurs when governments want to favor certain sectors of the economy (exporters trying to sell goods abroad) over other sectors (importers and consumers who benefit from cheap goods from abroad).

The result of sustained undervaluation is that the central bank will see its foreign exchange reserves grow. Having too many foreign exchange reserves may seem like a positive development that can help countries avoid the panic associated with running out of reserves that occurred in past episodes of currency crises. But undervaluation has adverse longer-term implications. When the central bank keeps handing out domestic currency for foreign currency, it is increasing the domestic money supply. Increases in the domestic money supply imply a rise in inflation as people bid up the price of domestic goods, services, and assets. It also means that the central bank has to manage its growing holdings of foreign exchange reserves. Additionally, foreign economies will exert substantial political pressure if they are unhappy with the fact that another country is using the exchange rate to favor its own exporters at the expense of foreign exporters.

> **revaluation**
> when a fixed exchange rate is adjusted so that the domestic currency is worth more than it used to be.

If the central bank feels like it has too many foreign exchange reserves, it will change the fixed rate to make the currency less undervalued, for example, by moving it from 15 units of foreign currency per unit of domestic currency to closer to 20 units of foreign currency. This is called a **revaluation** of the domestic currency, the fixed exchange rate

ECONOMICS *IN ACTION*

Currency Wars

One of the longest-running economic debates of the twenty-first century involves the exchange rate policy of China. China's remarkable economic transformation began in 1978 with the economic reforms instituted by Deng Xiaoping. These reforms were initially internally focused, transforming formerly collectively owned agricultural land into privately owned land, and gradually allowing farmers to sell their produce in markets at a price of their choosing rather than forcing them to sell to the government at a price of the government's choosing. These reforms gradually expanded to encourage foreigners to invest in the Chinese economy in designated "special economic zones" that were not subject to the same tight controls as the rest of the Chinese economy. This was the beginning of a change in Chinese policy toward achieving high rates of economic growth by focusing on exports and on attracting foreign direct investment (FDI).

A cheaper yuan would improve both exports and FDI, and thus the Chinese embarked on a series of devaluations in the 1980s as the yuan per dollar exchange rate changed from 1.5 in 1980 to 2.8 by 1985, 4.7 by 1990, 8.5 by 1995, and finally settling at 8.28 in the late 1990s. The rate then stayed unchanged at this level till the mid-2000s, as you can see from Figure 19-5. During this period, China's economy grew rapidly, with per capita gross domestic product (GDP) growth rates averaging around 7 to 9 percent. Even more impressive growth rates could be found in China's foreign exchange reserves, which increased from $19 billion in 1990 to $157 billion in 2000 to almost $700 billion at the time the 8.28 rate came to an end in mid-2005.

Although the rapid economic growth rates transformed China and brought hundreds of millions of people out of poverty, many countries (especially the United States) were unhappy with the exchange rate policy that was a key means to that end of rapid economic growth. A fixed exchange rate with rapidly rising foreign exchange reserves is the hallmark of an undervalued exchange rate, and as the reserves grew, pressure from the United States mounted as domestic political forces in the United States began to blame China for holding back the recovery of the U.S. economy from the 2001 recession. In February of 2005, Senators Schumer (NY) and Graham (SC) introduced a bill that would impose a 27.5 percent tariff on Chinese-made products as retaliation for what they considered to be unfair trade practices by China. This bill was later withdrawn after key U.S. policy makers told the senators that China would in fact allow their currency to increase in value.

Beginning in June of 2005, China allowed the yuan to appreciate in a tightly controlled fashion until it reached a value of 6.83 in September of 2008, an appreciation of around 17.5 percent. This appreciation did not completely placate the United States, especially because foreign reserves increased by almost $1 trillion during this period, reaching a level of around 1.7 trillion by September of 2008. In September, following the collapse of the Wall Street investment bank Lehman Brothers, the global financial system was plunged into crisis and GDP fell sharply in the United States during the fourth quarter of 2008. This crisis, in turn, had negative effects around the world, particularly in countries that relied on exports to the United States.

China responded by immediately halting the gradual appreciation of the yuan at a value of around 6.83 to the dollar and then embarking on a large stimulus package to ensure that the Chinese economy did not go into recession. The yuan did not appreciate much for almost 18 months, long after the recession had ended in mid-2009 and the sluggish recovery was under way. Finally, in late 2010, China allowed the yuan to appreciate again; by that time, China had added another trillion dollars to their reserve holdings, which now had reached $2.8 trillion. With 9 percent unemployment in the United States, policy makers were clearly unhappy with China. Treasury Secretary Tim Geithner made a series of speeches, beginning with his confirmation hearing before the Senate, in which he accused China of manipulating its currency, calling China's exchange rate policy "untenable," and threatening to file action at the World Trade Organization (WTO) accusing China of unfair trade practices. Even the Schumer–Graham bill from 2005 was dusted off and started circulating.

China has always been reluctant to allow its currency to appreciate in response to pressure from the outside world, especially from the United States. Furthermore, it believed strongly that export and FDI-driven growth was essential for the Chinese economy. But as we have read in this chapter, undervaluation poses serious long-term consequences, and especially undervaluation that has led to almost $3 trillion of foreign currency entering an economy. In 2010, news stories about asset bubbles in Chinese stock markets and housing markets, rapidly rising inflation, and concerns about the fall in the value of the dollar depleting the value of China's mountain of foreign exchange reserves became commonplace. Finally, it seemed like it was in China's best interest to let the currency appreciate, which in the end may be what it takes for the yuan to finally break free of its undervaluation and appreciate closer to its true value.

Figure 19-8

Foreign Reserves in China, 1990–2010

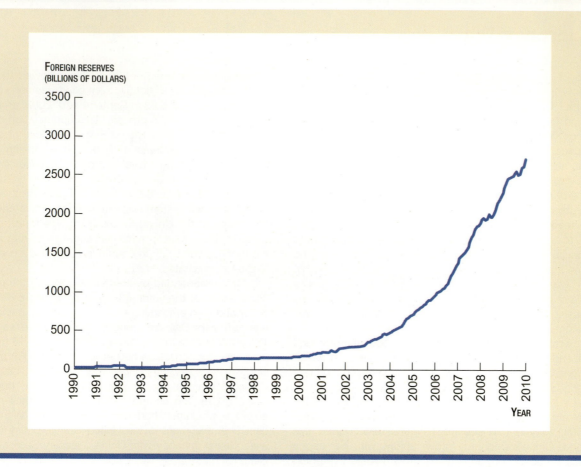

analogy to an appreciation. Foreigners will now want to rush into an economy when they can acquire another currency at a rate of 15, rather than waiting and paying 20 units per unit of domestic currency after a revaluation.

Similarly, people in the domestic economy who were looking to acquire foreign currency now will prefer to wait, because they can get only 15 units of foreign currency per unit of domestic currency today but potentially get closer to 20 units by waiting. This further decreases the supply of, and increases the demand for, domestic currency and drives foreign exchange reserves even higher. The central bank will be faced with ever-escalating problems from inflation and be more inclined to revalue its currency. This revaluation, in turn, will lead to an even more dramatic rise in the number of people wanting to acquire domestic currency, leading to another stampede, albeit to the entrance this time. This type of scenario is what China is facing today as it battles inflation and tries to control an overly rapid increase in the money supply.

Currency Unions

One of the most significant economic developments of the twenty-first century, and one that is frequently in the news, is the creation of the Eurozone, the Economic and Monetary Union (EMU) of the European Union. The Eurozone is the most prominent

REVIEW

- A flexible exchange rate policy allows the exchange rate to be freely determined in the foreign exchange market. In a fixed exchange rate policy, the government sets the exchange rate at which the central bank will exchange domestic currency for foreign currency.

- To implement a fixed exchange rate system, the central bank needs to have foreign currency reserves. The level of foreign reserves increases when the central bank hands out domestic currency in exchange for foreign currency and decreases when the central bank hands out foreign currency in exchange for domestic currency

- A government may choose to overvalue its currency by choosing a fixed exchange rate that makes the domestic currency artificially more valuable. Typically, this is done so that consumers and importers

- in the economy will benefit from having access to cheap foreign goods.

- A government, instead, may choose to undervalue its currency by choosing a fixed rate that makes the domestic currency artificially less valuable. A government may want to undervalue its currency to help exporters sell more goods to foreign buyers.

- A sustained overvaluation will cause a central bank to run down its foreign exchange reserves, set off a panicked rush to convert domestic currency into foreign currency, and lead to a currency crisis.

- A sustained undervaluation will lead to an increase in the domestic money supply, resulting in higher inflation. Foreign economies will exert political pressure if they are unhappy with the impact of the fixed exchange rate policy on their exporters.

example of a **currency union**, an arrangement whereby a group of countries adopt a common currency in place of their individual currencies. As of May 2011, the EMU is composed of 17 independent sovereign nations that have united to adopt a common currency (the euro) and a single monetary policy maker for the whole region (the European Central Bank, ECB). The Eurozone combines features of both fixed and flexible exchange rates: Because all member countries use the same currency, the euro, their exchange rates are strongly fixed to one another, but the value of the euro is determined by the forces of supply and demand in the foreign exchange market.

Many countries in the European Union—the Czech Republic, Hungary, Latvia, Lithuania, Poland, and Romania—have expressed interest in joining the EMU but have not yet been admitted. Other countries in the European Union—Denmark, Sweden, and the United Kingdom—would be admitted into the EMU easily but do not want to join. At the same time, rumors have circulated that some EMU member countries (Greece) want to leave the currency union. Why does a currency union lead to such a divergence of opinion among countries? We hope to answer this question by exploring how a currency union works and understanding the consequences of entering a currency union.

The origins of the EMU go back many years, but perhaps the most important development was the Treaty of Maastricht, which was signed in 1992. The Maastricht Treaty laid out the criteria that European Union countries would have to meet to enter the EMU and adopt the euro as the common currency. Among the criteria required were that all admitted countries have inflation rates that were within 1.5 percentage points of the three lowest inflation rates among member countries; that they have long-term interest rates that were within 2 percentage points of the three lowest interest rates among member countries; and that they have budget deficits that did not exceed 3 percent of GDP and government debt that did not exceed 60 percent of GDP. These conditions attempted to ensure that the economies of the member countries would converge to a similar state, in the hope that this would make the currency union function better.

On January 1, 1999, 11 countries embarked on what the *Economist* magazine then called "an awfully big adventure." The 11 founding countries that made up the EMU

currency union
an arrangement whereby a group of countries adopt a common currency in place of their individual currencies

were Austria, Belgium, Finland, France, Germany, Ireland, Italy, Luxembourg, the Netherlands, Portugal, and Spain. They were joined by Greece in January 2001, by Slovenia in January 2007, by Malta and Cyprus in January 2008, by Slovakia in January 2009, and most recently by Estonia in January 2011, making a grand total of 17 members. All domestic currencies have ceased to exist in these member countries.

The 17 countries that form the EMU have chosen not only to adopt the euro but also to cede monetary policy decisions to a central bank for the entire region. Since January 1, 1999, monetary policy-making decisions for the EMU have been vested in the ECB. The ECB together with the existing member central banks form a system known as the Euro-system. The member central banks took on a role similar to that played by the regional Federal Reserve Banks in the U.S. Federal Reserve System. The ECB is headquartered in Frankfurt. Wim Duisenberg, a Dutch central banker, was chosen as the first head of the ECB. He was followed by Jean-Claude Trichet, a French central banker.

As we discussed in Chapter 15, the ECB policy instruments are EMU-wide and do not relate to a particular country. In other words, the ECB cannot set one interest rate in Germany and a different interest rate in France. Instead, it decides on the appropriate euro-wide interest rates in setting monetary policy. This is an important feature of a currency union: Individual countries no longer have the ability to control their monetary policy, and the monetary policy appropriate for the region may not be appropriate for an individual economy. For example, shortly after the EMU's inception, the ECB embarked on an expansionary monetary policy because the region as a whole struggled during the global economic slowdown in 2000/01. But individual countries in the region, like Ireland, were growing fairly rapidly at the time and actually would have preferred a less expansionary policy than appropriate for the entire region. Conversely, in 2011, the ECB wanted to move to a less expansionary policy because of concerns about rising inflation. But this had adverse consequences for Greece, Ireland, and Portugal, which have been struggling with weak economic growth.

This type of disconnect is likely to be particularly problematic for smaller economies in the region because their economic outcomes will have little impact on the Eurozone aggregates that the ECB uses to set policy. Table 19-1 provides a set of weights

Table 19-1

Contributions of Each Member Country to Euro-Area Aggregates (consumption-based weights)

Country	Weight
Germany	25.9%
France	20.7%
Italy	18.5%
Spain	12.7%
Netherlands	4.8%
Greece	3.8%
Belgium	3.3%
Austria	3.2%
Portugal	2.2%
Finland	1.7%
Ireland	1.3%
Slovakia	0.7%
Slovenia	0.4%
Luxembourg	0.3%
Cyprus	0.3%
Estonia	0.15%
Malta	0.1%

ECONOMICS *IN ACTION*

Greek Lessons for America in its Debt Crisis

The future of the EMU may be contingent on what happens in Greece, where the debt crisis that resulted from poor budget management policies of the previous Greek government still lingers. The following news article summarizes some key lessons from this most recent Greek tragedy and draws parallels to the United States.

Greek lessons for America in its debt crisis

BY THE CHRISTIAN SCIENCE MONITOR EDITORIAL BOARD. REPRINTED WITH PERMISSION FROM THE MAY 11, 2011 ISSUE OF THE CHRISTIAN SCIENCE MONITOR. © 2011 THE CHRISTIAN SCIENCE MONITOR (WWW.CSMONITOR.COM).

Despite last year's bailout, debt in Greece continues to grow, and Athens is asking for another rescue package. As America nears the deadline to raise its debt ceiling, it should review its Greek lessons.

The Greek debt crisis that was supposedly solved a year ago is making a reappearance. This revives bad memories of shaken global financial markets. Hopefully, though, the Greek threat can also spur American politicians to cut US debt.

As Americans learned in "Greek Debt 101" last year, the US economy differs significantly from the Aegean version, but a debt problem left unchecked has serious repercussions for individual nations and the world.

In 2010, European governments and the International Monetary Fund (IMF) bailed out Athens with about $157 billion in loans. But it's now clear that total Greek debt is continuing to grow and Athens cannot meet its belt-tightening, deficit-reduction targets.

Hence, this week's downgrade of Greek debt by Standard & Poor's, a trip to Athens by European and IMF inspectors to review the situation, and another nationwide strike by Greek workers saying "enough" to austerity.

Given that Republicans and Democrats in Washington are trying to agree on a debt-reduction plan ahead of an August debt-default deadline, it's worth reviewing the lessons from Greece.

First, remember the pitfalls of putting off until tomorrow what should be done today. Last year, the Greek debt crisis was almost upon Europe before governments acted. They also had a hard time deciding what to do. The financial markets, including those in the United States, did not react well to the time squeeze and indecision. Watching Wall Street drop, American consumer confidence fell, slowing the pace of recovery and influencing the 2010 elections.

At least this time, Europeans recognize early a problem that's coming. Greece is now seeking debt funding for 2012 and 2013 as its European-IMF loan runs its course.

But will Europeans act in a timely manner? The biggest bankroller, Germany, wants to wait until after this week's European and IMF inspectors issue their findings in June. And who knows how long after that? The temptation is to put off a decision, because the options ahead—either more loans or a restructuring of Greek debt—are economically painful and not likely to sit well with voters.

Similarly, politicians in Washington may be tempted to put off the heavy lifting on a debt-reduction plan. For instance, they may put reforming costly entitlements such as Medicare aside until after the 2012 elections.

But remember, the financial markets have a highly sensitive nose that can sniff out half-baked solutions. And they don't like to be kept in suspense. Republicans and Democrats should not wait until the last minute to agree on a substantive plan to reduce deficits and raise the debt ceiling, which can be financed only until Aug. 2. After that, it's default time for America.

Even if Washington comes up with a meaningful plan, it must keep in mind whether a plan can actually be implemented. Greece has cut government salaries, pensions, and increased taxes—all requirements of the bailout—even in the face of stiff resistance and strikes.

But it has not finished its reforms, including privatizing public assets. Unions have delayed the consolidation of several hundred state organizations. Tax evasion is still a huge problem. Meanwhile, the austerity measures have contributed to economic contraction, reducing tax revenues to pay down debt.

Also, economic assumptions changed. Greek data were revised downward, which threw off the plan from the start. Then came the bailouts for Ireland and Portugal, which worsened financial market conditions in Europe.

Whatever plan America settles on will differ in the details from what's happening in Greece. But the US version must likewise be timely, substantive, and doable—all of which will require considerable political will and cooperation by both parties. The plan may also need adjusting in years ahead.

These are America's Greek lessons. May it learn them.

indicating the contribution of member countries to euro-area economic aggregates. These weights reflect the relative size of consumption in the economy. As you can see, Germany, France, Italy, and Spain together account for about three-fourths of the Eurozone and the remaining 13 countries combined count for as much as France does in terms of how much they contribute to euro-area aggregates. So a recession in a smaller economy, like Ireland or Greece, at a time when the large economies like France and Germany are growing rapidly will not result in any help for the smaller economies from the ECB and will lead to growing tensions within the union.

So why are so many smaller nations eager to join the EMU? Because many benefits accrue to these smaller economies, including greater trade and investment flows with a common currency. Moreover, uncertainty about future appreciation and depreciation is removed, as are transaction costs from exchanging one currency for another. This enhances travel and trade across borders.

These basic concepts help us understand why some member countries may want to leave the EMU and why some countries still want to join. To be sure, the EMU may not allow some of these countries to join because they have not met the convergence criteria laid down in the Treaty of Maastricht, and other countries are perfectly happy not to join because they value their own monetary policy autonomy.

REVIEW

- A currency union is an arrangement whereby a group of countries adopts a common currency in place of their individual currencies. The EMU is the most prominent example of a currency union in the world in the twenty-first century.

- The EMU began in 2001 when 11 countries that had met the convergence criteria laid out by the Treaty of Maastricht adopted a common currency (the euro) in place of their individual currencies and ceded monetary policy-making authority from their national central bank to the newly formed ECB.

- In a currency union, individual countries no longer have the ability to control their monetary policy. The monetary policy appropriate for the region may not be appropriate at all for the domestic economy. This is particularly true when a smaller economy in the region has conditions that diverge from conditions for the region as a whole.

- The primary benefits for a currency union are the prospects for greater trade and investment flows among the member countries because they all use the same currency. Another important change is the elimination of transaction costs from having to exchange one currency for another.

- In the near future, the EMU will have interesting developments because some countries may want to be admitted to the EMU, and at the same time, existing member countries may want to leave the EMU.

KEY POINTS

1. An exchange rate is a rate at which one currency can be exchanged for the other. The convention used in this chapter defines the exchange rate in terms of foreign currency units per unit of domestic currency.

2. Because the exchange rate is the price of domestic currency (in terms of foreign currency), we can use the supply–demand framework to understand how exchange rates are determined.

3. When there is excess demand for the domestic currency in the foreign exchange market, the domestic currency appreciates. When there is excess supply of domestic currency in the foreign exchange market, the domestic currency depreciates.

4. The supply–demand framework allows us to predict that the country whose interest rate increases will see an appreciation of their currency in the short run and that the country with a higher rate of inflation will see a depreciation of their currency in the long run.

5. In a fixed exchange rate system, the government sets the exchange rate at which the central bank will exchange domestic currency for foreign currency using reserves of foreign and domestic currency.

6. If the fixed exchange rate makes the domestic currency artificially more valuable, we say that the domestic currency is overvalued; if it makes the domestic currency artificially less valuable, we say that the domestic currency is undervalued.

7. A government may want to overvalue its currency so that consumers and importers in the economy will benefit from having access to cheap foreign goods. Conversely, a government may want to undervalue its currency so that exporters in the economy will benefit from their goods being more attractive to foreign buyers.

8. A sustained overvaluation will lead to a crisis situation in which the government runs out of reserves and is forced to take drastic action. A sustained undervaluation can lead to inflation in the longer term.

9. A currency union is an arrangement whereby a group of countries adopts a common currency in place of their individual currencies. The primary benefits for a currency union are the prospects for greater trade and investment flows among the member countries because they all use the same currency and thus avoid transaction costs related to the exchange of currency.

10. In a currency union, individual countries no longer have the ability to control their monetary policy. The monetary policy appropriate for the region may not be appropriate for all the economies in the region.

KEY TERMS

appreciation, 465

currency union, 477

depreciation, 465

devaluation, 474

exchange rate, 464

fixed exchange rate policy, 470

flexible exchange rate policy, 470

overvalued, 472

purchasing power parity (PPP), 469

revaluation, 474

the law of one price, 469

undervalued, 472

QUESTIONS FOR REVIEW

1. What is the relationship between the exchange rate and net exports?

2. How are exchange rates related to interest rate differentials in the short run?

3. How are exchange rates related to inflation differentials in the long run?

4. What does it mean when we say that a country has "fixed its exchange rate"?

5. Why might a country want to undervalue its currency?

6. What are the adverse consequences of a decision to undervalue?

7. Why might a country want to overvalue its currency?

8. What are the adverse consequences of a decision to overvalue?

9. Why did the countries that formed the Economic and Monetary Union have to satisfy the Maastricht convergence criteria?

10. What is the main advantage of joining a currency union? What is the main disadvantage?

PROBLEMS

1. Suppose a Toyota costs 2 million yen, and a Caterpillar tractor costs $300,000. If the exchange rate between Japan and the United States was 80 yen per dollar, calculate the price of the Toyota to someone in the United States and the price of the tractor to someone in Japan.

2. Now suppose the exchange rate changes to 100 yen per dollar. Which currency has appreciated? What happens to the price of the Toyota to someone in the United States and the price of the tractor to someone in Japan? Then redo this exercise, assuming the exchange rate changed to 75 yen per dollar, instead of 100 yen per dollar.

3. Draw a supply–demand diagram, like Figure 19-6, that provides a visual depiction of an exchange rate that is fixed at an overvalued rate. Suppose this country is in danger of running out of reserves so that investors begin to fear a devaluation is looming. Show the resulting impact on foreign exchange reserves on your diagram.

4. Now draw a supply–demand diagram, like Figure 19-7, which provides a visual depiction of an exchange rate that is fixed at an undervalued rate. Suppose this country is concerned about rising

inflation and investors have begun to expect that a revaluation is looming. Show the resulting impact on foreign exchange reserves on your diagram.

5. Why is a sustained undervaluation of a currency different from a sustained overvaluation of a currency, in terms of how quickly the policy maker will have to change the fixed rate?

6. What are some of the signs that can lead one to conclude that China's currency may be undervalued?

7. Using the information given in Table 19-1, explain why the European Central Bank may respond differently to a shock that hits an economy like Greece or Ireland (but not the rest of the euro area) than it would to a shock that hits an economy like Germany or France (but not the rest of the euro area).

8. Conduct an Internet search to find out which country is the most likely candidate to join the Economic and Monetary Union (EMU) next. What are the pros and cons for that country from joining the EMU, particularly in light of the travails of countries like Greece that are in the EMU currently?

45-degree line the line showing that expenditure equals aggregate income.

A

absolute advantage a situation in which a person or country is more efficient at producing a good in comparison with another person or country.

ad valorem tariff a tax on imports evaluated as a percentage of the value of the import.

adverse selection in insurance markets, a situation in which the people who choose to buy insurance will be the riskiest group in the population; analogous situations apply in other markets.

aggregate demand (*AD*) the total demand for goods and services by consumers, businesses, government, and foreigners.

aggregate demand (*AD*) curve a line showing a negative relationship between inflation and the aggregate quantity of goods and services demanded at that inflation rate.

aggregate hours the total number of hours worked by all workers in the economy in a given period of time.

aggregate supply the total value of all goods and services produced in the economy by the available supply of capital, labor, and technology (also called potential gross domestic product [GDP]).

antidumping duty a tariff imposed on a country as a penalty for dumping goods.

appreciation an increase in value of a currency.

asset something of value owned by a person or a firm.

asymmetric information different levels of information available to different people in an economic interaction or exchange.

automatic stabilizers automatic tax and spending changes that occur over the course of the business cycle that tend to stabilize the fluctuations in real GDP.

B

balanced budget a budget in which tax revenues equal spending.

bank a firm that channels funds from savers to investors by accepting deposits and making loans.

budget deficit the amount by which government spending exceeds tax revenues.

budget surplus the amount by which tax revenues exceed government spending.

C

capital the factories, improvements to cultivated land, machinery and other tools, equipment, and structures used to produce goods and services.

capital abundant a higher level of capital per worker in one country relative to another.

capital gain the increase in the value of an asset through an increase in its price.

capital income the sum of profits, rental payments, and interest payments.

capital intensive production that uses a relatively high level of capital per worker.

capital loss the decrease in the value of an asset through a decrease in its price.

capitalism an economic system based on a market economy in which capital is individually owned, and production and employment decisions are decentralized.

Cartesian coordinate system a graphing system in which ordered pairs of numbers are represented on a plane by the distances from a point to two perpendicular lines, called axes.

catch-up line the downward-sloping relation between the level of productivity and the growth of productivity predicted by growth theory.

central bank independence a description of the legal authority of central banks to make decisions on monetary policy with little interference by the government in power.

ceteris paribus "all other things being equal"; refers to holding all other variables constant or keeping all other things the same when one variable is changed.

checking deposit an account at a financial institution on which checks can be written; also called a checkable deposit.

choice a selection among alternative goods, services, or actions.

command economy an economy in which the government determines prices and production; also called a centrally planned economy.

commerce clause the clause in the U.S. Constitution that prohibits restraint of trade between states.

comparative advantage a situation in which a person or country can produce one good at a lower opportunity cost than another person or country.

complement a good that usually is consumed or used together with another good.

compound growth applying the growth rate to growth from the previous period; similar to compound interest.

consumer price index (CPI) a price index equivalent that calculates current price of a fixed market basket of consumer goods and services relative to a base year.

consumption purchases of final goods and services by individuals.

consumption function the positive relationship between consumption and income.

consumption share the proportion of GDP that is used for consumption; equals consumption divided by GDP, or C/Y.

consumption smoothing the idea that although their incomes fluctuate, people try to stabilize consumption spending from year to year.

controlled experiments empirical tests of theories in a controlled setting in which particular effects can be isolated.

Council of Economic Advisers a three-member group of economists appointed by the president of the United States to analyze the economy and make recommendations about economic policy.

countercyclical policy a policy designed to offset the fluctuations in the business cycle.

coupon the fixed amount that a borrower agrees to pay to the bondholder each year.

credit crunch a period when banks become cautious in making new loans.

cross-price elasticity of demand the percentage change in the quantity demanded of one good divided by the percentage change in the price of another good.

crowding out the decline in private investment owing to an increase in government purchases.

currency money in its physical form: coin and paper money.

currency union an arrangement whereby a group of countries adopt a common currency in place of their individual currencies

Current Population Survey a monthly survey of a sample of U.S. households done by the U.S. Census Bureau; it measures employment, unemployment, the labor force, and other characteristics of the U.S. population.

customs union a free trade area with a common external tariff.

cyclical unemployment unemployment resulting from a recession, when the rate of unemployment is above the natural rate of unemployment.

D

debt contract a contract in which a lender agrees to provide funds today in exchange for a promise from the borrower, who will repay that amount plus interest at some point in the future.

debt-to-GDP ratio the total amount of outstanding loans the federal government owes divided by nominal GDP.

deflation a decrease in the overall price level, or a negative inflation rate.

demand a relationship between **price** and **quantity demanded**.

demand curve a graph of demand showing the downward-sloping relationship between price and quantity demanded.

demand schedule a tabular presentation of demand showing the price and quantity demanded for a particular good, all else being equal.

demand shock a shift in one of the components of aggregate demand that leads to a shift in the aggregate demand curve.

depreciation the decrease in an asset's value over time; for capital, it is the amount by which physical capital wears out over a given period of time.

devaluation when a fixed exchange rate is adjusted so that the domestic currency is worth less than it used to be.

developing country a country that is poor by world standards in terms of real GDP per capita.

diffusion the spreading of an innovation throughout the economy.

diminishing returns a situation in which successive increases in the use of an input, holding other inputs constant, eventually will cause a decline in the additional production derived from one more unit of that input.

discount rate the interest rate that the Fed charges commercial banks when they borrow from the Fed.

discounting the process of translating a future payment into a value in the present.

discretionary fiscal policy changes in tax or spending policy requiring legislative or administrative action by the president or Congress.

disinflation a reduction in the inflation rate.

dividend yield the dividend stated as a percentage of the price of the stock.

division of labor the division of production into various parts in which different groups of workers specialize.

Doha Development Round the latest round of multilateral negotiations, opened in November 2001 in Doha, Qatar.

dual scale a graph that uses time on the horizontal axis and different scales on the left and right vertical axes to compare the movements of two variables over time.

E

earnings the accounting profits of a firm.

economic development the process of growth by which countries raise incomes per capita and become industrialized; also refers to the branch of economics that studies this process.

economic fluctuations swings in real GDP that lead to deviations of the economy from its long-term growth trend.

economic growth an upward trend in real GDP, reflecting expansion in the economy over time.

economic interactions exchanges of goods and services between people.

economic model an explanation of how the economy or part of the economy works.

economic rent the price of something that has a fixed supply.

economic variable any economic measure that can vary over a range of values.

economics the study of how people deal with scarcity.

efficiency wage a wage higher than that which would equate quantity supplied and quantity demanded, set by employers to increase worker efficiency—for example, by decreasing shirking by workers.

efficient market hypothesis the idea that markets adjust rapidly enough to eliminate profit opportunities immediately.

elastic demand demand for which the price elasticity is greater than one.

employment-to-population ratio the ratio (usually expressed as a percentage) of employed workers to the working-age population.

equilibrium interest rate the interest rate that equates the sum of the consumption, investment, and net exports shares to the share of GDP available for nongovernment use.

equilibrium price the price at which quantity supplied equals quantity demanded.

equilibrium quantity the quantity traded at the equilibrium price.

equilibrium risk-return relationship the positive relationship between the risk and the expected rate of return on an asset, derived from the fact that, on average, risk-averse investors who take on more risk must be compensated with a higher return.

equity contract shares of ownership in a firm; payments to the owners of the shares depend on the firm's profits.

excess reserves the amount of reserves over and above required reserves.

exchange market intervention purchases and sales of foreign currency by a government in exchange markets with the intention to affect the exchange rate.

exchange rate the price of one currency in terms of another in the foreign exchange market. We express the exchange rate as the number of units of foreign currency that can be purchased with one unit of domestic currency.

exchange rate the price of one currency in terms of another in the foreign exchange market. We express the exchange rate as the number of units of foreign currency that can be purchased with one unit of domestic currency.

expansion the period between the trough of a recession and the next peak, consisting of a general rise in output and employment.

expected return the return on an uncertain investment calculated by weighting the gains or losses by the probability that they will occur.

expenditure line the relation between the sum of the four components of spending ($C + I + G + X$) and aggregate income.

experimental economics a branch of economics that uses laboratory experiments to analyze economic behavior.

exports the total value of the goods and services that people in one country sell to people in other countries.

F

face value the principal that will be paid back when a bond matures.

factor-price equalization the equalization of the price of labor and the price of capital across countries when they are engaging in free trade.

federal budget a summary of the federal government's proposals for spending, taxes, and the deficit.

federal debt the total amount of outstanding loans owed by the federal government.

federal funds rate the interest rate on overnight loans between banks that the Federal Reserve influences by changing the supply of funds (bank reserves) in the market.

Federal Open Market Committee (FOMC) the committee, consisting of the seven members of the Board of Governors and the twelve presidents of the Fed district banks, that meets about eight times per year and makes decisions about the supply of money; only five of the presidents vote at any one time.

Federal Reserve System (the Fed) the central bank of the United States, which oversees the creation of money in the United States.

final good a new good that undergoes no further processing before it is sold to consumers.

financial crises disruptions to financial markets which make it difficult for people and business firms to borrow and obtain loans.

fixed exchange rate policy a policy in which a country maintains a fixed value of its currency in terms of other currencies.

fixed exchange rate policy a policy in which a country maintains a fixed value of its currency in terms of other currencies.

flexible exchange rate policy a policy in which exchange rates are determined in foreign exchange markets and governments do not agree to fix them.

flexible exchange rate policy a policy in which exchange rates are determined in foreign exchange markets and governments do not agree to fix them.

foreign direct investment (FDI) investment by a foreign entity in at least a 10 percent direct ownership share in a firm.

forward-looking consumption model a model that explains consumer behavior by assuming that people anticipate future income when deciding on consumption spending today.

free trade area (FTA) an area that has no trade barriers between the countries in the area.

freely determined prices prices that are determined by the individuals and firms interacting in markets.

frictional unemployment unemployment arising from normal turnover in the labor market, such as when people change occupations or locations, or are new entrants.

G

gains from trade improvements in income, production, or satisfaction owing to the exchange of goods or services.

gains from trade improvements in income, production, or satisfaction owing to the exchange of goods or services.

GDP deflator nominal GDP divided by real GDP; it measures the level of prices of goods and services included in real GDP relative to a given base year.

government failure the situation in which the government fails to improve on the market or even makes things worse.

government purchases purchases by federal, state, and local governments of new goods and services.

government purchases share the proportion of GDP that is used for government purchases; equals government purchases divided by GDP, or G/Y.

gross domestic product (GDP) a measure of the value of all the goods and services newly produced in an economy during a specified period of time.

growth accounting formula an equation stating that the growth rate of productivity equals capital's share of income times the growth rate of capital per hour of work plus the growth rate of technology.

growth accounting formula an equation stating that the growth rate of productivity equals capital's share of income times the growth rate of capital per hour of work plus the growth rate of technology.

H

human capital a person's accumulated knowledge and skills.

I

implicit rental price the cost of the funds used to buy the capital plus the depreciation of the capital over a given period of time.

imports the total value of the goods and services that people in one country buy from people in other countries.

incentive a device that motivates people to take action, usually to increase economic efficiency.

income elasticity of demand the percentage change in quantity demanded of a good divided by the percentage change in income.

increasing opportunity cost a situation in which producing more of one good requires giving up an increasing amount of production of another good.

inelastic demand demand for which the price elasticity is less than one.

infant industry argument the view that a new industry may be helped by protectionist policies.

inferior good a good for which demand decreases when income rises and increases when income falls.

inflation adjustment (IA) line a flat line showing the level of inflation in the economy at a given point in time. It shifts up when real GDP is greater than potential GDP, and it shifts down when real GDP is less than potential GDP; it also shifts when expectations of inflation or raw materials prices change.

inflation rate the percentage increase in the overall price level over a given period of time, usually one year.

informal economy the portion of an economy characterized by illegal, unregulated businesses.

innovation application of new knowledge in a way that creates new products or significantly changes old ones.

insider a person who already works for a firm and has some influence over wage and hiring policy.

interest rate the amount received per dollar loaned per year, usually expressed as a percentage (for example, 6 percent) of the loan.

interindustry trade trade between countries in goods from different industries.

intermediate good a good that undergoes further processing before it is sold to consumers.

International Monetary Fund (IMF) an international agency, established after World War II, designed to help countries with balance of payments problems and to ensure the smooth functioning of the international monetary system.

international trade the exchange of goods and services between people or firms in different nations.

international trade the exchange of goods and services between people or firms in different nations.

intraindustry trade trade between countries in goods from the same or similar industries.

invention a discovery of new knowledge.

investment purchases of final goods by firms plus purchases of newly produced residences by households.

investment share the proportion of GDP that is used for investment; equals investment divided by GDP, or I/Y. Sometimes called investment rate.

J

job rationing a reason for unemployment in which the quantity of labor supplied is greater than the quantity demanded because the real wage is too high.

job search a reason for unemployment in which uncertainty in the labor market and workers' limited information require people to spend time searching for a job.

job vacancies positions that firms are trying to fill, but for which they have yet to find suitable workers.

K

Keynesian multiplier the ratio of the change in real GDP to the shift in the expenditure line; the formula is $1/(1 - MPC)$, where MPC is the marginal propensity to consume.

L

labor the number of hours people are available to work in producing goods and services.

labor abundant a lower level of capital per worker in one country relative to another.

labor demand curve a downward-sloping relationship showing the quantity of labor firms are willing to hire at each wage.

labor force all those who are either employed or unemployed.

labor force participation rate the ratio (usually expressed as a percentage) of people in the labor force to the working-age population.

labor income the sum of wages, salaries, and fringe benefits paid to workers.

labor intensive production that uses a relatively low level of capital per worker.

labor supply curve upward sloping relationship showing the quantity of labor workers are willing to supply at each wage.

law of demand the tendency for the quantity demanded of a good in a market to decline as its price rises.

law of one price the notion that if transport costs are low, and people are not prevented from buying whatever they want, the same commodity in two countries will sell for about the same amount when measured in the same currency.

law of supply the tendency for the quantity supplied of a good in a market to increase as its price rises.

learning by doing a situation in which workers become more proficient by doing a particular task many times.

liability something of value that a person or a firm owes to someone else.

life-cycle model a type of forward-looking consumption model that assumes that people base their consumption decisions on their expected lifetime income rather than on their current income.

linear a situation in which a curve is straight, with a constant slope.

liquidity constraint the situation in which people cannot borrow to smooth their consumption spending when their income is low.

liquidity trap a situation in which increases in the money supply (liquidity) do not lower the interest rate any further; the interest rate is at or near zero.

M

macroeconomics the branch of economics that examines the workings and problems of the economy as a whole—GDP growth and unemployment.

marginal propensity to consume (MPC) the slope of the consumption function, showing the change in consumption that is due to a given change in income.

marginal propensity to import (MPI) the change in imports because of a given change in income.

marginal revenue product (MRP) of capital the change in total revenue because of a one-unit increase in capital.

market an arrangement by which economic exchanges between people take place.

market economy an economy characterized by freely determined prices and the free exchange of goods and services in markets.

market equilibrium the situation in which the price is equal to the equilibrium price and the quantity traded equals the equilibrium quantity.

market failure any situation in which the market does not lead to an efficient economic outcome and in which the government has a potential role.

maturity date the date when the principal on a loan is to be paid back.

medium of exchange something that generally is accepted as a means of payment.

microeconomics the branch of economics that examines individual decision making at firms and households and the way they interact in specific industries and markets.

minimum wage a wage per hour below which it is illegal to pay workers.

mixed economy a market economy in which the government plays a very large role.

monetary base currency plus reserves.

monetary policy rule a description of how much the interest rate or other instruments of monetary policy respond to inflation or other measures of the state of the economy.

money that part of a person's wealth that can be used readily for transactions; money also serves as a store of value and a unit of account.

money demand a relationship between the nominal interest rate and the quantity of money that people are willing to hold at any given nominal interest rate.

money supply the sum of currency (coin and paper money) and deposits at banks.

moral hazard in insurance markets, a situation in which a person buys insurance against some risk and subsequently takes actions that increase the risk; analogous situations arise when other markets have asymmetric information.

mortgage a loan to purchase a house.

movement along the curve a situation in which a change in the variable on one axis causes a change in the variable on the other axis, but the position of the curve is maintained.

multilateral negotiations simultaneous tariff reductions on the part of many countries.

N

national saving aggregate income minus consumption minus government purchases.

national saving rate the proportion of GDP that is saved, neither consumed nor spent on government purchases; equals national saving (S) divided by GDP, or S/Y.

natural unemployment rate the unemployment rate that exists in the absence of a recession and a boom and real GDP is equal to potential GDP.

negative slope a slope of a curve that is less than zero, representing a negative or inverse relationship between two variables.

negatively related a situation in which an increase in one variable is associated with a decrease in another variable; also called *inversely related*.

net exports the value of exports minus the value of imports.

net exports share the proportion of GDP that is equal to net exports; equals net exports divided by GDP, or X/Y.

nominal GDP gross domestic product without any correction for inflation; the same as GDP; the value of all the goods and services newly produced in a country during some period of time, usually a year.

nominal interest rate the interest rate uncorrected for inflation.

nontariff barrier any government action other than a tariff that reduces imports, such as a quota or a standard.

normal good a good for which demand increases when income rises and decreases when income falls.

normative economics economic analysis that makes recommendations about economic policy.

O

open market operation the buying or selling of bonds by the central bank.

opportunity cost the value of the next-best forgone alternative that was not chosen because something else was chosen.

opportunity cost the value of the next-best forgone alternative that was not chosen because something else was chosen.

outsider someone who is not working for a particular firm, making it difficult for him or her to get a job with that firm even though he or she is willing to work for a lower wage.

overvalued a currency is said to be overvalued if the fixed exchange rate system makes the domestic currency artificially more valuable.

P

peak the highest point in economic activity before a recession.

perfectly elastic demand demand for which the price elasticity is infinite, indicating an infinite response to a change in price and therefore a horizontal demand curve.

perfectly elastic supply supply for which the price elasticity is infinite, indicating an infinite response of quantity supplied to a change in price and therefore a horizontal supply curve.

perfectly inelastic demand demand for which the price elasticity is zero, indicating no response to a change in price and therefore a vertical demand curve.

perfectly inelastic supply supply for which the price elasticity is zero, indicating no response of quantity supplied to a change in price and therefore a vertical supply curve.

permanent income model a type of forward-looking consumption model that assumes that people distinguish between temporary changes in their income and permanent changes in their income; the permanent changes have a larger effect on consumption.

political business cycle a business cycle caused by politicians' use of economic policy to overstimulate the economy just before an election.

portfolio diversification spreading the collection of assets owned to limit exposure to risk.

portfolio investment investment by a foreign entity in less than a 10 percent ownership share in a firm.

positive economics economic analysis that explains what happens in the economy and why, without making recommendations about economic policy.

positive slope a slope of a curve that is greater than zero, representing a positive or direct relationship between two variables.

positively related a situation in which an increase in one variable is associated with an increase in another variable; also called *directly related*.

potential GDP the economy's long-term growth trend for real GDP, determined by the available supply of capital, labor, and technology. Real GDP fluctuates above and below potential GDP.

potential GDP the economy's long-term growth trend for real GDP, determined by the available supply of capital, labor, and technology. Real GDP fluctuates above and below potential GDP.

present discounted value the value in the present of future payments.

price the amount of money or other goods that one must pay to obtain a particular good.

price ceiling a government price control that sets the maximum allowable price for a good.

price control a government law or regulation that sets or limits the price to be charged for a particular good.

price elasticity of demand the percentage change in the quantity demanded of a good divided by the percentage change in the price of that good.

price elasticity of supply the percentage change in quantity supplied divided by the percentage change in price.

price floor a government price control that sets the minimum allowable price for a good.

price level the average level of prices in the economy.

price shock a change in the price of a key commodity such as oil, usually because of a shortage, that causes a shift in the inflation adjustment line; also sometimes called a supply shock.

price-earnings ratio the price of a stock divided by its annual earnings per share.

production function the relationship that describes output as a function of labor, capital, and technology.

production possibilities alternative combinations of production of various goods that are possible, given the economy's resources.

production possibilities curve a curve showing the maximum combinations of production of two goods that are possible, given the economy's resources.

productivity output per hour of work.

productivity curve a relationship stating the output per hour of work for each amount of capital per hour of work in the economy.

profit sharing programs in which managers and employees receive a share of profits earned by the firm.

property rights rights over the use, sale, and proceeds from a good or resource.

purchasing power parity (PPP) a theory that states that the exchange rate will adjust to equalize the price levels of two countries.

Q

quantity demanded the quantity of a good that people want to buy at a given price during a specific time period.

quantity equation of money the equation relating the price level and real GDP to the quantity of money and the velocity of money: The quantity of money times its velocity equals the price level times real GDP.

quantity supplied the quantity of a good that firms are willing to sell at a given price.

quota a governmental limit on the quantity of a good that may be imported or sold.

R

rate of return the return on an asset stated as a percentage of the price of the asset.

real business cycle theory a theory of macroeconomics that stresses that shifts in potential GDP are a primary cause of fluctuations in real GDP; the shifts in potential GDP usually are assumed to be caused by changes in technology.

real business cycle theory a theory of macroeconomics that stresses that shifts in potential GDP are a primary cause of fluctuations in real GDP; the shifts in potential GDP usually are assumed to be caused by changes in technology.

real gross domestic product (real GDP) a measure of the value of all the goods and services newly produced in a country during some period of time, adjusted for changes in prices over time.

real interest rate the interest rate minus the expected rate of inflation; it adjusts the nominal interest rate for inflation.

real wage the wage or price of labor adjusted for inflation; in contrast, the nominal wage has not been adjusted for inflation.

recession a decline in production and employment that lasts for six months or more.

recovery the early part of an economic expansion, immediately after the trough of the recession.

reinflation an increase in the inflation rate caused by a change in monetary policy.

rent control a government price control that sets the maximum allowable rent on a house or apartment.

rental price of capital the amount that a rental company charges for the use of capital equipment for a specified period of time.

required reserve ratio the fraction of a bank's deposits that it is required to hold at the Fed.

reserves deposits that commercial banks hold at the Fed.

return the income received from the ownership of an asset; for a stock, the return is the dividend plus the capital gain.

revaluation when a fixed exchange rate is adjusted so that the domestic currency is worth more than it used to be.

revenue tariff an import tax whose main purpose is to provide revenue to the government.

S

scarcity the situation in which the quantity of resources is insufficient to meet all wants.

scatter plot a graph in which points in a Cartesian coordinate system represent the values of two variables.

shift of the curve a change in the position of a curve, usually caused by a change in a variable not represented on either axis.

shortage (excess demand) a situation in which quantity demanded is greater than quantity supplied.

slope a characteristic of a curve that is defined as the change in the variable on the vertical axis divided by the change in the variable on the horizontal axis.

Smoot-Hawley tariff a set of tariffs imposed in 1930 that raised the average tariff level to 59 percent by 1932.

socialism an economic system in which the government owns and controls all the capital and makes decisions about prices and quantities as part of a central plan.

specialization a concentration of production effort on a single specific task.

specific tariff a tax on imports that is proportional to the number of units or items imported.

spending balance the level of income or real GDP at which the 45-degree line and the expenditure line cross; also called equilibrium income.

stagflation the situation in which high inflation and high unemployment occur simultaneously.

store of value something that will allow purchasing power to be carried from one period to the next.

structural surplus the level of the government budget surplus under a scenario in which real GDP is equal to potential GDP; also called the full-employment surplus.

structural unemployment unemployment resulting from structural problems, such as poor skills, long-term changes in demand, or insufficient work incentives.

substitute a good that has many of the same characteristics as, and can be used in place of, another good.

supply a relationship between price and quantity supplied.

supply curve a graph of supply showing the upward-sloping relationship between price and quantity supplied.

supply schedule a tabular presentation of supply showing the price and quantity supplied of a particular good, all else being equal.

surplus (excess supply) a situation in which quantity supplied is greater than quantity demanded.

T

target inflation rate the central bank's goal for the average rate of inflation over the long run.

tariff a tax on imports.

technological change improvement in technology over time.

technology anything that raises the amount of output that can be produced with a given amount of labor and capital.

technology anything that raises the amount of output that can be produced with a given amount of labor and capital.

time inconsistency the situation in which policy makers have the incentive to announce one economic policy but then change that policy after citizens have acted on the initial, stated policy.

time-series graph a graph that plots a variable over time, usually with time on the horizontal axis.

total amount of saving a measure of the amount of resources that a country has for investment, either in its own country or abroad.

trade balance the value of exports minus the value of imports.

trade creation the increase in trade resulting from a decrease in trade barriers.

trade diversion the shifting of trade away from the low-cost producer toward a higher-cost producer because of a reduction in trade barriers with the country of the higher-cost producer.

trade war a conflict among nations over trade policies caused by imposition of protectionist policies on the part of one country and subsequent retaliatory actions by other countries.

trough the lowest point of economic activity at the end of a recession.

U

undervalued a currency is said to be undervalued if the fixed exchange rate makes the domestic currency artificially less valuable.

unemployed person an individual who does not have a job and is looking for work.

unemployment rate the percentage of the labor force that is unemployed.

unemployment rate the percentage of the labor force that is unemployed.

unit of account a standard unit in which prices can be quoted and values of goods can be compared.

unit-free measure a measure that does not depend on a unit of measurement.

Uruguay Round the most recently completed round of multilateral negotiations, opened in 1986 and completed in 1993.

V

value added the value of a firm's production minus the value of the intermediate goods used in production.

velocity a measure of how frequently money is turned over in the economy.

W

working-age population persons over 16 years of age who are not in an institution, such as a jail or a hospital.

World Bank an international agency, established after World War II, designed to promote the economic development of poorer countries through lending channeled from industrial countries.

World Trade Organization (WTO) an international organization that can mediate trade disputes.

yield the annual rate of return on a bond if the bond were held to maturity.

INDEX